OXFORD EARLY CHRISTIAN STUDIES

General Editors

GILLIAN CLARK   ANDREW LOUTH

THE OXFORD EARLY CHRISTIAN STUDIES series includes scholarly volumes on the thought and history of the early Christian centuries. Covering a wide range of Greek, Latin, and Oriental sources, the books are of interest to theologians, ancient historians, and specialists in the classical and Jewish worlds.

TITLES IN THE SERIES INCLUDE

Irenaeus of Lyons and the Theology of the Holy Spirit
Anthony Briggman (2012)

Apophasis and Pseudonymity in Dionysius the Areopagite
"No Longer I"
Charles M. Stang (2012)

Memory in Augustine's Theological Anthropology
Paige E. Hochschild (2012)

Orosius and the Rhetoric of History
Peter Van Nuffelen (2012)

Drama of the Divine Economy
Creator and Creation in Early Christian Theology and Piety
Paul M. Blowers (2012)

Embodiment and Virtue in Gregory of Nyssa
An Anagogical Approach
Hans Boersma (2013)

The *Chronicle of Seert*
Christian Historical Imagination in Late Antique Iraq
Philip Wood (2013)

Christ in the Life and Teaching of Gregory of Nazianzus
Andrew Hofer, O.P. (2013)

Ascetic Pneumatology from John Cassian to Gregory the Great
Thomas L. Humphries Jr. (2013)

Contemplation and Classical Christianity
A Study in Augustine
John Peter Kenney (2013)

The Canons of Our Fathers
Monastic Rules of Shenoute
Bentley Layton (2014)

Gregory of Nyssa's Tabernacle Imagery in Its Jewish and Christian Contexts
Ann Conway-Jones (2014)

John Chrysostom on Divine Pedagogy
The Coherence of his Theology and Preaching
David Rylaarsdam (2014)

Cyril of Alexandria's Trinitarian Theology of Scripture
Matthew R. Crawford (2014)

The Practical Christology of Philoxenos of Mabbug
David A. Michelson (2014)

Law and Legality in the Greek East

The Byzantine Canonical Tradition, 381–883

DAVID WAGSCHAL

OXFORD
UNIVERSITY PRESS

OXFORD
UNIVERSITY PRESS

Great Clarendon Street, Oxford, OX2 6DP,
United Kingdom

Oxford University Press is a department of the University of Oxford. It furthers the University's objective of excellence in research, scholarship, and education by publishing worldwide. Oxford is a registered trade mark of Oxford University Press in the UK and in certain other countries

First Edition published in 2015

Published in the United States of America by Oxford University Press
198 Madison Avenue, New York, NY 10016, United States of America

British Library Cataloguing in Publication Data
Data available

Library of Congress Control Number: 2014936749

ISBN 978–0–19–872260–1

For my grandparents

Acknowledgements

This project began as a doctoral dissertation undertaken at the University of Durham from 2005 to 2010. Neither the dissertation nor this book would have been possible without the assistance and encouragement of many organizations and individuals.

Of the institutions that assisted me financially during my dissertation work I must first express my gratitude to the Social Sciences and Humanities Research Council of Canada and the (now sadly defunct) Overseas Research Students Awards Scheme. These organizations provided the bulk of the funding for my dissertation research. I am also very grateful for the conference and travel subventions extended to me by the Fellowship of St Alban and St Sergius and the International Society for Medieval Canon Law.

I continue to owe the deepest debt of gratitude to my doctoral supervisor, Prof. Andrew Louth. Throughout this project, from conception to publication, Prof. Louth provided me with expert guidance and critique, as well as endless encouragement and patience. His vast learning, his generosity with his time, and his perpetual optimism were indispensable in bringing this work to a successful conclusion. I am also exceptionally grateful for the encouragement and the suggestions offered to me by my examiners, Dr. Caroline Humfress and Prof. Lewis Ayres.

Many other scholars and individuals assisted me as I navigated the forbidding and obscure waters of Byzantine law. I am especially grateful to Dr. Ludwig Burgmann, Prof. Wolfram Brandes, and other members of the Max-Planck-Institut für europäische Rechtsgeschichte in Frankfurt, for their exceptionally warm welcome in April 2009; Dr. (Archimandrite) Grigorios Papathomas, for his hospitality and encouragement during my research trip to the Bibliothèque nationale in May 2008; Ms. Eleana Silk, librarian at St Vladimir's Seminary in New York, for her tireless assistance in helping me unearth rare Russian and Greek works; Deacon Andrei Psarev, instructor in canon law at Holy Trinity Seminary in Jordanville, New York, for his kind assistance with libraries in Russia; Dr. Evaggelos Bartzis for his guidance and skills as an interpreter during my visit to the canonists of Greece in November 2006; and finally the staff of the Pontifical Institute of Medieval Studies in Toronto for granting me access to their extraordinary collection in the final phases of my research.

On a more personal note, I also wish to thank Prof. Richard Schneider, Professor Emeritus of History at York University, Toronto. During my undergraduate years Prof. Schneider was instrumental in introducing me to the fascinating world of medieval history and in encouraging me to pursue my interests further. This work is in many respects the fruit of seeds that Prof. Schneider sowed many years ago.

Similarly, I wish to express my warmest gratitude to Mr. Peter Drobac, who generously commissioned the cover art for this volume.

Finally, I must thank my parents, Mark and Elisabeth, who have continued to show me extraordinary support, of all kinds, during both the original writing and revision of this work. This work is a testament to their unflagging belief in me, and their very great patience and love.

Contents

List of Figures

List of Tables

Abbreviations

ACO	E. Schwartz (ed.), *Acta conciliorum oecumenicorum 431–879*, 4 tomes in 14 vols. (Berlin, 1914–74)
Basilica	the *Basilica* (ed. H. Scheltema *et al.*, *Basilicorum libri LX*. Series A.1–8 (text); Series B.1–9 (scholia) (Groningen, 1953–88)
BNP	H. Cancik and H. Schneider (eds.), *Brill's New Pauly*, 15 vols. [trans. of *Neue Pauly*, 1996 ff.] (Leiden, 2002 ff.)
CJ	the *Code* of Justinian (ed. P. Krüger, *Corpus Iuris Civilis*, vol. 2 (Berlin, 1877); includes the introductory constitutions *Haec* (p. 1), *Summa* (pp. 2–3), *Cordi* (p. 4)
CJC	"Corpus Iuris Civilis," a 16th C designation, but a useful shorthand for Justinian's Code, Institutes, Digest, and Novels
Clavis	M. Geerard, *Clavis Patrum Graecorum*, 5 vols. with suppl. (Brepols, 1974)
Coll14	the *Collection in Fourteen Titles* (edns.: *Kormchaya*, *Pitra* 2.433–649, *RP* 1)
Coll25	the *Collection in Twenty-Five Chapters* (ed. G. Heimbach, Ἀνέκδοτα, vol. 2 (Leipzig, 1840), 145–201)
Coll50	the *Collection in Fifty Titles* (edn.: *Syn*)
Coll60	the *Collection in Sixty Titles* (not extant)
Coll87	the *Collection in Eighty-Seven Chapters* (ed. G. Heimbach, Ἀνέκδοτα, vol. 2 (Leipzig, 1840), 202–34)
CTh	the *Code* of Theodosius (eds. T. Mommsen and P. Meyer, *Theodosiani libri XVI cum Constitutionibus Sirmondianis et leges novellae ad Theodosianum pertinentes*, 2 vols. (Berlin, 1905)); trans. C. Pharr (Princeton, 1952)
Delineatio	N. van der Wal and J. Lokin, *Historiae iuris graeco-romani delineatio: les sources du droit byzantin de 300 à 1453* (Groningen, 1985)
DACL	F. Cabrol. *et al.* (eds.), *Dictionnaire d'archéologie chrétienne et de liturgie* (Paris, 1907–53)
DDC	R. Naz (ed.), *Dictionnaire de droit canonique* (Paris, 1935–65)
Digest	the *Digest* of Justinian (ed. T. Mommsen, *Corpus Iuris Civilis*, vol. 1 (Berlin, 1872); includes the introductory constitutions *Deo auctore* (pp. xiii–xiv), *Omnem* (pp. xvi–xvii), *Tanta/Δέδωκεν* (pp. xviii–xxvi); trans. A. Watson *et al.* (Philadelphia, 1985)
Ecloga	the *Ecloga* (ed. L. Burgmann, *Ecloga: das Gesetzbuch Leons III. und Konstantinos V.* (Frankfurt a.M., 1983))
Eisagoge	the *Eisagoge* [formerly *Epanagoge*] (ed. K. E. Zachariä von Lingenthal, *Collectio librorum juris Graeco-Romani ineditorum* (Leipzig, 1852), 61–217 = I. Zepos and P. Zepos, *Jus Graecoromanum* (Athens, 1931), 2.236–368)

Fonti	P.-P. Joannou (ed.), *Discipline générale antique (IVe–IXe s.)*, Pontificia Commissione per la redazione del Codice di diritto canonico orientale—Fonti, fascicolo IX, 4 vols. (Grottaferrata, 1962–4)
Historike	P. Menebisoglou, *Ἱστορικὴ Εἰσαγωγὴ εἰς τοὺς κανόνας τῆς Ὀρθοδόξου Εκκλησίας* (Stockholm, 1990)
Institutes	Justinian's *Institutes* (ed. T. Mommsen, *Corpus Iuris Civilis*, vol. 1 (Berlin, 1872); includes the introductory constitution *Imperatorium* (p. 2)); trans. P. Birks and G. McLeod (New York, 1987)
Kormchaya	V. Beneshevich (ed.), *Древне-славянская Кормчая. XIV титулов без толкований* (St Peterburg, 1906)
Mansi	J. D. Mansi (ed.), *Sacrorum conciliorum nova et amplissima collectio* (Florence–Venice, 1759–98)
MGH	H. vom Stein *et al.* (eds.), *Monumenta Germaniae Historica* (Hanover, etc., 1817 ff.)
N	Justinian's *Novels* (ed. R. Schöll and W. Kroll, *Corpus Iuris Civilis*, vol. 3 (Berlin, 1895))
NC14	the *Nomocanon in Fourteen Titles* (edns.: *Pitra* 2.433–649, *RP* 1)
NC50	the *Nomocanon in Fifty Titles* (ed. G. Voellus and H. Justellus, *Bibliotheca iuris canonici veteris* (Paris, 1661), 603–60)
NPNF14	H. Percival (trans.), *The Seven Ecumenical Councils*, Nicene and Post-Nicene Fathers, 2nd ser., vol. 14 (Oxford, 1900)
Peges	S. Troianos, *Οι Πηγές του Βυζαντινού Δικαίου*, 2nd edn. (Athens, 1999)
Pitra	J. B. Pitra (ed.), *Iuris Ecclesiastici Graecorum Historia et Monumenta*, 2 vols. (Rome, 1864, 1868)
PG	J. P. Migne (ed.), *Patrologia cursus completus. Series graeca* (Paris, 1857–66)
PL	J. P. Migne (ed.), *Patrologia cursus completus. Series latina* (Paris, 1840–80)
Prochiron	the *Prochiron* (ed. K. E. Zachariä von Lingenthal, *Ὁ Πρόχειρος Νόμος* (Heidelberg, 1837), 3–258 = I. Zepos and P. Zepos, *Jus Graecoromanum* (Athens, 1931), 2.114–228)
RE	A. Pauly and G. Wissowa (W. Kroll) (eds.), *Real-encyclopädie der classischen Altertumswissenschaft* (Leiden, 1894–1978)
RP	G. Rhalles and M. Potles (eds.), *Σύνταγμα τῶν θείων καὶ ἱερῶν κανόνων*, 6 vols. (Athens, 1852–59)
Sbornik	V. Beneshevich, *Канонический сборник XIV титулов со второй четверти VII века до 883 г.* (St Petersburg, 1905)
Sin	V. Beneshevich, *Синагога в 50 титулов и другие юридические сборники Иоанна Схоластика* (St Petersburg, 1914)
Sources	H. Ohme "Sources of the Greek Canon Law to the Quinisext Council (692): Councils and Church Fathers," in Hartmann and Pennington 2012, 24–114

Syn V. Beneshevich (ed.), *Ioannis Scholastici Synagoga L titulorum ceteraque eiusdem opera iuridica* (Munich, 1937)

TLG *Thesaurus Linguae Graecae*, online at <www.tlg.uci.edu>

Tripartita the *Collectio Tripartita* (ed. N. van der Wal and B. Stolte, *Collectio tripartita* (Groningen, 1994))

Notes to the Reader

CANONICAL CITATIONS

Canonical sources are cited by one- or two-word identifiers followed by canon number in Arabic numerals: e.g. "Trullo 23" = canon 23 of the council in Trullo; "Apostles 48" = canon 48 of the canons of the Apostles; "Dionysius 4" = canon 4 of Dionysius of Alexandria's canons. The identifiers are as follows:

Amphilochius	Amphilochius of Iconium (d. 394/403)
Ancyra	council of Ancyra (314)
Antioch	council in Antioch (traditionally dated 341; now thought to be *c.*328)
Apostles	canons of the Apostles (compiled *c.*380, perhaps in Antioch)
Athanasius	Athanasius of Alexandria (d. 373)
Basil	Basil of Caesarea (d. 379)
Carthage	the so-called *materies Africana*, a compilation of 4th and 5th C African material presented in the tradition as the council in Carthage 419
Chalcedon	council of Chalcedon (451)
Constantinople	council of Constantinople (381; with later supplements as per the canonical collections)
Constantinople 394	council in Constantinople (394)
Cyprian	council of Carthage (251; extracts from council presided over by Cyprian)
Cyril	Cyril of Alexandria (d. 444)
Dionysius	Dionysius of Alexandria (d. 264/5)
Ephesus	council of Ephesus (431; with later supplements as per the canonical collections)
Gangra	council of Gangra (*c.*340? 355?)
Gennadius	Gennadius of Constantinople (d. 471)
Gregory Naz.	Gregory of Nazianzus (d. 390)
Gregory Nyss.	Gregory of Nyssa (d. 395?)
Gregory Thaum.	Gregory Thaumaturgus (*c.*210–70)
Hagia Sophia	council in Constantinople (879)
Laodicea	council in Laodicea (before 380)
Neocaesarea	council of Neocaesarea (314/19)
Nicaea	council of Nicaea (325)
Peter	Peter of Alexandria (d. 311)

Protodeutera	council in Constantinople (861)
Serdica	council in Serdica (342)
Tarasius	Tarasius of Constantinople (d. 806)
Theophilus	Theophilus of Alexandria (d. 412)
Timothy	Timothy of Alexandria (d. 385)
Trullo	council in Constantinople "in Trullo," i.e. the Quinisext or *Πενθέκτη* (691/2)
II Nicaea	council of Nicaea (787)

If not specified, canonical texts are drawn from *Fonti*, and systematic rubric texts from *Syn* (for the *Coll50*) and *Kormchaya* (for the *Coll14*). Canonical numeration is according to *Fonti*. Page and line numbers are not specified for canons unless specially warranted.

Volumes, parts, pages, and (where present) line numbers for all sources are indicated through successive separations by full stops, e.g. *Fonti* 1.2.3.15–16 = *Fonti* volume 1, part 2, page 3, lines 15–16. Titles and chapters in the systematic indices are likewise indicated through successive full stops, e.g. *Coll14* 1.17 = *Collection in Fourteen Titles*, title 1, chapter 17. Manuscripts are cited as per convention, although locations have been anglicized and abbreviations have been kept as minimal as possible.

TRANSLATIONS

Length considerations, and the large number of canonical citations, have not permitted Greek and English to be provided for all texts. Translation has thus been approached pragmatically. Most lengthier texts, and passages where the Greek does not seem to clarify or reinforce the argument at hand or be in any way at issue, have been presented only in English. Occasionally, principally in Chapter 3, short citations made to demonstrate very specific lexical or grammatical points—for which knowledge of Greek is indispensable—have been left in Greek without translation. This is also sometimes true for texts cited in the footnotes. Otherwise both English and Greek have been supplied. Translations (and emphases) are the author's unless otherwise noted. For canonical texts, both *NPNF14* and *Fonti* have often been consulted.

LEXICAL DATA AND DICTIONARIES

At present no searchable electronic database exists for the entire Byzantine canonical corpus, although *Syn*, which includes the full texts of the Apostles, the 4th and 5th C councils, and sixty-eight canons of Basil, may be found on the *Thesaurus Linguae Graecae* (#2879). Outside of these sources, lexical data, particularly in Chapter 3, has been culled manually from *Fonti*, with reference to *Kormchaya* and *Pitra*.

A serious problem in the field of Byzantine law remains the lack of a lexicon of Byzantine legal Greek.[1] The standard works of Liddell–Scott–Jones 1996, Lampe 1961, and Sophocles 1860 do not give adequate coverage for late antique or Byzantine legal Greek. Supplementary lexical works consulted include Avotins 1989, 1992 (both supplements to Liddell–Scott–Jones from the *Novels* and *Code* of Justinian), Mason 1974 (a study of Roman Greek legal terms—concluding, unfortunately, with Diocletian), Pitsakis 1976, 387–424 (a short but exceptionally useful glossary of legal Greek appended to the author's edition of the *Hexabiblos*), Roussos 1949 (an invaluable Greek–Latin–French dictionary of ecclesiastical legal terms), and Preisigke *et al.* 1925–93 (with supplements, for the papyri). Du Cange 1688 has also proven useful on occasion. For classical (Athenian) legal Greek the glossary in Todd 1993, 359–402 is very helpful. All of these sources will be cited normally, as necessary. Occasionally, however, the author has had to manually backtrack words through the *Basilica* (a 10th C compilation of 6th C Greek translations and paraphrases of the *CJC*) to the Latin *CJC* and then to Latin legal dictionaries or textbooks (e.g. Berger 1953, Buckland 1963, Kaser 1955).

[1] As remarked in Stolte 2006, 3.

Introduction to the Law and Legality of the Greek East

The Byzantine Canonical Tradition, 381–883

The present work is an exploration into the cultural history of Byzantine law, and more specifically, the cultural history of Byzantine church law. Its central concern is to illuminate the fundamental perceptions, categories, values, expectations, assumptions, and structures that constituted the intellectual and cultural framework of Byzantine canon law—a set of dynamics that, borrowing loosely from Harold Berman, we may term Byzantine "legal beliefs."[1] In this, it seeks to complement more traditional legal-historical approaches which emphasize the history of legal institutions, legal doctrines, or, more recently, the manifold negotiations of power and identity in legal discourses. It is not, however, an attempt to illuminate the cultural history of Byzantium through law; it is an attempt to illuminate the cultural contours of Byzantine law itself. It is, in effect, an exploration into the Byzantine legal imagination.

Its particular task is to unfold the cultural contours of law and legality from a close reading of the central texts of the Byzantine canonical tradition AD 381–883. These texts include not only the Byzantine canons themselves, but also the principal prologues to the canonical collections and the tradition's first forays into systematization. From these texts, and for the most part from these texts alone, it will attempt to sketch a legal-cultural architecture of the system as a whole. This process is in part an experiment in legal-historical methodology, designed to gauge the extent to which such texts can be read to describe and "think" about their own legal world.

Two disciplines form the essential backdrop for this study. The first is the study of Christian law. In this field this work may be considered—albeit indirectly—a companion volume, or even sequel, to Hamilton Hess's *The Early Development of Canon Law and the Council of Serdica* and Heinz

[1] Berman 1983, vii.

Ohme's *Kanon ekklesiastikos: die Bedeutung des altkirchlichen Kanonbegriffes*.[2] These works, although focused on different questions, and employing very different methodologies, broach many of the same issues treated in this study. My examination, however, seeks to complement and expand these volumes by tracking developments far beyond the fourth and fifth centuries, if in only one major Christian tradition.

The second is Byzantine law. In this discipline my work has been conceived as primarily addressing a major lacuna: the lack of a modern comprehensive history of Byzantine church law, or even of Byzantine law more broadly conceived.[3] Since the early modern period the field of Byzantine law, secular and ecclesial, has been dominated almost exclusively by source surveys.[4] These studies describe the historical genesis and content of legal sources and legal collections and trace patterns of transmission and mutual influence among these texts. They do not, however, offer synthetic or thematic treatments of legal doctrines, legal institutions, sociological and political realities of the law, or legal-theoretical and legal-cultural patterns. This study seeks to take one small step beyond these surveys by developing a more synthetic treatment of at least one of these areas, the last.

In the context of both disciplines, this work also has a broader methodological goal: to delineate more clearly the problem of early medieval law as a topic of cultural historical research—something in itself rarely considered—and to further develop a "vocabulary" and set of techniques for its study. My hope is that this will not only contribute to the long-term development of a much more comprehensive account of Byzantine law and Christian law than currently exists, but will also ignite interest in a subject that remains neglected within the mainstreams of late antique and early medieval studies.

This project faces a number of challenges. Ironically, the most significant emerge as deeply ingrained prejudices within the scholarly disciplines of Byzantine and church law themselves. Two scholarly narratives in particular have played a prominent role, directly or indirectly, in stifling creative investigation of our subject. Their influence is both pervasive and pernicious.

The first is the old but omnipresent narrative of late antique/Byzantine legal decline and corruption.[5] This narrative has been especially characteristic of accounts of secular law, where the story of late antique and Byzantine law has

[2] Hess 2002; Ohme 1998.

[3] The only modern work to qualify as a comprehensive history of Byzantine law, of the traditional institutional and doctrinal variety, remains Zachariä von Lingenthal 1892.

[4] See the list in Ch. 1, n. 21. For comments on the state of the literature, Fögen 1987, 137; Kazhdan 1989; Simon 2005; Stolte 2005; 2009.

[5] The idea of late antique and Byzantine law marking a "decline" is so commonplace as to hardly need comment; see the discussions of this narrative in Garnsey and Humfress 2001, 53–5; Honoré 2004, 109–32; Humfress 2007, 2–3 (and Humfress 1998, 8–10 with more examples); Matthews 2000, 23–9; Pieler 1997a, 565–6.

been principally the story of a gradual falling away from the conceptual heights of the classical Roman jurists. Fritz Pringsheim voiced a central conviction of this narrative when he traced the narrative curve of Roman law as one of steep classical ascent and post-classical descent: "Roman classical law rises like a mountain above the common level of the [other ancient laws] and it slopes down again to the previous level in the Byzantine period."[6] For legal historians of this tradition the central problem of late antique and Byzantine historical research is precisely—and perversely—the apparent defectiveness of their subject in comparison to its classical predecessor (and, implicitly, medieval successor). The task of the historian thus becomes largely the enumeration and examination of all of the ways in which late antique and Byzantine law simply did not "work" as it should. The litany of complaints is long, and reflects the legal pieties of historians trained in modern continental law: doctrinal coherence and elegance seem elusive; the system was oddly rhetorical; jurisprudential activity ebbed; facts and law and law and morality became "confused"; equity and substantive justice tended to win over procedural regularity; legislation became embarrassingly ornate and conceptually clumsy; juristic autonomy (from political interference) and creativity waned; the rule of law was poorly observed; and laws generally lost their importance and efficacy as effective instruments of policy and of dispute resolution.[7] In light of these "failures," the central task of the legal historian becomes the exploration of the causes and results of this evident decline.

A more moderate version of this narrative appears in the tendency to cast Byzantine law as a significant subject of study only in its role as a static repository of ancient Roman traditions.[8] In this narrative it is conceded that the Byzantines preserved important legal knowledge, but that they themselves did not appreciate, understand, or develop this heritage: the Byzantines lacked the "spirit" of Roman law,[9] and their law possessed a "poverty" of content.[10] Implicit in this narrative is the idea that this heritage

[6] Pringsheim 1944, 60.

[7] For a flavor of these themes and assessments in the older literature, see e.g. Biondi 1952, 1.1–2; Jolowicz 1952, 517–38; Kunkel 1964, 150–4, 177–81. See the discussion in Pieler 1978, 351–5, 361–5 (with many further references); 1997a, 592–3; and Ries 1983, 167, 210–23. Among the Byzantinists see above all Simon 1973, and the references in nn. 26–30. Some of these characteristics, particularly the loss of classical doctrinal and terminological precision and sophistication, were the basis of Ernst Levy's famous, but now mostly defunct (in its technical aspects), notion of *Vulgarrecht*. On this concept, and the variety of its usages, see the summary treatment of Liebs 2008; also Wieacker 1988, 2.207–18 and the references in n. 5.

[8] For this view, common in the older literature, see the comments in Stolte 1998, 266–9; 2005, 58; 2009. Pieler 1997a, 566 stills opts for this view.

[9] Hammer 1957, 1; so also e.g. Stolte 2003, 92: "never in any moment of its history did Byzantine law manage to surpass the intellectual qualities of its great Roman ancestor, the 'classical' Roman law of Antiquity . . . the encyclopedia [the Digest] was never spiritually digested."

[10] Giaro 2006a, 285–6.

did become properly appreciated once more, namely during the great flowering of western medieval jurisprudence and, beyond that, in the European development of the *ius commune* generally—culminating, perhaps, in the 19th C German *Begriffsjurisprudenz* that forms the background of much 19th and early 20th C writing on Roman legal history. In any case, the history of Byzantine law becomes chiefly a story of transmission and anticipation, and thus of minor interest in and of itself.

This last tendency is one aspect of the second major narrative under which the modern study of Byzantine law labors: primitivism. This narrative is primarily a feature of the historiography of first millennium western law, this time more specifically ecclesiastical law, but its shadow falls over eastern developments as well. In this narrative, legal developments of the first millennium are consistently cast as a story of the slow but inevitable—almost providential—progress of law towards the 11th–12th C western legal developments. In canon law, the chief event is the transformation of canon law into an independent legal discipline on the model of the revived medieval Roman law.[11] This development is posited as the natural evolutionary endpoint of church law, and everything before this period is thus examined almost entirely, if perhaps unconsciously, in terms of the inchoate and "not yet," as simple prefigurations of later advances. Earlier developments are thus once again of little interest in themselves. Byzantine church law is rarely an explicit subject of these narratives, but it nevertheless suffers from association as the eastern counterpart to the first millennium western tradition, and from its own distinct lack of a medieval transformation comparable to that of the 12th C west. By implication, Byzantine church law remains only an example of a "primitive," pre-medieval, stunted legal world.

Both of these narratives have had a particularly crippling effect in the area of the cultural history of law. The logic is inexorable: if Byzantine law, secular or ecclesial, is simply the story of decline and decadence, and/or primitivism, it is precisely the intellectual and theoretical underpinnings of these historical realities that become least deserving of scholarly attention. Indeed, for the most part, until relatively recently, they have been almost completely ignored.

[11] Examples of this evolutionary reading of western canon law include Brasington 1994 (where prologues are studied as "evolving" towards the values of sophisticated jurisprudence); Cosme 1955a, 63 (with church law moving along the "way to internal perfection"); Fournier and Le Bras 1931, 75–7 (with systematic collections marking "progress" in the still "embryonic" science of canon law); Gaudemet 1994, viii (the first millennium characterized as "a slow ascension," moving towards the "golden age"), and Kuttner 1960, 1–3 (pre-12th C law as "dissonance" followed by "harmony"); see also Cosme 1955; Ferme 1998, 195–202; Kuttner 1976, 199–207. Sohm 1918, 3–8 provides many examples from the older literature of this narrative of the "Unentwickeltheit und Ohnmacht" of canon law for a thousand years. Such tendencies are much less marked in more recent surveys, such as Pennington 2007 and Reynolds 1986. See also the recent criticism of this type of narrative in Nelson 2008, 303.

Only a few countervailing currents in the older literature may be remarked. Two scholars in particular were almost unique in their attempts to present sympathetic accounts of late antique and/or Byzantine legal culture without pronounced recourse to the usual heuristics of legal decadence or primitivism. Each was interested not only in describing the cultural contours of the legal phenomena of this "dark age," but also in attempting to develop a set of categories and models for explaining and understanding these phenomena. Unfortunately, neither author has been particularly appreciated for his contributions in this regard.

In canon law the towering figure is Rudolph Sohm (1841–1917). A Romanist by training, Sohm turned his hand to the history of canon law in two major works: *Das altkatholische Kirchenrecht und das Dekret Gratians* (1918) and his two-volume study *Kirchenrecht* (1923). In these studies, particularly the latter, Sohm pursued the thesis that the "essence" of law is opposed to the essence of the church, and that therefore the history of church law has been mostly a long, sad story of a slow disintegration into secular legalism. For Sohm, the 12th C medieval developments, in particular, far from marking a moment of advancement and evolution, represented precisely the critical and catastrophic moment of "fall" into legal formalism—a kind of legal devolution.

This polemical Lutheran reversal of the standard Roman Catholic narrative led Sohm—almost accidentally—to reconsider the 4th–11th C developments in a more sympathetic light than virtually anyone previously. He even developed a model of early medieval church law as a proprietary 'sacramental" *altkatholisch* law, distinct (and superior) in many critical ways from the later medieval synthesis.[12] Estimations of this model vary, but the chief value of his work for our purposes is simply the attempt to consider this early medieval legal material as constituting a mature legal world worthy of detailed exposition in itself, on its "own terms," with its own values, preoccupations, and coherence.

Unfortunately the polemical, even homiletical, tone of his work, and the strained nature of some of his analyses (especially of Gratian's *Decretum*), have justifiably discouraged appreciation of his ideas by later legal historians.[13] Ironically, Sohm also introduced another narrative of decline into the scholarly mix, this time of the general devolution of all church law from an original charismatic, apostolic purity into the corrupt legalization and secularization of the post-Constantinian church. This narrative of decline-into-legalism has now become quite common in the literature, and is probably as detrimental

[12] See esp. Sohm 1918, 536–674; 1923, 2.63–86.

[13] For reflection, and extensive bibliography, on the tumultuous reception of Sohm's theories, especially among Roman Catholic canonists, see Congar 1973; also Brasington 2001. Berman 1983 represents something of a revival of Sohm in secular form.

to appreciating Byzantine developments as its secular counterpart.[14] Nevertheless, despite these problems, Sohm's brief treatment of early medieval church law remains among the most insightful assessments of pre-Gratianic law, eastern or western, ever committed to paper.[15] We will return to some of his exceptionally prescient formulations throughout this work.

A more respected, and better-known, work is Biondo Biondi's three-volume *Il diritto romano cristiano* (1952–4). This monumental study addressed almost all aspects of the transformation and appropriation of Roman law in the late antique Christian context. Although dated, it continues to be consulted as a point of reference for all manner of specific problems and issues of institutional and doctrinal development. The overall thesis of the work, however, has generally been neglected, even if it may be the most valuable and creative aspect of the whole study—certainly it is for our purposes. Biondi's central concern was to show that all of the traditional "failures" of late antique law can in fact be read as specifically Christian cultural reformulations and re-evaluations of the nature and purpose of law. Biondi thus tried to explore late antique legal developments in terms of cultural change, not simply cultural decadence, and therefore managed to produce a much more nuanced and sympathetic account of the late antique *Vorstellungswelt* than would otherwise be possible.

Unfortunately, like Sohm, Biondi's scholarship is directed by confessional concerns (this time Roman Catholic), and the scope of his argument (from late antiquity to the 20th C), along with his startling tendency to build arguments from late antique legal texts and modern Roman Catholic pronouncements in almost the same breath, can leave historians today a little nonplussed.[16] Nevertheless, his work—like Sohm's—retains its value simply because of its attempt to treat post-classical law as a subject worthy of careful cultural-historical examination and explanation in and of itself. Many of his observations remain fundamental.

Beyond these early figures, it is only very recently that the disciplines of late antique and Byzantine law as a whole have attempted to confront systematically the older narratives of decline and primitivism. The present work may be identified as another such attempt. Here, however, a certain methodological bifurcation may be remarked in how specialists in late antique law and Byzantine law have approached this problem.

The Byzantinists, particularly those associated with the Max-Planck-Institut für europäische Rechtsgeschichte in Frankfurt, have tended to address the problem of decline by completely rethinking the formalist cultural-legal

[14] This narrative is an aspect of the general (usually Protestant) narrative of the "Constantinian Fall" of the church. It can be felt quite tangibly in Erickson 1991a, Hess 2002, Ohme 1998.

[15] Sohm 1918, 536–674; 1923, 2.63–86.

[16] See e.g. Biondi 1952–4, 1.40–2.

paradigm that has generated the narrative in the first place. Instead of trying to fit the observed phenomena into a modern formalist mold, and to find various political or social rationales for its failures, they have tended to formulate a new paradigm to take account of the changes witnessed—that is, like Biondi, to attempt to read the "failures" as conforming to a new and very different cultural *ideal* of law.

The pioneering text in this regard is Dieter Simon's 1973 work *Rechtsfindung am byzantinischen Reichsgericht*.[17] In this study—still poorly known outside of specialist circles—the decisions of a judge of the Hippodrome, Eustathius, preserved in an 11th C Byzantine legal textbook, the *Πεῖρα*, are analyzed in terms of modern continental legal-scientific *Rechtsdogmatik*. Not surprisingly, Eustathius' decisions come off badly: terminology is varied for purely aesthetic reasons; decisions that could be based on laws are based upon equity; similar cases are treated completely differently and with reference to different laws; laws are sometimes sought after a decision to provide a predetermined penalty; and interpretative rules run wild.[18]

To explain these results, Simon does not, however, declare the *Πεῖρα* an example of primitivism or decline, nor even make recourse to the well-worn narrative of Byzantine political "corruption" or decadence.[19] Instead, he considers that the observed phenomena can be explained if we accept that rhetoric itself is the main dynamo of Byzantine *Rechtsfindung*, and that the laws are employed quite consistently if we consider them analogous to rhetorical topoi.[20] In effect—although these are not quite Simon's words—Byzantine law may be understood as functioning as a grand literary enterprise, focused on justice, and with laws constituting one (and only one) potential pool of literary tools for constructing and effecting justice. Other tools can also be employed, including any type of reasoned argument, a moral precept, or a citation from classical authors. Ultimately, as Simon puts it, one never so much argues "from" the law as "with" the laws.[21] Indeed, the author of the *Πεῖρα* at one point remarks that "for this decision he [Eustathius] *also* cited laws"[22] (apparently they are optional); and elsewhere a decision is praised first for its elegant and morally sound qualities, and *then* for the fact that it also included legal citations.[23]

[17] Simon 1973; and see esp. the discussion and expansion on Simon's work in Pieler 1978, 346–51.

[18] Simon 1973, 13–23.

[19] For a classic example of this last approach, see Beck 1981, who wishes to read—very anachronistically—variability in the application of Byzantine legal dogma in terms of *raison d'état*.

[20] On this particularly, see Simon 1973, 18–23.

[21] Simon 1973, 20.

[22] Cited without reference in Simon 1973, 21; emphasis Simon's.

[23] Cited without reference in Simon 1973, 13.

Simon notes that laws nevertheless remained important in this world, and he includes many examples of quite sophisticated technical rule arguing and application. The continued high status of laws, he suggests, may be explained by the fact that laws remain closely connected to the authority and person of the semi-divine emperor. Indeed, Simon observes, every Byzantine hearing could be considered an extension of the emperor's personal jurisdiction.[24] This, however, tended to heighten the degree of equity in the system, as the emperor's decision is beyond rational critique or the demand for juridical consistency—it is always a quasi-divine statement in the realm of the Just and the Good.[25] In effect, laws remain critical, but they must always be read in light of a substantive criterion: the emperor's sense of justice.

In very few pages, then, Simon turns on its ear any expectation of a Byzantine legal formalism of a modern variety (which I will define more extensively in a moment). Instead, he starts to sketch a reasonable alternative centered around the realization of the quasi-divine substantive justice of the emperor, and the ideal of the negotiation of legal rules in the context of a much broader set of literary and cultural values—all loosely governed by the expectations of an ancient rhetorical education. Modern continental civilian-legal values not only do not appear as ideals here, but they make little sense: conceptual consistency is overruled by concerns for aesthetically pleasing, rhetorically and morally consistent decisions, and judgments are *intended* to realize extra-juridical ideals of justice. The theoretical place for many other features of modern formalist systems—an independent and "creative" expert judiciary, forensic agonism, technical jurisprudence, the rule of law, the autonomy of law, and even the ideal of submitting to formal rules at all—is far from clear.

One may contest the details of Simon's conclusions, but his critical breakthrough is on the level of methodology: like Sohm and Biondi, Simon sees the "problems" of Byzantine law as an opportunity for charting an altogether different and rather fascinating legal world. By resisting the temptation to assume the hegemonic ideals of later western legal culture as absolute standards, he opens the way to a much more nuanced historical appreciation of the cultural dynamics of Byzantine law. In effect, he suggests that as long as one is willing to stretch one's legal imagination, Byzantine law emerges as not only an interesting legal phenomenon, but, taken on its own terms, one that is internally coherent and even rather sophisticated.

Numerous other studies in Byzantine law have since confirmed and built upon Simon's work. Investigation of other juridical decisions, for example, has tended to reinforce the low place of laws and technical-legal concepts in legal processes: general extra-legal moral or metaphysical considerations, and

[24] Simon 1973, 29. [25] Simon 1973, 29.

the rhetorical know-how of presenting them, are often more prominent than the juridical construction of justice.[26] John Haldon puts it well, commenting on 7th C law: "Judges were not . . . expected to fulfill their obligations through applying the law, in a modern sense. On the contrary, the law they applied was the morality of the society—this replaced the normative legal framework—interpreted through the prism of inherited legislation."[27] Law was essentially an exercise in applied morality.

The degree to which later Byzantine legislation disappoints as the policy instrument of an active modern-like positivist legislator has also become increasingly clear. Haldon again summarizes aptly: "the legal 'system' became less a practical instrument for intervening in the world of men . . . but more a set of theories which represented a desired . . . state of affairs. . . . Imperial action was thus not directed at emending laws to conform to reality, but rather at emending reality to conform to the inherited legal-moral apparatus."[28] Legislation thus emerges increasingly as a highly sacralized and symbolic project, more the product of God than a secular emperor, and with the task of providing a symbolic framework for understanding the world and impressing and internalizing moral and metaphysical lessons—not necessarily addressing "real" legal and political problems (although it did this too—at least occasionally).[29]

In this sacralized world, not surprisingly, standard legal abrogation principles such as *lex posterior derogat legi priori*—although known and understood—seem to have had disturbingly little meaning, and little consistent use (how do you abrogate a divine law?).[30] Similarly the rule of law and the relationship between secular law and church law can never seem to find clear conceptual articulation or delineation.[31] Consistent legal-dogmatic architecture of any kind is simply difficult to identify: legal concepts and techniques are known, and occasionally employed, but they are somehow not very important. As is constantly noted, Byzantine law seems strangely rhetorical, and untechnical.[32]

Byzantinists, then, in sum, have tended to confront the old narratives of decline and primitivism by rethinking the appropriateness of applying a formalist legal mold to this ancient law. By contrast, scholars in the field of

[26] e.g. Dennis 1994; Kazhdan 1994; Laiou 1994; Macrides 1990; 1992; 2005; Papagianni 2005; Pieler 1970; Stolte 2009.

[27] Haldon 1990, 278. [28] Haldon 1990, 249.

[29] In addition to Haldon 1990, see Fögen 1987; 1989; Lokin 1994; Simon 1994; also Lanata 1989a.

[30] As n. 29; also Fögen 1993, 67–8; Pieler 1978, 346; 1991; Stolte 1991; 1991a; 2008, 695; 2009, 85–8. Cf. also Triantaphyllopoulos 1985, 7–8 on the Greek principle of *lex* ***prior*** *derogat legi* ***posteriori***.

[31] See Fögen 1993, 68–72 for a summary of recent research; also Stolte 2009.

[32] Aside from Simon 1973, see Pieler 1978 and the excellent articulation of the problem in Stolte 1988.

late antique law have generally taken a very different tack. Here researchers have been more concerned to show that the "failures" of late antique law were simply not as bad, widespread, or meaningful as they sometimes appear: late antique law was not so corrupt as usually thought; jurists were still present and active; codification and legislation were still creative, even learned, and more doctrinally coherent than they are usually given credit for; juristic activity was not so closely controlled by the centralized state as sometimes supposed; the rhetoricization of legislation was not as complete, new, or significant as it seemed; the emperor was not so overwhelmingly in control of law as he appeared to be, nor as arbitrary, and participation in the legislative process was broader than often thought; laws were more efficacious than the old narratives allow; and (thank goodness!) there was still plenty of room for clever legal professionals to "play" the system.[33]

All of this is undoubtedly true for the late antique period. Nevertheless, it is difficult to shake off the disquieting sense that such studies are still "keeping up legal appearances." The unstated assumption of much of this research is that the only way late antique law might be possessed of a real legal cultural life is if it conformed to the demands of a modern-like formalist–positivist system (understood to be those of "proper" Roman law too), complete with an ongoing and quasi-independent scientific jurisprudence, a responsive and creative legislative center intent on effecting policy through laws, the rule of law, and a strong emphasis on resolving disputes through the consistent logical application of formal legal rules. Many of these studies thus appear to have internalized the legal-cultural preconceptions of the older generation of scholars. Certainly they have not taken the step that Byzantinists generally have, that is, to ask whether these assumed ideals corresponded to the actual legal-cultural ideals of late antique society in the first place. The deficiencies and problems of late antique law are thus addressed not in terms of the adequacy of our understanding of the legal-cultural model at play—which is in fact almost never raised as a direct topic of discussion in these studies—but in terms of the extent of our understanding of sociolegal praxis.

The reason for this difference is the distinctly sociohistorical turn of much recent scholarship on late antique law. Many scholars are simply no longer interested in exploring the intellectual architecture of late antique law, decline

[33] Among the scholars whose approaches reflect these concerns may be counted J. Harries, T. Honoré, C. Humfress, D. Liebs, J. Matthews, P. Pieler, B. Sirks, and W. Voss. Exceptions are mainly to be found in the older literature. Aside from Biondi himself, scholars such as Straux 1949 or Honig 1960, for example, and others engaged in the older conversation about the rhetoricization of Roman law, might be read as opening a door to a reassessment of the late antique conceptualization of law. In practice, however, this stream of research remained mostly confined to very narrow questions of the influence of specific rhetorical concepts on specific points of Roman juridical doctrine. For further discussion and references on this older literature, see Humfress 2007, 25, 81–6, *et passim*.

or no.[34] Instead, providing accounts of sociopolitical realities, and in particular the varieties of negotiations of power of which law is both part and vehicle, has taken center stage. Many recent studies thus treat intellectual-cultural issues, and often very perceptively, but their real argument is usually centered on affirming that, for example, late antique law can be read as an interesting, creative, and diverse set of sociopolitical interactions; legislative processes were informed by a surprisingly dynamic set of figures and influences; or that the rhetorical character of the legislation played an important role in broader patterns of power negotiation.[35] For all these topics, the matter of the intellectual or cultural "decline" of law, or indeed the intellectual and cultural underpinnings of these phenomena at all, is simply not a very relevant question, and can be sublimated into descriptions of social practice. Further, the cultural-historical problems that are raised, such as the construction of authority, perceptions of punishment, the textures of imperial propaganda, or the role of law in identity formation, tend to be more about the interface of law and culture than the ancient culture of law per se. In all cases, the specifically cultural-historical problems surrounding the idea of legal "decline," and the intellectual and cultural architecture of law and legality generally, are bypassed. As a result, the older cultural-theoretical models can easily persist unchallenged just beneath the surface.

This study is deeply indebted to the work of both late antique and Byzantine legal historians, but methodologically it finds its greatest affinity with the trajectory set by the Byzantinists. It too will attempt to confront the traditional narratives of decline and primitivism chiefly by re-examining the cultural-legal paradigms that have generated these narratives in the first place—and by further developing the new paradigm Simon and others have adumbrated. In particular, I will attempt to demonstrate that Byzantine canon law did constitute a distinct legal whole and that it possessed its own, sometimes even impressive, internal logic and coherence, albeit of a different kind than a modern lawyer might expect.

Other fields have also informed this work. A particularly important set of background problematics and insights has been furnished by eastern (Byzantine) Orthodox canon law.[36] This discipline remains largely unknown

[34] The paucity of trained lawyers among recent historians of late antique law may in part account for this difference of interest.

[35] See e.g. studies such as Harries 1999; 2000; Humfress 2007; or the contributions in Matthisen 2001.

[36] Recent overviews of some of the central issues of modern Orthodox canon law include Corecco 1992, Erickson 1991a, Meyendorff 1978, Ohme 1991, Patsavos 1981. No comprehensive survey of the modern discipline exists, although see Potz and Synek 2007, and the very brief treatment of Wagschal 2012. For a historical sketch of the Greek field, see Troianos 2001; for the Russian, see Tsipin 2002, 19–23; for the Romanian, see Stan 1974.

in the mainstream western study of legal history.[37] This is in part because the bulk of Orthodox canon law literature remains in languages that are not commonly known in the western academy. Equally important, however, is the fact that relatively little modern Orthodox canon law work is strictly historical in purpose or orientation. The dominant vehicles of the modern discipline have been technical canonical manuals.[38] Written in the categories and forms of the modern civilian tradition, these are orientated towards contemporary (and often highly regional) practice, and are therefore very synchronic in content and method. Even works written in a more historical vein tend to be directed primarily to contemporary problems in Orthodox church life, and are often very theological.[39]

Modern Orthodox canonical literature nevertheless remains of great interest for our topic, if simply because the central texts of the present study continue to function as the living legal corpus of the Byzantine Orthodox churches. As a result, much Orthodox canonical literature over the past century and a half represents a fascinating study in the appropriation of late antique and Byzantine legal thought in a variety of modern legal contexts. Directly or indirectly, Orthodox canonists have been confronting a problem not so dissimilar from my own: how to make sense of a pre-modern legal system in the context and categories of a very different, post-medieval legal culture.

The formulations offered by Orthodox canonists to "square the circle" of this difficult appropriation are varied. Broadly, two approaches may be identified. The first, and the dominant, is the "legal scientific" tradition, represented by most of the manuals. This tradition seeks to adapt the traditional texts to the forms and methodologies of modern continental civil law (and often modern Roman Catholic canon law). The degree of adaptation varies, but the typical concerns of representatives of this tradition—who usually have formal legal training of a western type—include how traditional texts can be read in terms of abstract categories of rights, duties, and powers; questions about the valid promulgation of legislation by competent authorities; the

[37] Exception include the many Orthodox scholars who have made distinguished contributions in the history of texts and ecclesial institutions, such as V. Beneshevich, P. L'Huillier, C. Pitsakis, and S. Troianos, to name only a few.

[38] No comprehensive list of the canonical manuals exists, although see Milaš 1902, 37–41 for 19th C bibliography. Those consulted here include Berdnikov 1889, Boumis 2003, Christophilopoulos 1965, Konidaris 2000, Milaš 1902 (one of the very few not restricted to one national tradition), Ostroumov 1893, Pavlov 1902, Rhodopoulos 2005, Sakellaropoulos 1898, Sokolov 1851, Troianos 2003a, Tsipin 2002. The only manual available in English is a modified translation of Rhodopoulos 2005 (Rhodopoulos 2007; but see also Patsavos 1975). All of these manuals are very similar to Protestant and Catholic canonical manuals of the 19th C. In Greece, the manual tradition divides roughly into "ecclesiastical law" (treating broadly secular law relating to the church, and its relationship with canon law; so Christophilopoulos 1965 or Troianos 2003a, for example) and "canon law" (treating the church's own law; so Boumis 2003 or Rhodopoulos 2005); for a list of Greek ecclesiastical law manuals, see Troianos 2003a, 19–20.

[39] e.g. Christopoulos 1972; L'Huillier 1996.

constitution of canon law as a valid branch of law; the disciplinary autonomy of law (versus theology); the formal mechanisms for legal change; the development of formal distinctions and definitions (for example, *ius sacrum* and *ius humanum*; "doctrinal" canons and "disciplinary" canons; validity and liceity; *potestas ordinis* and *potestas iurisdictionis*); and, above all, the consistency and comprehensiveness of canon law as a logical system of formal norms. Broadly, these concerns reveal a strong desire to mold the tradition into a modern legal science.

The second, much more amorphous, stream is mostly characterized by the conviction that modern legal categories—and particularly the formalist "legal scientific" model—are precisely *unable* to encompass or convey the textures of the traditional canonical materials.[40] Representatives of this "school," who are usually theologians, historians, or philosophers—not lawyers—point to the many dissonances between the expectations of a modern civilian jurist and the evidence of the texts. Typically, law itself is then rejected as a particularly helpful or useful concept for understanding Byzantine canonical phenomena. The canons, it is argued, must instead be understood as only expressions of deeper metaphysical realities. Characteristic is the assessment of Lewis Patsavos: "Although the holy canons constitute the Church's law, they nevertheless differ essentially from all other types of law . . . They are not to be understood as legal regulations, but as the practical application of the church's dogmas";[41] or Vladimir Lossky: "[The canons] are not, properly speaking, juridical statutes, but the applications of the dogmas of the Church."[42] In many cases the canons emerge as something to be bypassed or transcended: one must constantly strive to "go beyond 'canons' and 'canon law',"[43] or one must attain to a higher "canonical consciousness"[44] that is apparently above and beyond the canonical texts themselves.[45] Similarly, warnings abound against "legal mentalities"[46] and "reducing" canon law to legal categories.[47] Alternative

[40] Examples of this type of thinking, ranging from direct argumentation to passing expression, include Afanasiev 1933; 1936; Deledemos 2002; Erickson 1991a; Evdokimov 1959, 185–7; 1962, 181–3; Lossky 1944, 175; Meyendorff 1966, 111–12; 1978, 99–103; Patsavos (Kapsanis) 2003; Schmemann 1979, 33–4, 58–61; Yannaras 1970, 173–93. Afanasiev and Yannaras are perhaps this position's most prominent exponents. See also the trenchant—if not always well-informed—critique of such positions in Corecco 1992, 70–7; more balanced is Ohme 1991, 234–9. The context and origins of this "anti-legal" trend in Orthodox thinking have never been investigated at length, but important context, especially as relates to tendencies in 19th C Russian thought, is given by Nichols 1989, 1–33 and Walicki 1987, 9–104. The influence of J. Mohler (see Congar 1970, 415–23) and R. Sohm may be suspected frequently, when not explicitly acknowledged. On Sohm and Afanasiev in particular, see now Borbu 2009.

[41] Patsavos (Kapsanis) 2003, 186, 188. This ecclesiological perspective may be found most elaborately in Afanasiev 1933, 1936, and also Christopoulos 1972, 253–66.

[42] Lossky 1944, 175.

[43] Erickson 1991a, 21.

[44] A very frequently expressed concept, especially in Afanasiev.

[45] See Ohme 1991 on the hermeneutical difficulties of this type of theory.

[46] Deledemos 2002.

[47] e.g. Meyendorff 1978, 103.

formulations or hermeneutical concepts are then often proposed, including "jurisprudence of the Holy Spirit,"[48] or a narrative of a pre-Constantinian legal purity,[49] or various precepts of existentialist freedom,[50] or attempts at articulating a legal "via media" that is neither too legal nor too antinomian.[51] Not surprisingly, these positions often emerge in the polemical context of establishing a "non-legal" eastern Christian identity over and against the "legalist" west.

None of these formulae, which are more theological than historical in intention and content, will be the object of sustained discussion in this study, but many of the difficulties encountered by both schools, whether in trying to fit the traditional texts into modern molds or trying to devise some type of new formulation to describe the dynamics observed, serve as useful stimuli for my project of articulating a legal-cultural description of the Byzantine canonical world. I will occasionally return to the problems, insights, and formulations of this valuable literature.

To turn to methodology, this work is ultimately not closely aligned with any approach commonly employed in Orthodox canon law, the history of church law, or even late antique or Byzantine law (although Simon's work is a near parallel). Its approach may best be described as a kind of legal ethnography, albeit of a historical and literary variety. It will thus proceed by exploring how the central prescriptive texts of the Byzantine church—taken together as representing a distinct legal-cultural phenomenon—can be read as articulating the fundamental beliefs and categories of the Byzantine canon-legal world through their very structures, patterns of expression, definitions, strategies of composition, and even stylistic tendencies. It is not primarily an exercise in the history of ideas, that is, an inquiry into the meaning of particular concepts ("law" or "justice" or "canon") and their development over time. Explicit, conceptual assertions of legal belief and thought—definitions and statements of the nature of law and legality—will be considered, but equally important is the unstated, the unconscious, and the implicit. My conviction is that questions of ethos, predominant images, prevailing metaphors, and fundamental "shapes" of the law's expression and growth are as important as direct statements of legal theory in arriving at a nuanced and comprehensive description of the Byzantine legal imagination.

Such a methodology—details of which I will return to in a moment—has its limitations. I must in particular issue the caveat that, as a cultural-historical study, *this work is above all interested in how Byzantine canon law was designed or written to work* (consciously or unconsciously). That is, it is

[48] Meyendorff 1981, 207–8. [49] Erickson 1991a. [50] Yannaras 1970.

[51] See e.g. Erickson 1991a and his assessment of the tradition as composed of two poles: "legalists" and "anarchists"; similarly L'Huillier 1964 on the dangers of both *juridicisme* and *spiritualisme*.

focused broadly on how Byzantine canon law was *supposed* to work. This is not unconnected from how it *did* work. Expectations for the system's operation must be taken into account when one is evaluating evidence for its "real" operation, and vice versa. Nevertheless, this study is intentionally not directly concerned with the social or political-historical realities of the Byzantine system, except on a few occasions where they are essential for illumining specific problems of cultural perception. My chief emphasis is instead on what the legal anthropologists might call the "formalities" of law. Here a remark of Kenneth Pennington, commenting on the traditional figural representation of Justice, is not unhelpful: "social historians record the number of weights on [Justice's] scales but do not see justice through her eyes."[52] In this study I am very much trying to look through Justice's eyes, not count the weights on her scales.

Even as an exercise in cultural history, this study constitutes only one possible approach. Much can also be learned about Byzantine legal beliefs through investigation of legislative processes and institutions, the historical application of specific regulations, forensic practice, and references to law in non-legal literature. The first of these approaches, in particular, has dominated legal-cultural research within the field of church law, and has been very productive.[53] It examines the nature of canonical law and legality primarily through the eyes of its original producers, set firmly in their original contexts. My approach, however, is quite different. I wish to understand law not as encountered and constructed at its original point of production but as encountered in its principal textual manifestations in the later tradition, that is, in and as corpora of regulations in canonical collections. This is driven by the observation that law has a life that extends well beyond its original legislative contexts, and that the vast majority of Byzantines would have encountered and engaged with their canonical tradition as corpora of regulations gathered and arranged in collections precisely removed from their original contexts. As such, the assumptions about law and legality that these collections themselves embody and promote are critical, even central, to understanding Byzantine legal culture. Nevertheless, this focus is not exclusive of the more traditional approach, or any other, and illumines only one part of the picture.

To anticipate some criticism, this work is not directly engaging many of the concerns of the "new cultural history." This is intentional. Historians have become increasingly aware of the role played by forms of discourse in the negotiation of power among individuals and groups. Beliefs and ideals, it is

[52] Pennington 1994, 206. Justice, it will be noted, receives her blindfold only in the 15th C; see Curtis and Resnik 1987, 1755–6; Ziolkowski 1997, 18. Cf. Maguire 1994.

[53] So much so that the history of church law has at times become almost an adjunct to the history of church councils. See e.g. Hefele and Leclercq 1907, Halfond 2010, Hess 2002, *Sources*, Mardirossian 2010; it may even be felt in the source surveys, e.g. Gaudemet 1985. Cf. the comments of Halfond 2010, 159.

recognized, are both formed by, and serve to enforce and maintain, assertions of control and patterns of domination. Cultural historians have therefore become very sensitive to the problem of the interface and interrelation of cultural expressions with sociological and political contests. In this work, however, I am purposely, albeit artificially, bracketing cultural expressions from all broader sociopolitical matrices. This is not intended as an assertion of any particular historiographical dogmatics, but merely as an analytical tool for ensuring focus on Byzantine belief and theory *in se*, whatever their precise, if undoubted, interrelation with power dynamics. Although I would agree that a clear sense of the explicit and implicit goals, beliefs, assumptions, and aspirations of cultural phenomena is essential for any consideration of that phenomenon's sociological "existence," and vice versa, in this work the emphasis will be on the cultural half of this hermeneutic dynamic.

Following Simon's lead, I have placed at the core of my methodology a comparison of Byzantine and (a) modern legal culture. I might wish that I could approach the texts without a comparator, to allow the texts to describe and define "on their own" their sense of legality, with as little input or presupposition on my part as possible. But this is impossible. Some type of predetermined questions or criteria for identifying and examining "the legal" must be brought to the texts. In fact, one can only speak of examining the legal textures of the Byzantine canonical texts "on their own terms" if one understands this phrase as shorthand for the dialectical process of challenging modern preconceptions and expectations with the evidence from the historical texts—and as signaling a general willingness to refrain from an immediately negative valuation of any dynamics or tendencies that seem foreign or unusual. The success of this process is dependent precisely upon shedding any pretense of "presuppositionless" analysis. One must therefore be quite open about what type of legal questions and criteria one is bringing to the texts, that is, what legal-theoretical foil one is employing in the analysis. This requires a deconstruction of one's own legal-cultural presuppositions and categories.

Simon's foil was modern continental *Rechtsdogmatik*. He explored how the Byzantine texts conformed—or mostly, did not conform—to the doctrinal categories of modern legal science. This study's foil must be broader inasmuch as my scope of inquiry is broader. The concern here is not so much the operation of specific legal doctrines as the overall shape of the Byzantine legal imagination. The foil for this work must therefore be nothing other than a generalized description of modern legal culture itself—the set of expectations, values, categories, instincts, and images that make up the spoken and unspoken fabric of our modern western legal experience.

Any attempt to describe something as broad as "modern legal culture" is, of course, doomed to end in caricature and oversimplification. Nevertheless, if understood as a research heuristic and not a definitive cultural analysis, a reasonable working description of the broad cultural assumptions of modern western law can be constructed. Modern legal theory and modern legal anthropology and sociology have in fact already provided a rich vocabulary and set of categories for constructing just such a generalized portrait.[54]

Drawing on these disciplines, I will assert as my legal foil a composite construction of modern narratives, practices, and perceptions that may be termed legal formalism, or better, formalism–positivism.[55] This construction does not correspond to any real legal system—and certainly would not meet the approval of most legal theorists—but it is broadly descriptive of a set of practices and cultural ideals which have their immediate ancestors in 12th C western European readings of Roman law texts, and which have become characteristic of the official law of most modern western legal systems (especially continental).[56]

Law is first of all conceived as an independent and abstract project or field of learned endeavor concerned with the application of a formal system of mostly written rules to a wide range of dispute and order-related factual situations. These rules are conceived as, ideally, clearly established and defined by a competent legislative authority, and are treated as, and intended to form, a closed and coherent systematic whole.[57] The rules are intended to be as comprehensive as possible, even "gapless," and are meant to be able to address virtually any factual situation that may arise. To this end, they are often exceptionally lengthy and detailed, with many provisions, exceptions, and

[54] Legal anthropology and sociology, and the related field of comparative law, have been neglected by historians of Byzantine and church law but they are a fertile, and indeed indispensable, source of categories and concepts for describing and understanding our subject. Todd 1993, 18–29 awoke me to the importance of this literature, particularly legal anthropology. Among the works of legal anthropology/sociology, and comparative law, consulted for this study are the introductory works of Donovan 2007, Roberts 1979, and Rouland 1988, and the studies of Bohannan 1957, Diamond 1950, Glenn 2007, Gluckman 1955, Hoebel 1954, Hoebel and Llewellyn 1941, Maine 1861, Malinowski 1926, Pospisil 1971, and Weber 1925. Similarly stimulating has been the study of the cultural historian Walter Ong (Ong 1982, on orality and literacy, a work immensely useful for theorizing aspects of ancient legal thought), and works on law and literature, notably Posner 2009 and Ziolkowski 1997. Although of an entirely different nature, the opus of Pierre Hadot (e.g. Hadot 1995, 1995a) should also be mentioned here as containing many insights about the fundamental structures of late antique thought relevant to understanding late antique law—even if they have not yet been much tapped by legal historians. By way of caveat, of course, this work in no way pretends to be a work of legal anthropology or comparative law. I am, to borrow a phrase from Richard Posner (Posner 1993, xii), a consumer, not producer, of these fields.

[55] A very wide range of meanings can be attached to both these terms in modern legal theory. See the comments of Posner 1993, 9–26 (incl. n. 31); Wieacker 1952, 342 (incl. nn. 3, 5). My usage is proprietary and is defined by what follows.

[56] The following owes much to Berman 1983, 7–10; Glenn 2007, 118–52; Roberts 1979, 17–29; Watson 1995; Weber 1925, 61–4, 224–55, as well as numerous other works on legal theory and legal history found in the Bibliography. See also my preliminary delineation of these characteristics in Wagschal 2010.

[57] This does not require an actual code; Anglo-American law treats both statutory and case law as constituting a functionally coherent system—a "code"—of regulations, principles, and concepts.

qualifications—and there are usually very many of them. More importantly, the legal system is characterized by an advanced and sophisticated set of proprietary methods and techniques—a set of "secondary rules"—that governs the application and use of the "primary rules" and that tries to ensure that these rules can be applied as widely and consistently as possible.[58] These rules can even generate new rules as necessary.

Consistency and fairness of rule application is a central value of this system, and is related to the conviction that one can find a more or less "right" legal answer for any situation solely from the disciplined and predictable operation of logical legal principles and concepts (that is, the "forms" of the law can themselves produce correct answers—thus "formalism"). In effect, the rules *themselves* can be made to "think through" any situation. Because of this, the system places great emphasis on internal logical coherence, and is exceptionally concerned about establishing clear and precise definitions, concepts, and relationships between rules, and about eliminating any repetitions, irregularities, or contradictions. The system is thus often conceptualized as a "science." When the logical and consistent application of legal method and technique cannot find a proper legal answer, judicial "discretion" must be invoked—but, it is hoped, very rarely and in a very limited manner. It is much preferable for the system itself to produce an answer than to depend upon the whimsy of a fallible human judge. Indeed, the controlling metaphor of the system is technological: law is idealized as functioning as a quasi-mathematical mechanism of legal doctrine in which rules may be impartially—that is, mechanically—applied to different fact situations.[59] It is recognized that such a formalist rule mechanism will not always produce an obviously just solution for every problem, but this is understood as an unfortunate but necessary cost of the system. As a result, the critical distinction arises—and is accepted—between formal and substantive justice, that is, between a "legally" just solution (formally and procedurally correct) and a "really" just solution (according to the value judgments of a given observer or community). This can encourage a certain amoralism in law's practice, where participants are expected to function not so much as truth seekers but as skilled manipulators of a "rule game," defending "interests" in a strongly agonistic manner.

Not surprisingly, this complex structure of rules and rule logic is both operated and developed largely by a professional class of legal experts and academics, who are understood as an essential and natural aspect of the system. They function in the context of proprietary legal professional and academic infrastructures. These professionals tend to form a distinct caste in

[58] The concept of primary and secondary rules is borrowed here loosely from H. L. A. Hart (Hart 1961, 89–96), who borrowed it loosely from Wittgenstein.

[59] Justice's modern blindfold (see n. 52) is a perfect illustration: the *scale* is determining justice.

society, with its own forms of education, its own career paths, its own qualifications, its own professional language, its own dress, and its own standards of conduct—its own "ethos."

The presence of a well-defined and separate class of legal professionals is one aspect of another central motif: autonomy. Not only does law function as the domain of a clearly demarcated professional cadre, but law understands itself as a distinct field of human endeavor and study, separate from other fields and with its own language and special method of reasoning and thinking. It is, in particular, constantly concerned to differentiate itself from other types of normative systems and forms of social control. Especially characteristic is an ongoing preoccupation with distinguishing itself from ethics/morality and politics (and in canon law, theology). An extremely important aspect of this autonomous self-perception—and a critical aspect of its formalism *and* positivism—is the idea and ideal that law is able to function legitimately with as little recourse to "outside" narratives and values as possible. It wishes to remain sealed from all outside interferences, bound instead within its own well-defined legal rule world.

Finally, law is easily constructed and reconstructed as legislators or legal professionals shape and reshape it to conform to changing policies or values (this is the principal expression of the system's "positivism"). This may happen through a formal legislative process or through the application of philosophical or special legal-academic discourses (that is, a jurisprudence), whether deductive or casuistic in form. In all cases, however, the law is in this respect very "secular": it is very much a malleable human instrument or tool for the effecting of broader agendas or goals, whether these be the whim of a despot, the consequences of a natural-law theory, a policy of a democratic legislature, or a concern for greater systematic consistency. Provided that the correct formal procedures are followed (formalism again), rules may thus be dismissed, replaced, or modified quite easily. The law is thus typically always "progressing," "advancing," or "growing," adapting to new circumstances. Change, even profound change, is fairly easy, regular, and expected.

In summary, then, this legal world is characterized by detailed and comprehensive rules; an emphasis on systematic coherence and logical consistency; a strong assertion of autonomy from other normative discourses; very clear, almost mechanistic, processes for identifying and applying rules; complex structures of professionalism; and a high degree of legislative and jurisprudential malleability.

I must reiterate that this vision of the legal is a caricature, even a straw man. This particular image of law has long been recognized in both legal theory and legal anthropology as having no special claim as a source of universal categories to explore human law, nor even as embodying a particularly useful legal ideal.[60] Nevertheless, I employ it here because it is my conviction that it continues to quietly dominate the modern study of ancient law, secular and ecclesial, and more importantly, it remains, even if weakened, the functional *mythos* of modern western legal culture, however long ago modern legal theory may have left it in the dust. Indeed, even casual familiarity with legal textbooks or the rhetoric of the court system reveals that most lawyers, legislators, and judges in the western world tend to imagine their work in terms not so far from those just described. Similarly, most citizens of western countries, despite frustrations and dissatisfactions, understand and expect the processes, ideals, values, and struggles of this type of legal system. At the very least, then, this vision of law probably captures better than any other specific theoretical model the parameters and points of reference of our culture's baseline legal *imagination*, that is, our legal instincts and habits, the "cultural plot" of what law is about. It thus provides a heuristic backdrop of unparalleled richness and cultural density for any study of a non-western, non-modern legal system that aims to ferret out contrasts and similarities of legal-cultural belief.

This study is divided into four chapters. The first two treat the "framing" of the canonical tradition. In Chapter 1 I explore the tradition from a bird's-eye view, examining the overall textual shape of Byzantine canon law and the patterns of its historical development. Here I consider how the basic contours of these developments reveal the legal presuppositions of the "system" as a whole. In Chapter 2 I turn to how the Byzantines themselves introduced their own tradition and set the parameters of its operation through traditional prologues and prologue-like texts.

In the third chapter—in some respects the heart of this work—I turn to a careful reading of the Byzantine canons themselves as set within the Byzantine corpus. Here the literary orientation of the present work will become most evident as I analyze not so much the canons' substantive rule content as how forms, styles, and patterns of language reveal legal beliefs.

In the last chapter I move to the question of systematization. Here I consider in detail the origin, nature, and purpose of the first extant Byzantine systematic collections—the *Collection in Fifty Titles* and *Collection in Fourteen Titles*—as a means of exploring how the Byzantines conceived (or did not conceive) of the canonical tradition as an organized and interrelated system.

In the Conclusion I will consider how the various patterns and emphases that have emerged throughout the foregoing chapters might suggest a

[60] The extent that this model can claim universality for the definition of human law is the essential issue of the famous Gluckman–Bohannan debate in legal anthropology; see Donovan 2007, 100–22. In legal philosophy legal formalism–positivism of the type described here is strongly contested by virtually every modern school of legal theory, including—to name a few—sociological jurisprudence, legal realism, pragmatism, and critical law studies. To take but one example, see the comments of Stone 2004, 166–7.

coherent cultural-intellectual architecture of Byzantine canon law. I will attempt a description of this architecture or model and then consider what this might mean for our broader understanding of the history of Byzantine law, and what further problems it suggests.

A few other specific themes will be addressed throughout the study, even if they do not always emerge directly or obviously from the sources themselves. The most prominent is the relationship between Byzantine canon law and Byzantine secular law. This is a central question of the modern academic discussion of Byzantine law, and therefore deserving of special consideration. Here, however, my concern will be not the sociopolitical realities of this relationship, nor even so much the explicit theoretical articulations of this interaction (which are few in our texts, in any case), but rather the subtler textures of how the canonical texts locate themselves in relation to the secular law through patterns of shared nomenclature, diction, patterns of thought, compositional forms, genres, and images.

Throughout the work I will also occasionally employ comparisons with the Latin canonical tradition. This is both necessary and inevitable, given the western orientation of much modern canon law historiography: most of the basic models, categories, and narratives of the history of canon law have been developed with reference to the western experience. To fully appreciate the peculiarities of the eastern tradition I must therefore on occasion note points of similarities to and differences from the western tradition. I will also very occasionally look east, to the Syrian and "oriental" Christian worlds, considering ways in which Christian canon law can be read as a unified legal story. In both cases I will be attempting to take a few modest steps towards breaking the parochialism of much modern canon law historiography.

A number of limitations have been imposed upon this study. The first is chronological. The dates 381 to 883 have been chosen because the first corresponds (at least approximately) to the adoption of the so-called "Antiochian" corpus by the church of the recently triumphant Nicene orthodoxy, and therefore marks the emergence of the collection of texts that will become the core of the later Byzantine canonical tradition. The second marks the completion of the so-called Photian recension of the *Collection in Fourteen Titles*, which, in retrospect, marked the completion of the core Byzantine canonical corpus. These dates therefore encompass what may be considered the central period of development of the Byzantine canonical tradition, that is, the time during which the texts and text structures were produced that even to this day are considered the heart of the entire Byzantino-Orthodox canonical tradition. These dates are, however, symbolic; material outside of these dates will occasionally be considered to illustrate broader themes and patterns.

A limit has also been placed on the scope of material to be examined. As already remarked, I will mostly limit this study to the texts that emerge as the central corpus structures of the Byzantine canonical tradition. The definition and development of these "central corpus structures" will be examined in detail in Chapter 1, but suffice to say they include all of the canonical sources of the 883 recension of the *Collection in Fourteen Titles*, the introductory and rubrical structures of the two extant Byzantine systematic collections from this period (the *Collection in Fifty Titles* and the *Collection in Fourteen Titles*), and a number of other smaller texts from our period regularly found in the manuscripts. These texts are not exhaustive of the canonical material of this period, but they do constitute its most important and prominent elements.

The extent of historical contextualization has also been limited. The number of texts that could potentially illuminate the patterns and structures of Byzantine legal belief is enormous. I have therefore restricted my attention to those that may be considered primary parallels to or influences on the Byzantine canonical tradition *as a formal legal corpus*. This pool is still very large, and includes virtually all of the extant Greek and Roman secular legal collections of this period and earlier, as well as a wide variety of texts such as the Apostolic Church Order collections, classical literary or philosophical treatments of law, and scriptural legal texts. Naturally I will also from time to time make comparisons with later Byzantine legal sources.

Despite these limitations, the scope of this work remains extremely broad, encompassing over five centuries of developments. Some may find this breadth disconcerting. This scope is, however, necessary: the fundamental contours of legal belief can only be convincingly traced as they emerge over the cultural *longue durée*. It is only in the cumulative coherence, traced over centuries, of how the corpus takes shapes (Chapter 1), how the tradition explicitly frames its own endeavors (Chapter 2), how the central texts of the tradition implicitly describe their own legal world (Chapter 3), and how the tradition organizes and arranges itself (Chapter 4), that the nature of law and legality in the canonical collections begins to emerge with any clarity or persuasiveness. A more narrow study, or impressionistic anecdotal treatment, not only would not allow credible conclusions to be drawn about how the tradition as a whole was perceived—my question—but could even evade the challenge of considering the cultural whole in the first place.

One final caveat must be made. As noted, even as an exploration into Byzantine canon-legal culture, this work can be considered only one element of a much larger project. A broader range of sources must be consulted before we can make any claims to comprehensiveness. Two areas of study, in particular, must be singled out as standing in special need of scholarly treatment. First, Greek patristic thinking on law and legality is in need of much more thorough investigation than it has so far received.[61] A study on this topic must treat not only explicit discussions and expressions of legal

[61] On the Greek fathers and law, see the brief treatment in Stiegler 1958, 97–101, and more extensively Troianos 1992a. Now also McGuckin 2012.

theorization, but also the use of legal metaphors, images, language, and broader legal symbolism and iconology (and even architecture). In this it must explore the influence of both Jewish and Roman legal thinking. Comparison of similar dynamics in Latin patristic material, which has been much better served in these areas, would also be important.[62] Second, and perhaps more urgently, the discipline sorely needs a comprehensive analysis of texts conveying canonical forensic practice, similar to that performed by Dieter Simon on the *Πεῖρα*. Important texts would include conciliar *acta*, records of trials (for example, of Maximus the Confessor), and even epistolary exchanges on church-legal matters (for example, between Photius and Nicholas I). For our purposes, these texts need to be examined not so much for what they may or may not reveal about what "really happened" socially or politically, or the nature of legal structures of the day, but for the legal assumptions and values they assume and promote. Only when the results of these studies are taken into account will we begin to form a truly satisfactory and nuanced picture of the imagination and theorization of law and legality in the Greek East.

[62] For the Latin literature, see e.g. Biondi 1952, Gaudemet 1957, 163–76; 1958, 467–83, and with many further references Humfress 2007, 147–52.

1

The Shape of the Law

A. INTRODUCTION: THE SHAPE OF THE LAW

We first encounter Byzantine church law as a textual artifact, that is, as a set of texts in the manuscripts that we may identify as a distinct subject for editing, analysis, historical reconstruction, and other forms of interpretation. The formal contours of these texts, both as they now exist and as they may once have existed, are a critical point of departure for understanding the fundamental legal-cultural parameters of the Byzantine canonical tradition. How the texts are presented and arranged in the manuscripts, the quantity of texts, the way in which the texts constitute a distinct corpus, the structuring of this corpus, and the patterns and dynamics of growth and change in this corpus may all serve to illuminate the nature of legal texts, concepts of legislation and promulgation, strategies of legal change and interpretation, and how the tradition is conceived as a systematic whole. This chapter will thus begin our exploration of Byzantine canonical culture with a survey and analysis of the fundamental characteristics of the tradition's textual existence—its broadest physical shape.

B. MANUSCRIPTS AND EDITIONS: PRELIMINARY PROBLEMS

The starting point for such an analysis must naturally be the manuscripts themselves, and approached from one very particular perspective: how did the Byzantines themselves, at any given time, encounter their tradition? This requires information about the typical contents of a canon law manuscript, forms of publication, the extent of circulation, and typical layouts of texts. Unfortunately, none of this information is easy to come by. There are three reasons for this: the nature of the extant sources, the state of Byzantine legal codicology, and the general lack of interest among cultural historians in thinking about cultural phenomena codicologically.

The first two problems are the most serious in appearance, if not in substance. The problem with the sources is simple. The very earliest Greek canon law manuscript is usually dated to the early 9th C.[1] This is precisely the end of our period of examination. We thus have no direct codicological window onto most of our period. Fortunately, one of the fundamental characteristics of the Byzantine canonical tradition, as we will see, is its extreme conservatism and stability. As a result, if we combine the results of Vladimir Beneshevich's careful text-archeological reconstructions of pre-9th C recensions of the *Coll14* (and to a lesser extent, the *Coll50*), pre-9th C Latin and Syriac witnesses which reflect lost Greek originals, and other external witnesses, it is possible to make very good guesses about the basic shape of Byzantine canon law manuscripts prior to the 9th C. One can, with reasonable confidence, extrapolate back to fundamental patterns and dynamics of the manuscript tradition, if not specific forms.

More problematic is the state of modern Byzantine legal codicology. Thanks to the efforts of the research group Edition und Bearbeitung byzantinischer Rechtsquellen, founded in 1974 by Dieter Simon, virtually every known Byzantine legal manuscript, secular and ecclesiastical (at least until *c.*1600, but later ones have also been included) has now been microfilmed and gathered at the Max-Planck-Institut für europäische Rechtsgeschichte in Frankfurt.[2] An excellent and detailed manuscript-description project is underway. Unfortunately, only the first two volumes have been completed, and as a result it is still difficult to ascertain with absolute certainty fundamental information about codicological content (i.e. distribution of collections, predominate forms of collections, etc.). Until such time as this project is completed, one must complement the Frankfurt volumes that have appeared with a patchwork of older, sometimes unsatisfactory and incomplete catalogues, editions, descriptions, and source histories—and, of course, a sampling of the manuscript themselves.[3] This data is sufficient to allow basic conclusions

[1] Patmos 172. Stolte, however, has reported finding an early 8th C, possibly late 7th C, fragmentary palimpsest of the *Coll14*. Stolte 2002, 194, n. 16; 2010, 522–3.

[2] In total approximately 1,000 manuscripts; Burgmann *et al.* 1995, Schminck and Getov 2010. For a description of the project, see Burgmann *et al.* 1995, vii–xvii. The project is now formally based in the University of Göttingen.

[3] Of the approximately 500 extant pre-16th C Byzantine canonical manuscripts, roughly three-quarters contain recensions of collections relevant to our period. Two-thirds of these are the comparatively stable and homogeneous recensions of the 12th C commentators. The remaining manuscripts (approx. 130) contain "pure" recensions of the earlier collections, and have been the manuscripts of most importance to modern critical editions and the work of Beneshevich. Of these manuscripts, the following have been examined in microform: Athos Meg. Lav. B.93, Koult. 42, Pant. 234, Vatop. 555; Dublin Trin. 199; Florence Laur. gr. 10.10; Jerusalem Pan. Taph. 24; Milan Ambros. M.68 supp.; Moscow Syn. 398; Naples II.C.7 (= gr. 75); Oxford Barroc. 26, 86;

about the major contours of the tradition—adequate for our purposes—but many points of detail must remain tentative for the present.

Much more problematic for this investigation is a subtler set of issues surrounding how modern cultural-historical scholarship approaches ancient texts. The root problem is the strong, if mostly unconscious, habit of studying texts primarily as extracted and isolated from their traditional manuscript contexts. Cultural-historical analysis has typically begun with a topic or idea—for example, "Byzantine philosophy"—and then explored this topic through an examination of a set of genre-appropriate texts culled from the manuscripts. Rarely does one begin with the question of what a typical Byzantine "philosophical manuscript" looked like, what it contained, how it was structured, how commonly such a manuscript could be found and was read, or even if it existed at all—and *then* consider what this could mean for understanding "Byzantine philosophy" as a cultural phenomenon, and the Byzantine intellectual landscape more generally. Likewise, even in treating the reception of the works of a particular author, or tracking the development of a particular idea across various texts, rarely is the question raised how these texts were actually experienced: how often the texts were read and in what form, what they appear alongside of, what other types of texts might be equally relevant but are now neglected. As a result, any potential dissonance between a modern scholar's and an ancient reader's physical experience of a text tends to be downplayed or elided. The dissonance may not be significant in treating very specific problems or ideas, but it becomes highly problematic when we turn to macrocultural questions of the type broached in this study.

Oxford Laud. 39; Paris Cois. 36, 209, 211; Paris gr. 1319, 1320, 1331, 1370, 1371; Paris gr. supp. 614, 1085, 1086; Patmos 205; Rome Vallic. F.10, F. 47; Sinai 1112, 1113; Turin Bib. Naz. B.II.26; Vatican Barb. 578; Vatican gr. 640, 843, 1980, 1981; Venice Marc. app. gr. I.29 (= Nanian 22); Vienna hist. gr. 7; Vienna iur. gr. 5. Of the remaining manuscripts, reasonable (sometimes excellent) descriptions exist and were consulted for the following: Andros Pant. 6–7; Athens Eth. Bib. 1370; Athos Iver. 302; Athos Meg. Lav. B.93; Athos Pant. 141, 234; Athos Phil. 42; Cambridge Univ. Ee. iv. 29; Dublin Trin. 200; Escorial X.III.2; Florence Laur. gr 5.22, 9.8; Istanbul Panag. (Chalk.) 175; Jerusalem Cruc. 2; Metoch. 635; London BL Add. 28822, 34060; Milan Amb. E. 94 supp.; B. 107 supp.; D. 317 inf.; F. 48 supp.; G. 57 supp.; Moscow Arch. 3; Moscow Syn. 397, 432, 467; Munich Staat. Bib. gr. 122, 397; Naples Bib. Naz. II.C.4, II.C.7; Oxford Baroc. 185, 194, 196; Oxford Gr. misc. 4, 206; Oxford Rawl. G 158, Misc. 170; Oxford Seld. B.55; Paris Cois. 34, 35, 364, 1263; Paris gr. 1324, 1325, 1326, 1334, 1369; Paris supp. gr. 483; Patmos 172–3; Rome Vallic. F. 47; St. Petersburg GPB 66; Vatican Barb. 476; Vatican gr. 640, 827, 829, 840, 1142, 2060, 2184, 2198; Vatican Palat. 376; Sofia NCID 21; Venice Marc. 169, 170, 171; Venice app.I.29, III.2, III.17; Vienna iur. gr. 9; 11; Vienna hist gr. 56, 70. In total, 111 manuscripts or manuscript descriptions were examined. These include virtually all of the manuscripts consulted by Beneshevich and Joannou, and many of those listed (if not used!) by Pitra. Further, they include all of the manuscripts that may predate the second millennium, and representatives from all of Beneshevich's *Coll14* and *Coll50* recensions, as well as of the three known 11th C recensions (see Schminck 1998). They also include numerous instances of the synopsis, in various forms. Further details may be found in Wagschal 2010a, 269–73.

These problems become more apparent when we examine the two major disciplinary trends—almost habits—that drive this lack of codicological sensitivity. The first is modern historicism, which has tended to treat texts as anchored so firmly in original contexts that one can easily ignore their later textual settings, however important these settings may have been to the (possibly dominant) reading and perception of these texts throughout most of their history. Scholars have instead been encouraged to focus their studies on a text at one very discrete moment, usually the point of composition. The later appropriation, synthesis, and appearance of these texts—which raise questions of codicology—are treated as epiphenomena of the original creative act. Cultural histories thus tend to be written as narratives of a succession of discrete moments of creative acts of composition, instead of as descriptions of the broader frameworks of understanding that contextualize these discrete moments of creativity. For example, the history of early canon law tends to be written primarily as a history of councils, each analyzed for place, origin, date, and original context and purpose—and not as the unfolding of a complex of legal doctrines, beliefs, categories, practices, forms of expression, methods of reading, and the like. Similarly, histories of philosophy tend to be written as a history of a series of individual thinkers, instead of the history of a society's broader intellectual practices and concerns. For the former type of study, the codicological "life" of texts is quite secondary, only important to establish the best—that is, original—texts; for the latter, it is critical to the very essence of the topic.

The recent interest in reception history has moderated the excesses of this traditional fixation on point of composition and original contexts. Nevertheless, even reception histories tend to focus on the later effect of texts on other very specific texts at very specific points in time. They thus remain "punctiliar" in process, relatively immune to reflection on how texts form parts of larger intellectual-cultural wholes over the *longue durée.* Careful consideration of the physical shape and fortunes of the texts in the manuscripts is thus rarely in evidence.

The second trend, and closely related, is a general lack of critical evaluation, or even acknowledgement, of the biases of the modern critical edition. In particular, there is little awareness of the extent to which the idea of the critical edition has promoted an atomistic approach to texts in which the isolation and "disentanglement" of select individual texts from manuscript contexts is seen as the norm and even ideal. The result is that cultural historians almost never read whole manuscripts, or individual texts within the literal "con-texts" of the manuscripts. Instead, they are encouraged—in fact forced—by their critical editions to read single texts or even text fragments *across* different manuscripts. This discourages interest in how texts were physically synthesized and related to one other in the manuscripts and, by extension, in the cultural tradition itself. Further, and worse, it encourages resynthesizing and reordering these texts in relation to each other in ways that may have little resonance with the priorities, interests, or textures of the historical tradition in question. In effect, the networks or pathways of intertextual relations that governed the reading and interpretation of ancient texts are simply ignored, and can thus be unconsciously replaced by modern ones. Examples of this type of resynthesis are the many older "history of ideas" surveys of ancient theology or philosophy that systematically trace the development of various discrete concepts through a set of texts with little attention to whether the texts in question were ever much read at all, whether they were associated with each other, or whether they lent themselves to such systematic conceptual presentation in the first place. A specific example would be an exposition of Platonic philosophy in Byzantine thought that is theoretically rooted in a modern selection and chronological arrangement of Plato's dialogues, instead of the selection and progression of dialogues evident in Byzantine manuscripts. In the history of Byzantine church law, the 19th C Orthodox manual tradition represents a resynthesis of this type. These manuals systematically extract rule content from the traditional texts and reorganize this content under doctrinal headings and structures derived from western canon and civil law. These structures have little to do with the manuscript form or structure of the texts in the tradition itself. In this type of project the historical shape of the tradition is important only for clarifying and purifying the texts of the individual "sources" of this resynthesis, not for understanding the conceptual architecture of the historical tradition itself.

The extreme interest of critical editions in restoring only "original" texts—texts as found at one point in time, their origin—creates further problems, and reinforces the problems of historicism just raised.[4] Once again the historian is discouraged from considering how texts developed over time, and thus how the texts were related to each other and digested by the culture in question. Indeed, this privileging of "originals" means that editions present not what ancient readers were actually reading—the critical starting point of cultural-historical analyses such as our own—but what modern scholars think ancient readers *should* have been reading. As a result the great primary-source collections of modern scholarship in effect present the entire textual tradition of antiquity as a rather artificial montage of reconstructed, disembodied semi-hypothetical "originals" which both collectively and individually probably bear very little resemblance to what most historical subjects would ever have encountered.[5] Certainly they make contact with the "encountered" tradition of the texts extremely difficult.

[4] For broader critique of the concept of an "original" text, and the related ideas of "original meaning," see e.g. Epp 1999; Louth 1983, 104–9; McGann 1983.

[5] An excellent example is Christian scripture. Scholars who use modern editions can be quite surprised that the New Testament only rarely forms a single physical book in the Greek

A further unfortunate effect of this emphasis on "originals" is that variations, accretions, and manuscript paraphernalia are treated as problems that must be, and can be, penetrated, excised, and dismissed in order to get to the "real" or pure text. Sometimes this real text might not even be any given original, but simply those core elements of a textual tradition which are of particular interest to the editor. In Byzantine church law, Périclès-Pierre Joannou's edition of the canons, at present the best critical edition, provides an excellent example of this tendency.[6] It first disembodies or "cleans up" the tradition by stripping the canons of their traditional manuscript structures, appendices, indices, and scholia.[7] It then goes on to include a source that is not found in any Byzantine canonical manuscripts,[8] adds numerous rubrical headings not commonly encountered,[9] and boldly rearranges the sources in a form never encountered in the tradition, and quite contrary to its spirit.[10] The result is something that is neither particularly close to anything in the manuscripts nor, indeed, to any "original" collection. These actions make sense in light of Joannou's primary interest—providing modern Catholic codifiers with good texts of the most important individual Byzantine canonical sources—but they do not result in a particularly useful window onto the shape of the Byzantine canonical tradition as a whole.

In this respect, the older, and often inaccurate, edition of Jean-Baptiste-François Pitra is superior.[11] Although the overall form of the edition does not attempt to approximate any Byzantine manuscript, Pitra was careful to include the standard "framing" texts of the manuscripts (prologues, systematic indices), some of the introductory apostolic materials, some appendix material, and some scholia.[12] The much more accurate editions of Beneshevich are also more useful and reliable, inasmuch as they attempt to convey the whole of specific "originals," namely the original version of the *Coll50* and the "Tarasian recension" of the *Coll14*.[13]

manuscript tradition, or that, for example, the Catholic epistles almost always precede the Pauline. See Metzger 1981, 54–6; Parker 2008, 70–81. The physical object in their hands—their critical edition of the New Testament—bears little codicological resemblance to anything encountered by anyone before the 16th C.

[6] Turner 1899 is another example; the concern to compare texts of different recensions has made it difficult to determine the form of any one collection treated.

[7] Even one set of common "prologue" material, for Constantinople 381, is missing (*Fonti* 1.45).

[8] Constantinople 869 in *Fonti* 1.1.289–342. Joannou is careful to note, of course, that this is an addition.

[9] See Appendix A for more information on rubrics.

[10] Thus the Apostolic Canons are found prefacing the local councils (*Fonti* 2.1–53).

[11] Criticism of Pitra's text is widespread: see esp. *Sbornik* 24–5 and *Sin* 20–1 *et passim*, but also Funk 1905, 1.xxiii; *Sources* 27; Stolte 1998a, 184. Even casual use of the text reveals many small errors.

[12] Beneshevich is also quite critical of Pitra's edition of the scholia (2.642–55): "highly unsatisfactory" (*Sin* 250–1).

[13] *Syn* and *Kormchaya*.

Beneshevich was also concerned to convey scholia, albeit separated from the main body of the texts.[14] Curiously, however, the least critical of the modern editions, the so-called "Athens Syntagma" of Georges Rhalles and Michael Potles, is the edition most representative of the shape and texture of the historical tradition. It approximates very broadly the typical order and content of a full late Byzantine manuscript, with prologues, systematic index, full corpus with commentators, and appendix materials—although without scholia.[15]

The emphasis on producing purified originals (or specific recensions) can also entail the ingress of the subtler, but no less problematic, assumptions of modern printed-text culture.[16] This issue cannot be broached here at length, but suffice to say that these assumptions can distort the appreciation of the historical shape of the canonical tradition in a number of important ways. Print cultures, for example, tend to think of texts in terms of discrete recensions, on the analogy of the separate editions and printings of modern publishing houses. This encourages one to think about change in texts in terms of distinct moments of "official" publication, and thus in terms of very intentional stages of development. Manuscripts, however, suggest a much more gradual, continual, and indirect mechanism of textual change: each manuscript copying is in a sense a new recension or a new edition, and variation is easily found—and tolerated—manuscript to manuscript. Texts thus emerge as much more fluid, "living" phenomena than in printed-text cultures, subject to constant, multiform reworking by numerous agents. This reality consequently demands attention not simply to specific moments in the text's history but also to slow and gradual patterns and tendencies in textual shaping over time—something almost never considered when studying the history of printed texts. Such dynamics, however, are essential to any comprehensive description of the historical shape of an "encountered" pre-modern textual tradition.[17]

Further, the values and characteristics of print cultures, such as precision, accuracy, identity of texts, attention to detail, and intentional logical change, can

[14] *Syn* 157–90; *Sin* 250–68; *Sbornik* 145–9; *Sbornik* (Prilozhenie) 3–80.

[15] This edition serves as the vulgate text of the modern discipline of Orthodox canon law. On its contents, the circumstances of its creation, and its editors, see further Biener 1856; Deledemos 2002, 3–10; Narbekov 1889, 60–2; 1899, 1.244–7. The central corpus, volumes 1 to 4, is based upon a 17th C humanist edition (Beveridge 1672), but supplemented by (primarily) a very complete 14th C MS, Istanbul Topkapı 115 (via Athens EB 1372, an 18th C copy; see Menebisoglou 1982, 193–206). Like Beveridge it includes all three commentators in the corpus section, a combination never found in the manuscripts. Some traditional texts are omitted or placed in footnotes. The appendix material in volume 5 is based mostly on Leunclavius 1596, vol. 1.

[16] My inspirations for this paragraph are varied and diffuse, but see esp. Parker 1997, Eggert 1991, Jeffreys 2008, 92, Ong 1982, Stolte 1998a, 187 and 2010, 523 (on the "living" nature of the nomocanonical recensions) and the following note.

[17] For an important attempt to produce a "living" edition of canonical texts, see the Carolingian Canon Law Project, <ccl.rch.uky.edu>, directed by Abigail Firey.

easily obscure our appreciation of the dynamics of manuscript cultures: the gradual, the graded, the general, the similar, the subtle, the unconscious. This sensitivity is particularly critical in legal-cultural studies, where many of the values of modern legal culture (precision, strict definition, categorical application, logical systematization) would seem to be closely aligned with those of modern print culture.[18] An adequate description of the textual basis of the Byzantine canonical tradition must therefore be very careful not to project these values and expectations onto its subject material.

All of these complexities make the description and analysis of the textual shape of Byzantine canon law exceptionally difficult. It is not surprising, then, that real codicological analysis of Byzantine law, if not entirely neglected, is little in evidence.[19] Instead the study of Byzantine canon law, like the study of western canon law, tends to be centered around source surveys that take as their central and fundamental narrative unit the individual source or collection, extracted and reconstructed out of the manuscripts, understood as constituting a discrete published whole, and analyzed almost exclusively in terms of original compositional context (author, place, and date), discrete recensional stages, and narrowly conceived source relationships with other texts, that is, the derivation of individual texts.[20] As a result pieces of the manuscripts are privileged over wholes, compositional practices over reception and synthesis, and diversity and difference over continuity and formal similarity. In particular, broader morphological patterns across the manuscripts and collections, and how these patterns suggest a broader cultural-legal world—our precise concern—tend not to be considered at all. Likewise the dispositions of the relevant texts in their manuscript settings, such as how often they are found, where they are found, next to what and how often, in what form, with what breaks and with what scholia, are treated as only secondary, and optional, points of consideration. Editions too, as noted, have mostly been conceived as "snapshots" of collections as specific points in time and have not endeavored to convey a strong sense of how the texts *normally* appeared in the manuscripts and would have been most often encountered (with common variations noted). Further, stripped of common supplementary articles, customary orders, and other manuscript structures, the canonical texts are presented as sanitized versions of their historical selves.

[18] Changes in writing technology—including the invention of writing itself, the emergence of the codex, and the development of printing—have not infrequently been connected with changes in legal culture. See e.g. Gagarin 2005, 91–2, 2008; Heszer 1998; Kelly 1992, 9; Ong 1982; Thomas 2005, 50; Wieacker 1960, 93–119.

[19] A notable exception is Burgmann 2002; of the older studies, Mortreuil 1843–6 is probably the best at conveying the forms and contents of the manuscripts.

[20] So e.g. *Delineatio* and *Peges* for the east; Gaudemet 1985, Maassen 1871, Reynolds 1986, Stickler 1950 for the west.

At best, then, the editions only hint at the historical shape of the textual tradition; they do not convey it in its integrity.

C. A SURVEY OF THE TEXTUAL HISTORY OF BYZANTINE CANON LAW 381–883

In light of the many difficulties involved in describing the textual shape of Byzantine canon law, the best method of approaching our task is to present a narrative of the formation of the traditional corpus, and then, as much as possible, to distill from this narrative the fundamental dynamics and contours of the tradition as a textual artifact. Happily, considerable consensus now exists on the basic narrative of the development of the sources of the Byzantine canonical tradition both during and after our period.[21]

As is well known, the Byzantine—indeed, Christian—canonical tradition emerges as a coherent and distinct textual whole only in the fourth century. At this time earlier and more fluid patterns of written and customary regulation began to congeal around the increasingly regular institution of conciliar legislation. Local but ever more formal collections of written conciliar regulations (which start to be called *κανόνες* by the end of the 4th C) started to take

[21] The principal modern source surveys of Byzantine law are *Peges* and *Delineatio*, both of which treat secular and ecclesiastical law. Troianos 2012 is an English language reworking of the canon law sections of *Peges*. Beck 1977, 140–7, 422–5, 598–601, 655–62, 786–9 covers only church law, and is dated, but remain useful in its level of detail and as a guide to older editions. Pieler 1978 is restricted to secular material, but is exceptionally insightful. For the individual sources in the corpus, *Sources* is now the most up-to-date survey through to the council of Trullo, with extensive bibliography, but see now also Mardirossian 2010 on the Antiochian sources. The more comprehensive, but older, *Historike* is also invaluable. Other more specialized, but fundamental, discussions of the sources of Byzantine canon law texts include Schwartz 1936a, *Sbornik*, *Sin*, and Schminck 1998. Older studies often remain necessary when modern surveys do not fully rehearse older arguments. Of the 19th C surveys, Biener 1824, 1827, and 1856 are classic studies. Mortreuil 1843–8 is very dated but extensive, and still valuable because of its attention to the manuscripts and the early modern scholarship. Of Zachariä von Lingenthal's many fundamental works on Byzantine law, the most important for canon law are Zachariä von Lingenthal 1877 and 1885; 1839 remains useful. Carl Heimbach's lengthy survey in the *Allgemeine Encyklopädie der Wissenschaften und Künste* (C. Heimbach 1868) is the most comprehensive survey of the 19th C. The introductions of his brother, Gustav Heimbach, to his editions of various Byzantine legal texts also contain valuable material (G. Heimbach 1838). In Russian, the introduction to Narbekov 1899 is extensive and valuable. Early modern literature can also be consulted with interest. The most stimulating are Assemani 1762, Ballerini and Ballerini1753, and Doujat 1680; 1687. Many of these early modern works on canon law may be found conveniently compiled in Gallandius 1778. Brief bibliographical surveys and assessments of the early modern literature may be found in *Sbornik*, Mortreuil 1843, and Maassen 1871.

prominent place alongside the older customary and (pseudo-)apostolic traditions of regulation.[22]

Eduard Schwartz has proposed that sometime in the mid-4th C a small corpus of local conciliar material from Asia Minor, presumably of a type not uncommon elsewhere, began to rise to prominence.[23] Through a careful examination of the oldest Latin and Syriac material (the early stages of this process have left few traces in the Greek tradition itself) Schwartz has suggested a narrative of development that, although speculative, has been widely accepted. According to this theory, it seems that sometime between 360 and 378, likely under the direction of the Homoean Euzoius of Antioch (361–76), a small collection, probably Pontic in origin, was adopted in Antioch. It likely included Ancyra (314) and Neocaesarea (314/319), and perhaps Gangra (*c.*340? 355?), and later Antioch (*c.*328, although traditionally considered Antioch ἐν ἐγκαινίοις 341, even in the early 5th C[24]) and probably Laodicea (date uncertain; before 380).[25]

This early "Antiochian corpus," as Schwartz called it, seems to have been shaped primarily in an Arian milieu. With the accession of the Nicene Theodosius in 379, however, this collection was apparently adopted by the Nicene party, probably first by Meletius of Antioch, who was restored to his see in this same year. At this time—perhaps not so long before or after *Cunctos populos* (February 380), but at any rate by 381—the canons of Nicaea were added to the head of corpus. This move dramatically violated the chronological ordering of the sources that had prevailed thitherto (the councils of Ancyra and Neocaesarea were both known to predate Nicaea). Echoes of this unusual move may be found in special headings extant in the Greek, Latin, and Syriac traditions that explicitly justify this aberration.[26] Its effect was unmistakable: the Arian "Antiochian corpus" had become the "Nicene corpus."

[22] I bypass here the many complex issues surrounding the origin of formal church regulations. For good recent discussions, see Hess 2002, L'Huillier 1997, Mardirossian 2010, Ohme 1998. Schwartz 1910; 1911; 1936a remain foundational.

[23] The most recent and thorough discussion of the genesis of this corpus is Mardirossian 2010. Schwartz's conclusions are somewhat scattered, but see esp. in Schwartz 1936 and 1936a, with further references. Schwartz is building primarily on the foundation laid by Ballerini and Ballerini 1753. Other recent discussions of this early corpus may be found in *Delineatio* 24–30, *Historike* 21–32, L'Huillier 1976, Selb 1967.

[24] L'Huillier 1976, 59; Mardirossian 2010, 80–98; *Sources* 44–5, following Schwartz and Bardy; *contra*, *Historike* 356–66 (and also *Fonti* 1.2.100).

[25] On the dates of all of these sources, see Mardirossian 2010, 73–134; *Sources* 39–53. For the presence of Laodicea in the earliest collections, see *Historike* 23–5, L'Huillier 1976, 61. Note that Mardirossian 2010 now offers a slightly different picture of the Antiochian collection's compilation. He affirms much more strongly Euzoius' role in the creation of the collection—composed *in toto* under Euzoius' direction—and suggests that Antioch was originally placed before Gangra.

[26] Each version typically explains that Nicaea is placed before Ancyra or Neocaesarea because of its pre-eminent authority. For the Latin and Syrian, see most conveniently Schwartz 1936a, 174–5 (also Turner 1899, 2.1.19, 48–9, 116–17; Selb 1967, 377–8); for the Greek, see *Kormchaya* 229, 238. See also the later Greek scholion to the *Coll14*, *RP* 1.11–12, which again feels obliged to

The production of this Nicene corpus (a term I propose in order to restrict "Antiochian corpus" to the version of this body before its appropriation by the Nicene party) would prove to be a landmark moment in the development of Christian canon law. Within a century or so this corpus would constitute the undisputed canonical core of virtually the entire imperial church, whether Latin-, Greek-, or Syrian-speaking. Although this is a point that Schwartz did not much emphasize, its success must be attributable to a tacit understanding that, just as the Nicene creed was now the touchstone of Orthodoxy for all later doctrine, so the Nicene corpus—probably originally prefaced by the Nicene creed—was the standard for church order.[27] It seems to have become, in effect, the official Nicene imperial canon law book for the official Nicene imperial church. Although it will be subject to considerable reshaping and local variation as it passes west and east, it may be regarded as the first consistent and regular "physical" textual whole in the tradition.[28] This corpus seems to have passed into the Latin west very rapidly, and no fewer than three times in the 5th to early 6th C: first with the so-called Isidorian translation (a version of which is commonly referred to as the Freising-Würzburg version), perhaps the very collection sent west to Africa during the Apiarian affair (419; before 451 in any case); second, with the *Prisca* collection in Rome (*c.*451–500); third, and definitively, with the translations of Dionysius, also in Rome (*c.*500, perhaps as late as 523).[29] Through these three versions—and above all the *Dionysiana*, the most complete and accurate[30]—the Nicene corpus will go on to form the core of most major western collections, and many minor ones, for the next four or five centuries.[31]

explain the unusual prepositioning of Nicaea as "on account of its exceptional honour" (*διὰ τὸ τῆς τιμῆς ἐξαίρετον*).

[27] On the presence of the Nicene creed, see Ch. 2 B.1. Schwartz was aware of the symbolic significance of the Nicene prefacing of the Antiochian corpus (e.g. 1936a, 200), but does not consider its role in the broader—and extraordinary—spread of the collection. Mardirossian 2010, 253–5 (on the collection "*nicéanisée*") is now clearer on this point; see also Ohme 1998, 526–42.

[28] Perhaps the most significant change will be the later post-positioning of Nicaea after Ancyra and Neocaesarea (i.e. back in chronological order) in some significant streams of the Syrian and Arabic transmission. See Kaufhold, 2012 *passim*, Selb 1981, 88,107. This may also be occasionally observed in certain streams of the Latin tradition; see e.g. Maassen 1871, 76, 534.

[29] This is a simplification of what seems to have been a much more complex process of westward transmission. See esp. Maassen 1871, 65–130; also Hefele and Leclercq 1907, 3.1139–76. For this threefold transmission, see Gaudemet 1985, 77–9; 130–7, with references to earlier literature. Schwartz 1936a remains fundamental for the first transmission.

[30] On Dionysius and the *Dionysiana*, see now esp. Firey 2008 and Gallagher 2002, 9–18. Three redactions of the councils are known: "Dionysius I" (ed. Strewe 1931); "Dionysius II" (ed. Voellus and Justel 1661, 1.101–74 = *PL* 67.139–228); "Dionysius III," known only from its surviving preface (trans. Somerville and Brasington 1998, 49).

[31] Especially the *Dionysiana*, Cresconius' *Concordia* (a reorganized Dionysius II), the *Hispana*, the *Dionysiana-Hadriana*, and the so-called *Isidor Mercator* collection. It is also the underlying structure of the 6th C *Breviatio canonum* of Fulgentius Ferrandus, the 6th C *Capitula* of Martin of Braga, and many other smaller handbook-like collections. On all of these, see Gaudemet 1985, but esp. Maassen

The movement of the Nicene corpus into the Syrian east was likewise rapid and thorough, penetrating even beyond the imperial borders.[32] Perhaps already in 399 (or 410) the corpus through Laodicea was translated for the Persian church. Certainly the "western canons," translated or not, are formally listed and confirmed at the council of Yahballāhā in Seleukia-Ctesiphon 419/20, where the corpus is significantly described as the "laws that have been drawn up by the blessed fathers and bishops for the catholic church in the entire Roman empire"[33]: the universality of this "imperial" core is explicitly recognized. These canons were preserved even after the jurisdictional separation of the Persian Catholicosate from Antioch in 423, and this corpus, expanded to include Constantinople and Chalcedon, is attested at the synod under Mār Abā (539/40–552), and not infrequently thereafter.

The west Syrian tradition would also adopt (or maintain) the imperial corpus. Its tradition is more complex, evincing at least two major transmissions.[34] One tradition, exercising considerable influence on later material, is represented by a second translation, made *c.*500 in Hierapolis (Mabbūg), probably originally in Melkite circles.[35] This translation included the Nicene corpus through Chalcedon. Other manuscripts count the synodal canons through Ephesus, with Chalcedon listed later after a series of patristic canons. This ordering may date to a translation attested in 687. Other manuscripts show a number of other variants. In all cases, however, the basic Nicene structure at least through Constantinople is evident, dominating the west Syrian *synodika* as surely as the east Syrian.

Parallel processes of reception of the Nicene corpus will also be evident in other oriental traditions, where the same imperial core is easily evident in the major collections of the Alexandrian-Coptic, Armenian, and Ethiopic traditions (and later in the Georgian and Melkite traditions, closely connected with the Byzantine tradition).[36]

In the Greek east itself the reception of this Nicene corpus was rapid and complete—so much so, in fact, that the history of Byzantine canon law can quite reasonably be cast as the history of the expansion and development of this one collection. Already at Chalcedon (451), thirty years after the Persian

1871 and his concept of "general collections," which he defines precisely by the inclusion of this Greek core (Maassen 1871, 420–1; collections described pp. 422–797). Many of Maassen's systematic collections (pp. 798–900) also exhibit this core structure as an identifiable "backbone."

32 Overview in Kaufhold 2012, 295–313. Selb 1967, 371–83; 1981, 58–81, 83–94, 97–110; 1989, 86–173, esp. at 98–109, 139–49.

33 Selb 1967, citation at 374, without further reference, translated by Selb.

34 Overview in Kaufhold 2012, 238–55; Selb 1989, 103–10, 140–9.

35 Selb 1981, 89. Edition: Schulthess 1908.

36 For a sense of the diffusion of the texts, and editions, see *Clavis* 8000, 8501, 8504, 8513–27, 8536, 8554, 8570, 8600, 8603, 8604, 8607, 8717, 9008. The best survey, with extensive bibliography, is now Kaufhold 2012.

bishops had recognized that this collection was the "laws for the catholic church in the whole Roman empire," it is cited as a matter of course.[37] The Nicene corpus was clearly established as *the* collection of a formal imperial council. Chalcedon 1 thus confirms the collection: "We have judged it right that the canons set forth by the holy fathers in each synod until now are to remain in force."[38] Although the wording of this canon is vague, there is broad consensus today that it in fact refers to the Nicene corpus.[39] Certainly the regular and even casual citation of the Nicene corpus in the *acta* and the later absolute dominance of this corpus in the east should incline us to this view. The lack of specificity in this canon may even confirm the well-established nature of this Nicene corpus: everyone knew what "the canons" were.

Of course this Nicene corpus could not have immediately or completely supplanted other local collections and traditions, even in the Greek east. Other local traditions existed, and presumably continued to exist alongside the imperial corpus for some time. Traces of these earlier traditions may be detected within the later Byzantine corpus itself. The Apostolic Canons, for example, which take into account earlier conciliar legislation, were likely a local Antiochian collection of the late 4th C.[40] The canons of Basil and Gregory of Nyssa undoubtedly reflect local Cappadocian traditions. It is sometimes suspected that the large number of Alexandrian patristic sources in the later Greek corpus originally formed part of a local Alexandrian decretal collection.[41] Broadly, in fact, the later imperial corpus may be considered a compilation of earlier local traditions: Asian, Antiochian, Alexandrian, and Constantinopolitan (and eventually even African). One manuscript also contains traces of a small, separate collection, appended to the normal sources—a lone manuscript witness to earlier canonical diversity.[42] Other variants in the oriental collections, such as the frequent additions to Nicaea,[43] perhaps representing Greek originals, also point to earlier canonical variety.

Nevertheless, the general movement of the eastern tradition, as already evident at Chalcedon, was unmistakably towards the dominance and spread of *one* corpus structure, the Nicene corpus, and its later recensions. It is telling

[37] In-text citations at *ACO* 2.1.3.48, 60, 95–6, 100–1, 107; see also *ACO* 2.5.51. References from L'Huillier 1976, 54, and *Historike* 21–4.

[38] *Τοὺς παρὰ τῶν ἁγίων πατέρων καθ' ἑκάστην σύνοδον ἄχρι τοῦ νῦν ἐκτεθέντας κανόνας κρατεῖν ἐδικαιώσαμεν.*

[39] So *Historike* 25; L'Huillier 1976, 55–6; Mardirossian 2010, 253; Selb 1981, 84; 1989, 140; *Sources* 61.

[40] On these canons and their relationship to earlier councils, see Metzger 1985, 1.14–62; Schwartz 1936a, 199–200; Steimer 1992, 87–8; *Sources* 28–33.

[41] e.g. de Clercq 1937, 1172. Pitra notes that one could also group other, and often later, material into an "Asian" collection (*Pitra* 1.li–lii).

[42] The famous "Canonicon" of Palladius in Patmos 172. See *Sbornik* 235–40; Schwartz 1936a, 182–6; Turner 1914.

[43] On these canons, in the oriental tradition, see e.g. Graf 1944, 1.586–90; Riedel 1900, 178–80; Selb 1981, 100–1; also *Sources* 37. For another example, see Kaufhold 2012, 247.

that one must engage in considerable textual archeology to detect any indications of earlier diversity within the Greek material itself. Even the pre-Nicene existence of the Antiochian corpus had to be uncovered by Schwartz using archaic Latin and Syrian traditions, preserving, in effect, memories from around the periphery of the empire. At the center, the Greek tradition tends to present a picture of uniformity and homogeneity.

The corpus used by Chalcedon was continuously numbered. No Greek exemplar of this type is extant. Despite references in the *acta* of Chalcedon to this system, it seems to have passed out of all memory in Byzantium by the 9th C.[44] This numbering system does, however, survive complete in Latin and Syrian witnesses.[45] Variations in this system indicate that the early Nicene corpus was expanded at least twice, first with the *synodikon* of Constantinople 381 (that is, canons 1–4, outside of the continuous numbering in the collection used at Chalcedon, as in the Isidoriana; Constantinople is also absent in the 419 Persian listing)[46], and then with the twenty-seven canons of Chalcedon (outside of the continuous numbering in Dionysius II (*c*.500), but inside in London BL Syr. 14528 (500–1)).[47] After the addition of Nicaea itself, these are the first indications that the tradition was beginning to grow by the appending of newer sources to the older ones in one ever-expanding corpus structure. These "updates" evidently passed into the west and east very quickly.

After the Chalcedonian canons were added, the corpus began to develop in slightly different directions across the Christian world. The dynamic of growth, however, is everywhere the same: the core Nicene corpus is gradually expanded by the addition of later, often more local,[48] but sometimes more general, material.

In the east, conciliar legislation ceased following Chalcedon, not to be restarted for almost 250 years at the council in Trullo 692.[49] The eastern

[44] Photius is famously confused by a reference to Constantinople 2 as "canon 166" in a 6th C letter of Severus of Antioch. (*Bibliotheca* 228; reference from Schwartz 1936a, 159–60). See also *Historike* 31 n. 2. For the references in Chalcedon, see *ACO* 2.1.3.48 (canons "95" and "96" = Antioch 4, 5), 100–1 (canons "83" and "84" = Antioch 16, 17). Another reference may be found in a later letter dating to 457–8, *ACO* 2.5.51 (canon "83" again).

[45] See the useful schematics in *Historike* 23–5 or L'Huillier 1976, 60–2; for more detailed discussion of the enumeration of the Latin collections, see Maassen 1871, 126–30.

[46] On the absence of Constantinople in the Persian recension of 419, see Selb 1981, 88–9.

[47] *Historike* 23–5. See also Schwartz 1910, 200–1 on London BL Syr. 14526 and its omission of Chalcedon in the systematic index.

[48] I use the term "local" as a descriptive convenience for materials that do not pass out of their place of origin. These materials, of course, which will include papal decretals in the west, and later Greek and Syrian councils and fathers in the east, were not necessarily understood as of "local" significance by their authors or collectors.

[49] Not surprisingly a similar silence falls over the imperial west, i.e. in Italy and Africa, both in the slowing of the production of papal decretals (see Gaudemet 1985, 95–6), and in the number of local councils. Outside the empire, by contrast, in Gaul, Spain, and Persia, we see an explosion of conciliar activity during this period. Gaudemet 1985, 96–121; Selb 1981, 61–2, 111–14, 165–70.

corpus nevertheless continued to expand, but now through processes of consolidation and reception of earlier material. The chief agents—or perhaps witnesses—of this expansion seem to have been new "systematic" editions of the Nicene corpus that began to appear at the beginning of the 6th C, perhaps in connection with Justinian's secular codification (528–34).[50] These editions of the canons were prototypically a version of the expanded Nicene corpus preceded by a thematically arranged subject index (a "systematic index") of the canons. In the manuscripts, and the reconstructed earlier recensions, they tend to emerge in the following form:[51]

PROLOGUE(S) + THEMATIC INDEX + CORPUS + APPENDICES

The vast majority of extant Byzantine canonical manuscripts are systematic in form.[52] The prologues will be discussed in the next chapter. They can vary in number and sometimes prologues from different collections will be "stacked" one after another.[53] The thematic index is a series of individually numbered topics, usually called *τίτλοι* and/or *κεφάλαια* in Greek, with references to relevant canons. The "corpus" may be either in systematic form—in which case the entire thematic index is repeated and instead of simple references the full text of the canons is inserted under the subject titles—or in straight corpus form, that is, in which the texts are written out in their traditional source order, without any thematic headings. The *Coll50* is prototypically in the former form, the *Coll14* in the latter, but the reality of the manuscripts is more complex, as we will see in Chapter 4.

The "appendices" are a more fluid concept, still not thoroughly researched in the canonical collections, but well recognized as a phenomenon of Byzantine legal manuscripts generally.[54] It is thought, as we will see, that most Byzantine canonical collections were originally composed with at least one appendix of civil ecclesiastical legislation. In the extant manuscripts, however, appendix sections are often very large and varied, including later patriarchal or synodal decisions, secular laws, penitential material, question-and-answer tracts,

[50] For these collections generally, see esp. *Sbornik* and *Sin* as well as the recent surveys in *Delineatio* 51–4, 60–2, 66–70, 87–9; *Historike* 37–73 (with many references to the older literature); *Peges* 131–5, 142–8. Also important are Honigmann 1961; Stolte 1997; 1998. Still useful is Zachariä von Lingenthal 1877. These collections are discussed further in Ch. 4.

[51] See Burgmann 2002 for a broader discussion of the form of Byzantine legal collections.

[52] In fact, simple canonical collections are quite rare, and may often be accounted for by lost pages in surviving manuscripts. But see e.g. Oxford Baroc. 26, or Venice Marc. 171.

[53] e.g.the *Coll50* and *Coll14* prologues may both be found in Paris Coislin, 34, Florence 10.10, Milan D 317 inf, Oxford Baroc. 185, Paris gr. 1324, Sinai 1111, Vatican gr. 2184. Further examples in *Sbornik* 131–2.

[54] See esp. Burgmann 2002, 257, 261–4; Burgmann and Troianos 1979, 199–200. Burgmann notes regular appendix structures for the *Ecloga*, the *Synopsis Major*, the *Prochiron auctum*, the *Ponema* of Atteleiotes, the *Syntagma* of Blastares, and the *Hexabiblos* of Harmenopoulos. I discuss the concept of an "appendix" further in Section D. 5.

synodal histories, orders of sees, tracts on heresies, and similar disciplinary-legal material (doctrinal definitions, and even some liturgical material, also occasionally appear). Fairly stable "convoys" of such material have already been identified for a number of different recensions and collections.[55]

The first known Greek systematic collection, no longer extant, is the *Collection in Sixty Titles* (*Coll60*), usually dated to shortly after 534. It is known only from a vague description in the prologue of the *Coll50*, the next collection. It may have marked the first incorporation of the 85 Apostolic Canons, Serdica, a number of "canons" extracted from documents associated with Ephesus,[56] and Chalcedon into the eastern corpus.[57] Certainly the *Coll50* seems to include these sources as a matter of course, that is, as if they were already present in the tradition.[58]

The second, and first extant, systematic collection of the Greek tradition, the *Coll50* of John Scholastikos, is usually dated to *c.*550.[59] It includes the Apostles, the Nicene corpus expanded with Serdica, Ephesus, and Chalcedon, and now also sixty-eight canons of Basil the Great.[60] The introduction of the canons of Serdica, whether now or earlier, into the midst of the old Nicene corpus (between Ancyra and Gangra) no doubt explains the dropping of the old continuous-numbering system.[61] The addition of Basil marked the first formal and clear entrance of non-conciliar (or apostolic) material into the Byzantine corpus. Although such "patristic" material was likely circulating earlier in a variety of local traditions, perhaps as appendices, its inclusion in the *Coll50* clearly alongside the conciliar material seems to mark a new stage in the material's formal integration into the mainstream of Greek canonical literature.[62]

The next thematic collection, the *Coll14*, usually dated *c.*580, and perhaps authored by Patriarch Eutychius of Constantinople, included probably nine more patristic sources, maybe as many as eleven, and also added another letter

[55] See esp. Beneshevich *Sbornik* 130–77, *Sin* 26–9. I borrow the term "convoy" from Burgmann 2002, 257, 261–4.

[56] The "epistula universalis" (*Clavis* 8717) of Ephesus, divided into 6 canons, and at least one other extract from the *acta* seem to have been included in the original *Coll50* (some manuscripts however indicate 8 canons; see Beneshevich *Syn* 6); in the later Byzantine tradition two other *acta* extracts will also be added (see *Clavis* 8800). See *Historike* 219–26; *Sources* 55–7.

[57] Probably only 27 canons, as is often the case in early collections (e.g. the Dionysiana, the Syrian collections, and the *Coll50*); three other canons, all extracts from the council's *acta*, will be included in the *Coll14*, and always henceforth in the eastern collections. See *Historike* 256–75; Selb 1981, 61; 1989, 102; *Sources* 63–6.

[58] So *Delineatio* 42, *Historike* 38–9, *Peges* 131.

[59] Further discussion of date and authorship of the *Coll50* and *Coll14* may be found in Ch. 4.

[60] Letters 199 and 210.

[61] So *Delineatio* 53.

[62] On the possibility of a Syrian patristic collection of canons (translated from Greek, and including extracts from Ignatius of Antioch, Peter of Alexandria, Athanasius to Ammoun, and the full series of Basilian canons) predating even Chalcedon, see *Sources* 87, and *Fonti* 2.xvi–xvii, both following the data in Schwartz 1911, 322–3. The question is complex, however; see Selb 1989, 110–18, 145–9; Kaufhold 2012, 247–8.

of Basil.[63] Even more significantly, this collection saw the first—and last—admission into the eastern corpus of a major western canonical source, the so-called *materies Africana* or *codex canonum ecclesiae Africanae* (in the Byzantine tradition simply "the synod in Carthage").[64] This collection, an awkward translation of almost exactly the same compilation of African councils (with material from 345 to 419), used, and probably redacted or finalized, by Dionysius Exiguus in his second compilation, will become the single largest source in the eastern corpus.[65] Undoubtedly the recapture of Africa in 534 and the establishment of the Carthaginian prefecture facilitated this unusual eastward transmission.[66] A small excerpt from a council in Constantinople (394) was also probably added at this time.[67]

Many of the additions found in the 6th C Greek thematic collections also appear in the Latin and Syrian collections of the same period; indeed, we may envision a parallel process of updating taking place across the Mediterranean world throughout the 6th C and 7th C. In the Latin west, in one form or another, the Apostolic Canons (only the first fifty), Serdica, and the *materies Africana* will become a reasonably well-established part of many major canonical collections during this period.[68] They are already apparent in Dionysius, although he marks all three as still of uncertain reception.[69] In the Syrian world, the process of transmission and admission is obscurer, but Serdica will eventually enter the

[63] Athanasius (particularly his letter to Rufinianus), Gregory Naz., and Amphilochius are not always listed in the traditional tables of contents of the *Coll14*, nor in the thematic index references. Gregory Naz. and Amphilochius, in particular, were subject to particularly variable fates in the manuscripts, sometimes missing even in the corpus sections; see *Fonti* 2.xix–xx; also *Delineatio* 69, 129, 131; *Sbornik* 89–91;142–8; *Sources* 84–9. It is therefore suspected that all are later additions. Gregory Naz. and Amphilochius are in fact not securely attested in any canonical witness until Trullo canon 2—although a manuscript that may contain a pre-Trullan recension, Patmos 172, does contain them (*Sbornik* 236). In the later expanded *Coll50* recensions described by Beneshevich, Gregory Naz. and Amphilochius are also often missing (e.g. "Group A," "Group B," Paris Cois. 211). Stolte 1998a, 190 notes the possibility of an even smaller selection of fathers in the original *Coll14*. Unquestionably the fathers always constitute one of the "soft" spots in the corpus.

[64] Edition (Latin): Munier 1974. On this collection generally, see Cross 1961, Munier 1975, Gaudemet 1985, 79–83 (where the Greek translation is erroneously ascribed to John Scholastikos, following Munier 1974, 177), *Sources* 74–5. Two other, more minor, additions to the corpus, are also from the west: Serdica, already mentioned, may be considered western (see n. 163), and the short extracts from Cyprian's council, first attested in the east in the 7th C, are also African.

[65] On Dionysius and Carthage, see Cross 1961, 133–9; so also Hess 2002, 88.

[66] It may have passed east more than once, in fact; canon 81 is known in two different Greek translations. See *Sources* 75. In the manuscripts, a number of abbreviated or selected recensions are also known (see *Sin* 39–40, 100–1, *Sbornik* 247–9, 292–5).

[67] So *Historike* 62–3, *Delineatio* 61, *Sbornik* 86–7, *Sources* 76–7; see esp. Honigmann 1961, Stolte 1998a, 189. It is not mentioned in the collection's first prologue (see Ch. 2 B.4); however, it is cited under a chapter in the systematic index (9.13) that otherwise would be empty.

[68] See Maassen 1871, 50–65, 149–85, 408–10. The Apostolic Canons will be omitted in the *Hispana*, which is also notable for containing African material of a separate stream of transmission.

[69] Most notably in his preface to his (lost) third collection; trans. Somerville and Brasington 1998, 49.

west Syrian *synodika*, and Apostolic material, often expanded far beyond the eighty-five canons, will also be present.[70] Carthage seems to appear occasionally, in fragments or epitome.[71] A large degree of continuity across the Christian world is therefore still evident at this period. The textual shape of all traditions remains clearly centered around a Nicene corpus that has been expanded in very similar ways. The textual shape of the Christian canonical tradition may thus be conveyed at this point in a single formula:

Apostolic material + Nicene corpus [generally expanded to Chalcedon, and often including Serdica and some African material] + Local materials

At the same time, local material—and thus regional differentiation—begins to become more prominent. Some of the Greek patristic material will appear in Syrian canon law books, but not in precisely the same form; none will pass into the west.[72] In the west, in its place, other local Latin materials, notably the papal decretals, will begin to be found regularly in the collections. These, with the increasing number of local Spanish and Gallic councils, never pass east. In the Syrian east the *synodika* will continue to accrete their own proprietary traditions of local eastern councils and Syrian patristic canons.[73]

In the Greek east another important type of legislative material also begins to assume increased prominence at this time: imperial legislation.[74] The mid-5th to 7th C cessation of canonical legislation in the empire is often explained by the large quantity of secular ecclesiastic legislation produced during this hiatus, particular by Justinian.[75] Whether or not a true causal connection between these phenomena existed, there is no question that a central feature of the eastern canonical collections during this time is the admission of much secular ecclesiastical material. This material seems to have first entered the tradition in the form of discrete collections appended to the corpus. Three such eastern collections are known (all here given their 19th C names): the anonymous *Collection in Twenty-five Chapters* (*Coll25*), a collection of excerpts from the Greek sections of *CJ* 1.1–4 and four novels (these last later additions);

[70] Selb 1981, 104–10; 1989, 92–102, 140–5; also Schwartz 1910, 200–1 on the possibly very early admittance of some of apostolic material into the Syrian world. Serdica does not seem to be attested in the east Syrian *synodika*. On this material generally in the oriental collections, see Kaufhold 2012.

[71] See Kaufhold 2012, 233, 236, 274; Selb 1989, 102–4.

[72] The eastern patristic material in later western collections is mostly from different sources. On this material, see Munier 1957; also, Maassen 1871, 348–82. For Greek patristic material in the Syrian and other oriental collections, see Kaufhold 2012; also n. 62. It is never particularly prominent, and originates, I suspect, in independent lines of transmission.

[73] Kaufhold 2012 is the best survey; see also Selb 1981, 59–64; 1989, 110–32, 145–52.

[74] This is by no means a uniquely Greek phenomenon. Secular legislation will also find a place in later Latin and oriental collections. See de Clercq 1949, 669–80; Kaufhold 2012, 252–3, 283–7, 304–13, 323–5; Maassen 1871, 308–46, 887–900.

[75] A very useful reference remains de Clercq 1949; see also Alivisatos 1913; Pfannmüller 1902; van der Wal 1998.

the *Collection in Eighty-seven Chapters* (*Coll87*) of John Scholastikos, a more sophisticated topical collection of relevant Justinianic Novels, especially Novel 123; and the anonymous *Tripartita*, a set of topically arranged extracts from the *CJ*, *Novels*, *Institutes*, and the *Digest*.[76] In the extant manuscripts these collections tend to be found together, as a close adjunct to the canonical corpus, and in the order *Coll87*, *Coll25*, *Tripartita*.[77] However, because John Scholastikos is attributed with the authorship of both the *Coll87* and the *Coll50*, and in some manuscripts the two are closely associated,[78] and because the *Tripartita* sounds very much like a legal collection mentioned in the prologue to the *Coll14*,[79] and is used extensively as a source for the *NC14*, it is widely assumed that these two secular legal collections originally were attached as appendices to these two canonical collections.[80] By extension—following Karl Eduard Zachariä von Lingenthal—scholars often hazard that the *Coll25* (without the four novels) may originally have been an appendix of the lost *Coll60*.[81]

It is hypothesized that sometime between 612 and 629 material from the *Tripartita*, along with other antecessor material (i.e. 6th C translations and paraphrases of the Justinianic law books), was incorporated into the topical index of the *Coll14*—that is, under the topical headings—by an anonymous compiler now known to scholarship as "Enantiophanes" or the "Younger Anonymous."[82] The identity of this "Enantiophanes" (the name is taken from a later scholiast's confusing the name of the author with one of his books, *Περὶ ἐναντιοφανῶν*, "On Seeming Contradictions") is unknown. It has been suggested that he is the same author whose commentary on a *summa* of the *Digest* is preserved in anonymous scholia to the *Basilica*, and who wrote two secular legal monographs, but this is contested.[83] In any case he seems to have been a jurist of some note. The resulting collection has become known as the *Nomocanon in Fourteen Titles* (*NC14*).

At some point another collection of secular legal material, mostly drawn from the *Coll87*, was incorporated into the *Coll50*, to much the same effect. This collection, now known as the *Nomocanon in Fifty Titles* (*NC50*), which seems to have undergone two later recensions, the last as late as the 9th C, is

[76] See generally *Delineatio* 52–4, 61; *Peges* 137–42; van der Wal and Stolte 1994.

[77] Van der Wal and Stolte 1994, xiii–xiv.

[78] e.g. Paris supp. gr. 483 and Vatican gr. 843.

[79] *RP* 1.7; see Ch. 2 B.3.

[80] *Delineatio* 53–4, 61; *Peges* 137–42; van der Wal and Stolte 1994, xv–xvii; Zachariä von Lingenthal, 1877. See also Ch. 4 B.

[81] Zachariä von Lingenthal 1877, 614–16; the later four novels are often thought to have been added by Scholastikos when the *Coll25* and *Coll87*, in a second redaction, were added to the *Coll50*, perhaps *c.*565. See Beneshevich *Sin* 288–324; *Peges* 137–42; van der Wal and Stolte 1994, xv–xvii.

[82] See n. 50 for literature on the nomocanons; the most recent surveys are *Delineatio* 66–70; *Peges* 142–7.

[83] On this question, see *Delineatio* 63–8; *Peges* 145–6; Stolte 1985; van der Wal 1980.

attributed to John Scholastikos in the manuscripts; its earliest forms may indeed be his work.[84] Doubts, however, have long been raised about this attribution, principally because of the collection's rather clumsy composition.[85]

In the 11th C Michael Psellus, in a poem, will call these mixed collections "nomocanons" (*νομοκανών*, var. *νομοκάνονον*, *νομοκάνωνον*), as they comprise both *νόμοι* and *κανόνες*.[86] Originally, however, these collections seem to have had no special name, simply called by the variety of fairly generic terms shared by all canonical collections (*σύνταγμα*, *συλλογή*, *συναγωγή*). Byzantine terminology was in fact very variable for all of the canonical collections.[87] The first attestations of the term nomocanon, for example, which may date to as early as the 9th C, do not even clearly imply mixed civil-legal content.[88] Even well after the 11th C *νομοκανών* seems to have been a very broad term, applicable to a variety of other types of regulative collections, often including penitential collections and canonical collections clearly without civil law content.[89] Only in the later Byzantine period does the term seem to apply more regularly to the full *Coll14*, usually in its nomocanonical form, and sometimes called "the Great Nomocanon."[90] Nevertheless, the exclusive use of the term "nomocanon" for the Byzantine canonical-civil collections is characteristic only of modern scholarship. And even today, the terminology in the modern literature for these expanded indices can cause confusion, as the term nomocanon is sometimes

[84] *Sin* 292–321.

[85] So e.g. Biener 1827, 15–16; *Delineatio* 53, 67–8; Heimbach 1868, 289–91; Mortreuil 1843, 1.200–1. The authors of *Delineatio* believe that the collections were produced in the order *Coll50*, *Coll14*, *NC14*, *NC50*. Most other authors retain the sequence *Coll50*, *NC50*, *Coll14*, *NC14* (with perhaps the middle two switched), although scholars are often guarded about the *NC50*'s exact origin or author; e.g. Gaudemet 1965, 419, with older references; *Peges* 142–3; Pieler 1997a, 580.

[86] *Περὶ νομοκανόνου*, ed. Westerink 1992, 77–80.

[87] *Sbornik* 58–60, 104–15 and *Sin* ii–iii, 220–2 remain the fundamental discussions of terminology for the collections, and are the principal source of what follows. See also *Delineatio* 66; *Historike* 71 n. 4. On names of civil collections (with similar ambiguities), see Burgmann 2002, 258–9.

[88] Beneshevich (*Sbornik* 106) cites two instances: a question-and-answer response of Theodore Studite (9th C; Mai 1848, 147–8) and a passage in the Life of St Methodius (9th C; from chapter XV, ed. Lehr-Spławiński 1959, 119: "Тъгда же и номоканонъ рекъше законоу правило и отьуьскыя къннигы преложи."). The former, if genuine, most likely refers to only a straight canonical collection. The latter almost certainly refers to the earliest Slavonic *Coll50* translation which did not contain secular laws—although it may have had a civil law appendix, which could account for its name; see Maksimovich 2007, 9–10, also Gallagher 2002, 95–113. Beneshevich also notes (*Sbornik* 106–7) that the concluding epigraph of the *Coll50* in Moscow 432 (11th C) and Patmos 205 (12th C) refers to the proceeding work, without civil laws, as a *νομοκανών* (*Syn* 155). This may reflect post-10th C usage, but it nevertheless demonstrates how easily the "plain" *Coll50* could be called a *νομοκανών*.

[89] The best example is Aristenos' synopsis and commentary, frequently called a "*νομοκανόνον*" in its manuscript introductions (see those listed by Zachariä von Lingenthal 1887, 255–6); for others, see *Sbornik* 109 n.1; also Naz 1956, 1014). There is a vague possibility that *νομοκανών* did not originally mean "canons-and-laws" but "canon *of* the law." See the discussions in Wagschal 2010a, 274, based on Pavlov 1874, 39–42 and *Sbornik* 105 n. 4.

[90] *Sbornik* 109–11.

used to refer specifically to the thematic indices expanded with civil laws, while at other times it is used to refer to an entire collection in which such an index exists (i.e. prologue + thematic index with laws + corpus)—or, confusingly, like the Byzantine usage, to any systematic collection, even *without* civil laws.[91]

During the 6th or 7th C another important canonical sub-genre seems to have emerged for the first time: the canonical synopsis.[92] Only one such work exists, but in multiple recensions which witness to the gradual expansion and sometimes reordering of the material. All are straightforwardly abbreviated versions of the corpus, proceeding source by source, although all, except that to which the 12th C commentator Alexios Aristenos attached his commentary, omit some older or out-of-date canons, and show varying levels of renumbering and conflation.[93] The text of the individual abbreviated canons themselves, however, seems stable across the recensions.[94] The contents and orders of the canons in the three best-known (i.e. published) recensions are as follows:

In Voellus and Justel 2.673–709 (= PG 114.235–92),[95] under the name of Symeon the Logothete:	In Voellus and Justel 2. 710–48 (= PG 133.63–113),[96] under the name of Aristenos (also attributed to a "Stephen of Ephesus"):	The synopsis to which the 12th C commentator Aristenos attached his commentary. It may be found in Beveridge v. 2 (= RP 2–4, and PG 137 and 138).[97] Normal order of this version:
Apostles	Apostles	Apostles
Nicaea	Nicaea	Nicaea
Constantinople	Ancyra	Ancyra
Ephesus	Neocaesarea	Neocaesarea
Chalcedon	Gangra	Gangra
Ancyra	Antioch	Antioch
Neocaesarea	Laodicea	Laodicea
Gangra	Constantinople	Constantinople

[91] See the comments of Stolte 1989, 115.

[92] See *Delineatio* 68–9; Menebisoglou 1984; *Peges* 135–7, 245–8; Zachariä von Lingenthal 1887.

[93] See *Delineatio* 68.

[94] On this last, see Menebisoglou 1984, 78.

[95] From Paris gr. 1370. Also known in numerous other manuscripts. See *Sin* 63 n. 2, col. 2; Mortreuil 1843, 3.407; *Peges* 245 n. 53.

[96] From Paris gr. 1302. In the same order, but fragmentary (ending at Antioch), is a slightly different recension in Vienna theo. gr. 283, published by Kraznozhen 1911, 207–21. See also Mortreuil 1843, 1.200–1.

[97] The text here is not in normal manuscript order or appearance, distributed instead under the canons with the commentaries of Balsamon and Zonaras. Also, confusingly, the synopsis is labeled with Aristenos' name, and Aristenos' actual commentary is placed in subsequent paragraphs. For the manuscripts, see Mortreuil 1843, 3.408–10.

Antioch	Ephesus	Ephesus
Laodicea	Chalcedon	Chalcedon
Serdica	Serdica	Serdica
Carthage	Carthage	Carthage
Basil	Trullo	Constantinople 394
Trullo	Basil	Trullo
		II Nicaea
		Basil

Within the manuscripts, however, considerable further variation may be found. In its fullest and latest versions the synopsis contains all of the sources of the standard 9th C Byzantine corpus.[98]

In the manuscripts (and printed editions) these works are attributed to a variety of figures: Stephen of Ephesus, sometimes considered to be a 5th C bishop, but more likely a 7th C hierarch of the same name present at Trullo;[99] Symeon the Logothete, a 10th C author; and Aristenos, the 12th C commentator (no doubt because of the later attachment of his commentary to a later recension of the synopsis). Scholars vary in attaching these attributions to various recensions of the synopsis, and more research is required to clarify the text's history.[100] It is clear, however, that the recensions of the synopsis witness to ancient corpus configurations, including some not known from any other extant source. The recension attributed to Symeon is particularly interesting, as Trullo is placed after Basil, which strongly suggests that its source corpus was pre-Trullan.[101] Its placement of the four ecumenical councils at the head of Nicene corpus material is also extremely unusual in the Byzantine tradition, and likewise suggests an archaic configuration.[102]

[98] From the available editions the texts of the full form of the synopsis may be found by combining the synopsis entries under each canon in *RP* 2–4 together with the synopses of the Apostolic "Epitome" material and a few other para-canonical items published in *RP* 4.393–416. These last supplements are likely to have been composed in connection with the 11th C Bestes/ Michael recension of the *NC14*; see *Peges* 247–8, as well as the manuscript information in Mortreuil 1843, 3.408–16.

[99] *Peges* 136. The older literature often wished to see the 5th C Stephen as the author of earlier recensions of the corpus. See e.g. Voellus and Justel 1661, 1.16; Doujat 1687, 288–92; see the comments of Ballerini and Ballerini 1753, 99.

[100] See *Delineatio* 68–9; Menebisoglou 1984, 77–82; Mortreuil 1843, 1.200–1, 3.408–10; *Peges* 245–7.

[101] See *Delineatio* 68; *Peges* 136–7. Menebisoglou 1984, 79 believes that the earliest recension of the synopsis may predate Chalcedon.

[102] In *Delineatio* 77 it is stated in error that the Tarasian recension of the *Coll14* had such an order. It is clear in *Sborník* 260–88, to which the texts refer, that it did not. I know of only one other witness to this order: an incipit index to the *Coll50* found in Oxford Baroc. 86 43r–49r, as per Beneshevich's description *Sin* 60 (see also *Sbornik* 83 n.3). The four-council order is common in the west, where it had no little ideological significance: see the introductions to the *Hispana* and *Mercator*, translated in Somerville and Brasington 1998, 55–7, 82–91; also Congar 1960.

Conciliar legislation resumed in the empire in 691/2 with the publication of a code-like series of canons at the council in Trullo. These were followed a century later by the canons of the seventh ecumenical council, II Nicaea, in 787, and then by the "Photian councils" of Protodeutera (861) and Hagia Sophia (879). This "second wave" of legislation, distinct in many ways from the earlier "first-wave" material, was added to the corpus in stages. Again the principal agent/witness for corpus expansion seems to have been the thematic collections, but now via a succession of updated recensions of the *Coll14*—not the production of entirely new collections. Thanks to the work of Beneshevich, we can identify in the manuscripts a series of recensions in which Trullo, II Nicaea, Protodeutera, and finally Hagia Sophia seem to have been gradually added.[103] The *Coll50* likewise was gradually updated, although the stages in this process have not yet been carefully identified or correlated with specific events or dates—and typically the newer material is simply added after the older systematic corpus, not inserted into it.[104] But later versions of the *Coll50* tend to contain very similar material as contemporary *Coll14* recensions.[105]

A few other canonical sources also entered the corpus at this time. An extract from the council of Carthage in 255 under Cyprian appears in a pre-Trullan recension of the *Coll14* corpus, curiously placed after Nicaea 325 itself, that is, as the first of the councils save Nicaea.[106] It appears again in the corpus delineated by Trullo 2, now after all of the patristic canons. It is never especially common in the earlier manuscripts, and its fortunes will vary in later collections, often absent, or present but in different positions, for example at the end of the councils, or among the fathers, or in an appendix.[107] In Trullo 2 three other hierarchs also now make a definite appearance for the first time (Athanasius, Gregory of Nazianzus, and Amphilochius of Iconium), bringing the total of patristic sources to the symbolic number of twelve. The number and

Such an order is, however, suggested by *N* 131.1. A similar three-council grouping may be found in some non-Chalcedonian collections; see e.g. Riedel 1900, 124, 136.

[103] In each case "acceptance" into the corpus is marked by various combinations of entry into the corpus section, integration into the systematic references, and/or mentions and listings in prologue structures. See Section D. 5.

[104] On this last, see *Sin* 250, although Beneshevich notes a number of exceptions. Of these, see esp. Group G, *Sin* 179–85.

[105] For examples, see Beneshevich's Group C, D and G, Vienna hist. gr 7 (*Sin* 108–26), or Coislin 364 (*Sin* 150–65). There is considerable variation among these "expanded" versions. Compare e.g. Moscow Syn. 398, 432, Naples II.C.7, or Vatican 843. "Soft spots" in the *Coll50* tradition are similar to those of earlier recensions of the *Coll14*, and include Amphilochius, Gregory Naz., Cyprian, Hagia Sophia, and the full set of Carthaginian canons (selections are more common).

[106] In Patmos 172 (described *Sbornik* 230–6). On this canon generally, and its fate in the manuscripts, see *Delineatio* 69–70, *Historike* 81–2, *Fonti* 2.301–3 (esp. n.1), *Sources* 112–14.

[107] Compare its place e.g. in Beneshevich "Recensio Photio protoypa" (*Sbornik* 130–77), Jerusalem Cruc. 2, Florence Laur. 10.1, Oxford Laud.39, Rome Vallic. F.10, Vatican gr. 829.

order of the patristic sources listed in Trullo 2 will nevertheless vary throughout the manuscripts tradition, settling only after the 12th C commentators.[108]

Some of this second-wave eastern material passed west, as per tradition, but now much more sporadically. A thorough analysis of this transmission has never been performed, but some of the Trullan canons, and some of those of II Nicaea, were accepted into at least some western collections; some will appear in Gratian.[109] To my knowledge, neither council passed in any significant way into the eastern Monophysite or Nestorian collections, although they do, as we would expect, appear in later Arabic Melkite sources.[110] Curiously, Cyprianic material does appear in the east and west Syrian *synodika*.[111]

The recension of the *Coll14* that admits the Photian councils (or at least the first)—usually called the "Photian recension" although it is unclear that Photius had any hand in it—marked the closing of the Byzantine corpus of canons.[112] Datable to 883, it corresponds neatly with what will, in retrospect, be a cessation of imperial ecumenical councils, or at least imperial ecumenical councils producing canons. Official disciplinary legislation did not cease, but thenceforth will take the form of specific enactments of the ecumenical patriarchs and the Constantinopolitan ἐνδημοῦσα σύνοδος, or of imperial novels.[113] These will slowly be collected and added to canonical manuscripts, but neither they, nor any other "appendix" -type material added to the tradition, will truly penetrate the older canonical corpus itself, and be ranked with "the canons" proper in the same way as the older material—that is, be incorporated into the expanded *Coll14* or *Coll50* indices or tables of contents.[114] They will henceforth appear in the manuscripts as a more variable outer valence of appendix material, around the core, almost as an exegetical

[108] See *Fonti* 2.xiv–xx; *Sources* 84–9.

[109] For Trullo, see now Landau 1995; for II Nicaea, see the index of Gratian's sources (Friedberg 1879, 1.xx).

[110] Graf 1944, 1.598–600; Kaufhold 2012, 220–32; Riedel 1900, 9–10, 138–46 (who notes a certain degree of cross-pollination among Melkite and Coptic collections; see esp. the Collection of Macarius, described 121–9). Dura 1995, 238–40 claims a greater influence of later Greek synods in non-Chalcedonian circles.

[111] Selb 1981, 110; 1989, 102–4.

[112] Generally, *Delineatio* 87–9, *Historike* 83–91. The extent of Photius' participation in this recension is debated; see Deledemos 110–12, *Delineatio* 87–9, *Historike* 86–7, Meliara 1905–6, *Peges* 145, Petrovitz 1970, 34–8, Stolte 1997.

[113] Dölger and Wirth 1924–65 and Grumel *et al.* 1936–91 remain the standard repertories of the imperial and patriarchal material. No thorough survey, however, of the documents of this type typically found in canonical manuscript appendices—i.e. physically part of the canonical tradition—has yet to be produced. A selection of the most important may be found in *RP* 5; for the patriarchal decisions, a convenient list may be found in Milaš 1902, 157–65. *Peges* 232–40, 295–7 is the most recent overview.

[114] There are some exceptions; for example, the *Coll50* Group G does add some later appendix material under its references (*Sin* 179–85). Something similar may be observed in one chapter of the *Coll14* in Vat 827 (*Sbornik* 252). There are likely other examples, but such instances seem to have been quite occasional.

expansion of the earlier material—and indeed, in content most of this later material is devoted to sorting out details of the older tradition.[115]

Through the end of the empire no later collection of canons will ever come even close to replacing or displacing the 883 *Coll14* corpus. The later tradition is always written around this core, at most reorganizing it or presenting it in a more accessible form. Despite a constant blurriness around its edges,[116] then, the 883 corpus will emerge in the manuscripts as the regular and sealed "core" of the canonical tradition—a position it retains to this day in the modern Byzantine Orthodox churches.[117]

It is difficult to say, however, to what extent this closing of the corpus was perceived by contemporaries. Clearly, the *Coll14* corpus, in any redaction, was not immediately considered *the* authoritative statement of the corpus, even after the confirmation of an early form of it at Trullo in 691/2. Certainly the 883 recension was never "officially" promulgated or even defined.[118] In fact, it is curious how many witnesses exist to the very slow reception of the *Coll14* corpus. John of Damascus in the 8th C, for example, when describing "the canons," seems to cite the corpus of the *Coll50*.[119] In the 9th C, a letter of Pope Nicholas to Photius also refers to the *quinquaginta titulos* as the Byzantines' standard collection.[120] The synopsis tradition likewise seems more or less confined to the *Coll50* until approximately the 11th C—and even after it has absorbed Trullo, which prescribes the further *Coll14* patristic sources! Perhaps most telling, Michael Psellus, in a poem written for the to-be-emperor Michael VII—that is, in what we might expect to be a reasonably "official," or at least learned, statement of the corpus—will describe a corpus that is almost certainly an expanded *Coll50*, not the *Coll14*.[121] Even Aristenos in the 12th C does not comment on Protodeutera, Hagia Sophia, or any fathers aside from Basil—that is, his corpus looks like the *Coll50* corpus expanded with

[115] The supplementary nature of this later literature has been frequently remarked; see e.g. Beck 1977, 142–7; *Delineatio* 97; *Peges* 235. The later reception of much of this material could be quite slow and uncertain. See Burgmann 1985.

[116] The varying presence of Cyprian, Athanasius, Gregory Naz., and Amphilochius, and even Hagia Sophia are the chief examples of this "blurriness."

[117] There is widespread consensus on this point among Orthodox canonists, e.g. *Historike* 91–100; L'Huillier 1996, 7 n. 44; Meyendorff 1983, 80–1; Milaš 1902, 107–55; Tsipin 2002, 30–1.

[118] On the "official" promulgation of 920 sometimes asserted in the literature, see n. 224.

[119] *Libellus de recta sententia* 8 (*PG* 94.1432cd; *Clavis* 8046): [*ὄμνυμι*] *στοιχεῖν δὲ καὶ ἐμμένειν τοῖς ἁγίοις κανόσι τῶν ἁγίων ἀποστόλων, τῶν τε ἁγίων συνόδων, καὶ τοῦ ἁγίου καὶ θεοφάντορος Βασιλείου· ταῦτα πάντα φυλάξω*. Reference from *Sin* 326.

[120] Letter to Photius, Nov. 866 (*Mansi* 15.176.263 = *PL* 119, 1045–53, at 1051; reference from *Sin* 326; now Epistle 92, *MGH* Epp. 6.533–40, at 538). Deledemos is uncertain that this part of the letter is original, but he seems to cite the wrong letter (Deledemos 2002, 76 n. 183).

[121] Westerink 1992, 77–80. So Menebisoglou 1984, 88, *Peges* 249–50, *Sin* 327. *Contra*: *Delineatio* 106, who suggests it is the *NC14*, but this is almost certainly a mistake, perhaps a typographical error.

Trullo, II Nicaea, and the first letter of Basil.[122] Indeed, Zonaras and Balsamon do not seem to have commented on exactly the same 883 corpus either (although their collections contain all the canons): for example, Zonaras does not comment on Timothy, Theophilus, Cyril, or Gennadius, and neither Zonaras nor Balsamon comments on Amphilochius.[123]

A very strong conservative impulse, therefore, seems to have dominated the middle Byzantine period. It seems the core of the core, as it were, was viewed as something much closer to the original *Coll50* corpus. This does not mean that the later *Coll14* material, confirmed at Trullo, was not present, known, or used; indeed, by the end of the 11th C it seems to have become well entrenched.[124] But at least its outer edges, the patristic material in particular, and the most recent conciliar material, seem not to have "settled" into firm recognition for some time.

It was nevertheless clear, however, that the corpus would not substantially grow beyond its 883 revision. The next major recensions of the *Coll14*, those of Michael the Sebastos and Theodore the Bestes in the late 11th C, only slightly cleaned up and completed some of the corpus references of the 883 recension.[125] Substantial additions of new sources were made only to the secular legal material in the systematic section of the collection.[126] The canonical portion of the collection was thus already essentially frozen. The next major recension of the *Coll14*, that of Balsamon, would not venture even this: Balsamon appends his commentary to the secular material *after* the traditional nomocanonical texts, just as he does in the corpus section of the collection.[127] He does not seem to interfere with the existing tradition. As such, Balsamon, along with the other commentators, effectively seals—or at least witness to—the ultimate ossification of the 883 corpus and its secular legal material.[128] It is probably at this point, with the commentators, that the *Coll14* additions—seven centuries after their articulation—are finally accepted as beyond

[122] *RP* 2–4, checked against various manuscripts, including Moscow 237, Vatican 840, Vienna iur. gr 10.

[123] So *RP* 2–4, checked against Florence Laur. 5.1, Moscow Sin. 393, Vatican gr. 828, Venice app. 3.01, 3.03. The issue remains very muddy, however, because of the variability among the manuscripts and editions, and ambiguity in the ascriptions of individual commentary fragments. See Biener 1856, 179–82. A precise determination of this question must await new editions of Zonaras and Balsamon.

[124] *Peges* 241–2; *Sbornik* 109–11.

[125] It re-adds some Carthaginian and Basilian material that had been omitted, for example, along with other apostolic texts; see Schminck 1998, 379–83; and n. 147. According to Schminck, its basis seems to be Jerusalem Pan. Taph. 24, which had included the omitted canons in a catch-all chapter in Title 14. Schminck 1998 has revolutionized our knowledge of this recension—or rather, recensions. It was known to previous scholarship as the recension of "Theodore Bestes."

[126] Published as the *auctaria* in *Pitra*.

[127] I owe this observation to *Delineatio* 111.

[128] In his commentary on Trullo 2 Balsamon famously condemns the use of the *NC50*—although mostly, it seems, because of its selection of secular laws. *RP* 2.311.

question. The long-term success of the *Coll14* corpus as the immutable core of the entire tradition was assured.

D. MAJOR CONTOURS OF THE TRADITION

1. Unity, stability, continuity

The single most striking characteristic of Byzantine canon law as a textual phenomenon is its uniformity and stability. Contrary to the pervasive tendency in the modern literature to speak about Byzantine canon law as a succession of different collections,[129] or as otherwise quite varied and diverse,[130] the Byzantine tradition effectively consisted of only one canonical corpus. At the heart of this collection was the Nicene corpus, which was gradually subjected to various processes of expansion but never replaced or substantially or permanently modified (selected or interpolated). The textual history of the Byzantine canonical tradition is thus simply the story of the expansion, confirmation, and reissuing of this gradually growing and ever-ossifying central corpus structure. Indeed, the *idea* of a core-corpus structure is probably the central conceptual structure of the entire tradition.

This stability and uniformity become most obvious when one examines the extant Byzantine manuscripts. C. H. Turner long ago noted that "[t]he most obvious difference between Greek and Latin manuscripts of canons, taken in the mass, is the striking resemblance of the former among themselves contrasted with the almost infinite degree of divergence from one another which prevail in the latter. The contents of Greek canonical MSS are always more or less the same."[131] Indeed, by manuscript standards the Greek texts are strikingly uniform. Most complete manuscripts follow a very similar pattern.

[129] Everywhere the tendency is to speak of multiple collections succeeding each other, instead of the growth and development of one collection over time. Hess 2002, 54, for example, states very misleadingly that "[d]uring the sixth century the 'Antiochene Collection' was superseded by others, but it was fortuitously translated into Latin . . . before disappearing entirely from the Greek East." Similar expressions referring to the Antiochian or Chalcedonian collections may be found in Burgmann 2002, 241; Feine 1954, 83; Price and Gaddis 2005, 3.94 n. 6; Schwartz 1910, 195; 1936a, 159–60. See also how Plöchl 1959, 1.441 speaks as if Trullo defined a completely new self-standing collection (and so Ferme 1998, 81; Morolli 2000, 313).

[130] e.g. Nelson 2008, 299; Stolte 2008, 694; see also Plöchl's similar (273–4) but cryptic, and rather odd, statement (repeated in Ferme 1998, 78) that the sources of eastern church law reflect from the 6th C a fragmentation of the eastern church's unity (giving as an example the Acacian schism). This is part of an older narrative—appropriate when restricted to the west—that sees the first-millennium canonical tradition as a story of regional *Partikularismus* and fragmentation except, perhaps, where influenced by Rome; see e.g. Cosme 1955, 1955a, Fournier and Le Bras 1931, Stickler 1950.

[131] Turner 1914, 161.

They start with some type of prologue section, which is followed by a systematic index or two[132] (perhaps in nomocanonical form), followed by the corpus itself. The corpus in most extant manuscripts, whatever its exact form, usually approaches the full 883 recension in its selection of sources, perhaps with commentary and almost always followed by a selection of appendix-like materials.[133] In some manuscripts, effectively smaller *Hilfsmittel*-type works, the corpus will be replaced with the synopsis and the commentary of Aristenos—a kind of miniature version of the standard collections.[134]

The text of the canons themselves, as Joannou notes, is apparently remarkably stable, and with little regular omission, reordering, paraphrasing, or interpolation.[135] Likewise, the physical appearance and layout of the manuscripts, while slightly variable, almost never surprises. They are mostly quite plain and functional, with bland and unremarkable breaks between the sources,[136] simple marginal numberings for the canons, and, sometimes, marginal scholia. Some elements of the manuscript may be in slightly different order. For example, the corpus sometimes precedes the systematic indices.[137] Considerable variability can be noted in the appendix materials, and to some extent the prologue texts, although even the appendices tend to include broadly the same type of material.[138] The overall picture is thus one of regularity and consistency: there is a very recognizable and predictable "shape" to a Byzantine canonical manuscript.[139] In effect, in the extant manuscripts, to speak of multiple collections is really only to speak of different versions of the same collection.

There seems to be little reason to doubt that this stability and uniformity had obtained in the Byzantine east for some time before our earliest manuscripts (*c.*9th C). Not only do reconstructions of earlier recensions of

[132] See the list in *Syn* v–vi for pairings of the *Coll50* and *Coll14*, in various forms.

[133] Thus earlier collections, such as the *Coll50*, are generally found in the manuscripts updated to approach in their selection of sources the 883 corpus (so all of the major recensions described in *Sin*).

[134] e.g. Vatican gr. 840.

[135] *Fonti* 1.5; reaffirmed by L'Huillier 1996, 9–10. Such statements should be considered tentative, however; the internal state of the texts has not yet been sufficiently studied.

[136] Typically simple undulating lines, perhaps with some floral motifs, occasionally developing into more complex, but abstract, decorations in blank spaces or section headings (e.g. Sinai 1112, 4v or 77r; Rome Vallic. F 47, 23r). Further illustration and decoration (e.g. miniatures) in Byzantine canonical manuscripts seem otherwise very rare; see Hajdú 2003, 100–1 for an exception in Munich gr. 122 (small conciliar scenes), with further references. See also Paris supp. gr. 1085. See Stolte 1988 on the lack of imagery in Byzantine secular legal manuscripts.

[137] e.g. in a number of Beneshevich's "Group A" manuscripts of the *Coll50* (*Sin* 59). For the *Coll14*, see Vatican gr. 2198.

[138] See Appendix A, and the references in nn. 54–5.

[139] There are some exceptions, but before the 16th C, when more miscellaneous handbook-type manuscripts seem to become more popular, they tend to prove the rule; they are certainly very surprising when one stumbles upon them. Examples include Athos Vatop. 555 (12th C), Paris Cois. 364 (*a.* 1294), Vienna hist. gr. 70 (14th C), and Oxford Bod. gr. misc. f.4 (12th C).

collections in the east point to similar dynamics, but, more importantly, uniformity and stability are very evident across all of the major traditions of this period: Latin, Syrian, and Greek. From a "bird's eye view," in fact, stability and uniformity are probably the most striking characteristics of first-millennium canon law as a whole—which strongly inclines us to expect this within the earlier Byzantine tradition (probably the most conservative of all the traditions). This stability is rarely remarked in the scholarly literature, but from the narrative in the previous section it is clear that it manifested itself in two interrelated ways: in the general morphology of canonical collections, and in the content of a typical collection.[140]

In morphology, from the moment we first glimpse the Nicene corpus, all of the witnesses (the early western general collections,[141] the Syrian *synodika*, all the Byzantine sources) point to one central "textual idea" of what constitutes a full, proper canonical collection: a canonical collection conveys "the corpus." This corpus is a body of traditionally accepted legal sources, listed one after another, and with little or no significant selection or interpolation (this is particularly true in the Byzantine sources). The exact content and boundaries of "the corpus" will vary somewhat from place to place and time to time, but it is always an identifiable structure at any particular moment: faithfully transmitting a core corpus always seems to be the primary "point" of a full canonical collection.[142] Further, the options for presenting this corpus are few. Generally, east and west, collections will include some type of prologue or prologue sections, then perhaps a systematic index, then "the corpus" of canonical materials followed by (or fading into) a much more variable and idiosyncratic group of appendix materials.

[140] The lack of emphasis on this early unity is perhaps the single oddest characteristic of modern canon law historiography. It is well recognized, of course, that the Antiochian corpus is a central source of the entire Christian tradition. Schwartz and Maassen are well aware of this, and Cardinal Pietro Gasparri is often cited as noting the Antiochian corpus as *antiquarum collectionum fere omnium quasi principium et fons* (from his preface to the 1917 *Codex Iuris Canonici*; see e.g. Stickler 1950, 3; Gaudemet 1985, 76, also 41, 165; Mardirossian 2010, 13). Similar is Fournier's concept of *ancien droit* (1931, 1.3–126, especially 12–21), and Ferme's "common substrate" of early law (1998, 58). For Selb this fact is self-evident (e.g. 1989, 103–4), as for Mardirossian 2010. See also Bucci 1992, 94–8. Nevertheless, the atomistic presentation of early canonical collections, especially after the 5th C, as a kaleidoscopic array of regional variation with little reference to their morphological and substantive similarity, and each with their own special modern name, tends to render the unity of canonical culture in the first millennium only vaguely perceptible in many modern surveys (e.g. Gaudemet 1985; Reynolds 1986). This tendency is magnified by canon law historians of the high middle ages, who tend rely on a (medieval?) narrative of "dissonance" moving to "harmony," and thus rarely even consider whether the earlier period might have possessed any kind of standard text structures. See e.g. Brundage 1995, 22–3, 43; 2008, 97; Gallagher 2002, 121–2; Kuttner 1960.

[141] i.e. Maassen's "general chronological" collections.

[142] In the literature this point tends to be recognized for the older chronological collections, such as the Dionysius or the *Hispana* (e.g. Zechiel-Eckes 1992, 1.29–30; Mordek 1975, 3), but it is equally true for early systematic collections; see Section D.5.

Smaller collections do exist that are much more varied in even "core" material, and in these texts the canons may be abbreviated. These collections, however, are always clearly *Hilfsmittel* works, practical handbooks obviously constructed against the background of the proper, full *libri canonum*. Written to address a specific topic or problem, they are handbooks *to* the corpus, *from* the corpus, which always remains the tangible structure against which these smaller works are written. In the west, these minor collections are many, and will eventually become very diverse, especially north of the Alps, where the idea of "the corpus" will apparently become tenuous rather quickly;[143] in the east the only substantial examples in our period are the synopses.[144] However, these synopses follow the contours of the corpus of their day very closely, much like similar, early collections in the west such as those of Martin of Braga or Fulgentius Ferrandus.[145]

Contrary to the impression often given in the literature, early systematic collections, at least in the east, and certainly in the beginning in the west as well (most notably in the *Concordia* of Cresconius[146]), do not represent exceptions or major transformations or developments of this basic shape or "idea" of a collection. They are merely thematic recensions of "the corpus," which they convey in full. While they do mark moments in which new material is introduced into the corpus, and they play a critical role in defining the corpus, they are remarkably faithful in conveying all the material, complete and intact, that was clearly part of the tradition at their time of composition. Thus both the *Coll50* and the *Coll14* (and Cresconius) contain every canon of the corpus as it existed prior to their collection. As a rule they evidence pronounced selection (mostly in their references to the material under their topic headings) or abbreviation only in the material they have themselves (probably) just added to the corpus—that is, the newest, least traditional material, on the outer fringes of the corpus core.[147] In this, these collections

[143] Gregory Halfond (Halfond 2010, 174–8 *et passim*) has recently noted that already in the 6th–8th C it is difficult to detect any sense of a fixed corpus among Frankish bishops.

[144] Another example at the end of our period is the Slavonic translation of the *Coll50* made (probably) by Methodius for his mission (ed. Bartoňková *et al.* 1971). It is abbreviated and shows evidence of selection, no doubt for the convenience of the early Slavic mission; see Gallagher 2002, 95–113. An example of a manuscript containing only a short set of topical extracts (here mostly on clerical marriage) is Vatican Barb. 476.

[145] Gaudemet 1985, 137–8, 152–3.

[146] On the shape and content of the *Concordia*, see Zechiel-Eckes 1992.

[147] The *Coll50* in fact conveys every single canon of its corpus—and most only once (see Ch. 2, n. 77). It is almost literally a rearrangement of the corpus. The status of the editions does not yet permit precise conclusions, but comparison of the current editions of the *Coll14* reveal that the original *Coll14* systematic index seems to have omitted canons almost exclusively from two new sources: Carthage and the first letter of Basil (in particular Basil 15, 16, and Carthage 34, 51, 52, 64, 67, 69, 74, 75, 77, 78, 82, 85, 87, 88, 91–4, 97, 99–101, 105, 107–19, 127, and 134–8). The omitted canons seem to have been excluded because of their exclusively doctrinal or very local content. Notably, however, in the later 11th C recensions, these canons are all more or less

are very different from later western systematic collections, which ultimately emerge as moments of permanent substantive selection, synthesis, and sorting of any and all earlier material.[148] These early systematic collections are little more than glorified tables of contents *to* the corpus. It is for this reason that any tendency to speak as if the earlier Antiochian or Chalcedonian collections "disappear" from the Byzantine tradition is extremely misleading:[149] they simply morph into new, expanded versions. Likewise, the common narrative of an evolutionary transformation of canonical collections from "chronological" into "systematic" form (with the two almost competing)—borrowed from later western canonical historiography, where it is more applicable—is deeply problematic.[150] Eastern systematic collections, like their early western counterparts, *are* the old "chronological" corpora, but now merely with some level of systematic rearrangement or indexing; they are not in any way replacements of, or substantively discontinuous with, the earlier collections. The earlier structures are always preserved, and completely so. We will return to the extraordinary conservatism of these collections in Chapter 4.

As to content of these collections, "the corpus" is always—west and east—an identifiable recension of the Nicene corpus, in various stages of expansion.

added back into the collection in a separate chapter of title 14. See the descriptions in Burgmann *et al.* 1995, 47, 106. Cresconius likewise omits only some items from sources newer to the tradition: Carthage, and elements from the decretals (see Zechiel-Eckes 1992, 1.7,18). See Wagschal 2010a, 274–5 for more details.

[148] Gratian's *Decretum* is the ultimate example; see the index of his sources in Friedberg 1879, xix–xli. All of the Gregorian collections are of this type, however (Fournier and Le Bras 1931, 1.77: "les réformateurs subordonnent à leur programme le choix et l'ordre des canons"; descriptions in Fournier and Le Bras 1931, 2.3–54). On the creative potentialities and realities of the later western systematic collections, see esp. Mordek 1975, 6–7, Pinedo 1963, 291–2. It is difficult to pinpoint when western systematic collections shift from at least notionally transmitting an older corpus to actively choosing and selecting among the traditional texts. Western canon law historians do not tend to view this transformation as in need of special explanation. In light of the Byzantine experience, however, it is the single most peculiar aspect of western canon law. Halfond 2010 notes that general patterns of selection and modification are already very common north of the Alps in the 6th–8th C.

[149] For examples of this type of language, see n. 129.

[150] Assumed everywhere, but see briefly Zechiel-Eckes 1992, 1.29–31; Fransen 1973, 14–15; Maassen 1871, 3–4; Mordek 1975, 4–16; Somerville and Brasington 1998, 12–13. Fransen 1973, 14–15 can thus, for example, call the collection of (Ps.-)Isidor Mercator the "last" chronological collection in the west—and this is correct, as these collections do stop being widely copied in the high middle ages. But there is no "last" chronological collection in the east inasmuch as the systematic collections are little more than simple rearrangements of or indices to the chronological corpora. The traditional typology of collections as "chronological" and "systematic" is problematic in many ways (compare Fransen's use of "non-systematic," for example, and also the comments of Mordek 1975, 3), and should probably be abandoned. Better would be a general typology that could be employed east and west, and which Maassen already suggests, distinguishing (1) "general" or complete corpus collections, which, whether systematic or not, notionally convey a complete corpus structure faithfully, with little or no selection, interpolation, or modification within each source; and (2) partial or handbook collections, which either give only an abbreviated or selected taste of a corpus, or are addressed to specific questions.

The Nicene corpus is not therefore "a" Byzantine collection of the first millennium; it is *the* collection of the entire post-4th C Christian world. As already noted, its content from Nicaea and generally through Chalcedon, usually expanded with Serdica and some version of Carthage and the Apostles, is the common core of virtually all major "general" canonical collections of our period, certainly around the Mediterranean.[151] Even after the 6th C, when the Latin, Greek, and Syrian collections begin to develop along separate paths, later developments emerge mostly as gradual additions to this old Nicene corpus—and thus the Nicene core is itself remarkably persistent.

The tendency for the tradition to develop as a gradual expansion of the Nicene core is particularly pronounced in the east. Indeed, from the 5th C onwards, between any two collections one will always contain the entirety of the other, that is, the one is always simply an expansion of the other. Variations may exist among appendix-like materials, but no two collections can be found with entirely or even mostly different "core" materials—for example, one missing Ancyra, or Nicaea. This stability and uniformity of development is easily demonstrated in a chronological schematic of the corpora of the principal Greek collections (additions to each stage in boldface):

Antiochian corpus

[ANCYRA] + [NEOCAESAREA] + [GANGRA] + [ANTIOCH] + [LAODICEA?]

Nicene corpus (approx. as at Chalcedon 451)

[NICAEA] + [ANCYRA] + [NEOCAESAREA] + [GANGRA] + [ANTIOCH] + [LAODICEA?] + **[CONSTANTINOPLE I]**

Coll60 (c.534?)

[APOSTLES] + [NICAEA] + [ANCYRA] + [NEOCAESAREA] + **[SERDICA]** + [GANGRA] + [ANTIOCH] + [LAODICEA] + [CONSTANTINOPLE I] + **[EPHESUS?]** + **[CHALCEDON]**

Coll50 (c.550)

[APOSTLES] + [NICAEA] + [ANCYRA] + [NEOCAESAREA] + [SERDICA] + [GANGRA] + [ANTIOCH] + [LAODICEA] + [CONSTANTINOPLE I] + [EPHESUS] + [CHALCEDON] + **[BASIL (TWO EPISTLES)]**

Coll14 (c.580)

[APOSTLES] + [NICAEA] + [ANCYRA] + [NEOCAESAREA] + [GANGRA] + [ANTIOCH] + [LAODICEA] + [CONSTANTINOPLE I] + [EPHESUS] + [CHALCEDON] + [SERDICA] +

[151] North of the Alps things become more variable, and very quickly. For Francia in particular, see now esp. Halfond 2010, above n. 143. Early collections of very proprietary content that might have been considered "general collections" in their own contexts include the eccentric *Hibernensis*, in Ireland (see Sheehy 1982; ed. Wasserschleben 1885), and perhaps the *Vetus Gallica* (ed. Mordek 1975).

[CARTHAGE] + [**CONSTANTINOPLE 394**] + [BASIL (68 CANONS)] + [**NINE TO ELEVEN ADDITIONAL FATHERS, AND AN ADDITIONAL EPISTLE OF BASIL**]

Corpus of Trullo 2 (691)

[APOSTLES] + [NICAEA] + [ANCYRA] + [NEOCAESAREA] + [GANGRA] + [ANTIOCH] + [LAODICEA] +[CONSTANTINOPLE I] + [EPHESUS] + [CHALCEDON] + [CONSTANTINOPLE 394] + [SERDICA] + [CARTHAGE] + [**TWELVE FATHERS, INCLUDING BASIL**] + [**CYPRIAN**]

Corpus of 883 Coll14 (order as in Coll14 index ἐκ ποίων, Pitra *2.450–1)*

[APOSTLES] + [NICAEA] + [ANCYRA] + [NEOCAESAREA] + [GANGRA] + [ANTIOCH] + [LAODICEA] + [CONSTANTINOPLE I] + [EPHESUS?] + [CHALCEDON] + [SERDICA] + [CARTHAGE] + [CONSTANTINOPLE 394] + [**TRULLO**] + [**II NICAEA + TARASIUS**] + [**PROTODEUTERA 861**] + [**HAGIA SOPHIA 879**][152] + [APPROX. TWELVE FATHERS] + [CYPRIAN]

Corpus of 883 Coll14 ("systematic" or "Tarasian" order as typically found in Zonaras and Balsamon recensions)

[APOSTLES] + [NICAEA] + [CONSTANTINOPLE I] + [EPHESUS] + [CHALCEDON] + [TRULLO] + [II NICAEA] + [PROTODEUTERA 861] + [HAGIA SOPHIA 879] + [CYPRIAN] + [ANCYRA] + [NEOCAESAREA] + [GANGRA] + [ANTIOCH] + [LAODICEA] + [SERDICA] + [CARTHAGE] + [CONSTANTINOPLE 394] + [APPROX. TWELVE FATHERS]

Although this schema is simplified, and does not convey isolated variations among individual manuscripts, it nevertheless accurately illustrates the broad shape of the tradition as *one* collection that is slowly growing. It is interesting to note that even differences in ordering of the material are few and restrained.[153] Certainly, profound change to existing corpus material is not in evidence. Further, internally each of the sources will almost always be copied in full. In fact, we may formulate a striking rule: *once a canonical source is accepted into the core corpus, it never leaves.* This is true both of the sources as units within the corpus and their individual canons. Development thus will always tend towards accumulation, with concern for the scrupulous preservation of traditional sources, and not towards operations of sorting, revising, or selecting.[154] Even clearly obsolete or apparently rescinded canons tend to continue to be copied.[155]

[152] In fact, Hagia Sophia is not generally listed in the index ἐκ ποίων, even when found in the body of the MSS.

[153] See further Section D.5.

[154] This dynamic is frequently noted in Byzantine law more generally, e.g. Burgmann 2002, 263; Stolte 2008, 692–3.

[155] e.g. the rules in Apostles 37, Antioch 20 or Nicaea 5 on holding synods twice a year, despite the clear relaxation of the rule to once a year in Trullo 8 and II Nicaea 6; or Ancyra 10, which allows deacons to marry, despite the rejection of this exception in Trullo 6. Many other examples could be offered.

Of course, the process of the definitive reception of sources into the corpus takes time, and thus among different recensions and manuscripts a certain "softness" may be detected in the transmission of more recent or marginal sources. Carthage, for example, first added in the later 6th C, is often abbreviated in later expanded *Coll50* recensions, and the references to this source in the earliest *Coll14* thematic index are not complete.[156] Apparently this material was not yet inviolable at this point. Some of the later patristic canons, and also Cyprian, as noted, likewise will fade in and out of the corpus for some time. But these sources eventually became firmly established; the omissions in Carthage in the early *Coll14*, for example, will be remedied in a later recension,[157] and virtually all of the 883 patristic sources are well established after the commentators. Only in smaller handbook or extract-type collections are canons ever regularly abbreviated or omitted.[158] In larger collections such instances are not entirely unknown, but they seem very occasional.[159] Certainly such changes never turn into sustained, permanent selection or interpolation of material in the tradition as a whole: omitted corpus material can and will always eventually resurface in any collections with pretensions to completeness. The overall movement of the tradition is thus overwhelmingly towards the complete, faithful transmission of a unitary traditional corpus.

Real diversity among the Byzantine collections is thus always comparatively minor, at least by the standards of manuscript cultures. Between any two given manuscripts or recensions, diversity is mostly restricted to framing material and newer materials that form the outer valences of the core—and to slight variations in order. But these differences never extend to the point that one cannot recognize any two collections as fundamentally different versions of the same text. Substantially different "competing" corpora are present in the tradition only inasmuch as older and newer recensions of the Nicene corpus circulate alongside each other.

The face that the Byzantine tradition presents as a textual reality is thus highly hieratic and conservative, centered upon the concept and reality of one continuous, unified, central core corpus. This corpus structure gradually expands, and its edges may often be blurry, but at any given moment a core of inviolable material is always identifiable, and this traditional material is

[156] See nn. 66, 147. [157] See nn. 125, 147.

[158] See e.g. the synopsis under the name of Aristenos in *PG* 133.63–113 (although note that because of the unusual conflation and division of canons, the numeration is itself not an accurate guide to the degree of omission).

[159] Beneshevich occasionally notes some omissions, e.g. in Rome Vallic. F. 47 in Trullo (*Sbornik* 264). I have also observed some omissions in manuscripts, also in Trullo (e.g. in Oxford Laud. 39 157v; although the omission is noted by the rubricist). The true extent of such omissions—and whether or not they tend to be limited to sources perceived as new or less certain (which is possibly the case in these two examples)—will hopefully become more apparent when Schminck completes his survey. Regular and sustained patterns of omission, however, have not come to light.

never significantly or permanently modified or omitted. The central dynamics of this corpus-centered tradition are thus preservation, persistence, and agglutination. The Byzantine canonical tradition is the story of one text, its expansion, uses, and interpretation.[160]

2. A Greek phenomenon

The Byzantine canonical tradition is overwhelmingly a Greek phenomenon. The Byzantine canons are not only found in the extant manuscripts in—obviously—Greek,[161] but most were originally composed in Greek, and in the east.

This Hellenic orientation of the eastern canonical corpus highlights the relative impermeability of the tradition. In the entire history of Byzantine canon law, even until the end of the empire, only three sources from outside the Greek east were ever able to penetrate the Byzantine corpus.[162] All are from the west: Carthage, the "canon" of Cyprian, and Serdica.[163] Only the first is significant in terms of size, and all will exist for some time as "soft spots" in the manuscript tradition, sometimes omitted, abbreviated, or (most commonly) in slightly subordinate or uncertain positions.[164]

This admission of western conciliar sources highlights one absence in particular: papal decretals. This point requires emphasis only because of the overwhelming tendency of modern textbooks of canon law to speak as if canon law naturally has "two sources," even quite early: conciliar enactments

160 In this, Byzantine canon law mirrors, if in a much more dramatic and exaggerated way, the Byzantine secular tradition's attachment to the Justinianic corpus. Justinian's codification is never clearly replaced or abrogated in the Byzantine east, and always constitutes a symbolic touchstone for the whole tradition; see esp. Fögen 1993, 67–8; Haldon 1990, 258–64; Kunkel 1964, 181; Lokin 1994, 71–2; Pieler 1978, 449–50; Stolte 2008, 691–3; 2010, 79–80. See also Prinzing 1986, and for the older discussion on the later validity of Justinian's law, Wenger 1953, 720–3.

161 Although a few Latin marginal notations to Carthage seem to have made their way into Moscow 432 (*Sin* 86, 92).

162 A few other Latin items may occasionally be found as supplemental items, for example (fairly frequently) the letter of Leo I to Flavius on Eutyches (e.g. Athos Panach. 6–7, Cambridge Ee.4.29, Oxford Laud. 39, Vienna hist. gr. 7). But this text is doctrinal in orientation. The only major exception of a more canonical character is the Donation of Constantine, which will appear in Balsamon (*RP* 1.145–8) and as a regular item in the appendices to the 14th C secular collection, the *Hexabiblos* (Burgmann 2002, 262). Letters of Hadrian IV may be found in Milan Ambr. Q.76.sup., and (pseudo-)Innocent I in Paris supp. gr. 1280.

163 On the *status quaestionis* of the peculiar origin and transmission of the canons of Serdica, see *Sources* 66–71. The recent renewal in Hess 2002 of the Ballerinis' theory of a double edition of the canons, taken down by Latin and Greek scribes, has not received universal acceptance (*contra*: *Delineatio* 122), but seems likely. Whatever the case, the Serdican canons read in Greek as translationese, are in a typically western "parliamentary" form, and are generally treated as western material by the Byzantine tradition itself (e.g. in the scholion to the *Coll14* Ἰστέον *RP* 1.12, cited n. 201, or scholia 217a, 228 in *Sbornik* Prilozh. 28–30).

164 See further Section D.5.

and papal decretals. This double-source theory holds true in the west, but it is an entirely inadequate model for understanding Christian canon law as a global phenomenon. In the perspective of the history of Christian canon law as a whole, papal decretals are unquestionably a local Latin phenomenon. Even in the west this theory comes to complete realization only in the high middle ages, when papal legislation finally becomes a central vehicle of the development of western canonical law.[165] In our period the papal material sits at least formally in the western collections in a markedly appendix-like position, that is, parallel to the patristic canons in the east, after all of the conciliar canons, even very local ones, and often constituting one of the most variable parts of the collections.[166] Throughout our period canonical collections, Greek, Latin, or Syrian, are always primarily apostolic and conciliar in content and form—and then, in the Latin west, papal or, in the Syrian and Greek east, patristic/patriarchal.

The impermeability of the Byzantine tradition highlights another important dynamic in first-millennium canon law, one that is easily missed: the movement of canonical material is overwhelmingly from the Greek east *outward*. In this, Greek canon law is in a sense the "central" tradition of the first millennium. As we have seen, the core corpus of all Christian churches—at least in the empire—emerges from the east, and is largely updated from the east. This position as an active center of canonical production gradually fades but its legacy is clear: all major first-millennium Christian collections, at least within the (old) imperial sphere, and in Persia, contain as their clear core Greek apostolic material and the *sine qua non* Greek Nicene corpus. As a textual phenomenon, Christian canon law of the first millennium, in west or east, is at core a Greek imperial phenomenon.

This "Greekness" of canon law in the first millennium should not, perhaps, come as a surprise. The textual reality of canon law was simply following a well-worn path of Greek to Latin or Syrian cultural transmission, which scripture, much theology, monastic writings, and numerous other types of Christian (and before them, pagan) cultural expression had long followed.[167] It reflects the Greek origins of most early Christian literature and the continued political and cultural pre-eminence and vitality of the eastern empire throughout our period.

[165] A period Gaudemet terms "Le règne des Décrétales" (Gaudemet 1994, 375–407); significantly this material now becomes the "new law" of the church, in the phrase of Bernard of Pavia (d. 1213; Somerville and Brasington 1998, 219). See generally Brundage 1995, 53–6, 160; Fransen 1972, 11–14.

[166] See Fournier and Le Bras 1931, 30 (and n. 2); Fransen 1972, 17; Jasper and Fuhrmann 2001, 22–87; Zechiel-Eckes 1992, 1.7, 18; also Maassen 226–308 *et passim*.

[167] Henri Marrou reminds us that the image of antique culture as constituted by two parallel and equal Latin and Greek spheres is problematic: Latin culture is in many respects a subsidiary phenomenon of a broader Hellenistic reality (Marrou 1948, 242).

Nevertheless, this Greek character of canon law, even in the east, should give us some pause. The one aspect of Greco-Roman civilization that seems to have been the special preserve of Latin was precisely law and administration. Indeed, as Fergus Millar has recently strongly reiterated, the administration of the Greek east, at least at its higher levels and in formal expression, was still resolutely Latin throughout most of the 4th and 5th C—the time of the formation of the core first-wave material.[168] Legal judgments still had to be formally issued in Latin until 397, many Latin notarial formulae remained in use throughout the 5th C, and eastern imperial legislation starts to drift into Greek only slowly throughout the 5th C, not truly supplanting Latin until the 530s.[169] In this context it is a little surprising, then, even in the east, that the chief (internal) texts of order and administration of the 4th and 5th C imperial church were *not* in Latin. This is true even of the texts of the highest order, the ecumenical councils—precisely where, ironically, as Millar points out, it becomes evident how meager the eastern episcopate's knowledge of Latin really was.[170] Church order, therefore, was a distinctly Greek affair—something that may well have distinguished it from the civil order.

3. Size

Another important characteristic of the Byzantine textual tradition is its size. This emerges mostly in comparison with the western tradition. The Byzantine canonical tradition is remarkably compact. It is difficult to know how large early Byzantine canon law manuscripts may have been, and particularly how much appendix-type material, now lost, might have followed the various recensions of the corpus, but if one takes all of the extant pre-10th C canonical material—that is, everything that might have been prominent in a large manuscript of this time—the total is quite modest. It includes three prologues, two systematic indices, approximately 770 canons, a smattering of other material from the *Apostolic Constitutions*, the canonical synopsis, three comparatively short civil law collections (in total approximately 620 separate fragments, varying in length from a line to several pages), the civil law material of the nomocanonical recensions (largely overlapping with the previous collections), maybe some scholia,[171] and some other isolated jurisprudential

[168] Millar 2006, 84–107 *et passim*.

[169] See *Delineatio* 19; Jones 1964, 988–91; Krüger 1894, 312; Matthews 2000, 28–9.

[170] Millar 2006, 85, 97–107.

[171] See n. 14 for editions. Uncertainty about the dating and completeness of the published scholia—many of which, however, seem to be quite regular in the manuscripts, almost a small *glossa ordinaria*—have generally precluded their discussion in this work. See *Sbornik* 145, 161; *Sin* 22–3. Schminck and Getov 2010 are now systematically noting them in their manuscript descriptions.

material.[172] Exact calculations are difficult without electronic databases, but, taken together, this material—the full effective canonical corpus of the eastern empire—comprises approximately 150,000 words. This is roughly three-fifths the size of the *Hispana*—a major western collection from two centuries *earlier* that does not include western civil ecclesiastical law material, scholia, or other appendix or framing material![173] It is closer to a *third* of the size of the mid-9th C collection of (pseudo-)Isidore Mercator, likewise containing mostly pure canonical material.[174] And of course it goes without saying, if we extend the comparison more broadly, that this material is minuscule in comparison with the Talmud, or the secular Justinianic law corpus. The *Digest* alone is approximately 800,000 words.[175]

This distinction is equally evident in a comparison of the number of canons. The eastern core corpus, as defined by the 883 recension, will contain approximately 770 canons. The shortest version of the early 7th C *Hibernensis* had roughly 1,600 texts.[176] The systematic versions of the *Hispana* included approximately the same number.[177] Burchard's popular 11th C *Decretum* weighed in at 1,783 items and Ivo's *Decretum* at 3,760.[178] The standard edition of Gratian (only about half the 16th C Roman Catholic corpus, we may note) is usually counted to contain about 3,800 texts.[179]

Of course the division and nature of the texts and fragments in the western texts may not always be directly comparable with the relatively neat "canons" of the eastern collections, but the general disparity in size remains unmistakable.[180]

Other, more comprehensive comparisons also reveal this difference. At the end of the empire the full *NC14*, complete with secular material, prologues, corpus, and the three 12th C commentators (i.e. most of *RP* 1–4, estimated at about 500,000 words), is a little over three-quarters the length of the Friedberg edition of Gratian's *Decretum* and the decretal collection of Gregory IX,[181] that is, about three-quarters the size of the effective core corpus of the medieval church in the later 13th C. If one were to make a more accurate comparison, and include on the western side the post-Gregorian decretals, the ordinary glosses, and most of the major western commentators up until the 16th C, the difference would likely extend to at least a factor of ten, probably much more.

[172] See Section D.6.
[173] Estimated at 260,000 words from the González 1808 edition.
[174] Estimated at 500,000 words from the Hinschius 1863 edition.
[175] Honoré 1978, 186.
[176] Reynolds 1986, 403.
[177] Gaudemet 1985, 159.
[178] Gaudemet 1993, 83, 95.
[179] Gallagher 2002, 158; Gordley and Thompson 1993, xiii.
[180] Isidore Mercator is counted at 10,000 fragments! Gaudemet 1993, 32.
[181] Conservatively estimated at 650,000 words.

As a physical textual presence, then, the Byzantine canonical tradition is stable, conservative, linguistically homogeneous, *and small.*[182] Indeed, in the later tradition the full Byzantine nomocanonical corpus, plus the two most important commentators and numerous appendices—in a sense, most of the tradition—can be found in single manuscripts.[183]

4. Autonomy

Another simple but fundamental characteristic of the Byzantine canonical tradition is its textual autonomy: canonical texts exist in the extant manuscripts as a distinct and discrete physical textual tradition. That is, the tradition is mostly constituted by manuscripts that can be identified as "canon law manuscripts," that is to say, of which the sole, or at least predominant, content is formal disciplinary regulation. While the exact content of the extant manuscripts varies, particularly in the appendices, the basic structures and types of contents of these manuscripts are sufficiently regular and similar that one can always easily identify a canon law manuscript from, say, a scriptural or theological or philosophical manuscript. Canonical manuscripts thus comprise a distinct class or branch of the Greek manuscript heritage. Rare are manuscripts which profoundly mix proper canonical collections with other types of content—that is, in which a substantial part of the manuscript is given over to one topic and another part to canon law.[184] Manuscripts containing church law are usually purpose-made *as* canon law manuscripts, and almost exclusively as such.

Given references in Chalcedon and Justinian to canons being read from "a book" or "books of the canons" and the relative absence of more mixed or miscellaneous manuscripts—and certainly of traditions of such mixed manuscripts—we may tentatively assume that this textual autonomy obtained quite early.[185] Future work on the earlier Latin and Syrian manuscript traditions may help further illuminate this question.

[182] Despite occasional comments to the contrary, e.g. Nichols 1992, 416.

[183] So e.g. Florence Laur. 5.2 or Istanbul Topkapı 115. See Burgmann 2002, 260.

[184] On the general "purity" of Byzantine juristic manuscripts, see Burgmann 2002, 263. It is particularly difficult to find an example of a manuscript that combines a major non-canonical work—say a scriptural commentary, or philosophical treatise—with a canonical collection. The few exceptions, such as Athos Pant. 234 (12th–13th C), which is half biblical and theological manuscript and half *NC14* (and is not a composite of two separate manuscripts), seem to prove the rule. A later example is Oxford Baroc. 194 (15th C), essentially a grammatical manuscript with Zonaras appended. More common are manuscripts of very varying contents, perhaps devoted to a specific task or theme (e.g. anti-heresy or anti-Latin treatises, or a set of sermons), that happen to have sections citing a few canons (e.g. Vatican gr. 572, 720).

[185] In Chalcedon the canons are frequently read from "a book," *βίβλιον* or *βίβλος*: *ACO* 2.1.3.48, 60, 95, 96, 100 (references from *Historike* 21–2). See also *N* 6.4 for *τὰ βιβλία τῶν ἐκκλησιαστικῶν κανόνων*.

There is only one consistent exception to this autonomy: in the extant manuscripts civil and ecclesiastical legal materials do regularly appear together, and not simply in the form of civil ecclesiastical regulations within the canonical collections themselves. Often a major ecclesiastical canonical collection will also be accompanied by a short handbook of general civil law, for example.[186] It is not clear if this pattern was evident before the 8th C, when the earliest Byzantine civil law handbooks—the usual secular components—were first composed. Nevertheless, it seems that at least by the end of our period the Byzantine legal imagination could easily envision civil and ecclesiastical normative material sharing a common physical space.

Another type of autonomy may also be discerned in the relatively pure normative content of the Byzantine canonical collections themselves. The earlier Apostolic Church Order traditions evince a tendency towards encyclopedism: doctrinal/exegetical, moral, liturgical, and disciplinary texts are synthesized into one literary whole.[187] By contrast, in the imperial church these threads tend to be developed as separable and distinct textual traditions. This independence does not mean that the canons will be written as "pure" legal or disciplinary rules in a modern scientific-juridical sense, cleanly separated from theology or morality; indeed, quite to the contrary, their topics are quite varied, and as we will see later in this study, they frequently make juridically "inappropriate" recourse to doctrinal, moral, and even liturgical, realities. But they are not extensively interwoven with lengthy liturgical, doctrinal, or exegetical texts per se.

5. Structure, order, and patterns of growth

Structure in the Byzantine corpus of canons may be discerned in the ordering of its constituent sources (i.e. Nicaea, then Ancyra, then Neocaesarea, etc.). Witnesses to corpus orders may be found in five principal places: (1) the physical orders of sources in manuscripts; (2) the order of sources cited under thematic rubrics in the systematic indices; (3) the orders mentioned in prologues, canons, and other external sources (e.g. Psellus or John of Damascus' references); (4) the orders of sources in manuscript tables of contents; and (5) the orders of sources in synoptic or later commentary works. It is generally assumed that the source orders of the last four types of texts represent physical corpus configurations that at some point actually existed in manuscripts, and

[186] The most important of these are described in Burgmann *et al.* 1995; e.g. Athos Meg. Lav. B.93 contains the *Coll14* with the *Ecloga*, and Oxford Laud. 39 the *NC14* with the *Prochiron*.

[187] On the genre of the apostolic church orders, see Steimer 1992, 155–335; see also Metzger 1985, 1.33–54. The best example of such liturgical and disciplinary "mixing" is probably the *Didascalia apostolorum* (ed. Funk 1905). In the Byzantine period monastic *typika* to some extent continue this tradition, e.g. the Rule of Theodore Studite, trans. Thomas and Hero 2000, 84–119.

that these were later recorded and "frozen" in these witnesses. Whether or not this was always strictly true, certainly such witnesses suggest a structure which was at least conceivable to a given author. Taken together, then, all can be read as a series of witnesses to different stages of how the corpus developed over time as a text or at least as a textual concept.

Four fundamental patterns may be discerned in these witnesses.

The first is less of a pattern than a characteristic: the corpus *is* structured by sources. This may seem an obvious observation, but it is nonetheless important. The canons do not exist in the tradition as disembodied norms or abstracted rules. Instead, rules are consistently classed and designated according to their original source: canon 2 *of Nicaea*; canon 4 *of Gregory of Nyssa*. The canons are in effect always issuing from the mouths of their original legislators. The corpus as a whole thus always emerges as very much a self-conscious accumulation and compilation of traditional sources of canonical legislation. In this sense, it is broadly florilegic in character: it is a collection of traditional authorities on matters of church discipline.[188] This characteristic sets the Byzantine corpus apart from modern codes in which rules, deriving their authority from the issuer of the code, exist as more or less anonymous and rootless norms, and are easily subject to various levels of manipulation, reorganization, and rationalization—and are thus easily modified, added, or deleted. The Byzantine instinct is instead to keep the corpus as a collection of traditional sources which are themselves maintained more or less in their original form.[189] The authority of the sources is apparently linked to their issuance from their original, traditional source.

It is interesting to note that this general allergy to abstracting and presenting rules as detached from their traditional sources is also shared by the civil-legal tradition. The constitutions in the *CTh* and the *CJ*, even if excerpted and modified in many ways from their original (unlike the canonical material), all

[188] Cf. Gallagher 2002, 39–40, who rightly draws a (narrower) parallel between the use of florilegia in conciliar proceedings and the emergence of patristic canonical sources in the canonical collections. However, the entire canonical corpus may be considered florilegic in a broader sense. This tendency is enforced by the practice in some manuscripts of including short ὑποθέσεις before the listing of each source's canons (most notably Beneshevich's Group A recension of the *Coll50*, *Sin* 26–69). See Appendix A.

[189] The one apparent exception is the pre-6th C incarnations of the corpus as continuously numbered wholes. Here the rules do seem to be presented as much more anonymous and abstracted, referable to as "canon 166" or "canon 87," as in the *acta* of Chalcedon. However, even in these collections, the canons were still arranged by legislative source: Nicaea, Ancyra, Neocaesarea, etc. The canons were not rearranged or mixed in any way. More importantly, in the two principal extant witnesses to this enumeration, Dionysius II and the Syrian London BL syr. 14,528, the conciliar sources are still separated by headings indicating their original sources, and even conciliar introductions. Further, in BL 14,528 *both* continuous and source numbering systems are present (eds. *PL* 67.139–228 and Schulthess 1908; see *Delineatio* 26; Lietzmann 1921, 492; Mardirossian 2010, 59–60; Schwartz 1933, 3). Therefore the continuous enumeration runs through the different councils, but the individual identity of the councils is never lost.

retain attributions to their original legislators.[190] More surprisingly, even the fragments of the *Digest*, which are explicitly given their authority by Justinian as if issuing from his own mouth (*a nostro divino fuerant ore profusa*),[191] are still scrupulously sourced to their original (mostly pagan!) authors—and so even in the later *Basilica*.[192] The only real exception in the *CTh*/*CJC* literature is the *Institutes*: but it is merely a pedagogical handbook *to* the corpus. Real legislation always remains explicitly connected to traditional sources. Legal work in late antiquity is everywhere broadly florilegic/compilative—that is, traditional.[193]

The second pattern of structuring, already noted, is also the basic mechanism of growth in the tradition: accumulation. The structuring of the corpus over time reveals that one always only adds new material on top of older material. New material thus almost never physically replaces or ejects older material: older material, once well established in the corpus, is effectively eternal.[194] Older rules may fall out of use, and be clearly marked and recognized as such in the commentaries or scholia, but traditional sources, and even parts of sources, never actually exit the textual fabric of the tradition itself. We

[190] These could even be invented or reconstructed when the originals were no longer available. On the many complex problems surrounding the inscriptions and subscriptions of the *CTh* constitutions, see Matthews 2000; Harries and Wood 1993; Rougé *et al.* 2005. I am grateful to Caroline Humfress for bringing this to my attention.

[191] *Deo auctore* 6.

[192] In the *Digest* this is done quite explicitly on account of "reverence for antiquity" (*Tanta* 10).

[193] The preservative and compilative nature of late antique law is a commonplace of late antique source histories. See e.g. Pieler 1997a, 566–7, 580 (where he calls the *Digest* a "Florilegium of ius"), 591; see also the related narrative of (eastern) late antiquity's conservative and classicizing legal *Geist*, Kunkel 1964, 153–4; Schulz 1953, 278–85; Wieacker 1988, 2.263–6. These tendencies should be understood within the context of the broader late antique and Byzantine cultural penchant—almost cognitive tendency—for compilation and preservation. See, for a variety of contexts and epochs, Aerts 1997a, 648–9; Jenkins 1963, 47–50; Lemerle 1971; Louth 2002; Maas 2005a, 18–20; Odorico 1990, 1–7 (with a critical review of older literature on Byzantine "encyclopedism").

[194] The *idea* of more radically "cleaning" the corpus is not perhaps altogether absent. At least in Byzantine secular law the notion of a "cleaning," or "purifying," (ἀνακάθαρσις) of the law, including processes of clarification, paraphrasing, and even pruning of obsolete material, does emerge, although even here it perhaps implies mostly a movement of repristinization and renewal of older forms, not radical change (see *Delineatio* 81–7; Fögen 1987, 152–3; Pieler 1989; Stolte 2010). It is possible that a similar process was at times envisaged for the canons. The best candidate is the Edict of Alexios I, a.1107 (text and commentary Gautier 1973; see Magdalino 1996 and now also Schminck 1998, 367, who dates it to 1092). This text seems to suggest some type of legislative review of the nomocanon (Gautier 1973, 197), although it is far from clear that it is envisioning anything more than renewing canons that have fallen into disuse or perhaps fallen out of the nomocanon (Gautier 1973, 171; Schminck 1998, 368, esp. nn. 57, 58; also Macrides 1991, 590). If the intent truly was to purge the older canonical material, it clearly failed. As it turned out, the real Byzantine response to dealing with problems in the corpus was to add commentaries—i.e. to add a new interpretative layer—and not to restructure the tradition itself (a point inspired by Macrides 1991, 590, who suggests that the Edict of Alexios may have stimulated the creation of the commentaries).

may term this phenomenon "corpus persistence." A similar, if weaker, dynamic has also been occasionally observed in Byzantine secular legal literature.[195]

Third, the ordering of the corpus evinces an ongoing dialectic between hierarchical and chronological ordering. In the extant witnesses the default ordering strategy is clearly chronological, just as it is in the disposition of laws under titles in the imperial codices, or, for the most part, in the Florentine index of the *Digest* sources.[196] This default is nevertheless regularly violated, and each violation may be read as conveying some ideological message about the nature of the sources.[197] This hierarchization represents one of the very few ways in which the Byzantine corpus suffers—although quite superficially—a kind of systematic rationalization.

The first and prototypical violation, made at the tradition's onset, is the prefacing of the Antiochian corpus with the Nicene canons, despite the fact that Ancyra and Neocaesarea were known to be older. This is a very conscious, and explicitly marked, move, as already noted, and clearly indicated the appropriation of the collection by the Nicene party. No Greek manuscript exists that does not witness to this modification.[198]

The next consistent violation will be the relegation of Serdica (341) and Carthage (419) to places after Chalcedon (451) in the expanded Nicene corpus. This will become their standard position in the extant recensions of the *Coll14*, and finds resonance in older western and Syrian collections.[199] The *Coll50*, however, unusually placed Serdica in its chronological position, following Neocaesarea, and thus "within" the core Nicene collection.[200] In the

[195] See particularly the discussions of the lack of functioning principles of abrogation; references in Introduction, nn. 29, 30. Lokin 1994, 82 quite aptly compares this tendency to legal accumulation, with its lack of a functioning derogation model, to the accumulation of church dogmas.

[196] Published in *Digest* xxx–xxxii.

[197] As probably true for the privileging of Julian and Papinian on the Florentine list: the former is privileged as providing the model *digesta*, the latter as simply a particularly respected jurist. Schulz 1953, 145, 319.

[198] The only exception is perhaps Blastares' survey of the sources in his *Alphabetical Syntagma* (*a.* 1335; *RP* 6.6–2), but this is a historical treatment, akin to synodical histories, not a listing of the corpus per se. See n. 28 for exceptions in the oriental and Latin collections.

[199] Thus they appear in more marginal locations in the Syrian *synodika* (see Selb 1981, 104–10; 1989, 92–102, 140–5), and both are postpositioned after Chalcedon in Dionysius II, while in the non-extant Dionysius III both were apparently omitted explicitly because of doubts about their universal acceptance ("quos non admisit universitas"; Preface III, trans. Somerville and Brasington 1998, 49).

[200] Doujat, who thinks this recension can be attributed to Theodoret of Cyrrhus, ventures the curious suggestion that Serdica was added at this point—and we might assume placed in this unusually prominent position—because of Theodoret's need for the Serdican appeal canons in his conflict with Dioscorus at the council of Ephesus in 449 (Doujat 1687, 293–6). Like many of Doujat's suggestions this is probably fantastic, but it does highlight the problem of Serdica's curious prominence in the *Coll50*. If this position was the normal position of the "Ten Councils,"

Coll14 tradition, the subordinate placement of these councils is explicitly glossed as a relegation or marginalization because of their local character.[201]

The third violation is the placement of all patristic material after the conciliar material.[202] This was almost certainly intended to mark the subordination of the former to the latter, as made explicit in the first *Coll14* prologue.[203] It seems that at no point in the Byzantine tradition was the canonical material considered so homogeneous and generic that a true chronological corpus could emerge in which the patristic material could be mixed with the councils in one chronological series (for example, Ancyra, Neocaesarea, Peter, Nicaea, Athanasius, Gangra, Antioch, Basil, Laodicea, etc.). The patristic material itself tended to be arranged chronologically, as in Trullo 2, but other orders, sometimes evading explanation, are not unknown.[204]

The fourth major violation of chronological order involved the placing of all second-wave ecumenical conciliar material in a position immediately following Nicaea—that is, before the older Antiochian corpus sources (see the schema in Section D.1). This may be understood as an aspect of the general tendency to assimilate ecumenical material to Nicaea, and as an extension of the original Nicene prefacing. Its effect, however, was to create a new hierarchical distinction between "general" and "local" councils. In the Greek tradition, this ordering is first certainly witnessed to in II Nicaea 1 (787) and the recension Beneshevich associates with this council (the "Tarasian" or "systematic").[205] It becomes a regular order in the manuscripts only with Zonaras and Balsamon, although curiously even in these manuscripts it never entirely ousts the older order of the *Coll14* source listings inasmuch as the latter is still usually preserved in the traditional table of contents heading the *Coll14* portion of these very manuscripts, as well as in the references in the systematic indices. As a result, in a manner very characteristic of the Byzantine canonical tradition, the two orders (or even more) tend to coexist together in the same manuscripts—"piled" on top of each other—with the older order in

then it may also have been assumed by the original author of the *Coll14* prologue τὰ μὲν σώματα; see Ch. 2.B.4.

201 "The councils in Serdica and Carthage were chronologically prior to some of the other synods, but are placed after them because they set forth many ordinances relating to various local, that is, western places." Text from the scholion "ἰστέον" to the table of contents of the *Coll14* (*Pitra* 2.451).

202 Tarasius, however, generally follows II Nicaea in the manuscripts.

203 *Pitra* 2.446.

204 Joannou offers a brief survey, *Fonti* 2.xix–xx. For an example of an order by rank of church, see Paris Cois. 364 (described *Sin* 160–1); for an order in which Basil is favored, but otherwise the rationale for the order is difficult to discern, see Rome Vallic. F. 47 (described *Sbornik* 266–7).

205 The relevant section of II Nicaea 1 reads "we embrace the divine canons . . . of the all-praised apostles, and of the six holy ecumenical synods, and of the councils convened locally for setting forth such decrees, and of our holy fathers." The four-council order of the synopsis tradition associated with Symeon the Logothete may, however, represent an earlier version of this ordering strategy. See Section C.

the prologue sections and systematic references, and the newer one in the corpus itself.[206]

To return to the major structural patterns of the corpus, the most complex and important (the fourth) is a sustained pattern of differentiation between core material and appendix material. This dialectic, implicit in my discussion until now, consists of a series of techniques by which at any given moment one set of material in a collection or manuscript is marked as particularly standard, central, and inviolable in contrast to another set of material that is marked as newer, more peripheral, variable, and even optional—that is, more appendix-like. It is never a pattern that is articulated explicitly, nor does it lend itself to precise definition or suggest clear doctrinal consequences, but it nevertheless constitutes one of the most consistent and perceptible dynamics of the textual tradition as a whole. Its effect is to shape the material into a graded and diffuse spectrum of implied worth and value, with a small inner core distinguished from a series of successively larger core structures—rather as a series of multiple concentric rings, each ring gradually fading into the next. Although the exact boundaries between different levels of sources can be blurry, one can at any given moment identify at least some material that is clearly of the core and some that is not. It subsumes and presumes the dynamics of accumulation and hierarchization.

The markers of the core material are numerous, and change over time, but all function to distinguish certain sets of materials from others, older core material from newer additions. They often overlap and contradict each other, which produces the impression of a highly nuanced but messy spectrum of sources: the same sources may be marked as core in one way, and not in others. The following is a list of the main markers:

- numbering schemes
- presence and position of sources in prologues
- presence and position of sources in manuscript tables of contents
- presence and position of sources in systematic references
- presence and position of sources in definition canons (i.e. Trullo 2 and II Nicaea 1)
- descriptions in other literature
- presence and position of sources in the manuscripts themselves

The very earliest traces of this phenomenon—and a very good example—may be detected in the use of continuous numbering schemes in the original Nicene (and probably Antiochian) corpus, highlighted above. Here an earlier "core" of material may be understood as demarcated by continuous numbering.

[206] On this, see Stolte 1998a, 187.

Newer material appears with individual numbering, quite obviously marked as tacked-on or added, that is, appendix-like. Gradually, as noted, this material too is subsumed by the continuous numbering, in effect assimilated into the core.

In the 6th C the continuous-numbering system falls out of use in the Greek world, but a number of other markers function in a similar way. Thus the prologue of the *Coll50* refers clearly, and quite casually, to what is evidently already an established core structure—so much so in fact, that it even has a name: the "Ten Synods."[207] The sources included in this "Ten Synods" are enumerated in the *Coll50*'s "order of synods" (*τάξις τῶν συνόδων*). To this core is prefaced the Apostolic Canons—apparently already a standard addition—and postfixed the Basilian canons, which are not, however, enumerated with the councils. The result is a three-stage corpus structuring: first and foremost the Apostles, outside of the synodal list, which here probably implies precedence; then the neatly sealed Ten Synods; then, outside and after the synodal list, Basil—here probably implying subordination.

The first prologue of the *Coll14* also refer to the Ten Synods as a standard, accepted core of canons, and then goes on to give a relatively long explanation for three further additions, including (very briefly) the Apostles (apparently still controversial?), the "council of Carthage," and a large number of other fathers.[208] Both in the prologue itself, with its differentiation of the material (Ten Synods taken for granted; Apostles virtually for granted; Carthage and fathers in need of explanation), and in the traditional listing, the *πίναξ*, where Carthage, Serdica, and the fathers are placed after the older Apostles + Ten Synod core, a clear sense of core and "new core" material is again evident.

This pattern carries through in the patterns of references under the thematic titles of the *Coll14*. As already noted,[209] the original *Coll14* seems to have carefully cited every canon of the older core Apostotlic + Ten Synods + sixty-eight canons of Basil—i.e. the *Coll50* core. The only "selection" is in the newest stratum of material just attached to the core by the *Coll14* author, that is, in Carthage and the first letter of Basil. This material is thus subtly "downgraded" by this difference of treatment. Later, this material will be added back into the *Coll14* references—it has achieved higher "core" status.

Other patterns of core-appendix marking may then be found in the slow processes of corpus expansion evident in the later recensions of the *Coll14* (and *Coll50*). (Indeed, the recensions have been recoverable chiefly because the manuscripts contain different fossilized orderings of the corpus sources such that the newest sources are obviously outside an older "core," i.e. recensional form.) Only gradually are the new sources admitted into the older cores, slowly moving up through the hierarchy of sources.

[207] On this prologue, see Ch. 2 B.3.
[208] On this prologue, see Ch. 2 B.4.
[209] See Section D.1.

The fortunes of Trullo in the manuscripts provide the best illustration. In the very earliest witnesses, Trullo appears physically virtually outside of the corpus, even after the patristic material.[210] This pattern is mirrored in the *Coll14* source references under the thematic rubrics, where Trullo will appear distinctly "tacked on," following even patristic material.[211] Later, however, it may be found to have leapt in front of the patristic material, but still after all the earlier conciliar material, even the relegated Serdica and Carthage (and Constantinople 394).[212] This position will become its classical *Coll14* position; it has a difficult time penetrating beyond this earlier core structure. Nevertheless, in a few manuscripts attempts are made to do precisely this. In Venice Nan. 226, for example, Trullo is now pushed before Carthage (Serdica remains in the *Coll50* place). Similarly, in Oxford Baroc. 26 Trullo is placed after Serdica, but before Carthage, and in Venice Bess. 171 Trullo is placed immediately after Chalcedon (extremely unusually, Serdica and Carthage are here simply omitted).[213] These attempts to establish a higher place for Trullo may be viewed as failed experiments—they did not catch on. Nevertheless they demonstrate attempts to "push" Trullo more clearly into the core. Only with the hierarchical rearrangement of the corpus, in Beneshevich's Tarasian recension, will Trullo, as one of the general councils, finally physically appear immediately after Chalcedon—with all other councils following it. Trullo has "made it" into the core of the core.[214]

Similar "journeys to the core" may be suspected for II Nicaea and the Photian councils, although the evidence is a little less complete. For the former, in Oxford Laud. 39, which seems to contain one of the oldest recensions (and which may be a 10th C manuscript), one finds II Nicaea separated from Trullo (which it usually accompanies) by Cyprian.[215] In contrast, in another recension, Beneshevich's *Partes Distributa*, Cyprian has been gently pushed after II Nicaea.[216] Protodeutera and Hagia Sophia also take some time to be accepted into the collections—and the latter never seems fully integrated. Both are mentioned in the 883 prologue to the *Coll14*, but are missing, for example, in Oxford Baroc. 26 and Rawl. G.1.58 (both 11th C). In Vatican 2198 both are present but following Cyprian (after II Nicaea). Hagia Sophia, in particular, is often absent, for example in Vienna hist gr. 56 (*a.* 1000), or Oxford Baroc. 196 (11th C). In Athos Iver. 302 (14th C) Hagia Sophia is found, but curiously after Gennadius, which is after Protodeutera. Hagia Sophia in fact never seems to make it into the table of contents of even the

[210] Beneshevich's First Redaction (*Sbornik* 230–42); so similarly the Synopsis attributed to Symeon the Logothete, above, and also the corpus references in Beneshevich's *Coll14* index to the Tarasian recension (*Kormchaya*).

[211] e.g. *Coll14* 1.24, 4.14, 9.27,39 13.3, to note only a few (from *Kormchaya*).

[212] Beneshevich's Laudanian and Coislin redactions (*Sbornik* 177–88, 188–91).

[213] *Sbornik* 313–21.

[214] *Sbornik* 288–307.

[215] *Sbornik* 177–88.

[216] *Sbornik* 192–9.

Photian redaction, and only sometime later, certainly by the 11th C, do references to it enter the *Coll14* titles.[217] In the 12th C Aristenos still does not offer commentary on either council. These councils are thus not as regularly "marked" as core material. This only happens, it seems, with the commentators.

This whole phenomenon of the implicit creation of "cores" is very curious. One might expect that a chance 8th C manuscript might survive showing, for example, Trullo tacked on after the corpus for purely practical reasons—the newest legislation was simply added to existing manuscripts. But the fact that these manuscripts are much more recent and contain material following Trullo (II Nicaea, Protodeutera, etc.) indicates that Trullo is being left in a subordinate position more intentionally. It would have been exceptionally easy to have moved Trullo to a more prominent position in the corpus, perhaps after Chalcedon, or certainly before the fathers, in every subsequent manuscript recopying since the late 7th C. Instead, however, a much more hesitant, conservative, and gradual process of digestion and consensus building is evident in which the new material seems to pass through a succession of strata before it is certainly admitted to the older core.

Similar conservatism may be remarked in the persistence of the original *Coll50* core. As already noted, a number of external references suggest that this core remained a highly impermeable "core of the core" in the tradition for some time, long after the introduction of the *Coll14*. It seems that for John of Damascus and Michael Psellus, and even Aristenos, all of whom we may suspect had easy access to later materials (certainly Psellus and Aristenos), the older *Coll50* core somehow retained special standing. This sentiment is even implicit in the physical structure of the *Coll50* manuscript tradition in which later councils are usually only affixed after the systematic rearrangement of the corpus itself, thus visually marking a distinct difference between the original material—placed under the titles—and the later additions.[218] Also, as we just saw, the *Coll14* itself witnesses to the *Coll50* core as an established authority, adopting it almost wholesale, especially the Ten Synods, and carefully not selecting amongst its canons in its topical references. The *Coll50*'s ordering of the pre-6th C material, save only the location of Serdica, will also always be preserved in the *πίναξ* of the *Coll14*, even when the canons themselves will be rearranged in the manuscripts into the hierarchical general-then-local council order.

Both of the two principal corpus "definition" canons of the Byzantine tradition (Trullo 2 and II Nicaea 1) also obliquely evince a sense of the existence of a core corpus. Both list the traditional corpus, *but do not include*

[217] *Sbornik* 96–100. *Pitra* 2.450 does note one later manuscript (Vatican Barb. 568) that includes Hagia Sophia in the *Coll14* table of contents.

[218] See Section C and n. 104.

their own regulations in the listing. They thus make an implicit distinction between (1) the core, traditional corpus, and (2) their new canons. The latter are presented as only immediately following from and faithful to the former—which precisely mirror their physical position in the earliest recensions: right up against the older core, but outside of it.

A definitive core, as noted, will ultimately emerge as the corpus of the 883 recension of the *Coll14*. This status will be marked mostly by the hesitation of later recensions to add any more items to the *Coll14's* πίναξ or thematic references. The decision of the commentators to comment almost exclusively on this core undoubtedly functioned as the decisive factor in its demarcation. However, the boundaries between a given core and its "appendix material" are always fluid and open to some negotiation, and this will be true of the 883 corpus as well. (Indeed, the exact delineation of the 883 core is mostly a modern preoccupation.)[219] Thus the Michael/Theodore recensions recognize the 883 recension as definitive, but they also consider that the material of the Apostolic Epitome should be part of it.[220] As already noted, even the two major commentators will comment on slightly different corpora (and Aristenos' is quite different). Physically, in the manuscripts, some material that is generally "in," such as Cyprian, Gregory Naz., and Amphilochius, in fact tends to flit in and out of the manuscripts and indices, while material that is generally "out" can sometimes appear to enter the core. For example, the ἀποκρίσεις of Patriarch Nicholas, or the penitential canons of John the Faster or Nikephoros the Confessor, which become fairly regular appendix items in the later tradition, and often can be found following directly on the more traditional patristic material, can very occasionally be added under some systematic rubrics.[221] Similarly, Balsamon seems to have commented on the ἀποκρίσεις of Patriarch Nicholas.[222] A certain amount of material thus emerges as transitional material—it is either in the outer valence of the core, or the innermost stratum of the appendix material. It is "in" by the measure of some markers, or "out" by the measure of others.

Similar core–boundary "blurriness" may be detected earlier in various instances of "softness" in the corpus: Serdica and Carthage, the non-Basilian fathers, or even, at first, Trullo and the rest of the second-wave material.

This blurriness in defining the corpus is also reflected in the physical layout of the manuscripts. In my sampling of manuscripts, core material, by any definition, is not clearly and consistently distinguished from non-core

[219] e.g. *Historike* 91–100.

[220] In the longer prologue, text in Schminck 1998, 36; on the prologues of these recensions, see Appendix A.

[221] For an example of the latter, see *Sbornik* 252. Nikodemos Kallivourtsis, by including them in the *Pedalion* (Kallivourtsis 1800), an influential 19th C Orthodox edition of the canons, was thus following an old tendency in the manuscripts.

[222] *RP* 4.417–26 (but see p. 417 n.1).

material. For example, there is no exceptionally dramatic bar design or page break, or any other change of layout or style between the two. Only in manuscripts containing one or more of the commentators—where the cessation of commentary may be read as an obvious demarcation of the core—is the shift from core to appendix visually obvious. The core is instead marked by the prologues and their corpus listings, the systematic references, and sometimes a genre switch in the manuscripts (for example, from the canons to the ecclesiastical civil law appendices, and then back to purely ecclesiastical material, thus marked as somehow separate from the first set of ecclesiastical regulations).

6. Is something missing? Official definitions, jurisprudence, professionalization

Omissions or gaps in the textual shape and processes of shaping of the Byzantine canonical material may be as significant for our understanding of Byzantine legal culture as its positive characteristics. Three omissions stand out as particularly glaring: acts of official definition of sources, jurisprudential literature, and signs of professionalization.

The phenomenon of core formation may be understood as a very diffuse form of rule recognition.[223] That is, it is a mechanism which functions to define "valid" norms. This very indirect form of rule recognition by turns reflects, explains, and probably enforces the strikingly tenuous and desultory role of one very essential and normal element of most modern positivist theories of law: the clear definition of the valid sources of law by an "official" authority.[224]

Only once in the canonical tradition does something approaching a detailed official definition emerge: Trullo 2.[225] Yet it can only awkwardly and indirectly

[223] My immediate source for this concept is Hart 1961.

[224] This lack of a clear act of official definition of the 883 corpus seems to have so surprised modern Orthodox canonists that they felt compelled to find one where none existed. Thus N. Milaš considered that a very normal and unremarkable assertion of canonical fidelity in the concluding lines of the Tomos of Union 920 (*RP* 5.4–10; the passage at 10) effected an official recognition of the 883 corpus (Milaš 1902, 254). The text (*τοῖς ἐν καταφρονήσει τιθεμένοις τοὺς ἱεροὺς καὶ θείους κανόνας τῶν μακαρίων Πατέρων ἡμῶν . . . ἀνάθεμα*) in fact suggests no such official confirmation. Unfortunately, Milaš's 920 date was adopted by C. de Clercq in his influential *DDC* article on Byzantine canon law (de Clercq 1937), as well as by J. Gaudemet in his *RE* article (Gaudemet 1965), with the result that it has been asserted regularly ever since (e.g. *Fonti* 1.xvii; Morolli 2000, 314; Nichols 1992, 417; Rhodopoulos 2005, 84; innumerable encyclopedia articles). S. Troitsky seems to have first caught the error in the 1950s. See Žužek 1964, 25 n. 34, and now *Historike* 91–2.

[225] The definition in Chalcedon 1 is probably specific in intention, but not in form; II Nicaea 1 does little more than list the major types of legislation. Only one other more specific definition exists in the tradition, *N* 131.1, which confirms the dogmatic definitions and canons of the first

be cast as an exercise of true official definition, and certainly not as an act of official definition of law in its strongest (modern) positivist sense, that is, as implying an exercise of "sovereign" authority over the law.[226]

First, although rarely noted, this canon is primarily addressed to a very specific problem—the status of the *Apostolic Constitutions* in the corpus—and not to corpus definition per se. The lengthy corpus delineation itself reads as almost an afterthought, and should probably be understood as a consequence of the broader problem raised by the Apostolic Constitutions: the intrusion into the corpus of pseudepigraphal and false material. It is simply a reassertion of genuine sources in light of specific problems of falsification. The canon's conclusion, focused precisely on the issue of falsification, confirms the canon's primary orientation to this problem.[227] Interestingly, the synopsist also reads the canon as primarily about falsification in the apostolic material—the corpus listing is not even mentioned.[228] The canon is therefore not so much creatively or actively defining the law as a whole as clarifying a specific problem in the tradition, and in this process reaffirming the mainstream tradition (which already has authority).

Further, and as often noted, its corpus delineation is little other than an unremarkable confirmation of a corpus that had been in existence for at least a century: the canon more or less reads down the table of contents of the *Coll14* as it stood in the late 7th C.[229] The only source it may be adding is Cyprian, since it goes out of its way to justify and explain its presence; but even this canon seems to have been in the tradition earlier.[230] Most likely it is simply

four councils. It is updated in the 9th C in *Basilica* 5.3.2 to include the seven ecumenical councils. Even this imperial definition, however, is (1) not especially comprehensive; (2) it reads as only secondarily directed towards confirming the canons; and (3) it is mostly confirmatory in character—it sanctions and approves realities already established instead of formally promulgating rules not already in force. There is also little evidence in the texts that it played a particularly important role in defining the shape of the corpus per se. In particular, it is surprising how rare a four-council core structure, implied in *N* 131.1, is in the eastern tradition (see Section C and n. 102).

[226] Some modern Orthodox canonists, influenced by modern civil law doctrine, and in the context of modern attempts to codify Orthodox canon law, have been inclined to read Trullo in precisely this manner (e.g. Archontonis 1970, 20–1; Christopoulos 1972, 255–66; Gavardinas 1998, 136–8). This reading may be traced to the first Greek-language Orthodox canonical manual, *Δοκίμιον ἐκκλησιαστικοῦ δικαίου* of Apostolos Christodoulos (Constantinople, 1896; cited at length in Christopoulos 1972, 255–66), and is based upon a comparison of the concluding dispositive statements of Trullo 1 and Trullo 2. For discussion of this position, see Wagschal 2010a, 70, 279–80.

[227] "And no one is to falsify the preceding canons, nor set them at naught, nor receive any others against those set forth which have been composed spuriously by some who have attempted to traffic in the truth." (Trans. Nedungatt and Featherstone 1995, 68–9, modified.)

[228] *RP* 2.311–12. The synopsis reads in full: "Let that which has been fraudulently interpolated into the decrees of the Apostles through Clement be expelled."

[229] *Delineatio* 69–70; *Historike* 73–4; Ohme 2006, 32–3.

[230] See Section C.

confirming the place of Cyprian and generally solidifying the canon of patristic sources. Its content and tone are thus almost entirely traditional and deferential, "sealing" what has gone before.[231] Although it may be attempting to bolster the authority of the *Coll14* additions vis-à-vis the older *Coll50* core, or simply to clarify the general tradition, it is certainly not working to modify or dramatically shape this tradition, and it is not granting authority to something that had none before. In this respect it is interesting that the canon does not enumerate the canons for each source (aside from the Apostolic Canons, the canons at immediate issue)—they are presumably too well known.[232] It is thus more recognizing a law already well known than actively defining it. At most it is contributing to a broader process of definition and delineation, perhaps "tidying" around the edges, but mostly heightening and sharpening a previous and growing consensus.

The canon does still have a legislative function, but a comparatively rhetorical one. Its effect is to garner support for *Trullo's* own legislation: it is above all a proclamation of Trullo's fidelity to the canons, and thus the legitimacy of its own canons—and not of the canons' dependence upon its sovereign legislative "approval." In effect, Trullo is seeking the canons' approval for its legislation, not the other way around. It is above all a statement of allegiance to the established tradition.[233]

Finally, if Trullo 2 was intended as a definitive and categorical official definition of the law in something of the sense that we would expect today, it was certainly not very effective. It will never, for example, mark a particularly definitive corpus boundary (that is, there are few witnesses which embody the Trullan list as a definitive and obvious core[234]), and indeed the manuscripts and recensions often ignore its exact list and order of patristic

[231] The term "seal," *ἐπισφραγίζω* (*ἐπισφραγίζομεν δὲ καὶ τοὺς λοιποὺς πάντας ἱεροὺς κανόνας* . . .), may in part be responsible for the more positivist readings of this canon (see n. 226). This term can denote "ratify" in the positivist sense of putting into active force—but it can also mean seal in the sense of "confirm" or "recognize." (In the corpus, something approaching the former may be found in the *Προσφωνητικός* to Constantinople I, in *Kormchaya* 95; for an example of the latter, see Carthage 55; more generally Liddell–Scott–Jones 1996, 663 and Lampe 1961, 536–7). In the context of the previous canon, however, to which canon 2 is clearly written as an addition (*ἔδοξεν δὲ καὶ τοῦτο τῇ ἁγίᾳ ταύτῃ συνόδῳ* . . .), the latter meaning is much more natural: just as Trullo 1 proclaims its allegiance to the traditional doctrinal definitions of the church, so now the council proclaims its allegiance to the church's canonical traditions—and nothing more. Trullo 2 is no more truly putting into force or "defining" the canons than canon 1 is putting into force or defining the older doctrinal decisions. Most tellingly, Trullo 1 even uses the term *ἐπισφραγίζω*, among many others, obviously to "confirm" the older doctrines, and not to formally promulgulate them (Nedungatt and Featherstone 1995, 58.17). There is no reason to assume a different meaning in Trullo 2.

[232] Biener 1856, 196 makes this same observation.

[233] See Ch. 2 C.4.

[234] i.e. that contain the following corpus: Apostles, Nicene Corpus to Chalcedon, Constantinople 394, Serdica, Carthage, the Trullan patristic list, and *then* Trullo and later councils. Patmos 172 is very close.

fathers, its addition of Cyprian, and its prohibition of any other apostolic material aside from the Apostolic Canons. Certainly, when the final shape of the core corpus does emerge, as we have seen, it is defined not by Trullo 2 (or II Nicaea 1) but by a later anonymous recension of the *Coll14*. Finally, as we have seen, prominent later listings of the "the canons" recall the *Coll50* corpus, and not the *Coll14* at all, in any form, including that of Trullo 2! In short, no one seems to have been reading this canon as *the* official statement of the tradition.[235]

Some scholars have recently seen this curious lack of "official" effect as evidence for Trullo's late or tenuous reception into Byzantine canon law, and have suggested that Trullo was not truly in force until as late as the 12th C.[236] These readings, however, impose an excessively—and anachronistically—categorical and bivalent sense of legal validity and enactment, that is, the idea that a source is either absolutely in force or absolutely not, and that this status is meant to have immediate, consistent, and system-wide consequences, and that a particular person or organ can determine this. These interpretations thus tend to assume that, lacking complete adherence to its regulations in the broader tradition, Trullo must have suffered from a lack of recognition.

It is much preferable, however, to recognize that categorical, authoritative "official" statements of the law were simply not part of the Byzantine canonical-legal imagination. Indeed, they do not seem to be clearly a part of anyone's canonical-legal imagination before the high middle ages, and then mostly in the west.[237] "Validity" in the Byzantine world appears much more as a graded and fuzzy calculus of traditional weighting.[238] In this case, Trullo's effect and fortunes are perfectly normal, and even to be expected. New material, whatever its source, always starts outside the core of fully recognized traditional

[235] This author knows of only one reference where Trullo 2 is in some ways cited as a definitive list—in a 13th C letter of the Chartophylax Nikephorus (*RP* 5.401)—but even here it seems this is done mainly because it serves as a handy list of the local councils and fathers, not as an official, definitive list per se. Reference from Biener 1856, 196.

[236] *Sources* 86; *Fonti* 2.xv–xx; Ohme 1990, 332–44; 2006, 34. The background of this assertion is later medieval and post-medieval confessional concern about the "ecumenicity" of Trullo.

[237] "Prior to the thirteenth century, the very idea of a canonical compilation drawing its authority from a formal act of sovereign approval seems not even to have entered the mind of popes and canonists alike" (Kuttner 1947, 387). The seeds of this new idea are perhaps to be found in the Gregorian concern for the papal approval of genuine church legislation, as Kuttner goes on to discuss. The first moment when a collection appears explicitly and certainly to have received some kind of "official" approval is Innocent III's confirmation of the *compilatio tertia* of Peter Collivacina in 1209/10; the first collection composed by official order was Honorius III's *compilatio quinta* (1226). See Pennington 2008, 309–12. Gratian is not formally promulgated until the 16th C.

[238] See esp. Burgmann 2002, 252 n. 13, where it is noted that different levels of "officialness" could be encountered in the Byzantine secular collections. The traditional distinction between "official" and "private" collections in pre-modern law is problematic. See the comments in Firey 2008 on this problem in relation to the promulgation of the Dionysiana; also Mardirossian 2010, 62–3; Pieler 1978, 432–3, 452, 457.

material, and needs to slowly work its way in. In this sense it is true that Trullo is not fully "accepted" until the 12th C—that is, it is not absolutely clearly seen as itself expressive of the tradition until this point. But this does not mean that Trullo was not accepted per se as a real imperial ecumenical council, or that it had no canonical authority, any more than would be true for the early papal decretals in the west, on account of their variability in the manuscripts. The evidence for Trullo's general acceptance is quite the opposite.[239] By virtue of its newness, it is simply, and quite normally, a "softer" point in the tradition for some time. And so with the "definition" in Trullo 2.

In sum, therefore, a clear positivist action of sovereign legislative authority does not seem to have been operative in the Byzantine canonical tradition. Evident instead is a very different, much more diffuse—but no less real or effective—method of rule recognition. This method does not easily submit to legal-theoretical formulation. The best suggestion may in fact remain that of Rudolph Sohm, who noted that in this early medieval world authoritative positive legislators and moments of definition did exist, *but only in the past.*[240] Only after a period of time has elapsed can any type of legislative initiative become clearly recognized as authoritative. To phrase it differently, only when a legislative enactment becomes "traditional" can it assume real sovereign positive authority. As such, nothing *today* can acquire absolute recognition—no one living has authority *over* the rules. Instead, consensus must slowly build to identify the authority that "was" present in this or that legislative process. In practice, this process is thus very diffuse, indirect, and almost unconscious. In fact, curiously, this process's most direct agents are the parties involved with forming and transmitting the manuscript tradition itself. Copy after copy, recension after recension, "the corpus" is slowly and continually formed and defined through subtle practices of selection and ordering by innumerable, mostly anonymous, copyists and recensors.

The curious lack of instances of clear, official positive definition of the canonical sources points to a much broader and more conspicuous absence in the textual shape of the tradition: a jurisprudential literature. Largely missing in Byzantine canon law of our period is a literature of the technical juristic discussion of rules, their principles, their underlying concepts, and their logical relationships with each other.

Evidence of canonical jurisprudential activity per se is not hard to find.[241] Indeed, it is present in the canons themselves. As we will see in Chapter 3,

[239] e.g. its citation in II Nicaea, in Leo's Novels, at the council of 861; see Dura 1995; Troianos 1995. Even in the west it seems that serious objections to Trullo's validity as a whole were not raised until the Gregorian reforms—and even afterwards the council enjoyed a scattered reception (e.g. in Gratian). *Sources* 82–4; Landau 1995; Laurent 1965, 28–39.

[240] Sohm 1923, 2.75–7.

[241] Unquestionably, the early episcopal courts, in particular, attached to the civilian system, had constant contact with broader secular jurisprudential processes. On the *episcopalis audientia*

canons can sometimes be written in almost commentary-like style on older regulations, and can analyze in minute detail the nature and application of specific rules.[242] Some of this material may cautiously be considered instances of a very desultory "jurisprudential" literature.

Outside the canons themselves, the thematic collections and the synopsis also represent, as we will see, a modest level of jurisprudential activity. The former involve some sorting and classification, for example, and the latter do involve paraphrasing the canons. The extant scholia, if not all (or even mostly) within our period, witness to an ongoing process of explanation, reflection, and even dissection of the canons as a coherent body of rules. At the very end of our period Photius produces a set of canonical questions and answers,[243] and, just after our period, Arethas writes two short treatises on the transfer of bishops.[244] Earlier, Theodore of Studite had composed a number of letters that are more or less canonical answers.[245] A small work on the election of bishops, attributed to a certain Euthymius of Sardis, may also date to the early 9th C.[246]

But this production is very small, not particularly prominent in the manuscripts, and hardly constitutes a sophisticated and sustained project—certainly not a literature. Unquestionably, it pales in comparison with the extensive and advanced commentary work of the secular antecessors of the 6th C—to say nothing of the classical jurists—which seems to have included a number of different genres of lectures, paraphrases, and case examinations.[247] It is not even as creative or pronounced as the much more modest 7th–9th C Byzantine secular jurisprudential activity, which still sees the development of comparatively creative and novel manuals, compilations, and even monographs.[248] If parallel technical-juristic conversations about the canons were taking place, they have not left much of a trace.

The jurisprudential material that is extant is also usually practical and simple, hardly going much beyond clarification, indexing, and cross-referencing. Even the jurisprudence embedded in the patristic material and second-wave legislation does not emerge as in any way a sustained "scientific" or systematic endeavor. It seems much more ad hoc, employed to deal with a

generally, see now esp. Harries 1999, 172–211 and Humfress 2007, 153–73; also Wenger 1925, 337–44. On the gathering of episcopal judgments as precedents, see Garnsey and Humfress 2001, 77–8.

[242] See Ch. 3 C, E.1, and F.1.

[243] Grumel et al. 1936–91, #531, #539, #540, #542, #545. See *Peges* 253, also 154–6, 251, 256; Troianos 2003, 763.

[244] ed. Westerink 1968, 1.246–51. *Peges* 256.

[245] Epistles 40, 487, 489, 525, 535, 549, 552 (ed. Fatouros 1992). Troianos 2003, 763.

[246] ed. Darrouzès 1966, 108–15. *Peges* 156, 256.

[247] On the antecessors, the Greek schools, and their methods, see Collinet 1925, 243–56; Pringsheim 1921; Scheltema 1970; van der Wal 1953.

[248] *Delineatio* 63–6, 71–6, 78–87; Pieler 1978, 434–44, 452–69; Zepos 1958.

problem or two, but not part of a continued and sustained methodological enterprise.

This early absence of jurisprudential literature is thrown into particularly high relief by its later emergence. In the 12th C, in particular, a sustained jurisprudential literature does emerge in the shape of three corpus commentaries.[249] These join a number of increasingly detailed question-and-answer treatises and canon-legal monographs that had been growing in number throughout the 11th C.[250] Later practical handbooks and manuals also exhibit more creative patterns of selection and ordering, in line with broader Byzantine trends of excerpting and epitomizing.[251] There is no question that Byzantine canon law does eventually acquire a secondary literature of formal rule commentary and rule reasoning—even if never as extensive or sophisticated as parallel developments in the post-12th C west.

In light of this later development, the earlier jurisprudential silence becomes almost deafening. The sudden 12th C flurry of commentary work is particularly mysterious: why now and not earlier? It is hard to imagine that the need to explain some of the archaic canons of, for example, Ancyra or Carthage was so much more pressing in the 12th C than in the 9th C—or even the 6th C. Further, the 6th C Justinianic and 9th C Macedonian spurts of secular legal activity surely recommended themselves as sufficiently obvious moments for the stimulation of a real canonical jurisprudential literature as the (relatively obscure) 11th C revival in secular legal learning that presumably underpinned the 12th C canonical work.[252] Most critically, the canons themselves give evidence that canonical jurisprudential thinking and activity *were* taking place during these earlier periods, and there is every reason to believe that, on the model of the 6th C and 9th C literature, this could, if anything, have been more sophisticated and involved than what emerged later. But, again, if it existed, it simply did not form itself into a lasting and distinct body of work, that is, as a regular component of the physical tradition. The canonical tradition in our period overwhelmingly presents itself as simply a series of primary rules. A secondary discourse *about* these rules does not congeal in a textually significant way.

[249] Overview in *Delineatio* 108–12 and *Peges* 249–70 (see this last especially on a "fourth" commentary, a reworking of Balsamon). The only monograph remains Kraznozhen 1911. See also Gallagher 2002; Pieler 1991; Stevens 1969; Stolte 1989, 1991, 1991a.

[250] *Peges* 250–58, 303–6, 308–15 gives the most recent and thorough survey; for further references to the older literature, see Beck 1977, 598–601, 655–62.

[251] The best examples are the two 14th C collections, the *Syntagma* of Blastares (in *RP* 6) and the *Epitome* of Harmenopoulos (*PG* 150.45–168). The former adopts a method of organization known from earlier civil-law works (alphabetical listing of subjects; as found in the secular *Synopsis Major* and *Synopsis Minor*) and the latter proceeds through an exceptionally regular and rational progression of subjects.

[252] On the 11th C revival, see Angold 1994; *Delineatio* 98–104; Macrides 1990, 68; Wolska-Conus 1976, 1979.

This lack of a distinct jurisprudential literature is undoubtedly connected to another gaping hole in the "shape" of early Byzantine canon law: professionalization.[253] This is one of the few sociopolitical realities of Byzantine canon law to be broached in this work, but it is essential for explaining the tradition's textual peculiarities. Unfortunately, the topic of Byzantine legal professionalization remains a subject in need of further sustained research, even in the secular sphere, where research is more advanced. Nevertheless, a few central facts may be asserted with some confidence.

Byzantium did know secular legal professionalization, at least of a type. Late antiquity, with its well-known law schools and "bars," may even have marked something of the high-water mark of formal Roman legal professionalization, certainly on a scholastic level.[254] After the early 6th C, legal professionalization is notoriously difficult to trace in any detail, and the documentary trail at times fades to almost nothing, but there is little question that at least in Constantinople itself throughout much of Byzantine history one can detect professional notaries, advocates, and private teachers of law; at the very least, the *concept* of the legal professional is always present.[255]

By contrast, it is far from clear that even the concept of a professional "canonist" or "canon lawyer," parallel to the secular lawyers and jurists, ever existed in Byzantium. Without doubt it is elusive. Certainly the basic infrastructures of legal professionalization were not present: there were no "canon law" faculties in the Byzantine "universities" (such as they were), with dedicated "canon law professors"; there were no canon law qualifications; there were no clear and defined "terminal" (i.e. lifelong) career paths; there were no canon law associations or guilds, with admissions policies and standards of conduct; and while there were ecclesiastical courts, there seem to have been no regular and widespread dedicated "canon law" positions in the dioceses that were designed for their occupants to make a living primarily from their canon law knowledge.[256] Even terms such as "canon lawyer" or "canonical jurist" (for example, *κανονικοὶ σχολάστικοι, σόφοι τῶν κανόνων, νόμικοι τῶν κανόνων*) are not, to my knowledge, anywhere attested in the Byzantine tradition.

Instead of true canonical professionalization, one can detect overlapping patterns of (a) canonical *specialization* associated with certain ecclesial offices,

[253] On legal professionalization generally, and its connection to formal jurisprudential thought, see Weber 1925, 199–222.

[254] On the shape (and ambiguities) of late Roman legal professionalization, see Brundage 2008, 1–39; Garnsey and Humfress 2001, 41–55; Heszer 1998, 632–3; Honoré 1998, 7–10; 2004,119–24; Humfress 2007, 9–21; Jones 1964, 386–94, 499–516; Marrou 1948, 310–12; Matthews 2000, 23–36; Schulz 1953, 267–77.

[255] See now esp. Goria 2005; the literature, however, remains scattered. Haldon 1990, 254–79; Macrides 1994; Magdalino 1985; Pieler 1978, 429–31, 445–8, 473; Stolte 2002, 201–2; Wolska-Conus 1976, 1979; Zepos 1958.

[256] These criteria are drawn mostly from the post 12th C medieval western experience as explored by Brundage 1995a; 2008.

mostly attested in Constantinople itself; and (b) what we may term "borrowed professionalization." In both cases, however, the evidence is generally quite late. The best examples of the former are the patriarchal officers known as χαρτοφύλακες, essentially chief notarial and archival officers who seem to have become the *de facto* canonical experts of many administrations. Balsamon is the chief example of such officers, but others have left question-and-answer material.[257] A number of other offices—of which we know frustratingly little—also sound as if they may have at least in part required specialized knowledge of the canons.[258] But the pattern of specialization seems to be one of exceptional expertise in a particular set of text traditions—"canonical lore," as it were—and not mastery of an autonomous field of technical knowledge by which the officers were primarily making their living, and were formally qualified to pursue. These positions are better described as administrative positions demanding canonical specialization than canon-legal positions within the administration.

The pattern of "borrowed professionalization" is best exemplified by late antique ἔκδικοι (*defensores*).[259] They appear to have been charged with various aspects of their church's civil-legal relations, whether in defending its own interests in the civil courts, in assisting in the running of the bishop's own semi-civil jurisdiction (even functioning as a judge-delegate), or in acting as an advocate for the poor and widows. We must presume that most had extensive canonical knowledge—the canons themselves suggest a few duties for them.[260] But they nowhere appear as "canon lawyers" per se, that is, as specialized corps of proprietary lawyers of a quasi-independent ecclesial legal system. Instead they emerge as secular *advocati* with some type of professional secular legal training who could apply themselves to church affairs, including, probably, at times, canonical matters, but not as their primary task. These offices may thus be best described as civil-legal ecclesial positions. Much the same seems to be true of their shadowy Byzantine successors.[261]

This pattern of borrowed professionalization is also broadly assumed by the system as a whole: the many points of integration of civil-legal regulation and canonical regulation, whether in the nomocanons, the ecclesial courts, or even provincial administration, point to an ongoing need for civil law knowledge

[257] Darrouzès 1970, 19–28, 334–53; *Peges* 250–8.

[258] e.g. the πρωτονοτάριος, Darrouzès 1970, 355–9, Leontaritou 1996, 313–35. Darrouzès 1970 and especially now Leontaritou 1996 are the chief studies on Byzantine ecclesiastical offices.

[259] On the late antique ἔκδικοι, see now esp. Humfress 1998, 155–70; 2001.

[260] Chalcedon 23; cf. also canon 2.

[261] Darrouzès 1970, 323–32 *et passim*. It seems that at least in Constantinople a college of ἔκδικοι continued to exist, and the πρωτέκδικοι become fairly prominent officers in the patriarchate. A similar dynamic is probably to be assumed for the later ecclesial δικαιοφύλακες, an office that could be bestowed on civil or ecclesial officials. Darrouzès 1970, 109–10. See also Macrides 1990, 68–9.

within the church. Certainly formal—if not necessarily "professional"—civil legal training must always have been reasonably common in the higher echelons of the Byzantine ecclesial administration, as it was in the secular.[262] In our period we may also note that some of the most prominent figures associated with Byzantine canon law were evidently secular lawyers: John Scholastikos ("John the Lawyer")[263] is the most famous example, but the so-called "Enantiophanes" who seems to have composed the first nomocanonical recension of the *Coll14* was also evidently a learned jurist. Later, two of the canonical commentators, Aristenos and Balsamon, will be *νομοφύλακες*, a civil-legal position established in the 11th C, as well as, respectively, *πρωτέκδικος* and *χαρτοφύλαξ*. This pattern of the clergy using and exercising civil-legal knowledge will come to its apogee in the late Byzantine period, when the clergy virtually take over the operation of the secular legal system.[264] Yet even then this does not seem to have entailed the envelopment of the civil system "within" a parallel canonical system, or vice versa. The clergy are simply beginning to operate the civil-legal system. A curious result of this is that the only surviving patriarchal registers, from the 14th C, treat few properly canonical matters.[265] But we never see this borrowed professionalization morphing into a coherent parallel canon-legal professionalization.

This borrowed professionalization also does not seem to have involved a profound penetration of civil-legal juristic discourse into canonical discourse. It is thus revealing that the majority of canonical question-and-answer texts, in which canonical questions are directed from provincial bishops to isolated clerical specialists in the capital—and which are among the very few extant texts that provide a window onto the "real" operation of Byzantine canon law—are almost always very simple in content.[266] The answers sometimes contain technical civil-legal principles, but the overall pattern is of a fairly informal rule discourse informed by an occasional secular legal jurisprudential concept—and not of an ongoing, formal, and technical church-legal conversation carried on by a large network of even "borrowed" secular legal professionals dedicated to church matters. Even the canons themselves, and the thematic collections, while certainly evincing some technical stylizations redolent of professional legal composition, are in no way dominated by it.[267]

[262] As Wolska-Conus puts it (1979, 6), "tout fonctionnaire, dans la capitale ou dans la province, est un peu juriste."

[263] The epithet *σχολαστικός* does not inevitably denote legal training (Wolska-Conus 1979, 5 n. 17; also Humfress 1998, 75–6). However, John is referred to as *ἀπὸ σκολαστικῶν*, which certainly means "from the [professional] lawyers," "former lawyer." For his titles in the manuscripts, see *Sin* 220–1.

[264] Pieler 1978, 473–6; Fögen 1987, 157. Very often, however, it is unclear whether certain officers are meant to be treating primarily secular or canonical matters (or perhaps both equally).

[265] *Peges* 314.

[266] See Konidaris 1994.

[267] We may suspect they came into play mostly when civil-legal matters were broached. See Chs. 3 and 4.

Paul Magdalino has also recently surveyed a number of well-educated 12th C bishops and discovered very little evidence of advanced legal learning.[268] Civil-legal professional discourse did not seep far into the canonical tradition.

Generally, then, Byzantine canon law does not ever seem to have emerged as a distinct sphere of professional legal endeavor. Its professional or academic infrastructure, such as it was, appears only as a kind of appendage to either the ecclesial administrative system, mostly centered on Constantinople itself, and as marked here and there by officers especially learned in the canons, or to the civil-legal system, from which it seems to have desultorily borrowed legal expertise. But the real loci of the system's operation must have always been the much more "amateur" structures of the episcopal chanceries, and the figures of the bishops themselves, either individually or in synods, but always men of (if anything) very general education—a pattern not unfamiliar from the pre-12th C west.[269] Certainly the western explosion of canon-legal professionalization in the 12th and 13th C has no parallel in Byzantium.

E. ANALYSIS: THE LAW TAKES SHAPE

A survey of the broadest physical contours of the Byzantine canonical tradition reveals much about the intellectual parameters, priorities, and assumptions of Byzantine canon-legal culture. This culture is not entirely foreign, but little of what is revealed is particularly obvious or intuitive to the formalist legal sensibilities sketched in the Introduction.

The primary focus of the tradition can be identified as the collection and faithful transmission of a fairly small and specific set of traditional rule texts. The single-mindedness of the tradition in this regard, and the textual unity and stability achieved in the process, is striking. Although by the standards of modern (printed) codifications the Byzantine manuscripts and collections may seem quite "messy" and variable, the tradition nevertheless easily reads as centered around one gradually expanding set of core texts. The boundaries of this set of texts evince a curious gradation, and are subject to a constant, diffuse negotiation, but some type of core corpus is always discernible as the basic backbone of the entire endeavor. As a result, "the canons" (a phrase we will return to in Chapter 3) always have a reasonably concrete and unitary referent. Byzantine canon law thus presents itself as primarily a practice in the faithful transmission of a set of traditional texts—and not as an abstract jurisprudential project in which the corpus of rules might be variable,

268 Magdalino 1985, 171–2.

269 See Brundage 1995, 41, 120–1; 2008, 46–74.

contingent, or manipulatable. The focus is overwhelmingly on the "primary rules," to again borrow a concept from H. L. A. Hart.

Interestingly—although widely neglected in the surveys—this highly "corpus-centered" culture of canon law, if we may term it that, seems to have been surprisingly universal. When one looks west and east from Byzantium, the textual worlds of Latin and Syrian canon law look very familiar in both form and content. Everywhere canon law seems to be mostly about the collection and transmission of "the corpus," and "the corpus" is similar east and west, at least in its core, and certainly in its shape. At least until the 9th C, and throughout the Mediterranean, it is probably safe to speak of a common Christian canonical culture on the level of textual expression.

One of the chief characteristics of this culture, certainly in the Byzantine east, is its extraordinary conservatism. Over the long term, if a source makes it into the corpus, it is there to stay. On a physical level it will never disappear, and its integrity will never be successfully challenged—that is, canons never permanently drop out of the tradition or suffer permanent modification.[270] As a result, the system develops and is constructed almost exclusively through accretion. Indeed, the entire tradition seems to develop in an almost Talmud-like way, with each new layer simply placed on top of the old. Thus the patristic material and apostolic material are wrapped around the older synodal core; the systematic indices are then affixed to or gently placed around the corpus; and the civil legislation and second-wave materials are simply appended as yet two more layers. After our period this pattern will continue, with later synodal decisions and question-and-answer material simply stacked after the corpus, and finally, the writings of the commentators wrapped around the core corpus texts themselves.

This extremely conservative pattern of growth suggests an almost scriptural handling of the texts. Indeed, just as Byzantine (and all pre-modern Christian) "theology" is mostly an ongoing, cumulative, exegetical engagement with scripture, a sacred core corpus of traditional texts, so Byzantine canon law emerges as above all an ongoing engagement with another sacred—if growing—body of traditional texts.[271] And just as scripture will never be replaced or "edited" by later theological developments, so the core corpus of canons resists physical violation of any sort.[272]

[270] The formulation of Konidaris 1994, 133–4 that the canons are treated as "eternally valid" is an accurate description of the tradition's textual dynamics.

[271] See also Hadot 1995 on the broadly exegetical nature of all late antique philosophy.

[272] Cf. L'Huillier 1996, 10, who connects the stability of the texts with their attribution to divine inspiration. It is interesting that the fuzziness of the canonical corpus around its edges parallels, if to a greater degree, the fuzziness and variability of the Byzantine scriptural canon. For the variations in the Byzantine canonical lists of scripture, see the synoptic table in Boumis 1991, 1.205–7.

This quasi-sacral status of the texts may explain one of the most striking absences in the tradition: the lack of a sustained jurisprudential literature (and the requisite class of dedicated professionals to produce it). In a sacralized legal world the preservation of the sacred traditions is naturally the paramount concern. As a result, the development of an abstract secondary discourse that might exercise some type of power *over* the sacred rules, or provide the mechanism for their replacement, or otherwise actively reshape them (as we will see in the west with Gratian), would be quite unthinkable, and even nonsensical. The system must instead focus on the constant engagement with the core sacred rules themselves, not on "advancement" beyond them, or the construction of a more satisfying logical system that could potentially oust them. Jurisprudential discourse, inasmuch as it exists at all, must instead be comparatively ephemeral and occasional, working around the edges of the tradition, but not part of its core architecture—which is precisely what we see in the Byzantine tradition. Further, in a sacralized legal system of this type, the traditional starting points of constructive jurisprudence—contradictions and repetitions—are in any case mostly non-issues: sacred traditional laws cannot really contradict other sacred laws (certainly contradictions are more the reader's problem than the tradition's), and repetitions simply make traditions more traditional.[273]

The lack of even a relatively benign, non-constructive jurisprudential literature—that is, of a more exegetical type, like much traditional Roman jurisprudence, and certainly like the later Byzantine commentators—also suggests that the function of jurisprudence in assisting in the application and interpretation of the primary rules is being performed by other discourses. Despite its physical "autonomy," then, the textual shape of Byzantine canon law would seem to suggest that the tradition is deeply embedded in other regulative discourses which can provide it with the necessary secondary "rules about the rules." The identification and nature of these discourses will be a major focus of the next two chapters.

This intentional embeddedness is also implied by the small size of the corpus. The diminutive stature of the tradition strongly suggests that the system assumes the presence of other, external regulative discourses that can fill in the legislative gaps that must have been felt. Certainly the system assumes that it can function with a relatively small body of formal regulations. Since a sustained and comprehensive elaboration and creation of rules through either ongoing legislation or a technical jurisprudence are nowhere evident, other discourses must be at play.

Another absence that this emphasis on "law-as-sacred-tradition" vs. "law-as-jurisprudence" helps to explain is the lack of official definitions of the law,

[273] For similar observations in the literature regarding the sacrality of Byzantine laws and its impact upon legal doctrine, see the references in the Introduction, n. 30.

or indeed of any type of clear expression of sovereign positivist legislative authority over the law. This is among the most curious aspects of Byzantine canon law. However, as Sohm long ago noted, it may be explained if legal authority derives chiefly from tradition itself. Rules thus must always exist *as* traditional rules (that is, a canon is always a canon *of St Basil* or *of Nicaea—of* some traditional authority). This concept of legislative authority necessarily makes any "present" articulations of the law's shape, or assertions of radical change, rather awkward—and indeed we hardly find them. Instead, in the present, one is mostly expected to confirm the existing sacred tradition, that is, to recognize authoritative decisions that have already taken place. New rules can be added, but, as we see in Trullo (or II Nicaea 1—see Chapter 2), authority for new, "present" rules must be garnered primarily by firmly protesting one's loyalty to the past—that is, by placing new rules firmly in the trajectory of the old. One must "traditionalize" new rules to promulgate them. Critically, however, this never results in the physical jettisoning of older traditions, even if the new rules substantively contradict or modify the older tradition.[274] At best one can solve particular problems in the older tradition, and perhaps clarify a bit or neaten around the edges of the most recent additions. But assertions of comprehensive authority over the tradition, such as to radically modify or even to define categorically its shape, seem out of the question. The system instead relies upon very diffuse and indirect methods of selection and evolution within the manuscripts to define the tradition. The definitive promulgation of laws is mostly a very long, silent process of reception in which valid law "just happens" over time.

This method of traditional legislative promulgation has important implications for a critical, if often unremarked, characteristic of legal process: speed. In this world, fully promulgating law—or rather, waiting for the tradition to promulgate law—takes a very long time. The *Coll14* additions and Trullo, as we have seen, seem to have taken centuries to fully establish themselves in the traditional core. This slow pace of change undoubtedly impeded or precluded a number of legal processes that might be taken for granted today, most notably any attempts to overhaul the system as a whole, and any "instrumental" use of laws to effect immediate policy goals. The preferred, and more practical, course for addressing immediate policy problems would have been to look back to earlier articulations of a desired policy, and not to attempt to create entirely new legislation—which, of course, is broadly what we see throughout the late antique and Byzantine periods. It also implies the privileging of non-legal (i.e. political) methods of policy implementation.

Another formalist-positivist legal expectation—the precisionistic demand for bivalence in the assertion of validity—is also frustrated by this type of rule

[274] See n. 155 for some examples. See Glenn 2007, 65–6 for parallel observations about the nature of tradition in other pre-modern legal systems.

recognition. As strange as it may seem, the Byzantine textual tradition overwhelmingly presents its sources as constituting a *spectrum* of validity! That is, they emerge as a large array of diverse traditions marked in a variety ways to indicate their relative antiquity and acceptance. Although at any given moment one can broadly discern what material is "in" the corpus and what is "out," the exact line between the two is elusive. This strongly suggests, of course, that this line—that is, the categorical delineation of validity—is neither essential to the system nor even a priority. Certainly the tradition does not encourage, and probably does not require, inquiring very closely into this question. Decisions are to be made through a diffuse process of tradition weighing, not the application of a systematic source theory—which thus does not seem to have existed in the tradition. This suggests that we should be cautious about regarding the hierarchical rankings of the sources that are occasionally evident in the tradition (for example, councils before fathers, ecumenical councils before local councils) as legal-doctrinal in intent, that is, as constituting a formal scale of abrogation. They would seem more symbolic, one more indicator of relative "traditional weight."

In sum, then, the basic physical contours of the Byzantine canonical textual tradition, and the patterns and dynamics of its growth, already reveal, or at least imply, very much about the nature of Byzantine canon law as a legal phenomenon. Strikingly, many of the fundamental concepts, assumptions, and even instincts of formalism-positivism seem to be simply disregarded or contradicted—or at least very oddly implemented. One searches in vain for signs of a clear doctrine of positive sovereign legislative authority, or precise indications of validity, or even for a solid place for a technical professional jurisprudential discourse. Likewise, law is not particularly expansive and comprehensive, but brief and compact. Textually, it is not malleable, constructible, and instrumental, but rigid, conservative, and ossified. Its growth is not rapid, responsive, and intentional but slow, ruminatory, and almost unconscious. It is not highly variable and dynamic but generally uniform and static. It suggests not so much a doctrinally rationalized system as a florilegic repository of sacred traditions. It is not an autonomous rule system but a normative reality apparently deeply embedded in other rule discourses. Finally—although I have not dwelt on this aspect at length, and one must be cautious about assigning it immense significance—it is interesting to recall that its origin is not Latin, but Greek. In this sense, even our expectations of a "normal" late antique Roman law are frustrated. It is something really quite unusual.

2

Introducing the Law

A. INTRODUCTION: INTRODUCING THE LAW

The Byzantines composed relatively few texts that serve to frame or introduce their ecclesiastical legal tradition. Those texts that do exist are therefore extremely valuable as rare windows onto how the Byzantines consciously framed canon law—that is, how they imagined its nature, purpose, place, and scope. Unfortunately, little scholarship has been devoted to exploring how these texts shape and articulate a legal vision. Roman and Byzantine civil law prologues, as well as early western canon law prologues, have been the subject of legal-doctrinal investigation,[1] but Byzantine canonical prologues have as a rule attracted attention only inasmuch as they can help reconstruct the textual history of the collections to which they are attached.[2] The contents of the prologues that we may term (loosely) "doctrinal" have been largely overlooked in both eastern Orthodox and Byzantine law scholarship.

This is a serious oversight. By late antiquity prologues were quite consciously and explicitly marked as an important and even essential element of legal literature. The roots of this tradition run very deep.[3] Plato, as is well known, made it quite clear that prologues are a necessary part of the law: "the lawgiver must never omit to furnish preludes (προοίμια), as prefaces both to the laws as a whole and to each individual statute."[4] According to Plato, these prologues provide the "plain laws" (ἄκρατοι νόμοι) of normal legislation with the philosophical and pedagogical rationale necessary for their proper operation.[5] Plato's own *Laws* thus included a lengthy introductory section, and Cicero later

[1] In particular, and of most value to this study, Aerts *et al.* 2001, Brasington 1994, Fögen 1995, Honig 1960, Hunger 1964, Lokin 1994, Ries 1983, Scharf 1959, Simon 1994, Somerville and Brasington 1998.

[2] e.g. Menebisoglou 1989; Petrovitz 1970, 17–53; *Sbornik* 52–86; Stolte 1998a; Zachariä von Lingenthal 1877. Exceptions include Deledemos 2002, 79–82 and Viscuso 1989.

[3] For general discussions of ancient legal *prooimia*, see Hunger 1964, 19–35; Ries 1983.

[4] *Laws* 723b (ed. Burnet 1907).

[5] *Laws* 721b–d, and more broadly 718a–724b. See Fögen 1995, 1597–9; Laks 2000, 285–90; Ries 1983, 104–26, 212–23; Scharf 1959, 68 n. 2.

followed suit, championing Plato's theory.[6] Significant prologues will then be placed in the mouths of the semi-legendary lawgivers Charondas and Zaleukos. Philo, in his description of Moses as an ideal lawgiver, will likewise be careful to note that Moses understood the need to provide laws with prefaces and epilogues.[7] In Roman legal literature this aspect of legal composition will not come to explicit expression until the late principate, but thereafter imperial constitutions and legal collections regularly include ornate prologues and introductory-like sections.[8] Some elements of the early Apostolic Church Order material will also contain short prologues.[9]

This high estimation of prologues in late antique legal culture strongly commends such texts to our careful scrutiny. They are, in fact, often the only witnesses to Greco-Roman "legal theory" we possess from within the legal literature itself. Outside of this literature a number of highly theoretical philosophical or rhetorical treatments of law may be found, but within the legal tradition sustained general theoretical self-reflection is conspicuously rare.[10] The prologues—and more broadly, the introductory sections of the extant legal collections—are thus one of the very few places where ancient Greco-Roman legal literature has an opportunity to articulate its own scope,

[6] Cicero, *Laws* 2.6.14 (ed. Powell 2006); Ries 1983, 104–26, 212–23. Plato's prologue in the *Laws* may be considered to extend from 715e until 734e (and the *Republic* itself may be considered an enormous prologue).

[7] The *prooimia* of (ps.-)Zaleukos and (ps.-)Charondas are preserved in Stobaeus (ed. Wachsmuth and Hense 1884). For Philo, see *Life of Moses* 2.51 (ed. Cohn 1902, 119–268); cf. 2.46–8 on the purpose of Moses' historical introduction.

[8] See Ries 1983, 162–85. Three prologues from Diocletian seem to be our first substantial surviving examples (Fögen 1995, 1594). Most fully preserved novels from the 5th C onwards have *prooimia* structures. Hunger 1964 remains a critical study of these texts; more narrowly focused studies can be found in Biondi 1952, Honig 1960, Lanata 1984. For this study, texts examined include all of the *prooimia* attached to the 6th C novels treating primarily ecclesiastical matters (notably *NN* 3, 5, 6, 7, 9, 11, 16, 37, 40, 42, 46, 55, 56, 57, 58, 65, 67, 76, 79, 81, 83, 111, 117, 120, 123, 131, 132, 133, 137), the introductory materials connected to the Theodosian codification (*CTh* 1.1.5, 1.1.6, Novels 1 and 2 of the Theodosian novels, the full *Gesta* of the senate's reception of the *CTh*), and the Justinianic law books (for the *Codex*, constitutions *Haec*, *Summa*, *Cordi;* for the *Institutes*, constitution *Imperatorium*; for the *Digest*, constitutions *Deo auctore*, *Omnem*, *Tanta*/*Δέδωκεν*), the *prooimia* of the novels of Leo (which are estimated to comprise two-thirds of the Novels' full text; Fögen 1995, 1602, texts in Noailles and Dain 1944), and the general *prooimia* preceding the principal Byzantine law books (to the *Ecloga*, ed. Burgmann 1983, 160–7, to the *Eisagoge*, ed. Schminck 1986, 4–11, to the *Prochiron*, ed. Schminck 1986, 56–60, to the *Basilica*, ed. Schminck 1986, 2, and to the collection of Leo's Novels, ed. Noailles and Dain 1944, 4–9). Other structures of works that are broadly introductory in character have also been considered, including *CTh* 1; *Digest* 1.1–4 (and book one generally); *Institutes* 1.1–2; CJ 1; *Eisagoge* 1–10; and *Basilica* 1–6.

[9] Notably, and taken into account into this study, the short prefaces (and sometimes epilogues) of the *Apostolic Tradition* (and related sources), the *Constitutiones ecclesiasticae apostolorum*, the *Didascalia apostolorum*, and the *Apostolic Canons*. For editions, see Ch. 4, n. 105.

[10] i.e. the jurists themselves do not seem to have produced any works of Roman legal theory or legal philosophy. The lack of general theoretical reflection in the Roman legal tradition is commonly observed; see e.g. Johnston 2000; Schulz 1953, 69–70, 135; Stein 1995, 1539.

purpose, priorities, and nature. They become particularly valuable in the Byzantine period, when theoretical discussions of law of any type—philosophical or otherwise—become very rare.[11]

Introductory texts can take a number of different forms. For our purposes the Byzantine tradition of canonical introduction may be understood as constituted by virtually any text, or set of texts, that frames the canonical material. The most obvious and important of these are texts that directly and consciously introduce the tradition, that is, the formal prologues or epilogues attached to various collections. Also important are introductory letters prefacing individual canonical sources, and canons in the sources themselves or topics in the systematic indices that may be construed as broadly introductory in content or form. Many extant manuscripts also contain sets of articles that may be understood as introductory in character. These sets include not only the formal prologues, systematic indices, and tables of contents, but also a selection of other introductory-type texts such as excerpts from the Apostolic Church Order material, histories of the councils, listings of sees, and even doctrinal texts. A full schematic of the Byzantine canonical introductory tradition may be found in Appendix A.

The most substantial introductory texts of our period are the Nicene and apostolic prefaces, the prologue to the *Coll50*, the first two prologues to the *Coll14*, the Trullan introductory complex, and II Nicaea 1. These texts are distinguished by their prominence in the tradition (they have a regular and prominent place in the corpus and manuscripts structures), their detailed content, and/or their length. They will therefore be the focus of our examination. We will also, however, briefly consider some of the more minor introductory texts found throughout the corpus.

B. DESCRIPTION OF THE TEXTS

1. The Nicene creed

The first significant "prologue" to the canons may have been the Nicene creed itself. Presumably it was added at the same time as the Nicene canons.[12] It is to be found heading the canons in Schwartz's chief witnesses to his Antiochian

[11] On this last, see Aerts *et al.* (here B. Stolte) 2001, 145: "with the exception of the *prooimia*, there is no Byzantine reflection on law as a social and political phenomenon ... It is very hard to ascertain what the Byzantines thought about their legal system." See Fögen 1993, 72 on a similar state of affairs in Byzantine political theory.

[12] Schwartz 1936a, 161–2, 193–4, 200–1, 225; so *Delineatio* 26, and also Ohme 1998, who even suspects (527–42, 579) that a homoion creed may have prefaced the early Antiochian corpus, later replaced by the Nicene.

corpus, most notably London BL Add. 14,528 (*a.* 500/1) and the Isidoriana translation of the Freising-Würzburger manuscripts; other Syriac and Latin witnesses are not difficult to find.[13] We can therefore presume that it was a regular component of the earliest collections. In London BL 14,528, a particularly ancient witness, the creed is found amidst a number of other texts that head the collection:[14]

1. a note ascribed to Constantine
2. the edict of Constantine against the Arians
3. the Nicene creed
4. the Constantinopolitan creed
5. subscription list of Nicaea.

The presence of the Constantinopolitan creed is particularly interesting. It suggests that not only was the Nicene creed becoming a normal preface, but that a whole credal section was developing at the head of the corpus. This is quite logical: the *ὅροι* (to use the older terminology for church rules) of the faith are being placed together with the *ὅροι* of the disciplinary tradition.[15] Theological and disciplinary definitions form a natural pair.

This practice of credal prefacing does not, however, become normative in the later Greek tradition. Occasionally in later manuscripts creeds will be included among a number of introductory articles, but this does not seem to have been a widespread practice.[16] It does, however, find resonance in a much more general tendency of beginning collections, manuscripts, and sources with some type of faith or theological *topic*. This tendency is quite consistent throughout the tradition. Thus, for example, Title 1 of the *Coll14* starts with "theology" and "the faith" (imitating *CJ* 1.1), as do the canons of Constantinople, Carthage, and Trullo—and later the Epitome of Arsenius (12th C; title 1), and Blastares (14th C; *Πρόλογος περὶ τῆς ὀρθοδόξου πίστεως*).[17] Some manuscripts may also be found with series of doctrinal definitions, or *ὅροι*, if not creeds, stacked at their beginning.[18] This tendency should probably be

[13] See Turner 1899, 1.1.2.106–11, 154–5, 174–5. Compare the close association of the two in Carthage's Apiarian Dossier (*Fonti* 1.2.426–47), and various Syriac and Arabic witnesses (examples in Riedel 1900, 136–7, Selb 1989, 98 n. 71).

[14] In Schulthess 1908, 1–4, helpfully described by Schwartz 1936a, 161–2.

[15] See Schwartz 1936a, 193.

[16] One example may be found in Moscow Syn. 432 (where the creed is in Latin!); however, the creed can also appear with the Nicene canons in the corpus section, as in Athos Meg. Lav. B.93, or Oxford Rawl. G. 15.

[17] This last very explicitly treats faith outside of, and ahead of, the collection's alphabetical scheme because of its pre-eminence. *RP* 6.46–9.

[18] Cambridge Ee.4.29 (11th C) is an excellent example, containing, among other confessions, the *ὅροι* of Chalcedon, Constantinople 553, Constantinople 681, and Nicaea 787; see also Vat gr 2184 (with a few doctrinal letters of Cyril) or Paris supp gr. 1089 (with an article on the *filioque*, and a confession of faith). These types of doctrinal articles may also be very frequently found in manuscript appendices; see Burgmann *et al.* 1995, 264. Here also might be counted various

read as an instance of the much broader and older convention of beginning law codes with reference to the divine.[19]

2. The apostolic material

Apostolic Church Order material plays a number of subtle but important introductory and framing roles in the manuscripts and collections. The only element of this material to achieve a permanent place in the Greek corpus is the eighty-five Apostolic Canons from the eighth book of the *Apostolic Constitutions*. Placed prominently at the beginning of the corpus since at least the 6th C, these canons themselves function as a kind of apostolic preface: the later conciliar material now reads as flowing from and out of this original apostolic disciplinary "conversation." In effect, the canons are now cast as very literally an apostolic endeavor.[20] The Nicene corpus has become an apostolic corpus.

The Apostolic Canons also contain a short but dramatic epilogue in which the apostles themselves, speaking directly to the bishops, reflect upon the significance and purpose of their work:

> Thus have these things regarding the canons been prescribed for you, O bishops. If you remain steadfast in them, you will be saved [or "preserved safe": *σωθήσεσθε*] and you will have peace; but if you are disobedient, you will be punished and you will have eternal war with each other, earning the just recompense for your disobedience. God, the only unbegotten and maker of everything through Christ, will unify you through

liturgical introductory articles (short commentaries or other instructions, e.g. in Escorial Gr. X. III.2, Milan E.94.supp, Paris gr. 1263; Vatican gr. 640, Vienna Hist gr. 7). It is interesting that in the Greek *acta* of Chalcedon the canons, probably drafted in committee, are often placed as "session 7" after the credal statements in "session 6": faith/creeds and the canons again form a natural pair. See Price and Gaddis 2005, 1.xiv, 1.81 n. 277, 3.92–4.

[19] This pattern is very common in ancient Near Eastern and Greek legal literature, and may be observed in everything from the tendency of starting legislation with an invocation to the gods (the simplest version of which is the "*θεοί*" heading ancient Greek constitutions), to treating the divine legitimacy and origin of the legislator and his laws (e.g. Hammurabi 28–41, ed. Richardson 2004), to, as here, beginning with matters pertaining to the divine—"faith." Plato understands the prepositioning of divine matters as entirely natural (*Laws* 715e–718a; 723e, 732e), and it is very clearly expressed in Cicero's *Laws* 2 and Zaleukos and Charondas' *Prooimia*. We might also note that the Ten Commandments start with divine matters, as does, broadly, Deuteronomy (1–11), and Philo, *Special Laws* 1 (ed. Cohn 1906, 1–265), Josephus, *Antiquities* 3 (ed. Niese 1885–92), *CJ* 1, and the *Basilica*. See Hunger 1964, 29–31; Ries 1983, 11, 14, 20, 82, 88, 90, 98–9, 117–18, 120–1, 212–22.

[20] See Schwartz 1936a, 199–200. Many small literary techniques in these canons enhance the dramatic sense of these canons as emerging from the very mouths of the apostles. Thus, for example, in Apostolic 15, 26 "*we* ordain"; in 27 "*our* Lord"; in 29 "as Simon Magus was [cut off] by *me*, Peter"; in 82 "as *our* Onesimus appeared"; 85 (a listing of scripture) "*our* own books . . . and the Acts of *us* the apostles." On the techniques of apostolic pseudepigraphy generally, see Metzger 1985, 1.33–8; Steimer 1992, 130–3 *et passim*.

peace in the Holy Spirit, and will prepare you for every good deed [Heb. 13: 21] without deviation, blame, or reproach, and will make you worthy of eternal life with us through the mediation of his beloved son Jesus Christ, our God and savior, through whom is glory to the God of all . . . until ages of ages. Amen.[21]

This short text is sometimes lost in modern editions and translations,[22] and it seems to be absent in some of the later recensions,[23] but in the older manuscripts it is usually appended to the last canon, sometimes as part of it, or as slightly separated, and thus highlighted. It is perhaps most prominent in the *Coll50*, where as part of Apostolic 85 it is attached to the final title, and thus very consciously placed as the conclusion to the entire work.[24]

The content of this short piece is remarkable. It begins with an easily missed, but critical, piece of introductory information: the primary audience of the canons is the bishops. This pattern may be observed elsewhere in the few places where the expected audience of the canonical texts is made explicit. Bishops (and to a lesser extent the lower clergy) are understood as the primary readers of the canonical texts: canons are above all rules for bishops.[25]

As to purpose, the canons are written for "salvation" and "peace," and disobedience will bring suitable chastisement. This chastisement is perhaps understood chiefly as ecclesial disunity, but the implication that obedience leads to "eternal life with us," that is, with the apostles, suggests that a more eschatological horizon may be envisaged.[26] Clearly canonical adherence is not simply a matter of mundane discipline. The reference to "with us" also suggests that canonical obedience is part of an episcopal practice of apostolic mimesis. The canons are clearly a rather metaphysically charged "apostolic" aspect of episcopal administration.

Beyond the Apostolic Canons themselves, another set of apostolic material functions in the tradition in a quasi-introductory manner. It is almost invisible in modern editions and translations of the canons, but very evident in the manuscripts as an introductory structure. This body of material is known to

[21] Ed. Metzger 1985, 3.308–10.

[22] e.g. in *RP* 2.111 it is relegated to a footnote; Joannou's handling of it is excellent, placing a line break between it and Apostolic 85 (*Fonti* 1.2.52–3). The *Pedalion* (Kallivourtsis 1800) incorporates it into its introduction (pp. xix–xx).

[23] It seems to be absent principally in the recensions with commentary. So Beveridge 1672, 2.40 and *Pitra* 1.36; and so not in Istanbul Topkapı 115 or Florence Laur. 5.2. Unfortunately, most manuscript descriptions are not sufficiently detailed to make a clearer determination on the regularity of this omission (perhaps only when Balsamon and Zonaras are together in a MS?).

[24] See *Syn* 151–5.This is particularly evident in the versions of the work in which the canons are placed in corpus order under the titles (see Ch. 4 F): the Epilogue is here noticeably out of place.

[25] See e.g. the introductory epistles of Antioch and Gangra (in *Kormchaya*) as well as II Nicaea 2; Carthage 18 refers to bishops and clergy.

[26] Cf. the strong warning of eschatological punishment for ecclesial disorder in the opening section of the *Constitutiones ecclesiasticae apostolorum* (or "Apostolic Ordinances"), ed. Arendzen 1901, 60–1.

scholarship as the 'Epitome of Book Eight of the Apostolic Constitutions'.[27] Found only in canonical manuscripts, the Epitome is composed of five sections of excerpts from *Apostolic Constitutions*, book eight: (1) 8.1–2; (2) 8.4–5, 16–28, 30–1; (3) 8.32; (4) 8.33–4, 42–5; (5) 8.46. In essence it contains most of *Apostolic Constitutions*, book eight, save two large liturgical sections and the Apostolic Canons.[28] Like the Apostolic Canons, three of these fragments present themselves as common teaching of the apostles: (1) "Teaching of the holy apostles regarding χαρίσματα"; (2) "Constitutions (διατάξεις) of the holy apostles through Hippolytus regarding ordinations"; and (5) "Teaching of all the holy apostles regarding good order." The others are presented as rulings of individuals: (3) "Constitutions of the holy apostle Paul regarding ecclesiastical canons"; (4) "Constitutions of the holy apostles Peter and Paul."

The origin of these texts as a separate unit is not entirely clear, but it seems likely they hail from the 5th C, and that in the canonical manuscripts they originally formed a whole with the Apostolic Canons (which, comprising section 8.47 in the *Apostolic Constitutions*, would follow the fifth section of the Epitome).[29] In the extant manuscripts these extracts are among the most frequent introductory articles, often quite prominent as one of the very first items in a collection, even before the systematic collections' prologues.[30] Sometimes all five sections, in various levels of abbreviation, will be present in the manuscripts, sometimes fewer, and their order can vary.[31]

Their persistence in the manuscripts is quite remarkable in light of their mixed reception. By the 11th C they are sufficiently common that Michael the Sebastos chides earlier redactors for not including the rulings of "Peter and Paul," and he explicitly includes them in his redaction of the *Coll14*.[32] The expanded synopsis associated with Aristenos also contains some of them.[33] Other witnesses, however, are more negative. Trullo clearly approves only eighty-five Apostolic Canons—the only specific enumeration of canons in Trullo 2—and condemns the rest of the *Apostolic Constitutions*, including, presumably, these extracts. Zonaras later reiterates this disapproval.[34]

[27] ed. Funk 1905, 2.72–96, with discussion at pp. xi–xix. On the literature, see esp. Schwartz 1910, 196–213; Steimer 1992, 80–6. The synopsist's partial version may be found in *RP* 4.399–403.

[28] The text, however, differs from the received Apostolic Constitutions in a number of ways, which has led some scholars to doubt that it is a true "epitome." Its exact relationship to book eight of the *Apostolic Constitutions* remains a matter of debate. See Bradshaw 2002, 6; Metzger 1985, 42 n. 2.; Steimer 1992, 80–6.

[29] Schwartz 1910, 196–213; *Sin* 321; also *Sbornik* 172–4, 180–7. Schwartz believes that they may have been separated from the Apostolic Canons when the latter were integrated into the *Coll50*.

[30] See e.g. the recensions described in *Sbornik* 116–230 or *Sin* 70–103. Funk rightly refers to the "almost innumerable" manuscripts in which they appear (1905, xvi).

[31] Compare e.g. the selections described in *Sbornik* 131–2, 180–5. This internal variation marks these texts as a "soft" spot in the tradition.

[32] Schminck 1998, 361.

[33] *RP* 4.399–403.

[34] *RP* 2.110–11.

As introductory texts their primary function may be read as reinforcing the framing "message" of the Apostolic Canons: the canonical tradition is an apostolic project. Second, their content is broadly introductory. Reminiscent of the introductory *Amtsweisungen* elements of ancient law codes, in which the duties of various offices are detailed near the beginning of collections,[35] the Epitome's overriding, if not exclusive, concern is the description and delineation of positions, offices, and authority in the church. The first section is thus concerned to regulate the status of those possessed of special "gifts" (*χαρίσματα*), including the clergy, and the relationship of the clergy and the laity. It is in a sense a meditation on offices in general. Section two then details, in descending order, the forms for the ordination of the clergy: bishop, presbyter, deacon, deaconess, subdeacon, and so on. Sections three and four are much broader in content, but section five, "Teaching on Good Order" (*Περὶ εὐταξίας διδασκαλία*), a meditation on order in the church, returns to the general theme of hierarchical theory. Especially significant is the opening line of this text, which voices a central theme of Greco-Roman political thinking: "This we all [the apostles] in common enjoin, that each remain in the order (*τάξις*) given to him and not exceed its bounds."[36] In effect, a commonplace Platonic concept of justice, that each is to "do their [natural, class-restricted] thing,"[37] has been placed in the mouths of the apostles—and thus in an authoritative position at the head of the entire canonical tradition. This theme is then developed at length in this text, with many biblical citations enjoining each rank of Christian to adhere to their position.

The effect of this last text, and of the Epitome material in general, is therefore to act as a hierarchical manifesto, clearly setting the canons in the context of a worldview which sees order and justice—and so law—as stemming first and foremost out of proper maintenance and description of hierarchical authorities. This will resonate, as we will see in Chapter 4, with the tendency of the sources and systematic collections to order their material first with *Amtsweisungen*-like material.

3. The prologue of the *Coll50*: Οἱ τοῦ μεγάλου θεοῦ

The first extant formal prologue in the Byzantine canonical tradition is the *πρόλογος* of the *Coll50*, *οἱ τοῦ μεγάλου θεοῦ*.[38] Although short, it is a refined and erudite work, a rhetorical *tour de force* that is written in a Greek

[35] See Ch. 4 G. [36] Funk 1905, 92.

[37] i.e. *τὸ τὰ αὑτοῦ πράττειν*. See esp. *Republic* 433a–434c (and broadly from 369a onwards); also *Laws* 756e–757d. The core idea is that justice is realized when each part of the city/soul is functioning in its proper (hierarchical) place and order.

[38] Editions in *Sin* 214–18 and *Syn* 4–7, the latter slightly more complete, and my source here. On this prologue generally, see *Sin* 213–20; Menebisoglou 1989. An English translation may be

sufficiently sophisticated as to border on obscurity.[39] It even seems to evince a regular prose rhythm.[40] It may be divided into three sections: a general introduction with doctrinal and historical content (4.1–20)[41], a technical discussion of the method of composition of the *Coll50* (4.20–5.16), and a short introduction and listing of the canonical sources of the collection (5.17–7.2). These sectional divisions correspond to sentence divisions in the texts: the first section encompasses the first two sentences, 4.1–14 and 4.14–20; the second section, the third sentence from 4.20–5.16 (although this perhaps should be divided at 5.8 *οὐκ αὐτοὶ*); and the third, the remaining text from 5.17 until the end. Its author is presumably John Scholastikos.

The first part of the prologue, consisting of two lengthy periods, is an exceptionally rich and densely woven amalgam of images and ideas. Many of these become fundamental to the later tradition.

The elaborate first clause (1–3), initiating a period that resolves in line 6, introduces the agents of legislation: "The disciples and apostles of our great God and savior Jesus Christ and indeed those bishops and teachers of his holy church who succeeded them and were like to them..."[42] Here both the "disciples and apostles" of Jesus Christ and the "bishops and teachers" of his church who "succeeded and were like to" them (*οἱ μετ᾽ ἐκείνους καὶ κατ᾽ ἐκείνους*—a striking phrase[43]) are brought together as the common agents of the canonical task. Canonical legislation thus flows directly out of the evangelical and apostolic tradition, in a sweeping trajectory from Christ himself as its ultimate, albeit indirect, source, to the apostles and then, through an implied act of imitation, episcopal and pedagogical continuators. A similar sentiment will be expressed in another work ascribed to John Scholastikos, the introduction to the *Coll87*, *Εἰς δόξαν θεοῦ*, where the canons are described as "of the holy and blessed apostles and of those holy fathers who followed in their footsteps in each synod."[44] Canon law is thus an apostolic project continued by bishops meeting in synods—precisely as implied by the addition of the apostolic prefaces to the corpus, already remarked.

The basic context of this canonical work is then immediately made clear (4.3–5): the apostles and bishops have been entrusted "by grace" with shepherding the "multitude" of both the Jews and Gentiles who have "abandoned"

found in Appendix B. Russian translation: Zaozerski 1882; Latin: *Pitra* 2.375–8; partial German: Zachariä von Lingenthal 1877, 617.

39 On this point, see *Sin* 213. Beneshevich believes that this very complexity of diction and syntax may account for the text's stable transmission.

40 *Sin* 213 n. 1; some of Beneshevich's emendations are based on violations of this rhythm.

41 Page and line numbers are from *Syn*.

42 *οἱ τοῦ μεγάλου θεοῦ καὶ σωτῆρος ἡμῶν Ἰησοῦ Χριστοῦ μαθηταὶ καὶ ἀπόστολοι καὶ μὴν καὶ τῆς ἐκκλησίας αὐτοῦ τῆς ἁγίας οἱ μετ᾽ ἐκείνους καὶ κατ᾽ ἐκείνους ἀρχιερεῖς καὶ διδάσκαλοι...*

43 See Appendix B, n. 1 for an alternative translation.

44 ed. Heimbach 1838, at 208.

the "diabolical deception and tyranny" and have "of their own accord come to the King and Lord of Glory." The canonical task is thus firmly placed within a broad, indeed cosmic, narrative of salvation. The canons are part of the "shepherding" of the entire flock of the Christian people in their movement from the deception of the devil to the kingdom of God. Once again the strong metaphysical and eschatological horizons of the canons are apparent.

In 4.5–10, where we finally meet the main verb of the first sentence, the shepherd imagery is continued and now becomes the controlling metaphor. The apostles and bishops, far from seeking to harm wrongdoers, instead attempted to "brave dangers most readily for them" (προκινδυνεύειν δὲ μᾶλλον αὐτῶν ἑτοιμότατα). Here the Christo-mimetic imagery of the good shepherd laying down his life for the sheep is unmistakable, and quite remarkable, even paradoxical, as part of a reflection on the nature of the church's legal sanctions: instead of "harming," the bishops are supposed to be taking harm.[45] Canonical regulation is thus an aspect of self-sacrificial shepherding. The particular image and language here of προκινδυνεύειν, as a shepherding image, is not unknown in the literature, and will later appear in the 9th C *Eisagoge* as part of the ἴδιον, or "particular property," of bishops.[46]

Notably, the shepherd image is here developed with an explicit contrast with the civil laws: the civil laws harm wrongdoers, while the canons seek to guard, guide, and protect (4.5–7). The canonical project, as distinct from the civil laws, is essentially a pastoral task.

In the same phrase, language of pastoralism easily moves into road or way imagery: the apostles and bishops, "like the good shepherd," "hasten" to take care to guide and direct any wayward sheep that may be drifting from the straight path. The canons lead Christians on their correct way or path, a commonplace salvific image.

A smooth transition then occurs in the last clause of the first sentence from the image of legislators as good shepherds struggling (ἀγωνιζόμενοι) to keep their flock from harm to a set of medical images (4.10–14). In these images, probably still meant to stand in contrast with civil legality, the apostles and bishops are cast as interested only in the healing of spiritual illness, and the restoration of the sick to health. Just as the shepherd imagery is clearly biblical in its immediate inspiration, the medical imagery is also explicitly Christianized by an allusion to Ephesians 6: 17: the canonical legislator-healers wield "the knife of the Spirit, which is the word of God" (4.11). It is also notable that, at the same time, another figure, the Spirit, enters as a necessary coworker

[45] See John 10: 15 ff.

[46] *Eisagoge* 8.2. Other instances include Athanasius of Alexandria, *Apologia de fuga sua* 24 (4th C), Cyril of Alexandria, *Commentary on John* 2.235 (5th C), and Ignatius the Deacon, *Vita Tarasii patriarchae* 37 (9th C). A distant echo of the whole phrase may be found in Josephus, *Jewish Wars* 4.195.

with the fathers in the restoration of the sick: "Thus by the grace and co-working of the Spirit they restored to their first health those who were ill."

The next sentence (and the beginning of the third) turns to more mundane, but no less important, details of the "story" of the canonical legislators. We learn that the apostles and fathers have taken forethought for how those "after and like to them" (*μετ' ἐκείνους καὶ κατ' ἐκείνους*) might—to resume the pastoral purpose of the canons—keep those who are ruled "unharmed" (*ἀβλαβής*; 4.14–15). The means of this continuing pastoral care is made immediately clear: the convening of synods, which the "divine grace arranges" (*τῆς θείας χάριτος οἰκονομούσης*). The council is clearly assumed as the basic mode of legislation. "Grace" however, appearing here for the third time in the prologue, is an active agent in this process.

The fathers, the prologue continues, have thus at various times met in synods and there set forth certain "laws and canons, not civil but divine" (4.15–18). The terminology used for the legislation is significant: *νόμοι* and *κανόνες* are used virtually synonymously, and the former is clearly used to refer to ecclesiastical regulation (as also in line 4.21, and the rubric of *Coll50* 48). A distinction, however, is nevertheless once more made between civil and church laws, even if not as a terminological distinction between "laws" and "canons": the distinction is instead between "civil" and "divine."

The sentence ends with a series of short epexegetical phrases which gloss, or expand upon, the phrase "divine laws" (14.18–20). The first, "on what ought or ought not to be done" (*περὶ τῶν πρακτέων ἢ μὴ πρακτέων*), is a very stock phrase, a commonplace of legal definition broadly Stoic in origin and present perhaps most notably, and relevantly, in the second of the two Greek definitions of law in *Digest* 1.3.2 (that of Chrysippus): "the law . . . prescribes what ought to be done, and forbids what ought not to be done" (*ὁ νόμος . . . προστακτικὸν μὲν ὧν ποιητέον, ἀπαγορευτικὸν δὲ ὧν οὐ ποιητέον*).[47] Shorter versions, as found in this prologue, may be remarked in a variety of ancient authors.[48]

The glosses then continue with the assertion that the canonical work is directed towards the "life" (*βίος*) and "manner" (*τρόπος*) of each: its function is to rectify (*ἐπανορθόω*) both.[49] The canons thus have a very broad scope of action, encompassing life and morals. Road imagery then reappears as the canons "fortify" those on the "royal way," "punishing" those who "have fallen by the side." The verb "to punish," *ἐπιτιμάω*, may here already be a quasi-technical word for ecclesial punishment, although it and its nominal forms may be found as a reasonably normal word for "punish" or "penalize" in

[47] Frag. mor. 314, ed. von Arnim 1903, 3.77.

[48] See a list of such "Gebot–Verbot" phrases in Triantaphyllopoulos 1985, 82.

[49] For similar usage of this language in another regulative-legal context, see Demosthenes' definition of law cited below.

Greco-Roman literature.[50] In any case, although we learned earlier that the canons of the church do not aim to "harm" (*αἰκίζομαι*) wrongdoers (line 4.6), they do nevertheless punish or penalize them.

The first clause of the third sentence, the first part of the more technical section of the prologue, turns to the circumstances that have occasioned the present systematic work (4.20–1). The "laws and canons" are presented as having "of old" emerged as an essentially ad hoc activity: "issued by different men for different purposes and appropriate to different circumstances" (*κατὰ καιροὺς ὑπὸ διαφόρων πρὸς διαφόρους καὶ διαφόροις ἁρμόζοντες* [*οἱ νόμοι*]). This should probably be read as a very short but striking reminiscence of the topos of *varietas naturae* found in some legal prologues.[51] It has been suggested that this topos functions to justify legislative changes and developments.[52] Here, however, the phrase is used to justify John's *systematic* work: because of the variety of the laws, John needs to put everything in a more user-friendly form (4.22–5.2). This characterization of the canonical process is also significant in that the canons are not presented as the product of an intentional legislative program, but instead, as the prologue continues, as arising "as demanded by the emergence of matters at different times" (*ὡς ἀπῄτει τὰ κατὰ χρόνον ἀναφυόμενα*; see also a similar notion already in lines 4.15–16, *ἕκαστοι κατὰ καιροὺς ἰδίους εἰς ταὐτὸ συνιόντες*).

In the same sentence John quickly reviews the central sources of legislation, the apostles, the Ten Synods, and Basil (4.22–3), before continuing through to 5.16 with a more detailed description of his systematization. This section will be discussed in more detail in Chapter 4, but it may be remarked here that the overall tone of the section is curiously defensive. John not only seems to feel the need to stress repeatedly how chaotic the material is in origin (4.20–1, 24, earlier at 18, again in 5.3–4), but he strongly emphasizes—in a way difficult to capture in idiomatic English—how difficult it is to find anything (*ὡς ἐκ τούτου* ***δυσεύρετον*** *εἶναι* ***κομιδῇ*** *καὶ* ***δυσπόριστον*** *τὸ πρός τινων ἀθρόως περὶ κανόνος ἐπιζητούμενον*) and that he is not the first to do such a thing (*οὐκ* ***αὐτοὶ*** *τοῦτο* ***μόνοι*** *καὶ* ***πρῶτοι*** *ποιῆσαι τῶν ἄλλων ὁρμήσαντες*), but that because the previous attempt was defective, it nevertheless needs replacing (5.11–12). Once more, of course, everything, he notes, is done "by the grace of our lord and God and Savior Jesus Christ" (5.2–3). Most of these statements may be read as simple variations on justificatory and humility topoi, common for ancient introductions, but one may suspect a real unease in handling what was by this time already a very well-established and prominent corpus of texts. It seems that even the relatively innocuous work of systematization somehow

[50] Liddell–Scott–Jones 1996, 666–7, Lampe 1961, 537–8.

[51] e.g. in *Cordi* 4, *Tanta* 18, *N* 7.2.

[52] See Fögen 1987, 142; Honoré 1978, 27 n. 298, 299; Hunger 1964, 171–2; Simon 1994, 19. On the philosophical underpinnings of the topos, see esp. Lanata 1984, 165–87.

demands a defense. In fact Scholastikos' handling of the material in his collection is marked by extreme conservatism and scrupulous concern for completeness: as he is taking pains to stress, he will truly only make things easier to find.

The prologue concludes with a listing of its sources, including an "Order of Synods." As already noted, a rudimentary but clear hierarchy of sources is evident in this listing: the apostles are presented first, separate from the synods; then an "Order of Synods" with the synods listed by number; and then the legislation of Basil, also separate. The three are clearly distinct. The synods are in the Nicene order: Nicaea first, then everything else in chronological succession. Interestingly, within the synod listings, the canons are consistently described using the formula: "The canons [number] of the fathers in [a council]" (*Τῶν ἐν* [council] *πατέρων . . . κανόνες* [number]). As such, the agency of the "fathers" themselves is emphasized, and the difference from patristic regulations slightly elided. This is coherent with the usage of the rest of the prologue, where the agents of legislation are always either the "apostles" or the "fathers": the councils themselves are not agents. This curious literary feature—perhaps not of much significance in itself—may also be remarked in a set of iambic verses found concluding the *Coll50* in one manuscript ("The titles of the canons have thus ended/of the Apostles together with the Fathers"),[53] in the *Coll87* (cited above), and not infrequently elsewhere in the tradition.[54] The canons are prototypically of "the apostles" and/or "the fathers."

4. The prologues of the *Coll14*: Τὰ μὲν σώματα and Ὁ μὲν παρών

Three prologues (the last in two recensions) are associated with the *Coll14*. Two date from our period.[55] Their disposition in the manuscripts varies: the first may be found alone, the two may be found joined together, the two may be separated (in a variety of ways), or the second may be written as a scholion to the first.[56] In some editions they are printed as one text, in which case the first extends from *τὰ μὲν σώματα* to *μισθὸν ἀπενέγκασθαι*, and the second from *ὁ μὲν παρὼν* to *πρᾶξιν προήνεγκεν*.[57] It is generally accepted, following

[53] *Syn* 155, n. (a). [54] e.g. Chalcedon 1, Trullo 2, *N* 137.1.

[55] Sound critical editions do not exist for either. *Pitra* 2.445–51 remains the best. *Kormchaya* (1–4) also contains an edition of the first. There seem, however, to be no major variants among the MSS (Stolte 1998a, 187). An English translation of both may be found in Appendix B; Russian: Narbekov 1899, 2.7–19; Latin: *Pitra* 2.445–51; partial German: Zachariä von Lingenthal 1877, 619, 626–7.

[56] *Sbornik* 52–60, with examples. On the *Coll14* prologues generally, see Deledemos 2002, Menebisoglou 1989, Stolte 1998a.

[57] Most notably *RP* 1.5–9, as Voellus and Justel 1661, 2.789–95.

Beneshevich, that the traditional *Coll14* listing of the corpus sources, known by its incipit as ἐκ ποίων, was composed at the same time as Τὰ μὲν σώματα, but that the scholion ἰστέον ὅτι that is commonly found as part of the *Coll14* introductory complex and which discusses various violations of the chronological ordering of the councils in the list, namely the precedence of Nicaea, and the postpositioning of Carthage, Serdica, and Constantinople 394, was a later addition.[58] This scholion nevertheless became a regular part of the *Coll14* introductory tradition.

The first prologue presents something of a textual conundrum. Not all scholars are completely convinced that the text we have is the original.[59] The principal problem is that in its current form it seems to refer to the placing of the secular laws under their appropriate κεφάλαια or chapters—that is, in nomocanonical form (line 52[60]). If it is true, as is widely believed since the work of Zachariä von Lingenthal and Beneshevich, that the original *Coll14* was composed without any civil law placed under the titles, but only with some gathered in a separate work in an appendix (as the *Tripartita*), then the prologue as we possess it in all manuscripts must be interpolated. It is further curious that the dating of the council of Carthage (419) is incorrect (line 20). The council is presented as held under Honorius (r. 395–423) and Arcadius (r. 395–408)—clearly an error. This, however, is the correct dating for Constantinople 394 (dated according to consulships, while Theodosius was still alive),[61] a council that was very probably added to the corpus with the *Coll14*, but that is strangely not mentioned in the prologue. Here too, then, it seems possible that some type of elision or copyist error has occurred.[62] A subtler problem, not yet acknowledged in the literature it seems, is the prologue's assumption of the structure of the "Ten Synods" (lines 15–16). This structure, as known from the *Coll50*, placed Serdica after Neocaesarea and before Gangra.[63] Nowhere in the *Coll14* tradition, including the listing of the corpus sources in ἐκ ποίων, is such an ordering present.

None of these problems, however, is entirely decisive against the originality of the extant text. The reference to the κεφάλαια in line 52 does not absolutely need to refer to the *Coll14* titles. It is quite possible that it refers to the titles found in the *Tripartita* itself.[64] Further, although it is widely believed

[58] *Sbornik* 69–84.

[59] Most recently, Stolte 1998a, who draws attention to the following two points.

[60] Line numbers refer to the *Pitra* edition, counting down continuously, not including titles, headers, or footers.

[61] *Ἐπὶ ὑπατείας τῶν εὐσεβεστάτων καὶ θεοφιλεστάτων βασιλέων ἡμῶν, Φλαβίου Ἀρκαδίου, αὐγούστου τῷ τρίτῳ, καὶ Ὀνωρίου τῷ δευτέρῳ.* RP 3.625.

[62] So Honigmann 1961, 68–72; Menebisoglou 1989, 232–4; Stolte 1998a.

[63] *Syn* 4.22–3, 6.11.

[64] There was considerable controversy in the 19th C on how to read—and punctuate—this passage. See Narbekov 1899, 7–11, especially the references and discussion at p. 8 n. 2; more recently Menebisoglou 1989, 236–8 and Petrovitz 1970, 18–20, with further references. My

that the original *Coll14* was not nomocanonical in form, there is no absolute proof of this; it is still only a widely accepted assumption based upon the existence of some apparently very old recensions that do not contain civil laws.[65] Finally, the dating error of Carthage is not immense: the first *πράξις* is dated to Honorius and Theodosius (II)—the prologue only has the second name incorrect. Further, two of Carthage's *πράξεις are* dated to Honorius and Arcadius (those before canon 34 and 86). There is thus plenty of room for a simple slip. We need not imagine a major elision. As to the omission of Constantinople 394, it may have simply been considered too minor and innocuous an addition to mention (the additions mentioned explicitly by the prologue all have some controversy attached to them—this may not have been true of Constantinople 394), or it may have been added immediately after the prologue was composed. Finally, while the *Coll14* does not maintain the order of the Ten Synods, it does retain its content. Perhaps the order was insignificant. The extant prologue, then, may preserve the original text perfectly well.

In any case, the prologue clearly is pre-Trullan, and even if interpolated, it very likely dates at least to the early 7th C (i.e. the time of the proposed nomocanonical recension). Its author, like that of the *Coll14* itself, remains unknown.

The second prologue, happily, is dated explicitly to 6391, that is, 883 (lines 29–31). This is one of the very few firm dates that can be attached to any early Byzantine canonical collection. In some manuscripts this prologue is attributed to Photius; scholars are mixed in their acceptance of attribution. It is possible.[66]

The first prologue, *τὰ μὲν σώματα*, has the same basic structure as *οἱ τοῦ μεγάλου θεοῦ*. It begins with a "doctrinal" section (lines 1–17), moves to a technical discussion of the details of the collection's composition (lines 18–57), and then concludes with a list of sources (*ἐκ ποίων*). The second prologue consciously reads as an extension of the second, more technical part of the first prologue, but it does briefly reprise some "doctrinal" themes in its first sentence (lines 1–7) before turning to the practical details of its own additions (lines 8–50).

suggestion here seems resonant with Deledemos 2002, 92–3 and Menebisoglou 1989, 236–8, based on Zachariä von Lingenthal 1877, 619–20.

[65] Stolte 1998a, 186, 193 helpfully highlights this. Narbekov 1899, 5–8 *et passim* is perhaps the best discussion of the traditional arguments. My own investigation in Ch. 4 does confirm this assumption, inasmuch as I have discovered that Byzantine systematic rubrics are as a rule drawn very literally from the texts they subsume, and only in a very few cases do the *Coll14* rubrics seem to assume secular legal content—which strongly suggests that the systematic titles and chapters were constructed out of, and for, a canonical collection alone. See Ch. 4 F, esp. n. 78.

[66] References in Ch. 1, n. 112.

The doctrinal section of *τὰ μὲν σώματα*, like *οἱ τοῦ μεγάλου θεοῦ*, is written in a sophisticated Greek, albeit with fewer and less ornate periods. It unfolds as a series of two brief meditations on the law, both presented as the motivations for the collector's work.

The first (lines 1–11) is an extraordinary account of the anagogical ascent of the soul: in order for the soul to rise up towards "higher visions" (*ὑψηλότεραι θεωρίαι*), to enter the "heavenly vaults" and enjoy not just "shadows" but "truly good things" (*οἱ ὄντως ἀγαθοί*), and to have divine visions, it must be nourished with good thoughts and good deeds—which, it is implied, the canons promote.

No direct source in antique philosophical literature for the narrative as a whole, or even specific phrases, has yet been identified, but its content is an entirely conventional account of the soul's heavenly ascent, synthetic in orientation, but broadly (neo-)Platonic in diction, imagery, and ideas.[67]

The second section (lines 11–15) broaches the nature of law more directly. It is almost unique in the Byzantine tradition in providing something very close to a definition of the canons: the "divine decrees" (*θεσμοί*) are "a discovery and gift of God, the dogma of prudent and God-bearing men, the correction of willing and involuntary sins, and a secure rule for a way of living that is both pious and leads to eternal life."

There is nothing ambiguous about the ultimate source of this quotation: its pagan provenance is made quite explicit ("transferring to the divine statutes what was once said by one of the ancient *σόφοι*"). It is in fact a modified version of Demosthenes' famous definition of law in *Against Aristogeiton 1* 16.[68]

Like Chrysippus' definition of law, vaguely echoed in *οἱ τοῦ μεγάλου θεοῦ*, Demosthenes' definition may be found in Marcianus' *Institutes*, preserved alongside Chrysippus' in *Digest* 1.3.2. This does not mean that the *Digest* was the *Coll14* author's direct source for this passage.[69] True, a potential allusion to Chrysippus' definition in the last line of the sentence ("certain canon," *ἀσφαλῆ κανόνα*, not in Demosthenes, but recalling the *κανόνα δικαίων καὶ ἀδίκων* of Chrysippus), does perhaps point this way: both are held together in *Digest* 1.3.2, and both here. However, like the phrase of Chrysippus, Demosthenes' definition should be regarded as a legal commonplace. It may, for example, be found twice in the Hermogenian corpus of rhetorical works, the single most popular rhetorical corpus in the late imperial period—including once in the progymnastic exercise "Introduction of a Law" of Aphthonius, the most popular progymnastic handbook.[70] It will eventually

[67] Deledemos 2002, 79–80 detects a number of Platonic allusions, including *Phaedrus* 79b–e, 245–7; *Republic* 514–17 (and book seven broadly); *Timaeus* 90a–c.

[68] ed. Butcher 1907, 770–800.

[69] As Deledemos 2002, 81.

[70] Hermogenes, *On Ideas* 1.6 (ed. Rabe 1913, 213–413); Aphthonios, *Progymnasmata* 14 (ed. Rabe 1926, 1–51). In both places it is found in a truncated form, but it seems reasonably clear,

become a regular member of small groups of legal definitions in later Byzantine legal treatises.[71] Finally, it should also be recalled that Demosthenes himself was among the most important, popular, and well-read rhetors in the late imperial and Byzantine periods, and it is not impossible that the author took the extract directly from the original.[72]

In any case, the *Coll14* version of this definition differs from both the original and the form found in the *Digest*, as indicated in Table 2.1 (italics indicates modifications; boldface indicates additions):

Table 2.1 The Definition of Demosthenes.

Demosthenes *Against Aristogiton 1* 16	*Digest* 1.3.2 (compared with original)	*Coll14* (compared with original)
... πείθεσθαι προσήκει διὰ πολλά,	... προσήκει πείθεσθαι διὰ πολλὰ,	πεπεισμένος **τούτους**
καὶ μάλισθ' ὅτι πᾶς ἐστι νόμος εὕρημα μὲν καὶ δῶρον θεῶν,	καὶ μάλιστα ὅτι πᾶς ἐστιν νόμος εὕρημα μὲν καὶ δῶρον θεοῦ,	εὕρημα μὲν καὶ δῶρον **εἶναι** θεοῦ,
δόγμα δ' ἀνθρώπων φρονίμων, ἐπανόρθωμα δὲ τῶν ἑκουσίων καὶ ἀκουσίων ἁμαρτημάτων,	δόγμα δὲ ἀνθρώπων φρονίμων, ἐπανόρθωμα δὲ τῶν ἑκουσίων καὶ ἀκουσίων ἁμαρτημάτων,	δόγμα δὲ φρονίμων **τε καὶ θεοφόρων** ἀνθρώπων, ἐπανόρθωμα δὲ τῶν ἑκουσίων καὶ παρὰ βούλησιν ἁμαρτημάτων,
πόλεως δὲ συνθήκη κοινή, καθ' ἣν πᾶσι προσήκει ζῆν τοῖς ἐν τῇ πόλει	πόλεως δὲ συνθήκη κοινή, καθ' ἣν ἅπασι προσήκει ζῆν τοῖς ἐν τῇ πόλει.	καὶ πολιτείας **εὐσεβοῦς τε καὶ πρὸς ἀτελεύτητον** ζωὴν **ἀγούσης ἀσφαλῆ κανόνα**

Aside from a few minor stylistic features, the only substantial divergence of the *Digest* text from the original is the placing of "gods" in the singular. The *Coll14* text has also retained much of the substance of the original: the canons are ultimately divine in origin, they are the production of "wise men,"[73] and they correct the "wrongdoings" or "sins" of men. Nevertheless, a few important modifications have been made. First, the *Coll14* author adds "God-bearing" men. While laws are the decrees/judgments of wise men in general, the canons are those of God-bearing men, that is, of the Christian fathers who are saints.

especially in the first instance, that the author expects familiarity with the quotation. On this corpus in the later Greek east, see Jenkins 1963, 43–4; Kennedy 1983, 54 *et passim.*

[71] e.g. *Eisagoge* 1.1; *Epanagoge Aucta.* Proem.1; *Basilica* 2.1.13–14; *Ecloga Basilicorum* 2.1 13–14; *Prochiron Auctum* 40.53; Michael Attaliates, *Ponema* Proem.2; see Triantaphyllopoulos 1985, 10 for additional references.

[72] See his pre-eminence in Hermogenes' *On Style*, for example. Gibson 2002; Marrou 1948, 161–5; Kennedy 1983, 1994.

[73] We should probably not take this as a reference to Aristotelian "practical wisdom" (*Nic. Eth.* 6.5, 7). See Auberque 2008. Cf. however O'Meara 2003, 136–8.

Once again the canons emerge from the holy men of Christian tradition. More importantly, in the last phrase the notions of "life" and "city" take on a much more Christian ethical and theological/religious character. Gone is the notion of law as a "common agreement" (*συνθήκη κοινή*) for those living in a "city" (*πόλις*). Instead, the Chrysippian idea of law as a "rule" is invoked ("rule of what is just and unjust," *κανόνα τε εἶναι δικαίων καὶ ἀδίκων*)[74], but here, unlike in Chrysippus, it is a rule of a "pious," that is, properly religious, *way of life* (*πολιτεία*), that has an eternal end.

Across both parts of the introductory section of the prologue, then, the canons emerge as numinous and divine, sacred in origin, and clearly part of a dramatic eschatological ascent of the soul towards "higher visions"—and also oriented towards the whole moral "life" of their subjects.

After the Demosthenic definition the author rapidly moves to more practical issues, with the two preliminary meditations on the law presented as precisely the impetus and rationale for the author's eager endeavor in compilation: "considering these things . . . and persuaded that . . . I have with zeal attempted to gather . . . " (11–17). The description of the author's activities of compilation (15–18), although brief, is very similar to the corresponding section of Scholastikos, and may even suggest that a formula is being written to: the author (a) immediately turns to the question of sources, which (b) are introduced as arising in "different" times (with the same *διάφορος* vocabulary), and (c) the focus is the "Ten Synods." The author cannot resist, however, along the way, another quick epexegetical gloss of the purpose of the canons of these synods: they "confirm" the divine dogma of the church and are useful "teaching" for all (*ἐπὶ βεβαιώσει τοῦ σωτηρίου δόγματος καὶ χρηστῇ διδασκαλίᾳ πάντων ἀνθρώπων*). This could be read as a pairing of faith and moral discipline as twin subjects of the canons; in any case it again confirms the broad scope of the canons' potential subjects.

Unlike Scholastikos, the author then singles out three sources in a long source-critical aside: the apostles, Carthage, and the patristic material (18–41). Each seems to have excited some controversy, and the author feels obliged to justify their inclusion. Only the Ten Synods are admitted without question.

The Apostolic Canons are treated first, but quite summarily. The author simply notes that they will be included, "even if" some have thought them to be "controverted" (*ἀμφιβόλος*). Some hesitation about their authenticity is perhaps conceded: "the canons called 'of the holy apostles'" (*τοὺς* **λεγομένους** [*κανόνας*] *τῶν ἁγίων Ἀποστόλων*). The force of this phrase is hard to determine: does it denote "so-called" or simply "called"? In either case concerns about them are simply dismissed.

[74] *Digest* 1.3.2.

Carthage is treated at much greater length. The "synod in Carthage," the reader learns, is to be accepted, but only after a lengthy proviso on the local nature of some of its regulations, especially those regarding married clergy, which receive an elaborate critique (25–9). The general acceptance is explained, however, with an interesting aside: the author has found in them many things "that are able to contribute much that is useful for life" (*πολλά τε καὶ πόλλην ὠφέλειαν εἰσάγειν τῷ βίῳ δυνάμενα*) (21). Again, the scope of the canons extends to "life"—a very broad realm indeed.

Next, the propriety of accepting writings of individual fathers as canons is addressed (29–41). Their acceptance is clearly problematic, and the author admits knowing that both Basil and Gregory forbade canonical regulations from individuals: they should instead be issued by "many holy fathers coming together in the same place," testing and debating matters at length. Once again, then, as in the *οἱ τοῦ μεγάλου θεοῦ*, canons are clearly first and foremost conciliar canons; others must be justified. However, the author feels that patristic material contains much "piously said" that may still be regarded "in a certain way" as providing "a *typos* of rule" (*κανόνος τύπον*). A few reasons are offered. First, it is noted, the patristic writings often simply clarify the synodical material, and when they add something new they do not contain anything contradictory in either letter or meaning (56–62). (One may remark here the passing reference to the common rhetorical and legal hermeneutical categories of "letter" and "meaning," *κατὰ λέξιν ἢ νοῦν*.[75]) Furthermore—and this seems to be the clinching argument, built up in a series of dramatic clauses—patristic judgments are to be accepted because of the spiritual stature of the fathers, whose words "flash forth" with the light of the Holy Spirit (*ἔκ τε τῆς τῶν προσώπων ἀξιοπιστίας, ἔκ τε τοῦ πνευματικοῦ φωτὸς τοῦ κατ' ἐνέργειαν Θεοῦ τοῖς εἰρημένοις ἐπαστράπτοντος*) (39–41). Again, holiness of divine men and the action of the Holy Spirit emerge as key factors in legitimating canonical legislation.[76]

Having defended and outlined these three sources, the author then discusses the systematic work of dividing the material into fourteen chapters (41–57). Like Scholastikos, the author articulates this task with critical appraisal of "certain" forebears (*τινες τῶν πρώην*) (49–50). The author disapproves in particular of the tendency in older works to write out canons in full under the titles, instead of simply giving references to the appended

[75] On this very general rhetorical and philosophical concept, see Stroux 1949, Triantaphyllopoulos 1985, 23–4. Mitchell 2005 contains an interesting discussion of the concept in a patristics context.

[76] There is a certain irony here: the author's worry about the legitimacy of the patristic material is explicitly based in prohibitions from that very patristic material (Basil 47, Gregory 6). In a sense, the author assumes the authority of the canons whose authority he is debating. This once more confirms the overwhelming authority of tradition in the Byzantine legal world: tradition always trumps formalist niceties.

corpus. The former results in the repetition of canons, or even their fragmentation under different titles, which the author finds completely unjustified. This criticism is usually thought to refer to the *Coll50*, where canons are indeed written out in full under the titles instead of providing a straight corpus collection. However, it must be remarked that this is not a particularly good description of the *Coll50*. Scholastikos in fact very rarely repeats or divides a canon; he is much more remarkable for *not* repeating or dividing.[77] One may wonder then if these criticisms should be taken as more symbolic than concrete, a necessary element in a justification for anything new.[78] In any case, they do function to express a rather extraordinary conservatism vis-à-vis the integrity of the corpus: it is better to leave the corpus as it is, with only references in the titles.[79]

After a brief description of some secular-legal additions, the author concludes with a brief invocation for the success of the venture, with the help of God and the prayers of the saints (55–7). The author's assertion that his work is meant to provide "something useful," "mostly for himself," but also "for others," should be taken as a humility topos and not a doctrinal statement of the "private" nature of his collection.

The second prologue, *ὁ μὲν παρὼν πρόλογος*, written at least two centuries later, has as its main task the description of the additions of the 883 recension. It begins with a survey of the content of the first prologue. Echoing the first few lines of Scholastikos, the author portrays the canonical endeavor as constituting a continuous trajectory of development from the time of the apostles onwards (1–3). (The Apostolic Canons are accepted without comment, as we would expect by this time.) The original author is commended for diligence in gathering the synodal canons from apostolic times up until the "fifth" council—the priority of conciliar canons as "proper" canons is assumed—but the decision, and its criteria, to include some individual (*καθ' ἕνα*) authors is also approved (2–7).

[77] Variations exist across the manuscripts, but the following divisions or repetitions may be noted in the main text of *Syn*: Nicaea 6 is divided between titles 1 and 7; Serdica 3 is divided between titles 3 and 16, Serdica 11 is cited in full in title 3 and an extract is cited in title 47; the second part of Serdica 21 is cited in full in title 13 and the first part in title 48; Gangra 20 is cited with epilogue in 32 and without in 47; Antioch 2 is divided between titles 18 and 47; Basil 20 is repeated in full in titles 32 and 41; and Basil 62 is repeated in full in titles 41 and 44. In every case the divisions are very logical, and follow clean divides within the canons themselves (i.e. the canons address two different issues or contain two rules). Basil 62 is repeated because it contains the penalty referred to in Basil 63, which is found in title 44. The only true repetition is Basil 20 (on the case of a woman who leaves her husband), which seems to have been occasioned because of uncertainty about whether or not it refers to monastics in particular (because of the presence of the verb *ἀναχωρέω*), or is more general in scope—thus it is repeated under a monastic title, and a more generic marriage title.

[78] Cf. *Sin* 324–5, where Beneshevich sounds a slight note of hesitation about this attribution.

[79] I owe this point—the conservatism of the *Coll14* in comparison with the *Coll50* in the handling of sources—to unpublished comments of John Erickson.

Turning to its own content, a quasi-*varietas naturae* topos again briefly and obliquely emerges, with the typical διάφορος vocabulary. The author describes how since the first prologue many events "of life" have transpired, and synods have thus been convened for "various" reasons (8–9). Unlike the earlier prologues, however, this author now states that forebears will not be criticized—the author will instead happily follow in their footsteps, attaching the new material to the old.

The author then lists the edition's main additions: Trullo, II Nicaea, Protodeutera, and Hagia Sophia. The ordinal numbering is used for the ecumenical councils, and Trullo, as is common at this time, is termed "the sixth" council. One striking phrase emerges in the description of the contents of II Nicaea: its canons are presented as rectifying "the divine polity" (τὴν ἱερὰν πολιτείαν). It is tempting to hear in this phrase the conceptualization of the church as a "sacred polity," a state-like constitutional body. However, "sacred way of life," meaning the "Christian way of life" or "life of the church," is probably a more accurate rendering, and it may even refer to the life of the empire as a whole. Another possible reference is monasticism, as II Nicaea does contain an important series of monastic canons, from 17 to 22.[80] Whatever the case may be, if it does bear any of the stronger, more constitutional connotations of "sacred polity," it is one of the very few references of its kind in the canonical literature.[81]

The prologue concludes with a short mention of the addition of certain secular legal precepts, and a careful dating.

5. The Trullan complex

It is fitting that the first canonical legislation after a hiatus of almost 250 years should be prefaced by an elaborate introductory complex. In this respect, as in others, Trullo may be read as recapitulative and retrospective in tone, symbolically taking stock of the tradition as a whole up until the present, but now creatively re-expressing and reformulating it.

The introductory complex is threefold, containing a prologue-like προσφωνητκὸς λόγος and two introductory canons surveying orthodox doctrine (Trullo 1) and the canonical corpus (Trullo 2).[82] This structure is clearly evident as unified whole in the many manuscripts where canons 2 and 3 are

[80] See the similar usage in Diadochus, *Capita centum de perfectione spirituali* 51; John Climacus, *Scala paradisi* 26. The particular constructions in ὁ μὲν παρὼν—οὐκ ὀλίγους τῶν τὴν ἱερὰν πολιτείαν ἐπανορθούντων θέσμους—perhaps should incline us in this direction, as it suggests that the author is singling out one specific type of regulation.

[81] Another may be found in Blastares *RP* 6.1, although here too "way of life" or "life" may be a better translation; but see Viscuso 1989, 206–7.

[82] The best text is now Nedungatt and Featherstone 1995, a slightly corrected version of *Fonti*.

separated by the topical rubric "On priest and clerics" (περὶ ἱερέων καὶ κληρικῶν), referring to canons 3–39.[83] This gap breaks the introductory complex off from the main body of canons, and reveals the true structure of Trullo: a century of "proper" canons (3–102) prefaced by the λόγος and two introductory canons.[84]

The first element in the manuscripts, the προσφωνητκὸς λόγος (*Τῆς ἀῤῥήτου καὶ θείας χάριτος* . . .) is, in genre, a standard address to the emperor requesting his ratification of the council's work. It is modeled on the much shorter προσφωνητκόν found in the manuscripts before Constantinople I, which is cited verbatim at the conclusion of the Trullan text (54.18–55.7).[85] Although ultimately focused on the emperor and the matter of ratification, and thus not a prologue in quite the same sense as the previous texts, it nevertheless offers a dense and extended representation and contextualization of the council's canonical work.

Like the earlier prologues, the Trullan *logos* is characterized by a sophisticated literary style, with numerous complex periods. Its general composition, however, differs from these earlier works (and particularly the first *Coll14* prologue) in one fundamental way: unlike the earlier prologues, it employs scripture intensely, with numerous direct quotations and allusions.[86] It may, in fact, be characterized as chiefly an exercise in the scriptural glossing of the canonical process and its key agents: the bishops and the emperor. This difference finds an analogue in the much greater use of scripture and scriptural imagery in later Byzantine secular legal prefaces as compared with Justinian's prologues.[87] It is part of a much broader "scripturalization"—and especially "Old Testamentization"—of discourse sometimes noted in the late 6th and early 7th C, both east and west.[88]

The logos may be divided into four sections. In the first (45.17–49.12) the canons are set into a detailed narrative of salvation history, similar to that

[83] On these rubrics, see Ch. 4, n. 114.

[84] On the genre of the century, originally monastic in origin, see Louth 2007. That the λόγος and the first two canons were seen as forming a whole is witnessed by a 13th C letter of Nicholas the Chartophylax which casually refers to Trullo 2 as part of the "προοίμιον" of the sixth synod (*RP* 5.401: ὧν καὶ τὸ κατ' ὄνομα [referring to the list of the names of the local councils and patristic sources] ἐν τῷ προοιμίῳ τῆς ς' συνόδου . . . εὑρήσεις.). See also Mardirossian 2010, 261 n. 2 and Ohme 2006, 46 on these canons as introductory.

[85] Page and line references to Nedungatt and Featherstone 1995.

[86] It contains at least fifteen direct quotations, noted in Nedungatt and Featherstone 1995. The first "doctrinal" section of the *Coll14*, in contrast, aside from the reference to Demosthenes as one of those "from outside," contains virtually nothing overtly Christian. The *Coll50* prologue confines its scriptural texturing to allusions.

[87] It begins intensely with the *Ecloga*, and is very prominent in the introductions to the *Prochiron* and *Eisagoge*. See Scharf 1959, 70–2. For the more generic appeals to the divine in the Justinianic prologues, see the references in n. 119, below.

[88] In the west, see Kottje 1970; for the east, Pieler 1997 and also, with further references, the comments of Brandes 2002, 19 on the "Davidic ideology" of the Heraclean period.

glimpsed in *Coll50* (3–5), but now finding much fuller expression. The section begins with a brief summary of Christ's salvific work and its consequences: the truth has come to all, the first serpent, "the great mind, the Assyrian," has been captured, and proper worship established (45.17–47.10)—"in short, all has become new" (2 Cor. 5:17). "But" (47.11) the devil, enraged by our salvation, has not ceased from trying to attack us. His attacks are realized, in particular, by means of our passions (*τὰ παθή*) (47.21), and thus have a strongly moral dimension. But God, the author continues, has not overlooked our helplessness, and has raised up in "each generation" (48.6–7) those who "in the stadium of life" fight against the devil. These "leaders of the flock" (48.15)—at this point the author reprises the shepherd and road imagery, and the "spiritual knife," of *οἱ τοῦ μεγάλου θεοῦ*—draw upon the "knife of the spirit, which is the word of God," and wrestle with the evil one, shattering his "tyranny" and "setting us straight upon the road of the Lord," lest we slip (*διολισθάνω*) down the "cliff of lawlessness (*ἀνομία*)" because of "ignorance of the better" (48.15–19).

This last idea, that moral corruption is connected to ignorance, a standard Platonic notion, introduces the concept of canons-as-teaching, which the next sentence (48.20–49.12) develops in an even more manifestly philosophical direction: while we have been granted being (*εἶναι*) by God, it is also necessary that he show us the path to well-being (*εὖ εἶναι*), and this he has, in fact, done "through the luminaries and teachers of the church, who illuminate (*φωταγωγέω*) for us the ways of God and urge us towards the Gospel—and whose 'citizenship is in the heavens' [Phil. 3: 20], according to the divine apostle." Canonical work is thus the (philosophical) work of divine teachers, understood in highly moral terms, aimed at leading us to "well-being."

"Whence," the second section (49.13–51.12) begins, Christ, the "helmsman of that great ship of the present cosmos,"[89] has appointed the emperor as a pilot (*κυβερνήτης*) over us. We, it turns out, have been living "quite lazily" (*τὸν οἰκεῖον βίον διεξάγουσι ῥᾳθυμότερον*), and our virtue (*ἀρετή*) has been slowly stolen by the enemy (49.13–19). The emperor's office is then extensively glossed by a series of scriptural and standard Greco-Roman and Christian gubernatorial metaphors and epithets: the emperor is pious, "working judgment and justice in the midst of the earth," "walking in a blameless way" (Ps. 118: 1 LXX, significantly the beginning of the great "law Psalm"), born from wisdom, full of the divine spirit, the eye of the *oikoumene*, meditating on the law night and day (Ps. 1: 2), and so on. Finally the central point is made: given all of these qualities, the emperor is not only to look to his own life, but

[89] *ὁ . . . πηδαλιουχῶν . . . Χριστὸς*. This is the most likely source of both the title "Pedalion" and frontispiece image of the famous canonical edition of Nikodemus the Hagiorite (Kallivourtsis 1800), despite speculation of an origin from the Slavonic кормчая (on which, Černyševa 1998, Žužek 1964, 10–13).

to the preservation of all of his subjects from "turbulence of transgressions" and the "spirits of evil" (τὰ πνεύματα τῆς πονηρίας) (51.4–12)—that is, he is concerned to support the canonical task of the council. Metaphysical and soteriological concerns once again form the natural backdrop of canonical work.

In the third section (51.13–54.7) the transition is made to recent history, and the more concrete details of the council's request. The author begins by noting that the last two ecumenical councils had not issued canons, and the result has been corruption and decay (51.13–52.20). Then another of the very few quasi-definitions of the canons to be found in the tradition is offered:

> [the fifth and sixth councils did not write canons] through which the people might desist from their worse and lowly conduct and might be brought to a better and loftier life; and thence it follows that the holy nation, the royal priesthood [1 Pet. 2: 9] on whose behalf Christ died, is torn asunder and led astray by the many passions resulting from lack of order (ἀταξία) and is detached little by little and cut off from the divine fold, having slipped away from the achievements of virtue through ignorance and neglect; in the words of the apostle: "They have spurned the Son of God, profaned the blood of the covenant by which they were sanctified, and outraged the Spirit of grace" [Heb. 10: 29]. (52.3–20; trans. Nedungatt and Featherstone, modified)[90]

Again a rich tapestry of now familiar concepts of behavior, morality, life, virtue, and good order are cast as in the natural purview of canonical legislation. The absence of canonical regulation is notably quite serious: it results in behavior that treats the blood of the covenant as "common," and—with dramatic stress in the Greek, as here the main verb of the sentence is finally reached—it is an insult to the grace of the Spirit. The canons do not, evidently, treat of inconsequential and mundane matters.

The emperor, the treatise continues (52.20–53.16), in imitation of the Good Shepherd, has fortunately desired to gather again the "special people" (περιούσιον λαὸν; Deut. 14: 2/Tit. 2: 14) and persuade them to keep the "commandments and divine ordinances" (τὰς ἐντολάς τε καὶ τὰ θεῖα προστάγματα)—and thus he has called the ecumenical council. This vocabulary strongly suggests the assimilation of the canons to Old Testament regulations, and the emperor appears almost Moses-like. In the same passage, however, these commandments, as we read, also move in a New Testament valence: they "remove us from dead works," and "make us alive" (cf. Heb. 9: 14).

After a few more biblical glosses of conciliar process, the formal request for the emperor to ratify their canons is made (54.8–55.7), concluding the *logos*.

Trullo 1, the first introductory canon, is a lengthy survey of doctrinal heresy, and the history of its condemnation in the ecumenical councils. It is most interesting for its opening articulation of the precedence of doctrinal matters

[90] ed. Nedungatt and Featherstone 1995, 52.3–20.

in canonical regulation. It begins: "The best order when beginning any treatise or matter is to begin with God and to end with God, according to the words of the Theologian." This line is an explicit and literal borrowing from Gregory of Nazianzus.[91] Trullo must begin with properly "theological" matters, that is, doctrinal matters relating to God, and it does. The rest of the canon is a lengthy profession of faithfulness to tradition, listing and reaffirming the condemnations of every ecumenical council to date.

The second canon, already briefly discussed, is of most interest for our purposes. Indeed, as the only conciliar articulation of the Byzantine canonical corpus, this canon is one of the most commented upon in modern Orthodox canonical literature.

The canon begins as a continuation of the first: "And this also seemed good, that . . . " (*ἔδοξε δὲ καὶ τοῦτο . . . ὥστε . . .*). The two are, in a sense, written as a pair. Unlike the first canon, however, its stated primary intention is not to provide a general survey but, as already noted, to condemn the *Apostolic Constitutions* and to confirm and clarify the acceptance the Apostolic Canons. The criterion for the acceptance of these canons is entirely traditional: they have been "received" and "ratified" (*κυρωθέντας*) by the "holy and blessed fathers." Once more the canons are the product of the "divine fathers."

Within the initial section of this canon is a short, easily missed articulation of the purpose of the canons: "[the canons are] for the healing of souls and curing of passions" (*πρὸς ψυχῶν θεραπείαν καὶ ἰατρείαν παθῶν*) (64.20–65.1). Once again the discourse of healing emerges, along with the moral concepts of the "passions" and the "soul." This medical imagery will be briefly reprised at the very end of the canon: one who tampers with a canon will be subject to the penalty that canon pronounces, "thus being healed (*θεραπευόμενος*) by that in which he stumbles" (69.8–9).

Once the immediate subject of the canon is addressed, the canon moves on to "seal" the rest of the corpus: "we seal also the remaining sacred canons" (*ἐπισφραγίζομεν δὲ καὶ τοὺς λοιποὺς πάντας ἱεροὺς κανόνας*). A list of sources then follows, which, as already discussed, is little more than the table of contents of the *Coll14*. The councils are again listed in the form that stresses patristic agency, as in the *Coll50*: the canons of the "x" fathers, gathered in "y" place. In no case is the number of canons indicated: these are, it seems, too well known. (They are, in any event, enumerated in the traditional *Coll14* table of contents (*ἐκ ποίων*), which the canon likely presumes.)

[91] Gregory Naz. *Apologetical Oration* 2.1 (*PG* 35.408–513). The sentiment is something of a commonplace. See e.g. the opening lines of Charondas' *Prooimion* or of the (Ps.-)Pythagorean Golden Verses (ed. Thom 1995, with commentary and references pp. 104–6).

6. II Nicaea 1

The final major introductory structure within the corpus is also one of the most intriguing. Like Trullo 2 and Chalcedon 1, II Nicaea 1 is broadly a "confirmation" canon, affirming the corpus. Its emphasis, however, is even more obviously on confirming loyalty *to* the tradition than validating or authorizing the tradition per se. Its chief concern is to exhort the clergy to canonical obedience, an idea that is continued in II Nicaea 2, which mandates (among other types of knowledge) canonical learning for the episcopate.

Like Trullo's *logos*—but even more so—the canon is dominated by scriptural references. These references are artfully employed to assimilate the canons to the scriptural texts.

The canon begins with the assertion that "the patterns of the canonical constitutions are the testimonies and instructions for those who have received the priestly dignity" (*τοῖς τὴν ἱερατικὴν λαχοῦσιν ἀξίαν μαρτύριά τε καὶ κατορθώματα αἱ τῶν κανονικῶν διατάξεών εἰσιν ὑποτυπώσεις*). The term *μαρτύρια*, "testimonies," is a common biblical term for "laws": the canons are in effect biblical laws for the clergy. The biblical origin of the former term is made immediately explicit by a series of glosses from Psalm 118 (LXX) each of which mentions "testimonies" (vss. 14, 138, and 144 combined, and, allusively, 141):

> which [the "patterns of the canonical constitutions"] gladly receiving we sing to the master with the God-revealing David "I delight in the way of your **testimonies** as upon great wealth" and "you have commanded justice, your **testimonies** unto the ages; give me understanding and I will live forever" and "unto the ages" the prophetic voice has commanded us "to keep the **testimonies** of God and to live by them."

The clergy are thus exhorted to embrace "gladly" the canonical constitutions just as David embraced the testimonies (*μαρτύρια*) of the law—a message significantly conveyed by Psalm 118, the classical Davidic meditation on the law. Characteristics of the Old Testament law are also now subtly transferred to canon law: they are eternal and they pertain to justice and "life"—indeed, to eternal life ("I will live forever"). The effect is a quite blatant and striking assimilation of canon law to the Old Testament law. (The general association of law with "life" and "living," already remarked, is also worth noting again.)

This literary assimilation is heightened in the next line, where the clergy are exhorted to maintain the canons unchangeably,[92] "because the God-seeing Moses thus says 'it is not possible to add anything to them nor to take anything

[92] *ἀκράδαντα καὶ ἀσάλευτα*, "unshaken and unmoved." A very rare pair that, curiously, also occurs in Philo, *Life of Moses* 2.14, in precisely the context of describing Moses as the ideal lawgiver and his laws as eternal and unchangeable.

away from them.'" This citation comes from another significant Old Testament legal source, Deuteronomy, and is nothing other than Moses' injunction not to add to or take away from the law (Deut. 4: 2; 12: 32; note that the first, especially, is in a preface-like position in Deuteronomy; cf. also Rev. 22: 18–19). In Trullo 1 it had been applied only to doctrine, but here it is applied to the canons.

The climax of the section is reached when New Testament passages are applied to the canons. Here 1 Peter 1: 12 and Galatians 1: 9—"'into which things angels long to look' and 'if an angel should preach to you another gospel contrary to that which you received, let him be anathema'"—are cited. In their original setting these passages refer to the Gospel message. Here they are made to refer to the canonical regulations. The anathema reserved for those who preach a different gospel is now referred to those who violate the canons. The canons have been assimilated even to the Gospel.

In the second section, marked by "these things being so" (*τούτων οὖν οὕτως ὄντων*), the canon turns to its listing of the canonical sources, which the authors now "embrace to our bosom with gladness." Once again, however, a final reference to Psalm 118 is interjected, applied to the canons, now glossing the "embracing" of the canonical tradition by the council: "rejoicing in them as one who finds great spoil" (Ps. 118: 162). Then follows a listing of the elements of the corpus, but only in broad groups: apostles, six ecumenical synods, local synods, and fathers. (This is the first witness for the "Tarasian" order dividing general and local councils.) The church, the canon makes very clear, adheres to these in their completeness ("we hold fast to their commandment, complete and unshakable"), "for"—in another dramatic statement of the canonical sources' divine and spiritual origins—"they [the sources] have all shone forth from one and the same spirit." Inspired by the "same" spirit, all of the traditional sources are authoritative, and all must be adhered to in their integrity.

The canon concludes with a clever literary appropriation of a conciliar topos of loyalty to tradition. Throughout the conciliar tradition it is common to proclaim that, "as the fathers have condemned [such and such] . . . so we also condemn . . . "[93] This is an important way in which the councils articulate their fidelity to, and continuity with, traditional teaching, as the members of the councils are carefully locating their pronouncements within the trajectory of traditional articulations of the faith. Here, however, the canon creates a canonical version of these mimetic phrases, mimicking this formulation with the four most common canonical punishments: anathema, deposition, excommunication, and "penance" (*ἐπιτίμια*). Thus, the canon continues, "those whom they placed under anathema, so we anathematize, and those under

[93] e.g. in Trullo 1; but see e.g. *ACO* 1.1.7.66 or *ACO* 4.1.2.9.

deposition, so we depose, and those under excommunication, so we excommunicate, and those given over to penance, we subject to the same penance." The message is clear: the council of II Nicaea is entirely loyal to the ancient canonical tradition.

The canon then immediately concludes with a citation of Hebrews 13: 5: "for 'let your manner be free from love of money, content with what you have' (ἀφιλάργυρος γὰρ ὁ τρόπος, ἀρκούμενοι τοῖς παροῦσιν), clearly proclaims the divine apostle Paul, who ascended to the third heaven and heard unutterable words." The point of this concluding passage is a little obscure, and even the 12th C Byzantine commentators seem unsure what to make of it. Zonaras' suggestion, that it is meant ("I think") to imply that the canons are not to be added to, on the model of someone who is always grasping to add more money to their store, is quite likely.[94] This reading is coherent with the earlier citations from Deuteronomy, and the immediately preceding professions of mimetic loyalty. It is obviously not, however, intended as a categorical, doctrinal prohibition of future legislation: this canon is, it must be remembered, followed by twenty-one new canons. Instead, it is a simple admonition to continued loyalty to the traditional corpus. No *other* corpus is to be admitted, nor any other irregular additions. In this, it sums up the whole canon nicely: in accordance with scripture, one is to be entirely "content" with, and loyal to, that which has been handed down. The canons must be maintained and adhered to in a fashion appropriate to their dignity, which—the message of the canon as a whole—is nothing other than quasi-scriptural.

7. Minor texts

A few minor introductory structures may be found within the corpus. Some are little more than phrases in introductory sections of canons, while others are more substantial. All witness to important elements of the broader Byzantine conceptualization of canon law.

Within the conciliar sources, four texts possess formal introductory structures. The most elaborate of these is the oldest, a synodal letter from the bishops at Gangra to their brethren in Armenia. It includes both a section before the canons, and a closing epilogue. The former details the circumstances of the synod, listing the problems that provoked its disciplinary decisions (curiously, in a slightly different order than the canons that address these problems). This list concludes with a significant summary of the Eustathians' misbehavior: "For each of them, since they went out from the ecclesiastical canon (ἐπειδὴ τοῦ κανόνος τοῦ ἐκκλησιαστικοῦ ἐξῆλθεν), kept

[94] *RP* 2.559; Balsamon simply repeats Zonaras. Aristenos seems to paraphrase it in the same way, although his meaning is not entirely clear. *RP* 2.560.

their own individual laws (νόμους ἰδιάζοντας ἔσχεν), for there was no common opinion among them, but whatever each one conceived, this he added to the slander (διαβολή) of the church and to his own harm." The flow of associations is notable: to fall away from the general "ecclesiastical canon," here in the sense of a general rule of church order, is to set up "laws" for oneself (although νόμοι here may incline towards its sense of "customary practices") and to fall into individualistic ideas, which in turn leads to shame for the church and harm to oneself. Proper church order thus implies a unified and common set of regulations, and violations of this end in both slandering of the church and personal harm.

Following the canons, the lengthy epilogue (starting "we write these things," ταῦτα δὲ γράφομεν) clarifies the council's position: the bishops are not condemning asceticism per se, simply its excesses. One phrase is of particular interest. The council is condemning those who "are introducing novelties against both the scriptures and the ecclesiastical canons." The pairing of "scriptures" and "ecclesiastical canons" is significant: the two apparently constitute basic reference points for the question at hand, separate but clearly complementary. (The use of the singular, generic "ecclesiastical canon" in the preface, and the plural "ecclesiastical canons" here, is also notable; the two usages are obviously interchangeable, or at least not mutually exclusive, even if neither is necessarily referring to concrete written regulations.[95] The "canon" implies "canons" (I will return to this in Chapter 3)). Finally, all errors are innovations: καινισμοί. Right regulations are traditional. The whole sentiment is echoed again in the epilogue's concluding sentence: "and so, in summary, we pray that everything that has been handed down from the divine scriptures and the apostolic traditions be observed in the holy church." Proper discipline—as expressed by the council in its canons—is above all part of faithful adherence to scriptural and apostolic traditions.

The next introductory structure of the corpus, the letter prefacing Antioch, is notable most immediately for its very strong rhetoric of unity of mind and harmony (ὁμονοία and συμφωνία), all common concepts in late Greco-Roman discourse of governance and order.[96] The canons apparently both effect and presume harmony. Also prominent is a sense of the Spirit/God's agency: the "grace and truth" of Jesus are thus the immediate subject of the "correction" of matters in Antioch, binding the church together in unity with harmony and concord "and a spirit of peace"; indeed, "in everything" correction has been accomplished "by the assistance of the holy and peace-giving Spirit." The

[95] Cf. Ohme 1998, 401.

[96] The latter most famously in *N* 6pr; also e.g. *N* 132pr. On the former concept especially, see Schofield and Rowe 2000, *passim*. In the canonical literature ὁμονοία may also be found in the Prosphonetikos of Constantinople 381, Apostolic 34, and Carthage *acta* proceeding 66 (ἁρμονία here), *acta* proceeding 86, 134.

council has thus gathered as "believing in the grace of Christ and the Holy Spirit of peace, that you yourselves [the letter's recipients] will also be of the same spirit (*συμπνεύσητε*), united to us in and present together with the Holy Spirit and thinking the same thing with us... sealing and confirming that which has seemed correct to us by the concord of the Holy Spirit." Canonical legislation is overwhelmingly a task of the Holy Spirit, both in its formation and its acceptance.

The short *προσφωνηκτικόν* of Constantinople, requesting the emperor's ratification of the council's canons, is perhaps most notable for a short gloss to explain the purpose of the canons: "for the good order (*εὐταξία*) of the churches." The canons are for the "good order" of the church. The concept of *εὐταξία* is commonplace in Greco-Roman political discourse; *τάξις* language has in fact already been encountered several times in the foregoing texts. Also of interest is the basic subdivision of the council's work: first, the bishops explain, after "renewing harmony with each other" (harmony language again), they "ratified the faith" of Nicaea, and "anathematized heresies that have appeared against it," and then, "in addition to these things... we defined the said canons." Here once again "faith" or doctrine and "canons" appear held together as a pair as the two fundamental tasks of a council—the former, of course, clearly pre-eminent.

Carthage, a compilation of compilations, is quite complex in its historical composition.[97] Happily, it presents itself rather simply in the corpus, as a dossier of material from the council of 419 (treating the Apiarian affair) at which are "read" two series of canons, the first from the Apiarian council itself (1–33), and the second (34–133) a compilation of earlier African councils, separated by short introductory *acta* extracts.[98] The Apiarian *acta* themselves enclose these two "readings," before and after.

As a compiled whole, the most important introductory material is the first two canons, extensions of the first set of Apiarian *acta*. Their content is simple and unsurprising: the first, an assertion of Aurelius, the council president, exhorts the council to accept the definitions of Nicaea, creed and canons, just read in the proceeding acts; the second, the response of the bishops, confirms both that the faith/creed "handed down" is to be confessed, and "then," second, that the "ecclesiastical order" is to be maintained. Faith/doctrine and canonical order are thus once more held together as a natural pair for conciliar action. Here both canons cover, in a sense, the same ground as Trullo 1 and 2—confirmation of the faith and then canons—but in a very abbreviated form.

[97] See esp. Cross 1961; the synoptic table in *Fonti* 1.2.194–6 is extremely helpful.

[98] The first series is prefaced at *Fonti 1.2*.214.1–6 by *ἔπειτα τὰ ἐν ταῖς συνόδοις τῆς Ἀφρικῆς νομοθετηθέντα τοῖς παροῦσι πεπραγμένοις ἐντιθέμενα γινώσκονται*. The second at 1.2.249.3–5 by *ἀνεγνώσθησαν ἔτι μὴν ἐν ταύτῃ τῇ συνόδῳ διάφοροι σύνοδοι πασῆς τῆς τῶν Ἄφρων χώρας*. These headings likely originated in the Dionysian recension. See Ch. 1 C.

Finally, Chalcedon 1 may be read as a quasi-introductory structure. It too is a short confirmation canon: "We have judged it right that the canons set forth by the holy fathers in each synod until now remain in force." Its probable referent has already been discussed in Chapter 1. Introducing collections with a source discussion has already been remarked in Trullo 2 and II Nicaea 1, as well as the systematic prologues, and is, as we will see in Chapter 4, not unusual in the broader Greco-Roman legal tradition. Once more we may note the usage of referring to the canons as "of the holy fathers" *in* synods: the canons are always first and foremost productions of "the fathers."

Introductory structures of a sort may also be found within the patristic canons. Four sources are particularly significant in this regard: Cyril, Basil, Gregory of Nyssa, and Dionysius.

In Cyril, this "introduction" is simply a brief and elegant introductory sentence to his letter to Domnus, commenting upon the function of canonical order: "Each of our affairs, when properly transacted according to good canonical order (*κανονικὴ εὐταξία*), breeds for us no trouble and delivers us from the slander (*δυσφημία*) of any, but rather procures for us praise (*εὐφημίας*) from right-thinking men." Here again the language of *εὐταξία* emerges, but also now closely connected with shame/honor language: good canonical order brings *εὐφημία*, bad, *δυσφημία*.

The Basilian corpus contains three more substantial framing structures: a preface each to letters 188 and 199, and then canon 84 itself, the last canon in letter 217, which functions as an epilogue.

In both epistolary prefaces the central emphasis is teaching. The theme is only briefly treated in the simple and short preface to letter 199, where Basil commends Amphilochius' desire to learn—especially as Amphilochius (as a bishop) has been entrusted with teaching (2.117.5–16). The preface to 188 is more involved. Teaching is again the immediate focus, but now set in the (biblical) context of acquiring wisdom: "Wisdom will be reckoned to the foolish person who asks questions" (Prov. 17: 28). Amphilochius is asking a question in order to gain wisdom: canonical knowledge, the response, is apparently a matter of wisdom (*σοφία*), and it must be taught. Basil then notes that he too, in this process, becomes wiser in his efforts to answer, "learning many things I do not know" (*πολλὰ ὧν οὐκ ἐπιστάμεθα διδασκόμενοι*). Here Roy Deferrari has deftly detected an important allusion to a saying of Solon: "I grow older always learning many things" (*γηράσκω δ' ἀεὶ πολλὰ διδασκόμενος*).[99] Consciously, or even unconsciously, Basil is presenting himself and his work as an imitation of *the* great Athenian lawgiver—and, more so, in precisely the aspect as a learning/learned

[99] Deferrari 1926, 7 n. 1. The reference may be found in collections of apophthegmata attributed to Solon as one of the "seven sages" (ed. Mullach 1860, 219–35); it may also be found cited in Plato, *Laches* 189a, Plutarch, *Life of Solon* 31, and elsewhere.

lawgiver-sage. The basic theme of lawgiving as wisdom learning/teaching is thus subtly, but very effectively, enunciated.

The phrases "learning many things I do not know" is not simply a rhetorical flourish. Basil uses it to introduce his intended methodology in issuing his answers, revealed in the next few lines. Basil states that he is going to learn from Amphilochius' questions because he himself will try to "remember" if he had ever heard something on the questions from the "elders," and, if not, to reason out to similar conclusions from what he has been taught. Basil's wisdom-lawgiving activity is thus primarily about making recourse to the tradition, remembering it, and then reasoning from that tradition when it is silent on particular questions. Strikingly, many of Basil's canons do in fact read as conveying traditional regulations and commentating on those regulations.[100] His own work enacts the idea that law is very much about remembering and learning from tradition, and then talking around and about that tradition.

Gregory of Nyssa's canonical letter represents one of the most sophisticated and complex texts in the Byzantine canonical tradition.[101] Its lengthy introduction sets the canons in a dramatic context: the liturgical celebration of Pascha (Easter). Gregory begins by noting that one aspect of Pascha is that the church can "perceive the lawful and canonical *oikonomia* of those who have committed transgressions (*τὸ κατανοῆσαι ἡμᾶς τὴν ἔννομόν τε καὶ κανονικὴν ἐπὶ τῶν πεπλημμεληκότων οἰκονομίαν*), so that every spiritual weakness that has occurred by some sin may be healed." (*Fonti* 2.203.16–20). He explains further that Pascha, as the feast of the resurrection (*ἀνάστασις*) of the fallen, is thus also the moment of the rectification (*ἀνόρθωσις*) of those who have sinned, when not only the new catechumens are baptized, but penitents are reconciled to the church: "those who through repentance and turning from dead works return to the living road" and "are led to the saving hope." (204.10–19) In light of this, he concludes, it is his task to present a coherent and systematic account of the weaknesses that lead to penance, and how they may be healed. The rest of the letter proceeds through each of the faculties of the soul, prescribing the correct canonical medicine for each sin or "disease."

Gregory's letter thus presents canonical work as intimately intertwined with two major discourses. The first is the central salvific discourse of Christianity itself: death and resurrection, and particularly as mediated and experienced in the church's central liturgical experience, Pascha. The basic penal dynamic of the canons, excommunication, is thus significantly glossed as nothing other than a metaphorical movement from death to life, "a turning from dead works to the living road" (*ἐπιστροφῆς ἀπὸ τῶν νεκρῶν ἔργων εἰς τὴν ζῶσαν ὁδὸν*)

[100] Most notably Basil 1, 8, 9, 13, 18, 21, 30, 34, 47, 50, 51, 80. We may suspect, however, that much of Basil is in fact conveying local Cappadocian traditions. See also Ch. 3 C and 3.E.1.

[101] See Ch. 4 G for details of its structure.

(204.15–16). The familiar themes and images of "life" and "road"/"way" reappear. Here, however, they are set for the first time explicitly within the highly charged metaphysical and eschatological context of the new Paschal life of the resurrection. The penitential discipline of the church participates in the central Paschal dynamic of Christian theology.

The second discourse, raised at the end of the introduction, and the central focus of the letter, is that of medicine and of the healing of the soul. Developed at great length into the organizing scheme of the entire text, it casts the canons as addressing three fundamental types of spiritual diseases: the intellectual, the desirous, and the appetitive. The debt to Platonic psychology is obvious. Greco-Roman philosophy easily provides categories and vocabulary for framing the canonical project.

One of the oldest introductory elements in the corpus is the epilogue to Dionysius of Alexandria's canonical letter (*Fonti* 2.14.3–18). Here again the theme of teaching is prominent, although "negatively," as part of a humility topos: Dionysius has responded to the questions of Basilides, setting forth his mind "not as a teacher but with much simplicity, as befitting for us to converse with each other." Of course, Dionysius has been teaching Basilides, and the content of Dionysius' letter is exceptionally didactic.

This humility topos is interesting as it highlights another theme—almost a tonality—that runs through some of the introductory material. While Dionysius is in fact teaching Basilides, the tone of the epistle as a whole does nevertheless suggest some sense of bilateral conversation, or at least, of a sharing of opinions.[102] Dionysius is ostensibly offering his opinion to his brother bishop, Basilides, who is then exhorted to judge for himself, and write back should he consider another answer better (14.11–15). This sense of canonical writing as conversation may be detected elsewhere in the corpus as well, especially in the earliest legislation. In the letters in Antioch and Gangra, for example, the bishops are "asking" their brother bishops to adopt their canons. Another example is the almost "chatty" form of the parliamentary process embedded in Serdica and parts of Carthage—Hess's *dixit-placet* form.[103] The bishops are (at least notionally) "talking around" and agreeing about the issues, and the canons read as such. Even Basil and Gregory of Nyssa, although obviously writing as superiors to inferiors, retain a version of it: legislation emerges out of a kindly discussion between student and teacher, or father and son. Gregory of Nyssa's epilogue even makes clear that his work is composed in a spirit of fraternal concern (*Fonti* 2.226.12–17: "[I've composed these things] on account of the fact that it is

[102] Esp. *ταῦτα μὲν οὖν ὡς φρονῶ καὶ συμβουλεύω περὶ τούτων ἔγραψα* at *Fonti* 2.11.17–19; also perhaps at 12.4.

[103] Hess 2002, 24–9; he closely connects it with the concept of consensus at 72–4.

necessary to obey the commands of the brethren" (*διὰ τὸ δεῖν τοῖς τῶν ἀδελφῶν ἐπιτάγμασι πείθεσθαι κατὰ σπουδήν*).

This tonality becomes much less obvious later in the tradition, but a highly sublimated form of it may still be recognized in the subscription lists—which are functionally epilogues.[104] In these lists, every bishop individually attaches his name to the council's *acta*, sometimes adding his own personal statement of assent. The canons are thus framed as emerging very much as a communal effort, and having garnered widespread support. The effect of these lists can be fully appreciated today only when one flips through page after page of them in the manuscripts, marveling at both the amount of time such lists must have taken to create, and to copy. (It may also be noted that these lists serve to realize the "patristic" mode of referring to conciliar canons: the canons do in fact emerge *from the fathers* of the council.)

Even more abstractly, a kind of dialogue is perhaps present in the pervasive discourse of tradition: a dialogue with the dead. This is a discourse that will be explored in greater depth in Chapter 3, but already we can see that even Trullo and II Nicaea, self-consciously authoritative ecumenical councils, must speak out of and with reference to the "fathers" of the past, and indeed must emphatically profess their loyalty to the past in their introductory canons. Deference to tradition is, as we have seen, a theme of many of the texts examined above. This deference undoubtedly functions as a form of persuasion: the constant professions of faithfulness to the past evince a need to persuade, and appeals to tradition function to reassure and convince the reader of the legitimacy of the legislation.

This dialogical, persuasive tonality—a sense that law emerges out of a fairly polite discussion—should probably be understood in the context of broader antique traditions of *philia*, by which normativity and regulation tend to be stylized as a fairly polite affair, focused on consensus, friendship, and persuasion, and not coercion.[105] Today it is worthy of special note simply for its foreignness to the sensibilities of the formalist–positivist model proposed in the Introduction. Modern legislation usually shows little sign that law-writers feel they must dialogue with their audience or persuade their readers of their legitimacy in any way. Their authority and legitimacy are grounded not in an

[104] In the extant manuscripts, however, the only substantial list to be found is that attached (sometimes) to Trullo. See Ohme 1990. Carthage also contains numerous short lists amidst its *acta* excerpts (most notably *Fonti* 1.2.407–10). Earlier, they were more common, as Balsamon notes (*RP* 2.300–1), and as translations in older Syrian and Latin manuscripts attest. For a guide to these last, see the *Clavis* entries in Ch. 1, n. 36.

[105] See Brown 1992, 35–70, and more broadly Lendon 1997; also the references above (n. 5) on Plato's concept of the *prooimion*. On consensus in particular, see Hess 2002, 29–33. In light of these close connections between law, moral suasion, and consensus, Hess's attempt to oppose the first to the latter two (see 79–81, 89), part of his narrative of the "legalization" of canon law, is not persuasive.

ongoing conversation with their audience or with the past but the formally and absolutely defined powers of their office/institution. Normative writing can therefore be much plainer and more categorical. This is not so in antiquity.

C. CENTRAL THEMES, PRIORITIES, PROBLEMS

1. An initial problem: "rhetoric"

The texts described above set the Byzantine canonical tradition in a complex and rich matrix of images, concepts, and associations. These images and associations coalesce around a number of central themes and ideas that are deeply revealing of the Byzantine legal imagination. Underlying all of them, however, and in fact constitutive of their wealth and complexity, is a particular style and tone, or better, a mode of discourse, that demands preliminary consideration: their "rhetorical" character. Whereas crisp and precise conceptual prose might be expected of a modern code or legal introduction—modern Orthodox canonical manuals read this way, for example—the Byzantine introductions are written in an extraordinarily ornate, allusive, and imagistic manner, sometimes to the point of obscurity. This is particularly true of the doctrinal sections of the formal prologues, where the nature of church law is addressed most directly.

This rhetorical orientation of the introductions is not surprising within the broader context of late antique and Byzantine literature. However, whereas in theological, epistolary, historical, or philosophical texts we might expect and understand such a mode of writing, in legal literature it is more disconcerting. Yet it is very widespread: the rhetoricization of law is considered one of the stock "vulgar" characteristics of late antique and later legislation, and nowhere is it more pronounced than in the legal *prooimia*.[106]

This rhetorical style makes it exceedingly difficult for modern scholarship to read these introductions as seriously expository of legal realities. Indeed, in the literature such introductions tend to be consigned to merely subsidiary propagandistic or symbolic functions, perhaps important in themselves but somehow extrinsic to real legal concerns. They are thus explored as "mirrors" of imperial ideology, or as reflecting changes in political or social structures (mainly as part of the legitimization and enforcement of new structures), or changes in culture generally—but, strangely enough, not as *mirrors of the law*

[106] See esp. Ries 1983; Stolte 1988; Pieler 1978; also Corcoran 1996, 3–4; Fögen 1995; Honig 1960; Hunger 1964; Lanata 1989; Voss 1982. See also the Introduction.

itself.[107] In other words, rarely does anyone asks what it might mean for the nature of a legal system, on a theoretical level, to be so highly invested in such a literary form of self-fashioning.[108] Instead, the law itself is always assumed to be a technical-formalist reality underlying this rhetorical "decoration," and perhaps manipulated by it. At best, it seems, this outer layer of literary ornament is to be mined for bits and pieces of "real" legal doctrine that might be buried within it—as if the introductions really meant to be speaking like modern statutes or civil law textbooks, but just happened to be constrained by the (decadent) rhetorical mores of late imperial culture.

For the cultural historian of law, however, it is surely preferable to allow that the Byzantines might have been doing exactly what they wanted to be doing in these introductions: framing legal normativity in an intentionally ornate, literary manner, that is, "rhetorically." For the Byzantines (and their late antique forebears) the discourse of law was *meant* to be rhetorical.

If we adopt this perspective, one of the most basic and curious characteristics of these introductions—perversely enough—suddenly becomes their *lack* of interest in clear conceptual formulation of canonical jurisprudential "introduction." Nowhere in these introductions is sustained and clear theoretical articulation of fundamental legal distinctions, categories, principles, or other doctrines a clear priority. True, with a little effort it is possible to distill something of a source theory: supreme legislative authority is formally conciliar, sources should be authentic, validity may be universal or regional, and sources may be hierarchized (apostles, general councils, local councils, then fathers). Other quasi-technical-legal or legal-like concepts occasionally appear: the distinction between the "letter" and "mind" of the law (in *τὰ μὲν σώματα* 37),[109] or the idea of ratification (for example, *κυρο-* vocabulary in Trullo 2). But all of these concepts emerge only vaguely, are not pursued at any length or with much sophistication, and appear almost in passing: it is certainly not a primary concern of the tradition to provide a clear, consistent exposition of the sources of law,[110] or the criteria for formal validity, or the nature of legal interpretation.

Instead the energies of the introductions seem to be directed elsewhere, towards a much looser, much more ornate and literary presentation of the law.

[107] This is broadly true of the studies of Fögen 1995, Honig 1960, Hunger 1964, and Ries 1983. This is part of a much broader tendency to see any complex literary fashioning of legal texts as a de-legalizing of these texts. See also Honig 1960, 39–40 on the earlier work of E. Vernay.

[108] Stolte 1988, although brief, is an important exception. In the older literature, Stroux 1949 is also to some extent an exception (and following him Honig 1960, esp. at 40–1), but these treatments tend to be focused on the legal-doctrinal influence of specific rhetorical concepts and techniques, and not the texture of the system as a whole.

[109] See n. 75.

[110] Certainly nothing contradicts Stolte's judgment that "the Byzantines never reached a fixed theory of legal sources." Stolte 1991b, 545 n. 5; see also Stolte 1991a and Burgmann 2002, 252 n. 13.

This immediately raises the thorny question of what, from a legal-theoretical perspective, might be gained by framing and locating normativity in such a literary manner. The answer is simple. Functionally, this "rhetorical"—or better, literary—mode of presentation is very good at doing exactly one thing: embedding or enmeshing normativity in broader narratives. And in fact, although anathema to formalist instincts, this embedding of the law within a fluid, polyvalent literary framework is perhaps the single most obvious and central dynamic of the introductions. The introductions are therefore working within a legal framework in which the emphasis is placed on connectivity with external narratives, and keeping the normative processes firmly anchored in, and in a sense subordinate to, a broader, more generalized set of values and worldview. In this world, law becomes in effect one more aspect of broader narratives of right and wrong, of justice and injustice—and indeed, of ancient literary *paideia* generally. It has been suggested that the tendency in antiquity is to transform almost all realms of knowledge into a subset operation of general literary learning[111]—it seems that law is no different.

The results are conceptually messy by today's standards, but if understood within a worldview which places more emphasis on cultural and educational control of behavior than rule control, it is a strategy that is understandable and probably effective.[112] Certainly this tendency points towards an overall legal-theoretical orientation favoring the resolution of disputes and the maintenance of order via substantively equitable solutions and negotiations (as Weber's "substantive rational" systems, where the truly just solution to every problem is sought) and not via formally correct techniques, doctrines, and procedures that produce "legally" or conceptually correct solutions (as Weber's "formal rational" systems).[113] In such substantive rational systems the critical problem is not legal-conceptual coherence or consistent application of legal language, techniques, and doctrines, but maintaining consensus about the broad metaphysical narratives of justice that must be constantly invoked to demonstrate a given judgment is "just." For such systems the primary focus must thus necessarily be the constant reinforcing of these narratives and the repeated embedding of legal discourse in them—this is a *functional* requirement for the system. And this is precisely what the Byzantine introductions seem to be doing. Clear concepts and bare rule content may well exist in the Byzantine legal thought world, but they are not the primary concern of legal exposition.

The "rhetorical" character of the introductions should not, therefore, be considered extrinsic to their legal substance, but an essential element of it, and

[111] See esp. Marrou 1948, *passim*, but also, more broadly, Brown 1992; Carney 1971, 91; Morgan 1998, 94–5.

[112] See Brown 1992; Harris 2001; Lendon 1997.

[113] Weber 1925, 224–56 *et passim*.

indeed a critically important aspect of Byzantine canon law. The legal "message" of the introductions is precisely that law qua law is supposed to be rhetorically framed, that is, carefully embedded in broader value narratives.

Finally, we must not overlook a further implication of this literary stylization: law is supposed to be beautiful.[114] Although the tortuous periods of *οἱ τοῦ μεγάλου θεοῦ* or the Trullan *logos* may no longer read as elegantly as they once did, the intention is undoubtedly to fix the canons in a suitably high aesthetic setting.[115] This further emphasizes the belief that law not be considered a "plain" and technical formalist mechanism of rules, but as a part of a much broader cultural discourse where it is essential that good ordering and aesthetic expression be connected. We may also remark that the most "doctrinal" sections of the introductions, those set at the beginning of the formal prologues, for example, are generally the most ornamented and "beautiful." Today "rhetorical" tends to denote the insubstantial, but in the Byzantine world it would seem that the greater and more high-status the substantive content, the greater the rhetorical stylization.

2. Embedding the canons: fundamental contexts and referents

The Byzantine introductory tradition is thus best conceived as an attempt to embed the canon-legal endeavor within a number of significant contexts and narratives. As already noted, one of the most significant results of this process is that the introductions contain very little that is narrowly technical or specialized, legally or otherwise. Most of the terms employed are lexically unremarkable, and the contexts, images, and motifs invoked are commonplace. Even the few semi-technical-legal terms and concepts that are present (the *κυρο*-vocabulary, references to "word" and "mind" of texts mentioned above, and also perhaps the semi-technical "referring" language of *ἀναφέρω* in Constantinople and Antioch[116]) are hardly very technical, and probably well within the reach of anyone of a general education capable of reading these texts in the first place. They are certainly not technical in the sense of being produced by or understood solely by a professionalized cadre of legal specialists. The introductions are therefore not primarily inducting the reader into a

[114] See *Tanta* on the laws in the *Digest* coming to a *novam pulchritudinem* (liv.11), or *Deo Auctore* on the *Digest*: . . . *oportet eam pulcherrimo opere extruere* (xlvii.12); see broadly Pieler 1978, 351–62 ("Rechtsliteratur als Kunstform?").

[115] In this connection it is interesting that, as Beneshevich notes (*Sbornik* 145 n.2), the marginal notation *ὡραῖον* (beautiful, fitting, appropriate) may be found frequently in the manuscripts, apparently sometimes pointing out aesthetically pleasing constructions in the canonical texts. On this notation, see Montfaucon 1709, 370–3.

[116] The term *ἀναφορά* is often a translation for *suggestio* or *relatio,* an official petition or report to the imperial chancery. Its use in these canons is somewhat looser. See Roussos 1949, 45, and Ch. 3 E.1.

specialized and proprietary technical world. Rather, the movement of the introductions is towards the general and well known: the introductions are writing canon law *into* a common code of Greco-Roman and Christian learning, not out of it. They are certainly not demarcating a special, autonomous realm of discourse. The implication is clearly that understanding canon law requires above all being versed in a wide array of cultural associations, narratives, and allusions. Canon law is meant to be embedded in broader normative narratives.

If there is an overarching narrative into which the introductions wish to read the canons, it is the Christian "story" of salvation itself. As noted, this is most explicitly developed in Trullo, but it is also very evident in *οἱ τοῦ μεγάλου θεοῦ* and Gregory of Nyssa. The canons become an instrument in the great unfolding (Paschal) drama of salvation, of which the main players are God, Christ, the Spirit, the devil, and the saints. As such, as we have seen many times, the canons have a cosmic significance, with horizons easily opening up onto metaphysical realities and the next world—whether in a biblical key, as in the apostolic epilogue, for example, or in a more rarified Platonic form, as in *τὰ μὲν σώματα*.

In II Nicaea 1 the canons become woven so deeply into this Christian "story" that they emerge textually as quasi-scriptural: the canons can be cast as the OT law or even the NT "law," the Gospel. In this respect, however, II Nicaea 1 is only the acme of a much broader tendency of locating the canons firmly in a scriptural literary matrix, that is, of presenting scripture as the essential contextual reference point for understanding the content and nature of the canonical project. The simplest mechanism of this contextualization in the introductions is the constant appropriation of a number of obviously scriptural images: for example, the Good Shepherd, the language of the "royal way," and even the constant references to the canons/law being about "life," a common Old Testament theme.[117] Even very early in the tradition, canonical material or actions can be glossed directly by scripture: the image of the canons as the "knife of the Spirit" in *οἱ τοῦ μεγάλου θεοῦ* is an excellent example. Trullo, as noted, is filled with many more. The frequent pairing of scripture/faith and the canons is another form. Scripture and the canons clearly form a continuous trajectory of salvation and world ordering, with the canons rooted in and subordinate to scripture, but nonetheless of very similar substance and function.

Similar in effect is the tendency to cast the canons as first and foremost an apostolic project which has been continued by their holy successors, "the fathers," working in imitation of the apostles. The first line of *οἱ τοῦ μεγάλου θεοῦ* is perhaps the most explicit articulation of this idea, but the idea in Trullo of "each generation" of saints continuing the battle with the devil, or the tendency of speaking about the canons as prototypically "of the apostles and fathers,"

[117] For examples of this last, see Deut. 4: 1 or 5: 33.

conveys the same idea: the canons are always an apostolic-then-patristic endeavor. From the 6th C onwards this concept is even realized in the physical architecture of the corpus itself, when the apostolic legislation is placed at the head of the other canons: the canonical corpus itself has become, in effect, "apostolic."

Given these associations with the primary Christian agents of holiness, it is not surprising that the canons become easily cast as divine. Although not remarked systematically above, this is most obvious in patterns of sacral epithets. The canons are thus *θεῖοι νόμοι* in *οἱ τοῦ μεγάλου θεοῦ* (4.18), *θεῖοι κανόνες* in *εἰς δόξαν θεοῦ* (Heimbach 1838,208.3), *ἱεροὶ θεσμοί* in *τὰ μὲν σώματα* (12), *ἱεροὶ κανόνες* in Trullo (52.108.1 and Trullo 2), *θεῖοι κανόνες* in II Nicaea 1, and both *ἱεροὶ κανόνες* and *ἱερολογίαι* in *ὁ μὲν παρὼν* (27–8). Very characteristic of civil-legal terminology as well, these epithets are virtually formulaic by Trullo, after which they occur by default.[118]

The sacrality of the canons is equally evident in their divine and spiritual origin: they are defined directly as a "gift from God" in *τὰ μὲν σώματα*, the Holy Spirit himself has authored, or at least co-authored, them in *οἱ τοῦ μεγάλου θεοῦ* and Antioch (in the former "divine grace" also plays a role), and in II Nicaea 1 they all shine forth from "the same Spirit." Almost always, as just noted, they emerge from holy agents: the apostles or "the fathers." In this the canons are part of a very common, and increasingly pronounced, late antique and Byzantine pattern of casting law and legislation as divine and heaven-sent.[119] Some scholars[120] have suggested that this tendency wanes in

[118] For examples from the secular legislation, see Enßlin 1943, 73–4; also Wenger 1942, 98–100 with examples from Justinian of both laws and canons as "sacred." In the canons, see e.g. Trullo 26, 33; II Nicaea 10, 11; Protodeutera 10, 11. Earlier, Cyril 1.

[119] On the immense issue of the sacrality of law and the legislative process in Greco-Roman legal and political thinking, and its connection with the idea of a quasi-divine legislator, Dvornik 1966 remains the richest and broadest resource; see also Harries and Wood 1993, 147–8; Hunger 1964, 49–81; Kleinknecht and Gutbrod 1942, 1025–35; Ries 1983, 120–1, 221–2; Scharf 1959, 68–70. Sohm was well aware of this dynamic in first-millennium canon law, and identified it as an important element of his *altkatholisch* law (Sohm 1923, 2.68–77). On the increasing sacralization of even civil law in the Byzantine period—to the point that the emperor himself seems to become overshadowed by God as a real source of law—see esp. Fögen 1987 and Lokin 1994. This development may be viewed as a consequence of the increasing representation in the Dominate of imperial power as a semi-divine institution, mediating between heaven and earth—itself an old Platonic and Hellenistic theme; see the references in the Conclusion, n. 24. For ancient Near Eastern precedents, see the short summary with further references in Raaflaub 2000, 50–7. These concepts are, of course, present in the *CJC* prolegomena: see the famous dedication of *Tanta* (*in nomine domini dei nostri Ihesu Christi*) or the same prologue's blunt ascription of the law to heavenly authorship (*Tanta* pr); also *Deo auctore* 5, in which the digest is likened to a temple of justice (*quasi proprium et sanctissimum templum iustitiae consecrare*), and the same text's conclusion, at 14, in which the *Digest* is *deique omnipotentis providentiae argumentum*. A classical example of the emperor as divine legislator is *CTh Gesta* 3, where copies of the code are received from the emperor *manu divina*. See Enßlin 1943 for further examples.

[120] Notably Hess 2002, 76–7, writing *contra* Sieben 1979. Here Hess is over-anticipating a much later western medieval and post-medieval narrative of the separation of canon law from

canon law after the 5th C, but this is not supported by the evidence; in the Byzantine tradition at least, it remains constant and, if anything, especially in Trullo and II Nicaea, increases.

This divine and salvific nature of the canons is nuanced in one important way: a consistent pattern emerges of joining and assimilating, yet simultaneously subordinating, the canons to faith or scripture. This pattern of faith/scripture/doctrine first, and *then* the canons, is never a clear conceptual doctrine or distinction (like the later distinction between *ius sacrum* and *ius humanum*,[121] or between dogma and discipline), but it nevertheless emerges as a recurring motif, a kind of crease in the fabric of the tradition. Important examples include the various examples of the Nicene credal prefacing, the pairing of scripture and canons in Gangra, the division of conciliar work in Constantinople, the pairing of faith and order in Carthage 2, the pairing of Trullo 1 and 2, and the assimilation of the canons to scripture in II Nicaea 1. Indeed, this pairing probably represents the canons' fundamental self-situation within the tradition: the canons are always together with scripture/faith, with a similar goal and function, and assimilated to them, but nevertheless following them, and never totally identified with them.[122] We may suspect that the distinction and relationship between "theoretical" and "practical" knowledge (*θεωρητικά* and *πρακτικά*) in later Platonic philosophy is a critical context for this distinction.[123]

Another omnipresent discourse in the introductions is the casting of human organization and order in overwhelmingly moral terms, and particularly moral-psychological terms. For example, the practical effect and function of the canons is repeatedly expressed in moral and psychological terms of "rectifying the life and manner (*τρόπος*) of each" (*οἱ τοῦ μεγάλου θεοῦ* 4.18–19), of providing a "canon" of a "pious way of living" (*τὰ μὲν σώματα* 14), of leading the soul upwards to true good (*τὰ μὲν σώματα* 6), and above all—especially, but not exclusively, in *οἱ τοῦ μεγάλου θεοῦ*, Trullo, and Gregory of Nyssa—of curing and aiding the passions: "for the healing of souls and curing of passions" (*πρὸς ψυχῶν θεραπείαν καὶ ἰατρείαν παθῶν*) (Trullo 2). This tendency has deep roots in the Greek vision of law as a pedagogue to

theology and morality, and the clear doctrinal distinction between the *ius sacrum* and the *ius humanum*.

[121] Sohm 1923, 2.85–108, and so Afanasiev 1936, 55–7 and Patsavos (Kapsanis) 1999, 186, rightly view this distinction as a rather odd development from a pre-modern perspective; divinity is virtually a constitutive characteristic of ancient church law.

[122] For such pairings in the Justinianic legislation, see Wenger 1942, 125–9.

[123] See esp. O'Meara 2003, and particularly his emphasis on both as part of the ascent to ultimate *θεωρία*, as well as his notion of a constant ascending-descending interplay between the two, with the implication that neither an absolutely clear distinction between the two, nor a total assimilation, ever seems possible—very much as we see in the relationship between scripture/faith and the canons in the Byzantine tradition. See more broadly Hadot 1995a, 2002; Neschke 1995.

virtue, and expresses the idea that law is deeply and essentially intertwined with virtue and morality. Attempts to separate "law" and "morality"—as is normal today—are almost absurd in this type of tradition: the two are clearly, and intentionally, held together.[124] The medical imagery of the last quotation, an important subset of this discourse, finds its ultimate exposition in Gregory of Nyssa, whose concern to heal "every spiritual weakness" (*Fonti* 2.203.16–20) leads him to compose a lengthy treatise on penance as medicine of the soul. This medical theme too has a well-established ancient pedigree as a legal association.[125]

A notable part of this vision of the canons as moral and medical care is the constant emphasis on the canons as oriented towards "life." The canons lead one, for example, "to a greater and higher . . . life" (Trullo 52.5–7), and are able to provide "much benefit . . . for life" (*τὰ μὲν σώματα* 21). Evidently the scope of the canons is not limited to a narrowly defined legal arena: the canons are meant speak to human existence in a very broad sense. This idea of law treating "life" also has resonances in the broader antique legal tradition.[126]

Another persistent theme is teaching. This is also a major association of law in Greek literature, and closely related to the idea of law as the moral correction of the "life" of the body politic.[127] Law is essentially a realization of, and aimed at, the constant (moral) re-education of the person and society.

[124] When Plato asserts that the only aim of the proper legislator is total virtue (*Laws* 705d–e, also 630c), he sums up much of the tradition. On this ubiquitous ancient, and especially Greek, tendency to merge law, politics, and morality/values—and generally to assimilate the first two to the last—see e.g. Balot 2006, 11–14; Barker 1925, 352–3; Cohen 1995, 35–59; Dagron 1994, 30–5; Dvornik 1966; Jones 1956, 12–16; Schoefield and Rowe 2000 (*passim*); Gagarin (on Plato, in particular) 2002, 216; Troianos 1992a, 331–3. See also the Conclusion. One may cite also *Digest* 1.1: *ius est ars boni et aequi*; it is the art of the *good* and the fair. The tendency of Hess 2002, 80–5 to oppose morality and legality is again an over-anticipation of medieval developments. On the pedagogical aspect of law in particular, see n. 127.

[125] Law, government, and medicine are closely woven together in Greco-Roman thought, although it is a particularly strong association in the Platonic tradition (e.g. *Laws* 719e; the *Republic* largely casts law and government as therapy of the city/soul); see Dvornik 1966 (esp. the references to kings as physicians at 960); Hunger 1964, 103–9; 123–30; Lanata 1984; 1989a; O'Meara 2003, 107–10.

[126] It is especially common in Christian scripture, e.g. in Deut. 4: 1 or 5: 33, where the idea emerges of obeying the commands of the law "that you may live," a common refrain thereafter; but see also e.g. in *CTh Gesta* 4, where the law is a *magisterium vitae*, or in Leo's *Prooimion* to his novels (Noailles and Dain 1944, 5), where laws address *τὸ πολύτροπον τῆς τοῦ βίου καταστάσεως*.

[127] The association of law and teaching or gaining knowledge is central to ancient Greco-Roman thinking; see *CTh Gesta* 4 on the law as a *magisterium vitae*, or Plutarch's Lycurgus "attaching the whole task of legislation to education" (*Life of Lycurgus* 13; ed. Lindskog and Ziegler 1957). For Plato and Aristotle, in fact, law and politics are virtually an extended exercise in self- and city-education: law both is and assumes education. On this immense theme, see the references in n. 124; also Brown 1992, 35–70; Jones 1956, 5–8; Romilly 1971, 227–50; Ries 1983, 104–26; Too 2001. The concept of mimesis, by which rulers provide an example for their subjects for imitation, is an integral part of this dynamic; on mimesis in political thought, see Dvornik 1966, *passim*, with citations at p. 963.

Lawlessness in Trullo is thus, for example, about ignorance and "forgetting" of virtue (52.7–15) that must be corrected through the luminaries and teachers of the church (49.6–8). Elsewhere law itself is even defined as a "useful teaching" (*χρηστὴ διδασκαλία*) (*τὰ μὲν σώματα* 16–17), and a number of the *Apostolic Epitome* sections are significantly entitled "Teaching of . . . ". The theme is particularly evident, as we saw, in Basil, who presents his legislative work as above all an act of teaching—and being taught.

Finally, numerous other more specific images and concepts anchor the canons firmly within broader late antique legal-political discourses. Most of these images are sufficiently commonplace that they need no special comment. The canons, for example, are concerned with wisdom (*σοφία*), good order (*εὐταξία*), concord (*συμφωνία*), harmony (*ὁμόνοια*), and the prudent (*φρονιμόν*). Here we may also count the occasional emergence of honor/shame language, as well as the *Amtsweisungen*-like progression of the *Apostolic Epitome*. The broad contours of antique consensus, persuasion, and friendship language may also be detected. Even the conceptualization of the law in shepherd and "way" imagery (although in our texts both clearly as appropriated by Christians), and as divine, may be read as recognizable and quite regular elements of the symbolic and linguistic world of general Greco-Roman legal-political ideology.[128]

3. One special context: the civil law

A central question of much modern Byzantine legal scholarship is the relationship of canon law and civil law. This question was perhaps not quite so pressing for the Byzantines themselves. Trullo and II Nicaea 1, for example, are arguably more interested in establishing the canons' identity vis-à-vis the scriptural law than the civil (a concern, incidentally, shared by contemporary Byzantine secular prologues, and not, therefore, a substantive point of contrast with the secular law).

Nevertheless, this problem is not altogether ignored in our texts. In *οἱ τοῦ μεγάλου θεοῦ*, in particular, the civil law emerges almost immediately as a foil for understanding and defining the nature of church law. The prologue *τὰ μὲν σώματα* broaches the topic too, albeit more obliquely. In both cases, however, the relationship between the two laws is negotiated in a very nuanced and subtle way, and does not permit reduction to simple doctrines or clear principles. In fact, the treatment of this question in the prologues is a prime illustration of the conceptual "messiness" of the literary-rhetorical approach to

[128] For all these images and terms, see broadly Barker 1925, Dvornik 1966, Hunger 1964, Ries 1983, Schoefield and Rowe 2000.

shaping and imagining law that is so characteristic of the Byzantine introductory tradition.

The ambiguities of this negotiation are immediately evident in *οἱ τοῦ μεγάλου θεοῦ*. On the one hand, the prologue begins with an apparently strong and clear point of distinction between the laws: penology. According to Scholastikos, the civil laws seek to harm, while church law, guided by church leaders who function as good shepherds, seeks to protect, guide, and heal. A little later we also encounter another explicit distinction: the fathers did not decree "political" or civil laws but "divine" (*νόμους τινὰς καὶ κανόνας οὐ πολιτικούς ἀλλὰ θείους . . . ἐξέθεντο*).

These distinctions, however, within the broader context of Greco-Roman political-legal discourse, are less clear-cut than they may at first sound to modern ears. First, late antique civil law—and behind it the Greek civil-legal philosophical tradition—may easily speak of itself as protecting, guiding, and healing: neither medical nor shepherd imagery are especially foreign to it.[129] Scholastikos is thus in a sense distinguishing canon law from civil law with a pool of common "secular" legal images.

The use of "divine" as, apparently, a point of distinction from the "secular" laws is also strangely ambiguous. As noted, referring to civil laws as divine is an entirely normal convention of late antique civil law.[130] Indeed, the constant epithetizing of the canons as "divine" might elsewhere even be understood as precisely a means of assimilating church law to civil legislation! Here too, then, the canons are being distinguished from the civil laws, but with common "secular" legal concepts.

It is likewise curious that in the phrase cited above *νόμοι* and *κανόνες* are used synonymously. This is also true later in the prologue (4.21), and in Title 48 of the collection, where the canons are clearly referred to as *νόμοι*. Despite the fact, as we will see in Chapter 3, that *κανών* is already a reasonably technical term for church rules in the 6th C, and the term itself could be used to distinguish the ecclesial and secular laws—and elsewhere often does—the two terms here form a hendiadys. A potentially important terminological distinction between the two types of laws is thus quite noticeably *not* being made.

Another level of ambiguity emerges in the fact that this "divine" church law is immediately glossed by an allusion to a stock legal definition: "they [the fathers] set forth certain laws and canons, not civil but divine, regarding **what ought and what ought not to be done**" (*νόμους τινὰς καὶ κανόνας οὐ πολιτικούς ἀλλὰ θείους περὶ τῶν πρακτέων καὶ μὴ πρακτέων ἐξέθεντο*). Although applied here to "non-secular" divine laws, this is, as noted, an entirely conventional secular-legal definition. Its application to church legislation is

[129] See nn. 125, 128. [130] See nn. 118, 119.

thus an important example of legal-theoretical appropriation, and clearly locates canonical norms within the normal parameters of Greco-Roman legal thought. The ambiguity increases further—for the modern reader at least—as this definition is not exactly a proprietary technical or juristic legal definition in a conventional formalist sense: it is a general philosophical definition in its original form, and quite moral in tone. Thus the "divine" ecclesial laws are being defined by a secular-legal definition, but by one much broader than many conventional modern legal definitions.

In sum, then, the canonical legislation is distinguished from secular legislation with stock secular legal images, identified as non-secular with a common secular legal epithet (that does not sound secular today) while it is being referred to with common secular-legal terminology, and defined as non-secular with a common secular-legal definition (that does not sound particularly "legal" today)!

A similar set of problems may be found in the appropriation of the Demosthenic definition of law in *τὰ μὲν σώματα*. Again a common secular-legal definition of law is applied to the canons, which suggests a certain ease in locating canonical legality within mainstream secular-legal thinking. But the definition is modified, as we have seen, and in particular bleached of its more civil-legal connotations. The dynamic of this appropriation is thus very similar to that in *οἱ τοῦ μεγάλου θεοῦ*: the canons are actively distinguished from the secular law, but precisely, and ironically, through the appropriation of commonplace secular-legal concepts and images. At the same time, again as in *οἱ τοῦ μεγάλου θεοῦ*, a modern reader cannot help but notice that the definition employed is also rhetorical in origin, and extends far beyond the bounds of what the formalist–positivist vision of law sketched in the Introduction would tolerate; by such standards, it is hardly legal at all.

All of this results in something of a minefield for a modern legal historian. Perhaps the chief conclusion to be drawn is that the neat modern categories of "secular," "sacred," and even "legal" are not especially useful for understanding the complex negotiation of legal identity at work in these texts. A modern legal-doctrinal exposition of the distinction between the civil and ecclesiastical laws seems neither present nor possible. Indeed, the complex interweaving and stacking of philosophical, theological, and legal associations evident in these texts presume both a notion of legality and a process of doctrinal distinction that evade analysis by simple formalist legal heuristics of "secular" versus "sacred" or "civil" versus "ecclesial."

Nevertheless, the prologues do manage to communicate a coherent message about the relationship of the two laws. This message is not as neat and categorical as might be desired, and it assumes a notion of law much broader than a modern reader would expect—but it has a clarity of a sort. It has two aspects. On the one hand, both prologues are keen to point out a distinction in origin, function, and ultimate goal of the canons vis-à-vis certain aspects of secular (Roman) civil law: different penology; a difference, perhaps, in the type or degree of "divinity"; and probably a heightened eschatological, moral, medical, and pastoral orientation. These differences are not as categorical as traditional western legal theory would like, but the intention to make a distinction is still evident. On the other hand, church law does not emerge as an *entirely* different type of normativity: it is still firmly anchored within the general Greco-Roman symbolic world of "law." The difference between church law and secular law seems more one of degree. Nevertheless—and this point is critical—the points of similarity are located firmly within a conceptualization of law in very broad, almost philosophical terms—not within the technical terms of Roman law itself. In effect, church law is being predicated as a species of the genus "law," not as a species of the genus "(Roman) civil law" as a technical juristic whole. Canon law is thus not being constructed—as a modern reader might too easily assume—as a mirror image of Roman civil law, that is, as a parallel technical juristic discipline modeled on Roman law (as will emerge in the west in the middle ages). Canon law is "law" and civil law is "law," but law is something bigger than them both. In effect, the prologues only go so far as to identify the two laws as siblings of common parentage—but not as identical twins.

4. Sources and legislation

Of all the legal-introductory topics that we might consider conventional, the assessment and delineation of the canonical sources is the most prominent in the Byzantine introductions. This assessment naturally involves reflection, direct and indirect, on the nature of valid rule recognition and of the process of canonical legislation generally.

As already noted, some of this reflection approximates the contours of a modern source theory. Sources may be weighed in terms of origins and scope (local/universal), authenticity (genuine or not), hierarchy of type (conciliar/patristic), and even harmony of content (i.e. of patristic material with conciliar). The prologues are also obviously concerned with simply listing and delineating the canonical sources—that is, delineating the limits of a self-enclosed rule world.

Likewise, a process of legislation is clearly presumed that is both ongoing and even instrumental (in the sense of laws conceived as a means of addressing specific problems that arise), suggesting a certain positivism. Prototypically in *οἱ τοῦ μεγάλου θεοῦ*, legislation is depicted as emerging at many different times, for different reasons, to address different problems as they arise (*ὡς ἀπῄτει τὰ κατὰ χρόνους ἀναφυόμενα*) (4.20–4). This sentiment is echoed in *τὰ μὲν σώματα* (15–16), and especially *ὁ μὲν παρών*: many new problems arise "in life" (*ἄλλα τε κατὰ τὸν βίον οὐκ ὀλίγα ἐνεώχμωσε*) and synods are convened to address them (8–9). In Trullo the idea is expressed particularly strikingly, if a little obliquely, when Christ is portrayed as raising up "in each generation" (καθ' ἑκάστην . . . γενεάν) champions to wage war against the devil, shepherd the flock, and teach the wayward (104.3–105.12): Christ constantly raises up legislative leaders, such as the fathers at Trullo, to guide the church. Constant, responsive conciliar legislation is an expected, and normal, aspect of church law.

Any similarities with modern source theory and legislative process are nevertheless deceptive. The overall picture painted by the introductions remains quite foreign to the legal sensibilities delineated in the Introduction. As already noted, the dominant characterization of the canons is not as mundane instruments of a competent formal legislative authority created to enact policy, but as a highly numinous normative reality, authored by the Holy Spirit, and directly flowing from the apostles and "the fathers," the spiritual successors of the apostles, who are guardians and transmitters of the faith. Far from simple regulations of a purely disciplinary "good order," the canons are thus deeply embedded—quite obviously in Trullo—in broader Christian narratives of holiness and salvation. In this context, positivist-like concepts of source valuation and legislation process might be present, but they are not, as it were, the central point—and indeed, they have a markedly secondary place in the introductions. In effect they appear as only one element in the primary task of the introductions, which is the delineation of the divine and numinous tradition into which all legitimate normativity must be set. In this world, laws emerge as authoritative not so much through the application of formal criteria as through their substantive implication in specific metaphysical narratives of healing, teaching, saving, guiding, and so forth. Sohm thus quite correctly understood legislation in the pre-medieval church as fundamentally a "charismatic" process.[131] Formalist paraphernalia and processes may be present, but they are never particularly developed or coherent, as they do not need to be: they are simply one subordinate aspect of what is essentially a substantive process of determining normativity. To deploy the language of modern late antique cultural history, legislation emerges in the introductions as above all a function of the holy. As such, it may be categorized by formal criteria and it may display instrumentalism, but valid and relevant law ultimately emerges only as enacted by the holy, that is, as cast as coherent with accepted narratives of the holy, and according to the demands of the holy (mainly promoting the holiness of the community). Formal and instrumental treatment of regulations is thus present, but in a very different key than in modern formalist-positivist systems.

This charismatic aspect of lawgiving emerges above all in the peculiar traditionalism of the introductions. It is here that the dissonance with modern

[131] Sohm 1923, 2.63–86 *et passim.*

positivism becomes especially pronounced. As already noted in Chapter 1, in this world it seems that law is "validated" and legislative authority established mostly by reference to authorities in the past. The introductions are indeed oddly deferential and backward-looking: they stress remembering law, receiving it from the past, gathering it, confirming it, and pledging one's loyalty to it. There is surprisingly little expression of categorical, absolute sovereign authority *over* the laws, for one does not impute or "grant" authority, validity, or "force" to the traditional laws as much as recognize and affirm the authority, validity, and force that they already have—and then derive one's own authority therefrom. The best illustrations of this dynamic are Trullo 2 and II Nicaea 1: precisely at the moment of the exercise of one's "sovereign legislative authority"—in creating new laws—one is *most* concerned to carefully pledge one's adherence and allegiance to the received law as a sacral whole, and to forbid any tampering or modification of it. To legislate one must firmly and faithfully place one's texts in a traditional trajectory. Chalcedon 1 should also probably be read in this way: Chalcedon is here not giving authority to something that did not already possess this authority, but is instead affirming its own adherence to this tradition as part of its own legislative initiative. The prologue *ὁ μὲν παρών* is also very concerned to note that its additions follow very happily on the work of its predecessors: they are entirely coherent with what has gone before. Even the defensiveness of Scholastikos in *οἱ τοῦ μεγάλου θεοῦ* suggests that merely rearranging and thematizing the sacred corpus might be risky: the established tradition must be violated as little as possible for any new exposition or composition to achieve acceptance.

Curiously, however, this charismatic traditionalism does not seem to entail the casting of the tradition as a whole as rigidly immutable. The strict conceptual bivalence of "immutable" vs. "mutable" of later positivist systems is never articulated in the introductions. Although Trullo and II Nicaea both issue warnings against falsifying or omitting older material, as a whole the introductory tradition clearly assumes that one can always add newer material on top of the older, as circumstances require. One can also evidently clarify or even slightly modify the shape of the corpus and clean up around its edges (for example, in separating out the "local" from the "universal" councils, or in making judgments on Cyprian, or the *Apostolic Constitutions*), or express some formal evaluation of new elements (for example, *τὰ μὲν σώματα* on the patristic legislation), or, of course, rearrange the corpus under a thematic index (so the *Coll50*—although, as noted, this was one step too far for the *Coll14* author). None of this, of course, amounts to modern notions of law as a tissue of easily manipulatable and contingent legislative instruments subject to constant and radical positivist construction, deconstruction, and reconstruction. But neither does it promote the idea of complete ossification. The introductions always assume that the tradition is living and moving, albeit slowly. The very nebulosity and diffuseness of this charismatic and traditional mode of legislation seem to have allowed a certain movement and space for change, even if limited mostly to cautious accretion.

D. ANALYSIS: THE LAW INTRODUCED

The traditional introductions and framing structures of the Byzantine canonical tradition paint a picture of law that is complex and nuanced. We may summarize its chief features by noting its many points of coherence with the broader physical shape of the tradition traced in Chapter 1. For example, the extreme conservatism and stability of the textual tradition, which seems to suggest a quasi-sacral or even scriptural handling of the texts, finds an easy complement in the introductions' characterization of the canons as precisely sacred and quasi-scriptural. The curious absence of clear moments of categorical official legislative definition is echoed in the introductions' highly traditionalized and sacralized treatment of the sources: the Holy Spirit, the divinely inspired "fathers," "divine grace," and ultimately tradition itself are the real legislators/promulgators, not any "present" authority. The problem of the "missing jurisprudence" finds a parallel in the surprisingly untechnical and commonplace content of the introductions. The slow growth of the corpus by accretion is echoed in the traditionalist "source theory" of the introductions. Even the paralleling of civil and canonical material in the manuscripts—separate, yet still part of a larger whole—vaguely suggests the introductions' vision of the relationship of civil and canon law. Perhaps most dramatically, the curious way in which the physical tradition seems to imply that the canonical texts are embedded in broader regulative contexts and narratives finds very direct confirmation in the form and content of the introductions: one introduces the law primarily by embedding it in extralegal value narratives.

The "fit" between the physical reality of the tradition and its self-presentation is thus surprisingly good. The introductions, it turns out, are accurate "mirrors of the law." That this has not generally been recognized can be accounted for only by the overwhelming modern expectation that legal introductions, qua legal introductions, should delineate law as an autonomous field of technical-legal endeavor. Our authors, however, do not seem concerned with framing church law as an autonomous jurisprudential project at all. Their primary concern is to anchor law's normative authority firmly in the narratives of salvation/scripture, divinity, morality, philosophical enlightenment, and Greco-Roman political-legal ideals. The result is that law is cast much less as a mundane mechanism of consistent definitions, concepts, and techniques which govern a set of (malleable, human) rules than as a strangely numinous literary endeavor in which the central concern is providing the right "glosses" to understanding, internalizing, and applying a semi-sacralized body of traditional texts. Formalist legal definitions, concepts, and doctrines still exist in this world, but they are not its exclusive or even primary focus. In fact, we would exaggerate only slightly to suggest that these technical elements appear almost decorative in these introductions—the real legal content in this system is conveyed through the rhetorical interweaving of the canons into substantive narratives of tradition, justice, and truth.

3

The Language of the Law

A. INTRODUCTION: THE LANGUAGE OF THE LAW

Chapters 1 and 2 explored a variety of the ways in which the Byzantine canonical tradition presents and introduces itself as a normative system. I now turn to an analysis of how the canons themselves are written as normative texts and how they may be read to describe the beliefs, presuppositions, and priorities of their own legal world.

B. NOMENCLATURE

1. Naming the laws: terms for rules

The question of canonical nomenclature has been the subject of considerable scholarly attention, and rightly so. How the canonical tradition "names itself" potentially reveals much about the nature of the system as a whole, and how it relates itself to other normative systems. Naturally, most research has been directed towards the dominant term, *κανών*. In the Byzantine tradition itself Matthew Blastares (d. *c.*1350) considered it worthwhile in the *Προθεωρία* to his *Alphabetical Syntagma* to explain this term,[1] and short, stereotyped notices on its meaning and significance have since become a standard feature of eastern Orthodox canonical textbooks.[2] Similarly, modern histories of canon law rarely fail to note the origin and development of the term, and several articles have been devoted to its significance.[3] Classicists have also been interested in the term, and have produced two major studies of its use in

[1] *RP* 6.5–6; Zonaras earlier makes a very short comment (*RP* 4.81) with reference to the biblical canon. There is no definition in the *Suda*. In the west, explanations of this apparently unusual Greek term appear earlier, for example in the preface to the 7th C *Hispana* (trans. Somerville and Brasington 1998, 57).

[2] e.g. the *Pedalion* (Kallivourtsis 1800) xviii; Christophilopoulos 1965, 39; Milaš 1902, 11–12; Rhodopoulos 2005, 30; Tsipin 2002, 15–16.

[3] e.g. Erickson 1991a; *Fonti* 1.2.494–502; Hess 2002, 77–8; van der Wiel 1991, 11.

literary and legal contexts.[4] Recently, Heinz Ohme has published a comprehensive monograph on the Christian use of the term, particularly the phrase *κανὼν ἐκκλησιαστικός*. Ohme treats the concept from a highly synthetic viewpoint, taking into account the uses of the term in doctrinal, moral, scriptural, and canon-legal contexts through the early 5th C.[5]

The term *κανών*, however, is only one term used by the canons to refer to church rules. Table 3.1 is a survey of all substantives used for church norms within the traditional Byzantine corpus of canons.[6]

Table 3.1 Canonical Nomenclature I: Canons.

Term	Distribution (canons with one or more occurrences)
κανών (singular or plural, in sense of a specific church rule)	Ancyra 14*; Nicaea 5, 18*; Antioch 2**, 9*, 19; Constantinople 2, 6; Constantinople 394; Carthage 24, 134, 136, *Acta* 1; Ephesus 3, 8; Chalcedon 1, 5, 8, 19, 22, 24, 26, 28; Trullo 2, 3***,4, 6, 13***, 16, 18, 25, 26, 29, 30, 33, 34, 38, 40, 44, 49, 49, 51, 53, 54, 55, 61, 64, 94*, 96; II Nicaea 1, 2, 3, 5, 6, 10, 11, 12, 19; Protodeutera 2, 8, 9, 10, 11; Basil 1***, 3, 4**, 10, 21**, 47, 51, 88, 89; Gregory Nyss. 5, 7; Cyril 1; Gennadius; Tarasius (* possibly to be placed in following category) (** meaning shades into the quantitative sense of canon as "penitential tariff"[7]) (***meaning perhaps generic, as in "rule of prayer")
κανών (less specific, if still semi-technical, in sense of a synthetic concept of general Christian practice and normativity, verging on "tradition" or "custom")[8]	Neocaesarea 15, Nicaea 2, 6*, 9, 10*, 15*,16*, 18*; Antioch 2; Laodicea 1*; Cyprian; Basil 12; Gregory Nyss. 5 (* possibly to be placed in above category)
ὅρος (singular or plural, in sense of a specific church rule)[9]	Nicaea 15, 17, 18, 19; Antioch 1, 6, 21; Serdica 4, 15, 17; Carthage, 5, 18, 25/70, 86, 138; Chalcedon 4, 10, 14, 20, 28; Trullo 40, 81

(*continued*)

[4] Oppel 1937, Wenger 1942. [5] Ohme 1998.

[6] This survey covers all terms for any type of Christian rule, whether the rule is extant and/or in the corpus or not. It does not include very general references to Christian tradition, most references to custom (*ἔθη*, *ἔθος*, *συνηθεία*—on these see nn. 250–2), and the Greco-Roman parliamentary vocabulary of decision-making (i.e. "decision," "judgment," or "sentence" language, such as *ἀπόφασις*, *γνώμη*, *κρίσις*, *ἀπόκρισις*, *ψῆφος*—all of which occur in the canons). Further, it does not take account of the many verbal nouns used to refer to decisions and norms, such as *τὰ ὁρισθέντα* (frequent, especially in Carthage; see also *τὰ ὡρισμένα*, as Constantinople 2 or Antioch 19), *τὰ θεσμοθέντα* (Trullo 81), *τὰ δόξαντα* (fairly common, e.g. in Athanasius to Rufinianus), *τὰ ἐκδοθέντα* (e.g. Tarasius), *τὰ τετυπωμένα* (Ephesus 1), or *τὰ διατεταγμένα* (Trullo 28).

[7] Although this meaning may be considered simply a subset of the "specific" rule meaning, i.e. a specific rule of punishment. See then also Ancyra 24, Gregory Nyss. 4, Basil 1, 30, 79, 80, 81, 83.

[8] This usage is not, of course, to be confused with the sense of *κανών* as "register of clergy" (e.g. Nicaea 1, 16, 17, 18; Antioch 1, 2, 6, 11; Chalcedon 2; Trullo 5).

[9] The term *ὅρος* also appears with the sense of penitential tariff (in Ancyra 6, 19, 21, 23). Some of the instances noted in this category also have a strong sense of "measure," e.g. Trullo 40.

Table 3.1 Continued

Term	Distribution (canons with one or more occurrences)
διάταξις	Apostolic 3, 49 (but both referring to commands "of the Lord"); II Nicaea 1, 4 (but referring to scriptural commands of the apostles), 5, 10; Tarasius; Protodeutera 9
διάταγμα	II Nicaea 1 (for "ordinances" of the councils)[10]
διαταγή	Basil 88[11]
νόμος (referring to concrete church rule)[12]	Nicaea 13; Protodeutera 17; Hagia Sophia 3; Basil 24, 50; Theophilus 13 In Basil 24 (*ἀνδρὶ δὲ χηρεύσαντι οὐδεὶς ἐπίκειται νόμος*) and 50 (*τριγαμίας νόμος οὐκ ἔστιν· ὥστε νόμῳ τρίτος οὐκ ἄγεται*) the usage is vaguer, shading into "customary penitential tariff." This may be true for Nicaea 13 as well; nevertheless, in each case a fairly specific church rule seems to be envisaged. See also Basil 20 (*νομοθεσία τοῦ Δεσπότου*), 87, and Theophilus 14 where *νόμος* is more obliquely applied to church regulation as a whole.
θέσμος	Antioch 3, 11, 23; Ephesus 8; Chalcedon 12; Trullo 84; Hagia Sophia 2, 3; Basil 87; Cyril 3, 5 This term frequently, if not always, seems to refer to more general, unwritten rules;[13] once, in Antioch 11, it seems to approximate the synthetic singular use of *κανών*. Cf. also II Nicaea 7, with *θεσμοθεσία* for "written and unwritten" traditions of the church.
(*τύπος*)	(This term is never used as a general designation for church rules per se,[14] but comes close in its meaning as "formula" or pattern for penance or procedure in Nicaea 19; Carthage 49; Gregory Thaum. 5; Basil 3, 7, 76, 78; Theophilus 7, 12.)

We may also note, as Table 3.2 shows, the terms found in introductory material:

[10] Cf. Trullo 28 *διατεταγμένα*.

[11] This is the only instance where the term clearly applies to a specific church rule; in II Nicaea 1, however, it is applied to canonical regulation more generally (*ἐνστερνιζόμεθα καὶ . . . τὴν αὐτῶν [τοὺς κανόνας] διαταγὴν*), and in II Nicaea 20 to the monastic teaching of Basil; also, in Apostolic 85 it appears in the title of the "Apostolic Constitutions" (*αἱ διαταγαί*). The *διαταγ-* root seem to have been associated especially with the apostles; see the observations of Synek 1997, 71–3.

[12] Most instances of *νόμος* in the corpus refer to secular laws (e.g. Chalcedon 3, 18; Trullo 34, 71; Carthage 56 (*acta*), 93, 99, 102, 117, 119, 129; Protodeutera 6) or the Old Testament (e.g. Apostles 63, 41; Trullo 33, 70, 82; II Nicaea 6; Basil 3, 87). Gregory Nyss. 4 makes a passing reference to the "law of nature" (*ὁ νόμος τῆς φύσεως*).

[13] So Zonaras: *θεσμοὺς δὲ τοὺς ἀγράφους τύπους λέγει, καὶ τὰς ἀρχαίας παραδόσεις ἐνταῦθα, νόμους δὲ τοὺς ἐγγράφους* (*RP* 2.710).

[14] It seems to designate secular laws twice: Ephesus 8, Chalcedon 17.

Table 3.2 Canonical Nomenclature II: Introductory Material.

Term	Distribution (sources)
κανών (specific usage)	*Epigraphs and listings in traditional πίνακες*: all, without exception, where rule terms appear. *Traditional historical prefaces to sources* (from *Kormchaya*): Constantinople *Introductory structures (prosphonetikoi, letters)*: Constantinople, Trullo, Gangra (epilogue), Antioch, Carthage *Prologues*: *οἱ τοῦ μεγάλου θεοῦ, τὰ μὲν σώματα, ὁ μὲν παρών*
κανών (synthetic usage)	*Introductory structures*: Gangra (letter)
ὅρος	*Traditional historical prefaces to sources* (from *Kormchaya*): Laodicea *Introductory structures*: Constantinople (possibly only for doctrinal decrees); Gangra (letter), Carthage *Prologues*: *τὰ μὲν σώματα*
νόμος	*Prologues*: *οἱ τοῦ μεγάλου θεοῦ* (also in Title 48)
θέσμος	*Prologues*: *τὰ μὲν σώματα, ὁ μὲν παρών*

This data raises four questions: (a) which terms are used; (b) which terms are not used; (c) what is the significance of both of these phenomena; and (d) what changes in usage may be noted. Three immediate observations may be made.

First, it is clear that a variety of terms can be used to name church rules. Here a common tendency of the tradition to stack and juxtapose differing usages, one on top of another, is very evident. A disinclination to strict terminological rationalization is among the most obvious traits of traditional Byzantine canonical nomenclature.[15]

Second, it is equally clear that the term κανών becomes increasingly dominant. Its only serious competitor, ὅρος, fades almost completely by the second wave (i.e. Trullo and after).[16] By the 5th C, as is widely recognized, κανών has emerged as a quasi-technical term for specifically church rules.[17]

Third, despite a general congruence with standard Greco-Roman administrative and legal rule vocabulary (all of the above terms are attested in Greco-Roman legal literature), a number of prominent and formal late Roman

[15] This is true for later Roman secular (and papal) legislation as well; technical distinctions and "official" terms can be identified, but the overall picture is quite blurry. See Corcoran 1996, 198–203; Maassen 1871, 228–9; Mason 1974, 126–31; Jolowicz 1952, 478–9; Wenger 1953, 531; Wieacker 1988, 19. See Synek 1997, 48–52 for a brief overview of the similarly diversity in legal terms in the *Apostolic Constitutions*.

[16] Although its corresponding dispositive, ὁρίζω, becomes increasingly regular. See Section D. Further on ὅρος, see in this section, esp. at n. 53.

[17] See Ohme 1998 *passim*. See e.g. its regular and casual use throughout the *acta* of Chalcedon. In imperial legislation it becomes especially common from the 6th C onwards, but appears occasionally already in the 5th C. The first instance in the secular legislation where the term designates a church rule is *CTh* 16.2.45 (*a*. 421). Wenger 1942, 87–8 *et passim*.

secular terms for laws, most notably νόμος and διάταξις (*constitutio*), are conspicuously, if not totally, absent as terms for church rules.

These observations lead to a twofold conclusion. On the one hand, the pattern of terminological self-designation in the body of Byzantine church law clearly conveys a sense of the tradition's own self-conscious existence as a special body of rules with (increasingly) a proprietary nomenclature, that is, a method of reference distinct from civil law. In other words, the canons tend to talk about themselves as "the canons" in a sense close to the modern usage: as a coherent and demarcated set of church rules within Byzantine legal culture.

On the other hand, the data precludes the notion that the canons *cannot* think of themselves in any other way. This challenges any overly strict doctrinal readings of the significance of the term κανών for Byzantine church-legal culture. The impression is rather that the canonical tradition sees itself as part of a large and rich world of normative ordering whose terms the tradition may use freely, even if it generally does not.

The growing dominance of the term κανών is nevertheless unmistakable, and raises the questions of the meaning and significance of this particular term, as well as the reasons for its preference. This significance of the term has exercised the scholarly literature for some time. Broadly, two theses have become attached to the term, both of which make the word bear considerable—probably too much—weight in our understanding of the very nature and development of church law.

The first thesis, which we may term "canonical exceptionalism," is common in some modern eastern Orthodox presentations of canon law. This view tends to read the use of term κανών doctrinally, and almost ontologically: it is understood to mark church rules as distinct in their very essence from secular "laws" (νόμοι) and as thus signaling—at least early on—a fundamental difference between ecclesial and secular legal cultures, or even the lack of an ecclesial legal culture.[18] The precise nature of this difference of essence is often left undefined, but the implication is that canonical legality is not characterized by the patterns of legal formalism–positivism highlighted in the Introduction. Canon law, it is suggested, functions with its own distinct and special sense of normativity, and thus possesses its own distinct and special terminology for rules—thus the preference for κανών. In particular,

[18] Especially strong expressions of this stream of thought include Afanasiev 1936 and Deledemos 2002, 14–31, but it may be discerned as a diffuse background assumption or implication of much of the literature noted in the Introduction, n. 40, e.g. Erickson 1991a, 14–20, Yannaras 1970, 174–93. See, however, Archontonis 1970, 15–16, where this reading is rejected, and the comments of L'Huillier 1964, 112. Non-Orthodox literature can also voice this theory, notably Schwartz 1936a, 178. In all cases scholars are broadly standing in a trajectory of thought stemming from Rudolph Sohm, for whom "law" (i.e. modern formalist law) is considered antithetical to the essence of the church: "**Das Wesen des Kirchenrechtes steht mit dem Wesen der Kirche in Widerspruch**" (concluding line of Sohm 1923, 1.700; emphasis original).

κανών is understood to signal a more open, informal type of normativity than that conveyed by the term "laws": "guidelines" is a commonly proposed translation.[19]

The second thesis, which we may term "from the canon to the canons," has been the subject of more sustained exposition, most recently in the hands of John Erickson and, above all, Ohme.[20] This thesis suggests that early Christian rule culture was centered around a unified, synthetic concept of *the* canon of the church, the "ecclesiastical canon" (*κανὼν ἐκκλησιαστικός*), which encompassed dogmatic, behavioral/moral, and church-order normativity. Early synodal and patristic rules, it is argued, were self-consciously only specific expressions of this basic apostolic "canon of the church" (*κανὼν τῆς ἐκκλησίας*), as applied in concrete instances. They were thus prototypically *ὅροι* that instantiate *the* canon, and not *κανόνες* themselves. When *κανών* is found in more specific and plural uses in earlier texts, it was understood to refer not to concrete synodal decisions, as if they were pretending to the authority of "the canon," but to much more customary and traditional rules—which, it is argued, were understood as in their very essence rules of the Gospel or the apostles.[21] The concept of *the* canon thus precluded the ongoing creation of rules termed *canons* by positive (synodal) legislative authorities.

In the course of the 4th C, according to this theory, a fundamental change occurred. First in Antioch (330), and then more clearly in Constantinople (381), and forever afterwards, *κανών* began to refer to earlier synodal enactments, and even to synods' own enactments. Councils thus began to create "canons." This usage, Ohme argues, was encouraged by late antique legal schools' interest in secular legal *κανόνες* (*regulae*), short summary legal rules or principles which were becoming increasingly popular in the bureaucratized environment of late antique law.[22] Church regulations, it is suggested, were starting to take on both the form and name of these secular rules as they became increasingly conceptualized as short juridical legal rulings. This conceptualization was thus soon applied to the "Apostolic Canons," and would also find echo in the short, summary rules of late 4th C canonical sources such as Laodicea.[23]

[19] So e.g. Patsavos 1981, 108; Schwartz 1936a, 178.

[20] Erickson 1991a, Ohme 1998; Hess 2002, 60–89 adopts and develops Ohme's work. Mardirossian 2010 also stands in this trajectory, developing the thesis further in light of the doctrinal clashes of the 4th C.

[21] So Ohme 1998 reads, for example, the plural disciplinary usage of *κανών* in Origen (at 194–5), or the plural usage in Gangra (at 401), or the specific usage of *κανών* in Neocaesarea 14/15 (at 335–6), Nicaea 2 and13 (at 363–6).

[22] Ohme 1998, 497–8, 508, 580.

[23] In Ohme 1998 this development is tracked mostly in connection with the apostolic material, but later it is also connected with other epitomized collections (e.g. Ohme 2001, 775) such as Laodicea, or parts of Carthage. Hess 2002, 70–89 strongly emphasizes this theme,

The end result of this shift, it is claimed, was that the older idea of *the* canon of the church became eclipsed by this new more positivist/juridical reality—and indeed the earlier synthetic usage of the term fades in the later sources. Church rule culture, it is argued, thus recentered around positively defined conciliar (and patristic) canons, instead of the old synthetic scriptural and apostolic canon/canons. The distinction between apostolic ordinances and later synodal ordinances was lost. This opened the door to the onset of legal positivism in which law could be conceived as a closed system of constructed rules, and suggested a fundamental severance from the old Gospel-apostolic centered tradition of rule ordering.[24] By implication, the church's legal system had thus become secularized and legalized, and its own more native, Gospel-centered orientation lost: "Lost is the early Church's sense of canon as part of the tradition, absolute and universal, maximalist in its vision of church life. Instead, canons are understood to be laws on ecclesiastical matters duly made and promulgated in written form by the competent ecclesiastical authority."[25] Church rules, apparently, had gone from being based on broad moral consensus about the apostolic *κανών* to becoming legally binding dictates of sovereign authorities.[26] Their essential connectivity with the Gospel was severed by this new purely juridical orientation.

It is beyond the scope of this work to examine either of these theses, in any of their incarnations, in great detail. The latter, in particular, extends its discussion far beyond the parameters of our investigation. A basic problem with both, however—and they share the same weakness—may be quickly noted. It arises not out of what they do argue, but what they do not: neither investigates all the relevant phenomena to which their philological investigations pertain. The first thesis never closely examines the character or nature of legal discourse in the tradition as a whole, secular or ecclesial, to determine what or whether real differences in ecclesial or secular normativity existed, and particularly whether these were meaningfully attached to the use of *κανών*; and the second never verifies whether the juridical positivism it connects with the transformation in the use of *κανών* ever came into meaningful operation. If one does investigate these phenomena, it is clear that both theories are overstated.

The conclusion—or, at least strong implication—of the second thesis, that the late 4th C saw the onset of a canonical legal positivism, is particularly problematic, even anachronistic. In effect, Ohme and others have stepped from the 4th C directly into the 19th C, or at least the 12th C west. As already

detecting a generalized reconceptualization of canon law by the end of the 4th C on the model of "statute law."

[24] This conclusion is particularly evident in Erickson and Hess.

[25] Erickson 1991a, 19.

[26] See Hess 2002, 80–1 for this sense of "moral" versus "legal" rules.

noted, research in Byzantine law for the last forty years has shown that the operation and existence of a modern-like, or even medieval-like, formalist–positivist legal system is extremely difficult to locate in Byzantine society, at any time, even in the civil law.[27] In the present work, too, the picture of 4th C—and certainly post-4th C—Byzantine canon law emerging is already decidedly non-positivistic/formalistic: the entire system is built around embedding normativity in metaphysical and theological narratives, and most of the trappings and presuppositions of modern formalism (conceptualism, developed jurisprudence, professionalization, constructivism, and above all the clear assertion of categorical legislative authority) are strikingly absent. Indeed, many of the canonical system's central concerns—continuity with scripture, the apostles, and broader narratives of Christian order and morality—are precisely those that Ohme and others see as having been lost. Whatever the changes in terminology, the development of legal positivism that is purported to have begun in the late 4th C never in fact materialized—or if it did, only very briefly and tenuously.

The first thesis makes the same misstep. It too brings modern western legal positivism–formalism into late antiquity, but now as the unexamined straw man of all secular legality, and, further, as comprehensively embodied by the term *νόμος* and other ancient secular designators. Church law, quite correctly perceived to not function in such a formalist–positivist way, is thus radically distinguished from secular law or even *all* law, and this is attributed to a simple difference in terminology. But all law is not modern formalist law, and any distinction between *νόμος* and *κανών*, even if a conscious doctrinal distinction was intended, cannot automatically be read as a distinction between formalism and non-formalism: neither term can be shown to be a simple cipher for any type of legal conceptualization. Certainly one must also take into account the fact that the canons do cloak themselves in legal terminology and forms shared with and even derivative from the secular law—including the term *νόμος*. Conversely, *κανών* itself has a secular legal valence as *regula*. The negotiation of identity between the two types of regulations is thus much more complex than a simple doctrinal distinction based upon terminological difference allows. To read the use of *κανών* for church rules as a radical, ontological rejection of legal formalism–positivism then—or any type of secular legality—is to ask far more than the terminological data alone can support.

Despite these problems, both theses retain much value for understanding the significance of the term *κανών* in Byzantine church law. The central instinct of both is undoubtedly correct: we should not *properly* be thinking about church law in terms of modern legal formalism–positivism, and the use

[27] See the Introduction.

of the term κανών is in some sense indicative of this. The first thesis, in particular, is broadly correct in seeing κανών as distinguishing church regulations from secular laws. The distinction between secular νόμοι and ecclesial κανόνες, especially evident when the two are paired, is omnipresent from the 6th C onwards.[28] Further, just as church regulative enactments do not as a rule term themselves νόμοι or other related terms for secular laws, secular legal enactments, with some relatively small and technical exceptions, do not as a rule self-designate as κανόνες.[29] The latter rule is stronger than the former; as noted, it is always entirely possible to speak about church regulations as "laws," as is evident in the corpus itself.[30] But the church laws are *usually* κανόνες, and secular laws *usually not* κανόνες—and this is always true when the two are spoken of together.[31] There are two *Rechtsmassen* in Byzantium,[32] and they do tend to possess proprietary nomenclatures.

Ohme and others are likewise correct to draw attention to the hardening of canonical nomenclature in the term κανών in the late 4th C. Although one might quibble with details, Ohme is also correct to perceive a movement from earlier general and synthetic uses of ὁ κανών to more specific and concrete senses as clear written enactments. We may doubt that this witnesses to a true shift in legal mentality any more than the decreasing currency of the old doctrinal vocabulary of κανών τῆς ἀληθείας represented a fundamental shift in Christian belief, but it certainly reflected a movement towards greater definition of a fixed, bounded body of rules. This regular and concrete use of κανόνες for church regulations unquestionably heightens a sense of church normativity as existing as a clearly defined, autonomous body of ecclesial legal literature—which physically, as noted in Chapter 1, was probably finding increasing expression in dedicated canonical manuscripts. Thus, while the

[28] For examples of the pairing of the two in Justinian's Novels, see Wenger 1942, 123. Nineteen such examples in total may be found in the Novels. See also n. 17.

[29] Aside from technical tax usages, the major exception is the technical jurisprudential *regulae* which are translated as κανόνες; see Wenger 1942, 72–81. But normal imperial *leges* or ordinances are not called κανόνες (although the Latin usage of *regula* is a little broader; see Wenger 1942, 62–70). Significantly, as Wenger notes, even imperial regulations touching church matters do not call themselves κανόνες (Wenger 1942, 123).

[30] Outside of the corpus it is also not difficult to find instances of νόμος language—to say nothing of διάταξις or τύπος language—applied to ecclesial rulings. See e.g. Sozomen, *Ecclesiastical History* 1.23.2: *Ἡ δὲ σύνοδος* [Nicaea] *ἐπανορθῶσαι τὸν βίον σπουδάζουσα τῶν περὶ τὰς ἐκκλησίας διατριβόντων ἔθετο νόμους οὓς κανόνας ὀνομάζουσιν* (a particularly interesting example since the rules *are* laws, but are *called* canons); or Athanasius, *De decretis Nicaenae synodi*, 36.8; or John Chrysostom *Ad Innocentium papam* (epist. 1), or Theodoret *Ecclesiastical History* 1.7; more generally in Chalcedon *ACO* 2.1.3.104 (see Price and Gaddis 2.174 n. 12). Similarly, later scholia to Apostolic 27 and 38 will call the canons ἱεροὶ νόμοι (*Sbornik*, Prilozh. 7–8). A systematic examination of this question would, however, be useful.

[31] See Wenger 1942, 123. This is true throughout the Byzantine period. On the question of νόμοι and κανόνες and their relationship, see Beck 1981, Macrides 1990, Stolte 1991, Troianos 1991.

[32] Fögen 1993, 68–9.

onset of a full-fledged legal formalism–positivism is probably not to be imagined, the formalization and "hardening" of terminology is likely symbolic of a general pattern of formalization and standardization of earlier, more fluid patterns of customary regulation and definition. We may thus concede that the tradition took a step in a formalist/positivist direction, and the change in the usage of *κανών* reflects this. Certainly it signaled a sharpening of the reality that the church possessed its own proprietary written normative system.

In the end, however, neither thesis sheds much light on the broader problem of why the church settled so definitively on the term *κανών* in particular for its central written norms. Indeed, no one has yet to propose a completely convincing explanation. Ohme's suggestion (followed by Hamilton Hess) that a central influence was the secular legal *κανόνες* is weaker than it first appears.[33] Ohme is probably correct in noting that these secular legal *regulae*/*κανόνες* were increasingly prominent in late antique jurisprudence, particularly in the more academically inclined and teaching-oriented climate of 4th and 5th C Berytos—and that some Christian canonical writers were in touch with these developments.[34] However, the real connection of these *regulae* to the ecclesial canons—and certainly the implication that the former provided some type of model for the latter—is difficult to demonstrate. Ohme and Hess rely upon a very general point of formal similarity: both the canons of the late 4th C and the secular *regulae* are very short and mostly indicative summary statements of regulation.[35] However, the differences between the canons and these rules far outweigh these similarities. First, while there is a brief spurt of short indicative canonical regulation in the late 4th C, this is never a particularly typical form for canonical legislation; it is something of a passing "phase."[36] If this development must be attributed to the influence of the secular *regulae*, it is at the very least a very short-lived phenomenon. The canons in fact tend to become longer and longer as time goes on; and even very early they can easily tend towards the garrulous.[37] More telling, however, is the difference in the content and nature of the secular *regulae* and ecclesial canons. Most of the *regulae* are maxim-like principles and definitions of a technical jurisprudence. For example, *Digest* 50.17.3: "The power of refusal belongs to someone who is in a position to be willing"; *Digest* 50.17.9 "In matters that are obscure we always adopt the least difficult view"; *Digest* 50.17.196 "Some dispensations relate to things, some to persons, and so

[33] Ohme 1998, 497–8; so Hess 2002, 78.

[34] On the secular *regulae* generally, see Schulz 1953, 173–83, 295–6, 307–8; Stein 1966 (109–23 on the late classical period); Wenger 1942, 53–61.

[35] Ohme 1998, 497; Hess 2002, 69–89, as part of his "statute" form.

[36] The best examples are the canons of Gangra, Laodicea, the Apostolic Canons, and some of the shorter penitential regulations of Basil (e.g. 55–80).

[37] e.g. much of Nicaea and Antioch; even the brief Apostolic Canons are filled with decorative asides. For examples, see Section F, *passim*.

those which relate to things are transmitted to the heir; those which relate to person are not transmitted to the heir." This type of regulation is clearly part of a much larger technical-legal doctrinal superstructure—a technical rule-logic discourse. But this type of language and content, either as cited from the secular literature or as a product of a proprietary ecclesial jurisprudential discourse, is extremely—indeed conspicuously—rare in the canons.[38] To suggest that the type of summarization evident in the secular *regulae* is akin to that in even the briefest canons is thus a very misleading comparison. The canons represent "summaries" of the church rule world inasmuch as any type of legislation represents "summaries" of general social experience or value/ moral beliefs: but they are mostly non-technical brief statements of rules of a huge variety of types. The *regulae*, conversely, are a very technical type of doctrinal jurisprudential summary. They thus have very few true parallels in either the short 4th C canons, or almost any other type of eastern canon, before or after. The emergence in canon law of real *regulae*—very explicitly on the model of *Digest* 50.17—can only be identified as a coherent phenomenon in the 13th C west.[39]

In the end, then, neither in form nor in content do the canons look much like the secular *regulae*, and what similarities do exist become less pronounced over time. At most, perhaps, the secular jurisprudential use of the term *κανόνες* may have been one, rather vague, contributing factor in the adoption of this language—but if so, only alongside many other usages of *κανών*.

Ohme's broader research into the Christian ethical/philosophical discourse of *κανών* actually provides a better, if less specific, context for understanding the preference of *κανών* terminology. In Greco-Roman philosophy, as Oppel has shown, the term *κανών* clearly had a general ethical and epistemological meaning as a measure of the good or good behavior, or as a fundamental philosophical criterion of truth.[40] It is not difficult to see how these meanings could easily shade into more concrete meanings of the term as specific epistemological, stylistic, grammatical, or even moral, behavioral or legal rules or models—as indeed they did.[41] Likewise, in the Christian usage, as Ohme demonstrates, the well-known and well-established "canon of truth" language encompassed and synthesized not only a broad dogmatic hypothesis of the faith, a credal sense, but also moral and church-order normativity.[42] In church usage this more synthetic sense could also easily fade into a plural, specific sense. Thus already in Origin we read of "following the ecclesiastical canons" (*τοῖς κανόσι τοῖς ἐκκλησιαστικοῖς ἑπόμενος*) where the term *κανόνες*

[38] See Section E.1. [39] Naz 1965; Stein 1999, 46–51.

[40] Oppel 1937, 23–39, 51–7, 87–94.

[41] Oppel 1937, 34–5, 52–3, 64–6, 101–5. A good example of the first is Philo's "canons" for allegorical interpretation (see Oppel 1937, 64–6).

[42] Ohme 1998, 61–239 *et passim*.

is clearly used in a disciplinary sense for specific rules.[43] In the earliest canonical material itself it is likewise clear that, although not yet referring to concrete synodal enactments, *κανών* does refer to fairly specific traditional rules of a variety of types.[44] The term is thus clearly used for, as Hess puts it, "universally observed ecclesiastical standards," broadly of apostolic origin and character.[45]

Ohme thus demonstrates a continuity of normative meaning for *κανών* from its broadest synthetic doctrinal-regulative sense ("canon of truth") through to its later more specific sense of traditional disciplinary rules. The latter naturally flows from the former, as both encompass the idea of transmitting traditional apostolic norms. The step to understanding the later synodal *κανόνες* as simply extensions of this development would then seem very small: synods started using the term *κανών precisely because they understood what they were doing as producing "universally observed ecclesiastical standards," broadly of apostolic origin and character*. Inexplicably, however, Ohme feels that when this last step is taken, when concrete synodal enactments begin to be termed *κανόνες*, and particularly when these enactments are placed in the mouths of the apostles in the Apostolic Canons, a major break in semantic continuity has occurred, with the proper distinction between apostolic norms and later church decisions destroyed. He feels that the older and acceptable continuity between *κανών* and *κανόνες* was ruptured.[46] The opposite reading, however, is more likely, at least from the perspective of the synodal legislators themselves. The synods began to call their conciliar legislation *κανόνες* precisely as a terminological method for asserting the continuity of all legitimate church normativity with apostolic normativity—a continuity broadly asserted in the very shape of the tradition and the introductory material, as we have seen. In effect, for the synodal legislators, the *κανόνες* were understood as simply stating or realizing *ὁ κανών*, and *thus* the terminological continuity. The term was favoured not because of any loss of distinction between apostolic ordinances and later church ordinances, but because it is inconceivable that any legitimate church ordinances would not also be apostolic, that is, properly "canonical." In sum, *the κανών*, the traditional semi-written *κανόνες*, and the synodal *κανόνες* were all being asserted as part of the same continuous normative reality—which precisely explains the long-term preference of the term *κανών*.[47]

[43] Origen *In 1 Cor.Hom.*, frag. 4, discussed and cited in Ohme 1998, 194–5; further references at 217 n. 156.

[44] e.g. in Nicaea 2 or 6, or Gangra (Epilogue)—and here we might also count all of the early uses of the term for a penitential tariff or ruling in e.g. Peter or Basil (Ohme 1998, 296–312, 543–69).

[45] Hess 2002, 77.

[46] See Ohme 1998, esp. 379–407, 485–509, 510–42, 570–82.

[47] See Taylor 1980, 43–57 for a similar argument in terms of unwritten/written rules.

Another well-known suggestion to explain the use of κανών, made by Eduard Schwartz, is that the early use of κανών for a penitential tariff—reflecting the quantitative sense of the term underlying its employment for taxes or tables of values[48]—may have, in the context of the pressing problem of *lapsi* in the 3rd and early 4th C, provided a critical stimulus for the increased use, and ultimate dominance, of the term in the following post-Constantinian environment.[49] This is entirely possible, but, as Ohme points out, the tariff usage of the term κανών in the early penitential literature is rather less extensive than one might expect, and, in any case, the term ὅρος is more prominent than κανών for the earliest synodal decisions.[50] Penitential canons are also not a particularly dominant part of the tradition, earlier or later. Ohme is thus not wrong to suggest that this "tariff" use of κανών has little more to do with the later general usage than the use of κανών for a table of Easter dates or for the registry of clergy.[51]

None of these proposals is therefore entirely satisfying.

There may, however, be another possibility, but it requires that we take a different tack altogether. Most scholars have sought one or two principal semantic stimuli for the church's adoption of the term. It is possible, however, that the search for such narrow stimuli is itself the problem. In this respect Blastares' presentation of κανών, the only significant Byzantine treatment of the topic, is worth examining. His discussion stresses precisely the term's polyvalence. He understands the word as ultimately derived from the use of physical straightedge by builders, but he knows that it is used metaphorically (τροπικῶς) by the fathers for their "ordinances" (διατάγματα), as it is also used by "many different sages" (πολλοὶ ἕτεροι ἐπιστήμονες) of the "logical arts" (λογικαὶ τέχναι), including grammarians, philosophers, doctors, those who "reconcile the harmonies of the parts" (i.e. musicians), and, "indeed, what is more," by those who have gathered (or perhaps "composed," συντάσσω) the civil laws. All of them, he notes, use the term to separate and define, so that nothing incorrect or "base" (νόθος) intrudes itself. But in the end the term is used most properly, he suggests, for the ordinances of the fathers because of their particular goal (σκόπος), namely correct faith and the conduct of a God-loving life.[52]

From a modern lexical perspective, Blastares has indeed put his finger on the most important—and most certain—characteristics of κανών: its multiplicity of usages and its generality. The term κανών is notable precisely for the extraordinary number of regulative meanings and connotations it can signify:

[48] On this "table" usage, see Oppel 1937, 66–8; on the tax, see Wenger 1942, 24–47 (although the fiscal usage in Roman legal documents is attested only from the 4th C).

[49] Schwartz, 1936a, 177 *et passim*; Schwartz points mainly to the uses of κανών in this sense in Basil (cf. 1911, 316–33).

[50] Ohme 1998, 11–14; 582.

[51] Ohme 1998, 582.

[52] *RP* 6.5–6.

physical rulers, grammatical rules, musical rules, artistic and stylistic models, various types of mathematical tables and lists, types of taxes and tariffs, philosophical principles, and technical jurisprudential *regulae*. As such, it is a term that can potentially link to, and be glossed by, many different types of rule-realm associations. Although it does undoubtedly become a fairly technical designation for church regulation, it is not an inherently technical or narrow term.

In light of this polyvalence, it is worth considering whether the "problem" of why κανών emerges as the rule term for church legislation has been misconceived. We may just as likely ask why would it *not* have been chosen. If one were to seek a term for church regulations, and for whatever reason a "strong" secular legal term was not desirable and a more general term was needed, κανών is an obvious choice. In fact, there are not many other options.[53] Here it may be wise to consider further the extent to which by the Christian period κανών can be read as simply the normal Greek substantive for "rule," with something approaching the elasticity and generality—if not quite the banality—of the modern English term.[54] The foreignness that attaches to the borrowed term "canon" in Latin and in most modern European languages has perhaps unduly oriented our research to thinking of this term as exotic and proprietary, in need of special explanation. If the term means simply "rule," do we really need an elaborate explanation for its adoption?

[53] The other major possibility is ὅρος, a term also encountered in the earlier church legislation, but which later falls out of regular use. The reasons for this change are not entirely clear. The lack of extensive study of ὅρος comparable with that devoted to κανών makes speculation difficult. Schwartz's suggestion (1936a, 177 n. 3, 193) is perhaps the best: the term ὅρος eventually became associated with doctrinal statements, and so the need to distinguish doctrinal from disciplinary material meant that its continued use for the latter became inappropriate. At Chalcedon there is also an instance in which ὅρος, in the midst of a heated debate, is explicitly distinguished from a κανών, although the nature of the distinction is far from clear (*ACO* 2.1.1.91; see Price and Gaddis 1.157 nn. 111, 112). Erickson 1991a and Ohme 1998 (adopted by Hess 2002) wish to read ὅρος as substantively different from κανών (with the former originally denoting a more temporary, less metaphysically charged "rule," only an expression of the church's broader "canon of truth"), but I know of nowhere in the tradition where this distinction is clearly expressed, and these authors do not seem to take into account the extent to which the two terms can be found used virtually synonymously in Greek literature, often in *hendiadys* constructions (to take only a few examples: Demosthenes, *De corona* 296; Aristotle, *Protrepticus*, Frag. 39.1; Dionysius Halicarnassensis, *De Lysia* 18.4; Philo, *De Specialibus legibus* 3.164; Gregory of Nazianzus, *Apologetica* 35.477; Basil, *Sermon* 13 (31.876)). Oppel 1937, 28–9, 51–72 notably tends to treat them as more or less synonymous. Even in Roman legal literature ὅροι and κανόνες (*definitiones* and *regulae*) can often be very nearly synonymous (Schulz 1953, 66–7, 173; Stein 1966, 65–73 *et passim;* 1995, 1553–4). This overlap can even be found in the canonical literature itself, e.g. in Carthage *acta* 1, Chalcedon 28, *Τὰ μὲν σώματα*, or Antioch, where the terms are used synonymously in the very same text. The question of the use and nature of ὅρος, and any possible distinction with κανών, must therefore be considered open.

[54] As in modern Greek.

2. Naming the law? The missing concept of "canon law"

Scholarship's concern to identify the precise meaning and significance of κανών can easily distract us from a much more important observation: the Byzantine canonical tradition, and especially the central corpus of texts, seems to lack almost entirely the abstract expression "canon law" or "church law." When terms such as ὁ κανονικὸς/ἐκκλησιαστικὸς νόμος or τὸ κανονικὸν/ἐκκλησιαστικὸν δίκαιον appear, they almost invariably refer to individual, concrete laws, customs, or legal rights.[55] The more general and abstract senses attached to these terms in modern usage, referring to the physical body or collection of the canons as a whole, or "canon law" as a discipline, field, set of problems, or a jurisprudential project, are almost entirely absent.[56] To refer to canon law as a whole, or in any type of general way, the overwhelming tendency in the canonical literature is instead to resort to a plural concrete designator: "the canons," "the ecclesial ordinances," and so forth. This is the usage found in the prefaces, in the titles to collections, in manuscript rubrics, and in the commentaries. The singular terms *ius, lex*, ὁ νόμος, and τὸ δίκαιον can take on more abstract senses in other contexts, including the secular Roman law, and certainly in scripture (ὁ νόμος τοῦ θεοῦ), but this does not ever seem to have been transferred to the canonical realm.[57] There is no "canon law" in Byzantium.

[55] e.g. Nicaea 13, or Chalcedon 12.

[56] There are some passages outside of the canonical literature that approximate a more abstract usage, but it is rare that any of these instances convey with certainty our modern notion of "canon law" as a defined complex of positive legislation with its own jurisprudential processes/literature. Exceptions might include ὁ ἐκκλησιαστικὸς νόμος of Palladius' *Life of St John Chrysostom* 2, or ὁ ἐκκλησιαστικὸς νόμος καὶ θέσμος in Socrates' *Ecclesiastical History* 1.9. In both cases no specific law seems envisaged, as is normally the case. The phrase ὁ νόμος τῆς ἐκκλησίας, or very close variants, as found especially in Sozomon's *Ecclesiastical History* (1.3.6; 1.8.11; 2.4.7; 2.27.13; 6.17.2; 8.12.4), and occasionally elsewhere (Athanasius, *Apology to the Emperor Constantius* 31.5.3, or Theodoret's *Ecclesiastical History* 2.3), also sometimes seem to verge on a more abstract, jurisprudential sense of "church law," but in almost all cases the phrases probably denote something closer to "custom of the church," or "traditional rule of the church." It is interesting, however, that many of the most abstract-sounding uses of this phrase occur in historians who also happen to be lawyers (Socrates and Sozomen); on church historians and law, see Harries 1986. Theodore Studite will also later refer to the "divine law" (θεῖος νόμος; e.g. in Epistles 31.37 or 535.38), but here too this phrase seems to refer to a general rule of Christian living or ethical standard. Further study of the use of the singular "law" in Christian discourse would be profitable. It is clear, however, that an abstract jurisprudental sense of "church law" never became conventional in the Byzantine period—and certainly not within the core canonical literature.

[57] For secular *ius* in more abstract senses, see e.g. *Digest* 1.1–5, *Institutes* 1.1; for ὁ νόμος, see Dio Chrysostom, *Περὶ νόμου* (Oration 75; ed. von Arnim 1893). It is interesting, however, that classical Greek legal thinking does not have a term that corresponds precisely to *ius*: the term τὸ δίκαιον always reads awkwardly (see Triantaphyllopoulos 1985, 3). The phrase *lex Christiana*, encountered in the secular legislation—and not used in the Greek canonical tradition itself, as far

A more abstract usage of "canon law," *ius canonicum*, seems to appear first in the west, and apparently with frequency only after the 11th C, with the rise of canon law as a distinct field of study in the medieval universities, and patterned very clearly and directly on the newly rediscovered Roman law.[58] It seems that a similar mirroring or patterning of canon law on the Roman civil tradition did not occur in the east.

The significance of this point of usage is potentially immense, but has rarely been noticed or dwelt upon—even though the anthropological literature has long noted the phenomenon that "primitive" societies tend to have "laws," not "law."[59] In fact this observation accords well with the general shape of the tradition. As noted in Chapter 1, Byzantine canon law exists primarily as a collection of a concrete body of distinct legislative texts, "the canons," not as an abstract field of jurisprudential endeavor, "canon law": it is composed of a very conservative and stable set of traditional rule texts, and it lacks a sophisticated or elaborate jurisprudential literature or a significant proprietary academic or professional infrastructure to produce such a literature. Even in the later Byzantine period, the entire system will develop more as a huge exegetical meditation on "the canons"—as a comparatively concrete and specific body of texts—than as a systematic jurisprudential project implied by "canon law." By not referring to itself with an abstract term "law," the tradition reflects its substance quite accurately.

C. GENRE

By the standards of modern legal codifications the most prominent formal characteristic of the Byzantine corpus is its heterogeneity. In one sense, of course, the corpus may be read as mono-generic—that is, simply a collection of enumerated lists of rules either prohibiting or prescribing behaviors or actions—but the underlying literary media of these rules vary considerably. Five major genres may be identified: the conciliar pronouncement or record, the letter, the oration/treatise, the question and answer (*ἐρωταπόκρισις*), and the poem. Although some, even most, sources of the first genre were likely composed originally as enumerated lists of rules, most of the others clearly underwent later processes of division, extraction, and/or compilation to

as I am aware—seems to mean something more synthetic, along the lines of "Christian practice" or "way of life." On this difficult expression, see Humfress 2007, 196–201 and Pieler 1987.

58 Walter 1840, 1; also Gaudemet 1958, 478. Halfond 2010, 137–8 notes the phrase already in use in the Merovingian period. On the development of 12th C canonical *ius*, see Brundage 1995, Ghellinck 1948, Kuttner 1982, Sohm 1923, Southern 1995/2000.

59 e.g. Diamond 1950, 27; Donovan 2007, 114 (attributed to Gluckman without reference); Willetts 1967, 35 (citing Diamond).

produce their present enumerated forms. Sometimes these works still exist in unenumerated forms, and in many cases, even in the councils, variant enumeration schemes exist for the same source, which points to a gradual and variable process of corpus enumeration.[60]

The conciliar canons exist in three forms in the Greek manuscripts: (1) simple lists of regulations, with little or no introduction; (2) canons affixed to, or constituting, a synodical letter; and (3) extracts of records of conciliar *acta*. Ancyra, Neocaesarea, Nicaea, Laodicea, Chalcedon, II Nicaea, and the two Photian councils belong to the first group; Cyprian, Gangra, Antioch, Constantinople 1–4 (and in appearance 5–7), Ephesus 1–6, and Trullo to the second. The only sustained examples of the last are the two "western" sources, Carthage and Serdica, much of which reads as stenographic records of conciliar proceedings in the form Hess calls *dixit-placet* (εἶπεν-ἤρεσεν).[61] Carthage, however, is quite varied. Framed notionally as a case dossier, it contains a variety of different conciliar forms and texts, including letters and resolutions, and all punctuated by excerpts of conciliar minutes. Also in the form of an *acta* record or decision (ψῆφος, διαλαλία) are Constantinople 394 (*acta*), Ephesus 7–9 (decisions and a synodical letter), and Chalcedon 28–30 (a decision and two *acta* extracts).

The Apostles may be regarded as either a proprietary "apostolic" genre—as the tradition seems to treat it—or as a variant of the first type of conciliar document (that is, as the product of an "apostolic council," as it is presented in the *Apostolic Constitutions*)[62].

It is possible that some of the sources of the first two groups were originally in a form closer to the third, and what remains in the canonical collections reflects various processes of distillation and extraction from more elaborate parliamentary records. However, there is no clear evidence of this happening on a regular basis, or even that these sources were ever the subjects of real parliamentary debate or discussion.[63] It is particularly interesting in this regard that in the extensive *acta* of Chalcedon and II Nicaea the canons

[60] The Apostolic Canons are among the most variable, existing without numbers in the oldest known Latin translation (the *Fragmentum Veronese*), and, when enumerated, often showing considerable variation in order and number of canons in the manuscripts—both within the Greek tradition, and across the Latin, Greek, and Syrian versions (see *Fonti* 1.2.4–7; Metzger 1985, 3.12; *Pitra* 1.43–4; *Sin* 63 n.2; *Source* 31; Steimer 1992, 92; Turner 1899, 1.2.1.370–1). Elsewhere in the corpus instances of variations in order, division of canons, and degree of enumeration may easily be remarked; see *passim* throughout *Fonti, Historike, Kormchaya, Sbornik*, Schwartz 1936a (cf. also 1911, 324–6), *Sin, Sources*, and Turner 1899. On the division of the patristic canons into enumerated canons, see *Sources* 88.

[61] Hess 2002, 24–7, 61–89.

[62] See Metzger 1985, 34–5; also *Sources* 28.

[63] *Contra* Hess 2002, 69–72, who is inclined to see the language of *placuit*, ἔδοξε, ὁρίζω, or similar terms, at least in the first wave, as evidence of derivation or distillation of canons from earlier parliamentary records. This is possible, but, again, there is no direct evidence of it, and Hess has perhaps not appreciated the extent to which *placuit*-like forms can be quite generic

stand noticeably outside of the main body of record, precisely without much parliamentary scaffolding. This suggests that they were composed as an independent list, perhaps by a special committee, and later simply approved.[64] In Protodeutera, for which no *acta* are preserved, the presence of small narrative resumptives among the canons also suggests that the rules were originally written as a completely separate composition, as they now stand, and presumably adopted as a whole.[65] Only the three canons of Hagia Sophia may be found embedded in the council's *acta*, including with *dixit-placet* structures—although even here they were clearly composed beforehand and then read out in the council by the archdeacon.[66] (Trullo does not have extant *acta* beyond the subscription list and προσφωνητικὸς λόγος, and it is far from clear that such *acta* ever existed.[67]) We should therefore be cautious about understanding the conciliar canons as the direct product of true parliamentary processes, even as much as we see this in Carthage and Serdica. The parliamentary form may in fact represent something of a western peculiarity.

One distinction in style among the conciliar sources is sufficiently prominent as to amount to almost a difference of genre: the second-wave legislation tends to be longer, more rhetorically elaborate, more inclined to scriptural and patristic citations, and more interested in lengthy justifications and explanations than that of the first wave. It becomes at times almost homiletic in tone.[68] This distinction is always more quantitative than qualitative, and admits many exceptions, but the first-wave legislation is as a rule much shorter, simpler, and plainer.[69]

The patristic material shows even more formal variation than the conciliar legislation, although most sources are letters or letter-like, and are written as responses to specific inquiries. A key characteristic of these texts is that most, if not all, are consciously written to address specific disciplinary rule problems, and as such are expressly written as rule texts.[70] In this respect they are closely

Greco-Roman legislative stylizations. They cannot on their own be read as definitive evidence for a text's original embedding in a parliamentary record.

[64] On Chalcedon, and particularly on the idea that the 27 canons were composed by a small and separate committee, and perhaps never even formally approved, see Price and Gaddis 2005, 1.81 n. 277, 3.92–3. Certainly the canons do not seem to belong to any formal session. Instead they are tacked on in various places in the different versions of the *acta* (Price and Gaddis 2005, 1.xiv). The canons of II Nicaea likewise are simply appended to the final, eighth session of the council, with little comment; see *Historike* 314–17.

[65] *Fonti* 1.2.458.19–459.2; 474.13–475.16.

[66] *Mansi* 17.494–500.

[67] The point is debated; see Gavardinas 1998, 42–9; *Historike* 285–6; Ohme 1990, 25–7.

[68] Good examples include Trullo 45, 96; II Nicaea 2, 4; Protodeutera 10.

[69] Exceptions in the first wave include Nicaea 12, 18, Constantinople 6, and Chalcedon 4, all quite long and elaborate; Ephesus 8 is also quite elaborate, although it is a formal ψῆφος. Conversely, Trullo 15 and 58, and Hagia Sophia 3, are short and concise.

[70] For example, Basil's three classical canonical letters to Amphilochius are each a series of rules, and each of his individual letters addresses a specific disciplinary matter as its primary

akin to the papal decretals, yet quite unlike much of the later patristic material that appears in western collections from the 8th C onwards. The latter is the product of scouring general doctrinal, exegetical, homiletical, or other types of writings *not* originally written as rule texts, for rule content.[71] Such patristic "rule mining"—in fact a very creative jurisprudential process—is much less evident in the eastern tradition, if not entirely unknown.[72] The eastern inclination is instead to gather into the corpus ready-made patristic rule texts "as is," with little extraction or editing.

The majority of the patristic material may be loosely termed episcopal letters, generally from a bishop to some type of underling or underlings, often new or less knowledgeable bishops, and in response to various difficulties or questions.[73] In their manuscript prefaces, and/or in the *Coll14* source listing *ἐκ ποίων*, they are usually termed either simply "letter" (*ἐπιστολή*)[74] or, most often, "canonical letter" (*ἐπιστολή κανονική*)[75]—when a term is supplied at all.[76] One canon is presented as from a festal epistle (*ἑορταστική*)[77], and one is termed an encyclical (*ἐγκύκλιος*).[78]

The tone of the letters can vary from brotherly and consultative (e.g. Dionysius), to paternal and didactic (the most common; e.g. Basil to Amphilochius, Gregory of Nyssa, Timothy, Athanasius to Rufinianus), to administrative (e.g. Theophilus 2–11), to excoriating and admonishing (e.g. Basil to Paregorios or to "his bishops" [= canons 88, 90]). Some are written in a relatively discursive, almost meandering style, with considerable explanation, justification, and scriptural citation.[79] Others read more as a straightforward

concern; Peter is an oration "on repentance," but is nevertheless almost entirely written as a set of rules addressing specific problems; Gregory Nyss. is a systematic exposition of penance that is likewise almost entirely taken up with reviewing traditional penitential rules; Theophilus is a series of administrative rulings; Timothy is a set of rules in the form of "answers"; and so forth.

[71] The earliest major example of this type of operation may be found in *Hibernensis* (*c.*700; ed. Wasserschleben 1885, and see Sheehy 1987), although this activity does not seem to have become exceptionally common until the 11th C. See esp. Munier 1957; also Fransen 1973; Maassen 1871, 348–82. For the definitive western selection in Gratian, see Friedberg 1879, 1.xxxi–xxxvii.

[72] e.g. Peter 15 "from his treatise on Pascha"; the excerpts from Basil's *On the Holy Spirit*; the two scriptural canon poems; perhaps Athanasius to Ammoun and Theophilus 1. Most are comparatively late additions to the corpus. See also the more marginal patristic appendix items in *RP* 4.389–91 and *Fonti* 2.187–91.

[73] Peter, Gregory Thaum., Gregory Naz., and Amphilochius are without addressees. Cyril to Domnus of Antioch, although from one great see to another, is written as from a senior bishop to a junior. Tarasius, to Pope Hadrian, is the only source written to a notional superior.

[74] Basil 86 to Amphilochius, Theophilus to Menas, Cyril to Domnus, Cyril to the bishops of Lybia and Pentapolis, Athanasius to Ammoun and Rufinianus.

[75] Dionysius, Gregory Thaum., almost all of Basil's epistles, Gregory Nyss., Theophilus to Aphyngios, Tarasius.

[76] In the manuscript prefaces one will often find a simpler form of *τοῦ αὐτοῦ πρὸς* . . . or *τοῦ αὐτοῦ περὶ* . . . This is especially true of Basil's letters, and to some extent of Cyril and Theophilus.

[77] Athanasius 2. [78] Gennadius.

[79] Chiefly Dionysius, Gregory Thaum., Peter, Athanasius, some of Basil, Gennadius, Tarasius.

citation of traditional rules,[80] while at least one, Gregory of Nyssa, should be considered a small systematic treatise in the guise of a letter. One source, the ὑπομνηστικόν of Theophilus, as its name suggests, is a technical administrative document, a registry of episcopal chancery missals that briefly decide or provide for the decision of very specific matters referred to him (ὑπομνηστικά) in his jurisdiction.[81] Theophilus 13 and 14 are very similar in form, as are Cyril 4 and 5. Gennadius, although listed under the patriarch's name in the patristic material, is a general synodical encyclical subscribed by the Constantinopolitan *endemousa* synod. It is the only specimen in the corpus of a formal synodical epistle, a genre that is quite prominent in the canonical tradition after the 9th C (although Tarasius is similar).

A very few patristic canons are not letters, or at least not clearly. One, the answers (ἀποκρίσεις κανονικαί) of Timothy to "various" bishops and clerics, given at the council of Constantinople 381, is a formal ἐρωταπόκρισις, the only example of its type in the corpus. Many representatives of this genre will appear in the later appendix material.[82] Theophilus 1 is listed as a προσφώνησις, a public address. Peter of Alexandria's lengthy and involved tract is presented as κανόνες φερόμενοι ἐν τῷ περὶ μετανοίας αὐτοῦ λόγῳ—that is, in a λόγος, or treatise.[83] Likewise Peter 15 is presented as an extract from his λόγος on Pascha (Peter 15). Basil 91 and 92 are identified as from chapters 27 and 29 of his "writings" (γεγραμμένα) *On the Holy Spirit*. The two canons in verse form in the corpus, Gregory of Nazianzus and Amphilochius, are presented respectively as "from his metrical works" (ἐκ τῶν ἐμμέτρων ποιημάτων), and Amphilochius as "from his iambics to Seleucus" (ἐκ τῶν πρὸς Σελεύκον ἰάμβων). Their verse form, exceptionally curious for legal texts, is undoubtedly mnemonic in intention.[84] A few other examples of non-letters may be found in the common para-canonical patristic material just outside of the corpus proper, namely a few excerpts from John Chrysostom's *On the Priesthood* and his exegetical works, as well as a short sermon on the priesthood attributed to Basil.[85]

From this data we may make two general observations about canonical genre.

First, the corpus's handling of genre evinces one central instinct: the gathering and transmission of traditional rule texts *in their integrity*. In a phenomenon already remarked in Chapter 1, sources tend to enter the corpus in their original forms, with most of their original compositional paraphernalia intact,

[80] Much of Basil's three canonical letters to Amphilochius.

[81] See Dölger and Karayannopulos 1968, 82. [82] *Peges* 250–5.

[83] Although this "treatise" is really an encyclical letter, a point clearer in the Syriac, where more of its original heading has been preserved. *Sources* 91.

[84] Although Solon versified law, as reported e.g. in Plutarch, *Life of Solon*, 3.4. I am grateful to Caroline Humfress for this observation.

[85] *RP* 4.389–92.

and these forms tend to be preserved throughout the sources' later transmission. Ongoing processes of homogenization through abbreviation, modification, or the extraction of "pure" rule content from the sources—processes that would be routine in modern codification projects and which are very evident in the ancient civil codes—are very hard to demonstrate. The only ongoing editing operations we can detect are the division of all sources into numbered canons and the "trimming" of conciliar subscription lists or addressee sections.[86] Any other significant changes seem to have occurred before, or perhaps at, the source's first introduction into the corpus—not in the course of a source's transmission in the corpus. Thus Carthage is clearly a highly edited compilation of numerous earlier extracted sources;[87] Laodicea may be an abbreviation and compilation of earlier, longer texts;[88] and numerous patristic texts obviously represent only the answers to questions now lost.[89] But there is no evidence that much editing took place after these sources were included in the canonical manuscripts.[90] From the moment these and other sources definitively enter the corpus, the rule seems to have been the preservation of original form. Once again, then, the basic formula for codification is agglutination: the ongoing juxtaposition of traditional texts in their traditional form. The end result is a kaleidoscopic array of heterogeneous, semi-sacred, ossified sources.

Second, canonical legislation demonstrates both dissonance and resonance with the late Roman civil-legal tradition on the level of genre. Resonance is to be found in the preponderance of the letter form. Late antique and Byzantine secular legislation was surprisingly epistolary, and this seems to have become increasingly the case as time progressed.[91] General laws, and even many more specific command texts, were overwhelmingly dated missives sent to a high official, or a group of addressees.[92] Vestiges of this letter form are even preserved in the abbreviated redactions of the *constitutiones* found in the codices, where the addressees and dates are almost always retained.

[86] On these last, see Ch. 2 B.7 (esp. n. 104); also Appendix A. [87] See Ch. 1 C.

[88] On the structure and composition of Laodicea, see the overview in *Sources* 48–9; also L'Huillier 1976, 59–60.

[89] e.g. Theophilus, Basil.

[90] It seems that Carthage could on occasion be abbreviated, as already noted (Ch. 1, n. 66), but this seems to have occurred only early, when the source was not yet well established in the tradition. It will later be transmitted in its full form. This abbreviation does not in any case seem to have entailed stylistic homogenization.

[91] Millar 2006, 7–35 has recently emphasized this.

[92] As many edicts do in fact possess addressees (albeit general ones—e.g. *CJ* 1.2.1; 1.23.4), and can be understood to gradually blur with imperial law letters (see e.g. the comments of Corcoran 1996, 198–203), it is safe, with Millar, to assimilate them to the "letter" (and more so with the later pragmatic sanctions). For an overview of late antique and Byzantine legislative forms, see Dölger and Karayannopulos 1968, Pieler 1978 (*passim*, but esp. 351–61), 1997a; also van der Wal 1981.

Canonical legislation is likewise surprisingly permeated, if not quite to the same degree, by the form of the letter: not only are the majority of the patristic sources framed as letters, but so are a number of councils (especially Gangra, Antioch, Constantinople, and Ephesus; even Trullo, headed by its *προσφωνητικὸς λόγος*, could be viewed as such).

The dissonances are more striking. Despite the general preponderance of the letter, the absence of true *leges*-type law writing in the corpus is very conspicuous. Virtually no source in the corpus is written in clear imitation of a proper late Roman novel: that is, as a self-standing letter on a fairly unitary topic and, above all, with a clear structure of *protocol* (certainly with *inscriptio*, i.e. addressee, and perhaps *invocatio*), *prooimion, narratio, dispositio, sanctio*, and *eschatocol* (including subscription and dating, and publication instructions).[93] Individual canons may contain *prooimion, narratio, dispositio, sanctio* structures; indeed, in the second wave these structures can become quite pronounced, and may even reflect a certain assimilation to imperial law-writing form.[94] Even some conciliar sources as wholes, such as Antioch, Constantinople, or Trullo, with their addressees and (original) subscription lists, may vaguely suggest a novel-like structure. The letters of Gennadius and Tarasius are even closer: they are self-standing letters written on a specific topic, with a specific addressee, and under one name. But in all cases they lack, in particular, structures corresponding to the fairly stereotyped imperial protocols (with at least a generic addressee) and *eschatochols* (with at least a date), which clearly distinguishes the canonical law writing from the secular *constitutiones*, even when the latter are found in their abbreviated forms in the codices. Further, even the longest canons with *prooimion, narratio, dispositio, sanctio* structures only faintly recall the detail and extent of these structures typical of imperial novels. Some of the most common secular legislative dispositives are also rare.[95]

This dissonance becomes more glaring when we realize that ecclesial law writing that is much more obviously imitative of the secular novels is well known in late antiquity and later: the papal decretals.[96] Further, post-9th C Byzantine canonical legislation, in which synodical letters dominate, approximates the secular forms much more closely.[97] The earlier legislation thus emerges as a surprisingly distinct legal form.

[93] See above all Dölger and Karayannopulos 1968 (whence the terminology here), with summary at 48–9, also 77; also Pieler 1978, 355–61; 1997a, 571–3. (For some criticism of Dölger and Karayannopulos 1968, Bochove 1997, 159–60.)

[94] Some of Trullo, and much of II Nicaea and Protodeutera read as such. Trullo 79, II Nicaea 7, and Protodeutera 10 are particularly "full" examples of this form.

[95] See Section D.

[96] See Jasper and Fuhrmann 2001, 11–22; briefly Gaudemet 1958, 222–6. On the general modeling of papal authority on imperial administrative patterns, see Humfress 2007, 211–12 with further references.

[97] See the many samples in *RP* 5.1–185.

This highlights the troublesome fact that the canons as a whole, and the conciliar legislation in particular, do not in truth look much like *any* other type of contemporary civil-legal texts.[98] Broad resonances with parliamentary records and procedures (senatorial and perhaps provincial) have frequently been remarked, and there may be parallels to be made with municipal codes.[99] If one allowed comparison with much older texts (the Twelve Tables, in any reconstruction, the Pentateuchal material, or other extant ancient codes), further points of identity could be made.[100] Nevertheless—although the point is perhaps a bit fine—compared with the products of the only other major source of *living*, active, public written laws in most of our period, that is, the imperial government, producing its *constitutiones*, the canons as a whole, and particularly the conciliar canons, are effectively a proprietary legislative phenomenon, with a proprietary form. (The collective origin of the conciliar canons further distinguishes them dramatically from imperial laws.) The two public, living, empire-wide legislative *Rechtsmassen* of the late antique and Byzantine worlds thus do look quite different. They are not radically "other" from each other, certainly, but clear, comprehensive imitation is not evident.

It is also worth re-emphasizing that the only other major type of legal literature with currency in late antiquity and Byzantium, jurisprudential writing, also finds little real parallel in the canons on the level of genre. A comparison is often made between the patristic canons and the works of Roman jurisprudents, but this is misleading.[101] It is applicable only in the most general senses: the patristic letters are "responding" to questions or clarifying or communicating certain rules; they are written by individuals; Timothy's ἀποκρίσεις represent a genre known to be in use among the jurisprudents; the patristic material tends to be treated as secondary to and interpretative of the canons; and the patristic material is occasionally apt to sound as if it is expressing opinion rather than issuing true authoritative judgments. But these points of similarity are vague. Direct genre imitation and sustained textual similarities are few. In particular, the patristic writings do not form themselves as "books" in imitation of the Roman jurisprudential

[98] Of course the closest material in genre, tone, and style to the canons is the Apostolic Church Order materials; but these are "internal" texts of the Christian tradition, not our subject here.

[99] Hess 2002, 24–7, 69–75 surveys the recent literature on the senate and/or municipal councils as models for Christian conciliar procedure and publication, with a summary of procedure at p. 27. See also Dvornik 1966, 640–1, Harries 1998. Here we do not count the secular *regulae* as a properly "legislative" form—and, as noted, the canons do not much resemble them in any case.

[100] For the longer ancient edicts, see Johnson *et al.* 1961.

[101] This is unfortunately very widespread, e.g. *Fonti* 2.xiii; Hess 2002, 87; *Peges* 63–4; *Pitra* 1.li–liv; Schwartz 1936a, 178–9.

works listed in the Florentine index (for example, *βιβλία digeston*, *ὅρων*, *iuris civilion, regularion*, *ἐγχειριδίου*, *actionon, ad leges*, etc.), none emerge as formal commentaries on an established corpus structure such as the Praetorian Edict or the Sabinian corpus, and none are written with anything approaching the sustained, closed, technical, and well-defined conceptual textures for which the *Digest* is well known.[102] Only one patristic source—Basil—could be read as consistently recalling this literature, and only dimly. Basil does give the impression of commenting on an established (perhaps unwritten) Cappadocian corpus, and some of his canons are written in an unusually technical, quasi-commentary style, that is, in which a known rule is stated and then subjected to various processes of quasi-technical rule reasoning.[103] A few other instances of such technical or doctrinal semi-commentary, directed towards narrow points of law, may be found among the patristic sources.[104] But in all cases, even in Basil, such discourse is fairly desultory, ad hoc, and hardly beyond a level of technical sophistication expected of any well-educated rhetor. This type of writing is also not that much more characteristic of the patristic material than the conciliar—so there is no reason to draw the comparison specifically between the jurisprudential literature and the patristic material.[105] Further, none of the patristic authors explicitly, or even allusively, cast their work as comparable to that of the secular *σόφοι τοῦ νόμου* (the normal Greek term for the Roman jurists).[106] This is entirely correct: their works are in fact much more analogous to those of secular magistrates than the *prudentes* or assessors. A few first-millennium texts aside, the first instances in the Byzantine canonical tradition of a proper jurisprudential *literature* is the 12th C commentary tradition.[107]

Contrary to a common formulation, then, the conciliar canons do not look much like imperial laws, and the patristic canons do not look much like jurisprudential literature. Such a comparison finds a clear referent only in the post-12th C western canonical structure of papal decretals (= imperial *leges*) and the commentaries of the decretalists (= jurists).[108]

[102] Schulz 1953 remains an excellent overview of the literary and conceptual textures of this material. Pringsheim 1921 usefully dissects many techniques.

[103] See Ch. 2 B. 7 (esp. n. 100) and this chapter, Section E.1.

[104] Certainly parts of Gregory Nyss., Theophilus, and Cyril.

[105] Commentary-like texts and technical interpretative activity may be found in Trullo or Protodeutera—or even Nicaea. See Sections E.1 and F.1.

[106] The *Coll14* prologue *τὰ μὲν σώματα* perhaps suggests it (*Pitra* 2.446.11–2.447.3) but it is still notable that no direct assimilation of the fathers to the *σόφοι* are made—especially since the secular *σόφοι* are mentioned later in the prologue (*Pitra* 2.447.15). See van der Wal and Stolte 1994, xvii on the term *σόφος* for "jurist"/*prudens*.

[107] See Ch. 1 D.6.

[108] See generally Brundage 1995, 59–61, 154–74.

D. STRUCTURE AND DISPOSITIVE VOCABULARY OF THE CANONICAL RULES

The level of abstraction and categorical force of the canons, as well as the relationship of the canons to other types of normativity, may in part be determined by an analysis of the canons' basic structural features. These features may be defined as (1) the overall syntactical structure of the canon (for example, an "if... then..." case structure, or a straight apodictic prohibition "Let not...," or a formal compositional division such as *narratio, dispositio, sanctio*), and (2) the key dispositive, or normative, vocabulary employed (for example, "we order," "we command," "must").

A survey of both these features reveals that the Byzantine tradition is again characterized strongly by heterogeneity. This is true across the corpus as a whole, which we might expect, but also within individual sources. There are only two sources which show almost complete consistency in *both* form *and* vocabulary of rule expression: Gangra, which enunciates each of its short rules according to the schema *Εἴ τις* + optative (sometimes indicative, but optative readings may often be found in the manuscripts)... *ἀνάθεμα ἔστω*; and Protodeutera, which uses the dispositive formula *ἡ ἁγία σύνοδος... ὥρισεν...*, or the similar *ἡμεῖς... διοριζόμεθα* or simply *ὁρίζομεν*[109] in every canon but one (9),[110] to convey the canon's central rule content and/or punishment. In a few other sources, large stretches of texts are often very similar (which suggests a process of compilation of earlier works), but the consistency of expression in parts of these sources ultimately serves only to highlight the discontinuity of form in the whole of the sources.[111] Harmonization and uniformity were simply not priorities in Byzantine legal composition.

Most sources cycle through a variety of structures and dispositives, even if one or two forms may be particularly common. Nicaea, to take one example (and considering just the primary rule of each canon, or where this is unclear, the first rule; if supplementary rules were to be counted, the diversity would be greater), exhibits *εἰ* + imperative constructions in canon 1 and 8; *εἰ* + indicative in 9; *ἐπειδή* + *ἔδοξεν* in 2 and 20; *ἐπειδή* + imperative in 7 and 12; *ἐπειδή* + *δικαιόω* in 17; *ἦλθεν εἰς τὴν... σύνοδον* + imperative in 18; *ἀπαγορεύω μήτε* + infinitive in 3; *προσήκει* + infinitive in 4; *χρή* + infinitive in 16; *περί* + imperative in 5; *περί* + *ἔδοξε* in 8, 11, 14 (partially in 5); *περί* + indicative in 13, 19; *διά*+ *ἔδοξε* in 15; straight imperative in 6, 12; straight indicative in 10. This degree of variety is fairly typical.

[109] Canons 11, 12, 17.

[110] Where it is replaced with *ἡμεῖς οὕτω συμψηφιζόμεθα*, since canon 9 is merely repeating and strengthening an injunction of the apostles, Apostolic 27.

[111] See esp. Laodicea 1–19 and 20–59, as well as Constantinople 1–4, and, to a lesser degree, Basil 56–74, Carthage 35–47, 66–85.

When we turn to syntactical and compositional structures alone, one general pattern may be observed throughout the corpus: the canons are overwhelmingly casuistic. That is, the majority of canons can be understood to contain (and in this order) a functional protasis, in which a problem, behavior or circumstance is related, and an apodosis, in which the consequence of or determination for this problem is stated, often including or constituting a sanction. The classic form of this structure is an explicit "if . . . then" statement: "If anyone should pray with an excommunicated person, even in a house, let him be excommunicated" (Apostolic 10). But many variants are possible, and once again variety is the rule. A common type, easily converted to an "if . . . then" statement, is a nominative or accusative participial subject structure (in English usually rendered "He who . . . ," "Those who . . . "), such as Ancyra 19: "Those who having professed virginity disregard their profession, let them fulfill the penance of digamists" (Ὅσοι παρθενίαν ἐπαγγειλάμενοι ἀθετοῦσι τὴν ἐπαγγελίαν τὸν τῶν διγάμων ὅρον ἐκπληρούτωσαν). Examples of this form, or the previous one, are present in almost every canonical source, and are especially prominent in the first wave.[112] Also very common are casuistic structures beginning with ἐπειδή clauses or περί phrases[113] or preliminary *narrationes*.[114] These become more prominent in second-wave sources, although they are already important in the first wave (for example, in Ancyra and Laodicea). But the basic formula of all these rules, whatever their exact form, is "if in *x* situation, then *y*." This corresponds to a simple *narratio-dispositio* structure.

Not all canons are casuistic. Some—at least in their primary rule—are straight apodictic authorizations or prohibitions. An example is Apostolic 1: "Let a bishop be ordained by two or three bishops." Many of these apodictic regulations, essentially isolated dispositive phrases, do not specify sanctions. Those that do often must add a supplementary sanction in an "if . . . then . . . " form, and may be viewed as semi-casuistic. An example is Apostolic 5: "A bishop or presbyter or deacon is not to cast out his wife on the pretext of piety; if he does cast her out, let him be suspended; persisting, let him be deposed." Such non-casuistic rules may be found throughout the corpus, but by far the greatest concentration of rules of this type is to be found in Laodicea, and to a lesser extent Antioch (e.g. 1, 2, 7, 8, 9, 13, 19–25). They are clearly a subordinate type of regulation.[115]

The second major structural feature of canonical rules, dispositive vocabulary—that is, the phrases used in the dispositive acts of ordering and

[112] Principal exceptions include Laodicea and Constantinople.
[113] See e.g. the initial lines of Trullo 6 or Chalcedon 5.
[114] e.g. the first sentence of Protodeutera 7.
[115] Contrary to the impression given by Ohme 1998 and Hess 2002, who seem to present this type of legislation as an evolutionary end point of the church's "legalization."

legislating, and their grammatical mood (indicative, infinitive, imperative)—is also chiefly marked by variety and irregularity. Real consistency is the exception, within or across the sources. The only lengthy sources in which at least some elements of the dispositive vocabulary are almost entirely regular, aside from Gangra and Protodeutera, are Antioch (almost entirely "legal infinitives") and Laodicea (mostly *δεῖ* statements).

Most sources move through a variety of terms and grammatical forms. These include third-person imperatives or equivalents (i.e. third-person subjunctive aorists), as Apostles 23, *κληρικὸς ἑαυτὸν ἀκρωτηριάσας καθαιρείσθω*; second-person imperatives or equivalent (very rarely), as Basil 28, *ὥστε καταξίωσον διδάσκειν αὐτους τῶν ἀπαιδεύτων προσευχῶν καὶ ἐπαγγελιῶν ἀπέχεσθαι*; command or "legal" infinitives, in which the infinitive has no explicit governing auxiliary, as Apostles 35, *Ἐπίσκοπον μὴ τολμᾶν ἔξω τῶν ἑαυτοῦ ὅρων χειροτονίας ποιεῖσθαι*;[116] plain indicative statements of rules or practices, as Constantinople 7, *τοὺς προστιθεμένους τῇ ὀρθοδοξίᾳ... ἀπὸ αἱρετικῶν δεχόμεθα κατὰ τὴν ὑποτεταγμένην ἀκολουθίαν καὶ συνήθειαν*; impersonal modal constructions, of which *δεῖ* and *χρή* (and variant *χρεωστεῖ*) phrases are the most frequent, but including also *δίκαιόν ἐστιν, προσήκει, δύναται, ὀφείλει, ἔξεστι, ἀδεία ἐστίν, εὔλογόν ἐστιν*, simple *ἐστίν* (in the sense of "it is right/possible"), and a number of more complex phrases such as *τὸ ἔθος καὶ τὸ πρέπον ἀπαιτεῖ*... (Theophilus 1) or *ἔστω τύπος ὥστε*... (Theophilus 7); and, finally, a large number of "meta-dispositives," that is, indicative statements in which the legislators explicitly voice their own agency in the legislative process through statements such as "*we* decree," "*we* decide," "it seems good to *us*."

These last are collectively the most common, productive, and varied form of rule expression in the corpus. They are dominated by terms that denote deciding, decreeing, judging, or "judging good," such as *ὁρίζω* (the single most common term throughout corpus, very frequent from Chalcedon onwards[117]), *δικαιόω* (e.g. Nicaea 17; Ephesus 3, 4, 5, 9; Chalcedon 1), *δοκέω* (usually in the third-person form *ἔδοξε*, also very frequent[118]), *ἀρέσκω* (regularly in Carthage and Serdica as a translation for *placere* forms; also in Athanasius to Rufinus), *ἀποφαίνομαι* (Dionysius 1; Gregory Nyss. 5), *ψηφίζω* (Chalcedon 28,

[116] On this type of infinitive, especially prominent in Antioch, see Smyth 1956, 448.

[117] Chalcedon 3, 6, 7, 10,11, 12, 14, 16, 19, 20, 23, 27; Trullo 3, 6, 7, 17, 29, 30, 31, 36, 42, 45, 49, 53, 54, 56, 61, 62, 72, 79, 82, 84, 85(*διορίζω*), 86, 92, 94, 99; II Nicaea 2, 4, 7, 8 20; all Protodeutera; Hagia Sophia 1, 2. Earlier, it may be found in Apostles 74 (in the sense of measuring or apportioning out a tariff); Nicaea 6; Ancyra 21 (tariff usage); Serdica 7, 8, 11, 12, 15; Antioch 18; Laodicea 1; Constantinople Prosphonetikos; Ephesus 6, 7, 9; Basil 4 (for past decisions), 27 (tariff usage), 88; Theophilus 12 (for synod); Gregory Nyss. 4; and not infrequently in Carthage, especially after 50 (usually translating *statut- /constitut-* roots).

[118] e.g. Nicaea 2, 14, 15; Ancyra 1–4, 6, 7, 11, 12, 14; Antioch 10, 20; Ephesus 8; Chalcedon 25, 26; Trullo 2, 3, 12, 55, 60; Gregory Thaum. 2; Athanasius to Rufinianus; Basil 1; Gennadius.

itself a ψῆφος), θεσπίζω (Trullo 1, 8; Hagia Sophia 1), τυπόω (Basil 1; Trullo 3), νομοθετέω (Basil 18, 88; Trullo 12, 26, 36; Protodeutera 1), θεσμοθέω (Trullo 81), ἐπιτίθημι (Peter 5), τίθημι (Basil 8; Protodeutera 17), ἐκτίθημι (Basil 17, 51), διατίθημι (Basil 18), κρίνω (Basil 21, 24, 52; Gregory Nyss. 2, 5; Cyril 1), ἐκφέρω (Basil 81), διορθόω (Basil 90), καταδικάζω (Gregory Nyss. 7), δικάζω (Cyril 1), συνοράω (Trullo 3, 28, 33, 37, 39, 54), βούλομαι (Trullo 75), or θεραπεύω (Trullo 96). Closely related are "ordering" or "commanding" terms, such as προστάττω (e.g. Apostles 27, 41, 46; Ancyra 17, 21; Basil 34; Trullo 21, 63, 65, 73, 97, 100) and κελεύω (e.g. Apostles 15, 26; Ancyra 23, 25; Antioch 36; Constantinople 6; Ephesus 3; Basil 1, 24, 34, 51; Serdica 14, 18; Protodeutera 5), as well as permission and forbidding language such as ἐπιτρέπω (Apostolic 82; II Nicaea 14), ἀπαγορεύω (Nicaea 3; Trullo 51), or ἄδειαν δίδωμι (Protodeutera 6). Other expressions are confirmatory in character, including ἀνανέομαι (Trullo 3, 8, 25, 36, 49; II Nicaea 6, 7), κρατύνω (Trullo 1; II Nicaea 1), ἐπισφραγίζω (Trullo 1, 2), κυρόω and ἐπικυρόω (Trullo 1, 2; Protodeutera. 11), συνευδοκέω (Trullo 43), συμψηφίζομαι (Protodeutera 9, 11), and συμφωνέω (Protodeutera 11). In a number of sources, especially earlier patristic material, a number of "measuring" or "tariff" meta-dispositives are common. These are used specifically to indicate the length of particular penances, and include ὁρίζω (e.g. Basil 4; Gregory Nyss. 4), οἰκονομέω (Basil 62, 72; Gregory Nyss. 1; Theophilus 2), κανονίζω (Basil 77), συμμετρέω (Gregory Nyss. 2), and, once in this sense, δοκιμάζω (Gregory Nyss. 5). Similar are a number of "punishment" verbs including καθυποβάλλω (e.g. Trullo 79), ἐπιτιμάω (e.g. Trullo 67; Theophilus 2), κινδυνεύω περὶ τὸν βαθμόν (Chalcedon 2, 22), or ἀναθεματίζω (Trullo 81).

Individual sources may evince a higher concentration of one type of dispositive form than another,[119] but only one major pattern in the corpus as a whole may be discerned: the general councils are much more given to statements of rules with meta-assertions of the legislator's action than the other sources. There are exceptions. Ancyra, for example, contains numerous examples of meta-dispositives—although they are almost all ἔδοξεν, which might be regarded as an archaic form, as it rarely occurs in the second wave.[120] Both the early western sources, too, often as part of their parliamentary structures, contain a large number of meta-expressions. Antioch and Gangra do not contain meta-dispositives within their canons per se, but the canons are framed in the corpus by introductory structures that serve much the same

[119] Aside from those already mentioned, the Apostles and Theophilus have a very large number of imperatives; Ancyra favours ἔδοξε and imperative constructions; the western sources privilege ἀρέσκει clauses; Nicaea and Athanasius to Rufinianus contain a large number of ἔδοξε constructions; in Ephesus 1–6 δικαιόω is especially prominent; straight indicative statements are common in Basil; and Timothy is dominated by ὀφείλω.

[120] The exceptions are Trullo 3, 12, 55, and 60.

function. Conversely, Trullo contains numerous imperatives.[121] Nevertheless, on a canon-by-canon basis the pattern is fairly clear: the Apostolic Canons, much of the Antiochian corpus, and much of the patristic legislation (especially Basil) are dominated by simple imperatives, impersonal modals, and indicative statements, while the ecumenical councils prefer meta-dispositives. We may consider this pattern a quasi-chronological development, as much of the first group of material is written in the 4th C, and much of the second in the 5th C or later, although Nicaea and Constantinople are exceptions. This development is made all the more striking by the fact that this increase in meta-dispositives is accompanied by a gradual but unmistakable privileging of one term in particular: *ὁρίζω* (and variants). Already very prominent in Chalcedon, *ὁρίζω* phrases emerge in the second wave as virtually *the* dispositive formula for canonical legislation, far more frequent than any other individual term.[122] This development is also part of yet another, larger development, namely the general movement away from indirect meta-dispositives (*ἔδοξε*, *ἤρεσεν*), especially common in the 4th C sources and the western material, to direct dispositives, usually in the first-person plural or the third-person singular (with subject "the holy synod" or similar).

This broad shift towards meta-dispositives may represent an assimilation of canonical forms to imperial law writing. Imperial novels are almost always written with such meta-dispositives, and the solemnity of imperial conciliar legislation could call for precisely this type of imitation. Many of the later canons with these dispositives also contain prominent *prooimion–narratio–dispositio–sanctio* structures, which heighten the similarity with the secular *constitutiones*.[123] At the very least this shift witnesses to a gradual regularization—and formalization—of the legislative task.

In terms of the selection of dispositives, a broad continuity with Greco-Roman legislative language may be observed. The lack of systematic studies of secular dispositive terminology makes it impossible to draw precise conclusions, but vocabulary of, for example, *ἀπαγορεύω*, *ἔδοξε*, *ἔξεστι*, *δικαιόω*, *κελεύω*, *προστάσσω*, *ὁρίζω* (*διορίζω*, *προσδιορίζω*), *ψηφίζομαι*, and of course *δεῖ* and *χρή* are easily found in the Justinianic and Leonine novels.[124] Many of the simpler imperatival or indicative statement forms also find easy resonance in the secular codices and synopses, as well as in the biblical laws and moral tracts.[125]

[121] e.g. canons 5, 11, 13, 14, 15, 20, 21, 24, 27, 35, 40, 46, 47, 48, 52, 58, 59, 69, 70, 72, 83, 88, 98.

[122] See n. 117.

[123] See n. 94 for examples. It is true of virtually all lengthy second-wave canons.

[124] For Justinian, see the *vocabularia* of Archi and Colombo 1986 and Mayr 1923 (and both Justinian and Leo's Novels are searchable on the *TLG*). See also the brief comments of Dölger and Karayannopulos 1968, 75.

[125] To name only the most prominent examples: *CTh*, *CJ*, the *Ecloga*, the *Prochiron*, Exod. 20–3, and Deut. 12–26 (in the scriptural sources future statements and second-person imperatives or equivalents are particularly notable).

A few points of dissonance nevertheless exist. Most interestingly, two of the "strongest" secular legislative verbs are surprisingly rare in the corpus. The most conspicuous absence is *θεσπίζω*, probably the most common legislative term in the Justinianic material, and not uncommon in Leo.[126] It can be found in the corpus only four times.[127] The similarly strong term *νομοθετέω* (and variants), although not nearly so common as *θεσπίζω* in the secular material, also has a notably minor presence in the canonical literature, occurring only seven times.[128] Interestingly, in all but four instances of both of these terms the verbs are placed in the mouths of past legislators, that is, they are not real dispositive assertions by the source at hand.[129] It seems that the strongest legislative terms are most suitable in the mouths of previous, well-recognized legislators. A third term, *κελεύω*, is also much more prominent in the secular material than the ecclesial.[130] Is it simply too categorical or coercive for the canonical material?

Conversely, *ὁρίζω* vocabulary, used as a general dispositive, is hardly present in Justinian at all. It is more evident in the 9th C Novels of Leo, which may suggest that the term was growing in popularity in the later Byzantine period in both secular and ecclesial legislative writing. Nevertheless, its proportional predominance in later church legislation still points toward its ascendancy as a particularly ecclesial term.[131]

None of these differences, however, are enormous; they are mostly on the level of emphasis. The essential observation to be made about the shape of dispositive diction in the canonical literature remains its unexceptional nature: the canons are mostly written within the normal parameters of Greco-Roman legal rule writing.[132] The general avoidance of a number of "strong" imperial

[126] It may be regarded as virtually the standard Justinianic meta-dispositive, occurring approximately 300 times in the Novels, often in the formula "*θεσπίζομεν τοίνυν . . .*". It is also common in Leo, occurring 45 times. See Archi and Colombo 1986, 1334–49 and Mayr 1923, 199–200.

[127] Serdica 11; Trullo 1, 8; and Hagia Sophia 3.

[128] Basil 18, 88; Carthage 77; Trullo 12, 26, 36; Protodeutera 1.

[129] The exceptions are Basil 88, Carthage 77, Trullo 1, and Hagia Sophia 3. Even in Basil 88 it appears in a sentence which emphasizes that Basil was not the first to legislate on his particular topic: *οὔτε πρῶτοι οὔτε μόνοι, ὦ Γρηγόριε, ἐνομοθετήσαμεν γυναῖκας ἀνδράσι μὴ συνοικεῖν*. In Trullo 1 *θεσπίζω* is found in the rather rare circumstance of asserting a doctrinal confirmation, which may explain the unusual presence of such a "powerful" dispositive; but here too it may simply be an example of stylistic *variatio*, as Trullo 1 conspicuously, and rather elegantly, cycles through a number of different dispositives: *ὁρίζω*, *ἐπισφραγίξω*, *ἐπικυρόω*, etc.

[130] Over 200 examples of formal first-person forms of the simple root may be found in Justinian's Novels, and 20 in Leo's. See Archi and Colombo 1986, 1512–17 and Mayr 1923, 231. The canonical evidence—the examples above are virtually exhaustive—seems proportionally much sparser, and includes all forms of the root.

[131] For Justinian, see Archi and Colombo 1986, 2390–939; Mayr 1923, 329. Twenty-six instances of dispositive statements with *ὁρίζομεν* may be found in Leo's Novels.

[132] Cf. Pieler 1991, 606, 616–17 on Zonaras' ease in paraphrasing and discussing the ordinances of the canons with secular-like language and forms.

dispositives, particularly θεσπίζω, should be read as simply one more example of the canons' delicate and indirect negotiation of identity with the civil legislation: the two broadly exist in the same realm of rule language and form, with many resonances, yet with some subtle patterns of distinction.

Surveying the overall normative shape of canonical rules, both in structure and dispositive diction, we may conclude once again that the canons emerge as above all a heterogeneous collection of specific rule traditions. A strong concern for formal uniformity or rationalization is rarely evident (if not altogether absent), either in composition or compilation. Indeed, despite a certain gradual standardization in form and diction in the second-wave legislation, a distinct lack of concern for formal regularity is everywhere evident. The emphasis instead remains on the concrete and particular and thus the irregular. Here law is not conceived as a neat rational construct, a gapless system of homogeneous and strictly coherent norms: it is instead a sprawling collection of authoritative pronouncements, in many different forms, made in many different contexts.

The preponderance of casuistic rules in the corpus demands special comment. It once more reveals the strong inclination to "do law" in terms of specifics and the concrete. In this respect Byzantine canon law is very much like most other ancient legal systems.[133] In these systems law presents itself as concerned not so much with juristic abstraction or general principles built through hypotheticals and deductive reasoning as with the preserving and presenting of sets of traditional answers to specific problems. The system is thus built from the bottom up: one amasses many concrete details and then, through induction, builds analogies and abstractions as necessary. But in truth the system is not exactly "built" at all—and it is not really much of a "system" either. Expansion is above all about the gradual and unprogrammatic accumulation of ever greater quantities of specific regulations. Processes of induction and abstraction are no doubt occurring, but they do not take permanent or prominent expression in the literature itself. The "law" is again always primarily "the laws": induction and abstraction must be assumed, but they are not much articulated. They are not the central point.

[133] On this aspect of ancient Near Eastern law, and ancient law generally, see Westbrook 1988, 88–102 (where, however, the contrast with later Roman and Greek law is overdrawn), 2008. On Roman law's oft-remarked lack of interest in abstraction and deductive system building, Berman 1983, 121–41; Frier 1985, 158–70; Gaudemet 1986; Glenn 2007, 127–8; Schulz 1936, 41–65; Stolte 2003, 85; Weber 1925, 215–16, 276–7; and esp. Hezser 1998, 586–95, 629–31, where the observation of Roman "Gelegenheitsgesetzgebung" is also extended to Talmudic writing, with many further references. See also Tuori 2004 on the exaggeration of the extent and sophistication of early Roman "legal science," and the broader, but critically important, comments in Hadot 1995, 1995a on the minimal role of systematic thinking in ancient philosophy.

It is interesting to note, however, that while the majority of the canons are formally casuistic, they are rarely substantively casuistic—that is, they rarely contain explicit narration of specific historical events, cases, or decisions.[134] Most canons are written as generic rules in casuistic form. In this sense, the system tends to a fairly high level of generalization in terms of potential rule application—the "specificity" of the system is more formal than substantive. This serves as an important reminder that the casuistic orientation of the system—the seemingly ad hoc nature of the regulations—should not be taken to imply a lower level of categorical force, or a lowered expectation for general applicability, as if the canons were merely local statements of examples, "suggestions," or "guidelines," as sometimes is proposed in the literature.[135] Quite the contrary: Roman law, Mosaic law, and indeed most pre-modern laws are all built around the conglomeration of specific, casuistic rules of the very same type, and Byzantine canon law must not be understood as less categorical in intention or force than any of these. Here the coherence in diction and form of the canons with contemporary Roman law is also important. Despite subtle patterns of literary differentiation, the canons do not emerge in their rule structures or dispositive vocabulary as exceptionally unique: they are broadly written in same realm of law expression as the civil legislation, and presumably imply about the same level of categorical "legal" force.

E. THE LEGAL LANGUAGE OF THE CANONS

A critical—if often unstated—question of the modern literature is the degree to which the canons contain linguistic and conceptual phenomena that might be considered "legal." It is impossible to develop a set of heuristics by which this question could be answered in an absolute sense (this would require that we posit a universal human discourse of legality), but from the standpoint of the formalist-positivist legal culture sketched in the Introduction, "legal language" can be assigned a reasonably clear referent: it means "technical-legal discourse," and this in turn implies patterns of concepts and language that function as the specialized logical grammar—learned and operated by trained professionals—for the application of a closed and clearly defined body

[134] Important exceptions include, naturally, most of the *acta* extracts attached to Constantinople, Ephesus, and Chalcedon. Other instances, generally involving the naming of individuals or very specific cases, include Ancyra 25, Constantinople 4 and 5, all of Ephesus, Serdica 18 and 19, and a number of Carthaginian canons, most notably the framing Apiarian dossier. In the patristic material, most of Gregory Thaum., Theophilus, Cyril, and many of Basil's supplementary letters (after canon 85) read as specific cases; most of the rest, the majority, do not.

[135] See Section B.1.

of formal rules to a variety of fact situations. This discourse manifests itself in the use of specialized and proprietary vocabulary and stylistic tropes; a strong interest in terminological, conceptual, and definitional precision and consistency (and thus the heavy use of formulaic phrases); a tendency to schematize and proceed methodically through different aspects of a problem, usually with considerable attention to hypothetical dilemmas; a strong accent on detail and comprehensiveness in rule elaboration, including special concern for exceptions and what we might term "rule prophylacticism," in which rules attempt to foresee and forestall false interpretations, and thus make multiple, slightly different provisions for various types of circumstances; and finally, a concern to speak within and to the rules—that is, to refer to other rules often.[136]

In the canons almost all aspects of this type of technical-legal discourse may be detected. Sometimes it emerges in the passing citation of a noticeable phrase or term from technical civil-legal discourse, sometimes it may be manifest as a stylistic tendency, or at times it may appear as the sustained conceptual structuring of the rule material itself. Occasionally it emerges in its most dramatic form, when the system begins to sound as though it is operating as autonomous proprietary legal discourse: that is, evincing its own special concepts, terminology, and rule "grammar," as distinct from other Greco-Roman technical-legal discourses.

1. The legal parts

We may seek technical-legal discourse in the corpus under four headings: (1) terminology; (2) stylistic tendencies; (3) legal "turns of thought," which include the use or development of legal concepts, definitions, and principles; (4) examples of sustained or sophisticated rule logic. We will examine each in turn.

First, however, one canonical sub-discourse, combining elements of all four categories, is sufficiently distinct and self-contained to demand preliminary and separate treatment: penal provisions.[137] The system of sanctions in the canons is the single most prominent manifestation of technical-legal discourse in the corpus. Quite aside from the fact that the stipulation of clear, specific sanctions may itself be understood as a defining characteristic of law (versus other types of social or moral rules),[138] the canonical penal system evinces an unparalleled regularity and formulaic quality that strongly suggests "the legal"

[136] The inspiration for these characteristics may be found in the references cited in the Introduction, nn. 54, 56; also Mellinkoff 1963.

[137] On Byzantine canonical penal law, see esp. Panagiotakos 1962 and Rhalles 1907. For the graded penitential system, see Schwartz 1911.

[138] See Donovan 2007, 3–15; Freeman 2001, 207–19.

to modern ears. This is particularly noticeable in sources such as the Apostolic Canons (especially 42–4, 51–72), Gangra, Trullo, or Protodeutera, where the repetition of penal formulas is very conspicuous (e.g. ἢ παυσάσθω ἢ καθαιρείσθω; ἐὰν [one condition or subject] ἀφοριζέσθω, ἐὰν [another condition or subject] καθαιρείσθω; εἰ . . . ἀνάθεμα ἔστω). Curiously, this is even more prominent in the older penitential material (e.g. much of Basil's letter 217, Ancyra 1–9, most of Gregory Nyss.), which evinces a strong sense of technicality in its precisely defined and schematized penitential steps (mourners, hearers, supplicators, "standers"), and its interest in developing a detailed system of quantitative tariffs (one-year excommunication, three-year, etc.).

A legal-like standardization may also be noted in the types of penalties. Despite much variation in both content and terminology, a set of three basic sanctions may be distilled from across the corpus: excommunication (for laity) or suspension (for clerics), usually called ἀφορισμός;[139] deposition for clergy, generally termed καθαίρεσις;[140] and a stronger and rarer punishment of ostracism or permanent public damnation, more varied in content and terminology, but often conveyed with ἀνάθεμα, ἀπορίπτω, ἀποκηρύττω, or ἀποβάλλω language.[141] In addition, one will also occasionally hear of a fourth, less specific category of ἐπιτίμια ("penalties"), which overlaps somewhat with ἀφορισμός.[142] In the first wave these three (or four) categories are already standardized in the Apostles (e.g. 42–5, 62) and the *Coll14* 9.10–18, where they are schematized. By the second wave they are omnipresent, if not exclusive, and all three emerge twice in short overviews of canonical penalties, first in II Nicaea 1, which professes faithfulness to traditional provisions ἀνάθεμα, καθαίρεσις, and ἀφορισμός (it also speaks of other types of ἐπιτίμια), and Hagia Sophia 1, which confirms the reciprocal observation of Roman and Constantinopolitan canonical measures in these same three categories. Although different types of penalties will elsewhere be specified (loss of rank, loss of honor),[143] the comparatively regular presence of these three defined and distinct concepts strongly suggests a technical, methodical—that is, "legal"—conceptualization of sanctions.

Penal provisions also constitute one of the very few clear and consistent examples of a proprietary technical discourse in the corpus. Although the basic notions of suspension, demotion, and ostracism are not unique to the

[139] We may also observe paraphrases with ἀκοινώνητος language, e.g. Chalcedon 8 (ἔστωσαν ἀκοινώνητοι). On all three of these sanctions the best work is Panagiotakos 1962. For ἀφορισμός, see esp. Panagiotakos 1962, 295–6, 334–5.

[140] Related to, if not always identical with, the punishment of being in danger of losing one's βαθμός, rank, e.g. Chalcedon 2 τοῦ οἰκείου ἐκπιπτέτω βαθμοῦ. See Panagiotakos 1962, 4.264–70 for common paraphrases and further examples.

[141] See Panagiotakos 1962, 321–3.

[142] e.g. Chalcedon 3, 8, 14, 24; II Nicaea 16; Protodeutera 6.

[143] See Panagiotakos 1962, 4.264–340, Rhalles 1907, 43–134.

canonical tradition, the collection of these three terms as a regular set of penal provisions, and the relatively consistent use of the terms themselves, seem without obvious and regular parallels in the Greco-Roman legal world. Certainly the contemporary imperial legislation does not regularly express sanctions in this way. The Byzantines were in a sense conscious of this, inasmuch as they could speak about the distinction between secular and church law as lying precisely in the different character of their sanctions.[144] Church law clearly had its *own* penal system.

To return to the four types of technical-legal discourse found in the corpus more generally, the first, technical-legal terminology, is the easiest to detect. In principle we might expect to find technical terms borrowed from Greco-Roman civil law or scriptural law, or evidence of the formation of proprietary canonical terminology. In practice technical-legal terminology is confined overwhelmingly to borrowings from Roman legal and administrative discourse.

Among the most obvious and prevalent of these borrowings are a large number of terms for Greco-Roman institutions, offices, and legal instruments. Among the most prominent are terms for offices or positions, such as ἀξίωμα, τιμή, or ὀφφίκιον;[145] terms for legislation or documents such as νόμος, διαταγή, διάταξις, or λίβελλος;[146] the names of specific offices such as ἔκδικος (*defensor*);[147] administrative and legal institutions such as ἐγγύαι (securities),[148] ἐνέχυρα (pledges),[149] λόγοι (in the sense of financial accounts, *rationes*), and εὔθυναι (reports of administration);[150] terms for basic legal procedures such as the διάγνωσις (the standard translation of *cognitio*)[151] or an ἐξέτασις or ἀκρόασις ("examination," "hearing").[152] These borrowings have often been remarked in the literature, and all clearly evince the broad penetration of civil Roman forms into ecclesiastical administrative discourse.[153]

More intriguingly, and more germane to our investigation, is the subtler weaving of Roman legal phraseology into the very articulation of the canonical rules themselves. Procedure is a particularly fertile area for this type of borrowing.[154] Most of these borrowings are quite generic, common to both

[144] See οἱ τοῦ μεγάλου θεοῦ, discussed in Ch. 2 B.3.

[145] Common, e.g. Apostles 29; Nicaea 7, 8; Antioch 5; Serdica 20; Chalcedon 2, 4; Trullo 7; Hagia Sophia 2.

[146] For λίβελλος, see Ephesus 8, Cyril 3; Tables 2.1 and 2.2 for others.

[147] Carthage 75, 97; Chalcedon 23.

[148] Chalcedon 30.

[149] Tarasius at *Fonti* 2.326–7.

[150] Antioch 25, Basil 20.

[151] Serdica 14; Carthage 20, 100, 104 (rubric); Trullo 39; Protodeutera 13, 14 (συνοδικὴ διάγνωσις).

[152] e.g. Serdica 3, Cyril 1 (a κανονικὴ ἀκρόασις), Theophilus 6 (ἀκριβοῦς ἐξετάσεως γινομένης).

[153] On Christianity's general appropriation of Roman governance and legal forms, see Gaudemet 1958, 322–30, 378–407; Herrmann 1980, 23–92, 207–31, 290–306; Hunt 1998, 240–50; Humfress 2007, 196–211; Jones 1964, 874–94; Millar 2006, 133–40.

[154] It is often remarked that the most obvious Roman law borrowings in church law are in this area; see recently Humfress 2007, 208–9.

Greek legal usage and Roman law texts, and includes words like *ἔγκλημα/ἐγκαλέω*[155] or *αἰτία/αἰτιάομαι*[156] (both general Greek legal terms for charges or accusations, the former also a technical translation of *crimen*), *ὑπόθεσις* (case),[157] *δίκη* (penalty, punishment), *ἀπολογία/ἀπολογέω* (defense),[158] *κατηγορία/κατηγορέω* (accusation),[159] *ἐλέγχω* and *διελέγχω* (convict and prove),[160] *ἀποδίδωμι* (hand over),[161] *ἀποκατάστασις* (restoration or reversal),[162] *φωράω* (always in passive, to be caught in a crime),[163] *ἐκκαλέω/ἔκκλησις* (appeal),[164] *εὔθυνος* or *ἀνεύθυνος* and *ἔνοχος* or *ὑπεύθυνος* (guilty/innocent and liable).[165] Although individual instances of these terms may be unremarkable, the concentration or repetition of some of these terms can create a highly technical-legal ambience.[166]

Other procedural or quasi-procedural terms are even more strictly "legalese," that is, specific to technical Roman law writing. A good example is *προκρίνω*, as in Nicaea 10: *τοῦτο οὐ προκρίνει τῷ κανόνι τῷ ἐκκλησιαστικῷ* ("this does not prejudice the ecclesiastical canon"). Here *πρόκρινω* is a calque of the Latin *praeiudicare*, which denotes in legal texts any type of "prejudice," that is, impairment of, harm to, or attribution of liability to someone or something, including very often, as here, "harm" to the validity or applicability of some rule.[167] It is quite common in conciliar *acta* and may be found several times throughout the corpus.[168] Other procedure-oriented instances of

[155] Very frequent, e.g. Apostles 28 (where they are to be *φανερά*); Antioch 14, 15; Constantinople 6 (including in the very technical *ἐκκλησιαστκὸν ἔγκλημα*); Carthage 9, 11, 12, 43, 79, 129; Ephesus 9; Chalcedon 18 (directly appropriating the secular Roman condemnation of the crime of conspiracy, *τὸ τῆς συνωμοσίας ἢ φρατρίας ἔγκλημα*); Peter 12 (in the slightly more technical phrase *ἔγκλημα προσάγειν*), 13, 15; Basil 9 (*τὸ γὰρ ἔγκλημα ἐνταῦθα τῆς ἀπολυσάσης τὸν ἄνδρα ἅπτεται*), 21 (*ὑπάγειν ἐγκλήματι*), 24, 33, 37, 41, 53; Theophilus 3, 6, 9; Trullo 21 (*ἐγκλήμασι κανονικοῖς*), 98; Protodeutera 10, 13, 14.

[156] e.g. Laodicea 40; Cyril 1; Carthage 18, 20, 28; Constantinople 6.

[157] Chalcedon 9.

[158] e.g. Antioch 4, 6, 12; Serdica 4, 13, 21.

[159] e.g. Constantinople 6 (esp. *ἐκκλησιαστκὴ κατηγορία*), Basil 61, Carthage *passim*.

[160] e.g. Neocaesarea 8, 9 (and here "*φανερῶς*"); Basil 61; Gregory Thaum. 8, 9; Carthage 15, 27; Protodeutera 9; the latter, Cyril 1.

[161] e.g. Gregory Thaum 8, 9.

[162] Apostolic Epilogue; Antioch 13; Protodeutera 3.

[163] Very frequent, e.g. Apostles 54, 73; Ephesus 7; Basil 68, 70; Gennadius (*Fonti* 1.2.296); Trullo 12, 20, 33, 50, 53, 77, 79, 88; II Nicaea 10, 18; Protodeutera 4, 6, 7.

[164] e.g. Serdica 3, 5; Carthage 28, 125.

[165] Basil 42, Cyril 1, Theophilus 6 (*ἐγλκήματι πορνείας ὑπεύθυνος*), Carthage 26; Chalcedon 29, Trullo 21.

[166] So e.g. the repetition of *ἀπολογία* and *ἀποκατάστασις* as a quasi-legal formula in Antioch 4 and 12; or of *ἐὰν μὲν κατηγορηθέντες ἐλεγχθῶσι . . . ἐὰν δὲ ἑαυτοῖς ἐξείπωσι καὶ ἀποδῶσι* in Gregory Thaum. 8, 9; or of *ἐλεγχθῆναι φανερῶς* in Neocaesarea 8, 9; or of *εἰ μόνον ἐλεγχθείη* in Protodeutera 14, 15. Areas of high levels of concentrated procedural terminology include Constantinople 6, Cyril 1, much of Theophilus, and, above all, Carthage.

[167] Berger 1953, 644; cf. Avotins 1992, 181.

[168] Nicaea 10; Theophilus 3, 5; Carthage Introductory *acta*, 119; Constantinople 394; Trullo 37; Protodeutera 7.

legalese include κινέω and κινέω παρὰ (in the sense of instituting a lawsuit, probably a direct translation of *actionem* or *litem movere*),[169] παρανοχλέω or ἐνοχλέω (in the sense of *impetrare*, impetrating the emperor),[170] ἀναφέρω/ἀναφορά (= *suggestio* or *relatio*, a calque of the latter),[171] ὑπόθεσιν γυμναζείν (γυμνάζειν here as a calque of *exercere*, as in *exercere actionem/iudicium/litem*),[172] ἐνίστασθαι τὰς κατηγορίας/τὴν κατηγορίαν (= *institutere/deferre accusationem*),[173] ἐκδικέω (in its legal sense as "claim," i.e. as a translation for *vindicare*),[174] πράγμα ἔχειν πρός τινα (πράγμα here as a technical-legal denotation of the formal object of a case, a *causa*, in the sense of *qua de re agitur*),[175] τὰ τῆς δίκης συγκροτεῖσθαι (to discuss the matter, perhaps similar to *agitare causam*),[176] ἐκφέρειν ὅρον/ψῆφον/ἀπόφασιν (akin to *sententiam proferre*),[177] ἐμφανεία συνοδική (synodical court "appearance"),[178] and, in Ephesus 8, perhaps, a technical usage of διδάσκω (in a Greek and Roman sense of "teaching" the court one's position, here διὰ λιβέλλων).[179]

Closely related are a number of phrases from technical parliamentary discourse. For example, we encounter διαλαλέω/διαλαλία, in its usual role as a calque of the Roman *interlocutio*, that is, an "interlocutory judgment."[180] Formal decisions, judgments, or rulings are often rendered with ἀποφαίνω/ἀπόφασις or γνώμη, both standard translations for *sententia*.[181] Constantinople 394, a parliamentary extract, is full of such language, including a rare technical use of ἐμφανίζω (*insinuare*).[182] The same text also begins with a

[169] e.g. Nicaea 9; Carthage 15, 19; Chalcedon 17. See Avotins 1989, 87–9.

[170] Antioch 11, 12; Carthage 75. In the Antiochian canons, however, it is quite possible that the terms are meant in their more generic sense of "bother, annoy," which does generally fit the context (and the Dionysian translation of Antioch 11 and 12 uses *molest-* roots).

[171] Mostly in Carthage, e.g. 47, 48, 64, 99, 100; also somewhat more loosely in Chalcedon 28. See Du Cange 1688, 74, Roussos 1949, 45. See also Ch. 2 B.7.

[172] Chalcedon 9. See also Carthage 59 (here "exercising" a right). See Avotins 1989, 30–1; Berger 1953, 462.

[173] Constantinople 6. Berger 1953, 504; cf. Roussos 1949, 176.

[174] Nicaea 9 (perhaps); Serdica 14; Carthage 55, 56; Basil 1. See Pitsakis 1976, 397; Roussos 1949, 156. The term also has a more general legal sense of "exacting punishment for, avenging," as in Basil 2 ἐκδικεῖται οὐ μόνον τὸ γεννηθησόμενον, ἀλλὰ καὶ αὐτὴ ἡ ἑαυτῇ ἐπιβουλεύσασα.

[175] In Serdica 3, 5, 14; Chalcedon 9; see also the uses of πράγμα in Carthage 19, 30, 79, 87, 100, 120. See Berger 1953, 662, 676; Du Cange 1688, 1215; and esp. *Digest* 50.16.23.

[176] In Chalcedon 9. See Roussos 1949, 408.

[177] Serdica 4, 5, 20. See Berger, 1953, 701; Roussos 1949, 164.

[178] See Avotins 1992, 79–80.

[179] Cf. Avotins 1992, 63 q.v. "διδασκαλικός"; Too 2001, 111–13.

[180] Constantinople 394; Ephesus 7; Gennadius (*Fonti* 1.2.297). Avotins 1992, 58; Berger 1953, 512–13.

[181] e.g. Nicaea 5; Antioch 6, 14, 15; Serdica 4, 5, 14, 19, 20; Cyril 1; Theophilus 4; Gennadius (*Fonti* 1.2.298).

[182] i.e. *insinuare apud acta*, that is, "enter into the public acts," here in its somewhat broader sense of "formally exhibit/demonstrate before a court." See Avotins 1989, 53–4; 1992, 79–80; also q.v. "ἐμφάνισις."

curiously formal (and technical?) statement of Nectarius "seeing" before him the two bishops in disagreement.

Some technical-legal borrowings are not directly related to procedure or parliamentary process. Among the most prominent is δίκαιον/δίκαια, in its technical sense of legal rights (*ius/iura*). Thus, for example, in Ephesus 8 each province is to preserve its "inherent rights" (τὰ αὐτῇ προσόντα δίκαια); likewise in Chalcedon 12 there is a concern that metropolitans preserve their οἰκεῖα δίκαια ("own rights") during imperial divisions of the jurisdictions; in Trullo 37 various ἐκκλησιαστικὰ δίκαια ("ecclesiastical rights") are to remain unharmed.[183]

Similarly, the language of κύριος/ἄκυρος is reasonably common, corresponding to the common *ratus/irritus* of Roman law, that is, the language of validity and confirmation. Thus, for example, in Nicaea 4 we read of τὸ δὲ κῦρος τῶν γινομένων δίδοσθαι . . . τῷ μητροπολίτῃ ἐπισκόπῳ ("and the confirmation of these things is to be given to the metropolitan bishop").[184] Not every instance of this term should be regarded as an assertion of a complex technical doctrine of validity (it can simply mean "approved" or "firm"), but a strong technical sense of "validate" or "ratify" is sometimes unmistakable. For example, in Serdica 15 it is paired with ἀβέβαιος, which lends it a highly categorical and official tone: ἄκυρος καὶ ἀβέβαιος ἡ κατάστασις ἡ τοιαύτη νομίζοιτο ("let such a situation be considered invalid and of no force"). The term βέβαιος, *firmus*, can itself take on highly technical connotations.[185]

Technical Roman property language also emerges on occasion. A good example is the concept of ἐκποίησις, that is, *alienatio*.[186] Similarly the technical property phrase προσκυρόω, broadly related to *adiudicare*, to transfer ownership or assign, may be found in this highly legalistic phrase in Protodeutera 7: τὸ δὲ νεουργηθὲν [monastery], ὡς μηδὲ τὴν ἀρχὴν μοναστηρίου δίκαιον ἀπειληφός, ὡς ἰδιωτικὸν τῷ ἐπισκοπείῳ προσκυροῦσθαι ("the newly constructed [monastery], as having not received from the beginning the right [of construction] of a monastery, let it be transferred to the diocese as its own property").[187] It also appears in Carthage 121.

[183] Other examples may be found in Constantinople 394; Carthage 86, 99; Ephesus 8; Trullo 39; Protodeutera 7.

[184] Other examples may be found in Apostolic 76; Nicaea 15, 16; Antioch 13, 22, 23; Carthage 7, 8, 91; Constantinople 1, 4; Ephesus 8; Chalcedon 6; Trullo 1, 2, 72; II Nicaea 3, 12; Protodeutera 11. It often refers to the validity of an ordination, as well as the validity of decisions. Sometimes, e.g. in Trullo 72 or 85, it reflects a civil law regulation (i.e. on validity of marriage or manumission).

[185] Basil 42; Carthage 1, 2, *acta* before 86, 86, 91, 94, 135, 136; Chalcedon 30; Trullo 2, 37. See Pitsakis 1976, 393; Roussos 1949, 103–4.

[186] Cyril 2; II Nicaea 12.

[187] On προσκυρόω and *adiudicare*, see Berger 1953, 349; Avotins 1989, 137; Du Cange 1688, 1253.

Protodeutera also contains one of the very few Latin loan words in the (Greek)[188] canons: βρέβιον, found in Protodeutera 1 in the phrase βρεβίῳ ἐγκαταγράφεσθαι ("to inscribe in a brief [of erection of a monastery]"). The term is derived from *brevis*.[189] The verb ἐγκαταγράφεσθαι here is also redolent of "administrativese." Elsewhere, as noted above, we may remark ὀφφίκιον (*officium*) and λίβελλος (*libellus*); Nicaea 12 also contains a reference to βενεφίκιον (*beneficium*).

Proprietary technical terminology is much more difficult to identify, aside from the penal provisions noted above. The term κανών itself, as a regular term for an ecclesial rule, is among the best candidates. The technical cast of the term is most evident in the various adverbial and adjectival uses of the root, κανονικῶς or κανονικός: apparently the canons constitute a sufficiently specialized and autonomous rule discourse to speak "canonically" or of the "canonical."[190] Another proprietary phrase may be the usage in Trullo 41 and 46, in a monastic context, of the phrase μετ'εὐλογίας ("with blessing"), which seems to take on a technical meaning of "with permission" (a usage retained in the eastern churches today).

Aside from these, proprietary Christian terminology in the corpus relates only to specific ecclesiastical institutions. The most technical-sounding example is probably the concept of a σύνοδος τελεία (a full or "perfect" synod) in Antioch 16, 17, and 18.

More difficult to pinpoint than technical-legal terminology is our second type of legal discourse, technical-legal style or tone.

One of its more obvious incarnations is the terse and economic prose found in much of the first-wave legislation. This stylization, peremptory in tone and almost staccato in rhythm, lends a strong sense of force, comprehensivity, and generality to the rules. This style is particularly prominent in much of the Apostles, most of Gangra and Laodicea, much of Basil's third letter to Amphilochius (217), and Theophilus' ὑπομνηστικόν. In the last, the highly administrative prose is economic and dense to the point of obscurity.

Another distinctive legal stylization may be termed "legal pleonasm," which involves the rapid successive restating of a concept or action, but with the tense changed or sense slightly altered. It conveys a strong sense of authority, precision, and rule comprehensiveness. Never as common in the canons as in the secular *leges*, it nevertheless can be quite marked. Thus, for example, in Ephesus 7 we read that "no one is permitted to *bring forward* or *compose* or *construct* another faith"; in Constantinople 4, "Maximus did not *become* and *is*

[188] More may be found in Carthage, of course: βρέβιον (canon 34 and the proceeding *acta*); ἐμαγκιπατίωνος (35), πούβλικον (43); κομμονιτορίον (first *acta* extract, 51, 93, 134); κομιτάτον (93, 94, 97, 106, 134).

[189] See Avotins 1992, 46.

[190] e.g. Ephesus 9; Cyril 1; Trullo 21, 33; cf. Wenger 1942, 119–25.

not a bishop . . . and everything that that has been done *concerning him* and *by him* (τῶν **περὶ αὐτὸν** καὶ τῶν **παρ' αὐτου**) is declared invalid"; in Chalcedon 17, "and if a city *has been* erected or *afterwards will be* erected by imperial authority . . . " Sometimes, with pairs of near-synonyms, it is difficult to tell whether one is encountering merely stylistic hendiadys, or whether a real conceptual distinction is intended.[191]

Similar in effect is the repetition of formulae. The most common examples are the repetitions of penal formulae (already noted) and subject designators ("If a bishop, presbyter, or deacon . . . "), but more complex examples also appear, such as Protodeutera 12, where the ponderous phrase "those performing services in houses of prayer inside households" is repeated verbatim twice, then a third time in a slightly modified form. At other times a formula in repeated in canons in close proximity to each other. For example, in Gangra 12 and 13, 17, 18 we read repeatedly about actions committed "on account of supposed ascesis" (διὰ νομιζομένην ἄσκησιν).[192] In all cases this stylization conveys a strong sense of precision and categorical force.

Another similar, and very simple, legal stylization is the use of "aforesaid" (προειρημένος) phrases. Common in Roman civil legislation, the best example in the canons is Chalcedon 28: "and further the bishops in the areas of the barbarians of the *aforesaid dioceses* are to be ordained by the *aforesaid* most holy throne of the most holy church in Constantinople, it being clear that each metropolitan of the *aforesaid dioceses* with the bishops of the province ordains the bishops of the province as the canons prescribe. And, as said, the metropolitans of the *aforesaid dioceses* are ordained by the archbishop of Constantinople." This technique again lends a strong sense of precision and categorical force to the regulation. It is fairly common.[193]

Less common, although often combined with pleonasm, is the production of hyperbolic categoricals. For instance, in Ephesus canon 3 we find the phrase "[orthodox bishops are to be subordinated to non-orthodox] not *at all* at *no* place or time" (μηδ' **ὅλως** ὑποκεῖσθαι κατὰ **μηδένα** τρόπον ἢ χρόνον), and in Ephesus 9, "we have judged and defined without *any* controversy" (δικαιώσαμεν καὶ ὡρίσαμεν δίχα **πάσης** ἀντιλογίας). A similar effect is achieved by the repetition of μή-compounds in Chalcedon 6 "Let *no one* be ordained at

[191] See the instances of this type of stylization in Ephesus 1, 2, 3, 5, 9; Chalcedon 4, 27; Hagia Sophia 2; Protodeutera 1, 5, 6, and 13.

[192] Other examples include the heavy repetition of "such and such bishop said" and πάλιν/ὁμοίως ὡρίσθη/ἤρεσεν in much of Carthage, the introductory περὶ . . . statements of Theophilus' ὑπομνηστικόν, or even the repetition of "ἢ οὔ;"at the end of questions in Timothy 2, 4, 5, 7, 12, 15.

[193] Other examples may be found in Laodicea 34; Antioch 4; Constantinople 394; Trullo 1, 2, 16, 19, 37, 39, 40, 41, 62; Protodeutera 16; Hagia Sophia 2. A similar phenomenon may be found in Chalcedon 23, where the Constantinopolitan ἔκδικος, i.e. *defensor*, who is charged with the expelling of vagrant clergy, is mentioned twice, the second time with the precisionistic epithet "the same" (διὰ τοῦ ἐκδίκου . . . διὰ τοῦ αὐτοῦ ἐκδίκου).

large, *neither* a presbyter, *nor* a deacon, *nor* anyone in the ecclesiastical order."(**μηδένα** ἀπολελυμένως χειροτονεῖσθαι, **μήτε** πρεσβύτερον, **μήτε** διάκονον, **μήτε** ὅλως τινὰ τῶν ἐν τῷ ἐκκλησιαστικῷ τάγματι.)

Overlapping with legal stylizations are conceptual tendencies or patterns that we may term "legal turns of thought," our third category of legal discourse. The simplest and most obvious of these is the tendency to write with frequent reference to other, usually older, rules.[194] Although not always noticeably "legal" if examined in isolated examples, the cumulative effect of repeated rule references strongly conveys the idea that one is writing with a closed system of formal norms. Such rule referencing may be found throughout the corpus—as Table 3.1 indicates—but is especially intense in Gennadius, Basil, and virtually all of the second-wave material, in which canons can be entirely occupied with conveying or interpreting older rules.[195] It may even be found in the Apostles, which refers to earlier rules of the Old Testament, teachings of Jesus, or writings of the apostles.[196]

A much broader and multifaceted legal-conceptual phenomenon is the pattern of speaking and thinking in exceptional detail, with evident concern for precision and comprehensivity. This technique creates the impression that the rules are struggling to encompass as much of reality as possible and as carefully as possible—and that it is extremely important to know exactly how far the rules extend. Its most obvious manifestations are substantive provisions which evince almost pedantic attention to very narrow problems or provisions. A good example is the stipulation in Ancyra 14 that those who fast must at least occasionally taste meat, before they may abstain from it (to prove they are not reviling meat-eating per se). This stipulation also involves the specification of minimum rule requirement, another "legal" concern. Other examples include Timothy 8, which addresses the very specific problem of whether a woman on the verge of childbirth must fast during Holy Week Timothy 13, concerned with a minimal requirement for sexual abstinence (couples must abstain from intercourse at least on Saturday and Sunday); Basil 37, which rules that a man who has married again after his first marriage to another man's wife will be punished for adultery for the first marriage—but not for the second; or Theophilus 5, which focuses on whether the deacon Panuph married his niece before or after baptism.

A notable aspect of this type of concern to delineate the rule world in great detail is the frequent positing of exceptions to broader rules, often as asides. For example, Apostles 54 forbids clerics from eating in taverns—unless they

[194] See generally Table 2.1; also Section F.1.

[195] For examples of this last, see Basil 1, 3, 8, 9, 12, 24, 47, 50, 51, 80; Trullo 6, 8, 14, 16, 36, 90 (among many others; see *Historike* 294–5); II Nicaea 5, 6, 11; Protodeutera 8, 9. Tarasius is an example par excellence, as it is essentially a canonical florilegium on simony.

[196] See Section F.1.

must stay at an inn while on a journey. Laodicea 1 permits digamy, but only if there is no clandestine marriage. Chalcedon 3 forbids clerics from engaging in business affairs, but lists two exceptions: guardianship of minors or ecclesiastical administration. Protodeutera 5 rules that novitiates must be three years in duration, but then quickly inserts two exceptions: those who are sick or who are already living a monastic-like life. Many other instances of such provisos may be found.[197]

Another variation on this theme is the concern to work through different aspects of the same general rule or problem, either within one canon or across a series of canons. This technique leaves the impression of very careful concern for comprehensiveness and thoroughness, and often suggests an agonistic rule environment. Many of the instances of legal pleonasm cited above might be counted here, but a good general example is Gangra 7, which is careful to specify as problematic both the taking *or* giving of offerings against the will of the bishop *or* anyone entrusted with these things. Likewise, Ephesus 2 makes separate mention of both bishops who never condemned Nestorius, as well as those who did condemn him but then backslid. Ephesus 4 specifies that both private and public adherence to Nestorianism is forbidden. II Nicaea 10 is careful to stipulate that clerics may only come to Constantinople and serve in nobles' houses with the permission of both their bishop and the patriarch of Constantinople. Chalcedon 27 condemns not only those who participate in seizure marriages, but those who are party to the plan (*συμπράττοντας ἢ συναιρομένους*). II Nicaea 8, on fake Jewish conversions, is quite careful to note that such Jews may not: (a) take communion; (b) participate in prayer; (c) enter into a church; (d) baptize their children; or (e) either buy *or* possess a slave. Hagia Sophia 3 condemns anyone who strikes *or* imprisons a bishop without reason *or* for a contrived reason (*εἴ τις . . . τολμήσειεν ἐπίσκοπόν τινα τύψαι ἢ φυλακίσαι ἢ χωρὶς αἰτίας ἢ καὶ συμπλασάμενος αἰτίαν*). Gangra frequently addresses in different canons slightly different circumstances of the same problem: canons 14–16, on familial duties, carefully move through different types of kin, one after another; canons 1, 4, 9, 10, 14 all treat various circumstances that emerge because of the ascetic disdain for marriage; canons 5, 6, 9, 20 deal with a variety of issues relating to church assemblies; and 7 and 8 treat finances.[198]

This comprehensive rule provisioning is especially evident when it emerges in the form of a series of "stacked" conditional clauses, each expanding a rule with specific additional possibilities. Ancyra 18 is a good example. The basic rule is that if certain bishops (*εἴ τινες . . .*) are rejected from their own churches, they cannot interfere in other dioceses. The canon continues, however, by noting that if (*ἐὰν μέντοι . . .*) such bishops accept a seat among

[197] e.g. in Basil 13; Ancyra 11; Antioch 11; Chalcedon 4, 25; Trullo 68; Protodeutera 4.

[198] Other similar examples include Apostles 22–4, 42–3, 72–3; Ephesus 1–6; Serdica 3–5.

the presbyterate, they are welcome to take such a position. But it then adds an even further clause that if (ἐὰν δὲ . . .) such bishops then engage in any seditious activity, they will be expelled. Such εἴ-clause stacking may be remarked throughout the corpus.[199]

Even more revealing of a technical concern for detail—and reinforcing a strong sense of the rules operating within a well-defined body of regulations—are the various instances when a later rule fills in or corrects small details or gaps is earlier legislation. Basil 24, for example, addresses a rule gap in Pauline legislation: if widows who marry are to be overlooked in the distributions, what about widowers? Timothy 5 is a response to a question on the details of Paul's rules about couples' mutual sexual abstentions (the night before liturgy too?). Trullo contains a very large number of such instances. Canon 5 repeats prohibitions against clergy living with women (particularly Nicaea 3, but also Ancyra 19, Basil 88, and more vaguely Carthage 38), but now adds a clear punishment, and extends the rule to eunuchs as well. Trullo 6 cites Apostolic 26, that only readers and singers may marry, and reaffirms it by stating that presbyters, deacons, and subdeacons may *not* marry after ordination; the intention must be to counter attempts to assimilate subdeacons to the lesser clergy named in Apostolic 26. Canon 15 supplies a minimum age for ordination of subdeacons, which had been overlooked in the earlier legislation (just summarized in canon 14). Canon 49 may be trying to close a potential loophole when it cites, word for word, Chalcedon 24, against the transformation of monasteries into secular habitations, but then also adds that monasteries may not be *given* to seculars either. Canon 67, which repeats the food prohibitions from Acts 21: 25, may be meant to supersede Apostolic 63, which had included a number of extra food prohibitions from Leviticus 17: 14–15. Canon 90 gives more precise indications of what exactly kneeling "on Sunday" means: from Vespers on Saturday night to Vespers on Sunday night. Canon 93, on the reception of heretics, is a word-for-word reproduction of Constantinople 7, save that one more category of heretic is now added. II Nicaea 6, on synods, slightly extends the provisions of earlier canons by adding punishments for governors who hinder yearly synods and for metropolitans who fail to call them. Protodeutera 8 extends Apostolic 22–4, on castration, to include those who order others to be castrated.

This concern for detail and comprehensivity is sometimes accompanied by—or develops into—the creation of systematic schematizations and graded categorizations, as well as the marked use of formal distinctions, definitions, or principles. Both phenomena demonstrate the classical jurisprudential concern to explore how rules can be applied rationally to a varied set of fact situations.

[199] e.g. Apostles 74; Antioch 3; Constantinople 6 (a long example); Carthage 19, 118 (both extensive); Chalcedon 9; Timothy 4; II Nicaea 18, 22; Protodeutera 16.

Among the best examples of technical schematization and graded categorization are the *lapsi* schemata of Ancyra 1–9 and all of Peter. Both sources display a concern to draw careful distinctions and to systematize rationally in their methodical progression from higher-ranking subjects to lower-ranking subjects, or from less problematic to more problematic cases.[200] Similar are the detailed graded categorizations of heretics, primarily in Basil 1, Constantinople 7, and Trullo 95, but also in Nicaea 8 and 19, Laodicea 7 and 8, and Basil 54. A more localized example is the carefully graded distinctions in age and status of perpetrators of bestiality in Ancyra 16. The most sophisticated case, however, is Gregory of Nyssa's division of penitential rules into the Platonic schema of the faculties of the soul.[201] Here Gregory builds a multilayer branching set of divisions (sin is divided into three categories, each category is divided into further types of sins, and so on)—a "conceptual pyramid," as Manfred Fuhrmann calls it, rather like the *Institutes*.[202]

Elsewhere other legal-like distinctions and definitions appear. Particularly striking is the distinction between voluntary and involuntary actions.[203] Basil 8, on murder, explores this difference in great detail, considering a number of different scenarios. Elsewhere we find the distinctions of unwritten/written,[204] custom/law,[205] knowledge/ignorance,[206] or of a crime confessed/unconfessed[207]. Many of these distinctions emerge in the context of determining a penitential tariff, usually as potential mitigating or exacerbating factors. Related are a number of formal concepts concerning the circumstances of an act, such as a person's "intention" or "disposition" (*προαίρεσις*, *διάθεσις*, *πρόθεσις*)[208], or the presence of "need" or "force" (*ἀνάγκη*, *βία*).[209]

On occasion distinction and definition-making become a central focus of a text. This is particularly obvious in Gregory of Nyssa, just mentioned, where distinctions are explicitly named as *διαιρέσεις* and *διαφοραί*, terms with technical valences in both law and philosophy. Here extended discussions may be found on the differences between adultery and fornication (canon 4) or stealing and robbery (canon 6). Elsewhere in the corpus very specific, even proprietary, distinctions emerge as primary topics of regulation, including distinctions between self-castration and non-self-castration,[210] formed and unformed fetuses,[211] different degrees of sexual contact,[212] and widows and virgins.[213]

[200] Something similar may be found in Ephesus 1–6 and Protodeutera 13–15.
[201] For further discussion, see Ch. 4 G. [202] Fuhrmann 1960.
[203] Ancyra 22, 23; Gregory Nyss. 2, 5; Basil 8 (also called a *διαφορά* here).
[204] Basil 91, 92; II Nicaea 7. [205] Basil 87. [206] e.g. Basil 7, 27, 46; Trullo 79.
[207] Gregory Nyss. 4, 6; Gregory Thaum. 8, 9; Basil 61.
[208] Nicaea 12; Basil 8, 10, 11, 53; Gregory Nyss. 8; Neocaesarea 6, 12; Carthage 47 (although these last three are with specific reference to baptismal theology).
[209] e.g. Gregory Thaum. 1; Gregory Nyss. 3; Ancyra 3; Chalcedon 25; Trullo 41.
[210] Nicaea 1; Protodeutera 8. [211] Basil 2. [212] Basil 70. [213] Basil 18.

Similarly, some canons are almost entirely focused on whether a case may be subsumed under a certain definition. Basil 2, for example, treats the scope of application of the technical definition of murder: does it include abortion? (yes.) Basil 31 deals with the problem of whether a woman whose husband has gone away and who marries before assurance of his death is indeed an adulterer (yes). In a similar way, Protodeutera 9 revolves mostly around the meaning of the verb "to strike."

Very occasionally, real principles or maxims—*regula*-like material—are voiced. The best example is the biblical prohibition of double jeopardy, which is employed explicitly as a general principle three times in the corpus.[214] In Protodeutera 17, however, we can find a real Roman *regula*: "not making the exception in any way the law of the church" (*τό γε σπάνιον οὐδαμοῦ νόμον τῆς ἐκκλησίας τιθέμενοι*). The resonance with *Digest* 1.3.4 (= *Basilica* 2.1.5) is unmistakable.[215] Likewise Basil 40 should also probably be read as appropriating a Roman legal principle when he notes that a slave who has married without her master's consent is a fornicator, since "the contracts of those who are subject to another have no force."[216] Something similar is perhaps true for Apostolic 76, which explains that bishops may not appoint successors because the things of God may not become subject to inheritance. In this last case, the expression of the rule is quite general (*κληρονόμους γὰρ τῆς ἐπισκοπῆς ποιεῖσθαι οὐ δίκαιον τὰ τοῦ θεοῦ χαριζόμενον πάθει ἀνθρωπίνῳ· οὐ γὰρ τὴν τοῦ θεοῦ ἐκκλησίαν ὑπὸ κληρονομίαν ὀφείλει τιθέναι*), and the author may not have a specific *regula* of Roman law in mind, but the notion that *res sacrae* are outside normal human transactions is a common notion in Roman law.[217]

A few principles may be considered proprietary to the canonical tradition. Basil's formulation in canon 27 that a presbyter who has sinned sexually cannot serve liturgically, as "it is illogical for one to bless another who ought to heal his own sins," seems to have become accepted as a canonical principle at Trullo, cited as such in canon 3.[218] In Basil 26 we should also perhaps hear a proprietary canonical principle enunciated in "fornication is not marriage, nor the beginning of marriage."

Beyond these relatively simple or isolated uses of formal distinctions, definitions, and principles, certain sections of the canonical material evince

[214] Apostolic 25; Basil 3, 32. The principle is from Nahum 1: 9. Scripture perhaps provides one other principle, found in Basil 20, where Romans 3: 19 (*ὅσα γὰρ ὁ νόμος λέγει, τοῖς ἐν τῷ νόμῳ λαλεῖ*) is cited to void the professions of virginity of heretics.

[215] *Basilica* 2.1.5 reads: *Τοὺς νόμους ἀπὸ τῶν ὡς ἐπὶ τὸ πλεῖστον συμβαινόντων, οὐ μὴν τῶν σπανίως εἰσάγεσθαι δεῖ*. The text in Protodeutera could, of course, be an exact citation of another, now lost, antecessor paraphrase.

[216] See Buckland 1963, 419–20; Kaser 1955, 1.314.

[217] See *Institutes* 2.1.7 ff., 3.19.2; Berger 1953, 677, 679. Other possible examples of the employment of secular legal rules or concepts may be found in Basil 87, 91, 92; Constantinople 394; and Protodeutera 7.

[218] And again in Trullo 26 as part of a fuller citation of Basil 27.

even more sustained or sophisticated instances of "rule think." In these cases—the fourth and final of our categories of legal discourse—the "legal" or jurisprudential texture of the texts is unmistakable. Frequently these texts combine many of the foregoing elements.

Some of the most impressive examples involve the contradiction of an overly subtle interpretation of a canon or the closing of a loophole. Protodeutera 9, for example, is written to counter a sophistic evasion of Apostolic 27, which forbids clerics from striking wrongdoers. Apparently, clerics had been ordering *others* to strike wrongdoers. Protodeutera 9 therefore disallows this evasion and, in a fairly technical way, addresses the problem by clarifying the definition of "strike" in the canons. It ultimately opts for a simple but comprehensive meaning, that "the canon chastens simply 'striking'" (*τοῦ κανόνος τὸ τύπτειν ἁπλῶς κολάζοντος*). Similarly, II Nicaea 12, probably the most "legalistic" canon in its source, directly addresses a very narrow and ingenious rule loophole: seculars may not acquire church property directly *or* through an intermediary clerical possessor. Its argument is developed with considerable secular-legal terminology and stylization, and it bases its regulation on an older fixed rule (Apostolic 38).

Gennadius is also an extended example of an attempt to close a technical loophole. The letter is directed at the "sophistic"[219] attempt by certain Galatian bishops to wriggle out of the Chalcedonian condemnation of simony. Apparently the bishops were attempting to make fine distinctions regarding the time of the giving of the money. Gennadius—in technical-legal fashion—is quick to plug this loophole with a fine example of legal tense comprehensiveness: "but neither *before* the time of ordination, nor *after* the time of ordination . . . nor *at* the time . . . " He then formally renews Chalcedon 2 in a highly categorical way: "It seemed good to us too to renew again these things . . . to cut off the custom . . . without any scheming or any pretext or any sophism" (*ἔδοξε καὶ ἡμῖν αὐτὰ ταῦτα πάλιν ἀνανεώσασθαι . . . ὥστε δίχα* ***πάσης*** *ἐπινοίας καὶ* ***πάσης*** *προφάσεως καὶ* ***παντὸς*** *σοφισμοῦ τὴν . . . συνήθειαν . . . ἐκτεμεῖν*). Later he is also very careful to re-enumerate in a comprehensive way all of the possible subjects of this ruling (bishops, chorepiscopoi, *periodeutai*, etc.).

Sometimes the subtlety is more on a canon's own part than that of any targeted (mis-)interpretation. Trullo 13, for example, reads Carthage 3 and 25, on clerical celibacy, as properly referring only to sexual continence before the service of the liturgy—a fine distinction not entirely evident in the canons in question. Trullo 16, interpreting Neocaesarea 15, a canon which limits the number of deacons in a city to seven, draws a similarly subtle distinction between deacons who serve liturgically and the deacons of Acts who were

[219] The interpretation criticized is repeatedly characterized by the *σοφισ-* root (e.g. *δεῖ . . . μὴ σοφίζεσθαι τὰ ἀσόφιστα; . . . οὐδὲ σοφιστικῆς δεόμενον ἐξηγήσεως*).

specially appointed to address the needs of the community—again, a distinction not particularly evident in the source canon.

Many of the most sustained instances of technical "rule think" may be found in Basil, whose canons, as noted earlier, often read as virtual rule commentaries. Basil 1, which treats the rules of the reception of different types of heretics, is a particularly sophisticated example, representative of many of Basil's techniques and concerns.[220] Basil approaches the question by systematically researching older rules, making a technical distinction between three types of heretics (defining each type), weighing the value of traditional rulings—one of which, Cyprian's, he treats in full, going step by step through its rather fine, multistep logic—worrying about objections and complications (for example, what it means that the Encratites accept orthodox baptism), and then finally offering his own reasoned opinions on a number of topics. We thus find here the classical jurisprudential concerns of rule finding, precedents, distinctions, definitions, systematic classification, problems with authority of rules, problems of gaps in legislation, and ways of harmonizing conflicting rules. Perhaps most importantly, Basil is building his own conclusions primarily out of a careful, logical exploration of the rationale of older rules. In this we may detect one of the most important characteristics of "proper" jurisprudential thought: the logical generation of new rules from old ones, that is, in effect making the rule system *itself* create rules.

Another good Basilian example—and one of the most sustained examples of technical rule discourse in the entire corpus—is Basil 87, the letter to Diodorus. Here Basil explicitly targets a very fine interpretation of the Mosaic law, which justifies taking one's dead wife's sister in marriage on the grounds of Leviticus 18: 18: "You will not take your wife's sister, to uncover her nakedness, to rival her, while your wife still lives." The argument Basil opposes is that one could marry one's wife's sister once one's wife was dead. Basil, extremely annoyed at this "*σόφισμα*," responds angrily that everyone should know better than this, even without detailed reasoning—but that he will nonetheless provide arguments "from reason" (*ἐκ τῶν λογισμῶν*). He then goes on to analyze how—to take one example—"syllogizing from logical inference from the silence of a law is to make one a lawgiver, and not to let the laws speak" (*τὸ δὲ ἐκ τῆς τοῦ ἀκολούθου ἐπιφορᾶς τὸ σιωπηθὲν συλλογίζεσθαι νομοθετοῦντός ἐστιν, οὐ τὰ τοῦ νόμου λέγοντος*), and produces several pages of similar logical and exegetical arguments showing the absurdity of such reasoning, and the likelihood of his own interpretation. The whole argument is far too long to repeat in full, but there can be little question of Basil's readiness to argue a technical problem of rule interpretation at great length.

[220] Other very "jurisprudential" canons include Basil 8, 9, 10, 18, 21, and 63.

A different type of sophistication is evident in Athanasius 3, the letter to Rufinianus. Here sophisticated rule logic is not so much in evidence as a methodical clarification of a technical rule on a specific subject (the reception of lesser clergy who had submitted to Arian leaders). Despite many rhetorical flourishes, Athanasius' answer moves very carefully through (1) the source of the ruling; (2) the reasons for the ruling; (3) the nature of this formal exception; and (4) the criteria established by the ruling for its application.

Another lengthy and sustained foray into jurisprudential rule thinking—also too long to convey at length—is Constantinople 394. It is a record of a formal discussion on a technical matter: how many bishops are required to depose another bishop? The answer to this problem (an issue of a minimum rule requirement), replete with technical-legal diction, is arrived at through a careful weighing and discussing of various legal principles and the citations of older rules. The decision is significantly presented in terms of what is logical (ἀκόλουθον . . . ἀκόλουθος . . .).

A text like Trullo 40, by contrast, is notable not so much for the extent of its jurisprudential argument as its type of argument. Here a rule on the age of monastic profession is developed by employing a classical jurisprudential technique: analogy. The church earlier lowered the age of admission to the female diaconate, and so Trullo may now lower the age of monastic profession.[221] Elsewhere in the corpus a more generalized form of analogy may be found when secular regulations are presented as a model that the church should adhere to "all the more so" because of the church's spiritual nature (the *a minori ad maius* trope).[222]

Another example of brief but sophisticated conceptual reasoning may be found in Apostolic 76, already cited (that bishops may not appoint successors because the things of God may not become subject to inheritance). This canon is interesting not simply because it employs a general principle, but because the regulation as a whole is cast as following directly from that principle—that is, the rule is presented as produced purely through a deductive process. Ephesus 1 similarly notes that apostate metropolitans are not able to do anything against their bishops or participate in communion at all, "for already they have been cast out by the synod and are incapable of action" (ἤδη γὰρ ὑπὸ τῆς συνόδου ἐκβεβλημένος ἐστὶ καὶ ἀνενέργητος ὑπάρχει). On the face of it this is perhaps little more than the noting of a simple consequence of an earlier action, but it may suggest a more sophisticated doctrinal architecture: expulsion creates a state of "incapacity for action", and "incapacity for action" entails the consequence that metropolitans cannot do anything legitimately against their bishops.

[221] Similar examples of analogical rule creation or modification may be found in Basil 9, 18, and Gregory Nyss. 8.

[222] Chalcedon 18; Trullo 7.

2. The legal whole?

When the above instances of technical-legal language and thought are considered en masse, it becomes difficult to avoid the simple conclusion that technical-legal discourse does exist in the canons—that is, the canons are entirely capable of speaking and thinking in a manner consistent with modern expectations of a closed, formalist, and agonistic rule system. The large number of parallels, borrowings, and crossovers with secular Greco-Roman technical-legal discourse also demonstrates that canonical discourse could very easily adopt contemporary secular jurisprudential forms: the canons can engage in the "rule think" and "rule talk" of Roman law.

This first-blush consonance with modern expectations—and even Roman law—is nevertheless deceptive. Our amassing and categorizing of the technical-legal characteristics of canonical language in one place might leave the impression that this discourse is quite pervasive, but in fact the corpus as a whole does not read as a primarily or convincingly technical-legal text—certainly not by modern standards, and not even in comparison with the complex technical texture of the *Digest* or other contemporary Roman legal works (although here the difference may be more quantitative than qualitative). Many factors combine to create this dissonance.

First, although this was perhaps not immediately apparent in the previous section, technical-legal discourse is present only very unevenly in the corpus. Whereas modern technical discourse, virtually by definition, is programmatic, systematic, and above all consistent, this is not so in the canons. Technical-legal stylizations and characteristics—formulas, technical diction, high levels of details, use of principles, arguments from technical definitions, and so on—tend to fade in and out throughout the corpus. In some parts of the corpus they are very evident, such as in Antioch, Basil, Gangra, Protodeutera, many of the *acta* extracts, and above all Carthage.[223] But elsewhere sources evince hardly any technical-legal content at all—the two canonical poems of Gregory of Nazianzus and Amphilochius, and most of the very general letters of Dionysius and Gregory Thaumatourgus, are obvious examples. This unevenness is also true on the level of individual canons. Some canons may be exceptionally "legal," such as Protodeutera 9 on "striking," or the property-focused II Nicaea 12, or Basil 1 on heretic baptism, or (not mentioned above) Constantinople 6, a huge meditation on procedure, or Constantinople 394, a

[223] The technical-legal character of Carthage—which in its depth and extent is unrivaled in the corpus—warrants a study of its own. It is created primarily by a very heavy use of parliamentary and procedural terms, as well as a high level of detail and precision in many provisions (e.g. 15, 19, 48, 99, 106, 121, etc.). The effect would no doubt be amplified to the Greek ear by the cumbersome nature of the translation from Latin—recalling the awkward cadence of the translated Latin legal literature.

technical discussion of the number of bishops needed to ordain and depose another bishop, or Chalcedon 28, a very detailed canon filled with legal stylizations. But such rules must be placed alongside the distinctly un-legal Carthaginian doctrinal canons (109–16), or the Basilian exegetical canons (15–16), or canons such as the bizarre Neocaesarea 4 ("If anyone, desiring a woman, intends to lie with her, but his desire does not come to fruition, it is evident that he has been saved by grace"), or the homily-like regulations of Ephesus 9 or Trullo 96. Most often, in fact, rules are simple statements and prohibitions, embellished in various ways, but with hardly enough technical-legal stylization or content to distinguish them markedly from any other type of social or cultural rule.

It is also noteworthy that certain topics tend to attract more technical-legal stylization than others. Although it is a point that requires further study, it seems that topics that are akin to matters treated in contemporary Roman law (secular or ecclesiastical) attract the most technical elaboration: marriage, procedure, heretics, jurisdiction, finances, and interactions with the secular administration. Other topics show markedly less technical development.

Further heightening this sense of unevenness, sources that are quite technical are rarely technical or "legal" in quite the same way as other sources—and rarely are they technical in all aspects of their composition (style, thought, content). Gangra, for example, is technical in its precise, formulaic, and detailed language, but is otherwise quite simple and commonplace in diction and thought. Theophilus is technical in its very dense style and technical diction, but is rather "messy" in topic and presentation, a clear example of workaday administrative prose. Antioch is ponderously officious in tone and refers to a number of secular administrative institutions, but is garrulous and rhetorically ornamented. Athanasius is technical in its methodical approach to its subject, but is highly wrought rhetorically. Basil 1 or 87 show evidence of careful rule thinking, but are still very theological in content and tone. Protodeutera is often novel-like in its structures and legal stylizations, but also almost homiletic in style.

All such texts therefore feel distinctly "legalistic" in some particular way, but not consistently so—at least, not by modern standards, or even by the standards of a text such as the *Digest*. Totalizing patterns of technical rule writing are simply very hard to identify. Even the same type of legal stylization in an individual source is often quite irregular. Trullo 3 and 16, for example, show a high degree of rule logic, but other rules, such as Trullo 96, are little more than moral-rhetorical homilies. Most of Trullo's rules are simple prohibitions.

Many of the technical aspects of the canons are also revealed, upon closer inspection, to be not quite as technical as they first appear. The penal system, for example, while showing considerable consistency by Byzantine standards, is still in fact more notable—from a modern perspective, at least—for its variety of terminology, its lack of standardization, and its numerous gaps and ambiguities.[224] Many canons do not even specify punishments, or they are very vague.[225] It would have been comparatively easy to harmonize canonical penalties, but this was never done.

Likewise, the seemingly technical Basil 87 is revealed upon closer analysis to be an expression more of simple moral outrage than real jurisprudential logic: despite its jurisprudential ornamentation, its decisive argument is ultimately that one should not be acting passionately. Similarly, the principle against double jeopardy that is articulated three times in the corpus is also bluntly contradicted several times—apparently it was not consistently applied.[226] Gangra also seems to evince many formulae and a concern for detail, but its overall structure is chaotic, and shows little rational progression or concern for logical topic coverage—five canons, for example, scattered throughout the source, touch on virtually the same topic.[227] It is in fact a very haphazard composition. Many other examples of this type could be offered.

Revealingly, it is also often surprisingly difficult to determine whether a text, while "technical" in some respects, is legally so: the distinction of "canonical" books and "books that can be read" (*κανονιζόμενα* versus *ἀναγινωσκόμενα*) in Athanasius 2 is a good example: this is a technical distinction, but need we read it as a "legal" distinction? Even Gregory of Nyssa's interest in *divisio* is not for the most part particularly "legal" in texture—it is medical, psychological, and philosophical, and typical of elementary textbooks of many varieties.[228] Many of the distinctions noted in the texts (for example, "mind" versus "letter") may also be viewed as rhetorical commonplaces, and thus not necessarily "jurisprudential" in the sense of belonging exclusively to the vocabulary of a specialized legal caste. The technical-legal cast of some elements of the corpus is thus more apparent than real.

Also glaring are the many aspects of the canonical texts that can best be described—by modern standards—as instances of simple legal clumsiness. Frequently, unclear drafting will create unnecessary ambiguity, or rules will be asserted that simply seem inappropriate, irrelevant, or hopelessly vague. For example, Apostolic 60 rules that pseudepigraphal books cannot be read publicly "as holy works . . . to the harm of the people." Does this mean they could be read if not considered holy and/or not read so as to harm the people? In Laodicea 10 children are not to be married to heretics "indiscriminately" (*ἀδιαφόρως*). Could they be married to heretics with care? Gangra 1 condemns

[224] See the references in nn. 139–41.

[225] Much of Laodicea and Serdica are examples of the former; for the latter, see e.g. Chalcedon 3, 9, 14.

[226] e.g. Apostolic 29, Neocaesarea 1, Serdica 1.

[227] Abhorring marriage: 1, 4, 9, 10, 14.

[228] Including, but not restricted to, the *Institutes*. Fuhrmann 1960.

any ascetic who "reviles" a married woman "as if she were not able to enter the kingdom [of heaven]." Does this mean that reviling with another type of ideological intention might be permitted? Antioch 19 notes that it is "better" that a full synod elect a bishop, but not necessary. Why do we need to know what is "better"? Surely only the minimal rule should have been articulated. Neocaesarea 2 simply notes that penance for the spouse of a fraternal digamist will be "difficult" (!)—with no further comment. In Basil 53 a widow slave has "perhaps" (?) not fallen too greatly if she gives herself over to an abduction marriage. Many other examples of this type could be cited.

Finally, and perhaps most importantly, the canons are enveloped and pervaded by a huge quantity of not-so-technical discourse. They are full of material that would be considered entirely extraneous from a modern technical-legal perspective. This material includes moral and theological asides, scriptural exhortations, rhetorical decoration, and small harangues. These elements can easily submerge and obscure the more technical elements of rule articulation, and if read as part of technical rule articulation, they can create considerable ambiguity. They are the topic of the next section.

The overall complexion of technical-legal discourse in the canons is thus quite strange, and particularly when the corpus is considered as a whole.[229] On the one hand, technical-legal handling of the rules is clearly possible, and can even appear in quite serious and sustained ways. It would be a mistake to suggest that this legal world is unconcerned with comparatively narrow problems of rule interpretation and application, or logical consistency, or even the development and use of a technical "grammar" of terms, principles, and definitions. Quite to the contrary, the canons are capable of, and value, detailed "rule think."

On the other hand, this technical-legal discourse is clearly not the only or default mode of church rule exposition: it is not the controlling discourse of the system. There is no sense that the system as a whole is trying particularly hard to constitute itself as a convincing technical-legal mechanism, or that the canons are primarily being written for such a discourse.[230] Instead, technical-legal discourse tends to appear occasionally, almost opportunistically. It may be present in the corpus but it does not dominate it—it certainly does not constitute a fundamental framework for its operation. As odd as it may seem today, it is apparently only a *part* of a much broader, irregular, and variegated legal discourse—not an unimportant part, but only a part.

[229] And, note, we have for the most part not even been considering possible points of contradiction within the substantive provisions of the law.

[230] Cf. Biondi's conclusion that late antique "Christian-Roman" law is intentionally not particularly concerned to develop or employ technical-legal discourse. Biondi 1952, 2.525–9.

F. THE NON-LEGAL LEGAL LANGUAGE OF THE CANONS?

The fact that technical-legal discourse is only one part of canonical discourse immediately raises the question of what the other parts might be. Here it is helpful to consider the function of the canons. Their first and most obvious function is to convey rules. It is in this function that their technical-legal aspect is most prominent. To engage in an analysis of the canons simply as rules, however, we must first distill and extract their "pure" rule content from the canonical texts themselves as compositional wholes—which is precisely what we have done in the last two sections. In so doing, however, we have quietly ignored much other "extraneous" matter that is present in the canons. We have not, then, analyzed canonical-legal discourse in its full, native form. We have instead treated the canons as scholars typically, mostly unconsciously, treat ancient legal texts, as a messy quarry from which pure legal rules and doctrine might be, with care, and often some frustration, extracted. But in this process of "purification" it is very easy to overlook what else might be going on in these texts—and to fail to ask why they seem to be so full of "extraneous" matter in the first place.

Recently, in Byzantine law studies and elsewhere, a growing recognition has developed that laws can have not only a pragmatic rule function but also a symbolic function.[231] This realization has emerged from the need to explain the function of rules that otherwise seem to contain completely obsolete or impossible provisions—as is the case with much of later Byzantine law, which consists mostly of material recycled from the 6th C. In this view, it is recognized that laws can provide not only, and maybe not even primarily, a set of real-life rules, but also an interpretative framework for a society's self-understanding, that is, a means for expressing a culture's identity. As John Haldon puts it, they "enunciate a more or less consistent world view, a moral system . . . regardless of its practical relevance in day-to-day terms."[232] Such laws still provide normativity and regulation, but of a type that is geared more towards the internalization of broad narratives of social order and socio-cultural behavioral expectations than the development of a functional rule system per se.

In such a view, the presence of many "extraneous" ideological elements in the laws suddenly becomes less surprising. This is particularly true if we go one

[231] In Byzantine law, see esp. Fögen 1987; Haldon 1990, 258–64; see also Harries 1999, 56–9, and Nelson 2008, 309, on early medieval western collections as "totemic and inspirational as well as practical." The notion is common in the study of ancient Near Eastern law, where there is considerable controversy among those who wish to see the ancient codes as "real" law (i.e. practical rule systems of a formalist type) and those who see them as only symbolic/propagandistic, or perhaps academic, in orientation; see Westbrook 1985, Roth 2000.

[232] Haldon 1990, 258.

step further and accept that laws may be not simply *used* in a symbolic way in moments of cultural decline but also intentionally *composed* with such symbolic functions in mind. This is, in fact, precisely Plato's prescription for the composition of proper laws: a good law is symbolically dense.[233] In this world the "extraneous" elements, as in the prologues, are suddenly not so extraneous.[234] They are instead simply speaking to other normative dimensions of the text which are not necessarily any less essential or important than the pure rule content. Indeed, in this case it would be a mistake to consider these elements as extraneous to the nature of the texts as laws at all—a proper law qua law speaks "symbolically": it speaks to broader narratives of normativity.

There are in fact many broad indications that late antique and Byzantine legal writing was conceived in this symbolic way. Law in its most official, ideal form always seems to have been symbolically and rhetorically rich, filled with moral admonition, elegant turns of phrases, and imperial ideology. Of course the Romans and Byzantines were perfectly capable of extracting and abstracting pure rule content. The civil codifications (quite explicitly), the synopses, the systematic rubrics, the later Byzantine handbooks, even the *Institutes*, are all witnesses to such rule extraction and purification. Nevertheless, it is always quite clear that these texts are representationally a *secondary* form of the law: they are the practical handbooks and the aids for day-to-day operations. When one writes a real law in late antiquity and Byzantium—that is, a proper, full imperial novel—all of the "padding," the extraneous content, tends to resurface. Wulf Voss's work on law and rhetoric in late antiquity is in many ways the ideal illustration of this phenomenon. If he is correct that the late Roman imperial chancery tended to produce two types of texts for laws—coherent and regular "pure" rule texts for internal use, and rhetorically ornate versions embellished by the quaestors for publication—it is clear that the real or official, i.e. published—law *was the rhetorical version*. That is, this version of the law was the version marked as culturally important, high-status, and, in effect, complete. Anything else was partial and derivative, for quiet, technical in-house consumption.[235] Modern historians may still wish to evaluate and study this (murky) bureaucratic underworld of technical-legal work and pure rule expression as law's "real" life,[236] but it is quite clear that late Romans and Byzantines would have done the opposite. Law in its most ideal form, its most

[233] See *Laws* 721b–e, an extraordinary passage, where Plato gives an example of a law in a short, "pure" rule form (the wrong way of legislating!), and a longer, pedagogically and philosophically "padded" version (the correct way).

[234] Not simply "rhetorical decoration," as Fögen 1987, 147 puts it, making this very point.

[235] Voss 1982.

[236] This is a very pervasive tendency in the modern literature. To give but one example, see Honoré 2004, 119, where it is noted that contemporaries in late antiquity could "read between the lines" of their rhetorical legal texts to understand the real (legal) meaning. Honoré wishes to read *through* the rhetoric to reach the law, instead of reading the rhetoric as law.

proper form, was not conceived as coterminous with pure rule content. Real law was *supposed* to be profoundly implicated in broader cultural currents.

In this light, the careful analysis of the "extraneous" material in the canons suddenly becomes quite relevant. We may analyze these "extraneous" elements as consisting of sets of compositional features, themes, and intertextual references that accompany or envelope the pure and technical rule content. This material is best analyzed in two stages. First, we may identify three framework discourses. These represent the basic modes or strategies of presenting or referring to the "extraneous" material. Second, we may explore the most prominent assemblages of ideas, motifs, images, references, and intertextual connections employed or assumed by these strategies. These represent the fundamental intertextual referents of the canons.

1. Three Principal Discourses: Tradition, Pedagogy, Persuasion

Aside from conveying rules, the canons "do" three principal things. First, the canons tend to look backwards: they speak to and from tradition. The canons are constantly positioning themselves in relation to older rule material, and speaking to the present from the past. Second, the canons teach. The canons are constantly explaining, re-enforcing, or drawing out the broader consequences of the rule material. Third, and closely related to the second, the canons persuade and dissuade. The canons exhort and chastise, honor and dishonor, and generally employ numerous rhetorical devices to encourage or discourage certain types of behavior.

The discourse of tradition is extremely pervasive.[237] It functions to set rule content against a broader background of older regulative traditions. This positioning may entail a number of different relations. The dominant relation is that of coherence and adherence: one writes rules "according to" past authorities or as renewing older authorities. Clarification, interpretation, modification (often a relaxation), or extension are also not uncommon. For example, Ancyra 21 relaxes an "earlier rule" (*πρότερος ὅρος*) on women who engage in abortion, reducing the penalty from lifelong excommunication to ten years; Chalcedon 28 casts itself as developing further consequences of the patriarchal rights established in Constantinople 2; Trullo 6 clarifies that only readers and cantors may marry after ordination, slightly modifying and clarifying earlier rulings (Apostolic 26; Ancyra 10). At times this interpretative relationship may become so pronounced as to transform canons into virtual commentaries on older rules, especially when the traditional rule is listed at

[237] For some discussion of similar tendencies in the secular legal literature, see Honig 1960, 127–44, and Ch. 1 D.5. Humfress 2005, 171 is right to see even Justinian's legislation as presenting itself as fundamentally rooted in the past.

the beginning of a canon. This is true of many of Basil's longer rules, as already noted, but may also be found elsewhere.[238]

Sometimes older traditions are more or less rejected—although usually on the basis of yet other traditions. An example is Basil 1, which explicitly contests Dionysius of Alexandria and Cyprian's views on re-baptism with extensive argumentation from other traditions. Likewise Trullo 12 essentially overturns Apostolic 5, which permitted episcopal marriages, with reference to scriptural teachings.[239]

In all cases there are three primary traditional referents: (1) scripture; (2) specific canonical rulings; (3) vaguer "customs" or "traditions" "of the fathers." The last group, the most nebulous, includes references to "customs" (ἔθη), traditions (παραδόσεις), "the rule" (ὁ κανών, in its older, more synthetic sense), and similar concepts. Occasionally, especially in the second-wave sources, specific patristic and liturgical sources are cited.[240]

Scripture—the ultimate source of traditional Christian authority—is the most common and persistent traditional referent in the corpus as a whole.[241] The distribution of scriptural references in the corpus is nevertheless uneven. Its presence may be felt most intensely in the earliest material, especially the patristic writings of Dionysius, Peter, Gregory Thaumatourgus, and Athanasius (canon 1), as well as in the most recent material, that is, the second-wave material.[242] It is at its least intense, not surprisingly, in the very laconic legislation of Neocaesarea, Gangra, and Laodicea, and in narrowly administrative types of documents, such as Theophilus' "memorandum" (ὑπομνηστικόν). Even in the terser canons, however, it can occasionally emerge quite prominently (e.g. Neocaesarea 15). In the Apostles its presence is quite pronounced. This last is particularly interesting, as it demonstrates

[238] e.g. Nicaea 2, 5, 13; Basil: 2, 4, 7, 8, 9, 13, 18, 26; Gregory Nyss.; Chalcedon 28; Trullo 6; II Nicaea 3, 6, perhaps 12; Protodeutera 8–11.

[239] Trullo is particularly notable for its careful confrontation, to various degrees, of earlier rules. See canons 3, 12, 13, 28, 30, 32, 33, 40, 55, 65.

[240] Non-canonical or non-scriptural authorities are referred to explicitly in three Trullan canons: in canon 16 John Chrysostom's *Homily* 14 on Acts (*PG* 60.116) is invoked to reinterpret Neocaesarea 15; in canon 32 the appeal by Armenian apologists to the same father's Homily 82 on Mathew (*PG* 58.740) is rejected; in canon 64 Gregory of Nazianzus' *Oration* 32 (*PG* 36.188) is cited in support of the rejection of lay teachers. Canon 32 also counters the Armenian reading of John Chrsysostom by referring to elements from his liturgy, as well as from the liturgies of St James and St Basil. II Nicaea 2 cites Dionysius the Areopagite (*Ecclesiastical Hierarchy* 1.4; *PG* 3.389); 16 cites Basil's *Greater Asketikon* (*Regulae brev. tract.* 39; *PG* 31.977); canon 19 makes another citation of Basil's non-canonical writings, this time his treatise *On Fasting* (4; *PG* 31.192); and canon 20 contains a vague reference to Basil's monastic regulations. In Protodeutera 10 Gregory of Nazianzus is referred to loosely (cf. *Oration* 28; *PG* 36.45), almost in passing. Earlier use of non-canonical material to support rulings may be found in Cyprian and Timothy 9 (both liturgical references). All references are from *Fonti*.

[241] See further Section F.2.a.

[242] e.g. in Trullo see the use of scripture in 7, 12, 13, 16, 54, 60, 61, 64, 65, 67, 70, 72, 76, 83, 85, 88, 89, (somewhat less so) 100, and 101; and in II Nicaea 2, 4, 5, 7, 12, 13, 15, 16, 18, 22.

that even the apostles must "look backwards" and ground their decisions in even earlier tradition: Jesus' teaching, the Old Testament, and the apostles' own actions and writings in the New Testament.[243]

The second type of referencing, to earlier specific canonical rulings, is also very common. It is rarest in some of the shortest 4th C canons, but overall it is surprisingly consistent across the entire corpus. From beginning to end the canonical material is written—very consciously—against the background of a quite substantial and concrete rule world.[244] Table 2.1 is a good guide to its distribution. To give a few examples from the first-wave material, Nicaea 5 introduces its topic (*Περὶ τῶν . . .*) with the clear citing and affirmation of "the opinion according to the canon which forbids . . . " (*ἡ γνώμη κατὰ τὸν κανόνα τὸν διαγορεύοντα*). Antioch refers to the Nicene "definition" (*ὅρος*) of Easter in its first canon, and then in canon 3 to "the ecclesiastical ordinances" (*τοὺς θεσμοὺς τοὺς ἐκκλησιαστικούς*). In Antioch 9 a reference is made to "the ancient canon prevailing from our fathers" (*τὸν ἀρχαῖον ἐκ τῶν πατέρων ἡμῶν κρατήσαντα κανόνα*), in canon 21 to "the definition already earlier brought forward on this matter" (*τὸν ἤδη πρότερον περὶ τούτου ἐξενεχθέντα ὅρον*), and in canon 23 to "the ecclesiastical ordinance" (*τὸν θεσμὸν τὸν ἐκκλησιαστικόν*). Likewise, Constantinople 2, on the privileges of Alexandria, Antioch, and the Asian civil dioceses, is quick to assert its coherence with "the canons"—three times, in fact, twice with explicit mention of Nicaea. Constantinople 394 refers specifically to the Apostolic Canons. Chalcedon 19, on holding synods twice a year, legislates "according to the canons of the holy fathers" (*κατὰ τοὺς τῶν ἁγίων πατέρων κανόνας*), clearly intending Nicaea 5 or Antioch 20. Theophilus, in his letter to Agathos, charges a certain Maximus with "not knowing the laws of the church" (*ἀγνοῶν τοὺς τῆς ἐκκλησίας νόμους*). Basil 3 takes as a central point of discussion an "ancient canon" (*ἀρχαῖος κανών*), as does Basil 4, noting "they ordained a canon" (*ὥρισαν κανόνα*), here in the sense of a tariff, before going on to discuss its topic in terms of a usage (*συνήθεια*) which Basil has "received" (*κατελάβομεν*). In Carthage the entire Apiarian dossier is aimed at discerning the real rules of Nicaea. In Chalcedon 2 and Gennadius we see older canons being "renewed." Many other similar examples could be cited.[245] In some cases one may doubt whether a truly specific, concrete rule is being referred to, or whether perhaps the older, more generic use of "canon" is intended (e.g. in Nicaea 5 or Antioch 9),

[243] See e.g. Apostles 3, 25, 27, 29, 41.

[244] This has often been remarked for the early tradition; see e.g. *Fonti* 2.500–1; Hess 2002, 77–9; Schwartz 1936a, 179–81, 186–7. Broadly relevant to this phenomenon is the discussion of the interrelationship and dependence of norms in early canonical sources; see Mardirossian 2010, 65–72, 318–20 *et passim*; *Sources* 29–30; Ohme 1998. See too the notes to earlier sources throughout the Deferrari translation (1926) of Basil's canonical epistles.

[245] Explicitly in e.g. Constantinople 1, 2; Constantinople 394; Antioch 1; Chalcedon 28; Basil 88, Theophilus 12; Gennadius; Carthage 18c.

but the effect is the same: the canons are unquestionably written as if set firmly against an established rule background.

In the second-wave material such references become even more frequent, as is evident from Table 3.1. They are generally of the same type. Now, however, canons are also occasionally cited by number,[246] or, more often, quoted in part or even in full,[247] sometimes as part of being explicitly "renewed." This quotation of earlier canons, which sometimes results in canons that are compilations of older rules,[248] represents an acme of traditionalization: new rules are physically woven out of the old. The apogee of this type of rule repeating is Tarasius, a long canonical florilegium on simony. (Interestingly, this type of straight quotation of rules may also be found, or suspected, in some first-wave sources.[249])

The third, vaguer type of traditional referencing is hardly less frequent. The canons are littered with expressions such as "according to the ecclesiastical canon" (in a general sense; Laodicea 1); "the majority said that..." (Neocaesarea 9); "it has been judged by the fathers that..." (Gregory Nyss. 2); "the ancients judged that...it seems good to those from the beginning that...it seemed good to the ancients that...our fathers considered that..." (Basil 1, 18); "according to the prevailing usage [συνήθεια]..." (Constantinople 2);[250] "following everywhere the decrees of the holy fathers...according to custom..." (ἔθος) (Chalcedon 28);[251] or "according to a most ancient tradition..." (παράδοσις) (Trullo 69)[252]. Such references are usually professions of loyalty and continuity, but, again, sometimes older traditions are rejected.[253] In some cases entire sources are framed by such general professions of traditional loyalty, most notably Gangra, Carthage, Trullo, and II Nicaea, as already noted in Chapter 2.

[246] II Nicaea 16 refers to Chalcedon 2; Tarasius refers to Apostolic 29, Trullo 22, and Chalcedon 2; Protodeutera 8 to Nicaea 1, Protodeutera 9 to Antioch 5. Earlier, Carthage will sometimes refer to previous synods by name, e.g. as in canons 34, 48, 86, 94.

[247] Trullo 3, 6, 11, 12, 14, 25, 26, 34, 36, 38, 49, 84, 87, 94; II Nicaea 3, 5, 6, 7, 12; Protodeutera 8–12.

[248] The best examples are Trullo 93, 95, although neither explicitly notes its sources.

[249] It is perhaps most likely in some of the canons of Basil and Gregory of Nyssa which often read as simply conveying older rules. This includes canons of Basil that begin with (or are) a simple rule statement, as if Basil is simply conveying an established tradition (e.g. 2, 3, 5, 8, 25, perhaps most of Basil 51–84). The best first-wave examples are, however, the literal doublets shared between the Apostles and Antioch (*Sources* 29). Gennadius also contains explicit citations of earlier material.

[250] For further συνήθεια references, see Nicaea 7, 15, 18 (cf. 6 σύνηθες); Constantinople 2, 7; Carthage 70; Trullo 39; II Nicaea 15; Basil 3, 4, 21, 89, 91, 92; Gregory Nyss. 8.

[251] For further ἔθος references, see Nicaea 6; Ephesus 8; Chalcedon 30; Trullo 28, 37, 39, 62, 65, 90; II Nicaea 7, 14; Basil 87, 91, 92; Theophilus 1, 2, 3.

[252] For further παράδοσις references, see Nicaea 7; Gangra Epilogue; Carthage 3, 24; Chalcedon 8; Trullo 29, 69; II Nicaea 7; Basil 91–2; Peter 15; Gregory Nyss. 6.

[253] e.g. Nicaea 15; Basil 21; Gregory Nyss. 8; Trullo 28, 65.

The full force of all three types of traditional references is best illustrated by an example. Nicaea, despite its own sense of authority as a "holy and great council" (canon 8, 14, 15, 18), is particularly full of such references, as it constantly articulates its legislation with reference to past authorities. Thus, canon 2 begins by condemning ordinations "against the ecclesiastical canon" and immediately cites scripture (1 Tim. 3: 6–7) against the practice of ordaining neophytes; canon 5 introduces its topic very clearly with the citing and affirmation of "the opinion/decision according to the canon..." (ἡ γνώμη κατὰ τὸν κανόνα); canons 6 and 7 start, respectively, "Let the ancient customs prevail..." and "Since a usage and ancient tradition has prevailed..."; canon 13, very much like 5, treats its topic commentary-style, with an opening citation of "the ancient and canonical law" (ὁ παλαιὸς καὶ κανονικὸς νόμος), which is to be preserved "even now"; canon 15 treats the transfer of clergy as entirely a traditional problem, a matter of a bad usage (συνήθεια) that is "against the canon"; canon 16 starts by chastising those who neither fear God nor know "the ecclesiastical canon"; canon 17 takes as its starting point the fact that some have "forgotten" the scriptural rule against lending at interest (Prov. 26: 11); and finally canon 18 begins with condemning a practice by asserting that "neither the canon nor usage has handed down that...," a combination of three common tradition-vocabulary words (κανών, συνήθεια and the παραδιδ- root). In other Nicene canons traditional references are not quite so prominent but nevertheless present. Canon 9 mentions those "acting against the canon" and canon 10 does not permit ignorance to "prejudice the canon."[254] Many other sources—for example, Cyprian and Ephesus 8—contain similar levels of "traditionalizing."

Almost as pervasive as the language of tradition is the second major mode of canonical discourse, that of pedagogy. As already noted, pedagogy is hard-wired into the ancient conceptualization of law: law is virtually defined as pedagogy of the sociopolitical soul, and it in turn presumes patterns of social, spiritual, and moral formation.[255] For a modern reader, however, pedagogical stylization is one of the most peculiar aspects of ancient law, and an important factor in creating a sense of canonical rule discourse as distinctly foreign, archaic, and "messy."

Its most obvious manifestation is those sources which in their very genre, topic, and composition are primarily didactic or argumentative. The pedagogical aspects of these texts are so obvious as to require no comment: by their very act of providing careful arguments and rationales—something modern legislation generally does not feel obligated to do—they are teaching. Broadly, virtually all of the material in the form of a non-conciliar letter or an actual

[254] In both these cases, however, it is just possible that "canon" here should be read in the sense of "register of clergy."

[255] See Ch. 2 C.2.

treatise—that is, much of the patristic material—could be counted in this category.[256]

Pedagogical stylization is most disconcerting, and requires the most careful exploration, in material that is more conventionally legal in form, that is, most of the conciliar material, and the patristic material that closely approximates the conciliar style of legislation. In this material pedagogical discourse may be defined as any type of construction that is not strictly necessary for the articulation of the rule at hand (pedagogical constructions can generally be removed from a canon without any change in the canon's basic rule content or even grammar), but that provides some type of additional background, explanation, or rationale for the rule at hand. These constructions "unpack" some further consequence, context, motive, or principle of the rule content at hand. This elaboration may be moral, psychological, theological, philosophical, scriptural (here overlapping with traditional discourse), or even legal-doctrinal in tone. In all cases its effect is to make the canons speak to some type of reality beyond their mere rule content.

In practice, instances of pedagogical styling often takes the form of short epexegetical asides set off by ὡς, γάρ, ἵνα, ὅπως, ὥστε, or the like. A typical example is Apostles 22: someone who castrates himself cannot become a cleric, "*for* he has become a murderer of himself and an enemy of the creation of God." We thus learn not only the rule, but the rationale and the full implications of the behavior condemned. Similarly in Nicaea 5, a rule prescribing a pre-Lenten synod is accompanied by this rationale: "*so that* a pure gift might be offered to God with all small-mindedness taken away." Another, more extended example can be found in Ephesus 8, where the consequences of the Antiochian usurpation of Cypriot rights are drawn out at great length: "[the Antiochians are to give up the usurped province] lest the canons of the fathers be transgressed, or the vanities of worldly authority be brought in under pretext of sacred work, or we lose, without knowing it, little by little the liberty which our Lord Jesus Christ, the deliverer of all, has given us by his own blood" (trans. *NPNF14* 235, altered). Jurisdictional imperialism apparently implies a breaking of custom, worldliness, and a violation of the very salvific freedom given in the blood of Christ!

Very frequently a scriptural passage offers a short explanation or "lesson." Thus in Basil 41 a widow with authority over herself is permitted to live with a man, "since the apostle says: 'if her husband dies, she is free to marry whom she wishes; only in the Lord' [1 Cor. 7: 39]." Apostles 52 employs considerable

[256] The most didactic texts are Dionysius 1, Athanasius 1, Basil 87, 90, 91, 92, Gennadius, and Tarasius. They all contain definite rule content, but encased in extensive didactic scaffolding. Lesser examples include Gregory Thaum., Peter, the rest of Athanasius, Gregory Nyss., and much of Cyril. Pedagogical stylizations are much less marked in Basil's remaining canonical letters (although, as noted, they are introduced as highly didactic in tone and goal), Timothy, and Theophilus.

pathos when it deposes clergy who reject repentant sinners, "because it grieves Christ who said 'there is joy in heaven when one sinner repents' [Luke 15: 7]." Gangra 17 similarly cannot resist a (vague) scriptural gloss, and ponderous deduction, for why a woman must not cut her hair: "If a woman . . . should cut her hair, which God gave to her as a reminder of her subordination [cf. 1 Cor. 11], so that she would be setting aside the commandment of subordination, let her be anathema." Such short pedagogical glosses, scriptural or otherwise, are very common and may be found throughout the corpus.[257]

In the second wave some of the canons begin to approximate miniature didactic treatises, and pedagogical styling can become exceptionally pronounced and sustained.[258] II Nicaea 2, for example, on the educational requirements of bishops, begins with a framing scriptural exhortation to "meditate upon thy statutes," as well as the reminder that to do so is "saving" for all Christians, and especially the hierarchy. It later moves on to a patristic gloss on the necessity of learning scripture: "for the God-given oracles, that is, the true knowledge of the divine scripture, are the essence of our hierarchy" (*οὐσία γὰρ τῆς καθ'ἡμᾶς ἱεραρχίας ἐστὶ τὰ θεοπαράδοτα λόγια ἤγουν ἡ τῶν θείων γραφῶν ἀληθινὴ ἐπιστήμη*[259]), and closes with another scriptural passage warning of God's rejection of those who reject knowledge. A relatively simple rule has become a short sermon.

Opening and/or closing with small pedagogical contextualizations, as in II Nicaea 2, is particularly common. It is already evident in Trullo and II Nicaea, but is especially characteristic of Protodeutera, where it becomes the norm.[260] Protodeutera 1 is a good example. It begins with a moralizing commentary (a faux *narratio*) on the restoration of monasteries: "The restoration of monasteries has of old always been considered a sacred and honorable thing by our blessed and holy fathers, but today is seen to be practiced badly . . . " Further pedagogical styling continues as the canon gives an unflattering description of the motivations of its target, private owners of monasteries, as "contriving to consecrate to God only in name," before eventually concluding with a final condemnation-via-rhetorical-question: "for if one does not remain

[257] Ancyra, Gangra, and Theophilus contain only a few each. Most contain many more. They are especially prominent in the Apostolic Canons, where over half contain some type of similar explanatory aside or scriptural example/amplification: see canons 8, 9, 13, 16, 22, 23, 24, 25, 26, 27, 29, 31, 33, 34, 36, 38, 39, 40, 41, 46, 47, 49, 50, 51, 52, 53, 55, 59, 60, 63, 64, 68, 73, 74, 75, 76, 77, 78, 80, 81, 82, 83.

[258] In addition to the examples cited below, see esp. Trullo 7, 64, 73, 82, 88, 101, 102; II Nicaea 1, 4, 6 15, 22; and all of Protodeutera save 16.

[259] Dionysius the Areopagite, *Ecclesiastical Hierarchy* 1.4 (*PG* 3.389).

[260] See Trullo 40, 60, 73, 96; II Nicaea 1, 2, 4, 5, 7, 16, 18, 22; in Protodeutera, all canons but 9 and 14 contain some form of it. It may also be found occasionally in the first wave, e.g. in Serdica 1, which begins and ends with short moral harangues, or Ephesus 8, which begins with a lengthy meditation on the vagaries of pastoral leadership. For a similar phenomenon in Byzantine secular laws, see Hunger 1964, 191–203.

owner of those things which one gives to a man, how will one be permitted to seize ownership of those things which one consecrates and dedicates to God?" Bookended with didactic stylizations, the canon has become both rule and moral/theological lesson.

A much lengthier example is found in II Nicaea 5, which begins with this extensive preface:

> It is a "sin unto death" [1 John 5: 16] when people incorrigibly continue in their sin; but they sin more and deeply who proudly lifting themselves up oppose piety and sincerity, accounting mammon of more worth than obedience to God, and caring nothing for his canonical precepts. The Lord God is not found among such, unless perchance having been humbled by their own fall, they return to a sober mind. It behooves them rather to turn to God with a contrite heart and to pray for forgiveness and pardon of so grave a sin and no longer to boast in an unholy gift, for the Lord is near to them who are of a contrite heart. With regard, therefore... [the rule content begins]. (Translation from *NPNF14* 558–9, altered)

Usually such "theological" introductions are shorter. Trullo 40, for example, opens: "Since it is a very salutary thing to cleave to God on account of withdrawal from the tumults of life...;" and Trullo 73 begins with: "The life-giving cross has shown us salvation, and we ought thus with all assiduousness to render worthy honor to it, through which we have been saved from the ancient fall. Whence..."

Perhaps the most extraordinary example of pedagogical ornamentation is Trullo 96. It contains approximately two lines of rule content (highlighted) embedded in a lengthy quasi-homiletic treatment of the evils of extravagant hairdos:

> Those who through baptism have put on Christ have promised to imitate his life in the flesh. **In the case of those,** therefore, **who** to the detriment of those who see them **arrange the hair on their head in elaborate plaits,** offering allurement to unstable souls, **we shall treat them paternally, with an appropriate penalty,** educating them and teaching them to live prudently; so that once they have given up the error and vanity of material things they may direct their mind constantly toward the blessed and imperishable life, may preserve chaste behavior in fear of God, may draw near to God, in so far as possible, through pureness of life, and may adorn the inner rather than the outer man with virtues and honest and blameless manners; and thus they will bear in themselves no trace of the enemy's perversity. **If anyone behaves contrary to the present canon, he shall be excommunicated.** (Translation from *NPNF14* 406, altered)

A relatively simple rule is again turned into an extensive moral, philosophical, and theological object lesson.

The final mode of canonical discourse, the discourse of persuasion, is the least tangible in terms of direct, citable instantiations, but nevertheless constitutes an integral textual characteristic of the corpus as a whole. It frequently overlaps with the discourses of tradition and pedagogy, since most appeals to tradition are broadly intended to persuade the reader to obedience, and the pedagogical highlighting of motives, consequences, rationales, or requisite dispositions functions to persuade the reader to undertake or refrain from certain behaviors. Distinct elements of the discourse of persuasion/dissuasion may nevertheless be identified. Unlike the other two discourses, it is mostly a function of tone and style, created by patterns of hyperbole, amplification, deprecation, and laudation—and generally the rhetorical "charging" of language. Its effect is usually to induce a strong, often emotional complicity in the reader with a rule's intention and content. It is perhaps best termed the "discourse of moral outrage" after its most normal mode, although it can also take on more irenic or dialogical forms.[261]

One of its most dramatic incarnations is the casting of infractions as acts of insolence and impudence. Thus, in Antioch 1, for example, wrongdoers are constantly "daring" (*τολμέω*) to commit infractions: "All those who *dare* to set aside the decree... and if one of those who preside in the church... *dares* to act on his own... and those who *dare* to communicate with them..." Similarly, in Antioch 5 priests and deacons who separated themselves from their bishop are "despising" (*καταφρονέω*) him. Likewise, at the opposite end of the corpus, Hagia Sophia 3 speaks about laity "puffed up with authority" (*αὐθεντέω*) and "despising" (*καταφρονέω*) commands, "deriding" (*καταγελάω*) the laws of the church and "daring" (*τολμέω*) to strike a bishop. Similar instances are easily found elsewhere.[262]

The discourse of persuasion also appears in the form of hyperbole and the use of dramatic phrasing. In Antioch 16 a misbehaving bishop "hurls" (*ἐπιῤῥίπτω*) himself at a vacant church, and "snatches" (*ὑφαρπάζω*) its throne. Likewise, in Laodicea 36 one "hurls" (*ῥίπτω*, instead of a more typical *βαλ-* root word) clergy who are wearing phylacteries out of the church. In canon 35 of the same council those who engage in the invocation of angels dramatically "forsake" (*ἐγκαταλείπω*) Christ and the church. In Chalcedon 22 a cleric wrongfully "snatches" (*διαρπάζω*) the goods of a bishop. Protodeutera 1, just cited, also speaks of "snatching" ownership of monasteries (*ὑφαρπάζω*). Serdica, which contains a number of very highly wrought stylizations, begins its first canon with this piece of invective: "There is no more awful custom in need of being uprooted from its foundation than the most harmful, corrupt practice... [of transferring bishops]" (*οὐ τοσοῦτον ἡ φαύλη συνήθεια ὅσον ἡ βλαβερωτάτη τῶν πραγμάτων διαφθορὰ ἐξ αὐτῶν τῶν θεμελίων ἐστὶν ἐκριζωτέα*).

[261] See Lanata 1989 for examples of similar patterns in Justinian's Novels.

[262] e.g. Apostolic 28, 31, 74; Nicaea 1, 16; Gangra 3, 6, 11; Serdica 7, 11, 13, 21; Antioch 1, 4, 10, 11, 12, 13, and 22; Carthage 13, 48, 53, 54, 86; Constantinople 6; Ephesus 4, 7; Chalcedon 7, 8, 10, 12; Protodeutera 7, 10.

Similarly, the behavior of wrongdoers is often described in highly contemptuous terms. In Nicaea 2, for example, one who disobeys the council does so "audaciously" (*θρασύνω*). In Antioch 1 those opposing the decree of Nicaea do so "for love of strife" (*φιλονεικότερος*). Gangra 20 cannot help but note that those who disparage assemblies of the faithful do so "in a disposition of arrogance" (*ὑπερήφανος διάθεσις*), and in 12, 14, 17, and 18 it places the asceticism and piety of its targets in distinct quotation marks—their "supposed ascesis" or "supposed piety" (*νομιζομένη ἄσκησις, νομιζομένη θεοσέβεια*). Constantinople 6, especially in its introduction and conclusion, goes out of its way to paint a decidedly negative picture of the character of those it wishes to condemn: they act, for example, "with love of enmity and as false accusers" (*φιλέχθρως καὶ συκοφαντικῶς*), wishing to do nothing other than ruin the reputation of priests and whip up "troubles" (*ταραχή*) among the laity. Ultimately, they are simply "outraging (*καθυβρίζω*) the canons and ruining (*λυμαίνομαι*) good ecclesiastical order." Similarly, in Chalcedon wrongdoers often act "on account of" or "according to" negative dispositions: love of gain (*δι'αἰσχροκερδίαν*), love of money (*διὰ φιλαργυρίαν*), arrogantly (*κατ'αὐθάδειαν*), "on account of the desire of empty glory" (*διὰ δόξης κενῆς ἐπιθυμίαν*)—or once, in the case of good behavior, "on account of the fear of the Lord" (*διὰ τὸν φόβον τοῦ κυρίου*).[263] Serdica 1 concludes with a scathing assessment of the moral character and motivations of its subjects: "Whence it has come to pass that such persons burn with a flaming greed and are slaves to pretension so that they might appear to acquire greater authority" (*ὅθεν συνέστηκεν διαπύρῳ, πλεονεξίας τρόπῳ, ὑπεκκαίεσθαι τοὺς τοιούτους καὶ μᾶλλον τῇ ἀλαζονείᾳ, δουλεύειν, ὅπως ἐξουσίαν δοκοῖεν μείζονα κεκτῆσθαι*). Similar is Serdica 20, which contrasts characteristics of canonicity (salvific, coherent, fitting, pleasing to God—*σωτηριωδῶς, ἀκολούθως, πρεπόντως, θεῷ ἀρέσαντα*) with the uncanonical (shameful, pleasing to arrogance and pretension rather than to God—*ἀναισχυντία, τύφῳ μᾶλλον καὶ ἀλαζονείᾳ ἢ τῷ θεῷ ἀρέσαι*). In Carthage 53, a canon replete with such language, wrongdoers are acting out "tyranny" (*τυραννίς*), and are "puffed up" and "stupid" (*φυσιούμενοι και μωροί*). Somewhat differently, but to the same effect, Antioch 1 employs a strategy of piling one harmful consequence on top of another with "not only... but also..." phrases: "becoming a cause of sin *not only* to himself *but also* a cause of corruption and subversion to many, and it [the synod] deposes *not only* such persons from their service *but also* those who dare to commune with them" (*ὡς οὐ μόνον ἑαυτῷ ἁμαρτίας ἀλλὰ πολλοῖς διαφθορᾶς καὶ διαστροφῆς αἴτιον γινόμενον, καὶ οὐ μόνον τοὺς τοιούτους καθαιρεῖ τῆς λειτουργίας ἀλλὰ καὶ τοὺς τούτοις κοινωνεῖν τολμῶντας*). More typically, Trullo 7 characterizes deacons who sit above their position as "acting

[263] Chalcedon 2, 3, 8, 10.

with presumption and self-will" (*αὐθαδείᾳ καὶ αὐτονομίᾳ κεχρημένους*) and again "daring" to act with "tyrannical insolence" (*τολμήσει τυραννικῷ [χρωμένους] θράσει*). In II Nicaea 8 Jews who feign conversion to Christianity "mock" (*μυκτηρίζω*) Christ. In II Nicaea 9 the iconoclast writings are "childish playthings and maniacal ravings" (*μειρακιώδη ἀθύρματα καὶ μανιώδη βακχεύματα*).

At times this type of emotional and polemical "charging" can be sustained across an entire source. This is particularly evident in some of the longer patristic letters and treatises. A good example is one of the very earliest sources, Gregory Thaumatourgus, which evinces a very distinct buildup of anger and frustration. The letter begins with a very calm and moderate consideration of an initial problem (canon 1), but soon, in canon 2, tension mounts as Gregory notes that there is not enough room in one letter to convey all of the scriptural passages that denounce greed and robbery. He then launches into an angry scriptural exposé of how the wrath of God will fall upon the church if the sinners are not expelled. The rhetorical momentum builds as he then begins to shoot rhetorical questions at the reader—will not the wrath of God fall on his interlocutor as well? Did not the wrath of God fall on Achar (canon 3)? Did the wrath of God fall on Achar alone, or on others around him as well? And as to those who have stolen things on the pretext of "finding" them (now in canon 4)—well, "let no one deceive himself"—for in scripture one is not allowed to benefit from an enemy's misfortune in peacetime: How much less then now are Christians not to benefit from the misfortune of their brothers during war? In canon 6 the tension comes to a crescendo, as a report is received that is "unbelievable" (*ἀπηγγέλη δέ τι ἡμῖν καὶ ἄπιστον*): Christians are keeping Christian captives, escaped from barbarians, as slaves. An emissary is to be sent to address the problem, "lest indeed thunderbolts strike those doing such things" (*μὴ καὶ σκηπτοὶ πέσωσιν ἐπὶ τοὺς τὰ τοιαῦτα πράσσοντας*). Canonical wrongdoers can be struck by lightning!

More moderate, but similar, examples of the sustained buildup of irritation and tension may be felt in Cyril 1–3 or Basil 87, 90.

Gentler forms of persuasion also appear. In Ephesus 9 the reader is coaxed into agreeing with the council's decision through a deft weaving of images of the grief and troubles suffered by Eustathius. The council particularly recalls his inexperience and isolation, and employs the pathetic topos of a weeping and injured old man ("we all felt for this old man and considered his tears to be our own") who had made mistakes "far away from his home city and dwellings of his fathers for such a long time." Similar in effect are the lengthy, affective descriptions of the sufferings of noble *lapsi* (for example, Ancyra 3, 5, "shouting that they are Christians," "crying," "prostrating"), all employed to garner support for relaxed punishments.

A particularly curious form of persuasion may be found in Neocaesarea. This source has the strange habit of speaking directly to its reader, inviting the reader into complicity with its conclusions. The most obvious instance is canon 7, which forbids priests to attend banquets of digamists. This canon directly asks the reader to agree with its apparently obvious conclusion: "for if the digamist must do penance, what type of priest will he be who through his attendance approves the marriage?" Canon 14 likewise directs the reader to search in Acts to confirm that there ought to be seven deacons. More subtly, canons 2 (its last clause) and 4, perhaps originally answering specific questions, lack real rule content but seem to invite the reader to join them in thinking out loud: "But if the woman or man in such a marriage should die, penance for the survivor will be very difficult"; "If a man, desiring a woman, should intend to sleep with her, and his desire comes to nothing, it seems that he has been saved by grace."

Elsewhere in the corpus a similar effect is achieved by the occasional posing of rhetorical questions or the use of other short meta-narratival interjections.[264] Of these last, the best examples are the occasional use of "it is clear" or "obviously" (δῆλον, πρόδηλον), as found, for example, in Nicaea 1 and 6, or the *a minori ad maius* trope (if "*x*" is true, then "*y*" must be all the more true), as found in Apostolic 41 or Chalcedon 18. Both subtly encourage the reader's support for the canon's ruling.

2. Principal "Assemblages": the basic contexts

The discourses of tradition, pedagogy, and persuasion are all intertextual in function: they link the canons into broader networks of texts, ideas, value narratives, and images. We may identify six major assemblages of such texts or narratives: scripture, morality and metaphysics, honor and appearances, purity and defilement, medicine, and the divine presence.[265]

a. Scripture

The single most prominent text cited within the canons is Christian scripture, both Old and New Testaments. Over 180 canons contain at least one scriptural reference, often as a quotation.[266] This exceeds even the number of canons

[264] Rhetorical questions may be found in Apostles 46; Gregory Thaum. 2, 3, 4; Basil 27, 29, 48; Gennadius; Protodeutera 1, 3, 10.

[265] Many of the following may be identified in the contemporary secular legal material. In the literature they are frequently discussed as elements of the "rhetoricization," "ethicization," or "Christianization" of law; see esp. the studies of Biondi 1952, Honig 1960, Hunger 1964.

[266] By my own count; see also the index in *Fonti* 4, which lists approximately 380 scriptural citations in total (although this list is not complete). Akanthopoulos 1992, 26 notes 349 *canons*

(approx. 120) with more or less clear references to other canonical rules, the second most common type of referent.[267] (Patristic references and other legal references/allusions are a very distant third, at perhaps fifteen references.[268]) Scripture may thus—not surprisingly—be considered the pre-eminent textual referent of the canons.

It is beyond the scope of the present study to examine the use of scripture in the canons in detail.[269] Suffice to say that scripture's presence in these texts is highly variable in content, form, and function. Across the corpus as a whole its employment is neither systematic nor rationalized. Its overall function may be best described as a pool of highly flexible, infinitely relevant contextual referents that can be adapted and adopted for virtually any compositional need. Its effect is to create a broad literary coherence between the canons and scripture: the canons naturally and easily speak out of scripture, and with scripture. The canons become a broadly "scriptural" text.

Several types of references may be identified. Many provide a general principle or rationale for a rule.[270] For example, Apostolic 46 rejects heretical baptism, "for what agreement does Christ have with Belial, or a believer with an unbeliever?" (2 Cor. 6: 15). Others are more ornamental, in effect a means of stylization.[271] For example, when Neocaesarea 5 speaks about fallen catechumens becoming "hearers," it adds "sinning no more" (John 5: 14; 8: 11). Very rarely a canon will convey or apply a specific scriptural rule or an aspect of a specific scriptural rule.[272] For example, Basil 11 explicitly follows Exodus 21: 18–19 in determining criteria for voluntary and involuntary murders.

One use of scriptural rules is conspicuous by its absence. At no point are the scriptures systematically "mined" for rules which are then added to the corpus as self-standing regulations.[273] Such a process will develop in the Latin

which contain scriptural references, a number I account for only if, perhaps, every possible resonance and allusion is included. (Unfortunately Akanthopoulos's fuller treatment of scripture in the canons, *Ἱεροὶ Κανόνες καὶ μετάφραση τῆς Ἁγίας Γραφῆς* in *Εἰσηγήσεις Δ′ Συνάξεως Ὀρθοδόξων Βιβλικῶν Θεολόγων* (Thessaloniki, 1986), 189–90, has not been available for consultation.)

[267] Even if one includes broader references to tradition, "the fathers," and custom, the total does not much exceed 150 canons.

[268] See the aforementioned patristic citations (n. 240) and *regula*-type material (in Section E.1).

[269] The study of scripture in the canonical tradition is still in its infancy, especially for the eastern tradition. For a more detailed treatment, see Wagschal 2014; also Pieler 1997.

[270] These may be found throughout the corpus, but they are especially prominent in the Apostolic Canons, Trullo, II Nicaea, Gregory Thaum., Dionysius, Peter, Basil, and Tarasius.

[271] Rarer; these are most common in the Apostles, Trullo, II Nicaea, Protodeutera, Basil, and Gregory Nyss.

[272] Very uncommon; see Wagschal 2014 for the more important instances. Firey notes that this type of rule sourcing is also rather rare in the western Pseudo-Isidorian collections (Firey 2003, 290).

[273] The only major exception in the Byzantine legal tradition seems to be the 8th C *νόμος Μωσαϊκός*, a small compilation of rules from the Pentateuch (ed. and commentary, Burgmann

tradition, as is well known.[274] But in the east the direct sourcing of a canon in a scriptural rule is in fact comparatively rare and desultory—and exceptionally so when the scriptural rule is mostly constitutive of a canon.[275] In general, a concrete scriptural rule is cited as a principle, parallel injunction, or confirmation of a canonical rule.

This lack of direct rule sourcing signals an obvious but very important assumption of the canonical texts: scriptural rules stand on their own. They are not to be repeated, or extracted, since the canons already assume their presence. The canons thus seem to be understood as a different, and in fact lower, form of rule text, continuous with scripture and rooted in it, but ultimately a companion and supplement to, in effect, the real rulebook.[276] This is the impression given by the prologues, as noted in Chapter 2. It is once even almost brought to explicit articulation in the corpus itself.[277] Apparently scripture is understood as constituting a very real body of regulative material, assumed by the canons but separate from them.

In this relationship an assimilative pairing, and yet hierarchical ordering, of scripture and canons thus emerges once again. Both scripture and the canons constitute essential and "in force" pools of regulative texts, and both are interrelated, but the latter is clearly dependent upon, and subordinate to the former.[278] The canons thus do not replace scripture as the regulative texts, nor do they systematically extract and compile scriptural rules, but they are always intended to be broadly "scriptural" in texture, development, and intent.

and Troianos 1979; also Pieler 1997, 90; Schminck 2005; Troianos 1987). Although present in some canonical manuscripts as an appendix (see *Sbornik* 170), it seems to have had relatively little currency in the canonical tradition as a whole. In the manuscripts, however, other small *testimonia*-type appendix articles may occasionally be found in which scriptural passages are gathered to illuminate a specific topic, such as clerical oaths. One such collection is described for Paris supp gr. 843 in *Sin* 144; see also *RP* 4.415. The full extent of such excerpt collections is not known, but it does not seem great.

[274] In the west, systematically scouring scripture for rules to insert in canonical collections seems to have begun in early 8th C Ireland and then spread elsewhere. See Fournier and Le Bras 1931, 64–8; Gaudemet 1984; Kottje 1970; Sheehy 1987; Wasserchleben 1885, xiv–xvi. On scripture and the canons generally in the west, see Firey 2003 (with further references at n. 44), Gaudemet 1984, Helmholz 1995 (who at 1557–8 comments on the poor state of literature for even high medieval canon law), Le Bras 1938, Andresen 1980.

[275] The best candidate is Apostolic 63, conveying the dietary laws of Gen. 9: 4, Exod. 22: 30, Lev. 5: 2, and Acts 15: 29 (surprisingly, not exclusively Acts 15: 29, as in Trullo 67). Even it does not merely repeat one scriptural rule, but synthesizes material from several sources.

[276] Cf. Pieler 1991, 21 on the primary importance of scripture in Zonaras' commentary—equivalent, Pieler feels, to the position of imperial laws in secular juristic writings.

[277] In Carthage 5; see Wagschal 2014. So similarly in Gregory Nyss. 5 and 6.

[278] The statement in Beck 1981, 7 that the Bible has only a "subsidiary" role in Byzantine law is thus slightly misleading; the tradition clearly sees the canons as subsidiary rules to scripture!

b. Morality and metaphysics

If scripture is the pre-eminent textual referent for the canons, morality and metaphysics are their principal topical preoccupations. The canons constantly speak to moral and metaphysical realities beyond their basic rule content, both describing and prescribing the values, beliefs, and standards of behavior demanded by the rules themselves.

The canons are particularly eager to elaborate upon internal dispositions, attitudes, emotions, and motives. Canonical rules thus speak—strangely by modern standards—to both the "what" and the "how" of behavior. Indeed, the two seem to be closely linked. Uncanonical behavior is thus frequently cast as connected to some negative internal disposition, attitude, intention, or motive, and legal behavior to more positive internal states or faculties. Most often, wrongdoing is cast as a function of vice.

Many examples of this moralizing have already been offered, and include most of the language of "moral outrage" cited above (wrongdoers as "despising," "daring," and so forth), or the glossing of motivations as "on account of" various vices and evil dispositions.[279] In all of these cases it is clear that to commit canonical wrongs is to act in a morally defective manner. These "passions" are sometimes even explicitly named as such. Protodeutera 2, for example, condemns those who take up the monastic habit with vainglorious intentions ("so that by the reverence of the habit they might receive the glory of piety"), so as to "give their own passions (πάθη) abundant pleasure." See also Ephesus 8 ("passions," cited below), or the reference to "virtue" (ἀρετή) in Trullo 96, above.

Not surprisingly, vices and dispositions are even to be taken into account directly in investigations of wrongdoing. In Nicaea 5, for example, in cases of the excommunication of priests, the bishop is to be examined lest "meanness of spirit or love of strife or any such unpleasantness" is involved. Serdica 14 is very similar, directing that the anger of the bishop be investigated.[280]

Positive behavior is also sometimes described and prescribed in terms of correct internal attitudes, motivations, and dispositions. Thus, in Antioch 24 and 25 episcopal property management is to take place "with good conscience and faith" and "with all piety and fear of God." Gangra 3 is concerned that slaves are not to run away, but to continue to serve their masters "with a good mind" (μετ'εὐνοίας). Dionysius 2 justifies its prohibition on menstruating women's communion by reference to what "faithful" (πιστός) and "pious" (εὐλαβής) women would do. II Nicaea 1 depicts clergy as law-abiding "gladly" (ἀσμένως), and who, through the words of scripture, "delight" (τέρπω) and "rejoice" (ἀγαλλιάω) in the law, and "hug [the canons] to their chests" (ἐνστερνίζομαι).

[279] See Section F.1. [280] Cf. Carthage 134.

At times analysis of internal dispositions and vices/virtues can become quite sophisticated. Here the canons clearly adopt the theoretical discourse of ancient spiritual psychology. The pre-eminent example is Gregory of Nyssa's canonical letter, which, as an intentional attempt to classify penitential material according to the standard psychological schema of λόγος, ἐπιθυμία, and θυμός, stands in a class of its own. Canonical regulation as a whole becomes defined as a psychological-therapeutic practice. Serdica 1, cited above, much briefer, is equally notable for offering a short analysis of the psychology of bishops who transfer sees: the real motivation for the bishops is a burning lust for power, which leads them to be "enslaved" to the passion of covetousness. A similarly involved analysis is evident in Trullo 45, a canon that forbids ostentatious tonsuring ceremonies for nuns. A new nun, formerly bolstered by "untroubled thoughts" (λογισμοὶ ἀκλινεῖς), is disturbed by a "remembrance" (ἀνάμνησις) of the world she has left. As a result, the nun's soul is troubled (ἐκταράσσω) "as by waves churning and tossing this way and that" (δίκην κυμάτων ἐπικλυζόντων καὶ τῇδε κἀκεῖσε περιστρεφόντων). Tears are expected, and analyzed in some detail for their effect on observers. Trullo 100 likewise engages in a short exposition on how easily bodily sensations (αἴσθησις) corrupt the mind: "for the sensations of the body easily influence the soul" (ῥαδίως γὰρ τὰ ἑαυτῶν ἐπὶ τὴν ψυχὴν αἱ τοῦ σώματος αἰσθήσεις εἰσκρίνουσι).

References to the heart, grief, and (as in Trullo 100) tears feature surprisingly prominently in some canons. Emotional states are apparently well within the purview of canonical legislation. Tears, in particular, can appear quite prominently. Most frequently they arise as a substantive gauge of true repentance in *lapsi* canons, in the penitential material, and in clauses or canons that suggest some attenuation of a penalty.[281] Similarly, certain states of the "heart," as in Trullo 45, are also noted in the context of describing appropriate states of penance or sincerity.[282] The pathos of grief and inner pain also occurs, as in Apostolic 52 (where Christ is "grieved" (λυπεῖ Χριστόν)).[283]

Aside from dispositions, motives, and virtues, the canons can also invoke metaphysical doctrines, Christian or Greco-Roman. These references are usually made in support, as a source, or as a ramification of a specific rule.[284] Many—even most—of the short scriptural citations and short pedagogical glosses cited above are doctrinal/theological references of this sort. A good example is Apostolic 51. Clergy who abstain from marriage, meat, and wine, not because of asceticism but because of "abhorrence" (βδελυρία), have

[281] e.g. Ancyra 5; Basil 27, 77; Nicaea 12; Ephesus 9.

[282] See II Nicaea 8, Trullo 41, 89, Basil 10, 75.

[283] See also Cyril 1, 2; Basil 90; Ephesus 9.

[284] Here we are excluding those canons whose central topic is a doctrinal problem: e.g. a Christological or Trinitarian heresy (Constantinople 1, 5; Ephesus 7; Trullo 1), Donatist beliefs about original sin (Carthage 110–16), or certain exegetical matters (Basil 15, 16).

"forgotten" correct scriptural doctrine: "forgetting that everything is 'very good' and that God made man male and female." Likewise Laodicea, normally very laconic, does not hesitate to add in canon 34 that heretic martyrs are to be avoided, "for these are not of God"—a short theological explanation. In canon 48 the doctrinal effect of chrismation is briefly mentioned: "because it is necessary that those enlightened are chrismated after baptism with the heavenly chrism and become partakers of the kingdom of God." In Chalcedon 4 wandering monastics are to be confined "so that the name of God is not blasphemed"—a type of theological consequence. Trullo 4 dramatically glosses the violation of a consecrated woman as "having corrupted the bride of Christ." Trullo 90 provides some brief liturgical-theological commentary, explaining that the rule forbidding kneeling on Sunday is to begin on Saturday evening, "as in this way we celebrate all day and night the resurrection." II Nicaea 13, after offering a brief etiology of iconoclasm—it was caused "because of our sins"—concludes with a lengthy and dramatic scriptural exploration of the nature of the excommunication of those who have turned religious houses into taverns: "[they are excommunicated] as condemned by the Father and the Son and the Holy Spirit and assigned to where 'the worm does not die and the fire is not quenched' [Isa. 66: 24/Mark 9: 44], because they have opposed the voice of the Lord saying 'Do not make my Father's house a house of trade' [John 2: 16]."

Such theological or doctrinal glosses become especially notable when drawn out at length. II Nicaea 5 and Trullo 96, cited above, along with many of the longer, more elaborate examples of pedagogical styling evident in the second wave, and especially the many short "theological" introductions, are all especially good examples.[285] In each a broad set of metaphysical doctrines is both assumed and inculcated.

Especially interesting are the few occasions when relatively technical Greco-Roman philosophical language (aside from the technical psychological language already noted, as for example in Gregory of Nyssa) makes an appearance. This is particularly characteristic of Trullo, where, as observed, it is already evident in the *Προσφωνητικός*.[286] Thus, in Trullo 41 monastics seek solitude not for "empty glory" but for "the true Good" (*δι' αὐτὸ τὸ ὄντως καλόν*), and in Trullo 45 nuns are not to recall the things of their former life through the putting on of adornments of "this perishable and transient world" (*φθαρτοῦ τε καὶ ῥέοντος κόσμου*). Language of "materiality" (*ὕλη*) also emerges briefly in Trullo 96, in the phrase "giving up the deception and vanity of material things" (*ἀφέντας τὴν ἐκ τῆς ὕλης ἀπάτην καὶ ματαιότητα*), and again in canon 101, when those receiving communion with metal receptacles are chastised for preferring "inanimate and lower matter" (*τὴν ἄψυχον ὕλην καὶ ὑποχείριον*) to the image of

[285] See Section F.1. [286] See Ch. 2 B.5.

God (i.e. using one's hands). In all of these cases the broadly Platonic provenance of the language is obvious.

c. Honor and appearances

Another major assemblage of ideas and expressions relates to honor and appearances. This discourse, by prescribing and proscribing certain types of attitudes, moral standards, and ways of thinking about the nature and implication of infractions, may be considered a subtype of moral/metaphysical discourse. Its particular province, however, is the discourse of reputation, insult, mockery, respect, shame, suspicion, and generally "how things look." It is often a key component of the aforementioned language of moral outrage: infractions are not simply infractions of an impersonal rule, but personal insults; wrongdoing is not simply a matter of a neutral "mistake," but an act of insolence. Considering the well-known importance of such concepts in Greco-Roman political discourse and literature, its presence in the canons is not surprising.[287]

It is perhaps most noticeable as a subject of substantive regulation. Apostolic 8, for example, suspends clergy who do not reveal the reason why they are not receiving communion precisely since this may create suspicion (ὑπόνοια) among the laity as to the purity of the offering, and thus its cultic efficacy. Here the perception or appearance of wrong is a central part of the problem addressed. Even more directly, in Apostolic 53, 54, 84 people are condemned who "insult" (ὑβρίζω) bishops, presbyters, deacons, and the emperor or magistrates. Evidently dishonoring the clergy or civil officials must be directly regulated. (These rules should, of course, be read in the context of civil-legal regulation of hubris, that is, libel, a very serious charge.[288]) Interestingly, in Basil 45 a rule of somewhat unclear intention is issued that forbids "insulting" (ἐνυβρίζω) Christ. Not dissimilar is a canon like Laodicea 20, in which a provision is explicitly made for diaconal "honor" (τιμή): "the deacons are also to receive honor from the servers and all the clergy." Many other regulations may be found which treat the "honorable" appearance of Christians, including various types of insults and the problem of reputation and "suspicions" thereabout (especially regarding the good standing of plaintiffs).[289]

In a manner entirely coherent with normal late antique usage, honor language is also embedded in the language of institutional process, rank, and office.[290] In Nicaea 7, for example, change in jurisdictional status is phrased in

[287] See e.g. Brown 1992 and Lendon 1997, with many further references.

[288] e.g. *Digest* 47.10; *CJ* 9.35–6; *Institutes* 4.4.

[289] See e.g. Apostolic 74; Gregory Thaum. 1; Cyril 4; Nicaea 9; Constantinople 6; Ancyra 3; Laodicea 53; Carthage 9, 38, 44, 132; Chalcedon 21; Trullo 73; II Nicaea 16.

[290] See e.g. Jones 1964, 377–90 on the *dignitates* and *honores* of the late imperial administration.

terms of "honoring" (τιμάω) and an "order of honor" (ἀκολουθία τῆς τιμῆς), and the problem of a metropolitan retaining his "dignity" (ἀξίωμα, i.e. *dignitas*), that is, his rank or office. Constantinople 3 similarly addresses the institutional position of Constantinople in terms of "prerogatives of honor" (πρεσβεῖα τῆς τιμῆς). Earlier, such language may be found describing the difference between the metropolitan and his bishops in Antioch 9: "he will also exceed them in honor" (καὶ τῇ τιμῇ προηγεῖσθαι αὐτον). It may be found elsewhere in similar institutional/office functions, and may even be found in sanctions.[291]

Honorable action and the avoidance of, in particular, shame is likewise a very common topic of numerous supplementary glosses. Nicaea 17, for example, strongly textures its condemnation of clerical interest-taking with shame vocabulary (αἰσχρο- roots: αἰσχροκέρδεια, αἰσχροῦ κέρδους ἕνεκα). Chalcedon 2, on simony, likewise speaks of "shameful takings" (αἰσχρὰ λήμματα), and Chalcedon 3, on clerics engaging in secular business dealings, of "shameful gain" (αἰσχροκερδία). Chalcedon 4, conversely, begins its condemnation of busybody monastics by noting how the honor of the monastic schema does properly accrue to monks who are worthy of it: "let those who come truly and purely to the monastic life be deemed worthy of the appropriate honor" (τῆς προσηκούσης ἀξιούσθωσαν τιμῆς). The function of this line as the formal introduction to the canon is significant: honor constitutes a normal and prominent conceptualization for characterizing, rewarding, and promoting proper behavior. Similarly, Trullo 17 casts a relatively technical administrative matter in shame/honor language: a cleric who is registered in another church without letters of release is described as "bringing shame (καταισχύνων) upon the one who ordained him." Carthage 138 casts Apiarius' activities as his "shameful conduct" (αἰσχρότης) and his denials as "shamelessness" (ἀναισχυντία). In Serdica 20 the bishops are concerned that "the divine and most reverend name of the priesthood" is being brought into disrepute by the "shamelessness" (ἀναισχυντία) of a few. Similar concerns about shame, scandal, and "name" emerge elsewhere with some frequency.[292]

A particularly interesting subtype of honor/appearance language involves texturing infractions or their results as insults or acts of dishonor or mockery, often with the insult/hubris (ὕβρις) language already remarked as a topic of substantive legislation. Serdica 13 is perhaps the earliest example. This canon treats the problem of bishops communing with clerics excommunicated by another bishop, but describes such infractions in terms of hubris: "[a bishop]

[291] For examples of the former, Apostolic 76; Nicaea 8; Ancyra 18; Antioch 5, 10; Serdica 10; Carthage 6, 13, 57 (probably), 62, 104. For sanctions, see Ancyra 1, 2; Antioch 18; Chalcedon 12 for the punishment of losing the τιμή of one's office.

[292] See Serdica 6, 11; Carthage 60, 65; Trullo 12, 37, 47; II Nicaea 18, 20; Protodeutera 12.

ought not to inflict hubris upon his brother by offering him [the excommunicate] communion." Laodicea 27 likewise forbids a (somewhat obscure) disruption of church order "on account of the hubris that this inflicts upon the ecclesiastical order." Similarly, Carthage 138 speaks about the hubris inflicted upon the synod (*πάσῃ τῇ συνόδῳ διαφόρους ὕβρεις ἐπιφέρων*) by Faustinus' attempts to appeal to Rome. Other examples include Constantinople 6 (wrongdoers "insulting" (*καθυβρίζω*) the canons and good order); Chalcedon 6 (at-large ordinations are hubris to the one who ordains); Chalcedon 15 (a fallen deaconess "insults" (*ὑβρίζω*) God's grace); Trullo 13 (the Roman practice of clerical celibacy "insults" (*καθυβρίζω*) marriage); Trullo 42 (false hermits "insult" (*καθυβρίζω*) their profession); and Basil 1 (Montanists "insult" (*καθυβρίζω*) the Holy Spirit).

Another important aspect of honor/shame discourse consists of explicit expressions of concern about the public appearance of actions. Thus Laodicea 27 condemns mixed-gendered bathing in terms of the response it might evoke from pagans: "for this is the first reproach among the pagans." Cyril 1, as already noted, casts canonical order as essentially concerned with the avoidance of "slander from some people" (*τῆς παρά τινων δυσφημίας*) and the acquisition of "praise from right-thinking people" (*τὰς παρὰ τῶν εὖ φρονούντων εὐφημίας*). A very striking and self-conscious reference to the public audience may be found in Protodeutera 1, where it is noted that sales of consecrated property "provide astonishment and an abominable scandal *to those who see it*" (*θάμβος ὁμοῦ καὶ μύσος τοῖς ὁρῶσι παρεχόμενα*).

Sometimes the audience is less explicit, yet still tangible. Apostolic 40, on the need to keep personal episcopal and ecclesial finances separate, phrases its rule in terms of keeping everything "evident" (*φανερός*) for all to see: "Let the bishop's own property be evident . . . and that of the church" (*'Έστω φανερὰ τὰ ἴδια τοῦ ἐπισκόπου πράγματα . . . καὶ φανερὰ τὰ τοῦ κυριακοῦ*). In this same canon the audience even extends into the divine realm: "for this is just before God and people" (*δίκαιον γὰρ τοῦτο παρὰ θεῷ καὶ ἀνθρώποις*). The canon concludes with an unmistakable and typical concern for public scandal: its regulations are put in place lest "the death [of the bishop] be surrounded with slander" (*τὸν αὐτοῦ θάνατον δυσφημίᾳ περιβάλλεσθαι*). Serdica 20, on punishments for bishops, likewise includes a reference to a human and divine "audience": regulations are made "pleasing to God and to people" (*καὶ θεῷ ἀρέσαντα καὶ ἀνθρώποις*).

d. Purity, cleanliness, and defilement

Rarer than honor/appearance language, although sometimes connected with it, is the discourse of purity, cleansing, and defilement. It is closely related to the language of disease and contagion.

This discourse's most obvious presence is in the numerous substantive regulations that touch on physical purity:[293] restrictions on Eucharistic participation because of blood or semen (Dionysius 2, Athanasius to Ammoun, Timothy 7); regulations on sexual purity relating to the reception of the Eucharist after licit sexual activity (Timothy 5, 13); restrictions on ordination and liturgical service because of both licit and illicit sexual activity (Neocaesarea 8; Laodicea 55; Theophilus 4; Carthage; Basil 27; Trullo 3, 13); regulations of consanguinity (Basil 23, 67–8, 75, 76, 78, 79, 87; Trullo 53, 54); rules on the sexual defilement of women (Ancyra 11, Gregory Thaum. 1, Basil 22, 30, 38); rules about inappropriate types of sexual activities (homosexuality, bestiality, pornography—Ancyra 16; Basil 7, 63; Trullo 100; almost all the canons on fornication, adultery, and polygamy could also be included in this category); regulations on the defilement of sacred property and goods (Apostolic 73; Trullo 68, 97, 99; Protodeutera 10); regulations on food purity (usually condemning overzealous ascetics showing *βδελυρία*, loathing or disgust, as in Apostolic 51, 53, 63; Ancyra 14; Basil 86; Gangra 2; Trullo 67); and a provision on purification from demon possession (Apostolic 79).[294]

The language of purity in all these instances is pronounced, and needs no extensive exposition. One aspect of this discourse is, however, noteworthy: sexual purity is treated very much like a physical contagion or wound. In this sense, purity language blends into medical language. The classic example is Basil 27, where a cleric's engagement in illicit sexual activity, even in ignorance, is understood to impair completely his ability to serve liturgically: "it is illogical that one who should heal his own wounds can bless another; for blessing is the communication of holiness, but he who does not have holiness through a transgression of ignorance, how can he share it with another?" (*εὐλογεῖν δὲ ἕτερον, τὸν τὰ οἰκεῖα τημελεῖν ὀφείλοντα τραύματα, ἀνακόλουθον. εὐλογία γὰρ ἁγιασμοῦ μετάδοσίς ἐστι, ὁ δὲ τοῦτο μὴ ἔχων, διὰ τὸ ἐκ τῆς ἀγνοίας παράπτωμα πῶς ἑτέρῳ μεταδώσει;*). Impurity appears to impair almost physically a priest's very capacity for sacral activity. This logic—and even the phrases—will be repeated in Trullo 3 and 26.

Aside from a subject of substantive legislation, purity, corruption, and contagion emerge as an accepted, if not frequent, part of general canonical discourse. Thus in Antioch 1, celebrating Easter with the Jews becomes "the cause of much corruption for many" (*πολλοῖς διαφθορᾶς . . . αἴτιον*). Apostolic 8 speaks of the suspicion of clergy not offering the Eucharist sacrifice *ὑγιῶς*,

[293] On purity in Orthodox Christian canon law, see Synek 2006.

[294] Interestingly, one type of purity thinking is explicitly rejected: lack of physical wholeness. In Apostolic 77 and 78 physical defects that do not "impede the affairs of the church" do not disqualify from ordination, "for the defect of the body does not defile a man, but defilement of the soul" (*οὐ γὰρ λώβη σώματος αὐτὸν μιαίνει, ἀλλὰ ψυχῆς μολυσμός*). It is important to note, however, that this is not a rejection of the concept of purity per se—quite the opposite. It is simply the rejection of one extension of the notion. The idea of spiritual impurity is affirmed.

"healthily" or "soundly." (It is not entirely clear what this means, but we may suspect a purity issue; cf. *Apostolic Constitutions* 2: 20, 6: 18). Ephesus 7, a doctrinal canon, condemns Nestorius' doctrines as precisely "stained" or "defiled" (*μιαρά*). In the next canon the rights (*δίκαια*) of every province are to be preserved "pure and inviolate" (*καθαρὰ καὶ ἀβιάστα*). In Serdica 1 the botanical metaphor of a rotting plant is invoked when the custom of episcopal transfer is described as a "corruption that must be uprooted from the foundations" (*διαφθορὰ ἐξ αὐτῶν τῶν θεμελίων ἐστὶν ἐκριζωτέα*). In the next canon people are portrayed as "corrupted" by rewards and honors (*μισθῷ καὶ τιμήματι διαφθαρέντας*). In Carthage 86 ecclesiastical order (*ἐκκλησιαστικὴ κατάστασις*) is to remain "undefiled" (*ἀμίαντος*). In canon 138 Apiarius needs to "cleanse" himself from the charges (*ἐγκλημάτων καθαρθῆναι*), and later in his confession is spoken of "cleansing" his shameful stains (*ἐκ τῶν οὕτως ἐπαισχυνταίων σπίλων . . . καθαρθῆναι*) (both times *purgare* in Latin; *Fonti* 2.429–31). In Trullo 1, Macedonius is *βδελυρός*, "abhorrent," and the fathers of the fifth council themselves "abhorred" or "abominated" (*βδελύσσω*) the Three Chapters. We also saw corruption terminology in Trullo 45: the "perishable" or "corruptible" and transient world (*φθαρτοῦ τε καὶ ῥέοντος κόσμου*). Trullo 96 likewise commends ornamentation of the self not through cosmetic adornments but through moral "cleansing" in life (*διὰ τῆς ἐν βίῳ καθάρσεως*). In II Nicaea 16 iconoclasm is referred to as a "stain" or "defilement" (*μίασμα*), and the verb "to abhor" or "abominate" (*βδελύσσω*) is used to describe the iconoclasts' attitude towards the icons. Similarly, II Nicaea 22 includes the exhortation for us to "purify" our minds (*λογισμοὺς ὀφείλομεν καθαίρειν*).[295]

e. Medicine

Within the corpus of canons the language of medicine, healing, and disease is most prominent in Gregory of Nyssa's canonical letter and Trullo 102. Both, especially the former, are elaborate and explicit treatments of canonical penances as precisely medicines for the soul, a metaphor already found in *οἱ τοῦ μεγάλου θεοῦ*.[296] Together these canons represent the single most elaborate theoretical development of any metaphor in the canons, and may be regarded as coming close to providing the canons with a framing "theory" of canonical sanctions.

Aside from these canons, however, medical references are never exceptionally common. Basil is unusually rich. In canon 1 his definition of "schismatics," as opposed to heretics, involves ecclesiastical differences that are "healable" (*ἰάσιμος*). In canon 3 Basil states in a general discussion of clerical penalties that, "in general the truer healing is departing from sin" (*καθόλου δὲ*

[295] Reading with *Fonti*, against *Kormchaya* and *RP*, *καθαίρειν* instead of *καθαιρεῖν*.
[296] See Ch. 2 B.3.

ἀληθέστερόν ἐστιν ἴαμα ἡ τῆς ἁμαρτίας ἀναχώρησις). The same "healing" root appears in his introduction to canon 90, a letter on simony: this letter is to be received by the guilty "as a cure" (*ὡς ἴαμα*). The related language of "therapy" or healing/remedy language (*θεραπεία*) occurs earlier in Basil 29: rulers who swear to harm their subjects "ought by all means to be remedied" (*πάνυ θεραπεύεσθαι προσῆκε*), and "their remedy is twofold" (*θεραπεία δὲ τούτων διττή*). The same language appears in canon 38, where Basil notes that "it seems that what happened has received remedy" (*δοκεῖ θεραπείαν λαμβάνειν τὸ γεγονός*). A little differently, in Basil 27 the rationale for the suspension of a cleric's function is articulated in terms of "wounds" (*τραύματα*) that prevent the priests in question from exercising their function.

Similar language may be found elsewhere. Antioch 5, unlike its doublet, Apostolic 31, contains a brief phrase in which it is noted that a recalcitrant priest, having being summoned numerous times, is now to be deposed completely as having "no further remedy" (*καὶ μηκέτι θεραπείας τυγχάνειν*). Ephesus 8 contains a more extended (psychological) medical metaphor, speaking of passions, healing, and harm: "the common passions require greater healing as causing greater harm" (*τὰ κοινὰ παθὴ μείζονος δεῖται τῆς θεραπείας ὡς καὶ μείζονα τὴν βλάβην φέροντα*). In Trullo 1 the faith is to remain "without wound" (*ἀπαράτρωτον*). In Trullo 2, as already noted, the canons are written for the "remedy/healing of souls and curing of passions" (*πρὸς ψυχῶν θεραπείαν καὶ ἰατρείαν παθῶν*). The same canon ends by casting its own penalties as "remedy" or "healing": "being healed by that in which he fell" (*δι᾽ αὐτοῦ ἐν ᾧπερ πταίει θεραπευόμενος*). Later, Trullo 41 notes that it is necessary that eremites who leave their cells without permission must be "healed" with fasts and other hardships (*νηστείαις καὶ ἑτέραις σκληραγωγίαις . . . θεραπεύειν*). In canon 96 penal activity is described with healing/remedy language: "we paternally remedy with a fitting penalty" (*ἐπιτιμίῳ προσφόρῳ πατρικῶς θεραπεύομεν*). Protodeutera 3 contains a strong example: heads of monasteries are condemned who do not pursue runaway monks and treat them "with the fitting and appropriate treatment for their failing" (*τῇ προσκούσῃ καὶ καταλλήλῳ τοῦ πταίσματος ἰατρείᾳ*).

f. The divine presence and the sacred

The sacred is present in the canons in a variety of ways. The most profound is the least explicit, and has already been noted: the general scripturalization and traditionalization of canonical discourse. These literary strategies serve to root canonical legislation, both directly and indirectly, in Christianity's most fundamental referents for sacrality and holiness: scripture, the apostles, "the fathers," and the tradition generally. The many theological and metaphysical glosses we have noted also contribute to this effect, especially when they indicate the salvific function of the canons or their capacity to effect spiritual healing.

On occasion the canons are directly, or almost directly, named as sacred. This is particularly obvious when accomplished with the epithets θεῖος, ἱερός, and ἅγιος, already mentioned.[297] More subtly it may be observed in canons such as Theophilus 14, where obeying canonical order is presented as equivalent to drawing near to "the law of God"—the canons have become a kind of divine law.[298] Almost in passing, II Nicaea 5 also refers to canonical precepts as God's own canonical precepts: "considering mammon of more honor than obedience to God and not holding to *his* canonical precepts" (καὶ τῶν κανονικῶν **αὐτοῦ** διατάξεων μὴ ἀντεχόμενοι). In II Nicaea 2 the canons are also directly included in the concept of "holy scripture": "[bishops must diligently read] the sacred canons, the holy gospel, and the book of the divine apostle, and all other divine scripture." Something similar is already implied in Apostolic 85.

The most striking presence of the sacred in the canons is the instances in which God himself intrudes into the canonical realm. These intrusions take a variety of forms. They often involves invocations of (final) divine judgment as an essential context of penance, or appeals to God as an "audience" (as already noted above), or references to God as a participant in church justice and church administration. This type of texturing is often brief and formulaic, but its effect is unmistakable: God is himself always part of ordering and ruling. This phenomenon may be termed the "eschatological" or "theophanic" discourse of the canons.[299]

Gregory Thaumatourgus' letter is perhaps the most dramatic example of this discourse. As has already been noted, Gregory is quite explicit that the wrath of God itself may fall upon the community as a result of disciplinary disorder. In canon 7 the Holy Spirit is also brought directly into the penitential decision-making process: Gregory decides that the wrongdoers in question are to remain outside of even the hearing of the scriptures "until such time as the saints, gathered together, should in common reach a decision about them—and, before them, to the Holy Spirit" (μέχρις ἂν κοινῇ περὶ αὐτῶν τι δόξῃ συνελθοῦσι τοῖς ἁγίοις καὶ πρὸ αὐτῶν τῷ ἁγίῳ πνεύματι). Apparently the Holy Spirit—God—is a primary agent in deciding difficult penitential cases.

[297] See Ch. 2 C.2.

[298] Something similar occurs in Basil 20, where church regulations are assimilated to the "laws of the Lord."

[299] Similar patterns may be found in the secular laws, where God's presence or punishments are often assumed or invited. See e.g. *N* 5.9.ep.; *N* 7.5.pr., *N* 137.1. A particularly good example is Justinian's demand that the gospels be placed in courtrooms. The explicit rationale for this provision is that this will bring to bear the presence of God in the courtroom, which places the judge himself under judgment; see *CJ* 3.1.13.4 and 3.1.14.2. Cf. also the tradition of antique judicial cursing tablets, described by Humfress 2009, 387–90.

This particular connection between God's presence and the determination of penalties emerges with some frequency. A similar sentiment, for example, may be found in Theophilus 13, which calls upon God to assist in a decision regarding the exercise of lenience: Theophilus instructs his bishop, Agathon, to "do what God suggests" (*ὅπερ ὁ θεὸς ὑποβάλλοι σοι, τοῦτο ποίησον*). More obliquely, in Laodicea 2 God's beneficent will is to be taken into account when considering the reconciliation of repentant sinners to Eucharistic communion: they are to be received "on account of the pity and goodness of God" (*διὰ τοὺς οἰκτιρμοὺς καὶ τὴν ἀγαθότητα τοῦ θεοῦ*). In Carthage 66 a decision is reached to treat the Donatists leniently not only after considerable conciliar examination of the matter, but also with the Holy Spirit himself "nodding assent" and "becoming resonant" with the decision (*ἐπινεύσαντος καὶ ἐνηχήσαντος τοῦ πνεύματος τοῦ θεοῦ*).

Sometimes God's participation in forensic process is more far-reaching. Carthage 138, the final element of the Apiarian dossier, is a particularly good example. Here God intervenes quite directly and repeatedly in the trial of Apiarius. The narration begins by noting that three days into the process "God, the just judge," himself "cut off" (*ἔτεμε*) the delays of Faustinus and the prevarications of Apiarius—God is immediately involved as a judicial agent, and precipitates the trial itself.[300] It is then noted that God himself has revealed, even to the eyes of all, Apiarius' wrongdoing: " for our God pressed his conscience and . . . made public to all the things in his heart" (*τοῦ γὰρ θεοῦ ἡμῶν τὴν συνείδησιν αὐτοῦ στενοχωρήσαντος καὶ τὰ ἐν τῇ καρδίᾳ κρυπτά . . . πᾶσιν ἔτι μὴν τοῖς ἀνθρώποις δημοσιεύσαντος*).[301] God is clearly acting like an effective judicial prosecutor/inquisitor. Later in the same canon, on a slightly different note, the council articulates its rebuke to Pope Celestine very much in terms of the Holy Spirit's active participation in church affairs: the Nicene fathers decreed that all matters are to be decided in the place they arise, "for [the canons of Nicaea] did not think that the grace of the Holy Spirit was lacking to each and every pastoral charge" (*οὔτε γὰρ μιᾷ καὶ ἑκάστῃ προνοίᾳ ἐλογίσαντο ἐλλείπειν τὴν χάριν τοῦ ἁγίου πνεύματος*).[302] Later the council expresses a similar disbelief that anyone could think that God would inspire one man (the pope) with justice, and yet deny this to a whole synod: "unless there is someone who will believe that our God is able to inspire any one man or other with the justice of judgment, but deny it to an innumerable number of bishops gathered in synod?" (*εἰ μὴ ἄρα τίς ἐστιν ὅστις πιστεύσει ἑνὶ ᾡτινιδήποτε δύνασθαι τὸν θεὸν ἡμῶν τῆς κρίσεως ἐμπνεῦσαι τὴν δικαιοσύνην, τοῖς δὲ ἀναριθμήτοις εἰς σύνοδον συνηθροισμένοις ἱερεῦσιν ἀρνεῖσθαι;*).[303] God clearly himself "inspires" and participates in church judgments. Similar examples can be found elsewhere.[304]

300 *Fonti* 1.2.430.20–431.4. 301 *Fonti* 1.2.431.9–12. 302 *Fonti* 1.2.433.22–434.2.
303 *Fonti* 1.2.424.10–16. 304 Basil 10, 84; Cyril 2; II Nicaea 13.

In Carthage 93 the divine participates in the forensic arena in a slightly different way. Here, as part of a request to the imperial government that civil laws be enforced against the Donatists, the authors provide the following rationale: "so that at least in this fear [of imperial force] they will cease from creating schisms and the foolishness of heresy—they who have not suffered to be purified and corrected by awareness of eternal chastisement."[305] Apparently schismatics and heretics are expected to be deterred and corrected merely by the prospect of eschatological punishment—even if in this case it is not working. Eschatological chastisement is in effect part of the canonical system of sanctions: the horizons of the canons once again open up onto the afterlife.[306]

God's action is not restricted to forensic practice. He can also become involved in quite mundane administrative matters. In Apostles 38, for example, the bishop is exhorted to manage financial affairs "as if God is overseeing" (*ὡς θεοῦ ἐφορῶντος*). God is to be understood as supervising accounts. Guidelines are then given of what God expects, particularly that no appropriations for relatives are to occur of *his* things: "the things *of God* are not to be given to one's own relatives" (*μὴ ἐξεῖναι . . . συγγενέσιν ἰδίοις τὰ* ***τοῦ θεοῦ*** *χαρίζεσθαι*). Not surprisingly, in the canon's Antiochian doublet, Antioch 24, God is again "God who oversees and judges all" (*τὸν πάντων ἔφορον καὶ κριτὴν θεόν*). In this same source, in canon 21, God again appears briefly as an administrative agent, this time placing clergy in their appropriate churches: clergy are "to remain in the church which they were allotted *by God* in the beginning" (*μένειν δὲ εἰς ἣν ἐκληρώθη* ***ὑπὸ τοῦ θεοῦ*** *ἐξ ἀρχῆς ἐκκλησίαν*). Similarly, in Carthage 26 a bishop who has not taken the required steps of consultation before selling church goods is to be held "accountable" not just "to the synod," but also "to God" (*ὑπεύθυνος τῷ θεῷ καὶ τῇ συνόδῳ*).

God is particularly concerned about questions of hierarchical order. In Carthage 86 the order of precedence among bishops is formally put in effect with the permission of God: "this order . . . will be maintained by us by the permission of God" (*κατὰ συγχώρησιν θεοῦ*). Similarly, in Trullo 64 the clerical order of the church is strongly defended in terms of its origin from God: lay people are to "yield to the order handed down by the Lord" (*εἴκειν τῇ παραδοθείσῃ παρὰ τοῦ κυρίου τάξει*). The rationale given for this order—with allusion to Paul (e.g. 1 Cor. 12)—is that God himself has made different members into one church (*ἐν γὰρ τῇ μιᾷ ἐκκλησίᾳ διάφορα μέλη πεποίηκεν ὁ θεὸς*). Later, in II Nicaea 14, which states that only ordained readers should read in church, the scrupulous observance of church hierarchy is asserted to be "well-pleasing to God" (*θεῷ εὐάρεστόν ἐστιν*). Apparently order and hierarchy is an especially divine and numinous aspect of the law.[307]

[305] *Fonti* 1.2.350.16–20. [306] See n. 299 for similar examples from the civil law.

[307] Compare the role of order and hierarchy in Plato's legal and political thought, noted in Ch. 2 B.2.

3. The legal whole revisited

With the principal "extraneous" elements of canonical discourse now identified and reintroduced into the legal equation—the flesh put back on the bones, as it were—the overall complexion of the canonical rules changes considerably, and a much more satisfying picture of the "legal whole" begins to emerge. The canons no longer appear as a set of mere regulations of (strangely) uneven technical merit, but as a rich, multidimensional normative reality that is designed to speak to more than one aspect of human sociocultural ordering.

We may summarize the effects of these extra-*regula* discourses by noting how each reveals a different facet of the Byzantine notion of canonical law and legality.

In the discourse of tradition canonical legislation once again emerges as a conversation with the past. The character of this conversation is mostly confirmatory and deferential, although the precise relationship of new rules with the old can vary. In all cases locating new rules in some traditional trajectory is both normal and expected. In practice, the chief concrete referents for this tradition are (in order of importance) scripture, other canons, a variety of traditional ecclesial customs and usages, and, much less commonly, specific patristic and liturgical material. Individual canons can, of course, still be written almost like modern statutes, with little explicit reference to the past, but the "backward-looking" character of the corpus as a whole is quite pronounced.

The discourse of pedagogy reveals that laws are understood to speak naturally and easily to moral and metaphysical realities, and that laws are to be kept firmly embedded in these realities. The law is thus both pedagogical in its own action, and it presumes pedagogy: the law itself teaches, and it requires that its subjects be formed in specific cultural narratives. As we have seen, these last include specific ideas and ideals of morality, theology, honor, law-as-medicine, purity, and a strong conviction in the ongoing action of God in the disciplinary life of the community. Whereas the fundamental instinct of much modern positivism–formalism is to preserve the strict autonomy of legal discourse from "outside" value narratives (and certainly from God!), the Byzantine instinct is the exact opposite.

The discourse of persuading and dissuading has a similar effect: canonical normativity is to be embedded solidly in the realm of moral imperatives. Obeying or disobeying the law is not a simple and neutral question of adhering to or not adhering to a set of minimal rules. Law instead involves questions of character and appearance, and thus demands conformance to a very broad set of communal narratives of correct behavior and internal dispositions. In effect, the canons co-opt broader forms of social control (morality, shame, fear) for their own uses, both instilling and demanding certain dispositions.

This instinct too is almost opposite to that of modern positivism–formalism, which seeks to distinguish as cleanly as possible the moral and legal, and to keep law well out of the "internal forum." The canons quite intentionally weave morality and legality together, and they freely make claims on the conscience and emotions of their subjects.

The unifying thread of all of these discourses is a conceptualization of law as *necessarily embedded* in broader narratives of the just and the right, whether these be traditional normative authorities, specific metaphysical concepts, or particular types of correct behaviors and dispositions. Far from simply conveying straight rules, the canons are written as expressions or manifestations of all these narratives, and are quite inseparable from them. This legal world thus does not read as a bare system of instrumental rules dominated by a technical proprietary discourse of rule logic, closed off from other narratives of theology, values, and morals, or only touching them now and then and in a controlled manner. Instead, the rules are clearly written for a conceptualization of legal process in which the rules are always read and applied in a constant intertextual negotiation with many other external narratives. A technical-legal discourse, with its logical rule finding and conceptual formalism, exists in this world, but as only one thread in the canons' normative fabric. It is less the controlling framework for the laws' operation—as we might expect—than one tool among others in the realization of justice.

G. ANALYSIS: THE LANGUAGE OF THE LAW

A formal analysis of the literary and technical-legal textures of the canons reveals much about Byzantine legal-cultural perceptions and beliefs.

From our survey of canonical nomenclature, one vital observation emerges immediately: the Byzantine canonical rules were perceived as possessing their own name. The presence of a proprietary and even technical nomenclature strongly suggests a self-conscious sense of the canons' own autonomy as a rule world, particularly in distinction from the civil laws. There can be little doubt that the canons were consciously conceived as a delimited, proprietary body of rules, alongside of, but separate from, the civil-legal rules: Byzantium knew two basic *Rechtsmassen*, the *νόμοι* and the *κανόνες*.[308] This corresponds to the physical reality of the manuscripts and aspects of the prologues, as described earlier.[309]

It is extremely difficult, however, to draw any further conclusions from nomenclature alone about the nature of this autonomous mass of rules. Their

[308] Fögen 1993, 68–9. [309] See Ch. 1 D.4 and Ch. 2 C.3, respectively.

relationship to the civil laws is a case in point. The terminological autonomy of the *κανόνες* simply does not seem to have entailed clear doctrinal consequences, which suggests, for example, a completely different notion of normativity. The variability in canonical nomenclature itself suggests that this was the case, but closer examination of the broader textures of the canons—genre, patterns of dispositives, rule structures, technical language—confirms shifting patterns of assimilation and distinction vis-à-vis civil laws that render any overly neat conceptual distinctions impossible. Whatever they may be called, the canons never emerge as radically "other" or discontinuous from the norms of civil-legal writing, nor do they emerge as truly imitative. A constant pattern of similar-yet-different emerges in a negotiation of legal identity that is more literary than doctrinal in character. In a manner very similar to what may be observed in the manuscripts and implied in the prologues, the two types of norms share the same general normative "space," and participate in the same general world of normative expression—but neither is an exact image of the other. The *κανόνες* are a distinct, but not a fundamentally different, type of norm from the *νόμοι*.

Despite attempts in the modern literature to argue the contrary, changes in canonical terminology also cannot be used as a significant gauge of the system's investment in legal formalism or positivism. The literary contours of the canonical texts make it clear that one of the *sine qua non* concepts of positivism–formalism—the conceptualization of the legal system as a body of internally coherent rules that operates as autonomously as possible from external narratives of morality and values—is precisely and directly negated *throughout the tradition*. The canons are constantly engaged in a very "messy" process of embedding themselves into broader traditional value narratives, and this process largely precludes the characteristic operations and assumptions of formalist–positivist systems. This embedding is one of the canons' most striking characteristics and, if anything, it increases over time—whatever the canons may or may not be called at any given moment. At best, then, the gradual hardening of canonical terminology around plural, concrete *κανόνες* indicates a slight shift in the formalist direction, but this shift is negligible in the context of the canons' broader theoretical orientation.

Turning to the narratives and values into which the canons are embedded, here we may note that the narratives identified in this chapter are precisely those that the introductory tradition, explored in Chapter 2, highlights. The prologues state that the canons should teach and tap into broader metaphysical narratives, and the canons *do* teach and tap into such narratives; the prologues cast the canons as being addressed to "life," morality, and spiritual psychology, and the canons do speak directly to these issues; the introductions cast canonical activity as traditional in orientation, and the canons are written with considerable traditional stylization; the prologues describe the canons as sacred and scriptural, and the canons are permeated with the sacred and with scripture; the introductions presume a highly rhetorical and persuasive mode of presentation, and the canons are often composed as highly rhetorical and persuasive in form; the prologues feature images and language of medicine and divine order very prominently, and these same discourses appear in the canons. Many other more minor points of correspondence could easily be noted.

This harmony between theory and (textual) reality is extremely significant. The coherence remarked in Chapter 2 between the physical shape of the tradition and the prologues can now be extended into the textual reality of the canons themselves. On almost every major count—the law's nature, its scope, its form, its ideals—the physical shape of the tradition (Chapter 1), the prologues (Chapter 2), and now the textual fabric of the canons demonstrate a remarkable consistency of vision.

This vision has been very much overlooked in the scholarly literature, as legal historians have traditionally been interested in only one type of consistency: technical-legal consistency. But, as we have seen, technical-legal discourse has an only very tenuous and ambiguous place in this world. Technical language, stylizations, and rule operations clearly exist in Byzantine canon law. The corpus even conceives of itself as a self-referring pool of norms, with a proprietary nomenclature and some standardization of forms and concepts. And yet these features never coalesce into a truly consistent, rationalized framework for the tradition as a whole. Instead, technical-legal discourse appears in the canons in only a highly desultory, uneven, and undeveloped form. In effect it is only one part of a larger, more complex construction of the "legal." This suggests a very different notion of law and legality from that which underpins the legal culture sketched in the Introduction.

The essence of this difference is perhaps best illustrated by what may be the single most important observation of this chapter: the overwhelming absence in the Byzantine canonical tradition of the phrase "canon law." The Byzantine canonical tradition seems to think of itself as a distinct and proprietary rule world, *and yet not abstractly*. This is evinced in the casuistic and surprisingly concrete nature of the canons as rules, as well as in the overall formation of the corpus as an agglutinating accumulation of heterogeneous traditions preserved in their original forms. The tradition does not form itself as an abstract and homogeneous aggregate of generic rules and principles constituting a constructed and autonomous field of jurisprudential endeavor—a "canon law." Instead, it emerges as a set of variegated specific rules, in their original forms, inextricably embedded in broader sets of values and narratives, and thoroughly traditional in character—the "sacred canons." Here the traditional character of the discourse is particularly important: legal authority is always vested in older semi-sacred traditions, and therefore the legal system per se is never a *present* abstract reality constructed out of the past, but always a collection *of the past authorities themselves*. The assumption seems to be that if a law is a real law, it is a concrete traditional text. This leaves very little room for an abstract rationalized jurisprudential construction of "law" to emerge. "Canon law" must always remain "the canons." Inasmuch as there is a broader, more abstract concept of the church's "law," it can only be a much broader backdrop of normativity against which the canons are set: the aggregate of the broad Christian regulative "stories" of justice, moral progress, divine instructions, and eternal judgment. The canons are thus essentially traditional rule sayings which find their legal coherence, structure, and force in their very embeddedness in this broader framework.

4

Systematizing the Law

A. INTRODUCTION: SYSTEMATIZING THE LAW

In the previous chapter we explored how the canons may themselves be read to describe Byzantine legal beliefs. In this chapter we turn to the first major instances of the Byzantine tradition itself reading, shaping, classifying, and generally "handling" the canonical corpus: the creation of the thematic indices of the *Coll50* and *Coll14*. These indices represent the first and ultimately the definitive attempts to organize the Byzantine corpus into a shape and structure beyond that of a straight corpus collection.[1] They thus provide an invaluable window onto the nature of Byzantine canon-legal systematization: how and to what extent could the texts be shaped into a new whole? What shape could this whole assume, and under what influences? How could the canonical "parts" be related to one and other? How could the individual texts be manipulated, interpreted, and transformed in these processes? To what extent can Byzantine canon law be conceived as a legal "system" at all?[2] More generally the

[1] In our period the *Coll50* and *Coll14* thematic schemata have no competition whatsoever. In the 12th or 13th C another small handbook-like thematic collection emerges, the *Synopsis* of Arsenius, in 141 titles. It was apparently very local in significance, and is known from only one manuscript (Paris gr. 1371, ed. Voellus and Justel 1661, 2.749–84 = *PG* 133.9–26; see Menebisoglou 1984, 89–90; *Peges* 249, 301–2). In the 14th C two other thematic collections were produced, Blastares' *Σύνταγμα κατὰ στοιχεῖον* (*RP* 6), and Harmenopoulos' *'Επιτομὴ κανόνων* (ed. Leunclavius (1596), 1.1–71 = *PG* 150.45–168). Both circulated widely, particularly Blastares, which became extremely popular in the post-Byzantine east (Pavlov 1902, 75–6; *Peges* 297–301, 302–3). Even Blastares, however, never entirely supplanted the earlier thematic systems, particularly the *Coll14*, which, associated with the name of Photius, seems to have remained the authoritative touchstone for the entire tradition (although details of the *Nachleben* of the *Coll14* and *Coll50* during the 15th–18th C are not well known).

[2] The problem of legal systematization is critical in light of the widespread assumption in much modern, especially civilian, legal thinking that legal phenomena should constitute internally coherent juristic and legislative wholes. See Berman 1983, 7–10; Glenn 2007; Merryman 1969, 65–70; 13–15; Weber 1925. For broader historical context, see Kelly 1970, see Kelly 1992, Robinson *et al.* 2000, Wieacker 1952. The methods, techniques, and especially implications of canonical systematization in the early medieval period have never been investigated in depth. The most useful study remains Pinedo 1963, although see also Gaudemet 1991 and Mordek 1975. Sohm's (in-)famous study of the *Decretum*'s order (Sohm 1918, 19–61; 1923, 79–85) is also

collections are among our best witnesses to the very nature and scope of early Byzantine canon-legal jurisprudence.

B. ORIGIN AND DATING

A thematic or systematic collection (the two terms may be used interchangeably) may be defined as any canonical collection which contains a set of topical titles or headings under which relevant canons are subsumed, either cited in full, in part, or as simple canonical references (for example, "Nicaea 10," "Ancyra 4"). These types of texts first emerge with any clarity only in the 6th C.

The first such collection, although mostly unrecognized in the survey literature, seems to be the Syrian *Collection in Fifty-One Titles*.[3] It is attested first in a 7th C manuscript (London BL syr. 14,526), and its titles contain references to canons only through Constantinople, despite being found in manuscripts that contain later material. As such, as Schwartz suggests, it may well be pre-Chalcedonian (*a.* 451).[4] According to Schwartz it is a translation of a Greek original, but is unrelated to the *Coll50*.[5] Possible relationships with other later systematic collections have not been explored.

In the west, the first thematic collection is usually recognized as the handbook-like *Breviatio canonum* of Fulgentius Ferrandus, dated *c.*535–46.[6] It was followed by another short handbook, the *Capitula* of Martin of Braga, *c.*563–80, as well as the much more extensive *Concordia canonum* of Cresconius,

important, as he saw in precisely its structure a last gasp of his *altkatholisch* legal mentality; see Chodorow 1972, 10–16 and Congar 1973 for further references on this study's later reception (mostly rejection). Fortunately, secular legal systematization and codification in our period, and earlier antiquity, are better treated, including Burgmann 2002; Diamond 1950; Frier 1985, 158–71; Gagarin 2000 (and Lévy 2000); Gaudemet 1986; Harries 1998; Heszer 1998; Honoré 1978; Jones 1956, 292–4; Matthews 2000; Schulz 1953; Stolte 2003; and, in part, Weber 1925. Works on general patterns of Byzantine compilation and collection are also important, notably Lemerle 1971 and Odorico 1990.

[3] ed. Schulthess 1908, 17–27. Unfortunately, no translation of this collection has been made, and I rely upon descriptions by Schwartz 1910, 200–1, 218 n. 2 and a few notes of Schulthess 1908, viii–xi and Selb 1989, 95, 100–1, 133, 143. It is to be distinguished from the *capitulatio* of London BL Syr. 15,428, which seems to be similar in form (and content?) to the *capitulatio* preceding Dionysius II.

[4] Schwartz 1910, 200–1.

[5] Schwartz 1910, 200 n. 2; see also *Sin* 10–12.

[6] On the following collections generally, see Maassen 1871 and, more briefly but recently, Zechiel-Eckes 1992, Fransen 1973, Gaudemet 1985, and Mordek 1975. Occasionally another small collection, the so-called *Statuta ecclesiae antiqua* (5th C; ed. Munier 1963), is treated as the first western "systematic" collection (e.g. Gaudemet 1991, 167; Mordek 1991, 901; Zechiel-Eckes 1992, 1.31). However, this collection lacks a title-rubric structure, and is best regarded as a rather ordinary example of Apostolic Church Order material with implicit topical themes—and as such is no more "systematic" than most other examples of Apostolic Church Order literature (e.g. the *Didache*). On this collection, see Munier 1960; see also Gaudemet 1985, 84–6.

dating to perhaps the mid-6th C.[7] Other prominent early Latin thematic collections include the 7th C systematic recensions of the *Hispana*, the 7th C *Vetus Gallica*, and the early 8th C *Hibernensis*. This genre will slowly gain ground in the west, becoming virtually the norm for collections after the 9th C, and reaches its culmination in the sophisticated *Concordia* of Gratian.

The Byzantine canonical tradition of the first millennium knew only three systematic collections, all of which are thought to have originated in the 6th C. Only the *Coll50* and *Coll14* are extant. One other collection, the *Coll60*, is known from a brief description in the foreword to the *Coll50*.[8] The *Coll50* and *Coll14* traditions, particularly the latter, each underwent numerous expansions and reworkings in the following centuries, but the original thematic titles themselves do not seem to have been significantly modified in later recensions; their number and content remain fairly stable throughout the tradition, with or without civil-legal insertions.[9]

Only two points of chronology are reasonably secure for the Greek collections. The first version of the *Coll50*, consistently ascribed to John Scholastikos in the manuscripts, must have been composed sometime during his lifetime, that is, from *c*.525–30 to 577.[10] The first nomocanonical reworking of the *Coll14* is very likely to be located between 612 and 629, perhaps 612–19, as all manuscripts contain a law of Heraclius of 612, but an important law of 629 is quite obviously a later addition in some manuscripts, and another law of 619 is missing altogether.[11]

Aside from these ranges, dating becomes more speculative, often dependent upon the (somewhat hypothetical) connection of the various collections to civil-law appendices. Scholars tend to assume, however, with Zachariä von Lingenthal, that the *Coll60* was unlikely to have been written before the completion of Justinian's civil codification in 534, and thus place it

[7] The date and provenance of Cresconius' *Concordia* is controversial; see Gaudemet 1985, 138–9; Reynolds 1986, 400; Zechiel-Eckes 1992, 1.66–118.

[8] *Syn* 5. From the very general description of Scholastikos it does not seem possible to reconstruct the precise form of the *Coll60*; see Beneshevich's comments, *Sin* 219; also this chapter, n. 71.

[9] The matter has not yet been thoroughly examined, but in the editions of *Kormchaya* and Meliara 1905–6 (both of pre-Photian recensions) no chapter clearly owes its existence to a post-6th C addition. *Pitra* and *RP*, however, both include one later addition, chapter 13.41, which is derived exclusively from a post-6th C addition (Trullo 64). Title 14 also tends to gain some extra miscellaneous chapters in the manuscripts, as reported by *Pitra* 2.636, and evident in MSS of the 11th C recensions (e.g. in Jerusalem Pan. Taph. 24 and Athos Pant. 234; see Schminck 1998); so also in the older Paris gr. supp. 614 (10th C). The *Nachleben* of these chapters is, however, unclear; apparently they did not become regular in the later commentator recensions. In one instance title 14 seems to disappear (Vienna hist. gr. 70).

[10] On Scholastikos' birth date, see *Sin* 273–4.

[11] The likely authorship of "Enantiophanes" also confirms this general period; for more detail on all these points, see *Delineatio* 66–7.

around 535.[12] If this is correct, it may vie with Fulgentius as the first thematic collection in the Greco-Latin world. This dating might find further support if, as is widely believed, the *Coll60* included the *Coll25* as an appendix, since the original form of the *Coll25* seems to have lacked any post-534 legislation.[13]

John Scholastikos' collection is often placed after his ordination as a presbyter *c.*550, or at any rate before his tenure as patriarch of Constantinople (from 565 to 577), and possibly while he was still in Antioch.[14] In support of these assertions is one manuscript, now lost, which attributes the collection to "the presbyter John."[15] Further, the *Coll87*, very likely an appendix to the *Coll50*, and composed at very near the same time, seems to lack any material after 546—in particular, Novel 129, of 551, which touches on church matters.[16] Finally, the *Coll87* omits various regulations relating only to Constantinople—which thus supports an Antiochian provenance.[17]

Ernst Honigmann's ingenious proposal—the details of which I cannot repeat in full—that the first *Coll14* was produced by Patriarch Eutychius and the monk John (later John IV "the Faster" of Constantinople) is widely regarded as a reasonable, if not provable, suggestion, and has tended to fix a date for this collection at *c.*580.[18] Suffice to say that if the references in *τὰ μὲν σώματα* to a predecessor are in fact to the *Coll50*, then it must have been produced at least after the *Coll50*, and presumably after the death of Scholastikos (the then standing patriarch) in 577. Further, if the *Tripartita* is the secular collection referred to in *τὰ μὲν σώματα*—which seems very likely, as no other extant collection fits the description given—then the date of 580 is certainly possible, since the latest piece of legislation in the *Tripartita* dates to 572.

Whatever the precise dates of the collections, the relatively synchronous appearance of many of these collections in both east and west in or around the 6th C suggests a certain coherence—almost a "systematic movement." There is no evidence of an official project, but if one maps the pre-7th C collections geographically, they unquestionably constitute a surprisingly coherent imperial Mediterranean phenomenon. All but one of these collections, the *Capitula* of Martin, are written in imperial territories (Ferrandus and Cresconius, of

[12] So esp. *Delineatio* 52; see Zachariä von Lingenthal 1877, 615–6. *Peges* 132 places it at 535–45.

[13] Thus *Delineatio* 52.

[14] e.g. Beck 1977, 144; *Delineatio* 52–3; *Historike* 44–5; Honigmann 1961, 53; L'Huillier 1976, 55; *Peges* 132–3; Schwartz 1933, 4; Zachariä von Lingenthal 1877, 618. The question, however, has not been thoroughly reviewed within the last century.

[15] The so-called "Claromontensis," now known only through Voellus and Justel 1661 and two early catalogue descriptions. See *Sin* 196–8 and Zachariä von Lingenthal 1877, 618.

[16] *Sin* 288–9.

[17] *Sbornik* 205 n. 2.

[18] Honigmann 1961, 55–64; so *Delineatio* 60–1; *Historike* 68–71; *Peges* 134–5; Stolte 1998a; van der Wal and Stolte 1994, xx–xxi. The remainder of this paragraph is drawn from these sources; see also Zachariä von Lingenthal 1877.

course, writing in the newly reconquered African provinces—or for the latter, perhaps Italy). Even Martin of Braga, writing outside the empire, spent time in the eastern empire and became a monk in the Holy Land; he is very much *of* the empire, and his work is consciously directed towards making better known the imperial (Greek) corpus to a western audience.[19] The Syrian *Titloi*, although perhaps earlier, also likely hail from the empire.

These collections are also all very similar in both form and content. All are built around the same core (Greek) corpus of canons, and all contain more or less the same type of thematic index: simple rubrical headings that summarize canonical content. In particular, Cresconius' *Concordia*, the most advanced and complete of the early western thematic collections, is an almost exact morphological twin of the *Coll50*. It contains one level of systematic rubrics, and it treats its source (the Dionysian II corpus) in almost exactly the same way as the *Coll50* treats its corpus: absolutely comprehensively, omitting very little (only some canons from Carthage, as is often the case at this period).[20] If the mid-6th C date for this collection is correct, it is even approximately contemporary with the *Coll50*. The systematic elements of the 7th C *Hispana* (in their various forms) are likewise morphologically very similar to the *Coll14*: a thematic index comprised of a series of books divided into chapters, and the whole tending to preface a straight corpus collection—and apparently including most of the source material of the *Hispana*.[21] Ferrandus and Braga in size and selection have no direct counterparts in the east at this time, but are clearly small practical "handbook" versions of the same general type of collection.

Despite, then, the tendency to treat the emergence of the thematic collections in east and west as two isolated if parallel events, the extant collections instead suggest a certain legal-cultural unity, and are another indication of a common imperial canon-legal world running east–west across the Mediterranean through at least the 6th C: it is centered on the same corpus, and tends towards the same systematic forms.

The stimulus for the appearance of these thematic versions of the corpus is not entirely clear. The usual explanation is twofold: an internal pressure was generated within the tradition itself by the increasing unwieldiness of the growing canonical corpus, and the Justinianic codifications (528–34) provided an impetus for a parallel ecclesial development.[22] Neither explanation is entirely satisfying.

[19] Preface translated in Somerville and Brasington 1998, 53–4.

[20] On its contents and sources, see Zechiel-Eckes 1992, 1.5–28; the decretals may also be considered as somewhat selected.

[21] See Díez 1966, 2.1 and 2.2; this parallel is especially close with the *Tabulae*.

[22] e.g. *Peges* 131; Pieler 1997a, 579–80; van der Wiel 1991, 42.

The idea that the corpus naturally and necessarily evolved into a thematic form is a retrojection—and "naturalization"—of the path taken by later western medieval canon law.[23] In fact we need not see anything natural or "necessary" about this development. The growing size of the material, in particular, cannot be posited with absolute certainty as a direct cause. It is true that the addition of Basil in the *Coll50*, and of Carthage and the patristic material in the *Col14*, and Carthage and papal material in Dionysius, did considerably increase the size of the various corpora. It is also true that the prefaces do imply that the variety and quantity of the material was a primary motivation for their work (see below). But this last may be more of a topos of justification for the innovation of the collections, and as for the former, these additions to the 6th C corpora were hardly overwhelming—not enough to credibly strain a pre-modern memory. Certainly the full corpus of the 6th C *Coll14* is minuscule in comparison to the quantities of secular legal material that are much more convincingly put forward as factors in the initiation of Justinian's secular codification project. Further, the Syrian *Titloi* were clearly formulated before considerable corpus expansions. The systematic indexing of the corpus thus may have been more of a convenience than a necessity, and even suggests a certain artificiality. A more ideological explanation may be preferable.

One such explanation, the idea that Justinian's codification may have inspired the ecclesial development, is an obvious one, and most scholars take it for granted.[24] It is especially compelling if the Syrian collection is ignored, and the *terminus post quem* of the *Coll60* (and perhaps Ferrandus) is set at 534. Certainly the form of the systematic collections—divided into books and/or *titloi* and chapters—is highly reminiscent of the *CJ* and the *Digest*.

Here too, however, caution is advised. There is no direct evidence that Justinian's codification work provoked the systematic recensions. The authors of the new collections do not explicitly cast themselves as working on the model of this emperor's work, or of secular legal works in general, and there are no references in the 6th C literature to such an imitative ecclesial "program."[25] In fact, in the external literature, there are no references in this period to the collections as "systematic" collections at all, and hardly any to "the canons in [*x*] titles"; overwhelmingly the canonical collections are always simply "books of canons" or "the canons."[26] There is virtually no explicit

[23] See Ch. 1 D.1.

[24] e.g. *Historike* 38; L'Huillier 1976, 55; 1997, 141; *Peges* 131; Pieler 1991, 604 n. 18; Schwartz 1910, 195; 1936a, 160.

[25] A possible, and indirect, exception is the occasionally remarked (e.g. *Historike* 46) parallel of the fifty titles of the *Coll50* and the fifty books of the *Digest*. However, fifty, half a century, is also simply a very convenient, round number.

[26] An exception is the 9th C letter of Pope Nicholas to Photius, which mentions the "quinquaginta titulos." See Ch. 1, n. 120.

consciousness or discussion of canonical systematization outside of the collections themselves.[27]

Further, strictly speaking there is no hard-and-fast reason why the systematic canonical collections could not have emerged before Justinian. Here we must be careful about a potential circularity in dating the collections in *Coll60* and Ferrandus to after 534 on the grounds that they "must" have been inspired by Justinian—and then bringing them forth as evidence of a sudden post-Justinian boom in thematic collections. The Syrian *Titloi* may well be pre-Justinianic, and the *Coll60* and the *Breviatio* could be too. In this respect one curious aspect of the transmission of the *Coll50* is worth noting: the collection is not uniformly ascribed to John Scholastikos. In a few manuscripts some versions of the nomocanonical recension are ascribed to Theodoret of Cyrrhus (393–457).[28] The text's editor, Beneshevich, dismissed this tradition because of the much broader tendency of ascribing the text to John, including in the oldest manuscripts, as well as the lack of awareness of this "collection of Theodoret" in the oriental orthodox churches.[29] But even Beneshevich admits that it is difficult to determine why Theodoret's name would ever have entered the tradition.[30] Certainly it is odd that anyone in the 6th C or later would have mistakenly or intentionally ascribed anything to Theodoret following the Three Chapters controversy—especially anything that was intended to have authority.[31] On the other hand, it would be very easy to imagine that Theodoret—in the vicinity of Antioch, which was already associated with church-legal activity, and also near Berytos—may have composed some type of collection well before 534. Could not John Scholastikos, who was from Antioch, have brought this text with him to Constantinople, perhaps modifying it, or perhaps just attaching his name to it or a later recension (perhaps when the *Coll87* was added)? Alternatively, perhaps the attribution to Theodoret is a vestigial memory of Theodoret's authorship of an earlier collection, perhaps the *Coll60*?[32]

In any case, and more to the point, there is nothing in the basic technique of the ecclesial systematic collections that demands Justinian's codification as a precedent. The method of topical organization evident in the canonical collections may be found, for example, in the 5th *CTh* (books and titles) and elsewhere in earlier legal literature.[33] Further, it is not entirely clear that a legal

[27] This finds a parallel in the oft-remarked lack of interest of contemporaries in the Justinianic codification; see Pieler 1978, 402–3 nn. 13, 14, with further references. See Laiou 1994b for similar patterns in later Byzantine sources.

[28] London BL Add. 28,822; Venice Nan. 226; Paris gr. 1370; Turin BN 170 (see *Sin* 269).

[29] *Sin* 269–70, 322.

[30] *Sin* 269.

[31] *Clavis* notes only three works that seem to have been attributed spuriously to Theodoret: 6286–8.

[32] On this notion see Doujat 1687, 293–6; 304–5. See *Sin* 269–70, *Historike* 38 n. 5.

[33] For this material, see, among other source surveys, Pieler 1997a, 566–7, 573–9; Schulz 1953; Wenger 1953, 530–61; also the comments of Honoré 1978, 139.

precedent of any sort is necessary. Although it is probably correct to view the systematic "movement" as in some sense inspired by secular codifications—and even one way the canonical tradition broadly assimilated itself to Roman legal literature—other types of literature also evince rubric-reference organizing structures. Schwartz, for example, saw Basil's *Moralia* as the most obvious model for the Syrian *τίτλοι*, and such listings may be found in 5th C biblical manuscripts (the term *τίτλος* is not exclusively legal).[34] If anyone had cared to thematize the canonical material before the 6th C, ample models, from a variety of different sources, were available.

It is therefore probably unnecessary to imagine any one particularly pressing need, cause, or inspiration for the thematic indices. The 6th C "explosion" of these collections remains curious, and may well be related to Justinian's codification and the growth of the corpus, but we should be careful about being too dogmatic about any one explanation.

C. SELF-PRESENTATION

Whatever the precise occasion and date of the collections, a more important issue for our purposes is how the collections present their own work of systematization. All three authors of the prefaces to the *Coll50* and the *Coll14* provide some description of their method of systematization and organization. These descriptions, inevitably in the latter part of the prefaces, seem to constitute a conventional part of Byzantine canonical introduction, and find parallels in a number of secular prefaces.[35] They are exceptionally valuable as the only texts in which Byzantine systematizers directly reflect on the technical aspects of their task, that is, how the Byzantines themselves defined and thought about their own systematic *τέχνη*, or "technique."

The descriptions are above all characterized by brevity and simplicity. Indeed, their most striking feature is not what is present but what is not: they engage in virtually no sophisticated jurisprudential analysis. They do not discuss contradictions, repetitions, or obscurities, nor do they elaborate means or principles for treating these problems. Instead, they describe simple methods of compilation and organization oriented above all to the facilitation of convenient and thorough engagement with the canonical texts.

The main notes are sounded by John Scholastikos in *οἱ τοῦ μεγάλου θεοῦ*. The canonical legislation of the church, he explains, has been issued in a

[34] Schwartz 1910, 200 n. 2; Goswell 2009; see Pinedo 1963, 289 n. 18 for parallels in patristic and even Masoretic practices.

[35] e.g. *Deo Auctore* 6–9; *Tanta* 2–8; *Prooimion* to the *Eisagoge* 84–113; *Prooimion* to the *Prochiron* 42–83.

variety of different (*διάφορος*) places, for different reasons, at different times. As such, this material is not "in a certain order by subject matter" (*οὐ τάξει τινὶ πραγμάτων*), and it is thus difficult to discover all that the canons say on any given topic.[36] His task, therefore, is to gather (*ἀθροίζω*) the material into one and divide it into titles in which the similar are joined (*συναρμόζω*) to similar.[37] His goal, as stated, is thus quite simple: to make the "finding" (*εὕρεσις*) of that which is sought easy (*ῥᾳδία*) and toil-free (*ἄπονος*).[38] These points are enforced by criticism of the previous *Coll60*, which made it difficult to find all that has been set forth on any one topic. In his collection, by contrast, each title clearly indicates the content of that which it encompasses.[39] His table of contents, he notes, also makes it easy to identify the "order" (*τάξις*) of the canons in one place (*λίαν εὐσύνοπτος*).[40]

The first prologue to the *Coll14*, *τὰ μὲν σώματα*, likewise speaks of gathering the canons of the synods which took place at "various" (*διάφορος*) times into one place—but, the author remarks, in so doing the name of each council will be preserved.[41] Having gathered (*συνάγω*) "everything," the author continues, the content or "force" (*δύναμις*) of the material will be gathered into titles, and will be divided into chapters under which the references are "fitted" (*ἁρμόζω*) to the appropriate canons.[42] These references include source name and number. The whole produces—"as I think"—a collection that is easy to take in at a glance (*σύνταγμα εὐσύνοπτον*).[43] Like Scholastikos, the author engages in technical criticism of predecessors. In particular, as already noted, the author criticizes the tendency of placing the full text under the titles, since this produces an unwieldy collection and leads to the undesirable division of canons.

The author concludes by describing how and from which sources political legislation has been derived, "in short and summary" (*βραχέα τε καὶ συντετμημένα*).[44] The exposition of this material is to be "brief" (*σύντομος*), and is meant as both an aide-memoire and for the "perfect research" of the readers (*σύντομον ἐν συναγωγῇ ποιησάμενος ἔκθεσιν, ἅμα μὲν εἰς ἀνάμνησιν, ἅμα δὲ πρὸς τελείαν αὐτῶν τοῖς ἐντυγχάνουσιν ἔρευναν*).[45]

The second prologue to the *Coll14*, generally attributed to Photius, or at least to a redactor of *Coll14* tradition active during Photius' patriarchal tenure, follows a similar pattern. The author notes that since the appearance of the first version new synods have arisen to address several new issues, of various (*διάφορος*) causes.[46] Thus, the author continues, new material has been added, but the "chain" (*εἱρμός*) and order of composition of the older collection have

36 *Syn* 4.24–5.1. 37 *Syn* 5.5–7. 38 *Syn* 5.7–8.

39 Exactly what was wrong with the *Coll60* is, however, difficult to discern from Scholastikos' description. The description is quite opaque. See n. 71.

40 *Syn* 5.17–20. 41 *Pitra* 2.445.17–18. 42 *Pitra* 2.447.3–6.

43 *Pitra* 2.447.6. 44 *Pitra* 2.447.13–14. 45 *Pitra* 2.447.16–17.

46 *Pitra* 2.448.8–9.

been preserved.[47] This last is interestingly described as that which the first prologue's author "devised well" (ἐφιλοτεχνήσαντο)—a rare use of τέχνη language in the canonical tradition.[48]

Taken together, these three descriptions paint a quite simple, but coherent, picture of the basic Byzantine self-conception of canon-legal systematic τέχνη. It is composed of four conventional elements, each conveyed with similar terminology:

(1) a varied (διαφορ-) source material is gathered together (συναγ-; συλλογ-; συνταγ-; αἴθρο-; συναιρ-; [συν][προσ]αρμοζ-);
(2) this material is then divided (διαιρ-) into titles or chapters (or both);
(3) the purpose of this division is that it allows for clearer and more convenient finding (εὕρ-) of what one is seeking, such that this process is not "difficult" (δυσευρετ-, δυσποριστ-, or δυσαλωτ-) but easy (ῥᾳδ- and ἀπον-, ἀκοπ-);
(4) and the result is always that the material is more easily and clearly apprehended (σαφ-, εὐσυνοπτ-).

The *Coll14* preface τὰ μὲν σώματα supplements these terms with memory (μνημ-) vocabulary: the fathers and secular legal legislation are provided as aides-memoires.

The extreme simplicity of this "systematic" prescription is noteworthy. The Byzantine self-presentation of canonical systematization is one of a very elementary model of "law finding": systematization facilitates the literal "finding" of and engagement with traditional legal texts. To systematize law is to engage in a straightforward categorization of traditional material by which one might be easily brought into closer contact with the original texts. Issues of contradictions, distinctions, underlying concepts, or material coherence are not explicit topics: the notion of the law being "varied" does not seem to imply an idea of contradiction, nor does the vocabulary of harmonization or "easy apprehension" (ἁρμοζ- or εὐσυνοπτ-) imply any type of interpretative reconciliation.[49] It is instead directed towards coherence of topical classification. There is, therefore, no sense that systematization in any way implies the material reshaping of the substance of the law. The concern of the systematizers is simply: (1) to identify and gather the correct traditional material, and then (2) to place it in thematic categories. It is a process of topical indexing.

[47] *Pitra* 2.448.17–18. [48] *Pitra* 2.448.18.

[49] Compare this, for example, with the concerns of the famous and influential Prologue of Ivo of Chartres (*c.*1040–1115; trans. Somerville and Brasington 1998, 132–58), which precisely enumerates principles of harmonization and rationalization.

D. MORPHOLOGY

The prologues' presentation of systematization corresponds well to reality of the systematic collections. The systematic collections are little more than corpus collections prefaced or reorganized by a topical index, and these indices are little other than glorified tables of contents. Indeed, in terms of genre the classical table of contents is probably the immediate ancestor of these indices: both are constituted by a brief set of rubrics that summarize the contents of the work, and both are often in the form "*Περὶ . . .*", "'*Ὅτι . . .*", "*De . . .*".[50] The difference is simply that the rubrics of the thematic indices subsume a number of specific texts, and they do not (generally) follow the order of chapters, but instead follow their own thematic order.

The basic morphology of all early systematic collections, Latin and Greek, may thus be schematized as follows:

Prologue + List of Sources (perhaps as part of the prologue) + Systematic Index + Corpus

There are a few major variations among the collections. First, the systematic indices may be either one-tiered or two (or more)-tiered. In the former, there is only one level of rubrics in the index; in the latter there are two, with sets of primary rubrics encompassing more detailed secondary rubrics, which themselves encompass the canonical references. Second, as already noted, the corpus portion of the collections may be arranged either systematically or non-systematically. In the former, the systematic index is simply repeated, also with the subsumed canons written out in full under each rubric (not just as references). In the latter, the index is left as an index prefacing the corpus collection.

We may thus indicate a more comprehensive schema:

Prologue + List of Sources + Systematic Index (one or two-tiered) + Corpus (systematically arranged or non-systematically arranged)

The *Coll50* is formally a one-tiered systematic collection, and as a rule found with a systematic corpus[51]:

Prologue + List of Sources + One-tiered Systematic Index + One-tiered Systematic Corpus.

[50] See e.g. the tables of contents that preface Eusebius' *Ecclesiastical History* or Basil the Great's *Greater Asketikon*.

[51] The *Coll50* index may be found on occasion without a systematic corpus, i.e. prefacing a straight corpus collection, e.g. in Paris Cois. 364 or Rome Barb. 578 (see *Sin* 223 and *Syn* xviii for other examples). In Cresconius the thematic index can also apparently become detached and then added to other collections (Zechiel-Eckes 1992, 1.205–25, 261–7); see Maassen 1871, 817–8 for something similar with the systematic Hispana.

It sometimes lacks the initial systematic index, which is understandable, as this is repeated in the corpus section.[52] Its corpus, while originally systematic in form, often has later additions appended to it listed chronologically, as noted in Chapter 1, with the result that its corpus is in fact mixed systematic/non-systematic.[53]

Cresconius' *Concordia*, which contains a very similar selection of sources, is very similar in form. It too has a prologue, a one-tiered index, and a one-tiered corpus in systematic form. Cresconius' collection may, however, be regarded as more conservative or "primitive," in that its system of rubrics is one step closer to a simple table of contents: its rubrics, mostly derived from Dionysius, are structured according to the order of the Dionysian corpus (e.g. titles 1–50 start each with Apostolic Canons; 76–80 from Nicaea; 81–106 from Ancyra; 107–20 from Neocaesarea, and so on).[54] As a result, very few titles function as real thematic groupings.[55] Further, Cresconius' rubrics are true one-tier rubrics. The *Coll50* titles, by contrast, usually contain more than one rubric, and are thus functionally two-tier.

The *Coll14* is a two-tiered collection comprising fourteen primary groupings of secondary rubrics. The primary rubrics are called *τίτλοι*, the secondary rubrics *κεφάλαια*. According to its first prologue, its corpus is intentionally and explicitly left in unsystematic corpus form, and this is the usual, if not inevitable, state of affairs in the manuscripts.[56] It prototypically conforms to the following schema:

PROLOGUE (as many as three in the MSS) + LIST OF SOURCES + TWO-TIERED SYSTEMATIC INDEX + NON-SYSTEMATIC CORPUS.

As noted, certain versions of the systematic *Hispana* may be regarded as the morphological twin of the *Coll14*, containing a similar two-tiered initial index, and a non-systematic corpus.

In the Byzantine collections, when the secular laws are added, these are always added as a discrete section in the systematic indices, following the canonical references in the rubrics, and often announced with the heading "the law" (*ὁ νόμος*). The secular laws are never actually mixed with the canons themselves, and can therefore be extracted without difficulty. This allowed for the easy publication of the collections in either canonical or nomocanonical form.

[52] *Syn* 10 n. (a). [53] See Ch. 1 D.5.

[54] Zechiel-Eckes 1992, 1.29–48; see also Firey 2008 on Dionysius' own attempts to provide a proto-systematic index in his title listing.

[55] Zechiel-Eckes 1992, 1.49 counts only about twenty titles (of 300!) with substantial numbers of referents.

[56] On the intention to leave the corpus in chronological form, see the first prologue, *Pitra* 2.447. The *Coll14* is found with a systematic corpus in Paris Cois. 36, Moscow Syn. 467, and Vatican gr. 1142 (see *Sbornik* 307–13 on the last).

E. SOURCE SELECTION

As the Byzantine systematic collections present themselves as little other than glorified tables of contents, we might expect that they, like any table of contents, will be comprehensive—that is, that they will encompass all of the corpus material. In this, as already noted, they do not disappoint. The single most striking characteristic of the two principal Byzantine systematic collections is the almost total absence of any sustained process of selection vis-à-vis their stated sources: almost every corpus canon is referred to by the rubrics. The Byzantine systematic collections are simple rearrangements and indexings of the corpus. They are not filters. Consequently the systematic indexes do not represent the *de facto* creation of substantively new collections. Although the composition and publishing of the systematic collections may have marked important moments of corpus expansion, the systematic indices themselves are always developed *out of* the corpus that they have chosen to promote: the corpus sources are not shaped or modified to suit the indices themselves.[57]

This feature is particularly pronounced in the *Coll50*.[58] The *Coll50* is virtually a literal rearrangement of the corpus: one could write out each canon on a separate piece of paper and then simply rearrange the pieces under topical themes to arrive at something very like the *Coll50*. It omits nothing. Cresconius is very similar.[59] Even repetitions in both collections are few.[60]

The original *Coll14*, on the other hand, does seem to have omitted some canons under its original rubrics. However, as already noted, these are only from sources that the *Coll14* itself seems to have just added to the corpus; the material that was already established as "core" seems to have been scrupulously incorporated. Further, the concern to encompass faithfully the traditional corpus is in one respect more pronounced in the *Coll14* than in the *Coll50*: the *Coll14* includes many one-canon rubrics which seem to have been invented precisely to ensure topical representation for all canons. Some of these, in their very specificity, verge on the bizarre; for example, 13.38, "On those who attempt to set at nought the enactments of Ephesus: Ephesus 6." One can hardly imagine anyone searching for a general topic on those who set at nought the enactments of Ephesus. Such rubrics were clearly created solely for the purpose of comprehensively representing the entire core corpus in the index. In later recensions of the *Coll14*, as already noted, the missing canons will in any case be re-added, at least in a catch-all chapter in title 14.[61] The

[57] This is also broadly true of Blastares.

[58] See Ch. 1 D.1 and Ch. 2 B.4 at n. 77.

[59] See Zechiel-Eckes 1992, 2.801–7.

[60] For Cresconius, see Zechiel-Eckes 1992, 2.801–7. For the *Coll50*, see Ch. 2, n. 77.

[61] See Ch. 1 D.1, esp. at n. 125.

imperative driving the composition of the *Coll14* is thus the same as that driving the *Coll50*: to represent faithfully the canonical corpus.

F. THE NATURE AND CONSTITUTION OF THE RUBRICS

The essence of Byzantine canonical "systematization" is the subsumption of canons under topical, or thematic, rubrics. These rubrics are then arranged in a (more or less) logical manner. This process presupposes: (a) a careful reading of the canons to identify, distinguish, and choose significant content; (b) the invention and composition of categories and topics to subsume that content; (c) the association of canons similar to each other; and (d) the development of some type of overall structure. Each one of these steps provides opportunities for interpretation and even the reshaping of the substance of the law.[62]

In this section we will examine the first three of these steps, that is, the formation and design of the rubrics themselves, and how they relate to their subsumed canons.

In theory, the hermeneutic relationship of rubric and canons could be very complex. For example, rubrics could contain categories, terminology, and ideas introduced from elsewhere, and the traditional canons could then be made to conform to them, subtly reshaping their reading; or the rubrics could subsume and group certain material in unusual and hermeneutically significant ways; or the language of the rubric could imply specific readings of the canons; or the rubrics could abstract internal jurisprudential principles or concepts from the traditional material. The methodical creation of general categories could also highlight gaps in the legislation. For example, if one were to find enough material to stimulate the creation of a topic on "episcopal marriage," one might then consider finding (or inventing) material on "presbyteral marriage" and then "diaconal marriage" or "subdiaconal marriage," and so on.

In fact, as we might already expect, relatively few of any of these activities are present in the Byzantine thematic rubrics. The hallmark of the Byzantine rubricization is instead deep conservatism and traditionalism. This conservatism is manifested in two interrelated ways.

First, the thematic rubrics are overwhelmingly derived from the canons themselves. This is the governing principle of Byzantine rubricization. With only one significant exception (to be discussed in a moment), rubrics are not

[62] For some consideration of this type of method, see Pinedo 1963, 293–4, and the brief comments of Mordek 1975, 4–6.

imported from any outside source. This demonstrates the close affinity of the thematic indices to table of contents: the content of the canonical titles is broadly inductive or exegetical, in the sense of being pulled "up" and "out" of the canonical material. In the *Coll14* this process is in fact twofold: the chapters (*κεφάλαια*) tend to be summaries of the canons, and the titles (*τίτλοι*) summaries of the chapters. More advanced forms of rubricization, identified by Pablo Pinedo in later western collections, where a rubric is created as a thesis to be proved or endorsed by the canons (for example, rubrics on papal primacy in the Gregorian collections), or as a problem to be solved (constantly in Gratian), are hardly evident.[63] Likewise, there is almost nothing parallel to Bernard of Pavia's direct introduction of titles from the *Digest* into his decretal collection.[64]

Second, the thematic rubrics show very little evidence of jurisprudential abstraction. There is little independent distillation of legal principles or general legal concepts, little attempt to extrapolate from specific regulations to more general norms, little attempt to discern or establish distinctions not already present in the canons, little introduction of new terminology, almost no attempt (even indirectly) to address contradictions, no provision of tools for extended rules to cover gaps, no attempt to organize canons according to internal principles, and finally, little uniformity in the degree of topical generalization. Instead, the rubrics adhere very closely to the surface contours of the canons themselves. The majority of titles are thus either very close paraphrases, or even literal composites, of specific canons' contents, or very innocuous summaries focusing on one or two key words from the canons—what Pinedo has aptly called "résumé rubrics."[65]

The following is an example of a typical "résumé rubric" (*Coll14* 8.16):

Regarding that clerics ought not to feast with those getting married for the second time or those married illicitly. Neocaesarea 7 and Timothy 11.

Περὶ τοῦ μὴ ὀφείλειν κληρικοὺς συνεστιᾶσθαι τῷ δευτερογαμοῦντι ἢ παρανόμως γαμοῦντι. Συνόδου Νεοκαισαρείας κανὼν ζʹ. Τιμοθέου κανὼν ιαʹ.

These canons are as follows:

Neocaesarea 7: A presbyter is not to feast at the marriage of one getting married for the second time, for if the digamist must do penance, what type of priest will he be who through his attendance approves the marriage?

Πρεσβύτερον εἰς γάμον διγαμοῦντος μὴ ἑστιᾶσθαι, ἐπεὶ μετάνοιαν αἰτοῦντος τοῦ διγαμοῦντος τί ἔσται ὁ πρεσβύτερος, ὁ διὰ τῆς ἑστιάσεως συγκατατιθέμενος;

[63] Pinedo 1963, 291–2; see also Fournier and Le Bras 1931, 1.77. The best example of the former may be the *Dictatus Papae*, if, as has been suggested, they were originally the headings for a planned canonical collection. See Ferme 1998, 166–9; Kuttner 1947, 400–1.

[64] For these titles, see Pennington 2008, 297–8, and the table in Friedberg 1879, 2.xx–xxviii.

[65] Pinedo 1963, 289, 292–3.

Timothy 11: [Question: Can a cleric attend various types of dubious marriages?] Answer: "You have just said 'if the cleric hears that a marriage is illicit'; if the marriage is illicit, the cleric ought not to participate in the sins of others."

Ἀπόκρισις. Ἅπαξ εἴπατε· ἐὰν ἀκούσῃ ὁ κληρικὸς τὸν γάμον παράνομον. εἰ οὖν ὁ γάμος παράνομός ἐστιν, οὐκ ὀφείλει ὁ κληρικὸς κοινωνεῖν ἁμαρτίαις ἀλλοτρίαις.

In this example it is evident that not only is the rubric a simple summary of the content of the two canons, but even much of the language of the rubric is borrowed directly from the subsumed canons: *ἑστιᾶσθαι, ὀφείλει, γάμος παράνομος, κληρικός*.

Sometimes the rubric is virtually a straight citation of a canon. Thus *Coll14* 1.10 reads: "Regarding that someone is not to be ordained bishop or presbyter or deacon before all those in his house are orthodox Christians" (*Περὶ του μὴ χειροτονεῖσθαι τινὰ ἐπίσκοπον ἢ πρεσβύτερον ἢ διάκονον πρὶν ἢ πάντας τοὺς ἐν τῷ οἴκῳ αὐτοῦ χριστιανοὺς ὀρθοδόξους*). The sole canon subsumed, Carthage 36, differs only very slightly: "That bishops and presbyters and deacons are not to be ordained before they make all those in their house orthodox Christians" (*ὥστε ἐπισκόπους καὶ πρεσβυτέρους καὶ διακόνους μὴ χειροτονεῖσθαι πρὶν ἢ πάντας τοὺς ἐν τῷ οἴκῳ αὐτῶν χριστιανοὺς ὀρθοδόξους ποιήσωσιν*).

This literal, surface correspondence of the rubric to canons is often so close that when there are multiple elements in a rubric, one can generally trace each element to specific canons under the rubric. For example, in *Coll14* 1.12, "How a pagan or one in sickness or one newly baptized or one from a mean way of life is ordained a bishop or cleric" (*Πῶς ὁ ἐθνικὸς ἢ ὁ ἐν νόσῳ ἢ ὁ νεωστὶ βαπτισθεὶς καὶ ὁ ἐκ φαύλης διαγωγῆς χειροτονεῖται ἐπίσκοπος ἢ κληρικός*), four canons are subsumed, each treating some aspect of ordination. From Apostolic 80 comes the reference to "pagan" (*ἔθνος*) and "mean way of life" (*φαύλη διαγωγή*), from Nicaea 2 again "pagan" (*ἐθνικός*) and the problem of recent ordination (*νεωστὶ βαπτισθεὶς* paraphrasing *ἅμα τῷ βαπτισθῆναι*), from Neocaesarea 12 the reference to "sickness" (*νόσος*), and in Laodicea 3 again the problem of rapid ordination (*προσφάτως . . . προάγεσθαι*).

The same tends to be true of the relationship between the primary and secondary rubrics in the *Coll14*: each element of the rubric can often be fitted to sections of chapters, and often in a similar order. For example, title 3, "On prayers, psalmody, and readings, and anaphora and communion and apparel and services of readers, singers, and servers," may be divided into four rubrical fragments, each of which corresponds to a distinct section of chapters: on prayers (= chapter 1), psalmody and reading (= chapters 2 and 3), anaphora and communion (= chapter 4–22 to the conclusion of the title, with the terms from chapter 4). The last rubrical fragment, on apparel and services of readers, singers, and servers, is a little out of place—rarely is the fit perfect. It is still a literal quote, however, but from chapter 10, perhaps singled out because of its exceptionally specific content.

This surface literalism is particularly pronounced in the *Coll50*, where it provides the key to unraveling one of the text's most curious mysteries. The text's editor, Vladimir Beneshevich, long ago noted that there exist in the manuscripts two principal traditions of arranging the canons under each rubric: an arrangement according to the normal corpus order (citing first the Apostles, then Nicaea, then Ancyra, etc.), and a "systematic" arrangement, which is highly irregular.[66] Beneshevich was very careful to detail and schematize this systematic arrangement in both his 1914 study, and again in his 1937 edition of the *Coll50* (published only a year before the great scholar was killed by the Soviet authorities).[67] It seems he never changed his assessment in his first study: "To establish the grounds on which this [systematic] order of rules was constructed is extremely difficult, and even impossible."[68] Because of this obscurity, and especially because the "systematic" order only occurs in thirty-three of the titles, he decided that this order was unlikely to have been original.[69]

Once we realize, however, that these collections are constructed by distilling rubrics very directly from specific canons, and then grouping similar canons with these source canons, the nature of this systematic order becomes quite clear. In this method of ordering, the canons are simply being placed in the order that corresponds to the order of the rubrics in each title. For example, title 14 reads: "Regarding that a bishop or anyone enrolled in the clergy must not assume worldly and civil duties, unless he be compelled by the laws, nor may he at any time lend at interest or give surety, nor connive for himself a military position or [other] dignity" (*Περὶ τοῦ μὴ δεῖν ἐπίσκοπον ἢ ὅλως ἐν κλήρῳ καταλεγόμενον κοσμικὰς ἀναδέχεσθαι καὶ δημοσίας φροντίδας, πλὴν εἰ μὴ κατὰ νόμους ἀναγκασθείη, μήτε δὲ δανείζειν ἐπὶ τόκῳ ποτὲ ἢ ἐγγύαις ἑαυτὸν ἐκδιδόναι, μήτε στρατείαν ἑαυτῷ περινοιεῖν καὶ ἀξίωμα*). This title subsumes nine canons. In corpus order they are: Apostolic 6, 20, 44, 81, 83; Nicaea 17; Laodicea 4; Chalcedon 3, 7—and so they are listed (more or less) in most manuscripts of the non-systematic type. In the systematic manuscripts, however, they are in this order: Apostolic 6, 81; Chalcedon 3; Apostolic 44; Nicaea 17; Laodicea 4; Apostolic 20; Chalcedon 7; Apostolic 83. If we place the canons in this order alongside the rubrics of the title, we find the correspondence is perfect, as indicated in Table 4.1 (close literal correspondences in parentheses):

[66] Hybrids and variations exist as well; see *Syn* xvii–xx, 261–5.

[67] *Sin* 224–47; *Syn* xvii–xx, 261–5. On Beneshevich's life, see Burgmann 1988, and <www.nlr.ru/ar/staff/beneshe.htm> (accessed March 2013).

[68] *Sin* 244.

[69] *Sin* 224–5.

Table 4.1. Title 14 of the *Collection in Fifty Titles.*

Coll50 Title 14	Canons in "Systematic" Order
Περὶ τοῦ μὴ δεῖν ἐπίσκοπον ἢ ὅλως ἐν κλήρῳ καταλεγόμενον κοσμικὰς ἀναδέχεσθαι καὶ δημοσίας φροντίδας . . .	Apostolic 6 (*κοσμικὰς φροντίδας*) Apostolic 81 (*δημοσίας διοικήσεις*)
. . . πλὴν εἰ μὴ κατὰ νόμους ἀναγκασθείη . . .	Chalcedon 3 (*πλὴν εἰ μήπου ἐκ νόμων καλοῖτο*)
. . . μήτε δὲ δανείζειν ἐπὶ τόκῳ . . .	Apostolic 44 (*τόκους . . . δανειζομένους*) Nicaea 17 (*ἐπὶ τόκῳ . . . δανείζοντες*), Laodicea 4 (*δανείζειν καὶ τόκους*)
. . . ποτὲ ἢ ἐγγύαις ἑαυτὸν ἐκδιδόναι . . .	Apostolic 20 (*ἐγγύας διδοὺς*)
. . . μήτε στρατείαν ἑαυτῷ περινοιεῖν καὶ ἀξίωμα.	Chalcedon 7 (*ἐπὶ στρατείαν . . . ἐπὶ ἀξίαν . . .*) Apostolic 83 (*στρατείᾳ σχολάζων*)

Not all of the thirty-three titles with this type of ordering work quite so neatly—there is a certain "messiness" across the manuscripts. But most are close.[70]

When the logic of this order is revealed, Beneshevich's argument that the corpus-order arrangement is original becomes much weaker. The systematic order would seem to be much more in keeping with an original process of composition in which like canons were grouped together, rubrics derived from them, the rubrics then combined to form the extant titles, and the original groups of canons then listed in rubrical order underneath.[71] In the systematic form the collection is also certainly much easier to use, and more logical; without it, one has to search about for the canons pertaining to each rubric. Further, it seems much easier to imagine later copyists transforming the odd-looking systematic order into a much more normal corpus order than the opposite; the latter would have taken considerable analysis and work. It is also interesting that two of the four oldest manuscripts for the *Coll50* are in this order.[72] Finally, it is only partially true that only thirty-three of the titles seem to evince a systematic order. In many of the seventeen remaining titles the order of the canons still corresponds with the order of the rubrical fragments—it just happens that systematic order and the chronological order are identical.[73]

[70] The correspondences in titles 12, 20, 24, and 36 are particularly uneven.

[71] Some of the otherwise obscure details of Scholastikos' description of his work in the prologue make more sense if this is how the collection was composed. In particular, the repeated assertions of attaching "like to like" (*Syn* 5.11,14; and esp. 5.6–7) and thus making the "division of the canons" clearer "by a juxtaposition of the material" (*σαφεστέραν . . . τῇ παραθέσει τῶν ὁμοίων ποιῆσαι τῶν κανόνων τὴν διαίρεσιν*) (5.13–14)—unlike, apparently, the *Coll60*—seems to imply something like this process. Is the lack of this type of internal grouping by rubric precisely what Scholastikos finds objectionable about the *Coll60*?

[72] Paris Cois. 209 and Venice Nan.22 (both 9th–10th C).

[73] Not all titles work perfectly; there is still considerable "messiness" in e.g. titles 5, 6, and 11.

In any case, to return to the broader dynamics of Byzantine systematization, this basic compositional imperative—to extract the rubrical topics from the canons themselves—means that the systematic indices read much more as summary statements of the content of the corpus than as significantly rationalized jurisprudential interpretations or abstractions of that content. In both the *Coll50* and *Coll14* creative shaping of the material is still possible, and even evident, but as a rule it is uneven, occasional, and rarely significant. Instances are often so subtle that it is frequently not clear how conscious they are. They may be surveyed very quickly.

The introduction of new terminology represents one of the simplest ways in which the rubrics can interpret, and direct the reading of, the canons. In both collections, however, only very rarely does the language of the rubrics diverge significantly from a very close and literal representation of the subsumed canons. Most instances can be dismissed as paraphrases of the most innocuous type, modified for entirely pragmatic or stylistic reasons. For example, in *Coll50* 28 the clumsy Laodicean *θεωρίας θεωρεῖν* becomes *θεωρίας ὁρᾶν*; in Title 6 the brief *ἀποδημοῦντα* is used to convey the bulkier *πρὸς τῇ τελευτῇ τοῦ βίου τυγχάνῃ* of Antioch 23; in title 10 *εἰς ἣν καθιερώθησαν* replaces *εἰς ἣν ἐχειροτονήθη* of Antioch 18, probably for reasons of *variatio*, to avoid repeating *χειροτον-* roots excessively in the rubric; *Coll14* 1.38 changes Neocaesarea's *ἀφιέναι* to *λύεσθαι*; *Coll14* 3.22 changes Timothy 14 *ἑαυτὸν χειρώσηται* to the somewhat more standard *ἑαυτὸν ἀνελόντος*. And so on.

Sometimes paraphrases appear to be hermeneutically more noteworthy, injecting a significant new term or phrase into the canonical discourse. Very often, however, the "intruding" term may be found already present elsewhere in the corpus, often in a similar context. As such, these instances do not represent the ingress of truly "external" concepts. Thus, for example, *Coll50* 14, cited above, contains the curious phrase *μήτε στρατείαν ἑαυτῷ* **περινοιεῖν** *καὶ ἀξίωμα* ("devising" or "conniving" an office or dignity for oneself). Although in its context this phrase is clearly intended to be a summary paraphrase of Chalcedon 7 and Apostolic 83, the term *περινοιεῖν* does not appear in either canon. However, this apparently creative phrase finds its direct origin in Serdica 7, a canon from the previous title, treating a similar matter, which speaks of *κοσμικὰ ἀξιώματα καὶ πράξεις* **περινοιεῖν** *τισιν*. It seems this phrase has been unconsciously transferred. Numerous other examples of this type could be offered.[74]

Only very occasionally are truly significant terminological innovations to be observed. They are so rare that they are in fact quite conspicuous. Interestingly, the source of the external idea or term is invariably either the civil law or

[74] See e.g. *Coll50* 20 (*ἐφοδιάζεσθαι*, from Antioch 11), 25 (*καὶ περὶ τῶν ἐκ συναρπαγῆς χειροτονουμένων*, from Apostolic 33), 26 (*ἐν κυρίῳ γαμεῖν*, from Basil 41), 39 (*εἰδολοθύτου*, from Gangra 2).

scripture (or both). The best example is the term "patriarch" (πατριάρχης). Originally a biblical term, the title first emerges as a quasi-technical term for the incumbents of the principal sees of the empire in the 5th C, chiefly in secular legislation.[75] The term is, however, nowhere present in the pre-6th C canons. Its first entrée into the canonical tradition is in *Coll50* 1 (περὶ τῆς ὁρισθείσης τοῖς πατριάρχαις ἐκ τῶν κανόνων τιμῆς), and again in *Coll14* 1.5 (περὶ πατριαρχῶν), referring in both cases to canons treating the chief sees of the empire. In the *Coll14* 1.5 it is also joined by another new term, "primate," πρίμας (καὶ τῶν ἐν Ἀφρικῇ λεγομένων πριμάτων), a Latin loan-word found nowhere in the canons.[76] The introduction of both terms lends a degree of technical precision and formality to supra-metropolitan jurisdiction, otherwise very ill-defined in the canons themselves.

Another example is the introduction of "theology" (θεολογία) in *Coll14* 1.1: "Regarding theology and orthodox faith" (περὶ θεολογίας καὶ ὀρθοδόξου πίστεως). This term appears nowhere in the canons subsumed by the original *Coll14*. Some of these canons do mention "faith" (πίστις), which accounts for the second part of this rubric. But three canons, Apostolic 49, 50 (on baptism), and Constantinople 5 (on Trinitarian belief), do not, and thus, on the rule of summary-literal rubric formation, must somehow be subsumed by the first part. As it happens, however, these canons do use the phrase "Father, Son, and Holy Spirit." It is thus likely that "theology" here is meant to paraphrase "Father, Son, and Holy Spirit," that is, a statement of "theology" proper, Trinitarian doctrine (and not "theology" in its more modern, abstract sense). This is confirmed by the fact that this rubric, the first in the *Coll14*, is one of the very few modeled on an external source, in this case the very first title of the imperial codices: "On the most-high Trinity and the catholic faith" (*De summa trinitate et de fide catholica* in *CJ* 1.1; Περὶ τῆς ἀνωτάτω τριάδος καὶ πίστεως καθολικῆς in *Basilica* 1.1; Περὶ τῆς ἀνωτάτω τριάδος καὶ πίστεως καθολικῆς ἤτοι ὀρθοδόξου in *Tripartita* 1). In the *Coll14*, "theology" has simply been substituted as a shorthand for "the most-high Trinity" (ἡ ἀνωτάτω τριάς).

Coll14 1.1 raises the important issue of the introduction of rubrics from external sources. This chapter is in fact the first part of the only significant example of external rubrical borrowing evident in either Byzantine collection. Broadly, *Coll14* 1.1–6, and the rest of the title, can be read as modeled on the first book of the *CJ*. Although close linguistic parallels are not generally evident, the following correspondences are reasonably obvious: *Coll14* 1.1 (on theology and faith) = *CJ* 1.1, but by extension 1–13, a section on "the

[75] Fuhrmann 1953, 120–31; Liddell–Scott–Jones 1996, 1348; Lampe 1961, 1051–2. In the civil legislation, see e.g. *NN* 3, 109.

[76] This seems to be the first Greek attestation of the term; I can find no earlier reference in any lexical resource, or the *TLG*. The source is obviously intended to be Carthage, but the extant Greek text of these canons renders *primas* by its normal Greek counterpart, πρωτεύων (e.g. Carthage 17).

sacred"; *Coll14* 1.2–4 (on types of valid sources) = *CJ* 1.14–25; *Coll14* 1.5 ff. (on offices) = *CJ* 1.26 ff. *Coll14* 1 may thus be regarded as a miniature canonical version of *CJ* 1. This undoubtedly accounts for the comparatively organized and "rational" nature of *Coll14* 1.1–5, particularly the exceptionally technical concern for valid sources in *Coll14* 1.3, 4 ("Which canons must be obeyed" and "That ecclesiastical custom must be kept as law, and that we do not need to keep the law of Moses")—a concern nowhere else voiced in the tradition of the 6th C with such precision or vigor. As a point of interest, the similarity with the later *Basilica* titles is even more defined: *Coll14* 1.1 = *Basilica* 1; *Coll14* 1.2–4 = *Basilica* 2; *Coll14* 1.5 ff. = *Basilica* 3 (only on clergy, with the added emphasis in the rubric, like *Coll14* 1, on "ordination"). More broadly, of course, this resonance may be extended to any other civil-legal collections that begin with "faith" or general doctrinal matters and then "source" matters.[77] Curiously, just as the beginning of *Coll14* 1.1, "On theology and orthodox faith . . . ", seems to be a paraphrase of *CJ* 1.1, so likewise the second title, "On the making of churches, and on sacred vessels and offerings . . . ," is reminiscent of *CJ* 1.2: "On the most holy churches and the things and privileges of them."

The influence of the codex may also be vaguely detected in one other curiosity (although not a borrowing of a rubric per se): the strange inclusion in *Coll14* 12.5 of the name of Porphyry in a list of heretics. This name is nowhere present in the canons. It is presumably referring to the (pagan) Porphyry condemned in *CJ* 1.1.3.[78]

To return to terminological innovations in the indices, a number of Greco-Roman legal-administrative terms without any precedent in the (pre-7th C) canons also appear in the rubrics, notably *ἀντίδικος* in *Coll50* 15, paraphrasing various terms for "accuser" in Chalcedon 9; or *ὀφφίκια* in *Coll14* 1.24, summarizing various offices listed in Chalcedon 2; or most strikingly, in *Coll14* 9.6 *ἀναψηλάφησις*, used in its technical Justinianic sense as a calque for *retractio*, retrial/re-examination.[79] These terms effect a subtle, but tangible stylistic legalization of canonical discourse.

Biblical language and concepts also intrude occasionally into the rubrics. Aside from *πατριαρχής*, the best examples may be found in *Coll14* 3.18 and 4:16. Chapter 3.18 reads: "That a woman ought not to take communion

[77] See n. 115.

[78] Two other rubrics might evince dependence on secular legislation. In *Coll14* 9.27, the curious phrase *θέαις παρεμβαλλόντων* could hail from Athanasius' *Syntagma* of Novels 1.2.20, which addresses a similar topic (. . . *μήτε θέαις παρεμβαλλέτω* . . . ; cf. also 10.2.13), and in *Coll14* 13.8, the unusual *συνίστωρ* might be explained by some connection to the term's appearance in the translation of *CJ* 9.13.3 (on the same topic) referred to in *NC14* 9.30 (*RP* 1.216).

[79] See Liddell–Scott–Jones 1996, 127, Roussos 1949, 1.46 Although *ψηλαφάω* in the sense of *tracto*, "examine," may be found as translationese in Carthage (e.g *Fonti* 1.2.206.20–1, 208.11).

in the days of her purification (ἐν ταῖς ἡμέραις τῆς καθάρσεως αὐτῆς)."[80] Chapter 4.16 is identical, but on baptism. The two canons subsumed by both, Dionysius 2 and Timothy 7, refer respectively to "women in their menses" (αἱ ἐν ἀφέδρῳ γυναίκες) and "the custom of females" (τὸ κατ'ἔθος τῶν γυναικείων). The rubric's phrasing of "in the days of her purification" is drawn directly from Leviticus 12: 4, 6 and/or its New Testament parallel, Luke 2: 22. The reason for this change is probably stylistic, but it does pose a subtle problem of interpretation. In Leviticus and Luke it is quite clear that, strictly, this phrase refers to the period of purification following childbirth. The canons, however, refer to menstrual periods. This distinction is not, in the long run, significant—the two types of blood impurity are clearly assimilated to each other in scripture (Lev. 12: 2) and in later church tradition. However, could this rubric contribute to, or at least reflect, the blurring of the distinction?

Beyond the introduction of new terminology, the most basic interpretative operation of the rubrics is the provision of general topical categories. Here too only very rarely does the formulation of general topics evince any particular creativity, extending much beyond a basic and literal summary of the canons concerned—certainly it almost never entails the distillation of internal principles or concepts. In the *Coll50*, in fact, relatively few truly general rubrics are to be found at all. The majority of its rubrics are not so much topical rubrics ("On *x*," "On *y*") as summary rules, and as such can be quite specific. For example, title 3 reads: "That a bishop must not go beyond his diocese without being asked unless to attend to his property; and he must not ordain beyond his borders." This is a short rule, complete with an exception. Even the more properly "topical" rubrics tend to be quite long and complex. For example, title 10: "Regarding bishop or presbyters who are ordained and whose service is not accepted or received by the city into which they were consecrated, not because of their own doing but because of others, or those who after ordination neglect the people and the clergy." Here, as often, the *Coll50* reads almost as a summary statement of corpus rules, virtually an organized canonical synopsis.[81]

[80] See Wagschal 2014.

[81] Is the *Coll50* an organized synopsis? A preliminary examination has not revealed any clear or convincing relation of the extant Byzantine synopsis rubrics (or those preserved in Vienna hist. gr. 7, *Syn* 193–223) to the rubrics of the *Coll50* or *Coll14*. Further investigation of possible relationships with rubrics preserved in Latin and Syrian traditions would be worthwhile. Similarly there seems to be no convincing way of extracting a set of 60 formally distinct rubric fragments from the rubrics of the *Coll50*—i.e. to demonstrate that the *Coll50* may have been constructed out of the old *Coll60* rubrics. Cresconius' rubrics, however, are formed mostly from a pre-existing set of rubrical index titles (from Dionysius II; see Zechiel-Eckes 1992, 1.55; on Dionysius' index, see Firey 2008).

Occasionally more general, almost abstract, rubrics emerge in the *Coll50*, but these often prove to be narrower in scope than they first appear. In several titles the first rubric fragment seems to be the most general, and comes close to functioning as a general rubric for the title.[82] Title 33, for instance, begins with the rather general injunction that ascetics must obey their bishops: "Regarding that ascetics must be subordinated to the bishops . . . " (*Περὶ τοῦ δεῖν τοὺς ἀσκητὰς ὑποτετάχθαι τοῖς ἐπισκόποις . . .*). We might expect that the following fragments address specific requirements of monastic obedience to bishops. In fact, three of the following four rubrics (monks not leaving the place in which they are assigned, monastic properties not becoming secular again, and slaves not becoming monastics without the permission of their masters) have nothing to do with obedience to bishops per se. The real topic of the rubric is something more general, perhaps "on monastic discipline"—but this is precisely the kind of abstraction these titles do not evince. In this particular example, upon closer inspection, the first rubric turns out to be created by a normal process of surface résumé of Chalcedon 3, which includes the very language of "subordination" (*τοὺς . . . μονάζοντας ὑποτετάχθαι τῷ ἐπισκόπῳ*).

The avoidance of topical generalization and abstraction in the *Coll50* may be regarded as an instance of a pattern widely remarked of ancient thought generally, and especially of ancient Roman jurisprudence—and which we have already broached in Chapter 3.[83] Instead of explicitly distilling and reducing the texts to general rules or principles—or even creating general topical categories—there is a tendency merely to juxtapose traditional texts and allow the reader to make the interpretative inductions. This may be regarded as another aspect of the textual traditionalism of many ancient legal systems: the law *is* the traditional texts, and thus extrapolating from the laws to create more abstract principles is only a secondary, and therefore implicit, process. Such extrapolation must undoubtedly have been performed, but its results are in a sense ephemeral, and subordinate to the traditional texts themselves. The movement from the laws to law, as it were, is an inconspicuous and secondary process—so much so that even systematic summaries do not engage in it.

The *Coll14* contains at first blush more general and sophisticated topical rubrics. Examples of basic general rubrics include: "On the holy anaphora and communion" (3.4); "How one must baptize" (4.3); "On offerings" (6.1); "On lawsuits of bishops and clerics" (9.5); "For what reasons one is deposed" (9.14); "On those who divorce" (13.4); and even "On greed" (14.1). The *Coll14* also makes use of another type of generalizing rubric: the multiple-aspect rubric. In these rubrics various aspects of one or more provisions are

[82] See e.g. 18, 24, 25, 37, 48, 50.

[83] Ch. 3 D.

indicated through the use of multiple interrogatives: for example, "Regarding whom and where one ordains bishops . . . " (1.6), or "Regarding who, and how, and what type of things, one must sing" (3.2).[84]

Upon closer inspection, however, the quality of generalization in the work as a whole is very inconsistent, and at times downright odd. Take the question of the breadth of representation. Some rubrics are truly very broad in scope. Chapter 1.6, just cited, encompasses twenty-four canons that all, in one way or another, relate to the who and where of ordaining clergy. Chapter 9.14 ("For what reasons one is deposed") likewise contains fifty-three canons on this topic. Other rubrics, however, sound general but in fact encompass only a very few canons. Thus 6.1, "On offerings," subsumes only three fairly specific canons. Title 10.2 purports to gather all canons on "the administration of ecclesiastical affairs," but contains only seven canons, mostly those which actually use the same words "administration" (διοίκησις) and "affairs" (πράγματα). And title 14.1 "On greed" is purpose-built for *one* canon that explicitly discusses greed. Modern codifiers of the canons would have placed many more texts under each of these rubrics.

Very general rubrics are also counterbalanced by the presence of many (ninety-two[85]) single-canon chapters, almost 40 percent of the total. These can become bizarrely specific, as already noted.

Also contributing to the unevenness of the generalization in the *Coll14* is a curious pattern of subgrouping within the titles. Very general chapters are often followed by a series of much more specific chapters on the same basic topic, which often repeat the canons of the first general rubric. The best examples are the "punishment" rubrics in 9.10, 9.11, 9.14, 9.15, 9.16, 9.18, and 9.19—each listing the canons by punishment (deposition, excommunication, anathema, etc.). These are followed in 9.21–39 by rubrics that refer to many of the same canons again, but now in much greater detail, listing specific canonical infractions. Similar in function is chapter 1.6, a very general multiple-aspect rubric on the who, where, and how of clergy ordination. It effectively heads the rest of the title's chapters, each of which deals with some specific aspect of ordination—that is, that explores in detail the topic 1.6. Similar patterns are evident in titles 3, and 10, and more sporadically elsewhere.[86]

The effect of these subgroupings is to transform parts of the *Coll14* into a three-tier collection: title topics, subgroup chapter topics, chapter topics. The result, however, is that the *Coll14* represents not so much an even, general account of content of the corpus as a general *and* specific account. The *Coll14* therefore reads as equally (and oddly) specific and detail-oriented as the

[84] The *Coll50* contains only one such rubric, in title 49.
[85] Using the text in *Kormchaya.*
[86] Titles 6, 7, 8, 13.

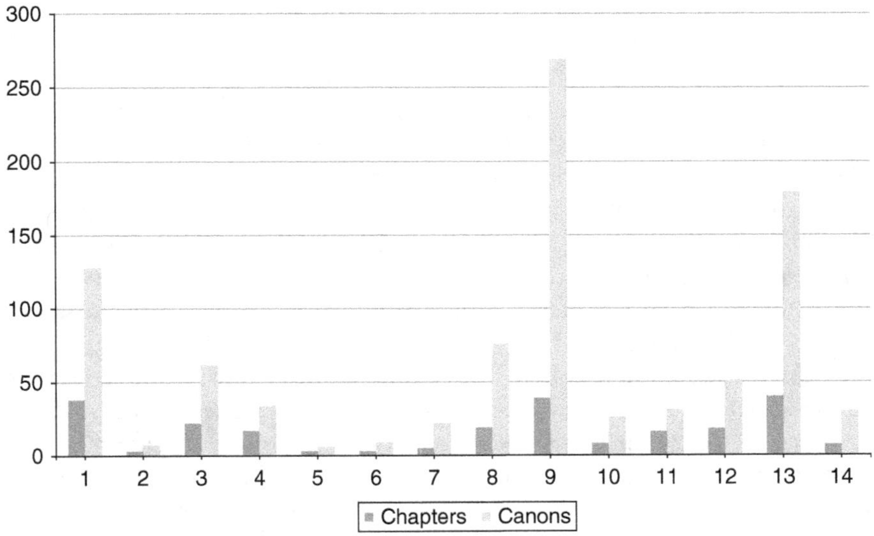

Fig. 4.1. Distribution of chapters and canons in the *Coll14*.

Coll50. For both collections the central imperative is clearly to convey as much of the surface content of the corpus as possible: not, in truth, to produce a neat and comprehensive set of general categories.

The unevenness and comparative irrationality of generalization in the *Coll14* is most evident in the wildly varying scope of the fourteen titles themselves. Titles such as 1 ("On theology, and orthodox faith, and canons, and ordinations"), or 9 ("On sins and cases of bishops and clerics and suspension and deposition and repentance and which sins ordination looses"[87]), or 13 ("On laity") sound very broad, and they do in fact encompass a large and varied number of canons. However, these titles sit alongside the much more specific titles 2 ("On the making of churches, and on holy vessels and dedications and clerics establishing sanctuaries against the will of their bishop"), and 5 ("On those who despise churches and synaxeis and memorials and those eating in church and on *agape*"), and 6 ("On offerings"), which each refer to only very few and much more specific rules. This unevenness of representation is well illustrated in the distribution of chapters and canons throughout the collection (see Fig. 4.1). Clearly there has been no attempt to devise a set of primary rubrics with approximately similar levels of topical generalization.

If topical generalization is uneven and desultory in both Byzantine collections one should not be sanguine about the presence of more sophisticated types of interpretation, rationalization, or legal innovation. Indeed, such

[87] This bizarrely specific final rubric, which refers only to 9.38, is an excellent example of the tendency to juxtapose very general and very specific rubrics.

instances are rare. Those present also often appear more creative and innovative than they actually are; as a rule, they only highlight or follow—and convey—a thread of thought already present in the corpus.

In almost no case, for example, does topical generalization sublimate into true doctrinal distillation—that is, very rarely does a rubric seem to name an abstract quality or underlying concept of a group of canons. Instead, as already noted, the instinct is simply to convey surface content or at most add different, if related, surface topics one after the other. Thus, for example, *Coll14* 3, which addresses numerous topics relating to "holy" matters and liturgical services, is not entitled "On holy matters," "On services in the church," or "On sacraments," any of which would have been appropriate, but "On prayers, psalmody, and readings, and anaphora and communion and apparel and services of readers, singers, and servers." Certainly nowhere does one find attempts to analyze the canons in terms of different types of powers or authority (for example, teaching, administrative, sacramental), or different types of rights or obligations. There is not even a branching categorization of the material into a genus-and-species "pyramidal" categorization as may be found in the *Institutes* tradition, and which seems to have been a standard method of systematic organization in rhetorical, philosophical, and grammatical manuals.[88] Even Gregory of Nyssa's categorization of canonical regulations into the three faculties of the soul had no impact on the collections. One can, in fact, perceive almost a resistance to the formation of rubrical topics that stray too far from the literal content of the canons themselves.

Two seeming exceptions are present in the *Coll50*. In titles 1 and 2 we read of "honor" being "defined" or "apportioned" for patriarchs and then metropolitans: (1) "Regarding the honor apportioned to the patriarchs from the canons . . . "; (2) "Regarding the honor apportioned to the patriarchs from the canons . . . ". The repetition of virtually the same phrase (*περὶ τῆς ὁρισθείσης τοῖς . . . ἐκ τῶν κανόνων τιμῆς*)—which is not derived from any specific canon—enhances a sense that "honor" (*τιμή*) is being turned into an abstract category to convey powers or rights granted by the canons. Likewise, in title 36 the final rubric, "and regarding the orthodox faith which one being enlightened must learn thoroughly" (*καὶ περὶ πίστεως ὀρθοδόξου ἣν ἐκμανθάνειν ἀνάγκη τὸν φωτιζόμενον*), might seem to suggest an abstract sense of "orthodox faith" in the sense of "collection of beliefs and doctrines"—especially as some of the subsumed canons treat matters of baptismal faith, and the Trinity.

In both cases, however, closer inspection of the subsumed canons reveals that the level of abstraction in these rubrics is at least partially illusory—almost accidental. A literal process of surface paraphrasis continues to drive the creation of these rubrics. Thus the relevant canons in titles 1 and 2 (Nicaea 7,

[88] Fuhrmann 1960.

Constantinople 4, Antioch 9, Chalcedon 3, 12) all mention the term τιμή more than once, and focus on matters of actual honor—that is, the title is addressing "honor" in a more literal form than seems immediately obvious. A more abstract usage of this word is still perhaps implied, but not to the degree a modern ear would perceive. Similarly, in title 36 the corresponding canons are clearly referring to learning the creed itself (thus ἐκμανθάνειν here almost certainly means "learn by heart"), and the rubric is in fact drawn directly from Laodicea 46 and 47, on learning the creed.[89] Other canons relating to the content of the faith are added (although the selection is odd, including the canons treating valid baptisms; having the words "Father, Son, and Holy Spirit" seems especially important), but the process of abstraction is again fairly limited: one rubric has been derived literally from the canons, and other material simply associated with it. This is perhaps a type of abstraction, but it does not entail the true distillation of conceptual categories.

Another opportunity for the creative interpretation of the canonical material could be provided by the inclusion of a canon under a rubric with which it does not have an immediate surface-topical relation, that is, with which there is no direct correspondence in content or language. Such an inclusion could imply a creative rereading of the canon, or a process of interpretive extrapolation. But the few instances where this might be suspected can usually be explained by other reasons. For example, Laodicea 42 reads: "That a hieratic [i.e. a member of the higher clergy] or cleric must not travel without the command of the bishop." This is placed, logically, under *Coll14* 8.2: "That a bishop or cleric must not travel at will from home to live in another diocese." Yet it is also placed under 8.5: "Regarding the reception of foreigners, and regarding letters pacific and commendatory." The collector may thus seem to be making an interpretative jump, extrapolating, perhaps, that the "command" in Laodicea 42 implies a letter, and that therefore this canon is appropriate under 8.5 as well; or alternatively, that a traveling cleric must be a "foreign" cleric. However, this same chapter contains Laodicea 41: "That a hieratic or cleric must not travel without letters of communion." One cannot help but wonder if its placement in 8.5 is therefore due to the fact that Laodicea 42 has simply been drawn into this chapter because of its direct proximity to Laodicea 41 in the corpus, and their broad similarity in topic. The motivation for the placement of Laodicea 42 in 8.5 is thus the accidental existence of a pre-made text link with Laodicea 41 in the corpus—and not a process of independent jurisprudential abstraction of possible rule application. The author is recognizing and following a textual link already present in the canons.

[89] The term πίστις, as found in the title and the canons, can simply mean "creed," instead of "faith" in the more abstract sense. See Lampe 1961, 1087. I owe this point to Price and Gaddis 2005, 2.202 n. 47.

Yet another type of jurisprudential rationalization that might be expected is the systematic and methodical organization of canonical content. Some parts of the collections do show concern for clear methodical progression and presentation. The best example is the penal rubrics of *Coll14* 9.11, 9.14, 9.15, 9.16, and 9.18, which ask "for which reasons . . . " different types of penalties are imposed, broadly progressing from least severe (suspension) to most severe (complete expulsion). A few encompass a huge number of canons (for example, all the canons for which one can be deposed). Similar in systematic rigor are the very many double (or even triple) rubrics in the *Coll14* which repeat certain canons under different titles to highlight different applications of the same rules. For example, Laodicea 30, which forbids "higher clergy, clerics, ascetics, . . . or any Christian or lay person" from bathing with women, is subsumed under three rubrics under three different titles: "Regarding higher clergy who bathe with women" (9.31—i.e. under the title on clergy); "That ascetics may not bathe with a woman" (11.07—i.e. under the title on monastics); "That men may not bathe with women." (13.25—i.e. under the title on laity). Very often, as in these last examples, only the subject of the rubric changes. At other times different material aspects of the same topic will be explored. For example, in 3.18 and 4.16, rubrics on menstruation, the first rubric conveys the rules in regard to the Eucharist, and the second, baptism.

All of these examples, made possible by the *Coll14*'s willingness to repeat canonical references, show a certain level of analytical sophistication, and, more so, the sense that similar analogous topics should be explored thoroughly for different circumstances. Nevertheless, very rarely do these analyses push beyond the surface of the canonical material itself, or evince any real creativity or material "advance" of the law. Thus, the penal categories in title 9 are already quite obviously present as categories in the canons—the *Coll14* is making no new divisions. Similarly, the divisions of multiple subject or object applicability are all very simple, following basic surface divisions in the canonical material itself.

In the *Coll50* a slightly more sophisticated type of methodical progression may be found in the first two titles. Although subsuming different sets of canons, each poses a similar rubrical "question" to different subjects, as indicated in Table 4.2:

Table 4.2. Titles 1 and 2 of the *Collection in Fifty Titles.*

Coll50 1	*Coll50* 2
Regarding the honor apportioned to the patriarchs by the canons	**Regarding the honor apportioned to the metropolitans by the canons** and metropolitan areas formed by imperial letters
and that none of them are to seize a province belonging to another . . .	**and regarding that they must not seize a diocese belonging to another . . .**

This is a small but significant attempt to apply a common doctrinal framework to different subjects, especially as the second highlighted rubric is not a literal extraction from any canon in either title (although it recalls Nicaea 16 and Antioch 16). One would almost expect a similar set of rubrics for bishops, and perhaps other clergy. However—characteristically—this attempt at methodical rubrical formation goes no further.[90]

Another place where the advanced analysis of rules might be sought is the extraction of rule content from a canon. This could suggest a subtle step towards the more abstract conceptualization of the canons as *containing* or expressing rules, instead of simply *being* the rules. However, most of the instances of this type of dissection follow obvious breaks within the canons themselves, and thus do not represent particularly creative acts of jurisprudential reading. In effect, the collector simply assigns different "parts" of the canons to different rubrics. The most obvious example is the dissection of the compound canon, Carthage 16, which contains five entirely disparate rules: that clergy cannot be procurators; that readers must decide about marriage at puberty; that clerics cannot take interest on loans; that deacons may not be ordained before they are 25 years old; and that readers may not bow to the people. In this case each rule is marked by clear literary markers in the canon: three *ἤρεσεν ἵνα/ὥστε* phrases, one straight *ἵνα* phrase, and one *καί* + third-person subjunctive phrase. When the collector cites the rule under five appropriate rubrics (*Coll14* 1.28, 8.11, 8.13, 9.27, 9.29), these pre-made divisions are simply being followed.

Sometimes the dissection of a canon is slightly more sophisticated. Chalcedon 25, for example, is concerned primarily with the prompt filling of vacant dioceses by metropolitans. It is thus assigned its own rubric on this very topic, *Coll14* 1.9. At the canon's conclusion, however, is found this supplementary regulation: "The revenue, however, of the widowed church will be kept secure with the steward of that church." As a result, the collector also subsumes this canon under 10.3: "Regarding the affairs and revenue of churches without bishops." This is a surprisingly helpful secondary categorization—this rule could otherwise be easily missed. Another good example is the extraction from Nicaea 8 (a canon on the reception of Novationists) of its final clause, " . . . that in one city there be not two bishops," by the canon's citation under *Coll14* 1.20 ("Regarding that there are not in one city two bishops"). Here, very unusually, a relatively passing epexegetical comment is elevated by the collector almost to the level of a general principle—it certainly is strongly emphasized.

The distillation of principles, and the identification of general distinctions and definitions, is another classic jurisprudential preoccupation that is not entirely lacking in the collections. The *Coll14* would seem to contain a

[90] It is more marked in the 14th C *Epitome* of Harmenopoulos (see n. 1).

surprising number. Thus definitions or distinctions can be found in at least five chapters: "Who are clerics or those belonging to the ecclesiastical order?" (1.31); "Regarding the difference between letters pacific and letters commendatory" (8.6); "What is heresy, what is schism, and what is *parasunagoge*?" (12.1); "What is a heretic?" (12.2); and the last element of "Regarding corruption, and marriage of a widow, and who is called a widow" (13.7).[91] Similarly, a principle of law is articulated in 9.17: "That one must not prosecute twice for the same case." The first rubric of 1.3, although a little less general, could also be considered a general rule: "That unwritten ecclesiastical custom should be kept as law . . . ," as can 1.4 "That canons are issued not by one bishop but by the commonality of bishops."

It is clear, however, that these few definitions and principles do not constitute a serious, systematic attempt to derive a complete set of definitions and principles from the material. They are far too infrequent. Further, and more importantly, only a few represent real jurisprudential analysis on the part of the collector. Most are entirely derivative from the subsumed canonical texts and thus represent only a slightly more sophisticated application of the normal surface-summary method of rubrical creation. Moreover, none entail the original distillation of a general rule from a wide selection of canons—they are instead relatively simple extractions or paraphrases of one or two canons.

Thus—to give only a few examples—the principle articulated in 9.17, ultimately derived from Nahum 1: 9 (οὐκ ἐκδικήσεις δὶς ἐπὶ τὸ αὐτό), is already stated *precisely as a principle* three times in the corpus (Apostolic 25, Basil 3, Basil 32). The collector is simply highlighting an aspect of the canonical text. Likewise, the definition in 12.1 is nothing more than a surface summary of the topic of Basil 1, and 8.6 is a simple summary of Chalcedon 11.

Sometimes a little more abstraction may be observed—but only just. For example, the question posed in 12.2 is not explicitly posed in the corpus. However, it follows very easily from the unusually schematic nature of Constantinople 7, which defines different categories of heretics. Likewise, 1.4 is not the central topic of the canons cited, but it is nevertheless clearly articulated within them as a specific problem. In both cases the collection is therefore still following the lead of the canons themselves, and not posing new jurisprudential questions to the material.

Other instances of substantive interpretation of the canons by the rubrics are uncommon, if not unknown. Rarely are they significant or unquestionably conscious. Most commonly a rubric might be read to restrict or expand the scope of a canon's application. For example, *Coll50* 8 affirms that the "laity" must be promoted through all the ranks before becoming bishop. The subsumed canon, however, Serdica 10, refers only to "someone wealthy or a

[91] See also 1.4, 8.17, 12.14.

lawyer from the agora" (τις πλούσιος ἢ σχολαστικὸς ἀπὸ τῆς ἀγορᾶς). *Coll50* 46 likewise refers to the illicit removal of "anything ecclesiastical" from the churches. However, the canons refer only to wax, oil, silver, gold, or textiles. *Coll14* 11.1 states that monasteries may not become private possessions (ἰδιωτικά). The subsumed canon (Chalcedon 24), however, only refers to monasteries becoming "worldly inns" (κοσμικὰ καταγώγια). The dissonance noted earlier between the "purification" rubrics *Coll14* 3.18 and 4.16 and their canons could also be included here.

Limitations or expansions of applicable subject are also common, often as a result of grouping together multiple canons that indicate different subjects. Thus *Coll50* 5, on episcopal duties, commands that bishops care for clergy in need; but Apostles 59, the relevant canon, had considered this a duty of presbyters too. *Coll14* 8.7, however, on the same issue, seems to extend the duty to deacons: "... and regarding bishops and presbyters and deacons who do not provide for ecclesiastical needs." *Coll50* 30 asserts that not only clergy but also lay people are forbidden from entering taverns; the relevant canons, Apostles 54 and Laodicea 24, refer only to clergy and lay monks (but many other canons of the same rubric do apply to both clergy and the general laity). *Coll14* 8.16, cited in full above, extends the Neocaesarean rule on attendance of digamists' marriage feasts from "presbyters" to "clerics."

Sometimes such "interpretations" are hardly more than clarifications. For example, in *Coll50* 22 the very odd κατασκευὰς τυρεύοντες ("curdling schemes," "conspiring") of Chalcedon 18 is regularized as κατασκευὰς ἀπεργάζεσθαι ("effect schemes"). In *Coll14* 9.25 φυλακτήρια ("phylacteries") in Laodicea 36 is changed into the more generic, and probably more understandable, περιάπτοι ("amulets").

Very occasionally more complex and definitive acts of interpretation may be observed. For example, Basil 32, "Clerics who sin the sin unto death are demoted from their rank...," is placed under title 27 in the *Coll50*, which treats clerical marriage regulations and, implicitly, sexual morality. As such, the collector has made a clear judgment on the meaning of the otherwise rather ambiguous Johannine concept of "sin unto death."[92] Likewise, in the *Coll14* 8.1 the τύποι of Chalcedon 17, which is sometimes read in modern translations as "forms,"[93] is clearly understood as "imperial enactments" (βασιλικοὶ τύποι). In one case—*Coll14* 1.3—we might wonder whether a new rule has been created. Part of the rubric of 1.3 reads "that we do not have need to keep the precepts of the Mosaic law." The source canon is almost certainly intended to be Basil's letter to Diodoros (Basil 87). Here Basil does cite Romans 3: 19, that the law speaks to those who are under the law, but his overall argument is subtler than the rubric suggests: for Basil, a *passionate*

[92] For the variety of later Byzantine interpretations of this phrase, see *RP* 4.173–5.
[93] e.g. *NPNF14* 280; similarly *Fonti* 1.1.83.

reading of the Old Testament law is inapplicable for Christians. The rubric 1.3, while not an impossible reading of the letter, is clearly an interpretation—possibly the boldest in the collection.[94]

Another, rather elementary, type of interpretative engagement may be sought in patterns of standardization of formulae across the thematic rubrics. The homogenization of dispositive terminology in the rubrics would be the simplest variety; more complex would be the standardization of the grammatical forms of rubrics or of the categories employed. The *Coll50* is particularly remarkable for the first. With only two exceptions, it articulates all of its rubrics with either δεῖ constructions or simple infinitives.[95] The subsumed canons, however, show a much greater variety, employing χρή, ἔξεστιν, ὀφείλει, ἀναγκαίον ἐστι, or third-person imperatives. By the standards of Byzantine systematization this is among the most striking and sustained instances of systematic rationalization in the entire tradition. But the *Coll50* does not usually standardize other terms, even when it would be useful to do so.[96] In the *Coll14*, dispositives are usually omitted in the rubrics or left as they are, that is to say, very diverse.

Other types of standardization are rarer. Only the first two rubrics in the *Coll50*, cited above, represent a serious attempt at the standardization of a formula. The many repetitions of similar rubrics across different titles in the *Coll14*, already noted, or the formulaic penal rubrics of 9.11–18, also lend a sense of methodical rubric formation. But these appear only irregularly. On the whole, rubrical standardization of any type is not pronounced.

A final test of the interpretative creativity of the collections is presented by the question of substantive representativeness: the extent to which the rubrics both individually and collectively reflect the content of their subsumed canons accurately and fairly. In other words, do the rubrics unduly emphasize or marginalize certain aspects of the tradition? Here caution is advisable: the history of interpreting patterns of canonical selection, compilation, or emphasis according to putative ideological agendas has never met with striking success.[97] It is also difficult to establish a neutral sense of what an accurate

[94] See also Wagschal 2014.

[95] The exceptions are titles 1 and 18.

[96] See e.g. the *Coll50*'s using both ἀσκ- roots or μοναχ- roots for monastics in titles 32–4, or the retention of many different paraphrases for ordination aside from χειροτον- roots (esp. titles 7, 8, 10, 19, 36, 39).

[97] It is difficult to think of even one such theory that has not met with serious difficulties (although it is too early to judge the success of Mardirossian 2010). These include the attempts to argue that the Apostolic Canons after 50 were not included in western collections because they were "anti-Roman" (rejected in *Sources* 33); the attempts to see the Slavonic translation of the *Coll50* as anti-papal (see the summary refutation in Gallagher 2002, 95–100, and esp. Žužek 1967); attempts to read the lack of Chalcedon 28 in Dionysius as a statement of its rejection by the west (but early eastern collections do not contain it either, as noted in *Fonti* 1.10; see L'Huillier 1997, 135–6); attempts to read Dionysius' selection of sources as supposedly motivated by church-political concerns (*contra*, see Firey 2008 n. 34); or attempts to read the Serbian

and fair reading of the canonical corpus should look like. Nevertheless, we may suspect a few instances of interpretative selectivity. Patterns of omission or marginalization are most obvious. The best example is *Coll50* 16. The title contains three rubrics: on bishops who are accused and those who may be accepted as accusers; that one who is unjustly deposed may travel to other cities; and that another bishop may not be appointed to a deposed bishop's see if the latter is still seeking an appeal. From these rubrics one may be surprised to find that this title contains all the Serdican and Antiochian appeal canons (3, 4, 5; 14, 15). Certainly they are not out of place here—the first rubric is so general as to subsume them easily by association, and the third rubric is derived from the Serdican canons, both in language and content. (The second rubric corresponds to another Serdican rule, canon 18.) The idea of "appeal" is also present. Further, the systematic order of canonical disposition in some manuscripts makes clear that the Serdican and Antiochian appeal canons are understood to be subsumed by the last two rubrics. It is nonetheless surprising that these canons are represented by only one very minor element of their provisions: the overly rapid appointment of replacement bishops. Nothing is said about the Roman see, neighbouring bishops, or other major procedural provisions. One may be tempted to read this as a Byzantine attempt to minimalize Roman jurisdiction, either for ideological reasons or simply because of their lack of applicability.

Another, more innocuous example is *Coll50* 23, which subsumes a number of specific regulations relating to deacons: giving communion to presbyters, sitting with presbyters, and receiving honor from lower clergy. Included among the canons, however, is Neocaesarea 14, which limits the number of deacons in any city to seven. Its provisions are nowhere present in the rubric. This absence may simply be carelessness or an example of excessively general associative grouping. Alternatively, it may represent the subtle marginalization of an awkward and archaic rule—in effect, an attempt at "hiding" it in the rubrics. (And this rule will later be modified by Trullo 16.)

Patterns of selective emphasis are more difficult to detect. The many single-canon rubrics in the *Coll14*, and the sometimes very specific rule rubrics in the *Coll50*, at times suggest that special emphasis is being placed on specific canons, but the phenomenon is too varied and random to suggest clear ideological patterns. Likewise, it is difficult to identify any particular category of organization or type of regulation that the rubrics themselves highlight or

Kormchaya as designed to reflect specifically Slavic concerns (contested by Burgmann 1995). Even the spotty western reception of Trullan canons is difficult to attribute to clear doctrinal motivations: the western reception seems almost random, and includes "anti-Roman" canons such as 13, 30, and 36 (Landau 1995; see Ohme 1990; 2006 for an important new reading of Trullo's western reception). As counterintuitive as it seems to the modern historian, canonical collections in the pre-modern period do not appear to select material for ideological reasons, at least not primarily or obviously.

"add" to the tradition. One exception, already mentioned, is *Coll14* 1.2–4, on valid canonical sources, generated through imitation of the civil codices. While formal validity is occasionally raised in the canons, the *Coll14* has noticeably highlighted them by both creating these chapters and placing them at the opening of the collection. In effect, the collector has added a new level of technical complexity to the tradition. *Coll14* 9.1–9, by clustering procedural rules together, with considerable quasi-technical-legal vocabulary, has a similar effect.[98]

Much more broadly, *Coll14* 2–7, and especially titles 2, 5, 6, and 7, may be read as unduly emphasizing "sacral" matters: construction of sanctuaries, prayers, sacraments, liturgical offerings. As Figure 4.1 demonstrates, these titles subsume very few canons. But the *Coll14* highlights these few canons by granting them especially prominent physical "title space." Similarly, the topic of "monastics" as a separate and distinct class of person and category of legislation emerges much more prominently in the systematic collections (*Coll50* 32–4 and *Coll14* 11) than in the 6th C source material itself (present really only in Gangra and parts of Chalcedon).

In all these cases the emphases are slight. If they are taken as a whole, there can be little doubt that the primary intention of both collections is simply to convey the traditional canonical content.

To conclude, the overall impression left by the formation and constitution of the thematic rubrics, and their various relationships with the subsumed canons, is one of marked conservatism. The central "agenda" of their formation seems to be the straightforward facilitation of engagement with the surface content of the canons themselves. The collections thus amount to little more than a basic recapitulation or unfolding of the traditional texts in organized, summary forms. Analytical and creative jurisprudential processes are not entirely absent, but their presence is tentative, desultory, and, we may often suspect, unconscious. Inasmuch as they are present, such processes function more to amplify and emphasize patterns that already exist in the source material than to reshape, develop, or otherwise substantively "advance" the tradition. As often is the case, what is not happening is more striking than what is: there is little distillation of general principles or doctrinal concepts; there are no sustained attempts to fill in gaps; and there are no hints of harmonization. There is, in short, little "scientific" juristic activity of any type. The canons instead seem to be treated in a very careful, almost hesitant, way that once again suggests a perception of the rules as a sacred body of texts which is to be transmitted and communicated as carefully and accurately as possible—an object of respect and veneration, not analysis or development.

[98] *κατηγορέω* (9.1), *καταμαρτυρέω* (9.2), *ἔγκλημα* (9.3), *δίκαι* (9.5), *ἀναψηλάφησις* (9.6), *δικάζω* (9.7), *κινέω παρά* (9.8).

G. ORDER AND STRUCTURE IN THE SYSTEMATIC INDICES

The manner in which the individual topical rubrics relate to the contents of their subsumed canons is only one aspect of how the thematic indices shape and "digest" the canonical tradition. Equally important are the larger structures and patterns into which the collections shape the canonical material by the creation, selection, and ordering of larger groups of individual rubrics. This type of structuring represents one of the most dramatic and literal ways in which the collections "shape" the law.

Scholarship has not been exceptionally interested in the order and structure of antique legal collections. As a rule, order and structure have become the focus of sustained study only when they assist in textual archeology or the reconstruction of the stages of a codification: for example, in recovering the original form of constituent texts, establishing the historical relationship of individual texts to each another, or in determining the mechanics of how a collection was composed.[99] Interest is much less marked in what the patterns of ordering themselves may tell us about attitudes towards law and legal thinking.[100]

The reason for this lack of interest is undoubtedly the extreme "fuzziness" of ancient ordering. Reading the canonical collections, one may well sympathize with Theodore Mommsen's observation—made with reference to the Praetorian Edict—that what order is to be found is more of a disorder.[101] But order may be found, of a sort. In contemporary legal science order tends to be sought in neat hierarchies of comprehensive categories of internal legal concepts. Strict logical coherence among parts, completeness of presentation, and the avoidance of gaps, repetitions, or contradictions are the central motifs. But in Byzantine canon law, as in most ancient sources, ordering is much more superficial, oriented towards simple associative grouping and arrangement according to surface content.[102] Its instincts are best captured by epithets

[99] So e.g. Bluhme's "masses" hypothesis, and more recently the detailed reconstruction of the creation of the *Digest* in Honoré 1978, 139–86. Broadly all of the emerging structural analyses of "palingenesia" projects could be counted here.

[100] As often, Sohm is an exception. Sohm 1918; 1923 wished to see in the order of Gratian's *Decretum* a last remnant of a mentality of "sacramental" law of the first millennium. The approach of Zechiel-Eckes 1992 is more representative. He does consider Cresconius' ordering system at length, but he is too struck by the system's "weakness" and "inadequacy" to consider its broader legal-theoretical implications (see esp. 1.51, 61–2).

[101] Cited in Schulz 1953, 151 (*Gesammelte Schriften* 1.164).

[102] For general comments on the nature of order and structure in pre-modern sources, see Tigay 1996, 449–59 (one of the best treatments, with discussion of other ancient Near Eastern sources and with many further references); Diamond 1950, 23–31 on Hammurabi; Honoré 1978, 174 on the *Digest*, the *Edict*, and Ulpian; Mordek 1975, 23 on the *Vetus Gallica*; Schulz 1953, 151 esp. n. 6, on the *Edict*, with further references; and Willetts 1967, 34 on Gortyn.

such as loose, digressive, agglutinative, irregular, and understated. Patterns and strategies of ordering are thus not absent, but they are subtle.

In surveying the structures of the Byzantine systematic indices, and indeed of the canonical sources themselves, only one pattern—or rather lack of a pattern—emerges with any clarity: almost nowhere can one detect the direct, sustained influence of any other legal ordering schema, Greco-Roman or otherwise. As noted, Bernard of Pavia in the 12th C will directly import *Digest* rubrics and structures into his Decretal collection, creating an order that will thenceforth become standard.[103] By contrast, almost nowhere in the Byzantine corpus does one find a comparable imposition of a pre-made, external schema onto the canonical material. The one exception, already mentioned, is *Coll14* 1.1–5, which seems to imitate the secular codices. But even here the imitation is loose, and brief. There may also be a connection between the strange *Coll14* 14.1 and the equally strange opening title of *Apostolic Constitutions* Book 1: both are *Περὶ πλεονεξίας*.[104] Otherwise, when one places the structures of the canonical sources and the systematic collections against similar patterns in the Apostolic Church Orders, the most prominent civil material, and literary/philosophical expositions of law, direct correspondences in the grouping and ordering of material are very hard to find.[105] This is true even where

[103] See Section F. On this order's long *Nachleben*, see Gaudemet 1991, 171–4; Fransen 1972, 21; Somerville and Brasington 1998, 218.

[104] Text in Metzger 1985, 1.100.

[105] The structures and orders taken into account for this comparison include those of the following texts.

For Roman law: *Twelve Tables* (as per Crawford 1996, 555–721 and, alternatively, Riccobono *et al.* 1940, 21–75, the latter with trans. Johnson *et al.* 1961, 9–18); Q. Mucius Scaevola's *Ius civilis* and the related Sabinian order, which may be considered one of two "backbone" structures of Roman legal literature (as per Lenel 1889, 2.1257–61, 1892, with analysis at 90–104; also, for the former, Liebs 1976, 223 and Watson 1974, 142–4, and generally Schulz 1953, 94–5, 157–8); the Praetorian Edict, the other backbone structure (as per Lenel 1889, 2.1247–56, with reference to Schulz 1953, 148–52); the *digesta* orders (essentially the Edict order plus a selection of appended *leges*, as per Lenel 1889, 2.1257–61, and with reference to Schulz 1953 *passim*); *CTh* (mostly a modified *digesta* order; see esp. Harries 1998, Matthews 2000); *CJ* (similar to *CTh/digesta*); *Digest* (a *digesta* order; see in particular Honoré 1978, 139–86; I also considered the order of the *Digest* described in*Tanta/Δέδωκεν*, and the orders of the educational curricula in *Omnem*); institutes literature, in structure generally related to the Mucian/Sabinian material, including Florentinus (as per Schulz 1953, 158–9), Marcian (as per Schulz 1953, 172–3), Gaius (ed. Seckel and Kuebler 1935), Justinian (*Institutes*). Many of the standard source surveys consider briefly patterns of ordering in the Roman collections, but Schulz 1953 is particularly helpful throughout. The table of Mommsen in *CTh* vol. 1 (Prolegomena) xiii–xxvii is invaluable for considering the Edictal order in relation to the *CTh* and *CJ*. Soubie 1960 is also helpful for the order and structure of the *Digest*.

For Byzantine law: the *Syntagma* (ed. Simon and Troianos 1989) and *Epitome* (ed. Simon and Troianos 1979) of Athanasius of Emesa; the *Ecloga* (see the important discussion of its order in Burgmann 1983, 7–8); the *Nomos Mosaikos* (ed. Burgmann and Troianos 1979); the *Eisagoge*; the *Prochiron*; the *Basilica* (order still mostly based on the Edict; see Lawson 1930, 494–500).

For late Roman/Byzantine civil treatments of ecclesiastical law: the order of topics in *CTh* 16; *CJ* 1.1–13; *NN* 5, 6, 7, 123, 131; *Coll87*; and the *Tripartita*.

patterning might be easily accomplished or suggested, for example in the ordering of criminal-like wrongs.[106]

Curiously, this lack of direct structural modeling is also evident *within* the canonical tradition. The two systematic collections do not show any clear evidence of trying to follow the order of topics found in, for example, Laodicea or the Apostles, or of each other. Even the second-wave material (generally much more tightly structured than the first-wave) does not show any strict or sustained dependence on the structures of the earlier thematic collections or the earlier corpus sources. This is true even where we might most expect it, in the structuring of the consciously code-like Trullo. This council is following the *Coll14* in its selection of sources, but, it seems, in no other way.[107]

For philosophical or literary legal discussions: the *Laws* of Plato (ed. Burnet 1907 with reference to the commentary of Schöpsdau 1994, 2003, especially the schematic 1993, 95–8); the *Laws* of Cicero (ed. Powell 2006 with reference to the commentary of Dyck 2004); Plutarch's description of Solon's and Lycurgus' legal activity in their *vitae* (ed. Lindskog and Ziegler 1957–80); the *Antiquities* of Josephus 4.197–292 (ed. Niese, 1887–92) and the same author's *Against Apion* 2.164–219 (ed. Niese 1889, 3–99) (both are reorganized presentations of the Mosaic law; see Altshuler 1982/3 and Geza 1982); *On the Special Laws* of Philo (ed. Cohn 1906, 1–265; essentially the Pentateuchal laws reorganized under the headings of the Ten Commandments); *Roman Antiquities* 2.1–29 of Dionysius of Halicarnassus (ed. Jacoby 1885; here a description of Romulus' constitution and laws).

For Christian scripture: Exodus (particularly chs. 20–40, with 20–3, 25–31, 35–40 as regulative discourses interspersed with narrative; this includes 20.22–23.33, the "Covenant Code" of modern scholarship); the Ten Commandments: Exod. 20: 1–17; Deut. 5: 6–21; Leviticus (as a whole, and as an extension of Exodus; the modern delimitation of 17–26 as the "holiness code" does not seem especially relevant for our period); Deuteronomy as a whole (particularly 12–26, perhaps with 4–11 as a lengthy introductory section; see esp. Tigay 1996, 449–59, with schematic); the Pentateuch as a whole; Matt. 5–7 (Sermon on the Mount); all Epistles with substantial regulative sections (including the "household codes" of modern scholarship): 1 Corinthians; Colossians; Ephesians; Titus; 1 Timothy; 1 Peter.

For Apostolic Church Orders material: *Didache* (ed. Niederwimmer and Attridge 1993); *Apostolic Tradition* (ed. Bradshaw 2002; see p. 15 for variant orderings) as well as its later forms, the *Testament of the Lord* (ed. Rahmani 1899), and the *Canons of Hippolytus* (ed. Bradshaw and Bebawi 1987); *Constitutiones ecclesiasticae apostolorum* or "Apostolic Church Ordinances" (ed. Arendzen 1901); *Didascalia* (ed. Funk 1905); *Apostolic Constitutions* (ed. Metzger 1985). Steimer 1992 provides the best overview of the Apostolic church order literature, with many further references.

For purposes of comparison, the orders of the following early western systematic collections were also considered: the *Statuta ecclesiae antiqua* (ed. Munier 1963), the *Concordia* of Cresconius (ed. Zechiel-Eckes 1992—including also the order of the "Gallican Cresconius" at 237–8) the *Breviatio canonum* of Fulgentius (ed. Munier 1974), the *Capitula* of Martin of Braga (*PL* 84.574–86), the *Vetus Gallica* (ed. Mordek 1975), the *Systematic Hispana(s)* (ed. Díez 1966), the *Dacheriana* (d'Achery 1672, 2.1–200), *Hibernensis* (Wasserschleben 1885), the *Anselmo Dedicata* (partial edition in Besse 1959), the *Collectio 9 librorum* (described Maassen 1871, 885–7), and the collection of Regino of Prum (Wasserschleben 1840).

[106] e.g. the progression through criminal-like material in *Coll50* 40–6 and *Coll14* 9.25–7, 13.20, 23 does not follow the progression of the exposition of crimes in *CTh* 9 or *CJ* 9, *Digest* 48, *Institutes* 4.8, or Plato, *Laws* 853d–910d.

[107] i.e. the order of topics addressed and the order of the older canonical sources used in no way follow the order of any of the topics or sources in the *Coll50* or *Coll14* indices. To give an example, if the Trullan canons were to follow the order of the infractions in the "clerical code" of

Nevertheless, if instances of direct and specific modeling are difficult to identify, general resonances and broad parallels are easily detected. This is true first within the canonical tradition itself. Almost every general topical grouping in the systematic indices has some precedent within the corpus sources. Just as the individual rubrics are in large measure derived directly and simply from the canons, so the larger groupings and associations of these rubrics depend upon pre-made associations within the corpus itself. In this respect the systematic indices once again do not represent any radical innovations in ordering or shaping the material: they are merely emphasizing and amplifying patterns already present.

Thus, for example, the systematic collections create a group for ordination material (*Coll50* 1–12; *Coll14* 1.6–28)—but so already Apostolic 1–2, 76–83, Ancyra 10–13, or Neocaesarea 8–12. Likewise the collections create groups for heretics, Jews, and pagans (*Coll50* 37–9; *Coll14* 12), but so already in Laodicea 29–39; likewise for procedure and penalties (*Coll50* 15–19; *Coll14* 9), so Serdica 3–9 (with 3–5 specifically treating appeal), Carthage 8–15, 27–30, 104–7, and 128–33, Antioch 11–15, and even Apostolic 74–5; or for liturgical, sacramental, and ritual matters (*Coll50* 46–7, 50; *Coll14* 2–7), so already in Apostolic 7–11 (paralleled in Antioch 1 and 2) or 69–73, Laodicea 43–52 (indeed, much of 20–52), or Carthage 3–7; or for marriage, women, family, and/or sexual matters (*Coll50* 41–4; parts of *Coll14* 13), so already in Ancyra 19–21 (maybe from 16), Gangra 13–17, Basil 3–7, Chalcedon 14–16, and much of Basil's second letter, especially 21–7, 30–42, 48–50; or for murder, sorcery, augury, violence, and theft (all broadly "criminal" matters, as *Coll50* 40–6 and parts of *Coll14* 9 and 13), so in Apostolic 21–7, Ancyra 22–5, or Basil 54–66 (perhaps 54–83).

Many of these groupings also find resonances in secular law codes or similar texts outside of the corpus sources. "Criminal" sections, for example, are frequently encountered in law texts.[108] Likewise, procedural sections are common,[109] as are marriage and family groupings,[110] or clusters of cultic and "sacred" matters.[111] More directly, works addressing specifically Christian matters often group heretics, pagans, and/or Jews together.[112]

Coll14 9.20–39, they would be in the following order: 67, 12–13, 61, 50, 24–5, 66, 10, 3–5, 92, 77, 9, 34, 102. Only the last canon (102) and chapter (9.39), on repentance, correspond.

[108] See n. 106. Other examples include the second half of the Ten Commandments, Josephus, *Antiquities* 4.266–91, and the second half of Philo's *Special Laws* 3–4 (as following the order of the second half of the Ten Commandments; especially those laws attached to 7, 8, 9).

[109] e.g. *Institutes* 4; *CTh* 2; *CJ* 2–3 (broadly); *Digest* 2–3 (or 2–5); Athanasius, *Syntagma* 4–5; Josephus, *Antiquities*; 4.214–22.

[110] e.g. Plato's *Laws* 772d–85b; *CTh* 3; Athanasius, *Syntagma* 10–11; Philo, *Special Laws* 2–3 (i.e. Ten Commandments 5, 6); Josephus, *Antiquities* 4.244–65.

[111] e.g. the Ten Commandments 1–4; Deut. 12–13; *Didache* 7–10; *Canons of Hippolytus* 19–38; Plato's *Laws*; *CTh* 16; *CJ* 1.1–13; Philo, *On Special Laws* 1–2; Josephus, *Antiquities* 4.199–213 (and broadly book 3).

[112] e.g. *Apostolic Constitutions* 6; *CTh* 16.5–10 and *CJ* 1.5–11; Athanasius, *Syntagma* 3.

The ways in which these rubrical groupings are then related to each other and structured in the collections also find numerous resonances both within and outside the corpus sources. Four ordering strategies are particularly prominent, even if all are sporadic, uneven, and often broken by digression.

The most obvious, and the dominant, pattern is the tendency to build structures around a hierarchy of personal subjects or offices. This type of structuring is especially prominent in the beginning of collections, and finds clear resonance in the many *Amtsweisungen* of the secular legal literature, as well as in some Apostolic Church Order texts.[113] Among the canonical texts the *Coll50* is especially notable for this type of structuring, particularly in titles 1–39, where the topics proceed down an exceptionally neat scale of clergy, laity, monastics, catechumens, schismatics, and finally heretics. The tendency in the Greek to place the subject very early in each rubric (in emphasis in Table 4.3 below) makes the sense of stepping down a descending hierarchy of subjects especially palpable. The rubrical *initia* shown in Table 4.3 below demonstrate this sequence:

Table 4.3 Rubrical *Initia* of the *Collection in Fifty Titles.*

Titles	Rubrical *initia*
1	*Περὶ τῆς ὁρισθείσης τοῖς* **πατριάρχαις** *ἐκ τῶν κανόνων . . .*
2	*Περὶ τῆς ὁρισθείσης τοῖς* **μητροπολίταις** *ἐκ τῶν κανόνων . . .*
3, 5, 6, 7, 12, 14, 15 [16], 19	*Περὶ τοῦ δεῖν* [or *μὴ δεῖν*] *τὸν* **ἐπίσκοπον** *. . .*
20	*Περὶ τοῦ μὴ δεῖν* **κληρικοὺς** *. . .*
21	*Περὶ* **χωρεπισκόπων** *καὶ* **πρεσβυτέρων** *. . .*
22	*Περὶ τοῦ δεῖν τοὺς* **πρεσβυτέρους** *καὶ πάντας τοὺς ἐν τῷ* **κλήρῳ**
23	*Περὶ τοῦ* **διακόνους** *μὴ δεῖν . . .*
24	*Περὶ χειροτονίας* **γυναικῶν** *. . .*
26	*Περὶ τοῦ* **ψάλτας** *καὶ* **ἀναγνώστας** *καὶ* **ὑπηρέτας** *καὶ* **ἐπορκιστάς** *. . .*
27, 28	*Περὶ τοῦ μὴ δεῖν* **ἱερέα** *. . .*
29–31	*Περὶ τοῦ μὴ δεῖν* **ἐπίσκοπον** *ἢ* **κληρικὸν** *ὅλως ἢ* **λαϊκόν** *. . .*
32–34	*Περὶ τῶν* **ἀσκούντων** *. . .* **ἀσκητὰς** *. . .* **μοναχῶν** *καὶ* **μοναστριῶν** *. . .*
35, 36	*Περὶ* **κατηχουμένων** *. . . Περὶ τοῦ μὴ δεῖν τοὺς ἄρτι* **φωτισθέντας** *. . .*

[113] Such structures are well known, and very common, in early codes and code-like literature. Solon—or at least the 403 BC Athenian "code"—is sometimes suspected of it (see the discussion, and doubts, in Ruschenbusch 1966, 27–31), Plato assumes it (*Laws* 734e; see Gagarin 2000, 218), Cicero does it (*Laws* book 3), and it is broadly true of Dionysius of Halicarnassus' account of Romulus' legislation (*Roman Antiquities* 1–29, ed. Jacoby 1885; part of a broader tendency, I think, of treating "constitutional" matters first). It is very evident in the first parts of *CTh*, *CJ*, *Digest*, *Eisagoge*, and the *Basilica*, and easily remarked in many examples of the Apostolic Church Order material, notably the Apostolic Tradition texts, the *Constitutiones ecclesiasticae apostolorum*, or the *Didascalia* (and thus the *Apostolic Constitutions*). The introduction to the *Eisagoge* even includes a rationale for this structure: see lines 91–4 (ed. Schminck 1986, 4–11). It is also quite clear in *NN* 123 and 131.

The progression is not, as ever, exact or mechanistic, and is disrupted numerous times by digressions. Thus, one might have expected 20 to follow 22—but the broader topic of 20 is a close continuation of 19. Similarly, it would seem that 27 and 28 should have been placed after 22, but the introduction of clerical marriage at the end of 26 (and the transitional function marriage plays in 29 and onwards) seems to have attracted both of these titles to their current place.

A similar pattern is evident in the *Coll14*, but in a more diffuse way. Title 1 begins the collection with regulations primarily on clergy, and its own chapters roughly proceed down the ladder of clerical offices, from patriarchs to deaconesses. After a long liturgical/sacral interlude (titles 2–7), the titles resume the treatment of (mostly) disciplinary matters relating to bishops and clerics (8, 9, and 10), then monastics (11), then heretics (12), then the laity (after heretics!) (13), and then "all people" (14). With titles 2–7 removed, a structured descent from clerics to monastics and then heretics and "others" is easily discerned.

Many individual corpus sources also show traces of this type of ordering. In the first wave it emerges especially clearly in the Serdican canons, which are neatly divided between regulations treating bishops (1–12) and those treating clerics in general (13–19). A much briefer instance is Ephesus 1–4, where we proceed from metropolitans, bishops, and then to clergy more generally. Similarly, Laodicea 20–8 is obviously focused on the clergy, while 29–39 is more general in scope (with either no subject or addressed to "Christians" in general). Elsewhere in the first wave hierarchical ordering is often more elusive, but it often remains just perceptible. Apostolic 1–59, for example, is mostly focused on the clergy, while later canons may be seen as more general in scope (although 76–83 represents a clerical reprise). Nicaea broadly works from clerical ordination and episcopal matters (1–8) down to more general or varied questions, and its *lapsi* regulations are treated in the order clerics, laypeople, catechumens (10, 11, 14). More briefly, Neocaesarea 1–4 treats the marriages first of clergy (1), then laypeople (2–4). Similar patterns may be discerned in parts of Ancyra, Neocaesarea, Antioch, Chalcedon, Serdica, parts of Carthage and Basil, and Peter.

In the second-wave sources hierarchical subject ordering becomes much more regular and obvious. II Nicaea moves (with some digressions) through emphases on bishops (2–7), clergy generally (10–16), and then monastics (17–22). Protodeutera, very curiously, reverses the hierarchy, moving from monastics and monasteries (1 to 6, or perhaps 7), up to clergy in general (7 or 8 to 12 or 13), and then on to bishops (13, or perhaps 14, to 17). Even Hagia Sophia proceeds distinctly through primates (1), bishops (2), and then laity (3). Trullo is exceptional in the corpus for containing short topical rubrics within its own canons which make the descending hierarchical organization of the collection explicit: "On priests and clerics" (*περὶ ἱερέων καὶ κληρικῶν*) before canon 3, "On monks and nuns" (περὶ μοναχῶν καὶ μοναστριῶν) before 40, and "On the laity" (περὶ λαϊκῶν) before 50.[114]

The second, and vaguer, pattern of structuring is the hierarchization of substantive topics. Also evident in non-canonical material, this pattern emerges most regularly in a tendency to place "high-status" matters of faith, general legal doctrine, clergy, and anything sacral near the beginning of a collection, and material that might be considered "lower status" near the end.[115] Thus, in the *Coll14* faith, clergy, and sacral matters clearly dominate

[114] These rubrics represent something of a textual mystery, and it is not entirely clear whether they are original. Their fortunes in the editions have varied. They are completely absent in Beveridge, and also (thus?) *RP* and the *Pedalion*. Pitra notes the presence of the first two in some MSS (*Pitra* 2.23 n. 1; 2.45 n. 1), but not the third, and does not include any in his main text. Beneshevich includes the first two in *Kormchaya*, without comment, but not the last. Joannou in *Fonti* (and thus Nedungatt and Featherstone 1995) includes them all without any textual notes at all, aside from asserting in his introduction that "the manuscripts divide the texts into three sections" (*Fonti* 1.98). Ohme 2006, 46 and Troianos 1992a, 10 mention them but do not indicate that they are part of the manuscript tradition. Confusion seems to have been created by an influential article by Vitalien Laurent (Laurent 1965) which speaks (20 n. 54) as if the rubrics were the invention of Pitra, a view that is echoed in Gavardinas 1998, 58–9, *Historike* 290, and Troianos 1992a, 10. In this author's examination of the manuscripts (see Ch. 1, n. 3) the first two rubrics are present very often, albeit sometimes in the margins, but the third is rare. It was found in only three manuscripts, Moscow Syn. 398, Patmos 205, and Vatican gr. 1980. The first and last of these, however, are quite old (10th–11th C). Of course, in all these cases the rubrics may still represent later additions. A full resolution of the problem of the rubrics' originality will have to await Ohme's edition for the *ACO*, in preparation. One may suspect that they are original, however, because they are strikingly accurate—especially by Byzantine standards. Canons 3–39 are all almost exclusively, and always primarily, addressed to the clergy; canons 40–9 form a very tight group of strictly monastic legislation; and the final section, 50–102, while more varied in subject, contains no canon that solely addresses the clergy or monastics or both—they either lack a specific addressee, contain multiple addressees that include the laity, or are addressed exclusively to the laity. Moreover, the divisions created by the rubrics are numerically quite neat (including the overall century which, by separating canon 1 and 2 from the rest, the rubrics make much clearer—a point also now suggested by Mardirossian 2010, 261 n. 2), which suggests that they are marking an intentional, and therefore probably original, compositional schema.

[115] There is a great deal of variation in the patterns of substantive ordering in the non-canonical legal literature. Nevertheless, sacral and general theoretical matters, or matters pertaining to prominent officials, or sources, are often first in a collection, and more distasteful criminal, sexual, or mundane financial-administrative matters emerge later. This pattern is broadly evident in all the *CTh* and *CJC* material, where high-status matters relating to doctrine, theory, sources, and high-ranking officials appear early (i.e. *CTh* 1, *CJ* 1, *Digest* 1, *Institutes* 1.1–2) and criminal material appears quite late (i.e. *CTh* 9, *CJ* 9, *Digest* 47–8—the "libri terribiles" of *Tanta* 8a—and *Institutes* 4). Within *CTh* and *CJ* the structures specifically dedicated to church matters (*CTh* 16, *CJ* 1.1–13) likewise place heretics, pagans, and other disagreeable subjects noticeably after doctrinal and cultic matters. The same pattern may be found in all of the Byzantine collections, with issues of faith, theory, and high officers placed early, as *Nomos Mosaikos* 1–2, *Eisagoge* 1–9, *Basilica* 1–7, Novels of Leo 1–17, and large criminal-penal sections last or near-last, as *Ecloga* 17, *Nomos Mosaikos* 42–50, *Eisagoge* 40, *Prochiron* 39, *Basilica* 60, Novels of Leo 58–66. This pattern is also apparent in Plato's *Laws* (clearly starting with religious matters and high offices in 715e–68e and much later moving on to criminal material in 853d–910d), as well as Josephus, *Antiquities* (4.199–213 vs. 4.266–91), and even the *Didascalia* (books 1–2 on general teaching and hierarchy, and its last on "schism"). Cicero's *Laws* are lost after book 3, but they also begin with religious and cultic matters (2.8) before moving on to

the first half of the collection (titles 1–7), while management, finances, and "criminal" matters dominate the latter half, along with more neutral topics on lower-status persons. A similar, if more diffuse, tendency may also be remarked within some of the *Coll14* titles.[116] Likewise, in the *Coll50*, topics become palpably more distasteful after title 36, where one starts to discuss schismatics, heretics, *lapsi*, astrologers/diviners, murder, fornication, marriage (!), aberrant sexual practices, thieves, perjurers, and sacrilege.

In the canonical sources themselves this pattern is most evident in the tendency to place faith, faith-like, and general questions about the canons as sources very early, as in Constantinople 1, Chalcedon 1, Carthage 1–2, Trullo 1–2, II Nicaea 1 (and 2). Sacral and liturgical matters also tend towards first position, as Apostles 1–9 (roughly), Antioch 1–9, Dionysius 1, Timothy 1–10, Theophilus 1 and 2, and II Nicaea 2–6. Likewise, matters treating more "criminal" matters, sexual issues, administrative and financial topics, or heretics/pagans, tend to cluster later in sources, as Ancyra 16–25, Laodicea 29–39, much of Antioch 10–25, Timothy 11–15, and II Nicaea 8–16.

Another important substantive hierarchy emerges in the structuring of topics according to growing or diminishing seriousness of offences, as, for example, in *Coll14* 9.10–18, or *Coll50* 39 onwards, or Gregory Thaumatourgus 1–8, which moves from less culpable actions to more culpable actions (especially if canons 3–5 are read as a digressive appendix to canon 2), or in the corpus's two main treatments of *lapsi*, Ancyra 1–7 and Peter 1–14.

Interestingly, some of the most common exceptions to the substantive hierarchies also seem to follow patterns—almost micro-traditions in themselves. One of the most prominent is a tendency to return to certain types of liturgical or sacral material—"high-status" matters—at the very end of a source.[117] Thus, various liturgical matters appear in the last title of the *Coll50*, as they do in Nicaea (18–)20, Gangra 18–20, Laodicea 14–19 (the end of what is often thought of as "first" Laodicea, from 1–19[118]), Laodicea

magistrates (3.1)—certainly they begin with high-status matters. This pattern is evident even in the Ten Commandments (1–5 on the identity of God and cultic matters, 6–10 on disciplinary and criminal matters)—and thus in Philo's *Special Laws* 1–2 and 3–4.

[116] Title 3, for examples, treats more general and generic matters pertaining to prayer and communion quite early (1–13 or so), but demoniacs (13), heretics and Jews (14–15, 20), menstruation, nocturnal emissions and sexual impurity (18–19, 21), and suicides (22) rather later. Similar, if far from exact, patterns are evident in titles 4, 6, 8, and 12.

[117] This phenomenon finds some parallel in extra-canonical texts where one may note a "recovering" of more respectable topics at the very end of a source. It is evident, for example, in *CTh* 16 (on religious matters), *CJ* with its last title on "dignities," and *Digest* 50.16–17, with its return to theoretical matters (general definitions and rules). The *Canons of Hippolytus* similarly conclude with Pascha.

[118] See L'Huillier 1976, 59; *Sources* 48–9. L'Huiller is right to detect even a third layer of sources.

58–9, and Peter 15. Similarly, the canon of scripture is mentioned last in the *Coll50*, as are the two listings of the content of scripture in the Apostles (canon 85) and Laodicea (canon 59). Finally, a general canon/rubric on repentance may be found at the end of Basil's third letter (canon 84), at the end of title 9 of the *Coll14* (chapter 39), and at the end of Trullo (canon 102).

Another curious exception is the placing of marriage-related canons very early in some of the oldest sources: Neocaesarea (1–3), Gangra (1), and Laodicea (1) are the most direct examples. If we except Ancyra 1–9 as a special pre-appendix section on *lapsi*, Ancyra's general canons are also headed by marriage regulations (10–11). Likewise, after two general canons on the faith, Carthage begins with marriage (3–4). The Apostolic Canons, after their initial ordination pair (1–2) and liturgical-altar pair (3–4), also move directly to the matter of clergy and their wives (5). This phenomenon may be connected with the next major ordering structure.

The third general strategy of ordering and structuring, and the most subtle, is to proceed according to a "life order," that is, to move through material in the order in which the topics would arise chronologically in the course of life. This pattern, not unknown in later Byzantine legal sources,[119] is very sporadic in the canonical literature, but still just perceptible. It may be felt dimly in the beginning of the *Coll50*, where in title 6 (or possibly starting at 4, with 5 as an associative digression) one begins with matters relating to the death of a bishop, and thus a vacancy. Then one moves to the manner in which a new bishop is to be elected (7), the time limit for the election and qualifications of new candidates (8–9), and finally a set of typical problems of ordination itself (10–12). The remaining titles all treat matters to be encountered once a bishop is ordained. In effect, the topics are tracking the stages of a bishop's career.

Another example may be found in *Coll14* 4, in which the chapters move from the acceptance to the catechumenate (chapter 1), to problems of catechesis for one in the catechumenate (2), to how the ritual of baptism is performed and how the catechumen must confess the faith at baptism (3–4), and finally to problems with particular types of baptismal candidates (5–10). The topics track the natural progression of entrance into the church. Chapters 11–14 then pass to issues that are post-baptismal: chrismation, rebaptisms, and reception of heretical baptisms. (Chapters 15–16 return to problems

[119] So Burgmann 1983, 7–8 on the order of the *Ecloga*. The pattern is never rigorous, but the *Prochiron* and *Eisagoge* also broadly move through matters of the beginning of (civil) life, i.e. marriage, then to matters during life (buying, selling, partnerships), then to matters relating to the end of life (inheritances, legacies). The *Eisagoge* is even self-conscious about this structuring—see its *Prooimion* 95–107 (Schminck 1986, 4–11). This order may also be perceived dimly in some Apostolic Church Order material, e.g. in the *Constitutiones ecclesiasticae apostolorum*, with a progression through catechesis, baptism, Eucharist, general prayer, and finally funeral matters (the *Basilica* and Plato's *Laws* also end with funeral matters). Cf. Plato's *Laws* 721a on codes following the "order of nature."

with candidates and catechumens, breaking the order—however, this section, entirely derived from one source, Timothy, may represent an appendix, added after the formation of the earlier rubrics to accommodate this later patristic source.)

"Life orders" may be suspected in some corpus sources. For example, a career-order progression is perhaps discernible in Antioch 17–25, a series of rules governing clerical, mostly episcopal, behaviors that otherwise seems to have little structure at all. The section starts with matters relating to the ordination of new bishops (17–19), proceeds to regulations on the behavior of bishops, especially with regard to other bishops and sees (20–2), and ends with matters of succession and finance that pertain mostly to the end of a bishop's life (23–4, with 25 as an extension of 24). A similar pattern may also underlie the otherwise mystifying opening structure of Nicaea: canons 1–2 treat problems relating to candidates for ordination, 4 treats the actual ordination of bishops, and 5–7 the consequent relations of bishops with each other (canon 3 on the *συνείσακτοι* intrudes as a digression). More clearly, in Protodeutera 1–4 another type of life order emerges as one moves from the construction of new monasteries (1), to the reception of postulants to monasteries (2), to problems encountered with those who have become monks (3–4).

The final major pattern of ordering and structuring—more an anti-pattern—may be termed the "miscellanizing pattern." It reveals itself in the surprisingly common tendency, evident in the civil literature as well, of proceeding from greater order to lesser order—with order again sometimes recovering at the very end of a source.[120] What "order" means can vary: perhaps clearer and more distinct subject hierarchies, more coherent topical groupings, more methodical categories, or more precise rubricization.

[120] Broadly, almost every external legal source examined (see n. 105), in different ways, is more ordered, logical, and structured in its very beginning than its later sections. This is particularly evident in collections that begin with any type of doctrinal-theoretical and/or *Amtsweisungen* section, which lends the first part of the texts a particularly clear and logical structure rarely replicated later in the same collections. Examples can be found in most extant secular Roman material, as well as in many of the Apostolic Church Orders. The reconstructions of the Twelve Tables likewise suggest a pattern of increasing disorder (especially in Tables 11 and 12). Plato's *Laws* also contains a notably miscellaneous end section (broadly 932–58), and the Deuteronomic code loses structure after Deut. 23: 10 (until 25). The Roman *digesta* pattern, and all sources dependent upon it, also evinces this tendency in another way, by following the Edict order rather carefully in the beginning, but then gradually descending into more miscellaneous public-law topics. Noailles and Dain 1944, xix likewise note such a pattern for the 113 Novels of Leo (ordered until 66 with distinct subject groupings, then becoming quite miscellaneous). In many cases Harries 1998, 78 is no doubt correct when she notes a similar pattern in the *CTh*, and attributes it to patterns of later modification and accumulation: "the ancient habit with law-codes was to set down what mattered most first, in an organized system, and then add modifications later, as required." This pattern of miscellanization, however, is too pronounced and widespread to attribute it solely to processes of later haphazard addition or alteration. It seems to be a true, general compositional characteristic of ancient legal texts, i.e. true of even first recensions.

This pattern is evident across the entirety of the *Coll50* and *Coll14*. Both begin quite distinctly with organized and detailed rubric groupings, but gradually dissolve into less precise and more variegated subject topics. In the *Coll14*, for example, faith and sacral matters are divided into seven comparatively precise titles, which, subsuming only about a quarter of the collection's references, are quite accurate and relay the canons' contents precisely. But the next topic, clerical discipline, is divided into only three titles; monastics, heretics, and, especially, laity then receive only one title each; and finally, the last title, title 14, "On common things of all" (*Περὶ κοινῶν πάντων ἀνθρώπων*), seems to function as a miscellaneous catch-all. In effect, the author seems to have become less ambitious and detailed in rubricization and categorization as the collection proceeded. This pattern is also evident within the individual titles. For example, 1.1–15 exhibits considerable structure, even imitating the *CJ*; but 1.16–38 evinces much less order, often without any discernible structure, or even coherent subject subgroupings. Similarly, 8.1–8 can be read as loosely centered on clerical travel, but 8.9–19 proceeds almost randomly. Title 12 begins with a clear introductory section treating preliminary definitions, "heretical books," and heretics (1–5; all as a "doctrinal" introduction, it seems), and this is followed by a well-defined sacral section (6–12), treating chiefly communion, entering churches, and praying together. The rest of the title, however, seems to lack any structure.

The *Coll50* is likewise most organized and regular in the first forty titles, with regular hierarchical progression, and fairly large, coherent groupings of related items. Titles thereafter become much more specific, unrelated, and illogical in progression: murder (40); fornication, marriage, and aberrant sexual practices (41–4); thieves and perjurers (45); removing items from church and appropriate offerings (46); liturgical matters (47); canons and repentance (48); synods (49); prayers, times, and calendar (50).

Similar "miscellanizing" is often evident within the corpus sources. Apostolic 1–15, for example, begins with considerable structure and logic, moving through the related sacral themes of ordination, altar service, communion, association with excommunicates, and letters for excommunicates. The rest of the text, however, evinces much less logic or order, progressing through marriage, surety, self-mutilation, criminal activities, marriage again, physical violence, liturgical actions of deposed clerics, simony, clergy rebelling, episcopal and synodal rules, dice, usury, baptism, eating in taverns, and so on. Similarly, Ancyra begins with two comparatively developed and defined sections on *lapsi* and ordination, 1–9 and 10–13, and then moves quickly through a kaleidoscopic array of other topics: abstention from meat, property of widowed churches, bestiality, reception of bishops, women and sex, murder, sorcery, and rape. The first section of Carthage, 1–33, begins, despite some digressions, with relatively coherent groups of canons on faith (1–2), sacramental matters (3–7), and then dispute resolution (8–15). From 16 onwards, however, the canons become much more mixed, moving through clergy and guardianship, reader marriage, clergy lending money, readers saluting the people, a primate for Mauretania, ignorance of the law, and so on. Trullo also starts with its very organized introductory canons and then a fairly coherent group on marriage and sex, but then loses almost any sense of topical order. II Nicaea also loses much coherence after about canon 16 (aside from the general monastic theme).

Beyond these four major patterns, a few other noteworthy, but isolated, ordering schemata must also be remarked. The most extraordinary is Gregory of Nyssa's canonical letter, the only truly systematic *aperçu* of church law in the Byzantine corpus—perhaps in the entire Byzantine canonical tradition. Using systematic medical τέχνη as his explicit model (ὡς δ' ἂν γένοιτό τις τεχνικὴ μέθοδος)[121], and proceeding through a branching process of *divisio* and distinction (with considerable concern for formal definition), Gregory creates a scheme based upon the common tripartite division of the faculties of the soul: the intellectual, desirous, and appetitive (λογικόν, ἐπιθυμητικόν, θυμοειδές).[122] Different canonical infractions are carefully classified into each group, and sometimes further subdivided through analysis of intention or other circumstances. Distinctions drawn include those between involuntary and voluntary actions, the level of coercion, whether one has turned oneself in or not, whether weaponry is involved or not, and the degree of harm done. One set of definitions is also established through an abstract analysis of effect: fornication and adultery are defined as, respectively, sexual acts which do not harm another and those that do.

Gregory thus provides an abstract hierarchical schema of categories and distinctions—largely external to any explicit concepts in the canons—for comprehending and interrelating the system as a whole. The classification requires the analysis of different infractions according to a set of underlying concepts, that is, types of psychological error, and not simply surface topics. Most remarkably, and characteristic of truly systematic approaches to law, the schema serves to reveal gaps in the existing legislation, as well as to challenge the consistency of existing concepts (both operations are possible because of the internal comparisons inherent in system building.) The former appears when Gregory notes (in canon 5) that, to his surprise, only one appetitive sin, murder, has been addressed at length by the fathers—despite the fact that other actions could be also considered appetitive (e.g. hitting, blasphemy). His categories have thus revealed/created a logical gap in the received penitential

[121] *Fonti* 2.205.13–14.

[122] For the general classical form of a hierarchical branching schema, see Fuhrmann 1960. This particular use of the psychological faculties as a principle of classification finds a parallel (and perhaps inspiration) in the division of rhetoric into the same three categories, e.g. as in Troilus, *Prolegomenon in Hermogenis artem rhetoricam* (ed. C. Walz, *Rhetores Graeci*, vol. 6 (Stuttgart, 1834), 42–55, at 54).

tradition. The latter emerges when Gregory observes (canon 8) that the traditional penance for sacrilege—a crime punishable by death in the Old Testament—is lighter than that for adultery. His systematic treatment has revealed a logical inconsistency. In both cases the systematic shaping of the material has encouraged substantive critique—and thus suggested a juristic "advancement" of the traditional regulations.

Despite its sophistication, however, the most remarkable aspect of Gregory's system is its almost total lack of influence on the later tradition. It is nowhere taken up as a model to be followed, even in the systematic collections. It merely becomes one more traditional rule text.

Another instance of a more sophisticated, but isolated, systematic ordering may be found in *Coll14* 9, on clerical infractions. This title, despite the relative disorder of the material after chapter 20, may be regarded as among the most sophisticated structures in the Byzantine canonical tradition. It employs a quasi-procedural order (a kind of specialized "life order").[123] The first eight chapters move through the steps of ecclesial actions, beginning with accusations against bishops (1–3), then trials themselves (5), and then retrials (6, and perhaps 8). (The technical-legal ring of these chapters is amplified by the high concentration of legal terminology.[124]) The title then moves to a set of unusually general rubrics on the types of punishment that might be imposed during such trials, broadly proceeding from least to most severe (10–19). The last half of the title (20–38) then treats all of the particular crimes covered by the canons, thus forming a substantive complement to the procedural beginning. Finally, the whole concludes with a very general collection of canons on repentance, chapter 39, which functions to address what to do after someone has committed any of the foregoing crimes and been assigned a punishment. The overall structure, even if implicit and loose, suggests a kind of mini criminal code for the clergy.

Despite these exceptions, however, when assessed as a whole, the basic mechanisms and strategies of structuring and ordering in the Byzantine canonical tradition remain very limited. For the most part structures are built only by clustering topics of similar surface content, and then placing these groups, almost always roughly, into very loose topical schemata. This method is often strangely associative, with connections made through sometimes only vaguely similar surface topics or similar phrases, and with a strong tendency towards digression.[125] It often seems almost opportunistic: connections are made mostly when easily made. The tradition seems to resist deeper internal analysis.

123 The best example of a procedural order in the secular material is that of the Praetorian Edict and its dependent traditions (see the references at n. 105).

124 See n. 98.

125 See n. 102 for further references on this phenomenon.

Interestingly, this associative method of grouping can occasionally create very tenuous pseudo-structures for parts of the material that otherwise seem to lack any obvious order. It can also sometimes account for odd breaks or transitions. Ancyra 10, 12, and 13, for instance, is a loose grouping of canons treating aspects of ordination. This grouping seems to be broken by canon 11, which treats betrothed girls who have been seized by others for marriage. However, this break should almost certainly be understood as an associative digression from Ancyra 10, which treats the status of ordination of deacons who have or have not made clear their intention to *marry* at the time of their ordination. The general matter of ordination is simply resumed in canon 12. Canon 11 has not really broken the grouping.

Sometimes association can be even vaguer, perhaps unconscious. A good example is an associative "chain" linking Apostolic 69–73, a cluster of canons vaguely centered around feasting, holy places, and behaviors appropriate to holy places. (The "chaining" concepts are in italics.) Canon 69 opens with the topic of *fasting* during Lent; the next canon then moves to *fasting* and *feasting* with *Jews*; the next, taking *oil* into *Jewish* synagogues during their *feasts*; the next, taking *oil* or wax out of the "*holy* church"; the next using any *holy* thing (i.e. out of a church) for one's own use. The progression develops through the associative chain of fasting–feasting–Jews/oil–holy items.

More common are associative transitional or "hinge" canons (or rubrics), in which a canon contains some type of superficial topical association with two different preceding and succeeding groups of canons.[126] For example, in Laodicea 49–54 four Lenten regulations (49–51) merge smoothly into two marriage regulations (53–4) through a regulation (52) that treats marriages during Lent. Or in II Nicaea, canon 7 functions to connect the "episcopal" section of 2–7 and the false belief/religion section of 7–9 by stating a rule that overlaps with both: the consecration of churches (an episcopal task) must be accomplished with relics, contrary to the heretical iconoclastic view. In some sources such associative transitions can be quite pronounced, running almost the entire length of a source.[127]

Such loose, semi-conscious associative structures do not, however, provide much "order" or structure by modern standards of rational systematization, and they are difficult even to detect. They point to what is in fact the single most important characteristic of Byzantine structuring and ordering: their absence. Very frequently in the canonical sources, and even in the systematic indices, there is not much order at all, and what does occur tends to be sporadic, localized, and elusive. Order tends to emerge occasionally, gingerly, and unevenly, and it is often difficult to determine the level of intention

[126] A phenomenon also remarked by Tigay 1996, 449–50.

[127] Most notably in Neocaesarea, much of Antioch, II Nicaea, and large stretches of the *Coll50* (perhaps also through *Coll14* 2–7).

involved. Rarely is any ordering sustained across the entirety of a source, or in exactly the same way. Indeed, lest the above examples mislead, in the corpus sources themselves, and in the systematic indices, large stretches of material can exhibit virtually no order at all. Both Chalcedon and Trullo, for example, but also much of Basil and Carthage show very little internal order; Nicaea is also very vague. Only with difficulty can one tease much structure out of *Coll14* 12 and 13 (despite some coherent subject groupings), and large parts of titles 1, 8, and 9 seem almost random; even the *Coll50* hardly constitutes a uniformly organized whole with truly predictable and consistent categories and forms. Its last half is particularly jumbled. In general, then, one of the key "methods" of canonical ordering is a non-method: one does *not* structure and order much.

The overall shape of order and structure in the systematic collections, as in the canonical sources themselves, is therefore mostly sporadic, tenuous, and simple. Like so many other aspects of Byzantine canon law, the collections evince a strong concern to adhere to and reflect the surface content and contours of the canons themselves, and therefore show little interest in sustained rationalization or abstract conceptual analysis, or any other type of structural creativity or initiative—despite occasional exceptions that demonstrate that such analysis and creativity were possible. Broadly continuous with patterns of ancient legal ordering, the hallmarks of Byzantine systematization are chiefly conservatism and minimalism.

H. ANALYSIS: SYSTEMATIZING THE LAW?

The first, and in many ways definitive, attempts of the Byzantines to "systematize" their canonical corpus do not today leave a powerful impression. They are ultimately little more than topical indices, the principal goal of which is to aid in the (literal) finding of canons on particular matters, that is, tools of "law finding" in the simplest sense. In their self-presentation, selection among their sources, creation of rubrics, and structuring of topics they show little inclination towards juridical abstraction, systematic creativity, or interpretative freedom. The overwhelming tendency in both the rubrics and broader patterns of structuring is to derive both content and form from the canonical sources themselves. The creativity and abstraction that can be found is thus more on the level of slight changes in emphasis than conceptual development—and it is revealing that this creativity must be searched for, often with some difficulty, and once found it is not always clear that it is intentional. Even relatively simple or obvious juridical reshapings of the material, such as in imitation of secular codices, are nowhere prominent (if not completely absent). The character of these works is thus best encapsulated in the phrase "organized surface summary": the collections provide a helpfully organized summary of the surface topics of the canons.

This method of systematization seems rather foreign, even odd, today. Since the early modern period most western European legal systems have tended to strive towards the ideal of the internally consistent, gapless whole: all rules, neatly defined and conceptually clear, are to relate seamlessly to one another in a clear and predictable manner, according to a strict internal logic. When a rule does not exist to address a certain situation, then the system is supposed to aid in creating one. The Byzantine systematic indices, by contrast, do not engage in even the precursor tasks to such systematization, such as casting canon law as a series of problems to be solved (gaps to be filled, contradictions to be resolved, or obscurities to be removed—all of which are evident in Ivo's *Prologue*[128] and Gratian's *Decretum*, or even the late antique secular codification projects), or the distillation of common concepts and principles. They also do not present the law as a synthetic whole even to the degree that the *Institutes* do, nor do they evince the sustained doctrinal thinking of the *Digest* fragments.[129]

Their conservatism and simplicity is thus quite striking, even unexpected. The canonical collections were created in a society, and during a period, possessed of many resources and models for far more penetrating systematic analysis and composition. The *Institutes* and *Digest* are the obvious examples, but the works of the Aristotelian commentators and the Neoplatonic and rhetorical pedagogical manuals might also be noted.[130] Indeed, Gregory of Nyssa's canonical letter reveals that the canonical tradition itself was perfectly able to think systematically in an abstract and creative manner. Yet Gregory's lead was never followed by the tradition as a whole. Here the odd place of technical formalist discourse in the canons, as explored in Chapter 3, finds a parallel in systematization: techniques and methods of systematization were available, known, and on occasion used, but somehow never constituted a central or compelling concern for the entire tradition.

This clear possibility for more advanced systematic work, yet its apparent rejection, makes it unwise to dismiss these collections as examples of legal primitivism. Instead, it may be best to consider that this phenomenon is simply evidence for a very different set of legal priorities. The nature of

[128] Trans. Somerville and Brasington, 1998, 138–58.

[129] Neither of which, by modern standards, does either task particularly well. On the inner "flow" of the *Digest* titles, see Stolte 2003, 89; Pieler 1997a, 581; see also Pringsheim 1921, 441 on the secular Greek scholiasts' concern for ἀκολουθία. On the general lack of internal systematic coherence in even the ancient secular codes—a commonplace observation—see Hezser 1998, 629–31; also Bretone 1999, 397–8; Gaudemet 1986; Schulz 1936, 53–66; Westbrook 1988. We do well to remember that it took the medieval glossators and commentators centuries to pull an internally coherent *usus* out of the *CJC*.

[130] On these, see Kennedy 1983, O'Meara 2003, and Westerink 2011, with further references.

these priorities may be discerned by considering the central function of the systematic indices—that is, what they are "doing." Their basic function is nothing other than to bring one into closer and easier contact with the canonical texts themselves—and in a fairly direct, literal way. They are connecting one as closely as possible to the actual textual contours of the canonical corpus. Thus, the collections do not select much among their sources, their rubrics do not stray far from the canonical texts themselves, and the arrangement of the texts hardly pushes beyond very simple and conventional patterns already evident in the structure of the individual canonical sources. The indices are consequently not trying to lead one beyond the canons, or to construct a doctrinal edifice into which the canons might then be fitted, or "advance" the law in any other obvious or dramatic way. They are not, in short, a step along the road towards creating "canon law." They are instead facilitating engagement with the original texts themselves, "the canons." To borrow a term from Zechiel-Eckes, they are deeply, and intentionally, *transparent* to the canonical texts.[131]

This concern for transparency is comprehensible if "law" is once again conceived as first and foremost a quasi-sacred body of traditional "laws," in the concrete plural—and not an abstract discipline or constructive project. Any movement away from, or any jurisprudential violation of, these laws is naturally avoided. Certainly any aspect of systematization that might suggest radical structural changes to the material would not make sense—and it is not, indeed, to be found. Juridical rationalization and abstraction, or any other type of systematic development, if not entirely absent, has then a very different place than we might expect today. It appears not as the controlling dynamic of the system as a whole, but as an occasional and tentative suggestion, mostly around the margins. This is especially evident in the overall structuring of the material, where the level of organization evident in the collections is only a slight step up from leaving things as they fall: the absolute priority remains the adherence to the surface contours of the legislation.[132] In effect, order and system are thus manifest only within the limits set by the canons themselves. At best a general coherence with the broader world of late antique legal ordering will be found, which occasionally, barely, verges on imitation. But strong, reconstructive juristic manifestations of systematic rationalization are neither in evidence nor expected.

The patterns of positive shaping that are evident—the assertions of "system" within and onto the material—may, as a result, be best described as symbolic. For example, the shaping of the material into various hierarchies of offices and topics does assert a symbolic, if not legal-doctrinal, sense of

[131] Zechiel-Eckes 1992, 1.37.

[132] Of all the early systematic collections, this is most evident in Cresconius' *Concordia*; see Section D.

systematic comprehensiveness: the rules, in effect, stretch from one end of the cosmic world order to another, and are a natural part of this quasi-sacred order. In this there is an implicit assertion of the canons' internal coherence, but not in a juristic or conceptual sense: the canons are instead "internally coherent" with the whole cosmic order.

More specific symbolic meanings might also be inferred from such structures. For example, the hierarchies of offices and substantive content suggest that canonical order must emerge from rightly ordered hierarchical officials, that disciplinary measures are subordinate to faith issues, or that some matters are more shameful than others. But these structural "messages" are not precepts of a purely juridical type. Instead, they function to embed the canons in specific metaphysical values which it is assumed (correctly) that the canons share and promote. Systematization is thus oriented less towards the advancement of a thorough and consistent application of rules to facts than towards the contextualization of the canons in external narratives of social and ideological ordering.

It hardly needs to be said, but this understanding of systematization remains strikingly coherent with the shape of the law already observed in the processes of growth and physical development of the corpus, the traditions of canonical introduction, and the concerns and textures of the canonical texts themselves. Byzantine legal systematization is above all marked by: (a) textual conservatism and an implicit tendency to treat the texts as sacred (and thus "system" emerges as deeply derivative and exegetical); (b) an identifiable kinship with civil texts, but with few instances of true imitation; and (c) a strong, if implicit, privileging of substantive value contextualization and embedding over autonomous technical juristic development.

Conclusions, Problems, Prospects

This study set out to describe the fundamental categories, values, expectations, assumptions, and structures of Byzantine canon-legal culture through a close reading of the central texts of the Byzantine canonical tradition 381–883. A surprisingly coherent picture of the Byzantine canonical imagination has slowly taken shape.

In Chapter 1 the shape of the law in its broadest, most literal sense—its physical structures and patterns of growth over time—reveals a legal world built around the transmission of an exceptionally unitary and stable body of traditional texts. Textually, Byzantine canon law emerges as the story of one unified collection of texts that slowly grows through the accumulation of sources in a succession of corpus "cores." Patterns of real diversity and radical, system-wide change are nowhere in evidence. Instead, the leitmotif of the system's growth is conservation and accretion, as newer traditions are simply affixed to older ones. The older traditions are almost never permanently lost or ejected: once a text has been accepted as part of the corpus, it is there to stay. Change occurs only through addition.

In this slow process of accretion sources are defined as "valid" or "official" through a very diffuse, mostly unstated process of rule recognition. Despite its vagueness, this process seems to have been remarkably effective. The definition of the corpus never seems to be particularly problematic. The unity and stability of the corpus means that at any given moment "the canons" have a fairly concrete referent. The uncertainty about valid or conflicting sources that we detect in the western tradition in the centuries immediately before the 12th C never finds a clear counterpart in the east: everyone always knows what at least the core corpus of "the canons" is, and this certainty seems, if anything, to have increased over time. Nevertheless, *precise* definition of the corpus is always elusive. The edges of the core are ragged and permeable, and it is surprisingly difficult to find any official definition of the corpus that has definitive, categorical force. The shape of the corpus ultimately seems to be determined through a multitude of implicit decisions of individual compilers and manuscript copyists.

This almost unconscious process of legal definition reflects an aversion to any clear expression of "sovereign authority" over the tradition. No authority ever emerges that claims the power to radically construct or reconstruct, or even definitively define, the corpus. Instead, authorities merely add material, index material, or perhaps clear up particular problems "around the edges." Their function is prototypically to confirm the existing tradition. Ironically, this is most evident in texts that come closest to defining the tradition officially, Trullo 2 or II Nicaea 1. Both define the corpus precisely through self-consciously traditionalist confirmations of long-established usages. Far from functioning as clear expressions of absolute legislative authority, they legitimize the new canons only by firmly anchoring them in traditional trajectories. And neither has the categorical force in the later tradition that one would expect. Their impact is felt only gradually, over time, when they themselves are well-established parts of the corpus. Thus, no clear mechanism of defining the tradition ever establishes itself, and no definitive corpus definition is ever made.

This wariness about expressions of positive authority has a counterpart in the curious absence of any type of sustained jurisprudential literature, or of a class of dedicated legal professionals to produce it. Although it is clear that a jurisprudential handling of rules can and does take place, this never coalesces in our period into a coherent and substantial discourse, nor does it establish itself as an important focus of the system. Byzantine canon law thus does not develop primarily as a jurisprudential construct: no attempt seems to be made to develop a coherent doctrinal architecture of "secondary rules" (to borrow once more a concept from H. L. A. Hart) that governs the interpretation and application of the canons. Jurisprudential principles are never given definitive leave to govern the shape of the law as a whole. Instead, the tradition presents itself as first and foremost a huge, extended project of preserving and faithfully transmitting a set of traditional "primary rules." Even the jurisprudential literature that does exist—and will later expand—is always self-consciously subordinate to the traditional texts, facilitative or exegetical in nature, and very much built *around* and *out of* the traditional canons. This handling of the texts strongly suggests a sense of the tradition as above all constituted by a body of traditional rules of a quasi-sacral nature.

In Chapter 2 the chief concern of the traditional introductions is quickly revealed to be the embedding of the canonical texts in extralegal narratives. The prologues cast the canons as above all part of broader scriptural and metaphysical "stories" of salvation, intimately speaking to and intertwined with questions of morality, virtue, and "life," and highly pedagogical and sacral in character. Technical jurisprudential themes are sounded from time to time, but they are neither especially elaborate nor prominent. The development of an independent jurisprudential discourse, autonomous from moral or metaphysical narratives, seems to be neither a value nor a goal. Value embeddedness is clearly the explicit theoretical objective and priority.

In Chapter 3 the canons can be seen to embody or enact the vision set out in the traditional prologues and implied in the physical shape of the tradition. The points of correspondence are many. In the prologues the canons are cast as highly traditional—and so the canons are written as constantly speaking to and from earlier traditions. In the introductions the canons are framed as oriented towards teaching and encouraging virtue, higher morality, and a proper way of life—and so the canons are frequently concerned with teaching and encouraging precisely these themes. The prologues cast the canons as quasi-scriptural and sacred—sure enough, the canons are littered with sacral self-designations and scriptural quotations, and frequently speak and act in surprisingly sacred registers. In the prologues technical-jurisprudential concepts and processes appear as only rather secondary and desultory concerns—in the canons technical-legal discourse has a similarly irregular and inconsistent place. In the broadest terms, the fundamental concern of the prologues is precisely that of the canons: to embed the rules in innumerable extralegal narratives. The autonomy of the rule system from extralegal narratives is neither an assumed, nor an evident, value. The canons presume that they are functioning alongside and as part of broader systems of normative control.

In the same chapter the lack of the phrase "canon law" emerges as a highly significant terminological peculiarity of Byzantine canonical nomenclature. The phrase's absence gives convenient expression to the historical shape of the tradition sketched in Chapter 1. The Byzantine legal tradition does not emerge as a sealed and well-delineated field of jurisprudential development or action, or as an abstract constructive legal project—all of which is implied in the modern notion of "canon law." Instead, it develops as primarily a diffuse accretion of concrete and plural law traditions. Canon law *is* "the canons." This reality is further reinforced by the Byzantine tendency, also remarked in Chapter 3, to stack different genres and forms one upon the other in the corpus, while the original forms of the sources are left mostly intact. It is equally evident in the highly variable, but mostly casuistic, nature of canonical rule expression. Everywhere it seems that the traditional texts are almost allergic to formal rationalization via homogenization, standardization of form, or most other types of jurisprudential abstraction. The concrete specificity of the traditions, as plural traditions, consistently trumps any homogenizing and rationalizing imperatives of a systematic jurisprudence. The canons never morph into canon law.

In Chapter 4 the deep conservatism of the tradition and its attachment to the traditional texts emerge with special force. The central point of early Byzantine canonical systematization seems to be "law finding" in its most elementary sense: the topical indexing of the canons with the goal of assisting in the locating of the traditional texts applicable to a given problem. Instead of representing complex processes of systematic interpretation or digestion of the tradition, the Byzantine systematic collections are thus deeply transparent to, and derivative from, the traditional texts, often to a surprisingly literal degree. The systematic rubrics thus do not, for the most part, represent attempts to abstract internal concepts or even implied topics or general questions from the canons. They instead adhere closely to the concrete surface contours of the canons themselves. Likewise, instances of interpretation and creative shaping of the material, if not entirely lacking, are mostly notable for their absence. Even the patterns of ordering imposed by the collections upon the corpus hardly represent dramatic reshapings of the tradition. Most are already present in the canonical sources, and are in any case conventional and unremarkable. Nowhere do we see a complex systematic rationalization of the material by internal concepts, in which, for example, gaps in the legislation might be highlighted and filled, or disparate elements of the system related to each other. At best, Byzantine systematization tends towards a symbolic function that, once again, serves ultimately to embed the canons in broader narratives of (cosmic) hierarchal order.

Across all four chapters the relationship of the canons to the civil law has been broached several times. Here another surprising consistency of vision emerges. On the one hand the canonical tradition frequently casts itself as comfortably part of the same general world of formal normativity as the civil law. The canons can share similar physical spaces (i.e. in the manuscripts), similar images, similar definitions, similar dispositive expressions, similar technical vocabulary, and similar forms of order and structure. On the other, the canonical material very rarely directly imitates the civil-legal material: the two laws are usually, if not rigorously, distinguished in nomenclature; their genres and forms are not exactly equivalent; their selection of dispositives is slightly different; the systematic orders of the collections are proprietary in details; and the two laws constitute distinct, delineated masses in the manuscripts. Further, the canonical tradition does at times theoretically distinguish itself from the civil law. As a result, both radical dissociation and radical assimilation are avoided: the canons emerge as neither an especially or radically "other" type of legal reality, nor an ecclesial mirror of the Roman civil system (as happens more clearly in the west during the high medieval period). The relationship between the two is always one of "similar, but not the same." This relationship, however, never finds clear doctrinal articulation. It is negotiated through indirect, literary means.

Surveying all of these observations, we may now attempt a description of the basic conceptual architecture of Byzantine canon law as a legal phenomenon. Three principal characteristics may be proposed. The first, and chief, is the concern to preserve, transmit, and exegete one core corpus of continuously fossilizing quasi-sacral traditional texts. These traditional texts *are* the law. They are not exactly sources of canon law, nor expressions of canon law, since "canon law" is not (or at least not primarily) an abstract project or doctrinal construct. Canon law is instead a concrete set of specific traditional texts gathered in a reasonably well-defined corpus, which may expand and grow but otherwise remains mostly invulnerable to change. The faithful "traditioning" and explication of these semi-sacred legal texts is the central concern and task of the system.

This emphasis on law in the plural, as an assemblage of concrete quasi-sacral traditions, is accompanied by a lack of interest in the development of a proprietary and sustained jurisprudential discourse. The absence of a complex legal-doctrinal architecture points towards Byzantine canon law's second major characteristic: Byzantine canon law is a "substantive justice system" (to borrow a category from Max Weber[1]). That is, the tradition is clearly oriented towards finding the truly just and correct answer to every problem, and not simply a formally correct legal solution. In such a "substantive" system, as Arthur Diamond has succinctly put it, "[t]he ruling internal principle (if it can be called such) is that justice should be done."[2] As a result, the system is not primarily designed as a coherent and predictable mechanism of legal concepts and techniques, safely isolated from "values" and any other external variables that might disturb its equilibrium, that is, its ability to produce a consistently correct "legal" answer. Instead, quite the opposite: the system is deeply and intentionally invested in embedding itself in broader narratives by which truly just decisions might be measured. In effect, then, the central instinct of the system is that to get law right, you must get scripture right, doctrine right, morality right, psychological dispositions right, Greco-Roman concepts of justice right, and so on. In a sense, the secondary rules of the system, the jurisprudential rules, principles, and definitions, which seem to be so lacking, are furnished—and quite intentionally so—by a huge set of broader cultural images and narratives of "the just." These are assumed to be reasonably stable, the subject of broad consensus, and easily accessible.

This substantive, embedded quality of Byzantine canon law explains the lack of professional canon lawyers. The system is clearly not written for a cadre of professional rule experts proficient at operating a complex and proprietary system of procedures and rules. Instead, it is designed for "culture experts," educated amateurs who are able to negotiate correctly the mass of cultural narratives that must be brought to bear on any particular issue. Technical aspects of legal reasoning are not absent, but they are not primary. Their place is analogous to that of the assessor in the late Roman courtroom: present, but off to the side, advising the judge, but not the judge.[3]

[1] See Ch. 2 C.1, esp. at n. 113. [2] Diamond 1950, 30.
[3] On the assessors, see Jones 1964, 499–507.

Finally, the entire system—not merely its textual life—is dominated by the notion of tradition.[4] Although never stated explicitly as such, this may be regarded as the system's controlling motif: tradition legislates, tradition adjudicates, and tradition interprets. First, as we have already noted, tradition, in the form of the traditional texts, is the law itself. Further, the prologues and canons constantly anchor the canonical task in a network of traditional references and sources: legitimate normativity arises primarily from linking laws into broader traditions of the just and right. Similarly, the exceptionally conservative nature of the systematic collections reveals a deep—at times almost bizarre—concern to adhere as closely as possible to traditional forms. Most remarkably, however, the dynamics of official definition reflect this instinct. Sohm long ago noted that, in the *altkatholisch* church, authoritative legislation always emerges from the past; more recent authorities, however exalted (council, pope, jurist, etc.), always remain subordinate to past traditions.[5] Indeed, as we have seen, changing and even adding to Byzantine canon law is strangely awkward: only time lends real confidence. Categorical assertions *in the present* of authority over the tradition are thus quite difficult to find. In particular, the two most common forms of asserting authority over the tradition—the idea of a "sovereign" positive legislative authority or of a rationalized jurisprudence that, through the application of juristic principles, has the ability to modify the tradition itself—are never particularly evident or explicit in the Byzantine texts. Additions, changes, and interpretations instead emerge warily, apologetically, and inconspicuously, often around the edges of the tradition, and often almost downplaying their own prominence. This strange evasiveness reflects the implicit assumption that tradition itself, as a diffuse process of consensus building over time, is the only real authority able to promulgate, modify, or ratify the law.

Curiously, however, this idea of "tradition" does not completely exclude modification or even confrontation. Throughout our period this is quite evident in the canons themselves, which frequently modify older rules. Likewise, as we have seen, the prologues assume explicitly the slow, continuous growth of the system. Tradition is not, therefore, a doctrinal principle with systematically stultifying consequences, as if it were a modern concept of the unchangeability of the canons or of their "infallibility."[6] Nor, for that matter, is it a category of legislative source (compare "customary law"). It is instead a

[4] The idea of the centrality of "tradition" in first-millennium canon law was already a major theme of Sohm's; see especially his idea of tradition, and not the church, as "infallible" (Sohm 1923, 2.65–7). Kuttner 1950, 357 also contrasts the "dialectical rationalization" of the 12th C and the "linear traditionalism" of the previous period. Cf. also Glenn 2007 for his fascinating account of the role of tradition in "chthonic" ("primitive") legal systems.

[5] Sohm 1923, 2.75.

[6] These concepts have much exercised modern Orthodox canon law. See (among others) Afanasiev 1936, Archontonis 1970, Boumis 2000, Ohme 1991.

cultural predilection towards the systematic downplaying of anything being done "now." It is more of an instinct than a principle.

These three characteristics—the emphasis on laws, not law; an orientation towards substantive justice; and the overwhelming dominance of the idea of tradition—constitute the three central pillars of Byzantine canon-legal "theory."

These pillars may be somewhat disconcerting to the modern legal historian. Is this what a European legal system of the Roman tradition is supposed to look like? The dissonance between this world and the formalist legal system sketched in the Introduction is certainly striking. In part, of course, the degree of dissonance may be an artifact of the present work's methodology. My constant counterposing of the phenomena in the Byzantine texts with a caricatured formalist "foil" has no doubt made the contrast particularly sharp. I may also have fallen unconsciously into the trap of orientalism, that is, of subtly favouring conclusions that present Byzantine culture as the shadowy opposite and "other" of the western experience.

Nevertheless, even if we allow for these possibilities, it remains difficult not to read Byzantine canon law as a very real counterpoint to the formalist instincts of mainstream civil-legal culture as it has developed in Europe since the high middle ages. In the latter, clear definition of the nature and domain of law as an autonomous field of social practice is critical, while in the former a "fuzzy" process of self-embedding in broader value narratives is the central concern. The one prefers clear, logical rules; the other messy, rhetorical ones. The one places high value on precision, internal consistency, and gaplessness, while the other is quite happy to tolerate high degrees of inconsistency, ambiguity, and legislative lacunae. The one is very wary about discretion and equity, while the other seems systematically to prefer and assume both. The one is deeply invested in professional infrastructure; the other is not. The one tends to be highly malleable, instrumental, and "secular," the other static, sacral, and inviolable. The one is centered on deriving legality and justice from the logical application of rules; the other is focused on deriving legality and justice from a polyvalent engagement with tradition. The one assumes a high degree of value plurality; the other assumes—and instills—a high degree of value uniformity. Very broadly, the one is "mechanical," almost technological, in operation and orientation, while the other is much more literary. Almost all of the most sacred doctrines of traditional formalism—of any flavor—are thus contradicted: autonomy, systematic coherence, predictability, constructability, and clear bivalence in rule recognition and application (valid vs. invalid). These points of contrast are too profound and systemic to be dismissed as merely a function of orientalist prejudice or the overly broad strokes of my presentation of formalism.

Of course we must not draw this contrast too sharply. The present work's investigation of canonical language and style has shown that the Byzantines were at times quite capable of engaging in formalist-like legal discourse. Indeed, Byzantine canon law, simply as a collection of formal written rules, does present itself as a "formalist" system in the most basic sense of presuming that a wide variety of factual situations can be addressed by a series of more or less general rules. One might quite suspect, in fact, that the vast majority of Byzantine canonical disputes were solved by reasonably straightforward application of rules in a manner that would not seem at all out of place in a modern formalist system. One only needs to quickly peruse the extant conciliar *acta* to become convinced of the ability of the Byzantine church to transact its affairs in quite technical, formalist-like ways.[7]

Nevertheless—and this is a critical conclusion of the present study—the system as a whole was clearly not *designed* or *written* as a formalist–positivist system. The structures and paraphernalia of legal formalism never constitute what we most expect them to: the basic framework of Byzantine canon law's conceptualization. Formalism and its values neither emerge as the clear ideals of the system, nor do they suggest themselves as in any way the locus of the system's central instincts, habits, intentions, or beliefs. In this sense, then, Byzantine canon law does represent a clear inverse of most modern western legal systems: the latter are conceived as fundamentally structured along formalist lines, but containing some substantive-justice elements. Byzantine law (at least church law) emerges as quite the opposite: it is fundamentally a substantive-justice system that contains some formalist elements. Further, and critically, this orientation is quite consistent across the whole system: in physical form, expressed theory, literary textures, and the systematic handling of the material. This orientation is not, therefore, explicable as an unintentional deviation or devolution from some other ideal: it is clearly how the system is *supposed* to work. It is an ideal in itself.

It is the very intentionality and consistency of these values that render narratives of decline, decadence, or primitivism unconvincing as models for the study of Byzantine canon law. In particular, the old paradigm of the eternal defectiveness of late Roman and Byzantine legal phenomena suddenly looks very much out of place—or at least beside the point—when the conclusions of this study are taken into account. It is precisely the odd and "defective" characteristics of Byzantine law that seem to be most valued by the Byzantines themselves. It is, therefore, preferable to read these characteristics as evidence for a very different set of cultural priorities. Likewise, the notion that Byzantine canon law was somehow superseded by a more "evolved" high-medieval successor is not compelling. From a Byzantine perspective—a perspective that does not seem to value formalism—it might even be possible, with Sohm, to consider these later formalist developments as something of a devolution! But

[7] Price and Gaddis 2005 offer an excellent platform for such a study.

clearly it is preferable not to engage in evolutionary/devolutionary modeling at all.

This unseating of formalism as a meaningful measure of "proper" legal culture suggests a reorientation of our legal-cultural questions. Traditionally, the "problem" or "mystery" of Byzantine legal history has been its deviation from formalist–positivist norms. The present work, following on that of Dieter Simon and others, suggests quite the opposite: the "problem" or "mystery" is now the formalist–positivist elements themselves! Why and to what extent do they emerge at all? What triggers them? When do they appear? Disappear? What exactly is their role and function within the system as a whole (since they are not the controlling or framework concepts)? And, perhaps mostly intriguingly, why does Byzantine canon law develop in such a different direction from Latin canon law in this respect?

A variety of social or political explanations may be offered to these questions. Here I will merely note how troubling this problem is from a theoretical perspective. The rub is that the Byzantines did understand and were capable of technical-legal discourse of a formalist–positivist variety. This precludes the usual "primitivism" explanation. Yet they did not systematically employ or prefer this discourse. This is extremely upsetting from a formalist perspective. The point (supposedly) of such formalist discourse is that it is meant to be employed regularly and consistently. In Byzantine hands, however, it often appears—ironically—as almost decorative, "rhetorical," or perhaps opportunistic and supplementary. Dieter Simon recognized this problem when he noted that, in the *Πεῖρα*, Eustathius does engage in very rational, even technically coherent arguments—but only sometimes.[8] He noted that particular cases will often be very well argued and internally coherent, but across the *Πεῖρα* as a whole legal argument is very inconsistent: certain technical terms and arguments will be employed in one place but not in a very similar context elsewhere.[9] Others scholars have noted similar phenomena, where technical-legal principles will be employed occasionally but not always, and not necessarily as a definitive argument.[10] Formalist rule reasoning is apparently possible, then, but not regular and sustained. I have come to the same conclusion: formalist discourse emerges occasionally, but it is strangely desultory. *It comes and goes.*

The best explanation for this phenomenon is perhaps to be extrapolated from Simon's suggestion that laws function as a kind of rhetorical instrument. In effect, formalist legal arguments and operations might be best conceived as one element among others in the Byzantine rhetorical toolbox, applicable where appropriate and necessary. This recalls Aristotle's famous, if disconcerting, classification of laws as a type of *proof*, not as structurally

[8] Simon 1973, 13–23 *et passim*. [9] Simon 1973, 27–9.

[10] For some examples, see the references in the Introduction, nn. 29–32, esp. n. 30.

determinative elements of the legal system as a whole.[11] Law is thus, in essence, a subset of rhetoric. "Rhetoric," however, needs to be understood here not so much as a technical art of persuasion but as a cognitive predilection for understanding the world through a formalized, aesthetic manipulation of a common pool of literary authorities, images, and narratives. Law and legal practice thus emerge as primarily a "literary" negotiation of conventional narratives of the just and the good, and only secondarily as a "science" of norms and their application. Formalist argumentation is thus employed only when these conventional narratives permit its use—in effect, only when it is in good taste.

Even if this is the case, understanding this "rhetorical" legal-cultural world is challenging—and probably will remain so for some time. Its instincts and emphases fit only very awkwardly within the horizons of traditional late Roman and European legal history. Future research will have to reach outside of these worlds, and their standard models, to find suitable categories and models.

Looking forward, one may identify several areas of research that need to become more prominent as we continue to chart the cultural landscape of this ancient legal world. One of these is legal anthropology. As noted in the Introduction, the description of Byzantine law that has emerged in this work is already much indebted to the legal anthropological theorization of so-called "primitive" legal systems.[12] But we have only scratched the surface of this field. Further, and deeper, engagement with this discipline will no doubt prove very fruitful.

Eastern Christian canonical literature also warrants more careful examination than it has received. Orthodox canonists have long been aware of the curious dynamics of their own legal system. This is particularly evident in their constant anxiety about whether the Byzantine canonical tradition can be considered properly "legal" from a modern (civilian-)legal perspective, and their consequent attempts to find formulations to describe the often uncooperative legal dynamics of the traditional texts. Many of their observations, although cast in theological form, resonate with the results of this work.[13] These cannot be explored in depth here, but among the most important are the notion that eastern orthodox church law cannot be separated from broader dogmatic narratives; that modern formalist juristic categories do not fit the traditional texts well; that change in the system does not happen as in modern legal systems; that the laws are surprisingly sacral in orientation; that the canons are very much concerned about morality, broader questions of life, and virtue, and are highly pedagogical in orientation; that the texts are strangely

[11] *Rhetoric* 1.15. [12] See the Introduction, esp. n. 54.

[13] Here may be mentioned esp. Erickson 1991, L'Huillier 1964, Meyendorff 1978a, Patsavos (Kapsanis) 1999, Phidas 1998. Cf. also now McGuckin 2012.

allergic to formalism; and that tradition is a central concept. In fact, eastern orthodox canonists have long known what this work has concluded: that the Byzantine legal world, if not totally "other," does not easily conform to modern formalist expectations. Formulae noted in the Introduction, such as "canonical consciousness" or "jurisprudence of the Holy Spirit," strive to convey this ambiguity.

We also need to investigate more carefully the influence of ancient Greek legal thought on Byzantine law.[14] This avenue of study is little in evidence today, but this is a serious oversight. While the image of law that has emerged in this work conforms in many respects quite poorly to our (traditional) formalist image of Roman jurisprudence, it is striking how well it echoes ancient Greek and Hellenistic patterns. Especially resonant is the rhetorical-literary texture of Greek law that has been emphasized so strongly in recent Greek legal scholarship.[15] Like Byzantine canon law, the entire classical Greek cultural tradition does not seem to privilege formalist or "scientific" jurisprudential work at all—and, as is well known, hardly contains any examples of it.[16] Indeed, one might detect in Hellenic legal literature a stigmatization of formal rule work and rule reasoning, and of rules generally. Plato's vision of law, for example, tends to cast laws as somewhat unfortunate necessities, ideally to be transcended, but if not, then justified only by their assimilation to educational tools and as the necessary instrument of the divine philosopher-king.[17] Strict rule adherence of straight commands is thus mostly a matter for slaves—not for the free, for whom law functions as yet one more means to the ethical education of the soul, and is to be persuasive and rational, not coercive.[18] Certainly, for Plato law is much more about virtue than rule adherence per se, subordinated to justice, and part of a much broader pedagogical program.[19] Greek rhetoric too, despite a developed forensic

[14] The influence of Greek law on Roman law has not infrequently been the subject of research, most notably in the work of Ludwig Mitteis and his school, but the tendency has been to seek Hellenic continuity in specific legal doctrines and institutions instead of in the overall conceptualization, stylization, and valuation of legal practices—where I suspect its influence is to be felt much more profoundly.

[15] See esp. the studies in Gagarin and Cohen 2005.

[16] e.g. Jones 1956, 292–308; Todd 1993, 10–17; Triantaphyllopoulos 1985, 31–5; Wolf 1975.

[17] On Plato's general legal theory, in a variety of contexts, Cohen 1995, 43–51; Dvornik 1966, 1.179–83 *et passim*; Jones 1956, 1–23; Kleinknecht and Gutbrod 1942, 1025–35; Laks 2000; Letwin 2005, 9–41; O'Meara 2003; Romilly 1971, 179–201; Rowe 2000; Schofield 2000. There are various ways of harmonizing Plato's sometimes contradictory statements about law, but there can be little doubt that the *Rechtsstaat* is a distinctly second-best solution.

[18] See esp. *Laws* 720–3. Cf. Lendon 1997, 236, where it is noted that the mechanical-like operation of a modern rationalized bureaucracy is better compared to a Roman slave workhouse than the Roman government.

[19] See e.g. Plato, *Laws* 630–1, 643e, 653b, 705d–6a; also Gagarin 2000. Aristotle's *Politics* tends in much the same direction.

tradition, with its unquestionable ability to function as a surrogate jurisprudence,[20] had a notably minor and even stigmatized place for real legal reasoning of a modern formalist flavor: argumentation is prototypically about questions of moral qualities of persons and substantive justice.[21] Even classical Greek procedure, embedded and preserved for late antiquity in the canonical rhetorical speeches, seems to have had a marked distaste for formalism, allowing considerable latitude to judges in arriving at decisions, unfettered by technical and strict rule adherence and even laws—very much as observed in the *Πεῖρα*, in fact.[22] All of this suggests that the rhetorical-literary character of Byzantine law, although disconcerting from some perspectives, might be read as quite coherent and expected within a broader Greek legal-cultural trajectory.

One may further wonder if this Hellenic trajectory informed even Roman civil-legal culture much more than is generally assumed. John Lendon and Peter Brown have demonstrated that imperial, and especially late antique, aristocratic power culture was dominated by relatively informal, yet deeply internalized, codes of *paideia*, friendship, and honor. Into this world technical, formalist dispute resolution fits only awkwardly.[23] Late antique legislation too, with its sacral epithets, morally and religiously charged language, and issuing from emperors who are themselves steeped in the Platonic/Hellenistic model of kingship as a semi-divine mediator between heaven and earth, the "law animate," hardly encourages the conceptualization of laws as the highly manipulatable and instrumental rules of a modern secular formalism–positivism. They seem much more like the numinous, divine mandates of a sacred law.[24] Certainly, the well-known rhetorical texture of late antique laws does not render the laws easily "computable" in a logical rule calculus. Instead, it implies a much more literary manner of employment in a complex and sophisticated set of value negotiations. All of this suggests that a "Greek" rhetorical or literary paradigm may be much more appropriate for understanding the broad dynamics of late Roman civil law than has generally been recognized.

[20] This is a commonplace observation. See e.g Calhoun 1944, 58–63; Jones 1956, 298–308. More broadly Bederman 2001; Brasington 1994, 227–8; Humfress 2007, 9–28, 62–132 (and pp. 3, 25 for references to the older debate of the influence of rhetoric on Roman law; also, Humfress 1998, 73–80); Winterbottom 1982. Ancient rhetoric, if far from suggesting a formalist legal science, is fully capable of providing a quasi-technical framework for the operation of legal argumentation, as stasis theory makes plain (see esp. Heath 1995).

[21] Heath 1995, 76–7, 141–2, 294; Morgan 1998, 234–5; Todd 2005; Yunis 2005, 202–4.

[22] Cohen 1995; Gagarin 2005a, 34–6; Lanni 2005; Sealey 1994, 51–7; Todd 1993, 58–60; Yunis 2005.

[23] Brown 1992, 35–70; Lendon 1997, 176–236.

[24] On this complex of images and concepts, its continuity and its (increasing) dominance in late antiquity, see Centrone 2000; Dvornik 1966, 2.672–723 (on the Christian usages; on the Greek, 1.132–277); Fögen 1987, 1993, 43–9; Garnsey 2000; Garnsey and Humfress 2001, 25–51; Kelly 1998; also Enßlin 1943.

Finally, and perhaps most importantly, we may need to expand our understanding of the broader Byzantine intellectual and conceptual world before we can further assimilate this strange world of law. At first blush, the self-representation of Byzantine canon law that has emerged in this work should not surprise the Byzantine historian. The law appears as sacral, unchangeable (certainly change is ponderously slow), florilegic, traditional, and hieratic. Its hallmarks are continuity and stability. These are all stereotypes of Byzantine self-representation. Indeed, like much Byzantine art and literature, Byzantine canon law seems strangely numinous and "unrealistic," suffused with symbolism, dogmatic and moral meanings, and stock *figurae*. The picture of law that has emerged from this work is thus, in a way, conventionally Byzantine.

And yet, even for the Byzantinist the picture of law delineated in this work may not be easily accepted. Whereas in artistic and literary works—iconography, hagiography, or even historiography—the strangely traditional, moralizing, and hieratic habits of Byzantine culture are not difficult to accommodate, in law these same characteristics are jarring. Our cultural instinct is to think of law as exceptionally secular, instrumental, and quasi-mechanical: law qua law is supposed to be a very human rule game, easily modified and reshaped, and often amoral in its operation—a nitty-gritty negotiation of competing power interests. And critically, *it is supposed to be understood as such by its practitioners.* But we cannot avoid the conclusion that the Byzantines seem to have been trying very hard not to see their canon law this way. They cast it instead as a very high-status, sacral matter: inviolable, aesthetically significant, and deeply rooted in the master narratives of Christian salvation and Greco-Roman philosophical advancement.

This dissonance is so great that our temptation is to downplay or to dismiss it altogether: "the Byzantines were *really* thinking of law as we do." Indeed, Byzantine cultural historians often are tasked with penetrating the static, sacral self-representation of the Byzantines in order to arrive at the more dynamic and mundane (and recognizable) reality underneath.[25] But here our challenge may be the opposite. Our task may be to try to understand how this self-representation *was* in some sense the Byzantine reality. In effect, we are being confronted with the possibility that the Byzantines had the cultural means—which we perhaps do not—of conceiving of something as real-world and mundane as law in a truly very different way than we do now. Since law is such a fundamental part of any civilization's sociocultural fabric, this dissonance is disconcerting. It certainly highlights the great distance between "us" and "them," the present and this long-dead world. But it challenges us to ask whether we have yet formulated a truly satisfactory

[25] Cf. Paul Lemerle's famous warning that "to represent Byzantium as immutable over a period of eleven centuries is to fall into a trap set by Byzantium itself" (*Cinq études sur le XIe siècle byzantin* (Paris, 1977), 251, cited in Magdalino 1999, 115).

paradigm for understanding how this strangely literary, associative, and rhetorically charged world of thought and belief actually "worked." And here, perhaps, the greatest difficulty is coming to terms not only with the points of difference, but with the unsettling combination of these differences with much that is familiar. The Byzantine icon does share features with modern portraiture; the Byzantine saint's life is not entirely unlike modern biography; the Byzantine declamation is akin to the modern political speech; the Byzantine history sometimes reads like a modern history—and Byzantine canon law is still recognizable today as law. And yet the overall complexion is very different.

APPENDIX A

Prefaces and Epilogues to the Byzantine Canonical Collections

Formal prologues may be found prefacing four Byzantine canonical collections:

Table A1. Prologues and Epilogues: Principal Collections.

Collection	Introductory texts, by incipit (with editions)
Coll50, *c.*550	Prologue: *Οἱ τοῦ μεγάλου θεοῦ* . . . (*Syn* 4–7) (Epilogue: the "Apostolic Epilogue," used to conclude the last title, may be considered the collection's functional epilogue; see Chapter 2 B.2)
Coll14 and later recensions, *c.*580 and later	Prologue I (*c.*580): *Τὰ μὲν σώματα* . . . (*Pitra* 2.445–7) Prologue II (*a.* 883): *Ὁ μὲν παρὼν πρόλογος* . . . (*Pitra* 2.448–50) Prologue IIIa (*a.* 1089): *Γέγονεν οὕτω καὶ ταῦτα* . . . (Longer version by the *σεβαστός* Michael) (Schminck 1998, 360–1) Prologue IIIb (*a.* 1092): *Γέγονεν οὕτω καὶ ταῦτα* . . . (Abbreviated version by the *βέστης* Theodore) (Schminck 1998, 359)
Σύνταγμα κατὰ στοιχεῖον of Matthew Blastares, *a.* 1334/5	"*Προθεωρία*": *Τὸ τῶν ἱερῶν καὶ θείων* . . . (*RP* 6.1–30) This is the most comprehensive prologue in the tradition, borrowing extensively from earlier introductory material, and incorporating a synodal history.
Ἐπιτομὴ κανόνων of Constantine Harmenopoulos, *c.*1346	"*Προθεωρία*": *Τῶν κανόνων οἱ μέν εἰσι* . . . (Leunclavius 1596, 1.1 unpaginated) = *PG* 150.45–50

Two smaller, supplementary collections also contain short prefaces:

Table A2. Prologues and Epilogues: Supplementary Collections.

Collection	Introductory texts (and editions)
Coll87, *c.*550	Epigraph: *Ἐκ τῶν μετὰ τὸν κώδικα* . . . "*Πρόλογος*": *Εἰς δόξαν τοῦ μεγάλου θεοῦ* . . . (Heimbach 1838, 2.280)
Σύνοψις τῶν θείων κανόνων of Arsenius of Philotheou, 12th or 13th C?	Short preface-heading: *Παρακειμένων ἑκάστῳ καὶ τῶν ἁρμοζόντων* . . . (Voellus and Justel 1661, 2.749 = *PG* 133.9)

The three classical 12th C commentaries contain introductory structure. Those of Zonaras and Balsamon are particularly extensive:

Table A3. Prologues and Epilogues: Commentators.

Collection	Introductory texts (and editions)
Aristenos, *c.*1130	Epigraph: *Νομοκάνονον σὺν θεῷ* . . . (Zachariä von Lingenthal 1887, 255–6)
Zonaras, after 1159	Epigraph: *Ἐξήγησις τῶν ἱερῶν καὶ θείων* . . . (*RP* 2.1) "*Προοίμιον*": *Ἡ δήλωσις τῶν λόγων σου* . . . (*RP* 2.1–2)
Balsamon, in stages, *c.*1177–93	Introductory verses: *Ἀστέρες ὡς πολύφωτοι* . . . (*RP* 1.1–3) *Τὰς κανονικὰς εὐσεβεῖς* . . . (*RP* 1.3–4) Epigraph: *Ἐξήγησις τῶν ἱερῶν καὶ θείων κανόνων* . . . (*RP* 2:31) Prologue: *Πείθεσθε τοῖς ἡγουμένοις ὑμῶν* . . . (*RP* 2:31–3) "*Ἐπίλογος*": *Τὴν Μωσαϊκὴν ἀναμετρήσας πλάνην* . . . (Horna 1903, 201)

Two other introductory texts may be found in the manuscripts:

Table A4. Prologues and Epilogues: Other.

Text	Edition
Verses prefacing Rome Vallic. F.10, 10th/11th C	*Νόμος μὲν αὐτὸς ὡς κανὼν ὡς εὐθύτης* . . . (*Pitra* 2.452 = *Sbornik* 244)
Epilogue following conciliar canons in Oxford Baroc.26, 10th/11th C	*Ἰδοὺ προεγράφησαν οἱ τῶν ἁγίων ἀποστόλων* . . . (*Sbornik* 318–19)

Many manuscripts contain broader introductory structures, i.e. sets of articles near the beginning of the manuscripts that usually accompany and are interwoven with the collection prologues and tables of contents. These have yet to be systematically studied.[1] The most common introductory texts seem to be the Apostolic Epitome material,[2] conciliar histories,[3] hierarchical lists of sees (*τάξεις προκαθεδρίας*),[4] and occasional doctrinal or liturgical articles.[5]

Within the corpus itself a number of sources contain prologues, epilogues, or canons that function in an introductory manner.[6] These are Dionysius (epilogue);

[1] The introductory items listed by Beneshevich for the recensions described in *Sbornik* 131–2, 192–3, 244–6 are quite typical.

[2] See Ch. 2 B.2.

[3] Burgmann 1999, 611 suggests that these are to be found in almost all canonical manuscripts (although not always in the introductory sections); certainly they are very common. See the data in *Sbornik*, *Sin*, and Munitiz 1974; 1978.

[4] See e.g. that of Vatican gr. 640 published in Beneshevich 1927, 131–55; see also more broadly Darrouzès 1981.

[5] See e.g. those in Cambridge Univ. Ee iv 29, Escorial X.III.2, Milan Ambros. E. 94 supp., Oxford Rawl G.1.58, Paris gr. 1263, Vatican gr. 640.

[6] Sometimes the epistolary introductions are removed, e.g. in Oxford Rawl G. 158, although here they are later re-added to the manuscript by a later scribe in a separate section. See also *Sources* 91.

Gangra (synodical epistle, including epilogue); Antioch (synodical epistle); Gregory of Nyssa (prologue and epilogue); Basil (epistolary introductions to letters 188, 199, 218; canon 84 is also epilogue-like); Constantinople (προσφωνητικόν); Carthage 1 and 2 (and more generally the framing Apiarian dossier); Cyril 1; Chalcedon 1; Trullo (προσφωνητικὸς λόγος and canons 1 and 2), and II Nicaea 1. Similarly, *Coll14* 1.1–3, treating theology, sources, and the force of unwritten law—very much in imitation of the opening sections of the civil codices—may be considered introductory in content.

In addition, canonical sources are usually prefaced in the manuscripts by short epigraphical notes indicating the name of the synod, its place, and sometimes the number of canons in the source, the number of fathers in conciliar sources, and/or a date. To judge from the current editions, and supplementary texts published by Beneshevich, these seem quite stable throughout the tradition, very often identical from manuscript to manuscript, or with only small variations, usually abbreviations.[7] Sometimes they may be found prefaced by short extended historical ὑποθέσεις; one set may be found in Beneshevich's Group A manuscripts of the *Coll50*, and the commentators provide another.[8]

Individual canons may also be prefaced by summary rubrics. Rather common in Latin canon law manuscripts,[9] these rubrics seems to be much less frequent in Greek manuscripts. From Beneshevich (*Kormchaya*, and descriptions in *Sbornik* and *Sin*), much of *RP*, and the author's own examination of the manuscripts, they seem to be regular only in Carthage and II Nicaea. Joannou, however, has systematically inserted rubrics into the entire corpus. His principal source is the manuscript Vienna hist. gr. 7, a rare reverse index to the *Coll50*, published as the *Index Vindobonensis* by Beneshevich (*Syn* 191–223).[10] Joannou has re-added these rubrics in the intriguing belief that this manuscript preserves rubrics originally present in the Antiochian corpus, since they are similar to Dionysius' rubrics (their relationship with the very early rubrics in London BL Syr 14,528 remains to be investigated). Mardirossian, however, is rather reserved on this point.[11] Occasionally the source of Joannou's later rubrics is not entirely clear (e.g. for Trullo or Hagia Sophia).

Finally, Michael Psellus' poem *Περὶ νομοκανόνου καὶ τῶν τοπικῶν συνόδων* may be considered an element of Byzantine canonical introduction, because it is not only one of the very few extant descriptions of a canonical work but also seems to be introductory in intent.[12] One other description of the tradition, in prose, and much simpler, may be found in Paris gr. 1182;[13] see also the description of the "Ten Synods" in Florence Laur. 5.22.[14]

[7] Compare those published in *Sin* and *Sbornik* (for the multiple recensions of the *Coll50* and *Coll14*), *Kormchaya*, *RP*, *Pitra*, and *Fonti*. In *RP* they are sometimes missing (e.g. Ephesus, II Nicaea) and often in footnotes (e.g. Ancyra, Nicaea, Chalcedon).

[8] *Sin* 33–67; *RP* 1–4.

[9] See Fransen 1973, 17, 33.

[10] Discussion in *Fonti* 1.1.8–10; also *Fonti* 2.1.xxiii–xxiv. On the contents of Vienna hist. gr. 7, see *Sin* 108–26.

[11] Mardirossian 2010, 261–2.

[12] ed. Westerink 1992, 77–80. *Peges* 249–50; cf. 206–7. It may be found as an introductory article in Vatican gr. 2184.

[13] ed. Heimbach 1838, 2.299–300.

[14] ed. *Sbornik* 83 n. 3.

APPENDIX B

Translations

Οἱ τοῦ μεγάλου θεοῦ [*c.*550]

[Edition: Syn *4–7]*

The disciples and apostles of our great God and Savior Jesus Christ, and also those bishops and teachers of his holy church who succeeded them and were like to them,[1] were entrusted by grace to shepherd in holiness the multitude of those from the Gentiles and Jews who had abandoned diabolical deception and tyranny and had of their own accord come in right mind and faith to the King and Lord of glory. These men did not think that they ought, as the civil laws do, to harm wrongdoers (for this seemed altogether simple-minded and very negligent), but instead were zealous to brave dangers most readily for their flock and to turn aright those who were going astray. Like the Good Shepherd, they hastened without hesitation after any who were wandering or veering from the straight path, and they struggled to draw up by all manner of means those who have already fallen headlong into the pit. With great wisdom and skill they cut off with the knife of the Spirit that which was already putrid and far gone, while that which was only damaged and weakened[2] they bound with various soft medicines and rational dressings.[3] Thus, by the grace and coworking of the Spirit they restored to their first health those who were ill.

In order that those who would succeed and be like to them might preserve unharmed those ruled by them, each thrice-blessed generation[4] has come together in its own proper time, when divine grace has arranged it and has gathered them into the assembly of each of their synods, in order that they may issue certain laws and canons (not civil, but divine) on what ought or what ought not be done, thus reforming the life and manner of each person. These canons fortify those who are journeying on the royal way, and penalize those who have fallen by the side.

Of old and at various times laws and canons of the church have been issued by different men for different purposes and appropriate to different circumstances (for there have been ten great synods of the fathers after the apostles, and in addition to

[1] *οἱ μετ' ἐκείνους καὶ κατ' ἐκείνους*. It is not entirely clear whether *κατ' ἐκείνους* should be translated in the sense "were like to them," i.e. acted in a way "according to them," "following their manner." Another, perhaps more likely, rendering would be "those at their time"—so Zaozerski 1882, 106 ("после них и при них бывшие") and *Pitra* 2.375 ("tam qui illorum temporibus, tam qui post illos fuere"). But this reads rather oddly in light of the order of the phrase ("those who came after them and those at their time"). We would expect the opposite, and indeed, Pitra has reversed it. It also makes little sense in this meaning when it reappears in 4.14, if Beneshevich is right, with some of the MSS, to reinsert the phrase here. The grammars do not seem to decide the question definitively, although the temporal meaning is probably more normal, especially with personal subjects (Kühner 1869, 2.1.411–14; Schwyzer 1939, 2.478–479; Smyth 1956, 380).

[2] Lit. "loosened" (*λυόμενος*). [3] *δεσμοὶ λογικοί*.

[4] *τούτων ἕκαστοι . . . οἱ τρισμακάριοι . . .*

these Basil the Great ruled on many matters). Naturally, because of this, the canons have been written by them in a scattered[5] manner, as demanded by the emergence of matters at different times, and not in a subject-matter order, divided among chapters. As a result it is altogether most difficult to find in one place the materials pertaining to one rule.[6] Because of this, by the grace of our Lord and God and Savior Jesus Christ, we have undertaken to gather together into one place their scattered regulations from different times, and we have divided them into fifty titles. We have not preserved a numerical order and progression—joining, as it were, the first canon to the second, to the third, to the fourth, to the fifth, and so on—but rather, as much as possible, have harmonized like matters with like, and woven the same chapter together with the same, and so have made it easy for everyone, I think, to find that which they seek without trouble. We have not been the only or first to have applied ourselves to this task, but have found that others have divided the material into sixty titles, neither joining the canons of Basil to the others, nor harmonizing like subjects to like. Because of this, one finds in the titles many canons under one chapter and it is difficult to grasp all the regulations on one subject. We have, as much as possible, made a clearer division of the canons by a juxtaposition of similar material, with, in addition, an inscription for each title which clearly indicates the content[7] of the subsumed material.

The order of the synods after the apostles, and how many canons each issued, and how many also Basil the Wondrous composed, is easily determined from what follows—for thus presented it is clear and very easily comprehended[8] for those who wish to read it.

The holy disciples and apostles of the Lord issued, through Clement, 85 canons. After them were their successors, as is here set forth in order.

The order of the synods.

1. Of the 318 fathers gathered in Nicaea in the consulship of the Illustrious Paul and Julian in the Alexandrian year 636 in the month of Desios before the 13th of the Calends of June: 20 canons.
2. Of the blessed fathers in Ancyra, whose canons were earlier than those of Nicaea, but which are placed second because of the authority, that is distinction[9], of the first ecumenical synod: 25 canons.
3. Of the holy fathers in Neocaesarea; this synod too was held earlier than Nicaea, and after Ancyra, but Nicaea, on account of its honor, is placed before it: 14 canons.
4. Of the fathers gathered in Serdica after the fathers in Nicaea: 21 canons.
5. Of the fathers gathered in Gangra, by whom were issued 20 canons.
6. Of the fathers gathered in Antioch, by whom were issued 25 canons.
7. Of the fathers gathered in Phrygian Laodicea, by whom were issued 59 canons.
8. Of the fathers gathered in Constantinople, by whom were issued 6 canons.
9. Of the fathers gathered in Ephesus, by whom were issued 7 canons.
10. Of the fathers gathered in Chalcedon, by whom were issued 27 canons.

There are also canons of the great Basil, 60 and 8 in number.

[5] *σποράδην.*
[6] *. . . δυσεύρετον εἶναι . . . τὸ πρός τινων ἀθρόως περὶ κανόνος ἐπιζητούμενον . . .*
[7] *δύναμις.* [8] *εὐσύνοπτος.* [9] Lit. "boldness," "forthrightness" (*παρρησία*).

Τὰ μὲν σώματα [*c*.580]

[Edition: Pitra *2.445–7]*

Bodies partake, as is appropriate for them,[10] of material nourishment, and so flourish and grow until they reach the limits in measure and duration set for these increases. Likewise, the rational soul is watered and increased by that which is kindred to it, reason, and it grows spiritually. While upon earth it seems to adhere to the body, but in many respects it ascends towards higher contemplations,[11] and enters into the heavenly vaults, in no way subject to the limits of measure and duration. There, above, it converses and shares citizenship[12] with the light-bearing powers and enjoys those things which are truly good, and not mere shadows of them.

Similarly it is proper here too [on earth] that the creator[13] has allotted that which is limitless to the immortal soul, and that which is perishable to the mortal body. Therefore it is seemly that the always moving element of the soul should ever accustom and attach itself to these limitless things, and not give opportunity to the soul to let go of genuine teachings and instead grasp hold of anything spurious. For if she [the soul] is occupied with good words and actions she will acquire divine visions[14] in sleep and in dreams.

Pondering these things, and applying a saying of an ancient pagan sage to the divine decrees, "convinced that they are a discovery and gift of God, the dogma of prudent and God-bearing men, the correction of willing and involuntary sins, and a secure rule for a way of living that is both pious and leads to eternal life," I have with zeal attempted to gather into one the God-befitting canons issued by the holy ten synods, which were convened at various times, and whose canons serve for the strengthening of the divine dogma and for sound teaching of all. I have placed the canons of each synod under the name of that synod. Furthermore, I have included the canons called "of the holy apostles," even if some believe them to be doubtful for certain reasons. I have also joined to the present work the sacred synod of Libyan Carthage that took place in the time of Honorius and Arcadius of pious memory. I have found that it decreed many things able to introduce much that is useful for life, even if some of them refer only to local matters and order and others are inconsistent with regulations issued both generally and specifically and with the ecclesiastical order prevailing in other dioceses or provinces. (One of these is the definition that those enrolled in the clergy above the rank of reader must abstain completely from their spouses lawfully wedded before their ordination. Among us it is not by command, but by free choice, that it falls to such people to practice either abstention on account of God-loving ascesis or undefiled intercourse on account of the honor of marriage—in neither case being liable to any sort of just reproach.)

I have also thought it good to make mention of the things piously spoken in personal letters, in questions and answers, by some of the holy fathers. These are in a certain way able to provide a kind of canon.[15] I am not unaware that both the great Basil and Gregory thought it right that one ought to call and judge "ecclesiastical canons" only those regulations which have been decreed not by one person by himself

[10] *καταλλήλως.* [11] *θεωρίαι.* [12] Or "dwells with" (*συμπολιτεύομαι*).
[13] Lit. "demiurge" (*δημιουργός*). [14] *φαντασίαι.*
[15] *. . . τινα τρόπον κανόνος τύπον παρέχεσθαι.*

but by common assent and with careful examination by many holy fathers gathered together in one place. However, I have considered that the pronouncements of these teachers either concern things already spoken of in synods, and so introduce something very useful for the clarification of those things that, apparently, seem to be hard to grasp for some; or they concern entirely new subjects which are in no way, in letter or meaning, present in the synodical enquiries and decisions. And I consider that those who have been so appointed judges of such things—from the worthiness of their persons and from the spiritual light that according to the energy of God blazes forth in these men—are able to produce judgments that are not only unimpeachable but indeed extremely praiseworthy.

I have therefore brought together the content[16] of all of the amassed material into fourteen titles, and divided each of these into different chapters. Under these I have then placed the regulations appropriate to each inquiry, making clear both the name of the sources where the regulations are found and the number through numerical figures. In this way I have, I think, produced a collection that allows for the easy discernment of the content of the material.[17] The reason that I have presented the material in this form—I mean, with numerical references, and not placing the appropriate word-for-word text under each chapter—is that I did not wish (on account of the needs of different inquiries) either to write out many times the same canon, and make the work unwieldy for readers, or to cut up and divide one canon that pertains to multiple chapters (which has been done by some in the past) and to then become liable among some for such fractioning to the just charge of ill-blessed license.[18]

If anywhere I have found that the civil legislation is usefully related to such canonical writings, I have taken from it short and concise extracts of regulations and placed[19] them under appropriate chapters in a separate section of this book. In this way I have put together in a collection a brief exposition of those regulations in both the imperial decrees and the interpretations of the jurists that pertain to ecclesiastical good order and that may serve as both an aide-memoire and for the full discovery of these regulations by the reader. If I have achieved my goal, with the help of God and the prayers of the saints, to provide something useful first for myself, but also for others, may I receive the reward of my eagerness and zeal.

Ὁ μὲν παρών [*a.* 883]

[Edition: Pitra *2.448–9]*

The present prologue [i.e. *τὰ μὲν σώματα*] set forth as its goal to gather into one the canons issued from the time when in the voices of the apostles the Christian teaching unfolded into the whole world until the fifth synod. The accomplishment of the things promised has been brought to a not unworthy conclusion. It has brought together into one the canons that the fifth synod and the preceding synods decreed, and, if the interval of this time has shown some other individuals among the sacred men to have arrived at such a height of virtue that they have been deemed trustworthy and their

16 *δύναμις.* 17 ... *εὐσύνοπτον ὡς οἶμαι κατὰ δύναμιν τὸ σύνταγμα πεποίημαι.*

18 ... *καὶ δικαίαν οὐκ εὐλόγου με τόλμης ἐπὶ τῇ τοιαύτῃ κατατομῇ παρά τισιν αἰτίαν ἀπενέγκασθαι.*

19 Lit. "attached them to," "fitted them to" (*προσαρμόζω*).

words have attained an equal honor and order to the canons, it has not rejected their works as adulterating that which is appropriate to this present task.[20]

The period following the fifth synod has brought forth not a few other novelties in life and has seen the convening of sacred synods for various reasons. We, however, not wishing to inflict indignities upon the works of the ancients—a rash act which many have been frequently driven to by the lack of recognition for their own efforts and which is meant to give the appearance of wisdom to the theft of others' works[21]—have instead lifted up in admiration and praise those who have made a beginning of any good thing in life, and thus we recognize as honored those whom we follow.

Therefore, maintaining inviolate the pre-eminence of the labors of these men, indeed increasing them, we have attached to what has gone before the things that have come after. What time has denied to them we restore with addition (paying damages, as it were),[22] and we present to them this labor of love, now complete with all that has transpired until the present.

The present book therefore contains all that the [first] prologue has described, as well as, in the same sequence, and in the same order of composition that those before us devised, the regulations which the sixth ecumenical council defined; and further those of the seventh, which is the second of the ecumenical councils convened in Nicaea. This synod condemned the iconoclastic madness and composed not a few ordinances of those that reform the sacred way of life.[23] In addition, it [this book] contains those regulations decreed afterwards by the first and second synod in Constantinople, which, when a certain strife was kindled, made the all-sacred temple of the apostles its hearing chamber for these affairs. Further, it contains those of a later synod which, convened for the common harmony of the church, sealed the synod in Nicaea, cast out all heretical and schismatic error, and added its canons to those of its brother synods.

Everywhere the here-mentioned labor of this book has also joined to the sacred writings certain legal excerpts—not neglecting their addition—which are in harmony with the sacred canons.

In order that one might know the year when the present material was added to the earlier, it is counted in thousands of years, increased sixfold, and exceeding even this, not stopping its course at three hundred more years, but driving on to the ninety-first year—this is the year that brought forth this present work under the sun's rays.

[20] *. . . οὐδὲ τούτων τοὺς πόνους, τῆς προκειμένης πραγματείας τὸ συγγενὲς οὐ νοθεύοντας, οὐκ ἀπεξένωσεν.*

[21] *. . . καὶ κλοπῇ τῶν ἀλλοτρίων ὀφρὺν ἀνασπάσαι σοφίας ἠπάτησεν.*

[22] *. . . ταύτην αὐτοῖς ἡμεῖς τὴν προσθήκην, ὡς ζημίαν, ἀποκαθιστῶντες . . . .*

[23] *ἡ ἱερὰ πολιτεία.*

Bibliography

I. Primary source editions and translations

Supplementary works only; principal editions and translations are listed in the "Abbreviations"

Arendzen, J. (ed. and trans.) (1901), "An Entire Syriac Text of the 'Apostolic Church Order'" [*Constitutiones ecclesiasticae apostolorum*], *Journal of Theological Studies* os 3: 59–80.

Arnim, H. von (ed.) (1893–6), *Dionis Prusaensis quem vocant Chrysostomum quae exstant omnia*, vols. 1–2. 2nd edn. Berlin.

Arnim, H. von (ed.) (1903), *Stoicorum veterum fragmenta*. 4 vols. Munich.

Barlow, C. (ed.) (1950), *Martini episcopi Bracarensis opera omnia*. New Haven, Conn. [replacing *PL* 84.674–586].

Bartoňková, D. *et al.* (eds.) (1971), *Magnae Moraviae Fontes Historici IV: Leges, textus iuridici, supplementa*. Brno.

Besse, Jean-Claude (ed.) (1959), "Collectionis Anselmo Dedicata Liber Primus," *Revue de droit canonique*, 9:207–96.

Beveridge, W. (ed.) (1672), *Synodikon Sive Pandectae Canonum*. 2 vols. Oxford.

Bradshaw, P. and Bebawi, C. (eds. and trans.) (1987), *The Canons of Hippolytus*. Bramcote.

Bruns, C. and Gradenwitz, O. (eds.) (1909–12), *Fontes iuris romani antiqui*. 7th edn. 2 vols. Tübingen.

Burgmann, L. (ed.) (1983), *Ecloga: das Gesetzbuch Leons III. und Konstantinos V*. Frankfurt a.M.

Burgmann, L. and Troianos, S. (eds.) (1979), "Nomos Mosaikos," in Simon 1979: 126–67.

Burnet, J. (ed.) (1907), *Platonis opera*: vol. 5, *Laws*. Oxford. Trans. R. Bury (1926), *Plato X–XI: Laws*. Loeb Classical Library 187,192. Cambridge, Mass.

Butcher, S. (ed.) (1907 [1966]), *Demosthenis orationes*, vol. 2.1. Oxford.

Cohn, L. (ed.) (1902 [1962]), *Philonis Alexandrini opera quae supersunt*. vol. 4. Berlin. Trans. F. Colson and G. Whitaker (1929–62), *Philo*. Loeb Classical Library 226, 227, 247, 261, 275, 289, 320, 341, 363, 379, 380, 401. Cambridge, Mass.

Cohn, L. (ed.) (1906 [1962]), *Philonis Alexandrini opera quae supersunt*, vol. 5. Berlin. (Trans. as Cohn 1902).

Crawford, M. (ed. and trans.) (1996), *Roman Statutes*, vol. 2. London.

D'Achery, L. (ed.) (1672), *Veterum aliquot scriptorum qui in Galliae bibliothecis . . . latuerant*. 2 vols. Paris.

Darrouzès, J. (ed.) (1966), *Documents inédits d'ecclésiologie byzantine*. Paris.

Deferrari, R. (ed. and trans.) (1926), *Saint Basil, the letters*. 4 vols. Loeb Classical Library 241–4. Cambridge, Mass.

Díez, M. (ed.) (1966–82), *La colección canónica hispana*. 4 vols. Madrid.

Fatouros, D. (ed.) (1992), *Theodori Studitae Epistulae.* 2 vols. Berlin–New York.

Ferrini, C. (ed.) (1884–97 [1967]), *Institutionum graeca paraphrasis Theophilo Antecessori vulgo tributa.* Darmstadt.

Friedberg, E. (ed.) (1879), *Corpus Iuris Canonici.* 2nd edn. Leipzig.

Funk, F. (ed.) (1905), *Didascalia et Constitutiones Apostolorum.* 2 vols. Paderborn.

Gautier, P. (ed. and comm. (1973), "L'Édit d'Alexis Ier Comnène sur la réforme du clergé," *Revue des études byzantines,* 31: 165–200.

González, F. (ed.) (1808), *Collectio canonum Ecclesiae Hispanae.* Madrid [= *PL* 84.93–848].

Gordley, J. and Thompson, A. (trans.) (1993), *The Treatise on Laws ([Gratian's] Decretum DD.1–20).* Washington, DC.

Heath, M. (trans. and comm.) (1995), [Hermogenes] *On Issues: Strategies of Argument in Later Greek Rhetoric.* Oxford.

Heimbach, G. (ed.) (1838–40 [1969]), *Ἀνέκδοτα . . . ex codicibus manuscriptis.* 2 vols. Leipzig.

Hinschius, P. (ed.) (1863), *Decretales pseudo-Isidorianae et Capitula Angilramni* [Collection of Ps.-Isidore Mercator]. Leipzig.

Horna, K. (ed.) (1903), "Die Epigramme des Theodoros Balsamon," *Wiener Studien,* 25: 165–217.

Jacoby, K. (ed.) (1885–1905 [1967]), *Dionysii Halicarnasei antiquitatum Romanarum quae supersunt.* 4 vols. Stuttgart. Trans. E. Cary (1937–50), *The Roman Antiquities.* Loeb Classical Library 319, 347, 357, 364, 372, 378, 388. Cambridge, Mass.

Johnson, C. *et al.* (trans.) (1961), *Ancient Roman Statutes.* Austin, Tex.

Kallivourtsis, N. [St. Nicodemus the Hagiorite] (ed. and comm.) (1800), *Πηδάλιον τῆς νοητῆς νηός...* Leipzig [repr. Athens 1841, 1864 ff.].

Lehr-Spławiński, T. (ed. and trans.) (1959), *Żywoty Konstantyna I Metodego.* Posnan.

Leunclavius, J. (ed.) (1596), *Iuris Graeco-Romani tam canonici quam civilis.* 2 vols. Frankfurt.

Lindskog, C. and Ziegler, K. (eds.) (1957–80), *Plutarchi vitae parallelae.* 2nd edn. 7 vols. Leipzig. Trans. [Romulus, Lycurgus, Numa, Solon] B. Perrin (1914; repr. 1998), *Plutarch's Lives I.* Loeb Classical Library 46. Cambridge, Mass.

Mai, A. (ed. and trans.) (1848), *Patrum Nova Bibliotheca,* vol. 5, part 2. Rome.

Meliara, K. (ed.) (1905–6), "*Μελέτη περὶ τοῦ Νομοκάνονος τοῦ ἁγιωτάτου πατριάρχου Κωνσταντινουπόλεως Φωτίου,*" *Νέα Σιών,* 2: 55–76, 343–55, 510–24, 878–93; 3: 11–27, 118–38, 250–6.

Metzger, M. (ed. and trans.) (1985), *Les Constitutions apostoliques.* 3 vols. Paris.

Mordek, H. (ed.) (1975), *Kirchenrecht und Reform im Frankenreich: die Collectio Vetus Gallica, die älteste systematische Kanonessammlung des fränkischen Gallien.* Berlin.

Mullach, F. (ed.) (1860 [1968]), *Fragmenta philosophorum Graecorum,* vol. 1. Paris.

Munier, C. (ed.) (1963), *Concilia Galliae, a. 314–a. 506.* Turnhout. [*Statuta ecclesiae antiqua* at 283–311.]

Munier, C. (ed.) (1974), *Concilia Africae a. 345–a. 525.* Turnhout.

Narbekov, V. (1889), *Толкование Вальсамона на Номоканон Фотия.* Kazan.

Narbekov, V. (intro. and trans.) (1899), *Номоканон Константинопольского патриарха Фотия с толкованием Вальсамона.* 2 vols. Kazan.

Nedungatt, G. and Featherstone, M. (eds.) (1995), *The Council in Trullo Revisited.* Rome.

Niederwimmer, K. and Attridge, H. (eds., trans., and comms.) (1993 [1998]), *The Didache: A Commentary*. Hermeneia Commentary Series. Translation from 2nd German edn. by L. Maloney. Minneapolis.
Niese, B. (ed.) (1885–92 [1955]), *Flavii Iosephi opera*. vols. 1–4. Berlin.
Niese, B. (ed.) (1889 [1955]), *Flavii Iosephi opera*. vol. 5. Berlin.
Noailles, P. and Dain, A. (eds. and trans.) (1944), *Les Novelles de Léon VI, le Sage*. Paris.
Powell, J. (ed.) (2006), *M. Tulli Ciceronis. De re publica; De legibus; Cato maior de senectute; Laelius de amicitia*. Oxford. Trans. C. Keyes. (1928), *Cicero De re publica, De legibus*. Loeb Classical Library No. 213. Cambridge, Mass.
Rabe, H. (ed.) (1913 [1969]), *Hermogenis opera*. Leipzig. Trans. M. Heath (1995), *Hermogenes On Issues*. Oxford.
Rabe, H. (ed.) (1926), *Aphthonii progymnasmata*. Rhetores Graeci 10. Leipzig. Trans. G. Kennedy (2003), *Progymnasmata: Greek Textbooks of Prose Composition and Rhetoric*. Leiden.
Rabe, H. (ed.) (1931 [1995]), *Prolegomenon Sylloge*. Rhetores Graeci 14. Leipzig.
Rahmani, E. (ed. and trans.) (1899), *Testamentum Domini nostri Jesu Christi*. Mainz. Trans. J. Cooper, A. J. Maclean (1992), *The Testament of Our Lord, an English Translation, with Introduction and Notes*. Edinburgh.
Riccobono, S. *et al.* (eds.) (1940–3), *Fontes iuris romani antejustiniani*, 3 vols. Florence.
Richardson, M. (ed. and trans.) (2004), *Hammurabi's Laws: Text, Translation, and Glossary*. London.
Ross, W. (ed.) (1957), *Aristotelis Politica*. Oxford. Trans. H. Rackham (1944), *Aristotle XXI: Politics*. Loeb Classical Library 264. Cambridge, Mass.
Schminck, A. (1986), *Studien zu mittelbyzantinischen Rechtsbüchern*. Frankfurt a.M.
Schminck, A. (1998), "Das Prooimion der Bearbeitung des Nomokanons in 14 Titeln durch Michael und Theodoros," in Burgmann 1998: 357–86.
Schulthess, F. (ed.) (1908), *Die syrischen Kanones der Synoden von Nicaea bis Chalcedon nebst einigen zugehörigen Dokumenten*. Berlin.
Seckel, E. and Kuebler, B. (ed.) (1935), *Gai Institutionum commentarii quattuor*. Leipzig.
Simon, D. and Troianos, S. (eds.) (1979), "Die Epitome des Novellensyntagma von Athanasios," in Simon 1979: 293–313.
Simon, D. and Troianos S. (eds.) (1989), *Das Novellensytagma des Athanasios von Emesa*. Frankfurt a.M.
Strewe, A. (ed.) (1931), *Die Kanonessammlung des Dionysius Exiguus in der ersten Redaktion*. Berlin.
Thom, J. (ed. and trans.) (1995), *The Pythagorean Golden Verses*. Leiden.
Thomas, J. and Hero, A. (trans.) (2000), *Byzantine Monastic Foundation Documents*. 5 vols. Washington, DC.
Trouillard, J and Segonds, A.-P. (eds. and trans.) (1990), *Prolégomènes à la philosophie de Platon (déb. VIe s.)*. Paris.
Turner, C. (ed.) (1899–1939), *Ecclesiae Occidentalis monumenta iuris antiquissima: Canonum et conciliorum graecorum, interpretationes latinae*... 9 vols. Oxford.
Voellus, G. and Justel, H. (eds.) (1661), *Bibliotheca Iuris Canonici Veteris*. 2 vols. Paris.
Vööbus, A. (ed. and trans.) (1975), *The Synodicon in the West Syrian Tradition*. 2 vols. Louvain.

Wachsmuth, K and Hense, O. (eds.) (1884), *Ioannis Stobaei anthologium*. 5 vols. Berlin. [Ps.-Charondas, Prooimion at 4.2.24; Ps.-Zaleucus, Prooimion at 4.2.19.]
Wasserschleben, F. (ed.) (1840), *Reginonis abbatis Prumiensis libri duo....* Leipzig.
Wasserschleben, F. (ed.) (1885), *Die irische Kanonensammlung* [Hibernensis]. 2nd edn. Leipzig.
Westerink, L. (ed.) (1968), *Arethae scripta minora*. 2 vols. Leipzig.
Westerink, L. (ed.) (1992), *Michaelis Pselli Poemata*. Stuttgart.
Willetts, R. (ed. and trans.) (1967), *The Law Code of Gortyn*. Berlin.
Zaozerski, N. (trans.) (1882), "Состояние канонического права в Доникейской церкви," *Чтения Общества Любителей Духовного Просвещения*, 2: 106–17.
Zechiel-Eckes, K. (ed.) (1992), *Die Concordia canonum des Cresconius: Studien und Edition*. 2 vols. Frankfurt a.M.

II. Secondary sources

See also "Abbreviations" for frequently cited reference sources.

Aerts, W. (1997), "Panorama des byzantinische Literature," in Lodewijk, J. *et al.* (eds.), *Neues Handbuch der Literaturwissenschaft. Band 4: Spätantike, mit einem Panorama der byzantinischen Literatur*. Wiesbaden: 635–709.
Aerts, W. *et al.* (2001), "The Prooimion of the Eisagoge: Translation and Commentary," *Subseciva Groningana*, 7: 91–155.
Afanasiev, N. (1933), "Les Canons et la conscience canonique," repr. in *Contacts*, 21 (1959): 112–27.
Afanasiev, N. (1936), "The Canons of the Church: Changeable or Unchangeable," trans. (anon.) and repr. in *St. Vladimir's Theological Quarterly*, 11 (1967): 54–68.
Akanthopoulos, P. (1992), *Θέματα κανονίκου δίκαιου*. Thessaloniki.
Alivisatos, H. (1913), *Die kirchliche Gesetzgebung des Kaisers Justinian I*. Berlin.
Altshuler, D. (1982/3), "On the Classification of Judaic Laws in the 'Antiquities' of Josephus and the Temple Scroll of Qumran," *AJS Review*, 7/8: 1–14.
Andresen, C. (1980), "Die Bibel im konziliaren, kanonistischen und synodalen Kirchenrecht," in Brecht, M. (ed.) *Text—Wort—Glaube: Studien zur Überlieferung, Interpretation und Autorisierung biblischer Texte*. Berlin: 169–208.
Angold, M. (1994), "Imperial Renewal and Orthodox Reaction: Byzantium in the Eleventh Century," in Magdalino, P. (ed.), *New Constantines: The Rhythm of Imperial Renewal in Byzantium, 4th–13th centuries*. Aldershot: 231–46.
Archi, G. and Colombo, A. (1986–9), *Legum Iustiniani imperatoris vocabularium. Novellae: Pars Graeca*. Milan.
Archontonis, B. (1970), *Περὶ τὴν κωδικοποίησιν τῶν ἱερῶν κανόνων καὶ τῶν κανονικῶν διατάξεων ἐν τῇ Ὀρθοδόξῳ Ἐκκλησίᾳ*. Thessaloniki.
Assemani, J. S. (1762), *Bibliotheca Juris Orientalis canonici et civilis*. 5 vols. Rome.
Auberque, P. (2008), "Prudence," *BNP* 12: 88–90.
Avotins, I. (1989), *On the Greek of the Code of Justinian: A Supplement to Liddell-Scott-Jones Together with Observations on the Influence of Latin on Legal Greek*. Hildesheim.

Avotins, I. (1992), *On the Greek of the Novels of Justinian: A Supplement to Liddell-Scott-Jones Together with Observations on the Influence of Latin on Legal Greek*. Hildesheim.

Ballerini, P. and Ballerini, G. (1753–7), *Sancti Leonis Magni Romani Pontificis Opera*, part 3 ("De antiquis tum editis tum ineditis collectionibus et collectoribus canonum ad Gratianum usque"), repr. in Gallandius 1778: 95–266.

Balot, R. (2006), *Greek Political Thought*. Malden, Mass.

Barker, E. (1925), *Greek Political Theory*. 2nd edn. London.

Beaucamp, J. (2005), "L'Histoire du droit byzantin face à la papyrologie juridique. Bilan et perspectives," in Burgmann 2005: 5–55.

Beck, H. (1977), *Kirche und theologische Literatur im Byzantinischen Reich*. 2nd edn. Munich.

Beck, H. (1981), *Nomos, Kanon und Staatsraison in Byzanz*. Vienna.

Bederman, D. (2001), *Classical Canons: Rhetoric, Classicism and Treaty Interpretation*. Aldershot.

Bellomo, M. (1995), *The Common Legal Past of Europe, 1000–1800*. Trans. L. Cochrane. Washington, DC.

Beneshevich, V. (1927), "Monumenta vaticana ad ius canonicum pertinentia," *Studi Byzantini*, 2: 127–91.

Berdnikov, P. (1889), *Краткий курс церковного права*. Kazan.

Berger, A. (1953), *Encyclopedic Dictionary of Roman Law*. Philadelphia.

Berman, H. (1983), *Law and Revolution: The Formation of the Western Legal Tradition*. Cambridge, Mass.

Berman, H. (2003), *Law and Revolution II: The Impact of the Protestant Reformations on the Western Legal Tradition*. Cambridge, Mass.

Biener, F. (1824), *Geschichte der Novellen Justinians*. Berlin.

Biener, F. (1827), *De collectionibus canonum ecclesiae graecae schediasma litterarium*. Berlin.

Biener, F. (1856), "Das kanonische Recht der griechischen Kirche," *Kritische Zeitschrift für Rechtswissenschaft und Gesetzgebung des Auslandes*, 28: 163–206.

Biondi, B. (1952–4), *Il diritto romano cristiano*. 3 vols. Milan.

Blumenthal, U. (ed.) (1983), *Carolingian Essays: Andrew W. Mellon Lectures in Early Christian Studies*. Washington, DC.

Bochove, T. van (1996), *To Date and Not to Date: On the Date and Status of Byzantine Law Books*. Groningen.

Bochove, T. van (1997), "*Οὐ κελεύομεν· συνεκεφαλαιώσαμεν καὶ ῥᾳδίαν ἔντευξιν παρέσχομεν*. Some remarks with respect to the nature of the preface to the Basilica," in Troianos 1997: 155–68.

Bodenheimer, E. (1974), *Jurisprudence: The Philosophy and Method of the Law*. 2nd edn. Cambridge, Mass.

Bohannan, P. (1957), *Justice and Judgment Among the Tiv*. London.

Bonner, S. (1977), *Education in Ancient Rome from the Elder Cato to the Younger Pliny*. Berkeley.

Borbu, S. (2009), "Charism, Law and Spirit in Eucharistic Ecclesiology: New Perspectives on Nicholas Afanasiev's Sources," *Sobornost*, 31(2): 19–43.

Boumis, P. (1991), *Οἱ κανόνες τῆς ἐκκλησίας περὶ τοῦ κανόνος τῆς ἁγίας γραφῆς*. 2 vols. Athens.

Boumis, P. (2000), *Τὸ κῦρος καὶ ἡ ἰσχὺς τῶν ἱερῶν κανόνων*. 5th edn. Athens.

Boumis, P. (2003), *Κανονικόν Δίκαιον*. 3rd edn. Athens.

Bouwsma, W. (1973), "Lawyers and Early Modern Culture," *American Historical Review*, 78: 303–27.

Bradshaw, P. (2002), *The Apostolic Tradition: A Commentary*. Hermeneia Commentary Series. Minneapolis.

Brandes, W. (2002), "Heraclius between Restoration and Reform: Some Remarks on Recent Research," in Reinink, G and Stolte, B. (eds.), *The Reign of Heraclius (610–641): Crisis and Confrontation*. Leuven: 17–40.

Brasington, B. (1994), "Prologues to Canonical Collections as a Source for Jurisprudential Change," *Frühmittelalterliche Studien*, 28: 226–42.

Brasington, B. (2001), "Canon Law in the 'Century of the Individual': Revolution and Continuity." Online only: <http://www.estig.ipbeja.pt/~ac_direito/melville2001new.doc> [accessed 1 May 2010].

Bretone, M. (1999), *Storia del diritto romano*. 7th edn. Rome.

Brown, P. (1992), *Power and Persuasion in Late Antiquity: Towards a Christian Empire*. Madison, Wisc.

Browning, R. (1983), *Medieval and Modern Greek*. Cambridge.

Brundage, J. (1995), *Medieval Canon Law*. London.

Brundage, J. (1995a), "The Rise of Professional Canonists and the Development of the Ius Commune," *Zeitschrift der Savigny-Stiftung für Rechtsgeschichte*, Kan. Abt. 81: 26–63.

Brundage, J. (2008), *The Medieval Origins of the Legal Profession: Canonists, Civilians, and Courts*. Chicago.

Bucci, O. (1992), "La genesi della struttura del diritto della Chiesa latina e del diritto delle Chiese Cristiane Orientali in rapporto allo svolgimento storico del diritto romano e del diritto bizantino," *Apollinaris*, 65: 93–135.

Buckland, W. (1932), *Roman Law and Common Law: A Comparison in Outline*. 2nd edn. Cambridge.

Buckland, W. (1963), *A Text-Book of Roman Law from Augustus to Justinian*. 3rd edn. Cambridge.

Burgmann, L. (1985), "Palatium canonibus solutum," in Burgmann *et al.* 1985: 19–32.

Burgmann, L. (1988), "Hommage à Vladimir Nicolaevic Benesevic," *Rechtshistorisches Journal*, 7: 3–12.

Burgmann, L. (1995), "Der Codex Vaticanus graecus 1167 und der serbische Nomokanon," in *Zbornik radova Vizantološkog instituta* 34: 91–106.

Burgmann, L. (1996), "Lawyers and Legislators: Aspects of Law-making in the Time of Alexios I," in M. Mullett and D. Smythe (eds.), *Alexios I Komnenos*, I: Papers. Belfast: 185–98.

Burgmann, L. (ed.) (1998), *Fontes Minores X*. Forschungen zur byzantinischen Rechtsgeschichte, Band 22. Frankfurt a.M.

Burgmann, L. (1999), "Die Gegenwart der Vergangenheit im byzantinischen Recht," in *Ideologie e pratiche del reimpiego nell'alto medioevo*, Settimane di studio del Centro Italiano di studi sull'alto medioevo, 46. Spoleto: 591–612.

Burgmann, L. (2002), "Juristische Buchproduktion in Byzanz," in V. Colli (ed.), *Juristische Buchproduktion im Mittelalter*. Frankfurt a.M: 247–67.

Burgmann, L. (ed.) (2005), *Fontes Minores XI*. Forschungen zur byzantinischen Rechtsgeschichte, Band 26. Frankfurt a.M.

Burgmann, L. and Troianos, S. (1979), "Appendix Eclogae," in Simon 1979: 24–125.

Burgmann, L. *et al.* (eds.) (1985), *Cupido legum*. Frankfurt a.M.

Burgmann, L. *et al.* (1992), *Bibliographie zur Rezeption des byzantinischen Rechts im alten Russland sowie zur Geschichte des armenischen und georgischen Rechts*. Frankfurt a.M.

Burgmann, L. *et al.* (1995), *Repertorium der Handschriften des byzantinischen Rechts*. Frankfurt a.M.

Calhoun, G. (1944), *Introduction to Greek Legal Science*. Oxford.

Cameron, A. (1991), *Christianity and the Rhetoric of Empire: The Development of Christian Discourse*. Berkeley.

Carney, T. F. (1971), *Bureaucracy in Traditional Society: Romano-Byzantine Bureaucracies Viewed from Within*. Lawrence, Kan.

Centrone, B. (2000), "Platonism and Pythagoreanism in the Early Empire," in Schofield and Rowe 2000: 559–84.

Černyševa, M. (1998), "Кормчая," in Burgmann 1998: 517–32.

Chodorow, S. (1972), *Christian Political Theory and Church Politics in the Mid-twelfth century: The Ecclesiology of Gratian's "Decretum."* Berkeley.

Christophilopoulos, A. (1957), *Θέματα Βυζαντινοῦ ἐκκλησιαστικοῦ δικαίου*. Athens.

Christophilopoulos, A. (1965), *Ἑλληνικὸν Ἐκκλησιαστικὸν Δίκαιον*. Athens.

Christopoulos, M. [Metropolitan Maximos of Sardes] (1972 [1976]), *The Œcumenical Patriarchate in the Orthodox Church: A Study in the History and Canons of the Church*. Trans. G. McLellan. Thessaloniki.

Clercq, C. de (1937), "Byzantin (droit canonique)", in *DDC* 2.1170–84.

Clercq, C. de (1949), "Corpus Juris Civilis," in *DDC* 4.644–80.

Cohen, D. (1995), *Law, Violence, and Community in Classical Athens*. Cambridge.

Collinet, P. (1925), *Histoire de l'école de droit de Beyrouth*. Paris.

Congar, Y. (1960), "La Primauté des quatre premiers conciles oecuméniques," in Botte, B. *et al.* (eds.), *Le Concile et les conciles. Contribution à l'histoire de la vie conciliaire de l'Église*. Paris: 75–109.

Congar, Y. (1970), *L'Église de saint Augustin à l'époque moderne*. Paris.

Congar, Y. (1973), "Rudolf Sohm nous interroge encore," *Revue des sciences philosophiques et théologiques*, 57: 263–94.

Corcoran, S. (1996), *The Empire of the Tetrarchs: Imperial Pronouncements and Government, AD 284–324*. Oxford.

Corecco, E. (1992), *The Theology of Canon Law: A Methodological Question*. Pittsburgh.

Cosme, R. (1955), "La unificación interna del derecho y las colecciones anteriores a Graciano," *Revista Española de Derecho Canónico*, 10: 353–82.

Cosme, R. (1955a), "Las colecciones canonicas en función de autenticidad, universalidad y unifación del derecho," *Revista Española de Derecho Canónico*, 10: 61–111.

Coussa, A. (1941), *Epitome praelectionum de iure ecclesiastico orientali*. Venice.

Cribiore, R. (2001), *Gymnastics of the Mind*. Princeton.

Crook, J. (1967), *Law and Life in Rome.* London.
Crook, J. (1995), *Legal Advocacy in the Roman World.* Ithaca, NY.
Cross, F. (1961), "History and Fiction in the African Canons," *Journal of Theological Studies*, NS 12: 227–47.
Curtis, D. and Resnik, J. (1987), "Images of Justice," *Yale Law Journal*, 96.8: 1727–72.
Dagron, G. (1994), "Lawful Society and Legitimate Power: 'Έννομος πολιτεία, ἔννομος ἀρχή," in Laiou and Simon 1994: 27–51.
Dain, A. (1964), *Les Manuscrits*, 3rd edn. Paris.
Darrouzès, J. (1970), *Recherches sur les ὀφφίκια de l'église byzantine.* Paris.
Darrouzès, J. (1981), *Notitiae episcopatuum Ecclesiae Constantinopolitanae.* Paris.
Deledemos, E. (2002), *Εἰσαγογὴ εἰς τὴν νέαν ἔκδοσιν.* Study prefacing vol. 1 of *RP*, Regopoulos edn. Thessaloniki.
Dennis, G. (1994), "A Rhetorician Practises Law: Michael Psellos," in Laiou and Simon 1994: 187–97.
Deslandes, J. (1934, 1935), "Les Sources du droit canonique oriental," *Échos d'Orient*, 32: 476–87; 33: 444–63.
Devreesse, R. (1954), *Introduction à l'étude des manuscrits grecs.* Paris.
Diamond, A. (1950), *Primitive Law.* 2nd edn. London.
Dölger, F. and Karayannopulos, J. (1968), *Byzantinische Urkundenlehre.* Munich.
Dölger, F. and Wirth, P. (1924–65), *Regesten der Kaiserurkunden des oströmischen Reichs von 565–1453.* 5 vols. Munich and Berlin.
Donovan, J. (2007), *Legal Anthropology: An Introduction.* Lanham, Md.
Douglas, M. (1966 [2002]), *Purity and Danger: An Analysis of Concepts of Pollution and Taboo.* London.
Douglas, M. (1986), *How Institutions Think.* Syracuse, NY.
Doujat, J. (1680), *Histoire du droit canonique.* Paris.
Doujat, J. (1687 [1748]), *Praenotionum canonicarum libri quinque.* Paris.
Du Cange, D. (1688), *Glossarium ad Scriptores Mediae et Infimae Graecitatis.* Paris.
Ducos, M. (1984), *Les Romains et la loi: recherches sur les rapports de la philosophie grecque et de la tradition romaine à la fin de la république.* Paris.
Dulles, A. (2002), *Models of the Church.* 2nd edn., expanded. New York.
Dura, N. (1995), "The Ecumenicity of the Council in Trullo: Witnesses of the Canonical Tradition in the East and in the West," in Nedungatt and Featherstone 1995: 229–62.
Dvornik, F. (1966), *Early Christian and Byzantine Political Philosophy: Origins and Background.* 2 vols. Washington, DC.
Dyck, A. (2004), *A Commentary on Cicero De legibus.* Ann Arbor, Mich.
Eggert, P. (1991), "Textual Product or Textual Process: Procedures and Assumptions of Critical Editing," in P. Cohen (ed.), *Devils and Angels: Textual Editing and Literary Theory.* Charlottesville, Va.: 57–77.
Enßlin, W. (1943 [1975]), "Gottkaiser und Kaiser von Gottes Gnaden," repr. in H. Hunger (ed.), *Das byzantinische Herrscherbild.* Darmstadt: 54–85.
Epp, E. (1999), "The Multivalence of the Term 'Original Text' in New Testament Textual Criticism," *Harvard Theological Review*, 92.3: 245–81.
Epp, R. and Lefebvre, C. (1981), *Le Droit et les institutions de l'église catholique latine de la fin du XVIIIe siècle à 1978: sources, communauté chrétienne et hiérarchie.* Histoire du droit et des institutions de l'Eglise en Occident 16. Paris.

Erickson, J. (1988), "Sacramental 'Economy' in Recent Roman Catholic Thought," *The Jurist* 38: 653–67.

Erickson, J. (1991), *The Challenge of Our Past: Studies in Orthodox Canon Law and Church History*. Crestwood, NY.

Erickson, J. (1991a), "The Orthodox Canonical Tradition," in Erickson 1991: 9–21.

Erickson, J. (1991b), "The Problem of Sacramental 'Economy'," in Erickson 1991: 115–32.

Erickson, J. (1997), "The Reception of Non-Orthodox into the Orthodox Church: Contemporary Practice," *St. Vladimir's Theological Quarterly*, 41: 1–17.

Erickson, J. (1998), "On the Cusp of Modernity: The Canonical Hermeneutic of St. Nikodemos the Haghiorite (1748–1809)," *St. Vladimir's Theological Quarterly*, 42: 45–66.

Evdokimov, P. (1959), *L'Orthodoxie*. Neuchâtel.

Evdokimov, P. (1962 [1985]), *The Sacrament of Love: The Nuptial Mystery in the Light of the Orthodox Tradition*. Trans. Gythiel, A. Crestwood, New York [originally published Paris].

Farrugia, E. (2000), *Dizionario enciclopedico dell'Oriente cristiano*. Rome.

Feine, H. (1954), *Kirchliche Rechtsgeschichte*. Weimar.

Ferme, B. (1998), *Introduzione alla storia del diritto canonico 1: Il diritto antico fino al decretum di Graziano*. Rome.

Firey, A. (2003), "Lawyers and Wisdom: The Use of the Bible in the Pseudo-Isidorian Forged Decretals," in C. Chazell and B. Van Name Edwards (eds.), *The Study of the Bible in the Carolingian Era*. Turnhout: 189–214.

Firey, A. (2008), "The Collectio Dionysiana." Online only:<http://ccl.rch.uky.edu/dionysiana-article> [accessed 26 April 2014].

Fögen M.-Th. (1985), "Horror iuris. Byzantinische Rechtsgelehrte disziplinieren ihren Metropoliten," in Burgmann *et al.* 1985: 47–71.

Fögen M.-Th. (1987), "Gesetz und Gesetzgebung in Byzanz. Versuch einer Funktionsanalyse," *Ius Commune*, 14: 137–58.

Fögen M.-Th. (1989), "Legislation und Kodifikation des Kaisers Leon VI," *Subseciva Groningana*, 3: 23–35.

Fögen M.-Th. (1993), "Das politische Denken der Byzantiner," in I. Fetscher and H. Münkler (eds.), *Pipers Handbuch der politischen Ideen. Band 2: Mittelalter. Von den Anfängen des Islams bis zur Reformation*. Munich: 41–85.

Fögen M.-Th. (1994), "Legislation in Byzantium: A Political and a Bureaucratic Technique," in Laiou and Simon 1994: 53–70.

Fögen, M.-Th. (1995), "The Legislator's Monologue. Notes on the History of Preambles," *Chicago-Kent Law Review*, 70: 1593–620.

Fögen M.-Th. (1998), "Reanimation of Roman Law in the Ninth Century: Remarks on Reasons and Results," in L. Brubaker (ed.), *Byzantium in the Ninth Century: Dead or Alive? Papers from the Thirtieth Spring Symposium of Byzantine Studies*. Aldershot: 11–22.

Fournier, P. and Le Bras, G. (1931), *Histoire des collections canoniques en Occident depuis les fausses décrétales jusqu'au décret de Gratien*. 2 vols. Paris.

Fransen, G. (1972), *Décrétales et les collections de décrétales*. Typologie des sources du Moyen Âge occidental, Fasc. 2. Turnhout.

Fransen, G. (1973), *Collections canoniques*. Typologie des sources du Moyen Âge occidental, Fasc. 10. Turnhout.

Freeman, M. (ed.) (2001), *Lloyd's Introduction to Jurisprudence*. 7th edn. London.

Friedmann, W. (1967), *Legal Theory*. 5th edn. London.

Friedrich, C. (1973), *The Philosophy of Law in Historical Perspective*. 2nd edn. Chicago.

Frier, B. (1985), *The Rise of the Roman Jurists: Studies in Cicero's Pro Caecina*. Princeton.

Fuhrmann, H. (1953), "Studien zur Geschichte mittelalterlicher Patriarchate: Teil 1," *Zeitschrift der Savigny-Stiftung für Rechtsgeschichte*, Kan. Abt 39: 112–76.

Fuhrmann, M. (1960), *Das systematische Lehrbuch: ein Beitrag zur Geschichte der Wissenschaften in der Antike*. Göttingen.

Gagarin, M. (2000), "Le Code de Platon et le droit grec," in Levy 2000: 215–22.

Gagarin, M. (2005), "Early Greek Law," in Gagarin and Cohen 2005: 82–94.

Gagarin, M. (2005a), "The Unity of Greek Law," in Gagarin and Cohen 2005: 29–40.

Gagarin, M. (2008), *Writing Greek Law*. Cambridge.

Gagarin, M. and Cohen, D. (eds.) (2005), *The Cambridge Companion to Ancient Greek Law*. Cambridge.

Gallagher, C. (1991), "Gratian and Theodore Balsamon: Two Twelfth-Century Canonistic Methods Compared," in Oikonomides 1991: 61–89.

Gallagher, C. (2002), *Church Law and Church Order in Rome and Byzantium: A Comparative Study*. Aldershot.

Gallandius, A. (1778), *De vetustis canonum collectionibus dissertationum sylloge*. Venice.

Garcia y Garcia, A. (1967), *Historia del derecho canónico*. Salamanca.

Garnsey, P. (2000), "Introduction: The Hellenistic and Roman Periods," in Schofield and Rowe 2000: 401–14.

Garnsey, P. and Humfress, C. (2001), *The Evolution of the Late Antique World*. Cambridge.

Gaudemet, J. (1957), *La Formation du droit séculier et du droit de l'église aux IVe et Ve siècles*. Paris.

Gaudemet, J. (1958), *L'Église dans l'empire romain IVe–Ve siècles*. Paris.

Gaudemet, J. (1965), "Nomokanon," in *RE* 87, Suppl.-Bd. 10.417–29.

Gaudemet, J. (1978), *Le Droit romain dans la littérature chrétienne occidentale du IIIe au Ve siècle*. Milan.

Gaudemet, J. (1983), "Collections canoniques et codifications," *Revue de droit canonique*, 33: 81–109.

Gaudemet, J. (1984), "La Bible dans les collections canoniques," in P. Riche and G. Lobrichon (eds.), *Le Moyen Âge et la Bible*. Paris: 327–69.

Gaudemet, J. (1985), *Les Sources du droit de l'église en Occident du IIe au VIIe siècle*. Paris.

Gaudemet, J. (1986), "Tentatives de systématisation du droit à Rome," *Archives de philosophie du droit*, 31: 11–28.

Gaudemet, J. (1991 [1994]), "Essais de systématisation en droit canonique," repr. in *La Doctrine canonique médiévale*. Aldershot, No. 2: 165–80.

Gaudemet, J. (1993), *Sources du droit de l'église en occident du VIIIe au XXe siècle*. Paris.

Gaudemet, J. (1994), *Église et cité: histoire du droit canonique*. Paris.

Gautier, P. (1973), "L'Édit d'Alexis Ier Comnène sur la réforme du clergé," *Revue des études byzantines*, 31: 165–200.

Gavardinas, G. (1998), *Η Πενθέκτη Οικουμενική Σύνοδος και το Νομοθετικό της έργο*. Katerini.

Geza, V. (1982), "A Summary of the Law by Flavius Josephus," *Novum Testamentum*, 24.4: 289–303.

Ghellinck, J. (1948), *Le Mouvement théologique du XIIe siècle, sa préparation lointaine avant et autour de Pierre Lombard, ses rapports avec les initiatives des canonistes; études, recherches et documents*. 2nd edn. Bruges.

Giaro, T. (ed.) (2006), *Modernisierung durch Transfer im 19. und frühen 20. Jahrhundert*. Frankfurt a.M.

Giaro, T. (2006a), "Modernisierung durch Transfer—Schwund osteuropäischer Rechtstraditionen," in Giaro 2006: 275–322.

Gibson, C. (2002), *Interpreting a Classic: Demosthenes and his Ancient Commentators*. Berkeley.

Glenn, H. (2007), *Legal Traditions of the World: Sustainable Diversity in Law*. 3rd edn. Oxford.

Gluckman, M. (1955), *The Judicial Process among the Barotse of Northern Rhodesia*. Manchester.

Gordley, J. and Thompson, A. (eds.) (1993), *The Treatise on Laws (Decretum DD.1–20)*. Washington, DC.

Goria, F. (2005), "Il giurista nell'impero romano d'Oriente (da Giustiniano agli inizi del secolo XI)," in Burgmann 2005: 147–211.

Goswell, G. (2009), "Early Readers of the Gospels: The *Kephalaia* and *Titloi* of Codex Alexandrinus," *Journal of Greco-Roman Christianity and Judaism*, 6: 134–74.

Graf, G. (1944–53), *Geschichte der christlichen arabischen Literatur*. 5 vols. Vatican.

Grumel, V. *et al.* (1936–91) *Les Regestes des actes du patriarcat de Constantinople*. 7 vols. Paris.

Hadot, I. (1984), *Arts libéraux et philosophie dans la pensée antique*. Paris.

Hadot, P. (1995), *Philosophy as a Way of Life*. Ed. and trans. Arnold Davidson. London.

Hadot, P. (1995a), *Qu'est-ce que la philosophie antique?* Paris.

Hadot, P. (2002), *Exercices spirituels et philosophie antique*. 2nd edn. Paris.

Hajdú, K. (2003), *Katalog der griechischen Handschriften der Bayerischen Staatsbibliothek München. Bd. 3: Codices graeci Monacenses 110–180, neu beschrieben*. Wiesbaden.

Haldon, J. (1990), *Byzantium in the Seventh Century: The Transformation of a Culture*. Cambridge.

Halfond, G. (2010), *The Archeology of Frankish Church Councils, AD 511–768*. Leiden.

Hammer, D. (1957), "Russia and Roman Law," *American Slavic and East European Review*, 16.1 (Feb.): 1–13.

Harries, J. (1986), "Sozomen and Eusebius: The Lawyer as Church Historian in the Fifth Century," in C. Holdsworth and T. Wiseman (eds.), *The Inheritance of Historiography: 350–900*. Exeter: 45–52.

Harries, J. (1988), "The Roman Imperial Quaestor from Constantine to Theodosius II," *Journal of Roman Studies*, 78: 148–72.

Harries, J. (1998), "How to Make a Law Code," in J. Harries and J. Smith (eds.), *Modus Operandi: Essays in Honour of Geoffrey Rickman*. London: 63–78.

Harries, J. (1999), *Law and Empire in Late Antiquity*. Cambridge.

Harries J. (2000), "Legal Culture and Identity in the Fifth-century West," in S. Mitchell and G. Greatrex (eds), *Ethnicity and Culture in Late Antiquity*. Cardiff: 45–58.

Harries, J. and Wood, I. (eds.) (1993), *The Theodosian Code: Studies in the Imperial Law of Late Antiquity*. Ithaca, NY.

Harris, W. (1989), *Ancient Literacy*. Cambridge, Mass.

Harris, W. (2001), *Restraining Rage: The Ideology of Anger Control in Classical Antiquity*. Cambridge, Mass.

Hart, H. L. A. (1961), *The Concept of Law*. Oxford.

Hartmann, W and Pennington, K. (eds.) (2012), *The History of Byzantine and Eastern Canon Law to 1500*. Washington, DC.

Hefele, C. and Leclercq, H. (*et al.*) (1907–), *Histoire des conciles d'après les documents originaux*. Paris.

Heggelbacher, O. (1974), *Geschichte des frühchristlichen Kirchenrechts bis zum Konzil von Nizäa, 325*. Freiburg.

Heimbach, C. (1868–9), "Griechisch-Römisches Recht im Mittelalter und in der Neuzeit," *Allgemeine Encyclopädie der Wissenschaften und Künste*, 86: 191–471; 87: 1–106.

Helmholz, R. (1995), "The Bible in the Service of the Canon Law," *Chicago-Kent Law Review*, 70: 1557–81.

Herman, É. (1957), "Jean III le scholastique," in *DDC* 6.118–20.

Herrmann, E. (1980), *Ecclesia in Re publica: die Entwicklung der Kirche von pseudo-staatlicher zu staatlich inkorporierter Existenz*. Frankfurt a.M.

Hess, H. (2002), *The Early Development of Canon Law and the Council of Serdica*. Oxford.

Hezser, E. (1998), "The Codification of Legal Knowledge in Late Antiquity: The Talmud Yerushalmi and Roman Law Codes," in P. Schäfer (ed.), *The Talmud Yerushalmi and Graeco-Roman Culture* I. Tübingen: 581–641.

Hoebel, E. (1954), *The Law of Primitive Man: A Study in Comparative Legal Dynamics*. Cambridge, Mass.

Hoebel, E. and Llewellyn, K. (1941), *The Cheyenne Way: Conflict and Case Law in Primitive Jurisprudence*. Norman, Okla.

Holland, J. and Webb, J. (2006), *Learning Legal Rules: A Student's Guide to Legal Method and Reasoning*. 6th edn. Oxford.

Honig, R. (1960), *Humanitas und Rhetorik in spätrömischen Kaisergesetzen. Studien zur Gesinnungsgrundlage des Dominats*. Göttingen.

Honigmann, E. (1961), "Le Concile de Constantinople de 394 et les auteurs du 'Syntagma des XIV titres'," in P. Devos (ed.), *Trois mémoires posthumes d'histoire et de géographie de l'Orient chrétien*. Brussels: 1–83.

Honoré, T. (1978), *Tribonian*. Ithaca, NY.

Honoré, T. (1994), *Emperors and Lawyers*. 2nd edn. Oxford.

Honoré, T. (1998), *Law in the Crisis of Empire, 379–455 AD*. Oxford.

Honoré, T. (2004), "Roman Law AD 200–400: From Cosmopolis to Rechtsstaat?," in S. Swain and M. Edwards (eds.), *Approaching Late Antiquity*. Oxford: 109–32.

Hove, A. van (1945), *Prolegomena ad Codicem juris canonici*. 2nd edn. Mechelen.

Humfress, C. (1998), "Forensic Practice in the Development of Roman Law and Ecclesiastical Law in Late Antiquity, with Special Reference to the Prosecution of Heresy." Unpublished thesis, Cambridge University.

Humfress, C. (2001), "A New Legal Cosmos: Late Roman Lawyers and the Early Medieval Church," in P. Linehan and J. Nelson (eds.), *The Medieval World*. London: 557–73.

Humfress, C. (2005), "Law and Legal Practice in the Age of Justinian," in Maas 2005: 161–84.

Humfress, C. (2007), *Orthodoxy and the Courts in Late Antiquity*. Oxford.

Humfress, C. (2009), "Law in Practice," in P. Rousseau and J. Raithel (eds.), *A Companion to Late Antiquity*. Oxford: 377–91.

Hunger, H. (1964), *Prooimion. Elemente der byzantinischen Kaiseridee in den Arengen der Urkunden*. Vienna.

Hunt, D. (1998), "The Church as Public Institution," in A. Cameron and P. Garnsey (eds.), *The Cambridge Ancient History, XIII: The Late Empire, A.D. 337–425*. Cambridge: 238–76.

Jasper, D. and Fuhrmann, H. (2001), *Papal Letters in the Early Middle Ages*. Washington, DC.

Jeffreys, E., *et al.* (eds.) (2008), *The Oxford Handbook of Byzantine Studies*. Oxford.

Jeffreys, M. (2008), "Text Criticism," in Jeffreys *et al.* 2008: 86–94.

Jenkins, R. (1963), "The Hellenistic Origins of Byzantine Literature," *Dumbarton Oak Papers*, 17: 38–52.

Johnston, D. (1989), "Justinian's Digest: The Interpretation of Interpolation," *Oxford Journal of Legal Studies*, 9.2: 149–66.

Johnston, D. (1999), *Roman Law in Context*. Cambridge.

Johnston, D. (2000), "The Jurists," in Schofield and Rowe 2000: 616–34.

Jolowicz, H. (1952), *Historical Introduction to the Study of Roman Law*. 2nd edn. Cambridge.

Jones, A. (1964), *The Later Roman Empire, 284–602: A Social, Economic, and Administrative Survey*. Oxford.

Jones, J. (1956), *The Law and Legal Theory of the Greeks: An Introduction*. Oxford.

Kaser, M. (1955), *Das römische Privatrecht*. 3 vols. Munich.

Kaser, M. and Hackl, K. (1996), *Das römische Zivilprozessrecht*. 2nd edn. Munich.

Kaster, R. (1988), *Guardians of Language: The Grammarian and Society in Late Antiquity*. Berkeley.

Kaufhold, H. (2012), "Sources of Canon Law in the Eastern Churches," in Hartmann and Pennington 2012: 215–342.

Kazhdan, A. (1989), "Do We Need a New History of Byzantine Law?," *Jahrbuch des österreichischen Byzantistik*, 39: 1–28.

Kazhdan, A. (1994), "Some Observations on the Byzantine Concept of Law: Three Authors of the Ninth through the Twelfth Centuries," in Laiou and Simon 1994: 199–216.

Kelly, C. (1998), "Emperors, Government and Bureaucracy," in A. Cameron and P. Garnsey (eds.), *The Cambridge Ancient History, XIII: The Late Empire A.D. 337–425*. Cambridge: 138–83.

Kelly, C. (2004), *Ruling the Later Roman Empire*. Cambridge, Mass.

Kelly, D. (1970), *Foundations of Modern Historical Scholarship: Language, Law and History in the French Renaissance*. New York.

Kelly, J. (1992), *A Short History of Western Legal Theory*. Oxford.

Kennedy, G. (1972), *The Art of Rhetoric in the Roman World, 300 B.C.–A.D. 300*. Princeton.

Kennedy, G. (1983), *Greek Rhetoric under Christian Emperors*. Princeton.

Kennedy, G. (1994), *A New History of Classical Rhetoric*. Princeton.

Kleinknecht, H. and Gutbrod, W. (1942 [1967]), "*Νόμος*," in G. Kittel *et al.* (eds.), *Theological Dictionary of the New Testament*. Trans. G. Bromiley. (Repr. Grand Rapids, Mich. 1964–76), 4: 1022–91.

Konidaris, I. (1994), "The Ubiquity of Canon Law," in Laiou and Simon 1994: 131–50.

Konidaris, I. (2000), *Εγχειρίδιο εκκλησιαστικού δικαίου*. Thessaloniki.

Kottje, R. (1970), *Studien zum Einfluss des Alten Testaments auf Recht und Liturgie des frühen Mittelalters (6.–8. Jahrhundert)*. 2nd edn. Bonn.

Kraznozhen, M. (1911), *Толкователи канонического кодекса Восточной Церкви: Аристин, Зонара и Вальсамон*. Yurev.

Krüger, P. (1894), *Histoire des sources du droit romain*. Trans. J. Brissaud. Paris.

Kühner, R. (1869), *Ausführliche Grammatik der griechischen Sprache*. 2nd edn., 2 vols. in 3. Hanover.

Kunkel, W. (1964 [1966]), *An Introduction to Roman Legal and Constitutional History*. Trans. J. Kelly. Oxford.

Kuttner, S. (1947), "Liber canonicus: A Note on Dictatus papae c. 17," in G. Borino (ed.), *Studi Gregoriani. Per la storia di Gregorio VII e della riforma gregoriana* 1–2. Rome: 387–401.

Kuttner, S. (1950), "Some Considerations on the Role of Secular Law and Institutions in the History of Canon Law," repr. in Kuttner 1990: 351–62.

Kuttner, S. (1960 [1993]), "Harmony from Dissonance: An Interpretation of Medieval Canon Law," repr. in *History of Ideas and Doctrines of Canon Law in the Middle Ages*. 2nd edn. London. No. 1: 1–65.

Kuttner, S. (1976), "Reflections on Gospel and Law in the History of the Church," repr. in Kutner 1990: no. 9: 199–209

Kuttner, S. (1982), "The Revival of Jurisprudence," repr. in Kuttner 1990: no. 3: 299–323.

Kuttner, S. (1990), *Studies in the History of Medieval Canon Law* [Collected Essays]. Aldershot.

Laiou, A. (1994), "Law, Justice, and the Byzantine Historians: Ninth to Twelfth Centuries," in Laiou and Simon 1994: 151–85.

Laiou, A. and Simon, D. (eds.) (1994), *Law and Society in Byzantium, 9th–12th Centuries*. Washington, DC.

Laks, A. (2000), "The Laws," in Schofield and Rowe 2000: 258–92.

Lampe, G. (1961), *A Patristic Greek Lexicon*. Oxford.

Lanata, G. (1984), *Legislazione e natura nelle Novelle giustinianee*. Naples.

Lanata, G. (1989), "Du vocabulaire de la loi dans les Novelles de Justinien," *Subseciva Groningana*, 3: 37–48.

Lanata, G. (1989a), "La Médecine et la loi: l'hippocratisme dans l'antiquité tardive," in G. Baader and R. Winau (eds.), *Die hippokratischen Epidemien: Theorie-Praxis-Tradition*. Stuttgart: 347–54.

Landau, P. (1995), "Überlieferung und Bedeutung der Kanones des Trullanischen Konzils im westlichen kanonischen Recht," in Nedungatt and Featherstone 1995: 215–27.

Lanni, A. (2005), "Relevance in Athenian Courts," in Gagarin and Cohen 2005: 112–28.

Laurent, V. (1965), "L'Oeuvre canonique du concile in Trullo (691–692): source primaire du droit de l'Église orientale," *Revue des études byzantines*, 23: 7–41.

Lausberg, H. (1963 [1998]), *Handbook of Literary Rhetoric: A Foundation for Literary Study*. Trans. M. Bliss *et al.* Leiden.

Lawson, F. (1930, 1931), "The Basilica," *Law Quarterly Review*, 46: 486–501 and 47: 536–56.

Le Bras, G. (1938), "Les Écritures dans le Décret de Gratien," *Zeitschrift der Savigny-Stiftung für Rechtsgeschichte*, Kan. Abt. 21: 47–80.

Lee, A. (2002), "Decoding Late Roman Law," *Journal of Roman Studies*, 92: 185–93 [review article].

Lefebvre, C., *et al.* (1976), *L'Époque moderne, 1563–1789: les sources du droit et la seconde centralisation romaine*. Histoire du droit et des institutions de l'Église en Occident 16. Paris.

Lemerle, P. (1971), *Le Premier humanisme byzantin: notes et remarques sur enseignement et culture à Byzance des origines au 10. siècle*. Paris.

Lendon, J. (1997), *Empire of Honour: The Art of Government in the Roman World*. Oxford.

Lenel, O. (1889), *Palingenesia Iuris Civilis*. 2 vols. Leipzig.

Lenel, O. (1892), *Das Sabinussystem*. Strasburg.

Leontaritou, V. (1996), *Εκκλησιαστικά αξιώματα και υπηρεσίες στην πρώιμη και μέση βυζαντινή περίοδο*. Athens.

Letwin, S. (2005), *On the History of the Idea of Law*. Cambridge.

Lévy, E. (ed.) (2000), *La Codification des lois dans l'Antiquité*. Paris.

L'Huillier, P. (1964), "L'Esprit du droit canonique orthodoxe," *Messager de l'Exarchat du Patriarche russe en Europe occidentale*, 12: 108–19.

L'Huillier, P. (1976), "Origines et développement de l'ancienne collection canonique grecque," *Messager de l'Exarchat du Patriarche russe en Europe occidentale*, 24: 53–65.

L'Huillier, P. (1996), *The Church of the Ancient Councils: The Disciplinary Work of the First Four Ecumenical Councils*. Crestwood, NY.

L'Huillier, P. (1997), "The Making of Written Law in the Church," *Studia canonica*, 31: 117–46.

Liddell, H. and Scott, R., rev. Jones, H. S. (1996), *A Greek–English Lexicon*. 9th edn. Oxford.

Liebs, D. (1976), "Rechtsschulen und Rechtsunterricht im Prinzipat," in H. Temporini (ed.), *Aufstieg und Niedergang der römischen Welt: Recht (Methoden, Schulen, Einzelne Juristen)* vol. 2.15. Berlin and New York: 197–286.

Liebs, D. (1987), *Die Jurisprudenz im spätantiken Italien (260–640 n. Chr.)*. Berlin.

Liebs, D. (1989), "Droit et littérature juridique," in R. Herzog (ed.), *Restauration et Renouveau: La littérature latine de 284 à 374 après J.-C.* Munich: 61–82.

Liebs, D. (2000), "Roman Law," in A. Cameron *et al.* (eds.), *The Cambridge Ancient History XIV: Late Antiquity: Empire and Successors, A.D. 425–600*. Cambridge: 238–59.

Liebs, D. (2005), *Römische Jurisprudenz in Africa mit Studien zu den pseudopaulinischen Sentenzen*. 2nd edn. Berlin.

Liebs, D. (2008), "Roman Vulgar Law in Late Antiquity," in B. Sirks (ed.), *Aspects of Law in Late Antiquity*. Oxford: 35–53.

Lietzmann, H. (1921), "Kirchenrechtliche Sammlungen," in *RE* 11: 488–501.

Lim, R. (1995), *Public Disputation, Power, and Social Order in Late Antiquity*. Berkeley.

Lokin, J. (1994), "The Significance of Law and Legislation in the Law Books of the Ninth to Eleventh Centuries," in Laiou and Simon 1994: 71–91.

Lokin, J. (1997), "The Novels of Leo and the Decisions of Justinian," in Troianos 1997: 131–40.

Lossky, V. (1944 [1957]), *The Mystical Theology of the Eastern Church*. London.

Lotte, K. (1999), *Canonical Collections of the Early Middle Ages (ca. 400–1140): A Bibliographical Guide to the Manuscripts and Literature*. Washington, DC.

Louth, A. (1983), *Discerning the Mystery: An Essay on the Nature of Theology*. Oxford.

Louth, A. (2002), *St John Damascene: Tradition and Originality in Byzantine Theology*. Oxford.

Louth, A. (2004), "Conciliar Records and Canons," in F. Young *et al.* (eds.), *The Cambridge History of Early Christian Literature*. Cambridge: 391–6.

Louth, A. (2007), "St John Damascene as Monastic Theologian," *Downside Review*, 125: 197–220.

Maas, M. (ed.) (2005), *The Cambridge Companion to the Age of Justinian*. Cambridge.

Maas, M. (2005a), "Roman Questions, Byzantine Answers: Contours of the Age of Justinian," in Maas 2005: 3–27.

Maas, P. (1958), *Textual Criticism*. Oxford.

Maassen, F. (1871), *Geschichte der Quellen und der Literatur des canonischen Rechts im Abendlande bis zum Ausgange des Mittelalters*. Gratz.

McGann, J. (1983), *A Critique of Modern Textual Criticism*. Chicago.

McGuckin, J. (2012), *The Ascent of Christian Law: Patristic and Byzantine Formulations of New Civilization*. Crestwood, NY.

McKitterick, R. (1985), "Knowledge of Canon Law in the Frankish Kingdoms before 789: The MS Evidence," *Journal of Theological Studies*, NS 36: 97–117.

Macrides, R. (1985), "Poetic Justice in the Patriarchate: Murder and Cannibalism in the Provinces" in Burgmann *et al.* 1985: 137–68.

Macrides, R. (1990), "Nomos and Kanon on Paper and in Court," in R. Morris (ed.), *Church and People in Byzantium*. Birmingham: 61–85.

Macrides, R. (1991), "Perception of the Past in the Twelfth-Century Canonists," in Oikonomides 1991: 589–99.

Macrides, R. (1992), "Bad Historian or Good Lawyer? Demetrios Chomatenos and Novel 131," *Dumbarton Oaks Papers*, 46: 187–96.

Macrides, R. (1994), "The Competent Court," in Laiou and Simon 1994: 117–29.

Macrides, R. (2005), "The Law Outside the Law Books: Law and Literature," in Burgmann 2005: 133–45.

Magdalino, P. (1985), "Die Jurisprudenz als Komponente der byzantinischen Gelehrtenkultur des 12. Jahrhunderts," in Burgmann *et al.* 1985: 169–77.

Magdalino, P. (1996), "The Reform Edict of 1107," in M. Mullett and D. Smythe (eds.), *Alexios I Komnenos*, I: *Papers*. Belfast: 199–218.

Magdalino, P. (1997), "The Non-Juridical Legislation of Leo VI," in Troianos 1997: 169–82.

Magdalino, P. (1999), "The Distance of the Past in Early Medieval Byzantium, VII–X Centuries," in *Ideologie e pratiche del reimpiego nell'alto medioevo*, Settimane di studio del Centro Italiano di studi sull'alto medioevo, 46. Spoleto: 115–47.

Magie, D. (1905), *De Romanorum iuris publici sacrique vocabulis sollemnibus in graecum sermonem conversis*. Leipzig.

Maguire, H. (1994), "From the Evil Eye to the Eye of Justice: The Saints, Art, and Justice in Byzantium," in Laiou and Simon 1994: 217–39.

Maine, H. (1861), *Ancient Law*. London.

Maksimovich, K. (1998), "Aufbau und Quellen des altrussischen Ustjuger Nomokanons," in Burgmann 1998: 477–508.

Maksimovich, K. (2006), "Byzantinische Rechtsbücher und ihre Bedeutung für die Rechtsgeschichte Osteuropas," in Giaro 2006: 1–31.

Maksimovich, K. (2007), "Byzantine Law in Old Slavonic Translations and the Nomocanon of Methodius," *Byzantinoslavica*, 65: 9–18.

Malinowski, B. (1926), *Crime and Custom in Savage Society*. London.

Mardirossian, A. (2004), *Le Livre des canons arméniens (Kanonagirk Hayoc) de Yovhannes Awjneci: église, droit et société en Arménie du IVe au VIIIe siècle*. Leuven.

Mardirossian, A. (2010), *La Collection canonique d'Antioche*. Paris.

Marrou, H. (1948 [1956]), *A History of Education in Antiquity*. Trans. G. Lamb. New York.

Mason, H. (1974), *Greek Terms for Roman Institutions: A Lexicon and Analysis*. Toronto.

Matthews, J. (2000), *Laying Down the Law: A Study of the Theodosian Code*. New Haven, Conn.

Matthisen, R. (1997), "The 'Second Council of Arles' and the Spirit of Compilation and Codification in Late Roman Gaul," *Journal of Early Christian Studies*, 5: 511–54.

Matthisen, R. (ed.) (2001), *Law, Society, and Authority in Late Antiquity*. Oxford.

Mayr, R. (1923), *Vocabularium Codicis Iustiniani*. 2 vols. Prague.

Meliara, K. (1905–1906), "*Μελέτη περὶ τοῦ Νομοκάνονος τοῦ ἁγιωτάτου πατριάρχου Κωνσταντινουπόλεως Φωτίου*," *Νέα Σιών*, 2: 55–76, 343–55, 510–24, 878–93; 3: 11–27, 118–38, 250–6.

Mellinkoff, D. (1963), *The Language of the Law*. Boston.

Menebisoglou, P. (1982), "*῾Ο κώδιξ τῆς Τραπεζοῦντος τοῦ ἔτους* 1311," *Ἐκκλησία καὶ Θεολογία*, 3: 193–206.

Menebisoglou, P. (1984), "*Συνόψεις καὶ ἐπιτομαὶ ἱερῶν κανόνων ἐν Βυζαντίῳ*," in *Μνήμη Μετροπολίτου Ἰκονίου Ἰακόβου*. Athens: 77–95.

Menebisoglou, P. (1989), "*Οἱ πρόλογοι τοῦ συντάγματος-νομοκάνονος εἰς δεκατέσσαρας τίτλους*," in *Αναφορά στην μνήμη του Μητροπολίτου Σάρδεων Μαξίμου*. Geneva: 227–51.

Merryman, J. (1969), *The Civil Law Tradition: An Introduction to the Legal Systems of Western Europe and Latin America*. Stanford, Calif.

Metzger, B. (1981), *Manuscripts of the Greek Bible: An Introduction to Greek Palaeography*. Oxford.

Metzger, M. (1985), *Les Constitutions apostoliques*. 3 vols. Paris.

Meyendorff, J. (1966 [1983]), "One Bishop in One City," repr. in *Catholicity and the Church*. Crestwood, NY: 111–20.

Meyendorff, J. (1978), "Contemporary Problems in Orthodox Canon Law," in *Living Tradition: Orthodox Witness in the Contemporary World*. Crestwood, NY: 99–114.

Meyendorff, J. (1981), *The Orthodox Church: Its Past and its Role in the World Today*. 3rd edn. Crestwood, NY.

Meyendorff, J. (1983), *Byzantine Theology: Historical Trends and Doctrinal Themes*. 2nd edn. New York.

Milaš, N. (1895–6 [1911]), *Правила Православной Церкви с толкованиями*. Trans. I. Palmov. St Petersburg.

Milaš, N. (1902 [1906]), *Τὸ ἐκκλησιαστικὸν δίκαιον τῆς Ὀρθοδόξου Ἀνατολικῆς Ἐκκλησίας*. Trans. M. Apostolopoulos (from German edn., 1905). Athens [also in German: *Das Kirchenrecht der morgenländischen Kirche*. (1905). Trans. A. Pessić (from 2nd Serbian edn.). Mostar].

Millar, F. (2006), *A Greek Roman Empire: Power and Belief under Theodosius II*. Berkeley.

Mioni, E. (1973), *Introduzione alla paleografia greca*. Padova.

Mitchell, M. (2005), "Patristic Rhetoric on Allegory: Origen and Eustathius Put 1 Samuel 28 on Trial," *Journal of Religion*, 85: 414–45.

Mitteis, L. (1891 [1963]), *Reichsrecht und Volksrecht in den östlichen Provinzen des römischen Kaiserreichs*. Leipzig.

Montfaucon, D. Bernardi de (1709), *Palaeographia Graeca*. Paris.

Mordek, H. (1975), *Kirchenrecht und Reform im Frankenreich: die Collectio Vetus Gallica, die älteste systematische Kanonessammlung des fränkischen Gallien*. Berlin.

Mordek, H. (1977), "Kirchenrechtliche Autoritäten im Frühmittelalter," in P. Classen (ed.), *Recht und Schrift im Mittelalter*. Thorbecke: 237–55.

Mordek, H. (1991), "Kanonessamlungen," in R. Auty *et al.* (eds.), *Lexikon des Mittelalters*, 5: 900–3.

Morgan, T. (1998), *Literate Education in the Hellenistic and Roman Worlds*. Cambridge.

Morolli, D. (2000), "Fonti canoniche della chiesa constantinopolitana," in Furugia 2000: 313–16.

Morolli, D. (2000a), "Fonti canoniche della chiesa copta," in Furugia 2000: 310–13.

Morolli, D. (2000b), "Fonti canoniche della chiesa etiopica," in Furugia 2000: 316–18.

Mortimer, R. (1953), *Western Canon Law*. London.

Mortreuil, J. (1843–6), *Histoire du droit byzantin*. 3 vols. Paris.

Müller, W. (2006), "Introduction: Medieval Church Law as a Field of Inquiry," in W. Müller and M. Sommar (eds.), *Medieval Church Law and the Origins of the Western Legal Tradition: A Tribute to Kenneth Pennington*. Washington, DC: 1–14.

Munier, C. (1954), "Les Sources patristiques du droit de l'église," *Revue de droit canonique*, 4: 184–92.

Munier, C. (1957), *Les Sources patristiques du droit de l'église*. Strasbourg.

Munier, C. (1960), *Les "Statuta ecclesiae antiqua."* Paris.

Munier, C. (1975), "La Tradition littéraire des canons africains," *Recherches augustiniennes*, 10: 1–22.

Munitiz, J. (1974), "Synoptic Greek Accounts of the Seventh Council," *Revue des études byzantines*, 32: 147–86.

Munitiz, J. (1978), "Synoptic Greek Chronologies of the Councils," *Revue des études byzantines*, 36: 193–218.

Naz, R. (1949), "Droit canonique," in *DDC* 4.1446–95.

Naz, R. (1956), "Nomocanon," in *DDC* 6.1014.

Naz, R. (1965), "Règles," in *DDC* 7.541–5.

Nedungatt, G. and Featherstone, M. (eds.) (1995), *The Council in Trullo Revisited*. Rome.

Nelson, J. (2008), "Law and its Applications," in T. Noble and J. Smith (eds.), *Early Medieval Christianities c. 600–c. 1100*. Cambridge: 299–326.

Neschke-Hentschke, A. (1995), *Platonisme politique et théorie du droit naturel: contributions à une archéologie de la culture politique européene*. Louvain.

Nichols, A. (1989), *Theology in the Russian Diaspora: Church, Fathers, Eucharist in Nikolai Afanas'ev*. Cambridge.

Nichols, A. (1992), "Afanas'ev and the Byzantine Canonical Tradition," *Heythrop Journal*, 33.4: 415–25.

Odorico, P. (1990), "La Cultura della *Συλλογή*," *Byzantinische Zeitschrift*, 83: 1–21.

Ohme, H. (1990), *Das Concilium Quinisextum und seine Bischofsliste*. Berlin.

Ohme, H. (1991), "Zur Diskussion um das kanonische Recht in der neueren orthodoxen Theologie," *Kerygma und Dogma*, 37: 227–56.

Ohme, H. (1998), *Kanon ekklesiastikos: die Bedeutung des altkirchlichen Kanonbegriffes*. Berlin.

Ohme, H. (2001), "Kanon" in D. Betz *et al.* (eds.), *Religion in Geschichte und Gegenwart*. 4th edn. Stuttgart: 4.774–6.

Ohme, H. (2006), *Concilium Quinisextum = Das Konzil Quinisextum*. Turnhout.

Oikonomides, N. (ed.) (1991), *Το Βυζάντινο κατά τον 12ο αιώνα: κανονικό δίκαιο, κράτος και κοινωνία/Byzantium in the 12th Century: Canon Law, State and Society*. Athens.

O'Meara, D. (2003), *Platonopolis: Platonic Political Philosophy in Late Antiquity*. Oxford.

Ong, W. (1982), *Orality and Literacy: The Technologizing of the Word*. London.

Oppel, H. (1937), *ΚΑΝΩΝ. Zur Bedeutungsgeschichte des Wortes und seiner lateinischen Entsprechungen–regula, norma*. Leipzig.

Orsy, L. (1992), *Theology and Canon Law: New Horizons for Legislation and Interpretation*. Collegeville, Md.

Ostroumov, M. (1893), *Введение в православное церковное право*. Charkhov.

Panagiotakos, P. (1962), *Σύστημα τοῦ ἐκκλησιαστικοῦ δικαίου: τὸ ποινικὸν δίκαιον τῆς Ἐκκλσίας*. vol. 3. Athens.

Papagianni, E. (2005), "Un témoin de la réalité juridique byzantine: la jurisprudence patriarcale au XIVe siècle," in Burgmann 2005: 213–27.

Papastathis, C. (ed.) (2001), *Byzantine Law: Proceedings of the International Symposium of Jurists, Thessaloniki, 10–13 December 1998*. Thessaloniki.

Parker, D. (1997), *The Living Text of the Gospels*. Cambridge.

Parker, D. (2008), *An Introduction to the New Testament Manuscripts and Their Texts*. Cambridge.

Patsavos, L. (1975), *The Canon Law of the Orthodox Catholic Church*. Typewritten course manual of Holy Cross Theological Seminary, Boston. Brookline, Mass.

Patsavos, L. (1981), "The Status of Canon Law in the Orthodox Church Today," in D. Constantelos (ed.), *Orthodox Theology and Diakonia: Trends and Prospects*, Brookline, Mass.: 103–14.

Patsavos, L. [Kapsanis, G.] (1999), "The Interface of Pastoral Ministry and the Holy Canons," *Kanon*, 15: 179–95. [Adaptation of G. Kapsanis *'Η ποιμαντικὴ διακονία κατὰ τοὺς ἱερούς κανόνας*, Piraeus 1976.]

Patsavos, L. (2003), *Spiritual Dimensions of the Holy Canons*. Brookline, Mass.

Pavlov, A. (1874), "Замечания о грузинском номоканоне," *Записки Императорской Академии Наук*, 25.1: 39–42.

Pavlov, A. (1902), *Курс церковного права*. Holy Trinity-Sergei Lavra.

Pazdernik, C. (2005), "Justinianic Ideology and the Power of the Past," in Maas 2005: 185–212.

Pennington, K. (1994), "Learned Law, Droit Savant, Gelehrtes Recht: The Tyranny of a Concept," *Syracuse Journal of International Law and Commerce*, 20: 205–15.

Pennington, K. (2007), "The Growth of Church Law," in A. Casiday and F. Norris (eds.), *Cambridge History of Christianity. Vol. 2: Constantine to c. 600*. Cambridge: 386–402.

Pennington, K. (2008), "Decretal Collections 1190–1234," in W. Hartmann and K. Pennington (eds.) *The History of Medieval Canon Law in the Classical Period, 1140–1234: From Gratian to the Decretals of Pope Gregory IX*. Washington, DC: 293–317.

Perentides, S. (1979), "Les Scholies juridiques des manuscrits byzantins," *Revue de l'histoire du droit francais et étranger* (ser. 4), 57: 51–60.

Petrovitz, B. (1970), *'Ο Νομοκάνων εἰς ιδ' τίτλους καὶ οἱ Βυζαντινοὶ σχολιασταί*. Athens.

Pfannmüller, G. (1902), *Die kirchliche Gesetzgebung Justinians hauptsächlich auf Grund der Novellen*. Berlin.

Phidas, V. (1998), *Droit canon: une perspective orthodoxe*. Geneva.

Pieler, P. (1970), "Die Entscheidungen des Patriarchalgerichts von Konstantinopel in zivilrechtlichen Streitfällen und das System der Quellen des byzantinischen Rechts," in *Österreichische Landesreferate zum VIII. Internationalen Kongreß für Rechtsvergleichung in Pescara*. Vienna: 7–16.

Pieler P. (1978), "Byzantinische Rechtsliteratur," in H. Hunger (ed.), *Die hochsprachliche profane Literatur der Byzantiner* II (Handbuch der Altertumswissenschaft, XII,5,2). Munich: 341–480.

Pieler, P. (1987), "Lex Christiana," in D. Simon (ed.), *Akten des 26. Deutschen Rechtshistorikertages*. Frankfurt a.M.: 485–503.

Pieler, P. (1989), "*Ἀνακάθαρσις τῶν παλαιῶν νόμων* und makedonische Renaissance," *Subseciva Groningana*, 3: 61–77.

Pieler, P. (1991), "Johannes Zonaras als Kanonist," in Oikonomides 1991: 601–20.

Pieler, P. (1997), "Das Alte Testament im Rechtsdenken der Byzantiner," in Troianos 1997: 81–113.

Pieler, P. (1997a), "Spätantike Rechtsliteratur," in E. Lodewijk and H. Hofmann (eds.), *Neues Handbuch der Literaturwissenschaft*, Wiesbaden: 4.565–600.

Pieler, P. (2000), "Die justinianische Kodifikation in der juristischen Praxis des 6. Jahrhunderts," in S. Puliatti and A. Sanguinetti (eds.), *Legislazione, cultura giuridica, prassi dell'impero d'oriente in età giustinianea tra passato e futuro*. Milan: 211–27.

Pinedo, P. (1963), "Fragmentación, titulación y sistema," in *Homenaje a Don Ramón Carande*. Madrid: 1.285–97.

Pitsakis, C. (1976), *Πρόχειρον νόμων ἢ Ἑξάβιβλος*. Athens.

Plöchl, W. (1959), *Geschichte des Kirchenrechts*. 5 vols. Vienna.

Posner, R. (1993), *The Problem of Jurisprudence*. Cambridge, Mass.

Posner, R. (2009), *Law and Literature*. Cambridge, Mass.

Pospisil, L (1971), *Anthropology of Law: A Comparative Theory*. New York.

Potz, R. and Synek, E. (2007), *Orthodoxes Kirchenrecht: eine Einführung*. Freistadt.

Preisigke, F. *et al.* (1925–93), *Wörterbuch der griechischen Papyrusurkunden I–IV*, Supp. I–IV. Berlin–Wiesbaden–Marburg.

Price, R. and Gaddis, M. (2005), *The Acts of the Council of Chalcedon*. 3 vols. Liverpool.

Pringsheim, F. (1921), "Beryt und Bologna," in *Gesammelte Abhandlungen*, 1: 391–449.

Pringsheim, F. (1944), "The Unique Character of Classical Roman Law," *Journal of Roman Studies*, 34.1–2: 60–4.

Prinzing, G. (1986), "Das Bild Justinians I. in der Überlieferung der Byzantiner vom 7–16 Jhdt.," in D. Simon (ed.), *Fontes Minores VII*. Forschungen zur byzantinischen Rechtsgeschichte, Bd. 14. Frankfurt a.M: 1–99.

Raaflaub, K. (2000), "Poets, Lawgivers and the Beginnings of Political Reflection in Archaic Greece," in Schofield and Rowe 2000: 11–59.

Reynolds, R. (1986), "Law, Canon: To Gratian," in J. Strayers *et al.* (eds.), *Dictionary of the Middle Ages*, New York: 7.395–413.

Rhalles, C. (1907), *Ποινικὸν Δίκαιον τῆς Ὀρθοδόξου Ἐκκλησίας*. Athens.

Rheinstein, M. (1938), "Law Faculties and Law Schools: A Comparison of Legal Education in the United States and Germany," *Wisconsin Law Review*, 5: 5–42.

Rhodopoulos, P. (2005), *Ἐπιτομή Κανονικού Δικαίου*. Thessaloniki.

Rhodopoulos, P. (2007), *An Overview of Orthodox Canon Law*. Rollinsford, NH [adapted from Rhodopoulos 2005].

Richard, M. and Olivier, J. (1995), *Répertoire des bibliothèques et des catalogues de manuscrits grecs de Marcel Richard*. 3rd edn. Turnhout.

Riedel, W. (1900), *Die Kirchenrechtsquellen des Patriarchats Alexandrien*. Leipzig.

Ries, G. (1983), *Prolog und Epilog in Gesetzen des Altertums*. Munich.

Roberts, S. (1979), *Order and Dispute: An Introduction to Legal Anthropology*. Harmondsworth.

Robinson, O. (1997), *The Sources of Roman Law: Problems and Methods for Ancient Historians*. London.

Robinson, O. *et al.* (2000), *European Legal History: Sources and Institutions*. 3rd edn. London.

Romilly, J. (1971), *La Loi dans la pensée grecque des origines à Aristote*. Paris.

Roth, M. (2000), "The Law Collection of King Hammurabi," in Levy 2000: 9–31.

Rougé, J. *et al.* (2005), *Code théodosien—Livre XVI*. Paris.

Rouland, N. (1988 [1994]), *Legal Anthropology*. Trans. P. Planel. Stanford, Calif.

Roussos, E. (1949), *Λεξιλόγιον ἐκκλησιαστικοῦ δικαίου*. 2 vols. Athens.

Rowe, M. (2000), "The *Politicus* and Other Dialogues," in Schofield and Rowe 2000: 233–57.

Ruschenbusch, E. (1966), *Σόλωνος Νόμοι: die Fragmente des Solonischen Gesetzeswerkes, mit einer Text-und Überlieferungsgeschichte*. Wiesbaden.

Sacra Congregazione Orientale (1932), *Codificazione canonica orientale*. Fasc.8. Fonti: Studi storici sulle fonti del diritto canonico orientale. Vatican.

Sakellaropoulos, M. (1898), *Ἐκκλησιαστικὸν Δίκαιον τῆς Ἀνατολικῆς ὀρθοδόξου Ἐκκλησίας μετὰ τοῦ ἰσχύοντος νῦν ἐν τῇ Ἐκκλησίᾳ τοῦ Πατριαρχείου καὶ ἐν Ἑλλάδι*. Athens.

Savigny, F. (1831 [1975]), *Of the Vocation of our Age for Legislation and Jurisprudence*. Trans. A. Hayward. New York.

Scharf, J. (1959), "Quellenstudien zum Prooimion der Epanagoge," *Byzantinische Zeitschrift*, 52: 68–81.

Scheltema, H. (1970), *L'Enseignement de droit des antécesseurs*. Leiden.

Schmemann, A. (1979), "The 'Orthodox World,' Past and Present," in *Church, World, Mission: Reflections on Orthodoxy in the West*. Crestwood, NY: 25–66.

Schminck, A. (1986), *Studien zu mittelbyzantinischen Rechtsbüchern*. Frankfurt a.M.

Schminck, A. (1998), "Das Prooimion der Bearbeitung des Nomokanons in 14 Titeln durch Michael und Theodoros," in Burgmann 1998: 357–86.

Schminck, A. (2005), "Bemerkungen zum sog. 'Nomos Mosaïkos'," in Burgmann 2005: 249–68.

Schminck, A. and Getov, D. (2010), *Repertorium der Handschriften des byzantinischen Rechts*. vol. 2. Frankfurt a.M.

Schofield, C. (2000), "Approaching the Republic," in Schofield and Rowe 2000: 190–232.

Schofield, M, and Rowe, C. (eds.) (2000), *The Cambridge History of Greek and Roman Political Thought*. Cambridge.

Schöpsdau, K. (1994), *Nomoi (Gesetze) Buch I–III*. Göttingen.

Schöpsdau, K. (2003), *Nomoi (Gesetze) Buch IV–VII*. Göttingen.

Schulte, J. (1875), *Die Geschichte der Quellen und Literatur des canonischen Rechts*. 2 vols. Stuttgart.

Schulz, F. (1936), *Principles of Roman law*. Trans. M. Wolff. Oxford.

Schulz, F. (1953), *History of Roman Legal Science*. Rev. edn. Oxford.

Schwartz, E. (1910), "Über die pseudoapostolischen Kirchenordnungen," *Gesammelte Schriften*, 5: 192–273.

Schwartz, E. (1911), "Bußstufen und Katechumenatsklassen," *Gesammelte Schriften*, 5: 274–362.

Schwartz, E. (1933), "Die Kanonessammlung des Johannes Scholastikos," *Sitzungsberichte der Bayerischen Akademie der Wissenschaften*. Phil-hist. Abt. 6: 3–6.

Schwartz, E. (1936), "Über die Sammlung des Cod. Veronensis LX," *Zeitschrift für die neutestamentliche Wissenschaft und die Kunde der älteren Kirche*, 35: 1–23.

Schwartz, E. (1936a), "Die Kanonessammlungen der alten Reichskirche," *Gesammelte Schriften* 4: 159–275.

Schwyzer, E. (1939–53), *Griechische Grammatik*. 3 vols. Munich.

Sealey, R. (1994), *The Justice of the Greeks*. Ann Arbor, Mich.

Selb, W. (1967), "Die Kanonessammlungen der orientalischen Kirchen und das grieschische Corpus canonum der Reichskirche," in H. Lentze and I. Gampl (eds.), *Speculum Iuris et Ecclesiarum*. Vienna: 371–83.

Selb, W. (1970), "Kodifikation im älteren orientalischen Kirchenrecht," in F. Schwind (ed.), *Wiener Rechtswissenschfltiche Studien*, 8: 17–23.

Selb, W. (1981), *Orientalisches Kirchenrecht. Band I: Die Geschichte des Kirchenrechts der Nestorianer*. Vienna.

Selb, W. (1989), *Orientalisches Kirchenrecht. Band II: Die Geschichte des Kirchenrechts der Westsyrer*. Vienna.

Sheehy, M. (1982), "The Collectio Canonum Hibernensis—a Celtic Phenomenon," in H. Löwe (ed.), *Die Iren und Europa im früheren Mittelalter*. 2 vols. Stuttgart. 1: 525–35.

Sheehy, M. (1987), "The Bible and the Collectio Canonum Hibernensis," in M. Richter and N. Chatháin (eds.), *Irland und die Christenheit: Bibelstudien und Mission*. Stuttgart: 277–83.

Sieben, H. (1979), *Die Konzilsidee in der Alten Kirche*. Paderborn.

Simmonds, N. (2008), *Central Issues in Jurisprudence: Justice, Law and Rights*. 3rd edn. London.

Simon, D. (1973), *Rechtsfindung am byzantinischen Reichsgericht*. Frankfurt a.M.

Simon, D. (ed.) (1979), *Fontes Minores III*. Forschungen zur byzantinischen Rechtsgeschichte, Band 4. Frankfurt a.M.

Simon, D. (1994), "Legislation as Both a World Order and a Legal Order," in Laiou and Simon 1994: 1–25.

Simon, D. (2005), "Wozu?," in Burgmann 2005: 1–4.

Sirks, A. (2007), "Rechtswissenschaft und Recht im spätantiken Gallien und Afrika," *Legal History Review*, 75: 39–46.

Sirks, A. (2007a), *The Theodosian Code: A Study*. Norderstedt.

Smyth, H. (1956), *Greek Grammar*. Rev. edn. Cambridge, Mass.

Sohm, R. (1909), *Wesen und Ursprung des Katholizismus*. Leipzig.

Sohm, R. (1918), *Das altkatholische Kirchenrecht und das Dekret Gratians*. Munich.

Sohm, R. (1923), *Kirchenrecht*. 2 vols. Munich.

Sokolov, I. (1851), *Опыт курса церковного законоведения*. St Petersburg.

Somerville, R. and Brasington, B. (1998), *Prefaces to Canon Law Books in Latin Christianity: Selected Translations, 500–1245*. New Haven, Conn.

Sophocles, E. (1860), *A Glossary of Later and Byzantine Greek*. 2 vols. London.

Soubie, A. (1960), *Recherches sur les origines des rubriques du Digeste*. Tarbes.

Southern, R. (1995, 2000), *Scholastic Humanism and the Unification of Europe*. 2 vols. Oxford.

Stan, L. (1974), "Contributions des théologiens roumains aux problèmes de droit canon et leur position dans ce domain," in *De la théologie orthodoxe roumaine: des origines à nos jours*. Bucharest: 382–421.

Steimer, B. (1992), *Vertex traditionis: die Gattung der altchristlichen Kirchenordnungen*. Berlin.

Stein, P. (1966), *Regulae juris: From Juristic Rules to Legal Maxims*. Edinburgh.

Stein, P. (1980), *Legal Evolution: The Story of an Idea*. Cambridge.

Stein, P. (1984), *Legal Institutions: The Development of Dispute Settlement.* London.

Stein, P. (1988), *The Character and Influence of the Roman Civil Law: Historical Essays.* London.

Stein, P. (1995), "Interpretation and Legal Reasoning in Roman Law," *Chicago-Kent Law Review,* 70: 1539–56.

Stein, P. (1999), *Roman Law in European History.* Cambridge.

Stevens, G. (1969), *De Theodoro Balsamone analysis operum ac mentis iuridicae.* Rome.

Stickler, A. (1950), *Historia iuris canonici latini: institutiones academicae. Vol. I: Historia fontium.* Turin.

Stiegler, A. (1958), *Der kirchliche Rechtsbegriff: Elemente und Phasen seiner Erkenntnisgeschichte.* Munich.

Stolte, B. (1985), "The Digest Summa of the Anonymous and the Collectio Tripartita, or the Case of the Elusive Anonymi," *Subseciva Groningana,* 2: 47–58.

Stolte, B. (1988), "(No) Pictures for Lawyers: Some Considerations on Image and Word in Byzantine Legal Literature," *Byzantine and Modern Greek Studies,* 12: 297–30.

Stolte, B. (1989), "Balsamon and the Basilica," *Subseciva Groningana,* 3: 115–25.

Stolte, B. (1991), "Civil Law in Canon Law: A Note on the Method of Interpreting the Canons in the Twelfth Century," in Oikonomides 1991: 543–54.

Stolte, B. (1991a), "The Past in Legal Argument in the Byzantine Canonists of the Twelfth Century," in Oikonomides 1991: 199–210.

Stolte, B. (1997), "A Note on the un-Photian Revision of the Nomocanon XIV Titulorum," in Troianos 1997: 115–30.

Stolte, B. (1998), "Not New but Novel: Notes on the Historiography of Byzantine Law," *Byzantine and Modern Greek Studies,* 22: 264–79.

Stolte, B. (1998a), "In Search of the Origins of the Nomocanon of the [*sic*] Fourteen Titles," in Papastathis 1998: 183–94.

Stolte, B. (2002), "The Challenge of Change: Notes on the Legal History of the Reign of Heraclius," in G. Reinink and B. Stolte (eds.), *The Reign of Heraclius (610–641): Crisis and Confrontation.* Leuven: 191–204.

Stolte, B. (2003), "The Corpus Iuris Civilis: Codification and the Encyclopedia of Legal Knowldege," in A. MacDonald *et al.* (eds.), *Learned Antiquity: Scholarship and Society in the Near-East, the Greco-Roman World, and the Early Medieval West.* Leuven: 81–99.

Stolte, B. (2005), "Balancing Byzantine Law," in Burgmann 2005: 57–75.

Stolte, B. (2006), "Recent Developments in Byzantine Law Studies," contribution to International Byzantine Studies Congress, 2006. Unpublished.

Stolte, B. (2008), "Justice: Legal Practice," in Jeffreys *et al.* 2008: 691–8.

Stolte, B. (2009), "The Social Function of the Law," in J. Haldon (ed.), *The Social History of Byzantium.* Malden, Mass.: 76–91.

Stolte, B. (2010), "The Organization of Information: Observations on the Manuscripts of the Nomocanon XIV Titulorum," in A. García and I. Martin (eds.), *The Legacy of Bernard Montfaucon.* Turnhout: 521–32.

Stone, M. (2004), "Legal Formalism: The Task of Judgement," in J. Coleman and S. Shapiro (eds.), *The Oxford Handbook of Jurisprudence and Philosophy of Law*. Oxford: 166–205.

Stroux, J. (1949), *Römische Rechtswissenschaft und Rhetorik*. Potsdam.

Synek, E. (1997), *"Dieses Gesetz ist gut, heilig, es zwingt nicht . . . ": Zum Gesetzesbegriff der Apostolischen Konstitutionen*. Vienna.

Synek, E. (2006), *"Wer aber nicht völlig rein ist an Seele und Leib . . . ": Reinheitstabus im Orthodoxen Kirchenrecht*. Egling.

Szegedy-Maszak, A. (1978), "Legends of the Greek Law Givers," *Greek, Roman and Byzantine Studies*, 19: 199–209.

Taylor, J. (1980), "Canon Law in the Age of the Fathers," in J. Hite et al. (eds.), *Readings, Cases, Materials in Canon Law*. Collegeville, Md.: 43–61.

Thom, J. C. (1995), *The Pythagorean Golden Verses*. Leiden.

Thomas, R. (2005), "Writing, Law and Written Law," in Gagarin and Cohen 2005: 41–60.

Thomson, F. (1965), "Economy," *Journal of Theological Studies*, NS 16.2: 368–420.

Thür, G. (2005), "The Role of the Witness in Athenian Law," in Gagarin and Cohen 2005: 146–69.

Tiftixoglu, V. (1991), "Zur Genese der Kommentare des Theodoros Balsamon. Mit einem Exkurs über die unbekannten Kommentare des Sinaiticus gr. 1117," in Oikonomides 1991: 483–532.

Tigay, J. H. (1996), *Deuteronomy: The Traditional Hebrew Text with the New JPS Translation*. JPS Torah Commentary Series. Philadelphia.

Todd, S. (1993), *The Shape of Athenian Law*. Oxford.

Todd, S. (2005), "Law and Oratory in Athens," in Gagarin and Cohen 2005: 97–111.

Too, Y. (2001), "Legal Instruction in Classical Athens," in Y. Too (ed.), *Education in Greek and Roman Antiquity*. Leiden: 111–32.

Triantaphyllopoulos, I. (1985), *Das Rechtsdenken der Griechen*. Munich.

Troianos, S. (1987), "Zum Kapitel 45 der russischen Kormčaja Kniga: Ursprung und Wesen des Nomos Mosaikos," repr. *Historia et Ius*, 1: 485–93.

Troianos, S. (1991), "Nomos und Kanon in Byzanz," repr. *Historia et Ius*, 2:199–222.

Troianos, S. (1992), *Η πενθέκτη οικουμενίκη σύνοδος και το νομοθετικό της εργό*. Athens.

Troianos, S. (1992a), "Das Gesetz in der griechischen Patristik," repr. in *Historia et Ius*, 2: 313–37.

Troianos, S. (1995), "Die Kanones des Trullanum in den Novellen Leons VI. des Weisen," repr. in *Historia et Ius*, 2: 493–506.

Troianos, S. (ed.) (1997), *Analecta Atheniensia ad ius Byzantinum spectantia I*. Forschungen zur byzantinischen Rechtsgeschichte. Athener Reihe, 10. Athens-Komotini.

Troianos, S. (2001), "Die Entwicklung und der aktuelle Stand des kanonischen Rechts und der Kanonistik in der griechischen Orthodoxie," repr. *Historia et Ius*, 2: 739–58.

Troianos, S. (2003), "Kanonistische Antworten und Abhandlungen in der Ostkirche (9. - 15. Jh.). Eine Übersicht," repr. in *Historia et Ius*, 2: 759–82.

Troianos, S. (2003a), *Εκκλησιαστικό δίκαιο*. 2nd edn. Athens-Komotini.

Troianos, S. (2004), *Historia et Ius* [collected works]. 2 vols. Athens.

Troianos, S. (2012), “Byzantine Canon Law to 1100” and “Byzantine Canon Law from the Twelfth to the Fifteenth Centuries,” in Hartmann and Pennington 2012: 115–214.

Tsipin, V. (2002), *Церковное право*. Klin.

Tuori, K. (2004), “The Myth of Quintus Mucius Scaevola: Founding Father of Legal Science?,” *Tijdschrift voor Rechtsgeschiedenis*, 72: 243–62.

Turner, C. (1914), “Canons Attributed to the Council of Constantinople, AD 381, together with the Names of the Bishops, from Two Patmos POB’, POΓ’,” *Journal of Theological Studies*, os 15.58: 161–78.

Vaillant, A. (1963), *Manuel du vieux slave*. 2nd edn. 2 vols. Paris.

Vessey, M. (2003), “Sacred Letters of the Law: The Emperor’s Hand in Late Roman (Literary) History,” *Antiquité Tardive*, 11: 345–58 [review article].

Viscuso, P. (1989), “A Late Byzantine Theology of Canon Law,” *Greek Orthodox Theological Review*, 34: 203–19.

Voss, W. (1982), *Recht und Rhetorik in den Kaisergesetzen der Spätantike: eine Untersuchung zum nachklassischen Kauf- und Übereignungsrecht*. Frankfurt a.M.

Wagschal, D. (2010), “Canon Law without Gratian,” in P. Erdo and S. Szuromi (eds.), *Proceedings of the Thirteenth International Congress of Medieval Canon Law: Esztergom, 3–8 August 2008*. Vatican.

Wagschal, D. (2010a), ‘The Nature of Law and Legality in the Byzantine Canonical Collections 381–883.’ Unpublished thesis. Durham University.

Wagschal, D. (2012), “Orthodox Canon Law: The Byzantine Experience,” in A. Casiday (ed.), *The Orthodox Christian World*. Abingdon: 383–97.

Wagschal, D. (2014), “Early Modern Period: Orthodox Canon Law,” in *The Oxford Encyclopedia of the Bible and Law*. Oxford: forthcoming.

Wal, N. van der (1953), *Les Commentaires grecs du Code de Justinien*. The Hague.

Wal, N. van der (1980), “Wer war der ‘Enantiophanes?’,” *Tijdschrift voor Rechtsgeschiedenis*, 48: 125–36.

Wal, N. van der (1981), “Edictum und lex edictalis. Form und Inhalt der Kaisergesetze im spätrömischen Reich,” *Revue internationale des droits de l’antiquité* (3e sér.), 28: 277–313.

Wal, N. van der (1998), *Manuale Novellarum Justiniani: aperçu systématique du contenu des Nouvelles de Justinien*. 2nd edn. Groningen.

Wal, N. van der and Stolte, B. (1994), *Collectio tripartita. Justinian on Religious and Ecclesiastical Affairs*. Groningen.

Walicki, A. (1987), *Legal Philosophies of Russian Liberalism*. Oxford.

Walter, F. (1840), *Manuel du droit ecclésiastique de toutes les confessions chrétiennes*. Trans. A. Roquemont. Paris.

Watson, A. (1974), *Law Making in the Later Roman Republic*. Oxford.

Watson, A. (1985), *The Evolution of Law*. Baltimore.

Watson, A. (1992), *The State, Law and Religion: Pagan Rome*. Athens, Ga.

Watson, A. (1995), *The Spirit of Roman Law*. Athens, Ga.

Weber, M. (1925 [1954]), *Max Weber on Law in Economy and Society*. Trans. E. Shils and M. Rheinstein, from *Wirtschaft und Gesellschaft*, 2nd edn., with introduction and annotations by M. Rheinstein. Cambridge, Mass.

Wenger, L. (1925 [1940]), *Institutes of the Roman Law of Civil Procedure.* Trans O. Fisk. New York.

Wenger, L. (1942), *Canon in den römischen Rechtsquellen und in den Papyri, eine Wortstudie.* Vienna.

Wenger, L. (1943), "Über canon und regula in den römischen Rechtsquellen," *Zeitschrift der Savigny-Stiftung für Rechtsgeschichte*, Kan. Abt. 32: 495–505.

Wenger, L. (1953), *Die Quellen des römischen Rechts.* Vienna.

West, M. L. (1973), *Textual Criticism and Editorial Technique applicable to Greek and Latin Texts.* Stuttgart.

Westbrook, R. (1985), "Biblical and Cuneiform Law Codes," *Revue Biblique*, 92: 247–65.

Westbrook R. (1988), "The Nature and Origins of the Twelve Tables," *Zeitschrift der Savigny-Stiftung für Rechtsgeschichte*, Rom. Abt. 105: 74–121.

Westbrook, R. (2008), "The Laws of Biblical Israel," in F. Greenspahn (ed.), *The Hebrew Bible: New Insights and Scholarship.* New York: 99–119.

Westerink, L. (2011), *Anonymous Prolegomena to Platonic Philosophy.* 2nd edn. Westbury, Wilts.

Wieacker, F. (1952 [1995]), *A History of Private Law in Europe with Particular Reference to Germany.* Trans. T. Weir. Oxford.

Wieacker, F. (1960), *Textstufen Klassischer Juristen.* Göttingen.

Wieacker, F. (and J. Wolf) (1988–2006), *Römische Rechtsgeschichte.* 2 vols. Munich.

Wiel, C. van der (1991), *History of Canon Law.* Louvain.

Williams, J. (1996), "Use of Sources in the Canons of the Council in Trullo," *Byzantion*, 66: 470–88.

Winterbottom, M. (1982), "Schoolroom and Courtroom," in B. Vickers (ed.), *Rhetoric Revalued: Papers from the International Society for the History of Rhetoric.* New York: 59–70.

Wolff, H. (1975), "Greek Legal History: Its Functions and Potentialities," *Washington University Law Quarterly*: 395–408.

Wolska-Conus W. (1976), "Les Écoles de Psellos et de Xiphilin sous Constantin IX Monomaque," *Travaux et Mémoires*, 6: 223–43.

Wolska-Conus, W. (1979), "L''École de droit et l''enseignement du droit à Byzance au XIe siècle: Xiphilin et Psellos," *Travaux et Mémoires*, 7: 1–107.

Woodhouse, S. (1932), *English-Greek Dictionary: A Vocabulary of the Attic Language*, 2nd edn. London.

Wortman, R. (1976), *The Development of a Russian Legal Consciousness.* Chicago.

Yannaras, C. (1970 [1984]), *The Freedom of Morality.* Trans. E. Briere. Crestwood, NY.

Yunis, H. (2005), "The Rhetoric of Law in Fourth-Century Athens," in Gagarin and Cohen 2005: 191–209.

Zachariä von Lingenthal, K. (1839), *Historiae juris Graeco-Romani delineatio, cum appendice ineditorum.* Heidelberg.

Zachariä von Lingenthal, K. (1840–94 [1973]), *Kleine Schriften zur römischen und byzantinischen Rechtsgeschichte.* 2 vols. Ed. W. Peek *et al.* Leipzig.

Zachariä von Lingenthal, K. (1877), "Die griechischen Nomokanones," repr. in *Kleine Schriften*, 1: 614–31.

Zachariä von Lingenthal, K. (1885), "Über den Verfasser und die Quellen des (Pseudo-Photianischen) Nomokanon in XIV Titeln," repr. in *Kleine Schriften*, 2.145–85.

Zachariä von Lingenthal, K. (1887), "Die Synopsis canonum," repr. in *Kleine Schriften*, 2.247–63.

Zachariä von Lingenthal, K. (1892), *Geschichte des griechisch-römischen Rechts*. 3rd edn. Berlin.

Zechiel-Eckes, K. (1992), *Die Concordia canonum des Cresconius: Studien und Edition*. 2 vols. Frankfurt a.M.

Zepos, P. (1958), "Die byzantinische Jurisprudenz zwischen Justinian und den Basiliken," in *Berichte zum XI. Internationalen Byzantinistenkongreß*. III/2 Munich: 1–27.

Zimmermann, R. (2001), *Roman Law, Contemporary Law, European Law: The Civilian Tradition Today*. Oxford.

Ziolkowski, T. (1997), *The Mirror of Justice: Literary Reflections of Legal Crises*. Princeton.

Žužek, I. (1964), *Kormçaja Kniga: Studies on the Chief Code of Russian Canon Law*. Rome.

Žužek, I. (1967), "The Determining Structure of the Slavic 'Syntagma of Fifty Titles'," *Orientalia christiana periodica*, 33: 139–60.

Žužek, I. (1969), "A Code for the Orthodox Churches," *Concilium*, 8.5: 74–9.

Index

The manufacturer's authorised representative in the EU for product safety is Oxford University Press España S.A. of el Parque Empresarial San Fernando de Henares, Avenida de Castilla, 2 – 28830 Madrid (www.oup.es/en or product.safety@oup.com). OUP España S.A. also acts as importer into Spain of products made by the manufacturer.

www.ingramcontent.com/pod-product-compliance
Lightning Source LLC
LaVergne TN
LVHW011910200926
848484LV00002B/587

* 9 7 8 0 1 9 8 7 2 2 6 0 1 *